INTELLECTUAL PROPERTY, COMPETITION LAW AND ECONOMICS IN ASIA

This book results from a conference held in Singapore in September 2009 that brought together distinguished lawyers and economists to examine the differences and similarities in the intersection between intellectual property and competition laws in Asia. The prime focus was how best to balance these laws to improve economic welfare. Countries in Asia have different levels of development and experience with intellectual property and competition laws. Japan has the longest experience and now vigorously enforces both competition and intellectual property laws. Most other countries in Asia have only recently introduced intellectual property laws (due to the Trade-Related Aspects of Intellectual Property Rights (TRIPS) Agreement) and competition laws (sometimes due to the World Bank, International Monetary Fund or free trade agreements). It would be naïve to think that laws, even if similar on the surface, have the same goals or be enforced similarly. Countries have differing degrees of acceptance of these laws, different economic circumstances and differing legal and political institutions. To set the scene, Judge Doug Ginsburg, Greg Sidak, David Teece and Bill Kovacic look at the intersection of intellectual property and competition laws in the United States. Next, country chapters on Asia are written, jointly, by two authors (one a lawyer, the other an economist). The country chapters outline the institutional background to the intersection in each country, discuss the policy underpinnings (theoretically as well as describing actual policy initiatives), analyse the case law in the area, and make policy prescriptions.

Intellectual Property, Competition Law and Economics in Asia

Edited by
R Ian McEwin

Visiting Professor of Law
National University Of Singapore
Chulalongkorn University, Bangkok

BLOOMSBURY
NEW DELHI • LONDON • OXFORD • NEW YORK • SYDNEY

BLOOMSBURY INDIA
Bloomsbury Publishing India Pvt. Ltd
Second Floor, LSC Building No. 4, DDA Complex, Pocket C–6&7,
Vasant Kunj, New Delhi 110070

BLOOMSBURY, HART PUBLISHING INDIA and the Diana logo are trademarks of
Bloomsbury Publishing Plc

First published in India 2022
First published in 2011

Published in the United Kingdom by Hart Publishing Ltd
16C Worcester Place, Oxford, OX1 2JW

Published in North America (US and Canada) by
Hart Publishing
c/o International Specialized Book Services
920 NE 58th Avenue, Suite 300
Portland, OR 97213-3786
USA

This edition published with permission from Bloomsbury Publishing Plc,
50 Bedford Square, London, WC1B3DP, UK

British Library Cataloguing-in-Publication Data
A catalogue record for this book is available from the British Library.

Library of Congress Cataloging-in-Publication Data
A catalog record for this book is available from the Library of Congress

ISBN: 978-93-93715-06-7

For sale in the Indian subcontinent only

Typeset by Compuscript Ltd, Shannon
Printed at Manipal Technologies Limited, Manipal

Bloomsbury Publishing Plc makes every effort to ensure that the papers used in the manufacture of our books are natural, recyclable products made from wood grown in well-managed forests. Our manufacturing processes conform to the environmental regulations of the country of origin.

To find out more about our authors and books
visit www.bloomsbury.com and sign up for our newsletters

PREFACE

This book presents papers presented to a conference held in Singapore in September 2009. The idea behind the conference was to examine the differences and similarities in the intersection between intellectual property and competition laws in Asia. The conference was divided into two sessions. First, eminent speakers were asked to provide a context to the interface from the perspective of the United States—the country with the most innovation and the most sophisticated jurisprudence dealing with the intersection. They were former Chairman of the United States Federal Trade Commission, Bill Kovacic, Judge Doug Ginsberg, until recently Chief Judge of the US Federal Court of Appeals for the DC Circuit in Washington and Greg Sidak and David Teece, long-time critics of the current approach to dynamic competition taken by competition law authorities.

Next, an economist was teamed up with a lawyer to write chapters on most countries in Asia. They were asked to outline the underlying economic and legal institutional background to the intersection in their particular country. This was to include background country economics—including a description of, and statistics on, industry structure, the amount spent on research and development, types of research, government policies towards innovation, industrial development policies, etc. Next, the competition law and intellectual property laws in each country were to be discussed and a description of how the intersection is dealt with by government (if at all), for example compulsory licensing. This was to be followed, where possible, with a discussion of how the intersection should be treated in that country. For example, the appropriate balance—does it make more sense to focus on dynamic or static efficiency given each country's level of development, institutional capacity, etc and the criteria used to determine the balance? Finally, authors were asked to make policy recommendations—including recommended changes to existing laws, how to deal with institutional aspects including limitations (eg training judges).

Country authors were given the freedom to determine the issues with which they would deal. Naturally, their choice depended on the extent to which the intersection had been examined by policy makers, regulators or courts, either in general or with respect to specific issues such as compulsory licensing or mergers. For many country authors this was the first time they had worked with an economist or lawyer. Sometimes difficulties arose as to the issues to be discussed, writing style, etc. However, this was anticipated. An important reason for the conferences was to make economists and lawyers more aware of each other's approach to competition law issues dealing with innovation. It is only through collaboration between economists and lawyers that competition law will improve economic outcomes.

I am grateful for the financial support provided by the Competition Commission of Singapore (CCS), the National University of Singapore (NUS), and Microsoft Corporation. My thanks in particular to the Chairman of the CCS, Mr Lam Chuan Leong, the Dean of the Law School at NUS, Professor Tan Cheng Han, and Mr Mike Yeh of Microsoft.

TABLE OF CONTENTS

AUTHOR BIOGRAPHIES

Part 1: Setting the Scene

William E Kovacic has served on the Federal Trade Commission since January 2006, and served as Chairman from March 2008 until March 2009. Kovacic was the agency's General Counsel from 2001 through 2004, and he worked for the Commission from 1979 until 1983, initially in the Bureau of Competition's Planning Office and later as an attorney advisor to former Commissioner George W Douglas. Before he became a Commissioner, Kovacic was the EK Gubin Professor of Government Contracts Law at George Washington University Law School, where he began teaching in 1999. He had taught at the George Mason University School of Law since 1986, after practicing antitrust and government contracts law for three years at Bryan Cave's Washington, DC office. Earlier in his career, Kovacic spent one year on the majority staff of the US Senate Judiciary Committee's Antitrust and Monopoly Subcommittee. Since 1992, Kovacic has been an advisor on antitrust and consumer protection issues to the governments of Armenia, Benin, Egypt, El Salvador, Georgia, Guyana, Indonesia, Kazakhstan, Mongolia, Morocco, Nepal, Panama, Russia, Ukraine, Vietnam, and Zimbabwe. Kovacic received a bachelor degree from Princeton University in 1974 and a law degree from Columbia University in 1978.

Douglas H Ginsburg has been a Judge of the United States Court of Appeals for the District of Columbia Circuit since 1986; he was Chief Judge from 2001 to 2008. He is also Visiting Lecturer at the University of Chicago Law School and Visiting Professor at University College London, Faculty of Laws. Judge Ginsburg was previously a Professor at Harvard Law School (1975–83); Director of the Office of Information and Regulatory Affairs, Office of Management and Budget (1984–85); and Assistant Attorney General in charge of the Antitrust Division of the US Department of Justice (1985–86). Judge Ginsburg is a graduate of Cornell University and of the University of Chicago Law School, where he was the Articles Editor of the *Law Review*. He serves on the Advisory Boards of *Competition Policy International*; the *Journal of Competition Law and Economics*; the *Journal of Law, Economics and Policy*; the *Supreme Court Economic Review*; the Law and Economics Center at George Mason University School of Law; and the Jevons Institute for Competition Law and Economics, University College London; as well as the *Harvard Journal of Law and Public Policy*; and the *University of Chicago Law Review*. He is a member of the American Law and Economics Association and of The Mont Pelerin Society.

Eric M Fraser is the Executive Director for Research at the Committee on Capital Markets Regulation in Cambridge, Massachusetts. He was a law clerk for Judge Douglas H Ginsburg of the United States Court of Appeals for the District of Columbia Circuit. Eric holds a BA in Physics from Pomona College; an MBA with High Honours from the University of Chicago Booth School of Business; and a JD with High Honours from the University of Chicago Law School, where he was awarded the John M Olin Prize in Law and Economics and was a Comments Editor of the *Law Review*, the John M Olin Scholar, a Bradley

Fellow, and an MVP2 Student Fellow. He also worked at the law firm Osborn Maledon in Phoenix, Arizona, and in the Worldwide Licensing and Pricing group at Microsoft Corp in Redmond, Washington.

J Gregory Sidak is the founder and Chairman of Criterion Economics, LLC in Washington, DC and the Ronald Coase Professor of Law and Economics at Tilburg University in The Netherlands. He is an internationally recognised expert on antitrust, intellectual property, regulation of network industries, and complex economic litigation. Professor Sidak has testified as an expert witness in scores of proceedings before courts, regulatory commissions, international commercial arbitration panels, and committees of Congress. He has served in the US Government as both an economist and a lawyer. Professor Sidak has been a consultant to the Antitrust Division of the US Department of Justice, the Republic of Mexico, and the Competition Bureau of Canada, as well as to major corporations in North America, Europe, Asia, and Australia. Professor Sidak edits the *Journal of Competition Law & Economics* for the Oxford University Press and has written extensively on antitrust, intellectual property, and regulation. His books and articles have been cited by the Antitrust Division, the Federal Trade Commission, the Federal Communications Commission, the Supreme Court of the United States, the Supreme Court of Canada, the European Commission, the US Court of Appeals for the DC Circuit, the Supreme Court of California, and many other courts and regulatory commissions. Professor Sidak has taught at the Yale School of Management and the Georgetown University Law Center. He was educated at Stanford University and clerked for Judge Richard A Posner.

David Teece is Thomas W Tusher Chair in Global Business and since 1994, Director of the Institute of Management, Innovation and Organization (IMIO) at the University of California, Berkeley. He was co-editor and co-founder of *Industrial and Corporate Change*, and a member of the Editorial Board of *Long Range Planning*. He has been Chairman of LECG Corporation and a Member of the Board of Directors, The Atlas Group and Board of Trustees, Atlas Insurance Trust. His books have included *Managing Intellectual Capital: Organizational, Strategic, and Policy Dimensions* (Oxford, Oxford University Press, 2000) and *Antitrust, Innovation and Competitiveness* (Oxford, Oxford University Press, 1992) (with Thomas M Jorde, eds). He was identified by Accenture as one of the World's Top 50 Living Business Intellectuals and listed by Science Watch (November/December 2005) as one of the 10 most cited scholars worldwide in economics and business, 1995–2005. He has honorary doctorates from St Petersburg State University, Russia, the Copenhagen Business School, Denmark, and the Lappeenranta University of Technology, Finland. He has a BA and M Comm from the University of Canterbury in New Zealand and an MA and PhD in Economics from the University of Pennsylvania.

Part 2: Country Chapters

Australia

Bob Baxt is Partner with Freehills in Australia. Before that he was Chairman of the Australian Trade Practices Commission and prior to that, the Dean of the Monash University Law Faculty. Professor Baxt has been an advisor to governments and clients on the impact of the Competition Policy Reform Act 1995, the Trade Practices Act 1974 and related legislation. Professor Baxt was honoured in the Queen's Birthday Honours

Awards in 2003 by being awarded an Order of Australia for services to the law. He is also a Professorial Fellow at the University of Melbourne.

Henry Ergas spent a decade as a micro economist at the Organisation for Economic Co-operation and Development (OECD) in the 1980s and headed the Secretary-General's Task Force on Structural Adjustment, which concentrated on improving the efficiency of government policies in a wide range of areas. Since leaving the OECD, he has focused on competition policy and regulatory economics. He has been closely involved in dealing with regulatory issues in a range of industries, including telecommunications, electricity, aviation, surface transport, and financial services. He chaired the Intellectual Property and Competition Policy Review Committee for the Australian Government in 1999–2000, and was a member of the Prime Minister's Export Infrastructure Task Force in 2005 and of the Defence Industry Consultative Group in 2006. He is currently the Chairman of Concept Economics, an economics consultancy firm with offices in Canberra and Sydney. He is also an Honorary Professor in the Faculty of Economics at Monash University in Melbourne, and a Lay Member of the New Zealand High Court.

China

Michael Jacobs is Distinguished Research Professor of Law at the DePaul University College of Law. In 2000 he held the Fulbright Distinguished Chair for Italy. He has been practicing, teaching and consulting in the field of antitrust since 1972, and has written dozens of articles, book chapters and books on various aspects of the topic. During the past five years, his research and writing has focused on the intersection between intellectual property and antitrust. Since 2001, he has taught and consulted regularly in China, with government, academic, and judicial groups. He has advised the Australian Competition and Consumer Commission, and for the past 11 years has been a Special Counsel to the Sydney firm of Blake Dawson. Professor Jacobs is a graduate of Dartmouth College and the Yale Law School.

Xinzhu Zhang was deeply involved in the drafting process of the Chinese Anti-Monopoly Law and the pre-merger notification policy for the State Council and Ministry of Commerce (MOFCOM) of PR China. Dr Zhang also has advised governments and private companies on the market implications of regulatory reform. He has also consulted in a number of cases in the payment card industry, electricity industry, telecommunication industry, and various consumer products industries. He has a BS from Xiamen University, an MS from Shanghai Jiaotong University and a PhD from the University of Toulouse.

Japan

Steve Harris practises antitrust law with Baker and McKenzie in Washington and has had considerable experience, including class actions and cartel and merger investigations, before US and international courts and agencies. He also represents financial institutions in complex regulatory and commercial litigation. Steve has extensive experience in Asia and serves as the Firm's Asia competition law coordinator. Steve is editor-in-chief and co-author of the two-volume treatise *Competition Laws Outside the United States*, published by the American Bar Association. He has served as the international officer of the ABA Section of Antitrust Law, as well as a member of its Council, as vice chair of the Inter-Pacific Bar Association, and as a member of the International Bar Association Competition

Law Committee. He speaks and writes frequently on antitrust topics. Steve is a Life Fellow of the American Bar Foundation and a member of the advisory board of the BNA Antitrust & Trade Regulation Report. He has a JD from Columbia University and an AB from Cornell University (magna cum laude).

Hiroshi Ohashi is Associate Professor at Graduate School of Economics and Graduate School of Public Policy, University of Tokyo. His areas of research include empirical industrial organisation and international trade policy. Dr Ohashi previously taught at Sauder School of Business, University of British Columbia, Canada, and held a visiting associate professorship in Ludwig-Maximilians-Universitat Munchen, Germany. He is also a chief researcher at Competition Policy Research Center at Japan Fair Trade Commission, a Faculty Fellow at the Research Institute of Economy, Trade & Industry, and a Head Research Officer at the National Institute of Science and Technology Policy in the MEXT. He holds a PhD in Economics from Northwestern University, and an MA and BA from University of Tokyo.

India

Vinod Dhall set up the Competition Commission of India from its inception in 2003 and was, until recently, the single member and its Acting Chairman. Prior to that he was Permanent Secretary to the Government of India's Department of Company Affairs. He has a law degree from Delhi University and a Masters degree in Mathematics from Allahabad University. He has also edited a book *Competition Law Today* (Oxford, Oxford University Press, 2007).

Augustine Peter is currently Economic Adviser with the Ministry of Commerce and Industry, Department of Commerce, Government of India. He is a member of the Indian Economic Service (IES) and has post graduate degree qualifications in Economics from Indian and UK universities. He specialises in areas such as Competition Policy, Multilateral Trade and Investment, with experience spanning over 30 years in banking and in various economic departments of government as well as in the United Nations Industrial Development Organization (UNIDO). He understands and speaks English, Hindi and French. Views expressed are personal.

Indonesia

Ningrum Sirait is Professor of Law, University of North Sumatera in Medan, Indonesia. Since 1989, she has lectured in both undergraduate and graduate subjects in the Law School, including competition law, contract law, corporation law and consumer protection. Professor Sirait has written extensive articles (both in Indonesian and international journals) and several books in the area of competition law. She has been a visiting researcher and scholar in Germany under a DAAD scholarship and given talks at various international seminars in Singapore, Hong Kong, Germany and Washington DC. Professor Sirait obtained her Master's degree from the University of Wisconsin in the United States in 1996 where her major field of study was economic law. She completed her Doctoral degree in 2003 at the University of North Sumatera with a dissertation in competition law, receiving a Fulbright Fellowship to help her finalise her dissertation.

Cento Veljanovski established and is Managing Partner of CASE Associates, London. He has been a director/partner of several management and economics consulting firms and on the board of listed public companies. The *Global Competition Review* 2006 survey voted

Cento one of the most 'highly regarded' competition economists. He has over 30 years' experience assisting lawyers and companies in responding to investigations by the European Commission under articles 81 and 82 of the EC Treaty, and the EC Merger Regulation, national competition authorities, national regulatory authorities, and in court proceedings in EU Member States and other countries in Europe, Australia, New Zealand and North America. He has been advisor to the Microsoft Monitoring Trustee on the pricing of protocols under commitments set out in the EC *Microsoft* (2004) decision. Cento has degrees in economics and law (BEc (Hons), MEc, DPhil) and is an associate member of the Chartered Institute of Arbitrators (ACIArb). After a short period at the Australian Federal Department of the Treasury, Cento held a Research Fellowship at the Centre for Socio-Legal Studies at Oxford University. He has also held academic positions at the University of London, Monash University (Australia), York University (United Kingdom), and Universities of Toronto, New York, and Miami.

Singapore

Ashish Lall is Associate Professor in the Lee Kuan Yew School of Public Policy at the National University of Singapore. He has published extensively in the areas of productivity and efficiency measurement in the aviation industry and on trade and competition policy issues. He has been a consultant for a number of Singapore Ministries, the World Bank, UNDP and the World Trade Organization. Ashish is a member of the Singapore Competition Appeal Board. He has a PhD in Economics from Carleton University in Canada.

Daryl Lim is an Assistant Professor at the John Marshall Law School. Prior to this, Daryl was the inaugural Microsoft Teaching and Research Fellow at the Fordham Law School Intellectual Property ('IP') Law Institute, where he taught courses on US patent law, copyright law, and the interface between IP and antitrust law and European IP law. He is a frequent speaker in the US and abroad, and has spoken on the intellectual property and antitrust laws of the United States, European Union, Japan, China, India and Singapore.

His book, *Patent Misuse: An Empirical Study,* will be published by Edward Elgar in 2011. His articles have been published in leading IP law reviews and books in the US, Europe and Asia. His recent publications include the chapter in this book, an essay, 'Post-eBay: A Brave New World?' (*European Intellectual Property Law Review*, 2010), and an article, 'Misconduct in Standard Setting: The Case for Patent Misuse' (IDEA: The Intellectual Property Law Review, 2011). The latter article won the grand prize in the 2009 International Essay Writing Competition of the International Association for the Advancement of Teaching and Research in Intellectual Property ('ATRIP'). Daryl delivered the paper at ATRIP's annual meeting in Stockholm in 2010.

Daryl has graduate law degrees from Stanford University and the National University of Singapore ('NUS'). He also has undergraduate degrees in law from NUS as well as another in economics and management from the London School of Economics. Previously, Daryl was in private practice at the IP & Technology Department of Allen & Gledhill LLP, Singapore's largest law firm. Daryl was a residential scholar at the Max Planck Institute for IP, Competition and Tax Law and later at the Queen Mary IP Research Institute.

He has served as an intern on the staff of Commissioner William E Kovacic at the Federal Trade Commission and in the chambers of Chief Judge Randall R Rader of the Court of Appeals for the Federal Circuit.

South Korea

Sang-Seung Yi is Professor of Economics, Seoul National University (SNU). He specialises in industrial organisation and was advisor to the Korea Fair Trade Commission from 2003 to 2005. In 2004 he received a Citation by the Chairman of the Korea Fair Trade Commission for contributions to the development of antitrust policy in Korea. He has a BA in economics from Seoul National University (Summa Cum Laude) and a PhD in Economics from Harvard University.

Seong-Wook Heo is Associate Professor of Law at Seoul National University. He has a BA in Economics, and an LLM and PhD in Law from Seoul National University. He specialises in law of economic regulation and antitrust law and teaches administrative law and law and economics at Seoul National University. He served as a judge of Seoul Central District Court in Korea before becoming a professor in 2006.

Thailand

Sakda Thanitcul is Associate Professor of Law and Dean at Chulalongkorn Law School. He holds an LLB from Chulalongkorn, an LLD from Kyoto University 2004, an LLM from Kyoto University, Japan, where he is also a PhD candidate in international law. He received a PhD in Asian Comparative Law from the University of Washington, USA. Professor Thanitcul has conducted extensive research in International Economic Law as well as Business Competition Law.

Ian McEwin is Visiting Professor of Law, National University of Singapore, a Senior Economic and Regulatory Advisor to Rajah and Tann in Singapore and a member of the Copyright Tribunal in Singapore. He has consulted widely on competition matters in Australia, New Zealand and Europe (including as an expert witness in major litigation). In 2004 he took up a position as economics advisor to the Department of Trade & Industry on the development of Singapore's new competition law. When Singapore's Competition Commission (CCS) was established, he joined it as its inaugural Chief Economist. He was founding Director of the Centre for Law and Economics at the Australian National University. He has a law degree and PhD in economics from the Australian National University.

Vietnam

Doan Tu Tich Phuoc is Deputy Director of Unfair Competition Division, Vietnam Competition Authority. He has worked at the Competition Authority of Vietnam since the very beginning of the entity and took part in more than 30 cases under the Vietnam Competition Law. From 2005, he joined several legislation projects and was a member of editorial boards for the Competition Law Guidelines 2005, the Intellectual Property Law's guideline 2010 and the Consumer Protection Law 2010. Doan is also a visiting lecturer in the Centre for Competition and Consumer Protection Law, Hanoi University of Law. He has an MA in Law from the Vietnam National University (Hanoi).

Bui Nguyen Anh Tuan is the Economic Expert of the Competition Policy Division, Vietnam Competition Authority (VCA). He joined the Authority in 2007 and has become a key expert in economics since then. Bui has been the main author of VCA's annual reports on national economic concentration from 2008 to the present day and plays an active role in competition law advocacy. He has a BA in Economics from the Foreign Trade University (Vietnam) and an MA in Economics, University of Leeds (United Kingdom).

TABLE OF CASES

Indonesia

Japan

Singapore

South Korea

United Kingdom

United States

Vietnam

TABLE OF LEGISLATION

Domestic Legislation

Australia

Canada

China

Regulations and Rules

India

Indonesia

Japan

Guidelines

Singapore

Guidelines

South Korea

Guidelines

Thailand

Notices

International Treaties and Conventions

1

Setting the Scene

1

Editor's Introduction

R IAN MCEWIN

I. Background

Innovation is the main driving factor in economic growth. Innovation includes the generation, diffusion, absorption and application of new ideas, knowledge and technologies, which leads to new or better goods and services, production processes, marketing methods (distribution, etc) and better forms of business organisation. Innovation is a major source of economic growth for both developed and developing countries.

Asia has experienced rapid economic growth and development since the end of the Second World War. To begin with, many Asian countries industrialised by developing import-substituting industries such as food processing, textiles, footwear, etc that built on their agricultural strengths. South Korea and India also focused on developing medium and heavy industries. Japan concentrated on rebuilding its industries through exports and by opening, to a degree, its economy to trade and investment. The Japanese approach was followed by China, South Korea, Singapore, Taiwan and Hong Kong. Later, Indonesia, Malaysia, Thailand and the Philippines introduced similar export-oriented policies that led to their rapid growth from the 1980s.

Technology was important, to varying degrees, in Asia's export success. Growth was fueled mainly by technology derived from imported capital equipment. As Brahmbhatt and Wu in a World Bank Report pointed out:

> While the econometric evidence is mixed, a rich body of case study literature argues that East Asian firms may have derived significant technological benefits from exports under longer term Original Equipment Manufacturing (OEM) contracts, as part of the global production networks of foreign multinationals … Here evidence for technology transfers through 'vertical' relationships between local firms and MNC affiliates (another form of supplier–oriented upgrading) is more convincing than for other channels that have been suggested.[1]

Almost 80 per cent of the world's research and development (R&D) is carried out in the developed world. For most countries, innovation means catching up with developed countries. However, even developed countries rely on imported technology for growth. Eaton and Kortum have estimated that foreign sources of technology account for at least 80 per

[1] Miland Brahmbhatt and Albert Hu, 'Ideas and Innovation in East Asia' (2009) *The World Bank Research Observer*, November 1, 4.

cent of domestic productivity growth in most Organisation for Economic Co-operation and Development (OECD) countries—except for the United States and Japan.[2]

However, the ability to introduce technology from abroad depends on a country's ability to learn and absorb the technology, which depends on scientific and technical skills within the country in universities, public and private research bodies, and the willingness of multinational companies to invest in training local staff.

Weak intellectual property rights (IPRs) reduce the returns from domestic R&D. However, for countries at an early stage of economic development, with little local R&D, there is little to protect. Copying allows local industries to grow—at least in markets where easy copying is possible. As a country develops and starts to develop its own indigenous research, IPR protection becomes more important. For example, new products increasingly come from innovation in large, fast-growing developing countries such as China, India and Brazil. Initially these new products were developed for domestic consumers but now increasingly they are for export to developed countries.[3] Industries engaged in indigenous research will argue for better local intellectual property (IP) protection and will clash with domestic industries that thrive on copying.

IP laws are mainly concerned with innovation. As Schumpeter puts it '... to survive in capitalist competition, incumbents must withstand a perennial gale of competition in the form of the new consumer goods, the new methods of production or transportation, the new markets, the new forms of industrial organization.'[4]

IPRs provide an economic incentive to innovate but they differ in their importance across industries. Mansfield[5] concluded in 1985 that patents were only essential in chemical industries and pharmaceuticals, but more recent work by Maskus[6] finds that patents are also important in newer technologies such as biotechnology and plant genetics.

IPRs do not exist in a policy vacuum. For example, the importance of IPRs in promoting innovation is affected by a country's complementary endowments and policies. Government commitment to education and skills training is more likely to lead to greater innovation—and so IPR protection becomes more important when combined with a policy emphasis on education. Similarly, the relationship between competition law and IPRs does not exist in a vacuum. Countries that are closed to trade, and so face little import competition, will find IPRs create greater market power than they would in an open economy. Thus, competition regulators may need to play a greater role.

IPRs promote innovation by allowing firms to protect their ideas or expression—so leading to new products or new forms of expression for which consumers are willing to pay. IPRs do not necessarily confer market power but they might. Where IPRs designed to promote innovation create substantial market power, they may conflict with competition law that tries to ensure new ideas and expression are disseminated at least cost as widely as possible. Put more technically, there may be a clash between IPRs, designed

[2] Jonathan Eaton and Samuel Kortum, 'Trade in Ideas: Patenting and Productivity in the OECD' (1996) 40 *Journal of International Economics* 251.

[3] See 'Innovation—the New Two-way Play' Knowledge@Wharton. Available at http://knowledge.wharton.upenn.edu/article.cfm?articleid=2684.

[4] Joseph A Schumpeter, *Capitalism, Socialism and Democracy* (London, George, Allen and Unwin, 1943) 84.

[5] Edwin Mansfield, 'Patents and Innovation: An Empirical Study' (1986) 32(2) *Management Science* 32, 173.

[6] Keith E Maskus, *Intellectual Property Rights in the New Economy* (Washington, Institute for International Economics 2000) 43.

to encourage optimal innovation over time (dynamic efficiency) and competition law, designed primarily to promote efficient short-term resource allocation (static or allocative efficiency where goods and services are supplied at least cost to consumers prepared to pay for them). Countries may face difficult policy choices in trading off conflicts between these two kinds of efficiency (ie optimal innovation over time versus the cost-justified use of innovation).

Many believe dynamic competition to be more important than short-term price competition. For example, McKenzie and Lee argue that economic models of price competition (ie static models) 'exaggerate the economic harm done by real-world monopolies in real-world markets' and that 'some degree of monopoly is good because without some monopoly presence no economy can ever hope to maximize human welfare over time'.[7]

Yet, modern competition law enforcement around the world (following the United States) continues to be concerned, mainly, with short-term economic efficiency and to apply economic models of short-term *price* competition. So, for example, in defining markets for competition law purposes, the focus is on price competition by using a price elevation test that looks at the extent to which consumers switch product as a result of an increase in price. However, competition in new product or process markets is often on the basis of product characteristics, not price. So markets defined for competition law purposes solely on the basis of price competition may not reflect competitive realities in either developed or developing countries.

II. Intersection between IPRs and Competition Law

Over the last 20 years, the United States has been at the forefront of the development of the policy and jurisprudence of the intersection between competition law and IP law. Typically, the United States has focused on the trade-off between domestic innovation (in the United States) and domestic dissemination of ideas and expression (again in the United States). The policy debate has been concerned with whether the traditional approach to competition law enforcement, with its focus on price competition, should be changed to accommodate situations where innovation and IPRs are important.

US regulators started to seriously consider the importance of dynamic competition from the early 1990s. For example, in their joint 1995 'Antitrust Guidelines for the Licensing of Intellectual Property', the Department of Justice and the Federal Trade Commission (FTC) stressed that: the common purpose of intellectual and competition laws; intellectual property was like any other type of property; IPRs did not necessarily create market power; and that licensing is generally pro-competitive.[8] The 1995 Guidelines also said that while licensing was pro-competitive, a licensor could limit a licensee's use of its technology in the same way that the licensor could if it exploited the IPR itself. So there is no obligation to promote competition in licensing one's own IPR.

[7] Richard B McKenzie and Dwight R Lee, *In Defense of Monopoly: How Market Power Fosters Creative Production* (Ann Arbor, The University of Michigan Press, 2008).

[8] US Department of Justice and Federal Trade Commission, 'Antitrust Guidelines for the Licensing of Intellectual Property' (Washington, 1995) s 2.

The 1995 Guidelines also identified three kinds of markets relevant to dynamic competition. First, an *innovation market* that involves R&D aimed at improving products or processes. Second, a *technology market* where the IPRs themselves are bought and sold (eg IPR licenses and the competing technologies that constrain any market power the licensor/licensee may have). Finally, the *goods market* which consists of the goods and services comprising the IPRs.[9] This characterisation has been questioned. For example, Hay and others wonder whether *innovation markets* are new or simply a new name for potential competition from new technologies.[10]

Most in the United States now agree that competition laws should incorporate dynamic competition into the existing approach. For example, in 2007, the US Antitrust Modernization Committee concluded that '[c]urrent antitrust analysis has a sufficient grounding in economics and is sufficiently flexible to reach appropriate conclusions in matters involving industries in which innovation, intellectual property, and technological change are central features'.[11]

The US approach to the intersection of IP and competition laws has been largely followed in Europe, Australia, etc. Competition law guidelines dealing with the intersection have largely followed the United States. However, is this approach appropriate to other countries, with different business practices, legal systems and levels of innovation, IPR regimes and stages of development? This book provides an overview of the relationship between IPRs, competition law and policies in Asian countries. The goal was to consider their intersection within a broader economic and legal context than just a domestic trade-off between innovation and static efficiency as in the United States. For example, for countries with little or no innovation there is no trade-off.

III. Competition, Innovation and Welfare

In the short-term, competition improves consumer welfare and contributes to economic growth by forcing firms to work in consumer's interests. Firms that fail to serve customers with the products they want at the lowest price lose out to firms that do. Competition drives price down towards cost promoting efficient resource allocation. However, to be competitive firms must be internally efficient. So competition also forces internal efficiency. As Holmes and Schmitz pointed out in a recent survey of competition and productivity:

> We have reviewed a new literature that has examined industries experiencing dramatic changes in their competitive environment. Nearly all the studies found that increases in competition led to increases in industry productivity. Plants that survived these increases in competition were typically found to have large productivity gains, and these gains often accounted for the majority of overall industry gains.[12]

[9] The stress on innovation markets followed Richard J Gilbert and Steven C Sunshine, 'Incorporating Dynamic Efficiency Concerns in Merger Analysis: The Use of Innovation Markets' (1995) 63 *Antitrust Law Journal* 569.

[10] George A Hay, 'Innovations in Antitrust Enforcement' (1995) 64 *Antitrust Law Journal* 7, 9. See also other contributions in the same volume.

[11] Antitrust Modernization Commission, *Report and Recommendations* (Washington, 2007) 38.

[12] Thomas J Holmes and James A Schmitz, 'Competition and Productivity: A Review of Evidence' (Federal Reserve Bank of Minneapolis, Research Department Staff Report 439, February 2010) 33. Available at www.minneapolisfed.org/research/sr/SR439.pdf.

While competition seems to improve what economists call X-efficiency or internal or within-plant efficiency, some argue that too much competition might also reduce dynamic efficiency and so longer-term economic growth. Schumpeter argued that economic change depends on innovation, entrepreneurship, but also on market power. Market power is beneficial, he said, if it is derived from innovation and provides better outcomes for consumers than price competition. While innovation may create monopoly power, rivals and imitators soon compete away these monopoly profits. Temporary monopolies, he argued, were necessary to provide the important incentives necessary for firms to develop new products and processes. Competition that reduces a firm's ability to capture monopoly profits discourages innovation and so long-term growth.

Evidence on the relationship between competition and innovation is mixed. For example, Blundell, Griffith and Van Reenen found a strong positive relationship between product market competition (eg the number of competitors) and productivity growth and innovation.[13] Others, like Michael Porter, argue that product market competition promotes growth because firms are forced to innovate or go out of business.[14] Factors that limit competition such as barriers to entry are also important—if there are barriers to firms introducing new technology then there is a reduced incentive to innovate.

Firms innovate because they believe they can make profits from R&D. This depends on the economic environment and the market conditions in which a firm operates. A firm is more likely to invest in R&D if it believes it can develop a major innovation that limits post-innovation competition (by making competitors' products obsolete or too costly). If an innovation is relatively trivial (and so only slightly differentiates the product from others) then it is likely that monopoly profits will be negligible. So, the likely level of post-innovation competition will be an important factor in deciding whether to engage in R&D.

However, innovation might be driven, also, by an attempt to pre-empt the R&D of a competitor or possible new entrant. R&D decisions also need to take into account the impact of any innovation on any existing monopoly profits (ie where innovation 'replaces' existing products). To the extent that new innovation cannibalises existing profits, the incentive to innovate will be diminished.[15] So, the dynamics of competition are more complicated than Schumpeter believed.

In 2007, Richard Gilbert surveyed the theoretical and empirical literature on competition and innovation[16] and stressed that there are many factors that affect the relationship between incentives to innovate and market power.[17] These factors include:

— Property rights system. How much protection is there? Are IPRs easy to invent around? Can innovation be protected outside the IP system?
— Nature of the invention—does it involve a new product or process innovation that reduces production costs? Is it a minor advance or does it replace existing products?

[13] Richard Blundell, Rachel Griffith and John Van Reenen, 'Dynamic Count Data Models of Technological Innovation' (1995) 105 *Economic Journal* 333.

[14] Michael Porter, *The Competitive Advantage of Nations* (New York, The Free Press, 1990).

[15] William F Baxter, 'The Definition and Measurement of Market Power in Industries Characterized by Rapidly Developing and Changing Technologies' (1984) 53 *Antitrust Law Journal* 717.

[16] See also chapter four in this book by Sidak and Teece.

[17] Richard J Gilbert, 'Competition and Innovation' (Berkeley, Competition Policy Center, Institute of Business and Economic Research, Competition Policy Research Centre, UC Berkeley, 2007) 9. Available at http://escholarship.org/uc/item/9xh5p5p9.

— Extent of competition pre and post-innovation—is a highly competitive situation before the innovation likely to be replaced by less competition afterwards, etc? Is competition mainly on the basis of price or product? Are there significant barriers to R&D? Is the inventor also the innovator, or does the inventor expect to license the innovation to someone else?
— The dynamics of R&D competition. Are outcomes of R&D predictable? Can firms collaborate to avoid duplication of R&D?

Gilbert went on to conclude that:

> The large body of economic theory and empirical studies on the relationship between competition and innovation fails to provide general support for the Schumpeterian hypothesis that monopoly promotes either investment in R&D or the output of innovation. The theoretical and empirical evidence also does not support a strong conclusion that competition is uniformly a stimulus to innovation.[18]

Studies by Blundell, Griffith and Van Reenen,[19] Greenhalgh and Rogers[20] provide some evidence that oligopoly may provide better innovation outcomes than more competition. Aghion and Griffith have empirical evidence supporting their argument that there is an inverted U-shaped relationship between competition and innovation.[21] That is, patents rise as competition increases but then a point is reached at which increased competition leads to a falling off in patent rates.

The complex factors that affect the relationship between competition and innovation are likely to differ not only across markets in a single country but more so across countries. Countries need a range of capabilities to allow firms to successfully exploit innovation. Teece first stressed the importance of complementary assets.[22] Assets such as skilled labour, information, financing opportunities, ability to use IPRs, the availability of sophisticated legal and accounting services are all important—and particularly important for an innovative firm in a developing country whose innovation is to be exploited in a developed country.

Given the uncertainties in the relationship between competition and the incentives for innovation, it seems likely that the relationship between competition law and IP will differ between countries.

Not only will the impact of one law on the other be different due to local economic circumstances, but countries may have different policy objectives towards both laws. National interests become important to any trade-off. For example, a country might use compulsory licensing to force overseas technology transfer to a local monopoly and then either regulate the price or protect it against imports as part of an industrial policy aimed at developing local industry or local vested interests rather than promoting domestic

[18] Ibid 24–25.

[19] R Blundell, R Griffith and J Van Reenen, 'Market Share, Market Value and Innovation in a Panel of British Manufacturing Firms' (1999) 66 *Review of Economic Studies* 529.

[20] Christine A Greenhalgh and Mark Rogers, 'The Value of Innovation: The Interaction of Competition, R&D and IP' (2006) 35(4) *Research Policy* 562.

[21] P Aghion and R Griffith, *Competition and Growth: Reconciling Theory and Evidence* (Cambridge, MA, MIT Press, 2005).

[22] David Teece, 'Profiting from Technological Innovation' (1986) 15(6) *Research Policy* 285.

competition. Competitor collaboration in setting standards may also be directed at protecting an indigenous technology rather than promoting consumer interests.

IV. Asian Legal Systems

Of course, the way IP and competition laws are enforced and their effectiveness depends on a country's legal system. Even where substantive laws are the same, different legal systems may enforce IP or competition laws differently. This may be due to differences in policy goals or procedural differences (the way or sophistication in which economic evidence is dealt with by regulators or courts for example). Asian legal systems vary but, in general, law in Asia is not as important as it is in the West. Glenn describes Asian legal systems in the following way:

> It is law which is secular in origin, yet greatly limited by its formal version, by its reach and effect. In China the limits are the secular ones of Confucianism; elsewhere, Asian religions have done the same work of limiting the role of the lawyers. Everywhere in the Asian tradition … there is denial of the primary role of secular law-makers and denial of the idea of a sweeping religious law. In short there is denial everywhere of a primary role for what is usually known as law. It is a secular, largely informal, legal tradition, though informed by great learning.[23]

Still, Asian law has been greatly influenced by the West. Japan looked to Europe in the early twentieth century. China followed. However, the US occupation after the Second World War impacted Japanese law and led to a US style competition law in 1947. Dutch, English and French law initially influenced law in South East Asia, but its influence declined in Cambodia, Laos and Vietnam post-independence. Common law is still important in Brunei, Hong Kong, Malaysia and Singapore.

V. Why Should Countries Introduce Competition and IPLaws?

Countries will only introduce (or enforce if forced on them) competition law and IPlaws when they yield tangible, positive, benefits. Both IP laws and competition law are highly technical, particularly where complex issues involving innovation and dynamic competition are concerned. Their successful introduction requires the kinds of skills that are limited or non-existent in developing countries. So some time may be needed to develop the necessary skills and expertise to identify whether a patent application is novel or whether business conduct is anti-competitive—and whether an anti-competitive practice can be realistically improved by intervening

Governments may give a low priority to protecting IPRs to ensure their citizens have low-price access to patented or copyrighted products. For example, a number of developing countries allow the importation or domestic production of generic drugs despite

[23] H Patrick Glenn, *Legal Traditions of the World*, 2nd edn (Oxford, Oxford University Press, 2004) 309.

patent protection. Preventing anti-competitive practices may be also given a low priority by governments. Well organised groups such as wealthy families who control legislatures may benefit considerably from government-protected cartels. Competition laws may threaten that wealth and so they may wield their political influence to prevent the introduction of competition laws. Or, a government may believe there are greater benefits from focusing on general competition policies such as reducing tariffs or opening up markets by reducing government-imposed entry barriers than introducing a competition law.[24] Domestic competition may be restricted as part of an export-oriented industrial policy. For example, local collaboration between competing firms may be allowed in order to develop sophisticated products for export in the longer term.

However, countries in Asia have increasingly introduced competition and IP laws. Sometimes they have been forced on them as part of a financial bail-out from the International Monetary Fund (IMF) or World Bank or introduced as a *quid pro quo or* for access to developed country markets (under Trade-Related Aspects of Intellectual Property Rights (TRIPS) or free-trade agreements). Sometimes this has been resented—particularly as sometimes the terms imposed have been more onerous than for similar recent assistance to developed countries in Europe.

VI. IP Laws, Competition Law and Economic Growth

How important are intellectual and competition laws to economic growth? This is a difficult issue to resolve both theoretically and empirically. Also, the evidence of the effect of both is mixed. A recent study by Falvey, Foster and Greenaway examined the relationship between IPRs and economic growth. They concluded:

> The relationship between the strength of a country's intellectual property rights (IPRs) regime and rate of growth is ambiguous from a theoretical standpoint, reflecting the variety of channels through which technology can be acquired and their differing importance at different stages of development. We investigate the impact of IPR protection on economic growth in a panel of 79 countries using threshold regression analysis. We show that whilst the effect of IPR protection on growth depends upon the level of development, it is positively and significantly related to growth for low- and high-income countries, but not for middle-income countries. This suggests that, although IPR protection encourages innovation in high-income countries, and technology flows to low-income countries, middle-income countries may have offsetting losses from reduced scope for imitation.[25]

For competition law, Crandall and Winston conclude that competition law enforcement track should be limited to 'the most egregious anti- competitive violations'.[26] On the other hand, in a study undertaken for the Directorate General for Economic and Financial Affairs of the

[24] Simeon Djankov, Rafael La Porta, Florencio Lopez de Silanes and Andrei Schleifer, 'The Regulation of Entry' (2002) 117(1) *Quarterly Journal of Economics* 1.

[25] Rod Falvey, Neil Foster and David Greenaway, 'Intellectual Property Rights and Economic Growth' (2006) 10(4) *Review of Development Economics* 700.

[26] Robert W Crandall and Clifford Winston, 'Does Antitrust Policy Improve Consumer Welfare? Assessing the Evidence' (2003) *J Econ Perspectives* 1, 3.

European Commission, Buccirossi, Ciari, Duso, Spagnolo and Vitale empirically investigated the impact of competition law on total factor productivity (TFP) growth for 22 industries in 12 OECD countries over the period 1995–2005. They found a positive impact. In particular they found the relationship was particularly strong with respect to the quality of enforcement. They note that 'The effect is strengthened by good legal systems, suggesting complementarities between competition policy and the efficiency of law enforcement institutions.'[27]

For East Asia, Brahmbhatt and Wu conclude that:

> Given the limited empirical evidence, it is probably unwise to draw firm conclusions for policy in East Asian or other developing countries. But a few observations can be hazarded. First, increased competition has many potential benefits … other than the impact on innovation, for example on firm efficiency and overall productivity growth (Ahn, 2002). Conclusions about the role of competition policy need to be based on an assessment of all of these effects. Second, the balance of empirical work cited finds a positive association between more competition between incumbent firms and innovation. While the study by Aghion, Bloom, Blundell, Griffith and Howitt (2005) reaches more qualified results, it too suggests that more competition is favorable for innovation when competition is low to start with—that is, when lack of competition is most likely to be of concern to policymakers.[28]

VII. IP and Competition Laws: The Experience in Asia

While there are differences in IP laws between countries, competition laws tend to be similar and cover anti-competitive agreements, abuse of dominance and anti-competitive mergers. However, in Asia there are differences between competition laws. For example, some competition laws include 'fair competition' provisions, consumer protection and, sometimes, IP provisions. While multi-lateral agreements exist on IP laws (eg the TRIPS Agreement), there is no equivalent for competition law.

Japan and South Korea have the longest experience in Asia with both laws. Recently, both have started to vigorously enforce their competition laws, including in situations involving possible conflicts with IPRs. However, most other countries in Asia have only recently introduced IP laws—due mainly to the TRIPS Agreement. However, enforcement is limited. Most Asian countries have now introduced competition laws—sometimes under external pressure. Recently, all countries in the Association of South East Asian Nations (ASEAN) committed to introducing competition laws by 2015, but it is unlikely that competition laws will be fully operational by then in Cambodia, Laos, Myanmar and perhaps the Philippines.

Countries concerned with overall welfare should develop policies towards competition and IP laws (and their intersection) that reflect their own particular circumstances. However, where they have been introduced as part of an international agreement or for financial aid, countries have generally copied the competition and IP laws of developed countries. It is arguable whether countries necessarily need either comprehensive competition laws or even

[27] Paolo Buccirossi, Lorenzo Ciari, Tomaso Duso, Giancarlo Spagnolo and Cristiana Vitale, 'Competition Policy and Productivity Growth: An Empirical Assessment' (Berlin, WZB Working Paper No SP II 2009 12, 2009, iii). Available at: http://economix.u-paris10.fr/pdf/seminaires/lien/Duso-v2.pdf.

[28] Brahmbhatt and Hu, 'Ideas and Innovation in East Asia' (2009) (n 1) 32.

the same laws for abuse of dominance or mergers, or, regulate the intersection between competition and IP laws in the same way.

Business reaction to IP and competition laws will determine their effect. Asian business is usually conducted on the basis of long-term relationships with little recourse to law to settle disputes. So there is considerable interaction between executive, legislature and judiciary. As Michael Backman, an Australian expert on Asian business practices, says:

> Those in business in Asia need to know about Asian politics because Asia's politicians and governments typically are highly intrusive in business. They need to know about family structures and behaviour in Asia because families run most Asian business. They need to know about imperfections in the law because the rule of law is weak in many parts of Asia. And they need to know about what interests the locals because nowhere more do people and personalities count in business than they do in Asia. Business in the West might be about companies and corporations. But in Asia it is about people and personalities. In the West the demarcation between the business and non-business worlds tend to be well defined. In Asia its not.[29]

Backman goes on to point out that Asian family firms exist, apart from providing income, to: provide honour for the family and ancestral founders, to keep the family together and to provide them with jobs. Corporate structures are complex and lack transparency mainly to make it harder for family members to leave the family company. So '[a]ppeals for reform based on efficiency, transparency and better corporate governance in general are likely to fall on deaf ears in such cases.'[30]

Importantly, Backman also concludes that for many Asian businesses economic return is not important—in fact some Asian family-run business groups are not profitable, nor expected to be. To the extent that this is so then there may be implications potentially for competition law. For example a dominant family business may, to preserve the business, be more likely to price below cost or to use competition law to prevent a good takeover offer.

Reflecting the close reflections between government and business in Asia, corruption is rife. The World Bank Worldwide Governance Indicator's project gives aggregate and individual governance indicators for 213 economies over the period 1996–2009. The World Bank ranks East Asian countries as follows in terms of control of corruption in 2009 (from best to worst): Singapore; Hong Kong; Brunei; South Korea; Macao; Malaysia; Thailand; Vietnam; China; Indonesia; Philippines; Laos; Cambodia and Myanmar. For rule of law in 2009 the rankings were almost the same: Singapore; Hong Kong; South Korea; Brunei; Macao; Malaysia; Thailand; China; Vietnam; Philippines; Indonesia; Laos; Cambodia and Myanmar.[31] Competition and IP law enforcement may reflect these vested-interest relationships rather than economic or other goals pursued in the national interest.

However, pressure from membership of international organisations like the World Trade Organisation (WTO) has increased pressures for Asia to rely less on informal relationships and more on economic governance through legal rules by lawyers and by judges (a process called 'juridification'). The importance of 'rule of law' to development has been

[29] Michael Backman, *The Asian Insider: An Introduction* (New York, Palgrave Macmillan, 2004) 3.

[30] Ibid 13.

[31] World Bank, *World Governance Indicators*. Available at http://info.worldbank.org/governance/wgi/index.asp.

extensively discussed (See Carothers,[32] and Gillespie for example.[33]) Two important areas discussed have been the importance of enforcing property rights (including IPRs) and reducing bureaucratic discretion in the economic system via increased transparency and accountability within legal constraints (and so predictability).

Whether IP or competition law is enforced depends on the strength of traditional relationships and political institutions. Political systems in Asia range from military dictatorships to those controlled by elites to a small number of democracies. The degree of economic sophistication also differs considerably.

VIII. Do Asian Countries Pursue Different IP and Competition Law Goals?

Some countries may not see the development of indigenous R&D as a national priority. Instead, reflecting past experience, attracting technology via foreign direct investment might be preferred because it yields more immediate economic benefits (and this is consistent with the evidence presented above). IP law protection is only necessary where the IP protected goods and services are sold. So a foreign investor or an innovator in the local country may not be concerned with local IPR protection if the goods are fully exported (or the secrets are mainly protected by *trade secrets*). However, where there is also a domestic market for those goods or services, then host country IPR protection is important to the foreign investment decision. However, R&D does not depend solely on the ability to appropriate the fruits of innovation. Technological opportunity, government R&D subsidies or tax policies are also important to location decisions.

Similarly, competition law should be seen in a broader policy context. Industrial policies that promote domestic monopolies to protect against potential foreign dominance of an important industry (important either because of strategic importance or because the wealth created to particular groups or families with political influence) will affect likely competition law enforcement. Competition law could be used to target dominant foreign companies—for example, correcting 'abuses' such as refusals to supply by forcing them to transfer technology

As mentioned previously, in the United States (and the approach is generally followed in Europe and Australia) it is generally accepted that IP and competition laws share the same goal. As the United States Department of Justice and FTC puts it:

> Over the past several decades, antitrust enforcers and the courts have come to recognize that intellectual property laws and antitrust laws share the same fundamental goals of enhancing consumer welfare and promoting innovation ... Consequently, antitrust and intellectual property are properly perceived as complementary bodies of law that work together to bring innovation to consumers: antitrust laws protect robust competition in the marketplace, while intellectual property laws protect the ability to earn a return on the investments necessary to innovate.

[32] T Carothers (ed), *Promoting the Rule of Law Abroad: In Search of Knowledge* (Washington, Carnegie Endow Int Peace, 2006).

[33] John S Gillespie, *Transplanting Commercial Law Reform: Developing a 'Rule of Law' in Vietnam* (Burlington, VT, Ashgate, 2006).

> Both spur competition among rivals to be the first to enter the marketplace with a desirable technology, product, or service.[34]

However, developing countries place priority on national development goals which may mean the two laws serve different goals and are enforced differently. If so, there will be conflict between them. For example, competition law may be used to force technology transfer to indigenous firms and IP standards set to benefit indigenous firms. The kinds of conflict that arise are likely to be different depending on the underlying policy objectives and stages of development in each country.

As economic interdependencies increase and technology becomes more important to economic growth, the relationship between IP and competition laws in Asian countries will become increasingly important. The interface between them has been considered mainly in the United States and European Union within competition law not IP law. Both IP and competition laws are national in scope. So the policy choices made and the recognition of IPRs and competition laws are country-specific, subject to international treaties.

IX. The Conference Background Papers

The conference was divided into two sessions. First, three presentations from experienced distinguished speakers from the United States provided the context for the conference. The United States has the most sophisticated jurisprudence dealing with the interface and has a strong emphasis on assessing the economic effect of alleged anti-competitive business conduct. William Kovacic, former Chairman of the US Federal Trade Commission, spoke about the interface from a regulator's perspective. Doug Ginsburg, former Chief Judge of the US Federal Court of Appeals for the DC Circuit and Eric Fraser, Executive Director of Research for the Committee on Capital Markets Regulation in the United States, looked at the importance of economics in US competition law jurisprudence. Gregory Sidak, the Chairman of Criterion Economics and David Teece, Director of the Centre for Global Strategy and Governance in the Haas Business School at the University of California, Berkeley, spoke on deficiencies in the way dynamic efficiency is treated in US competition law.

Kovacic, who has been involved in the introduction of many competition laws around the world, focused on the challenges facing competition law regulators. Reflecting the emphasis on consumer welfare in the United States, he stresses that ' … a competition agency should direct its enforcement resources toward those practices posing substantial dangers for consumers, the cessation of which promises the largest rewards for society'. However, this task requires considerable expertise and 'industry-specific knowledge because the role that IP rights play in competitive processes varies substantially from industry to industry'. For example:

> many biotechnology companies … conduct basic research to identify promising products then partner with a pharmaceutical company to test and commercialise the product. Patent protection can be essential to attract funds from capital markets, and facilitate licensing and joint venture arrangements.

[34] US Department of Justice and the Federal Trade Commission, *Antitrust Enforcement and Intellectual Property Rights: Promoting Innovation and Competition* (Washington, 2007) 1.

A regulator should not just be concerned with competition law enforcement but also with other policy tools such as research, advocacy and education.

Kovacic stresses the importance, from a policy perspective, of considering the IP–competition law interface from a broader perspective than just competition law. For example, in some circumstances it might be better to improve outcomes through the IP system. This was the approach taken in a report by the US FTC in 2003 that recommended judicial and legislative reforms and changes in the way the Patent and Trademark Office operated in the United States. Kovacic discusses a number of the recommendations, including the issuing of questionable patents, publication of patent applications, etc. The FTC Report not only identified how the patent system undermined the ability of competition to promote innovation, but also stressed the importance of economics in setting policy dealing with the intersection.

Ginsberg and Fraser discuss the role of economic analysis in competition law both in regulatory bodies and the courts. They suggest that other countries should look to US competition law experience 'both to avoid repeating its mistakes and to emulate its successes'. For developing countries in Asia who lack expertise in economics and in dealing with the interface this is a particularly important point. Business needs to be confident that its competition regulator is acting predictably. To ensure bipartisan political support, policy makers may need to be assured that competition law decisions made are in the best economic interests of the country. Crucial to whether competition law improves actual economic outcomes depends not only on whether the focus is on economic outcomes but also whether regulators and judges are proficient in economics.

Ginsberg and Fraser point out that, initially, US agencies subordinated economists to lawyers. This led to a situation where

> … the economists were routinely put in the position of trying to explain why a case the lawyers said they could win should not be brought for lack of economic merit. When economists and lawyers within an agency took diverging views on a particular issue—a common occurrence—the lawyers typically won.

This situation started to change in the mid 1960s. Reflecting the increased use of economics by the regulatory agencies, the US Supreme Court became less concerned 'with vague social and political goals' and so 'the scope of antitrust liability narrowed; the Court condemned only those transactions and practices that economic analysis showed to be inimical to consumer interests'. So the focus shifted away from protecting inefficient producers, especially small inefficient businesses. As a result, Supreme Court decisions became more predictable and the 'degree of agreement among the nine Justices steadily increased'. So, economics contributed '… to predictability and stability in the law, which are essential elements in a rule of law regime'. This is an extremely important lesson for new competition law regimes, particularly in complicated fact situations involving IPRs. To improve economic outcomes, regulators should understand the likely effects of any intervention. However, good economists skilled in industrial organisation are thin on the ground in Asia, even, at least initially, in developed economies like Singapore. Sound economic analysis is even more important when highly complex issues like the impact of competition law on innovation are involved.

Sidak and Teece are critical of current approaches to competition law. They argue that 'using static analysis to address antitrust issues in a dynamic economy is unlikely to improve consumer welfare and that a more dynamic analytical framework increases the likelihood of helping rather than hurting consumers.' They argue that there is little evidence that innovation is related to market concentration and so 'framing competition issues in terms of monopoly versus competition appears to have been unhelpful'. They say that innovation depends on rivalry but market concentration does not necessarily impact rivalry. So there is more to innovation than just competition and monopoly. As innovation is risky, costly and requires access to capital, then access to capital either externally of internally (from a multi-product income stream, for example) are also important. They point out that traditional static analysis focuses on detecting market power in product markets, but that dynamic analysis of competition stresses the process and less the outcomes.

Unlike the US Modernisation Commission, which concluded that dynamic competition could be accommodated within existing competition analytical frameworks, Sidak and Teece argue that the tools of static analysis should be used sparingly, if at all, because static analysis could lead to decisions that impede dynamic competition. In particular, they argue that the presumption that more competitors are always better is wrong—the goal is not just to lower price, but also to protect innovation. In markets where innovation is important, market conduct does not primarily depend on market structure but on internal organisational factors: standard operating procedures, investment strategies, and improvement routines. As a consequence, market concentration is likely to be an outcome of market selection, which in turn depends on the uneven exploitation of learning opportunities. Thus, they argue, concentration has little to do with market power.

Focussing on dynamic competition, they argue, eases the tension between IP and competition law. They are better harmonised if competition law focuses on innovation as its primary goal. So they conclude:

> Antitrust scholars must confront an inconvenient truth: innovation drives competition as much as competition drives innovation. Thus, antitrust analysis must recognize that advancing dynamic competition will benefit consumers most, certainly in the long run if not also in the short run.

X. Country Chapters

Next, papers on most countries in Asia were delivered. Each country paper was co-authored by both an economist and a lawyer. As the intersection is likely to be different in each country, authors were given the discretion to deal with the issues in the intersection as they thought fit. However, authors were asked to provide a paper that incorporated the following: some background country economics including: the amount spent on R&D, types of research, government policies towards innovation, industrial development policies etc; some background to the competition law and IP laws and how the intersection is dealt with (if at all) and how the intersection should be dealt with in that country.

Three major themes emerged from the chapters. First, that IP statutes should also deal with competition law concerns. Second, the increasing importance that compulsory licensing is playing in the intersection in Asia (particularly for pharmaceuticals). Third, the considerable institutional constraints countries in Asia face in implementing both IP and competition laws. Of particular importance is whether an IP authority should defer to the competition authority or vice versa.

A. Australia

Bob Baxt (a lawyer and former Chairman of Australia's competition regulator) and Henry Ergas (an economist who chaired an Australian Federal Government Inquiry into the intersection) look at the policy trade-off in Australia. They conclude that IPRs do not necessarily lessen competition but rather 'It is the ambiguities and inconsistencies between the two legislative regimes that limit innovation and distort competition.'

In the first part of the chapter, Ergas argues that the debate about the intersection has been about exemptions from IP statutes rather than seeing competition issues within IP statutes. He says that

> it seems reasonable to embody competition concerns in the IP statutes when those concerns form an intrinsic part of the eligibility tests for the right … however, the provisions themselves and the tests they embody ought to reflect the competition tests more widely in the economy.

So he believes there needs to be more consideration given to designing competition issues within IP statutes.

Baxt then looks at the treatment of joint ventures in Australian competition law. He points out that Australia 'does not adopt a rule of reason in dealing with anti-competitive agreements' which can impact on ventures involving IPRs. As cartel offences are now subject to criminal sanctions, he says 'that limiting the operation of an appropriate rule of reason in the context of joint venture activity, may unintentionally provide further impediments to joint ventures generally, and in particular the development of intellectual property rights though joint venture activities'. He goes on to point out that there is some 'indecision' in relation to the interaction but

> [o]ne consolation is that … the ACCC rarely faced problems surrounding the interface of competition policy and intellectual property. Perhaps that is because parties are not willing to risk pursuing arrangements that pose competition policy concerns with the ACCC.

B. China

Michael Jacobs, an academic lawyer from the United States and Xinzhu Zhang, an academic economist from China, look at the US and EU approaches to compulsory licensing. They conclude that they are different 'not because they ascribe to different schools of economic thought, but because the different political and cultural beliefs that inform and animate them lead inevitably to different answers'. Hence they are skeptical of international convergence 'around a single approach to complicated antitrust questions'. They then examine the experience in China. They conclude that the issue of compulsory licensing is so complicated that it is

> … too soon to recommend any specific approach … [h]owever, certain preliminary steps should be taken. First, the Chinese authorities regulating issues involving IP and competition law should issue specific regulations and guidelines to clarify the meaning and likely application of the legal rules guiding law enforcement. Second, the administration of law enforcement should be improved to facilitate the co-ordination of enforcement agencies, avoid conflicts between them, and ensure their independent decision making on compulsory licensing. Finally, efforts on capacity-building in law enforcement should be stressed.

C. India

Vinod Dhall, a lawyer and the single member (and acting Chairman) of the Competition Commission of India from its establishment in 2003 until 2008, and Augustine Peter, an economist and Economic Adviser in the Competition Commission of India (CCI) examine the intersection in India. Interestingly, they point out that both India's competition and IP laws contain provisions dealing with the intersection. For example,

> ... where during the course of a proceeding before a statutory authority (that would include an IP authority) a competition law issue is raised by any party, the authority may make a reference to the CCI for its opinion. The CCI shall give its opinion within 60 days. Thereafter, the statutory authority shall consider the opinion and give its finding recording the reasons for the same. The reference can also be made suo moto by the statutory authority. A mirror image of this provision exists in ... the Competition Act allowing the CCI to make reference to a statutory authority to obtain its opinion and consider it before passing orders in the case.

They note that India now is a more mature economic with 'greater capability within the economy for technological innovation and for operationalising innovations' and so the 'need for a balanced approach that will protect competition but not disincentivise innovation is quite clear'. As markets are likely to be more concentrated with high entry barriers, lower labour and other costs in developing countries, they advise that IP authorities be 'mindful of the competition perspective in the grant of patent and other IP rights lest these create monopolistic positions and deny access to essential knowledge and skills'. They do suggest that the Competition Commission of India should 'exercise forbearance and defer, as far as possible, to the powers given to the IP authorities under their respective jurisdictions'.

D. Indonesia

Cento Veljanovski, an economist with extensive experience in competition law in Europe and elsewhere, teamed up with Ningrim Sirait, a Professor of Law in Indonesia and one of the country's most prominent competition law commentators. They stress that:

> [i]n developing economies and especially those with low R&D investment and innovation such as Indonesia ... another layer of issues arise. There are basic questions regarding the legitimacy and coherence of both IPR and competition laws, the effectiveness and integrity of the enforcement agencies and courts, and the way the law is enforced. Further, since many developing economies are net importers of technology and goods and services protected by IPRs, there are distributional issues associated with the terms of trade and pricing of IPRs.

Article 50(b) of Indonesia's competition law exempts 'agreements related to intellectual property rights such as licence, patent, trade brand, copyrights, industrial product design, integrated electronic series, and trade secrets, and contracts related to franchises'. The Indonesian competition regulator (KPPU) issued guidelines on the intersection in 2010. They go on to point out that Indonesia's competition law has 'multiple objectives with very unclear guidance as to how these are to be balanced in any overall assessment'. To date there have been three competition law cases involving IPRs. The most recent case involved a breach of several competition law sections including price-fixing, a prohibition on cartels, restrictive agreements with foreign parties and abuse of dominant position. The parties argued that because the products involved were patented they were exempt from competition law. However, the KPPU ordered the companies involved 'to revoke certain supply agreements, cease further communications, and that Pfizer lower its price of Norvask by 65% and PT Dexia Medica its price of Tensivak by 60%'. They conclude that while Indonesia's IP and competition laws are increasing in significance, of crucial importance in the future is the way the art 50(b) exemption is applied.

E. Japan

Steve Harris, a lawyer from the United States with considerable international competition law experience and Hiroshi Osahi, an academic economist, examine the interface in Japan. First, they note that there is a general exemption within Japan's competition law for IP, ie art 21 says, 'The provisions of this Law shall not apply to such acts recognizable as the exercise of rights under the Copyright Law, the Patent Law, the Utility Model Law, the Design Law or the Trademark Law.'

However, they point out that the 'exercise of an IP right is not automatically exempted from the AMA'. In fact, the Japan Fair Trade Commission (JFTC) has issued several guidelines on the extent to which the The Act on Prohibition of Private Monopolization and Maintenance of Fair Trade (AMA) may be applied to IP-related activities—the most recent and most comprehensive in 2007.

They note that:

> The IP Guidelines do not contain several of the criteria that the European Union has imposed to limit the applicability of antitrust law in refusals to grant access to essential facilities, including IP licenses, which are intended to limit interference with independent decisions on which counterparties to deal with to only 'extraordinary' cases.

However, they conclude that JFTC decisions 'are consistent with the IP Guidelines, but are too sparse in analysis and too few in number to provide much needed detailed guidance on JFTC enforcement policy in this complex area.'

F. Singapore

Ashish Lall, an academic economist and Daryl Lim, an academic lawyer and writer on Singapore, note that Singapore is in the process of a government-sponsored transition towards an innovation-driven economy. It has a strong electronics sector (particularly in semiconductors) and is promoting new sectors in biotechnology, clean technology, nanotechnology and interactive digital media. In less than 20 years, Singapore has moved from a jurisdiction with little IP protection to a very strong IP protection regime. Recently, it also introduced a competition law based on that of the United Kingdom/European Union. The Competition Commission of Singapore has issued guidelines on the intersection based largely on those of the Office of Fair Trading in the United Kingdom. They conclude that:

> Singapore will benefit from the experience elsewhere but must decide how best to address the Interface, either from within the IP system or within competition law, or a cocktail of both. But 'competition law is an area of where law in which there is little scope for absolute concepts or

sharp edges'[35] and the actual contours of the law will not be known until Singapore courts have had opportunity to decide on cases dealing with the Interface.

G. South Korea

Sang-Seung Yi, an academic economist and Seongwook Heo, an academic lawyer, evaluate the Korean Fair Trade Commission's (KFTC) merger decisions in South Korea over the last 30 years through the lens of dynamic competition. South Korea's IP law and competition laws are mature. While they say that the KFTC over 30 years has had remarkable success in cartel enforcement and competition advocacy, their approach to mergers is appropriate only where domestic consumers are involved. They suggest an alternative model should be used in reviewing mergers involving more than one country. They argue the KFTC should:

> … consider the total national social welfare standard over *all* geographical markets combined (which considers gains in the foreign markets as legitimate efficiencies to be weighed against anti-competitive losses in the domestic market) as the proper welfare standard in evaluating mergers.

Attempts to 'restore competition to the pre-merger level in the *domestic* market through structural remedies runs the risk of jeopardizing the entire merger, when the synergy effects are linked between the domestic and foreign market operations'. Instead, they argue that '*actual* foreign competition in foreign markets serves as a stimulant for dominant domestic firms (which compete in foreign markets) to undertake innovative activities that ultimately benefits domestic consumers (although they suffer short-term losses at any point of time).'

H. Thailand

McEwin, an academic economist/lawyer and Thanitcul, an academic lawyer (and a former Member of Thailand's Trade Competition Commission (TCC)), look at the intersection via the compulsory licensing of pharmaceuticals in Thailand. Driving policy differences in health are differing perceptions of the role of IPRs. Health groups argue a 'privilege' view which sees IPRs not as property rights but granted by government to promote public policy goals like health as well as innovation. At the opposite end are those who believe that IPRs are *uber-rights* or rights that are stronger than other property rights—who see compulsory licensing as theft.

Compulsory licensing is used by both developed and developing countries. Thailand has granted compulsory licenses for medicines on the basis of public use 'to allow universal access to essential medicines'. The reaction of one multinational pharmaceutical company, Abbott Laboratories, whose drugs were subject to compulsory licensing, was to refuse to continue to register new drugs in Thailand. This *cross-border refusal to supply* was challenged on competition law grounds in Thailand. Elsewhere, a domestic refusal to supply would have been resolved in two possible ways—by examining whether the refusal to supply was a misuse of patent law or whether the refusal by a dominant firm breached competition law. However, there are differences in the way refusals to supply are treated in the

[35] *Racecourse Association v OFT* [2005] CAT 26, Case Nos 1035/1/1/04 at [167] ('[C]ompetition law is not an area of law in which there is much scope for absolute concepts or sharp edges'.).

United States and European Union. The United States is reluctant to intervene in refusal cases (including in cases involving IPRs) because of the possible impact on innovation). This reflects the fact that the United States is the most innovative nation. On the other hand, in Europe, there is more of a concern with whether the refusal distorts markets and harms competitors, perhaps reflecting a lesser concern with innovation.

In 2007, the TCC found the withdrawal of the drug registrations did not breach the Thai Competition Act because Abbott was not a dominant business operator. In 2008, the new Minister of Public Health reviewed the compulsory licenses and recommended that they remain in place but that the licenses could be revoked by the Minister of Commerce, the Minister responsible for competition law. Whether Thailand's compulsory licensing decision chilled R&D in Thailand is difficult to determine. The intervention was mainly to reduce drug prices in Thailand (although some argue it was to promote a generic drug industry in Thailand). The impact on other industries in terms of reduced foreign direct investment or reduced access to export markets is yet to be seen.

I. Vietnam

Doan Tu Tich Phuoc and Bui Nguyen Anh Tuan, both staff members of the Vietnam Competition Agency, look at the intersection in Vietnam. They point out that 'innovation is not currently regarded as part of Vietnam's core development policy'. For competition law they note that while

> the main purpose of the law was to create an environment of fair competition and to promote a competitive market structure ... some people believe that one of the main reasons ... was the government's concern about threats from larger multinational companies that could enter the domestic market ... on the basis that in many countries, competition law had proved itself as an effective tool in deterring market power and protecting local SMEs as well as consumers.

Regulations governing compulsory licenses were first introduced into the Civil Code in 1995 and developed further within the Intellectual Property Law 2005 which allowed for compulsory licensing to deal with anti-competitive practices. While there is regulation of licensing contracts (including provisions that prevent IP owners from misusing or abusing their IP rights), there are no specific provisions dealing with horizontal agreements like patent pools or cross licensing. As a result, anti-competitive horizontal agreements involving IPRs can be exempt if reduced costs and the promotion of technological advances enhance the competitiveness of small and medium sized enterprises (SMEs), etc.

Although compulsory licensing is available it has not been used (except for Tamiflu in 2005, where the patent owner was not able to supply Vietnam and essentially agreed to the licence, but no action was necessary as the bird flu epidemic was soon over). Different government agencies handle compulsory licensing in their areas of responsibility. The authors say that 'inadequacies in the laws regarding the intersection have led to inadequate enforcement where no compulsory licensing cases have been reported in 15 years for inventions and plant varieties. Meanwhile, other IPRs such as trademarks may be abused to deter competition'. They conclude that despite 25 years since the 'economic renovation', Vietnam is still a developing country dependent on agricultural or labour-intensive exports, with negligible R&D.

2

A Regulator's Perspective on Getting the Balance Right

WILLIAM E KOVACIC[1]

I. Introduction

Discussions among antitrust specialists about the relationship between competition policy and intellectual property (IP) policy focus predominantly on the appropriate design and application of antitrust rules to the accumulation and exercise of IP rights.[2] For that reason, the term 'antitrust' is typically equated with the enforcement of prohibitions against anti-competitive business practices.[3] The traditional focus of most competition agencies, including the Federal Trade Commission (FTC), is to bring cases against such practices.[4] Prosecuting antitrust cases is a vital element of a competition policy system. In devising a law enforcement strategy, a competition agency should direct its enforcement resources toward those practices which pose substantial dangers for consumers, the cessation of which promises the largest rewards for society.[5] Identifying such practices often requires extensive study and industry-specific knowledge, because the role that IP rights play in competitive processes varies substantially from industry to industry.[6]

Although important, prosecuting antitrust cases is not the only vital element of a competition policy system. For any specific issue, antitrust enforcement might not always be the sole or even best instrument to use.[7] Properly understood, sound competition policy

[1] The views stated here are the author's alone. I am grateful to Suzanne Michel and to the participants in the NUS Symposium for many useful comments and suggestions.

[2] See, eg, ABA Section of Antitrust Law, Antitrust Law Developments 6th edn (2007) 1077–1168.

[3] See William E Kovacic, *Institutional Foundations for Economic Legal Reform in Transition Economies: The Case of Competition Policy and Antitrust Enforcement* (2001) 77 *Chicago Kent Law Review* 265, 281 (describing the tendency in some commentary to equate competition law and policy with the prosecution of statutes that forbid various forms of business conduct).

[4] See William E Kovacic, *The Modern Evolution of US Competition Policy Enforcement Norms* (2003) 71 *Antitrust Law Journal* 377, 407–10 (discussing and criticising the case-centric conception of competition policy).

[5] See Timothy J Muris, *More Than Law Enforcement: The FTC's Many Tools—A Conversation with Tim Muris and Bob Pitofsky* (2005) 72 *Antitrust Law Journal* 773, 777 (discussing appropriate priorities for FTC antitrust law enforcement).

[6] See William E Kovacic and Andreas P Reindl, *An Interdisciplinary Approach to Improving Competition Policy and Intellectual Property Policy* (2005) 28 *Fordham International Law Journal* 1062, 1089–90 (discussing the importance to competition agencies of pursuing a research and analysis agenda concerning IP issues).

[7] For example, improving the rigor of the mechanism by which IP rights such as patents are granted may be a superior way to correct competition problems, rather than using lawsuits premised on theories of monopolisation or attempted monopolisation in order to mandate access to what are arguably improvidently granted IP

encompasses a larger collection of policy tools, such as research, advocacy and education.[8] One of the most important contributions of a competition policy system is to serve as an advocate within the Government and the country at large for reliance on pro-competition policies.[9] This is true, for instance, when the root of an observed competition policy problem resides in other government regulatory programmes that distort the competitive process.[10] In that case, the competition agency's aim should be to identify first-best solutions, which may involve reforms to the regulatory regimes. These considerations motivated the FTC's 2003 report on the patent system and its recommendations for judicial and legislative reforms and adjustments to the operations of the United States Patent and Trademark Office (USPTO).[11]

The FTC undertook its study of the patent system at a time when the interdependency of competition policy and intellectual property regimes was becoming more apparent due to the growth and increasing commercial significance of high technology and other IP-intensive industries.[12] There is broad agreement that the two systems are complementary in their efforts to promote innovation and consumer welfare.[13] Most observers also agree that the two systems use different methods to promote these goals and are not always equally successful in doing so.[14] Better coordination is needed to ensure that both can more effectively encourage innovation and competition.

IP regimes (and in particular the patent system) and competition law and policy intersect—and therefore require coordination—in at least two areas. On the one hand, competition enforcement affects how patent owners can use their rights. Poorly functioning antitrust law at the patent interface can harm IP driven innovation. The FTC and the Department of Justice (DOJ) Antitrust Division released a joint report in April 2007

rights. See ibid; Kovacic and Reindl, *Interdisciplinary Approach* (2005) 1066–67 (arguing that improvements in the rights-granting process is a superior, first-best solution to problems sometimes addressed through the litigation of antitrust monopolisation cases).

[8] See William E Kovacic, 'The Federal Trade Commission at 100: Into Our 2d Century' 110–43 (January 2009) (discussing application of varied tools to solve competition policy problems); William E Kovacic, *Measuring What Matters: The Federal Trade Commission and Investments in Competition Policy Research and Development* (2005) 72 *Antitrust Law Journal* 861 (discussing the importance of policy instruments other than litigation).

[9] See James C Cooper et al, *Theory and Practice of Competition Advocacy at the FTC* (2005) 72 *Antitrust Law Journal* 1091 (2005) (discussing accomplishments of the FTC's competition advocacy programme).

[10] See Kovacic and Reindl (n 5) 103, at 1064–66 (discussing how imperfections in the system for granting IP rights can distort competition).

[11] Federal Trade Commission (FTC), 'To Promote Innovation: The Proper Balance of Competition and Patent Law and Policy' (Report) (2003). Available at www.ftc.gov/os/2003/10/innovationrpt.pdf (hereinafter FTC IP Report (2003)).

[12] Proceedings conducted by the FTC in the mid-1990s identified this interdependency as a matter of increasing commercial significance. See Federal Trade Commission, Anticipating the 21st Century: Competition and Consumer Protection Policy in the New High-Tech Global Marketplace, Vol I (May 1996).

[13] See *Atari Games Corp v Nintendo of Am., Inc* 897 F.2d 1572, 1576 (Fed Cir 1990) (stating that even though 'the aims and objectives of patent and antitrust laws may seem, at first glance, wholly at odds ... the two bodies of law are actually complementary, as both are aimed at encouraging innovation, industry and competition'.) (citing *Loctite Corp v Ultraseal Ltd* 781 F.2d 861, 876–77 (Fed Cir 1985)).

[14] See, eg, Michael A Carrier, *Resolving the Patent-Antitrust Paradox Through Tripartite Innovation* (2003) 56 *Vanderbilt Law Review* 1047, 1049–53 (discussing the different approaches to innovation taken by patent and antitrust law); Timothy J Muris, 'Remarks Before the American Bar Association Antitrust Section Fall Forum 2' (November 15, 2001) (transcript available at www.ftc.gov/speeches/muris/intellectual.htm (discussing limitations of the antitrust and IP regimes as policy tools)).

examining these issues.[15] On the other hand, systemic problems in the rights-granting process can also distort competition and chill innovation. This latter issue is the subject of the FTC report on the patent system on which I will focus in this article.

II. The Need to Balance Patent and Competition Policy

Patents stimulate innovation by providing incentives to develop and commercialise inventions. Without patent protection, innovators that produce IP may not be able to appropriate the full benefits of their innovation when competitors are able to 'free ride' on the innovator's efforts. In the pharmaceutical industry, for instance, patents enable companies to cover their fixed costs and regain the high levels of capital they invest in research and development (R&D).[16] Following the initial innovation, patent rights often allow inventors to attract funding and develop relationships needed to commercialise the invention. Many biotechnology companies, for example, conduct basic research to identify promising products and then partner with a pharmaceutical company to test and commercialise the product.[17] Patent protection can be essential to attract funds from capital markets, and facilitate licensing and joint venture relationships.[18] Moreover, the public disclosure of scientific and technical information made through a patent can stimulate further scientific progress.[19]

Competition also plays an important role in stimulating innovation and spurs invention of new products and more efficient processes. Competition drives firms to identify consumers' unmet needs and develop new products or services to satisfy them. In some industries, firms race to innovate in hope of exploiting first-mover advantages. Companies strive to invent lower cost manufacturing processes, thereby increasing their profits and enhancing their ability to compete.[20] Representatives of computer hardware and software companies reported that competition, more than patent protection, drives innovation in their industries.[21]

To optimally foster innovation, patent and competition policy must work together. Errors or systematic biases in how one policy's rules are interpreted and applied disrupt the other policy's effectiveness. It is important to note that the FTC Report confirms that patents play an important role in promoting innovation.[22] Nonetheless, it also raises concerns about the ability of those patents of questionable quality—those that are invalid or overly broad—to distort competition and harm innovation in several ways.

[15] US Department of Justice and Federal Trade Commission 'Antitrust Enforcement and Intellectual Property Rights: Promoting Innovation and Competition' (Report) (2007), available at www.ftc.gov/reports/innovation/P040101PromotingInnovationandCompetitionrpt0704.pdf.

[16] FTC IP Report (2003) ch 3, 11–12.

[17] Ibid ch 3, 17.

[18] Ibid ch 3, 15, 17–18.

[19] Ibid ch 2, 3–7.

[20] Ibid ch 2, 9–12.

[21] Ibid ch 3, 31–32, 46.

[22] Ibid Executive Summary 3.

First, they may slow follow-on innovation by discouraging firms from conducting R&D in areas that the patent improperly covers.[23] When firms fear that they will infringe a questionable patent, the substantial costs and risks of litigation may persuade them to direct their resources into other areas. For example, biotechnology firms reported that they avoid infringing questionable patents and therefore will refrain from entering or continuing with a particular field of research that such patents appear to cover.[24] Such conditions deter market entry and follow-on innovation by competitors and increase the potential for the holder of a questionable patent to suppress competition.

Second, patents that should not have been granted raise costs when they are challenged in litigation.[25] If a competitor chooses to pursue R&D in the area covered by the patent without a license, it risks expensive and time-consuming litigation with the patent holder that wastes resources.[26] Questionable patents may also raise costs by inducing unnecessary licensing. If a competitor chooses to negotiate a license and pay royalties to avoid costly and unpredictable litigation, the costs of follow-on innovation and commercial development increase due to the unjustified royalties and transaction costs.[27] Questionable patents particularly contribute to increased licensing costs in industries with 'patent thickets'.[28]

Finally, firms facing patent thickets may spend resources obtaining 'defensive patents', not to protect their own innovation from use by others, but to have 'bargaining chips' to obtain access to others' patents through a cross-license, or to counter allegations of infringement. Some hearing participants believed that companies spend too many resources on creating and filing these defensive patents, instead of focusing on developing new technologies.[29] This is especially true when defensive patenting is conducted in response to, or results in, questionable patents.[30]

[23] Carl Shapiro, 'Navigating the Patent Thicket: Cross Licenses, Patent Pools, and Standard-Setting' in Adam B Jaffe, Josh Lerner and Scott Stern (eds), *Innovation Policy and the Economy* (Cambridge, MA, NBER Books, MIT Press, 2001) 119, 126.

[24] FTC IP Report (2003) ch 3, 21–22.

[25] Ibid ch 3, 6–41. 'Large and small companies are increasingly being subjected to litigation (or its threat) on the basis of questionable patents.' *United States Patent and Trademark Office Fee Modernization Act of 2003: Hearing Before the Subcomm. on Courts, the Internet, and Intellectual Property of the House Comm. on the Judiciary*, 108th Cong 2 (2003) (Statement of Michael K Kirk, Executive Director, American Intellectual Property Law Association), available at www.aipla.org/Content/ContentGroups/Legislative_Action/108th_Congress1/Testimony2/Testimony_on_Fee_Legislation.htm.

[26] If litigation does take place, it typically costs millions of dollars and takes years to resolve. The median costs to each party of proceeding through a patent infringement suit to a trial verdict are at least $500,000 when the stakes are relatively modest. When more than $25 million is at risk in a patent suit, the median litigation costs for the plaintiff and the defendant average $4 million each, and in the highest stakes patent suit, costs can exceed this amount by more than fivefold. The National Academies Press, 'A Patent System for the 21st Century' (National Academies' Board on Science, Technology and Economic Policy, 2004) 68, available at www.nap.edu/html/patentsystem [hereinafter, NAS Report (2004)]; see also FTC IP Report (2003) ch 2, 7–8; ch 3, 20–26, 33–41, 50–55; ch 5, 2–4.

[27] Mark A Lemley, 'Rational Ignorance at the Patent Office' (2001) 95 *Northwestern University Law Review* 1495, 1517 (noting that 'patent owners might try to game the system by seeking to license even clearly bad patents for royalty payments small enough that licensees decide that it is not worth going to court'). See Shapiro, 'Navigating the Patent Thicket' (2001) (n 23) 125; FTC IP Report (2003) ch 2, 7–8; ch 3, 20–26, 33–41, 50–55; ch 5, 2–4.

[28] A 'patent thicket' is a 'dense web of overlapping intellectual property rights that a company must hack its way through in order to actually commercialize new technology'. See Shapiro (n 23) 120.

[29] FTC IP Report (2003) Executive Summary 6–7, citing Greenhall 2/27, 377, 420.

[30] Ibid ch 3, 34–40, 52–53.

III. Recommendations of the FTC IP Report

The FTC Report went beyond identifying ways in which flaws in the patent system undermine the ability of competition to promote innovation. It also recommended changes to help restore the balance of patent and competition policy. The courts have implemented some of these changes. Features of other recommendations have been incorporated into the pending patent reform legislation and rules changes proposed by the USPTO.

Just as significant as the Report's specific recommendations, however, is its central theme on the need for patent policy to consider the value of competition in promoting innovation. Policymakers are increasingly incorporating that theme into the public debate on the appropriate scope of patent rights, as can be seen in a string of Supreme Court cases decided since the report's release.

A. Recommendations to Minimise Issuance of Questionable Patents

The goal of a first group of recommendations was to minimise the issuance of questionable patents. In particular, the Report recommended a tightening of the legal standards used to judge when a patent is obvious. The Supreme Court's decision in *KSR Int'l Co v Teleflex Inc*,[31] directly addressed this issue.

As the Supreme Court explained in a seminal case, *Graham v John Deere Co*,[32] the goal of the statutory non-obviousness requirement is to provide a 'means of weeding out those inventions which would not be disclosed or devised but for the inducement of a patent', and allow a patent only on those.[33] As it serves a crucial role as the primary gatekeeper preventing the issuance of trivial patents having negative effects on competition and innovation, it is essential that the obviousness standard is not compromised.

The FTC Report identified the Federal Circuit's 'teaching, suggestion, or motivation test' as a doctrine that compromised the obviousness standard when it required concrete suggestions to make a patented invention beyond those actually needed by a person with ordinary skill in the art. For that reason, the Report recommended that the obviousness analysis should better take into account the creativity and problem-solving skills of that person of ordinary skill, including the ability to combine and modify the prior art.[34]

In *KSR*, the Supreme Court rejected the 'teaching, suggestion or motivation test', calling it a 'rigid rule that limits the obviousness inquiry' by overemphasising the importance of published articles, but failing to take account of the common sense and creativity of patent law's 'person of ordinary skill in the art'.[35] Affirming the role of the marketplace in promoting innovation, the Court stated that '[i]n many fields it may be that there is little discussion of obvious techniques or combinations, and it often may be the case that market demand, rather than scientific literature, will drive design trends'.[36] Applying a common sense approach, the Court explained that if a person of ordinary skill in the art pursues a

[31] *KSR Int'l Co v Teleflex Inc* 127 S Ct 1727 (US 2007). (Staff editors will change this to US Reporter.)

[32] *Graham v John Deere Co* 383 US 1 (1966).

[33] Ibid 11.

[34] FTC IP Report (2003) Executive Summary 11–12; ch 4, 15.

[35] *KSR* 127 S Ct 1741–43.

[36] Ibid 1741.

'predictable solution' and attains 'anticipated success', the result is likely not the product of 'innovation but of ordinary skill and common sense'.[37]

In reaching this holding, the Court discussed the detrimental effects of obvious patents on innovation and the need to maintain the proper balance of patent and competition policy. An obvious patent withdraws from the public what is already known and diminishes the resources available to support innovation.[38] The Court warned that 'the results of ordinary innovation are not the subject of exclusive rights under the patent laws. Were it otherwise patents might stifle, rather than promote, the "progress of useful arts" contemplated in our Constitution.'[39]

Two other FTC recommendations that sought to minimise the issuance of questionable patents focused on the USPTO. The first was to provide adequate funding for the USPTO.[40] This recommendation, more than any other, received universal support from the patent community. The second recommendation suggested modifying USPTO rules to help get additional and better information to patent examiners.[41] The basis for the recommendation recognised the time constraints under which patent examiners must work and the fact that patent applicants often have more knowledge of the technology and prior art than examiners do. Finding more efficient procedures for sharing that information with examiners would improve patent quality, to the benefit of everyone.

B. Recommendations Supporting the Elimination of Questionable Patents

A second group of recommendations sought to bolster a challenger's ability to eliminate questionable patents after they issue.[42] A key recommendation in this category suggested legislation to create a new administrative procedure for post-grant review and opposition to patents.[43]

The Report argued that the existing means for challenging questionable patents were inadequate. Patent prosecution is *ex parte*, involving only the USPTO and the patent applicant, even though third parties in the same field as a patent applicant may have the best information and expertise with which to assist in the evaluation of a patent application. To enhance third-party involvement, Congress established limited *inter partes* reexamination procedures that allow third parties to participate in patent reexaminations.[44] Recent amendments have improved those procedures, but they still contain important restrictions

[37] Ibid 1742.

[38] Ibid 1739.

[39] Ibid 1746.

[40] FTC IP Report (2003) Executive Summary 12.

[41] Ibid 13.

[42] One recommendation falling in this category proposed legislation specifying that validity challenges be decided based on a 'preponderance of the evidence' rather than 'clear and convincing evidence'. That controversial proposal has not been considered in legislation but challengers have raised it in court. See Petition for Writ of Certiorari in *Microsoft Corp v z4 Technologies, Inc* 507 F.3d 1340 (Fed Cir 2007), cert. dismissed, 128 S Ct 2107 (No 07-1243). See also *KSR* 127 S Ct 1745 (finding it 'appropriate to note' that the rationale underlying the Federal Circuit's 'clear and convincing "standard" that the USPTO, in its expertise, has approved the claim-seems much diminished' when a defence of invalidity rests on evidence that the USPTO never considered).

[43] FTC IP Report (2003) Executive Summary 7.

[44] Optional *Inter Partes* Reexamination Procedure Act of 1999, Subtitle F (Optional *Inter Partes* Reexamination Procedures) of Tit IV (American Inventors Protection Act of 1999), §§ 4601–08 of Intellectual Property and Communications Omnibus Reform Act of 1999, Pub L No 106–13, Division B, Appendix I (S 1948), 106th Cong,

and disincentives for their use.[45] Once a questionable patent has issued, the most effective way to challenge it is through litigation, but that path is extremely costly and lengthy. It is not an option unless the patent owner has asserted the patent against the potential challenger.

For these reasons, the FTC Report recommended institution of a meaningful post-grant review and opposition procedure and identified several characteristics that might contribute to its success. To be meaningful, post-grant review should be allowed to address important patentability issues, including novelty, non-obviousness, written description, enablement, and utility. An administrative patent judge should preside over the proceeding, which should allow cross-examination and carefully circumscribed discovery. Proceedings should be subject to a time limit and the use of appropriate sanctions authority. Patent applicants must be protected against undue delay in requesting post-grant review and against harassment through multiple petitions for review. The review petitioner should be required to make a suitable threshold showing. Finally, settlement agreements resolving post-grant proceedings should be filed with the USPTO and, upon request, made available to other government agencies.[46]

The recommendation to institute a post-grant review process received broad support throughout the patent community, even though there is some disagreement on the details on how the process should work.[47] Patent reform legislation pending in both the House and the Senate contains provisions establishing post-grant review.[48]

Although not related to a specific FTC recommendation, a second development is worth mentioning because it demonstrates the Supreme Court's awareness of the need to consider competition principles in forming patent policy. Just as the Court's *KSR* decision emphasised the importance of avoiding the issuance of questionable patents, the Court's decision in *MedImmune v Genetech*[49] recognised the harm caused by those that do issue and the need to eliminate them. *MedImmune* allowed a patent licensee to challenge a patent's validity through a declaratory judgment action because the harm of paying royalties on an invalid patent would generate a 'substantial controversy between parties having adverse legal interests', and so would satisfy the Constitutional standing requirement.[50] As the Court explained in *Lear v Adkins*,[51] an earlier case which allowed a licensee to challenge patent validity, allowing such challenges to questionable patents vindicates 'the important public interest in permitting full and free competition in the use of ideas which are in reality a part of the public domain'.

1st Sess, 113 Stat 1501A–521, 1501A–567 through 1501A–572 (29 November 1999), *inter alia*, adding 35 USC ch 31, §§ 311–18.

45 FTC IP Report (2003) ch 5, 15–17.

46 Ibid ch 5, 17–24.

47 See United States Patent and Trademark Office 21st Century Strategic Plan, *Post-Grant Review of Patent Claims* (USPTO, April 2, 2003), available at www.uspto.gov/web/offices/com/strat21/action/sr2.htm; AIPLA Response to the October 2003 Federal Trade Commission Report (AIPLA Response to FTC IP Report), available at www.aipla.org/Content/ContentGroups/Issues_and_Advocacy/Comments2/Patent_and_Trademark_Office/2004/ResponseToFTC.pdf; NAS Report (2004) 95–103.

48 Patent Reform Act, HR 1908, 110th Cong (2007); S. 1145, 110th Cong (2007).

49 *MedImmune v Genetech* 549 US 118, 127 S Ct 764 (2007).

50 Ibid 771 (*quoting Maryland Casualty Co v Pacific Coal & Oil Co* 312 US 270, 273 (1941)).

51 *Lear v Adkins* 395 US 653, 670 (1969).

C. Recommendations Supporting the Disclosure Function of Patents

A third group of recommendations sought to promote the disclosure, teaching and notice functions of patents. Providing reliable and early notice of the subject matter a patent covers enhances business certainty for competitors who wish to avoid infringement. The Report recommended that Congress enact legislation to require publication of all patent applications 18 months after filing.[52] Both the House and Senate versions of patent reform legislation contain such a provision.[53]

To promote the disclosure function of patents, the FTC Report also recommended that Congress establish two alternative predicates for finding willful infringement. The patentee must show either actual written notice of infringement from the patentee sufficient to support declaratory judgment jurisdiction, or deliberate copying of the patentee's invention. This recommendation was necessary because some firms complained that they did not read their competitors' patents out of concern for treble damage liability.[54] Failure to read competitors' patents can harm innovation and competition by undermining one of the primary benefits of the patent system—the public disclosure of new inventions. This encourages wasteful duplication of effort, delays follow-on innovation that could derive from patent disclosures, and discourages the development of competition. Failure to read competitors' patents also thwarts rational and efficient business planning and can jeopardise plans for a non-infringing business or research strategy. The FTC's recommendation would permit firms to read patents for their disclosure value and to survey the patent landscape to assess potential infringement issues, yet retain a viable willfulness doctrine that protects both wronged patentees and competition.[55] Both the House and Senate versions of patent reform legislation contain such a provision.[56]

In recent years, the Federal Circuit has raised the threshold for willful patent infringement. In *In re Seagate Technologies, Inc*, the Court abandoned the nearly 25-year-old 'duty of due care' standard and held that proof of willful infringement requires 'at least a showing of objective recklessness'.[57] To establish entitlement to treble damages, a patentee must show that the accused infringer knew or should have known of an objectively high likelihood that its actions constituted infringement of a valid patent. This case significantly decreases the likelihood that any firm will be found liable for willful infringement. Whether legislation is still needed will depend on whether firms are now sufficiently comfortable that they will read patents for their disclosure value.

Another recommendation of the FTC Report that related to the disclosure function of patents and rational business planning addressed continuation applications. By filing a continuation application, a patent applicant literally 'continues' the prosecution of an application after an examiner either finally rejects or allows a patent application. Patent applicants frequently use continuation applications to pursue additional patents having claims of different scope than those previously allowed or rejected by the examiner. However, some applicants have used multiple continuations as a strategy to continue

[52] FTC IP Report (2003) Executive Summary 15.
[53] HR 1908; S 1145.
[54] FTC IP Report (2003) Executive Summary 16–17.
[55] Ibid ch 5, 38–41.
[56] HR 1908; S 1145.
[57] *In re Seagate Technologies, Inc* 497 F.3d 1360, 1371 (Fed Cir 2007).

patent prosecution so that they can later add claims based on new products discovered in the marketplace. The FTC proposed legislation to establishing prior user rights to protect the manufacturer of the new product in that situation.[58]

D. Recommendation to Consider Economics in Setting Policy

The final recommendation encouraged consideration of competition and economics in shaping patent policy. Many of the changes and proposed changes to the patent system that I have mentioned do exactly that. Although it does not relate to a more specific FTC recommendation, another important example of an analysis that considers economics stems from the Supreme Court's decision in *eBay v MercExchange*.[59] In *eBay*, as in *KSR* and *MedImmune*, the Court again demonstrated a concern for the balance between patents and competition as the best means to promote innovation.

In *eBay*, the Court rejected the prevailing rule that courts must issue permanent injunctions against patent infringement except in exceptional circumstances. The Court held instead that 'familiar principles of equity apply' in patent cases.[60] Those principles require a patent owner seeking a permanent injunction to satisfy the traditional four-factor equitable test that examines irreparable injury, the adequacy of money damages, the balance of hardships, and the public interest.[61]

The content and flexibility of this test plays directly to the central theme of the FTC Report—the need to restore balance between competition and patent policy. The test allows consideration of the role of exclusivity and competition in promoting innovation, and the need to appropriately compensate patentees in order to provide incentives to innovate without unduly burdening competition. Analysing these issues requires understanding of the place of patents in the economic landscape faced by the parties, a topic that the FTC Report examines in depth.

In many cases, the patent owner's right to maintain control over the invention by obtaining an injunction is critical to its ability to appropriate the invention's value. A patent owner's goal may be to exclusively commercialise its own invention, as is often the case in the pharmaceutical industry.[62] Alternatively, a patent owner's goal may be to license its patent to another firm exclusively so that the licensee will have sufficient incentives to develop and commercialise the invention, as is more common in the biotechnology industry.[63]

In other cases, however, the threat of an automatic, permanent injunction can cause 'hold-up'. 'Hold-up' typically arises when a patentee asserts its patent after the accused infringer has sunk substantial costs into design, development, and commercialisation without knowledge of the patent. The threat of an automatic injunction following expensive patent litigation increases the patentee's leverage in the licensing negotiations beyond the value of the patent's inventive contribution and leads to higher royalties. This dynamic

58 FTC IP Report (2003) Executive Summary 16.
59 *eBay Inc v MercExchange LLC* 547 US 388 (2006).
60 Ibid 390–91.
61 Ibid 391.
62 FTC IP Report (2003) ch 3, 11–12.
63 Ibid ch 3, 15, 17–18.

can be especially problematic when the patented invention is only a small component of the infringing product.[64] Justice Kennedy's concurrence, joined by three others, noted these problems and cited the FTC IP Report in support.[65] The concurrence explains that, for patent owners proposing non-exclusive licenses, 'an injunction, and the potentially serious sanctions arising from its violation, can be employed as a bargaining tool to charge exorbitant fees to companies that seek to buy licenses to practice the patent'.[66]

Since the Supreme Court issued its *eBay* decision, district courts have applied its equitable test in deciding whether to award a permanent injunction to a patent owner more than 40 times.[67] They have taken variable approaches to the analysis, and the law in this area is still developing.[68]

IV. Conclusion

Much has changed in the world of patent law and policy since the FTC released its Report in 2003. More changes seem likely. Perhaps the most significant change, however, is the increased awareness that to promote maximum levels of innovation, we must understand the complex mechanisms through which patents and competition work together to drive innovation, consumer welfare, and our nation's prosperity. Policymakers seem to have reached a consensus that allowing more patents to have greater breadth in more industries is not the best way to achieve our common goals.

However, the questions raised by the quest to achieve the optimal balance of patent and competition policy are complex and always changing. They require continual study as industry dynamics shift, new business models emerge and the law evolves. For that reason, the FTC has continued to study the role of patents and competition in promoting innovation, for the dual purposes of informing our antitrust enforcement actions and identifying opportunities for advocacy on patent issues.

In 2008, the FTC held a workshop to examine the changes to the patent system since the Report's release and the implications of those changes for the Report's recommendations.[69]

[64] Ibid ch 2, 29; ch 3, 37–38, 40.

[65] *eBay* 547 US 388, 396 (2006) (Kennedy J concurring). The United States' amicus brief, prepared with input from FTC staff, iterated these points. Brief for the United States as Amicus Curiae Supporting Respondent at § *I.C, eBay Inc v MercExchange LLC* 547 US 388 (2006) (No 05–130). Available at www.usdoj.gov/atr/cases/f215700/215790.htm.

[66] Ibid.

[67] See www.thefireofgenius.com/injunctions/ (listing court decisions to grant or deny an injunction in patent cases).

[68] In some cases, courts have simply held that irreparable harm exists, without further discussion, where a firm offers an infringing product in direct competition with the patent holder. See *O2 Micro Int'l Ltd v Beyond Innovation Technology Co Ltd* 2007 WL 869576 (ED Tex 2007) (Permanent injunction granted. Without further explanation the Court stated, '[t]he availability of the infringing products leads to loss of market share for plaintiff's products'.). In others, they demand a full showing of harm, complete with economic analysis. See *Praxair, Inc v ATMI, Inc* 2007 WL 906704 * 3 (D Del 2007) (Injunction denied because plaintiff did not provide any 'specific sales or market data to assist the court, nor has it identified precisely what market share, revenues, and customers Praxair has lost to ATMI'.).

[69] See FTC Announces First in Series of Hearings on Evolving Intellectual Property Marketplace (6 November 2008). Available at www.ftc.gov/opa/2008/11/ipmarketplace.shtm.

A report on the results of the workshop appeared in March 2011.[70] This report examined the role of technology markets and patent markets in innovation today, documented increasing activity and complexity of business models in markets for patents that do not involve the transfer of technology, and made recommendations for adjustments to legal rules and policies governing patent notice and remedies.[71]

The publication of the FTC's latest report is a further step toward realising a vision of policy making that engages competition agencies in the application of diverse, complementary instruments to address complex economic phenomena. Much like the FTC's 2003 Report *To Promote Innovation*, the 2011 study seeks to address problems at their roots—in this case, by repairing flaws in law and policy that govern patent notice and remedies. The pursuit of first-best solutions avoids excessive reliance on a tool (lawsuits to apply the antitrust laws) which otherwise might occupy the attention of an agency with a significant law enforcement mandate. The successful competition agency of the future will not be a single-dimension institution. Instead, it likely will be a body that has a broad portfolio of policy instruments, has research and analytical capacity to diagnose accurately the causes of market and regulatory failures, and devise solutions that draw upon the best possible mix of advocacy and enforcement.

In all of these endeavours, an agency's indispensable ally is a commitment to periodic assessment and refinement of its policies. The evaluation of past initiatives ought not to be a response to external shocks or crisis. Rather, it should be routine practice embraced by each generation of leadership. Only by carefully considering the road we have travelled can we formulate the best plan for moving forward.

[70] Federal Trade Commission, The Evolving IP Marketplace: Aligning Patent Notice and Remedies with Competition (March 2011), available at http://www.ftc.gov/os/2011/03/110307patentreport.pdf.
[71] Ibid, 1–5.

3

The Role of Economic Analysis in Competition Law

DOUGLAS H GINSBURG AND ERIC M FRASER

I. Introduction

From 1890 into the 1970s, competition law in the United States was not economically coherent. As a result, in all but the prosecution of cartels, enforcement was close to random. New business practices were viewed with suspicion, particularly when introduced by large firms, and mergers were interdicted without any understanding of their likely effects for good or ill. Indeed, in 1966 one Justice of the Supreme Court correctly observed, 'The sole consistency ... in [merger cases is that] the Government always wins.'[1] Beginning in the 1970s, however, the agencies charged with antitrust enforcement and then later the courts began to use economic analysis in order, respectively, to decide what cases to bring and to review the merits of those cases. Today, economic analysis plays a vital role in the enforcement of antitrust laws at all levels. We discuss the evolving role of economists and economic evidence in both the antitrust agencies and the courts. Our account demonstrates how the predictability of economic analysis supports a rule of law regime, but we also recognise the difficulties involved in interpreting and applying increasingly complex economic analyses to the facts in competition cases.

Countries with relatively young competition laws and enforcement agencies may be able to draw from the experience of the United States, both to avoid repeating its mistakes and to emulate its successes. To this end, we first discuss the role of economic analysis within a competition agency, recounting the evolving role of economists and economic evidence in competition agencies in the United States and suggesting what lessons newly formed competition agencies in other countries might draw from the experience in the United States. Next we examine how an increased emphasis upon economic analysis affects the relationship between competition agencies and courts. We then chart the path of the United States Supreme Court's embrace of economic analysis. Finally, we discuss how reliance upon economic analysis in evaluating competition cases both strengthens and challenges the rule of law.

[1] *United States v Von's Grocery Co* 384 US 270, 301 (1966) (Stewart, J dissenting).

II. Economic Analysis and Competition Agencies

The role of economists and of economic analysis in an agency designed to enforce competition laws is not predefined. In this section we first recount the experience of the agencies in the United States, which came only gradually to rely upon economists and economic analysis. We then discuss, in light of the experience in the United States, how a relatively new agency might best think about organising and staffing itself.

A. Experience in the United States

Competition agencies in the United States were born and grew up with few economists and little desire to focus upon economic analysis. Eventually, however, those agencies recognised the value of both economists and of economic analysis. The Federal Trade Commission (FTC) employed few economists in the first few decades after its creation in 1914. Beginning only in the 1970s did the FTC staff its Bureau of Economics primarily with PhD economists, who now number about 70.[2] The Antitrust Division of the Department of Justice (DOJ) hired its first economist in 1936,[3] and now employs about 60 economists.

Before 1983 when the agencies did hire economists, they made them subordinate to the lawyers. In the DOJ, for example, the economists reported to the Chief Economist, who in turn reported to the Deputy Assistant Attorney General (DAAG), who oversaw the legal staff that investigated mergers and other potential enforcement actions; the DAAG in turn reported to the Assistant Attorney General (AAG), who made the final decisions. See Figure 1.

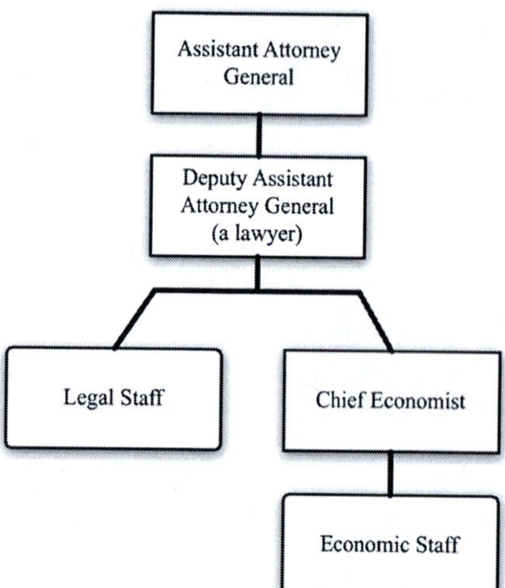

Figure 1: Pre-1983 Organisation of the Antitrust Division in the United States Department of Justice

[2] Michael Salinger and Paul A Pautler, 'The Bureau of Economics at the US Federal Trade Commission' in Global Competition Review (2006) *The 2006 Handbook of Competition Economists*, 3–5, also available at www.ftc.gov/be/recruit/06beover.pdf.

[3] 1936 Att'y Gen Ann Rep 22.

As a result, the advice of the Chief Economist was usually filtered through a lawyer, the DAAG; when the Chief Economist was able to communicate the economists' views directly to the AAG, it was only after the legal Deputy had presented the case to the AAG. It is therefore not surprising that in 1971 Judge Richard Posner described the Antitrust Division's economists as 'handmaidens to the lawyers, and rather neglected ones at that'.[4]

The structure in which economists played second fiddle to lawyers created organisational tension. Because the economists made their recommendations either through or after the lawyers, the economists were routinely put in the position of trying to explain why a case the lawyers said they could win should not be brought for lack of economic merit. As a result, agency lawyers long viewed economists unfavourably as 'case killers' who did not understand the law and who relied upon concepts and jargon the lawyers did not understand.

When economists and lawyers within an agency took diverging views on a particular issue—a common occurrence—the lawyers typically won. Perhaps this is because in disputes within a bureaucracy, the larger group usually wins; at both the FTC and the DOJ, the lawyers were by far the larger group. Another explanation for the 'case killer' view is that, prior to 1981, the ultimate decision makers at the FTC (the Commissioners) were almost always and at Justice (the AAG) were invariably lawyers[5] and therefore more inclined to understand and to favour the views of staff lawyers over those of staff economists.

This situation began to change in 1965, when Donald F Turner, who was both a lawyer and a PhD economist, became head of the Antitrust Division at the DOJ. Turner created the position of Special Economic Assistant to the AAG and staffed it with a distinguished economist who reported directly to him. Professor Oliver Williamson, the second Special Economic Assistant, observed that creation of that position 'signaled that economic analysis would [] be featured more prominently in the decision to bring cases and in the manner in which the cases were argued'.[6]

In 1968 Turner introduced the first 'Merger Guidelines', which were based upon economic rather than legal principles. Before then it is not clear whether there was any consistent analysis prescribed for the staff's evaluation of a proposed merger. The 1968 Guidelines classified markets using four- and eight-firm 'concentration ratios', that is, the percentage of sales in the merging firms' market that, after the merger, would be made by the four largest and the eight largest firms in the market. Under the Guidelines, if the top four firms after the merger would have a projected market share in excess of 75 per cent, then the merger would be scrutinised in greater detail. Under this heightened scrutiny, if the acquiring firm had, for example, a 10 per cent market share and the acquired firm had two per cent or more of the market, then the Antitrust Division would ordinarily challenge the merger.[7] The Guidelines reflected the 'conduct-structure-performance' paradigm then dominant in industrial organisation economics[8] and already influential in the Supreme Court.[9] The idea was simple: A high level of concentration in a particular market would

4 Richard A Posner, 'A Program for the Antitrust Division' (1971) 38 *University of Chicago Law Review* 500, 532.

5 See William E Kovacic, 'The Quality of Appointments and the Capability of the Federal Trade Commission' (1997) 49 *Administrative Law Review* 915, 935 (from 1949 to 1981 'the twenty-nine FTC commissioners had all been lawyers').

6 Oliver E Williamson, 'Economics and Antitrust Enforcement: Transition Years' (2003) 17 *Antitrust* 61, 62.

7 1968 Merger Guidelines § I.5.

8 Frank H Easterbrook, 'Allocating Antitrust Decisionmaking Tasks' (1987) 76 *Georgia Law Review* 305, 308.

9 See *United States v Philadelphia National Bank* 374 US 321, 363 (1963) ('a merger which produces a firm controlling an undue percentage share of the relevant market, and results in a significant increase in the concentration

facilitate and therefore make more likely actual collusion or at least tacit agreement among the market participants to avoid vigorous competition, particularly with respect to prices.[10]

In 1973, Professor Tom Kauper, then head of the Antitrust Division, created the Economic Policy Office. As he later recalled, 'A greater capacity for economic analysis was needed both in terms of the development of specific cases ... and in the development of an overall program that made economic sense.'[11]

In 1981, when the Reagan Administration took office, there was a sea change in the policies and practices of both the Antitrust Division and the FTC. William F Baxter, a professor of law who had been thoroughly converted to economic analysis of law in general and of antitrust in particular became head of the Antitrust Division.[12] James C Miller, III became the first PhD economist (and non-lawyer) to chair the FTC since its creation in 1914.[13]

In 1983, the lead author of this essay became Baxter's deputy and in 1985 succeeded him as AAG. As part of an overall reorganisation of the Antitrust Division to reflect its downsizing from a staff of 1,100 to about half that number, he elevated the position of the Chief Economist to that of a DAAG, thereby putting him at the same level as the senior-most lawyer reporting to the head of the Division (see Figure 2).[14] This structure remains in place today.

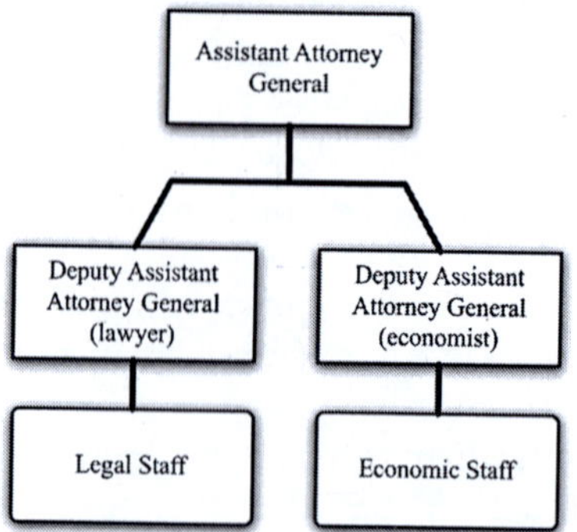

Figure 2: Post-1983 Organisation of the Antitrust Division in the United States Department of Justice

of firms in that market, is so inherently likely to lessen competition substantially that it must be enjoined in the absence of evidence clearly showing that the merger is not likely to have such anticompetitive effects').

[10] See generally Joe Staten Bain, *Industrial Organisation* (New York, John Wiley & Sons Inc, 1959) 297–98; Tibor Scitovsky, 'Economic Theory and the Measurement of Concentration' in National Bureau of Economic Research *Business Concentration and Price Policy* (Princeton NJ, Princeton University Press, 1955) 101, 102–10.

[11] Thomas E Kauper, 'The Role of Economic Analysis in the Antitrust Division Before and After the Establishment of the Economic Policy Office: A Lawyer's View' (1984) 29 *Antitrust Bulletin* 111, 119.

[12] Baxter had been active in the creation of the Neal Report, a controversial document submitted to President Johnson that 'recommended new federal legislation designed to attack instances of high market concentration regardless of conduct patterns'. Richard Schmalensee, 'Bill Baxter in the Antitrust Arena: An Economist's Appreciation' (1999) 51 *Stanford Law Review* 1317, 1320; see White House Task Force Report on Antitrust Policy, Antitrust & Trade Reg Rep (BNA) No 411, Special Supplement II (27 May 1969) (Neal Report). He later retreated from that position. See William F Baxter, 'Posner's Antitrust Law: An Economic Perspective' (1977) 8 *Bell Journal of Economics* 609, 613 ('Everything that has been learned in the intervening years has dragged me to the reluctant conclusion that Posner's ... probably represents the sounder position.'). As Schmalensee described it, 'Bill essentially learned economics a second time.' (1999) 51 *Stanford Law Review*, 1320–21.

[13] See Kovacic, 'The Quality of Appointments and the Capability of the Federal Trade Commission' (1997) 49 *Administrative Law Review* 935.

[14] Douglas H Ginsburg and Derek W Moore, 'The Future of Behavioral Economics in Antitrust Jurisprudence' (2010) 6 *Competition Policy International* 89, 91–92.

By the early 1980s not only were economists fully integrated into these agencies, but at least some of the agencies' lawyers had been exposed to economics in law school. The introduction of economics and of PhD economists into law faculties had originated at the University of Chicago in 1939, when Henry Simons joined the faculty, followed by Aaron Director in 1948. For many years Director co-taught antitrust with Edward Levi in an unusual format whereby Levi would teach cases four days a week and on the fifth Director would show why the legal doctrine made no sense from an economic point of view.[15] The tradition of analysing legal rules and institutions from an economic point of view persisted at the University of Chicago and became much more widespread with the publication in 1974 of then-Professor Richard Posner's *Economic Analysis of Law*.[16] By 1980, virtually all the leading law schools had appointed economists, some of whom also had a law degree.

The introduction of economics into antitrust analysis was particularly thoroughgoing. By the end of the decade Robert Bork's seminal work *The Antitrust Paradox* (1978) had appeared.[17] That same year the first three volumes of the Areeda and Turner treatise, *Antitrust Law*, were published; the next two volumes, which dealt with mergers, followed in 1980.[18] All these works integrate price theory and college-level microeconomics into antitrust analysis. All of them were written by lawyers literate in economics; Turner was actually a PhD economist as well as a lawyer. As a result the books were accessible to and well understood by lawyers with even the most modest prior exposure to economics.

The 1982 Merger Guidelines reflected this greater economic sophistication developing in antitrust law. For example, the four- and eight-firm concentration ratios were replaced by the Herfindahl-Hirschman Index (HHI), which measures concentration using the whole market rather than looking only at the few largest firms.[19] The HHI is more sensitive because it gives more weight to firms with larger market shares.[20] The 1982 Guidelines also employed the Hypothetical Monopolist–SSNIP test, which defines the relevant market by asking whether a hypothetical monopolist could profitably impose a 'small but significant non-transitory increase in price'[21] or if such a price increase would be frustrated by consumers switching to other products. The Guidelines looked not only to market structure and concentration—on which lawyers had traditionally focused but whose value has been proven neither theoretically nor empirically—but also to more theoretically and empirically established considerations, such as the likely competitive effects, entry, and efficiency gains associated with a merger.

As the lawyers within the agencies generally became (1) more comfortable with economic analysis of law and (2) more convinced of its relevance to antitrust law, they

[15] See Johan Van Overtveldt, *The Chicago School* (Agate, 2007) 73, 157–58.

[16] Posner has continued to refine and update this book, most recently in 2011. See Richard A Posner, *Economic Analysis of Law*, 8th edn (New York, Aspen Publishers, 2011).

[17] The most recent edition of Bork's book was published in 1993. See Robert H Bork, *The Antitrust Paradox*, 2nd edn (New York, Free Press, 1993).

[18] For a discussion of the treatise, see generally Herbert Hovenkamp, 'The Areeda-Turner Treatise in Antitrust Analysis' (1996) 41 *Antitrust Bulletin* 815.

[19] The HHI measures the concentration of an industry by summing the squares of the market shares of each firm: $H = \sum_{i=1}^{N} s_i^2$, where s_i represents market share of the ith firm in a market with N firms. See Albert O Hirschman, 'The Paternity of an Index' (1964) 54 *American Economic Review* 761, 761; see also 1992 Horizontal Merger Guidelines § 1.5.

[20] See 1982 Merger Guidelines § III.A.

[21] Ibid § III.B.

became less resistant to the recommendations of staff economists. Once viewed as case killers, economists came to be respected by lawyers because their work had become highly relevant, indeed usually essential, to the final decision whether to challenge a merger.

Today in the Antitrust Division, at least one staff economist is assigned to every civil investigation, including every merger investigation. Thus could Charles James, who headed the Antitrust Division in the early 2000s, say:

> Our economists are an integral part of our investigations from beginning to end, and it is impossible for me to imagine the Department operating without them.... [E]conomists are involved not just in the decision-making functions of the Department, but in all phases of our inquiries.[22]

B. The Lessons of Experience

A country may organise its system of antitrust enforcement and review in many different ways. Indeed, the Appendix to this chapter reveals that the countries represented in this volume are diverse in this respect. Regardless of the structure, the newly created competition authorities in those countries are at a distinct advantage in that they can learn from the unfortunate history of antitrust enforcement in the United States and thereby avoid repeating the mistakes that were made there. In particular, it is easier for an agency to integrate economists and economic analysis in every phase of competition policy enforcement during its formative early years, before a different way of operating becomes entrenched and fosters incumbent interests that will resist change. Although the integration of economics and economists into a law enforcement setting may be unfamiliar and unwelcome in a legal culture that is not used to the idea, competition policy is one of the fields in which the argument for integration is at its strongest. Most observers would agree it would be peculiar for an environmental agency not to employ environmental scientists and it should, when the argument is laid out, seem equally strange for economists not to play a central role in the work of a competition authority. Competition was, after all, an economic concept before it was the subject of laws.[23]

The integration of industrial organisation (IO) economists into the work of a competition agency raises a number of questions about the internal organisation of that agency. The fundamental question is whether the economists should report directly to the person or group of persons who make the enforcement decision or, alternatively, be embedded in the legal staff that alone reports to the decision maker(s).[24] Experience suggests the former organisation works well, probably better than the alternative, but it does require that an economist from one chain of command and lawyers from the other be integrated into each ad hoc team conducting an investigation or pursuing a case, as illustrated below in Figure 3.

[22] Charles A James, 'Antitrust in the Early 21st Century: Core Values and Convergence' at the Program on Antitrust Policy in the 21st Century (15 May 2002), available at www.justice.gov/atr/public/speeches/11148.htm.

[23] *Cf* Richard A Epstein, 'Pleadings and Presumptions' (1973) 40 *University of Chicago Law Review* 556, 560 (1973) ('"Legal concepts" are those that the law regards as material to the decision of legal issues. ... "Cat" is not generally thought to be a legal concept, but it would become one if it were made an operative term in a Uniform Cats Act.').

[24] See Luke M Froeb, Paul A Pautler and Lars-Hendrik Röller, 'The Economics of Organizing Economists' (2009) 76 *Antitrust Law Journal* 569 (2009).

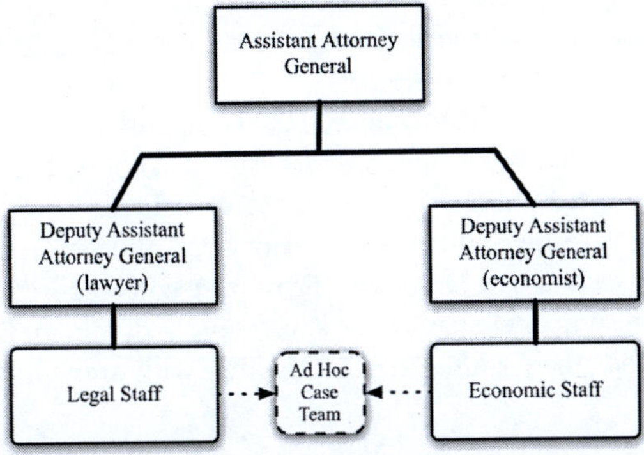

Figure 3: Ad hoc Case Teams in the United States Department of Justice

A related question is how a law enforcement agency should recruit and retain a high-quality staff of IO economics considering the different cultures in which lawyers and economists are trained and typically employed. In the United States at least, the best IO economists tend to teach at the university level rather than work for industrial or consulting firms, although they may well do some part-time consulting work. The key to assembling and retaining an excellent staff of economists in a competition agency, therefore, is to fit employment at the agency into the career path of first class IO economists. That means the economist's experience at the agency must help advance his academic career rather than be a detour from that path.

The experience of the Antitrust Division shows it is possible to attract high quality staff economists by providing a working environment that to some degree replicates the intellectual environment of an economics faculty. Of course, the economist's principal activity in the competition agency is the economic analysis of real world situations in real time, whereas his or her principal activities in a university are teaching and research. Still, agencies can provide some benefits of the academy to their economists by giving them a certain amount of time for their own research and writing, publishing a series of 'working papers', hosting a lecture series in which academic economists present their work, and so on. Perhaps the essential ingredient, however, is that the Chief Economist be a highly-respected academic for whom service at the competition agency is more like a fellowship at another university than time out of the academy altogether. By attracting a series of leading IO economists to serve in that role, the Antitrust Division has been able to attract high quality junior economists who know they will benefit from working under the distinguished Chief Economist and who realistically expect to leave the agency within some years in order to take up an entry-level academic post or to join a consultancy. This pattern of hiring newly minted PhD economists who will in time depart keeps the agency in touch with current economic thinking. There may well be other ways to organise a competition agency that are better suited to the local circumstances of different countries, but the point remains that the competition agency can and should be staffed by the best economic talent, as opposed to permanent bureaucrats of the sort too often found in other government offices.

Relatedly, in the last decade or two it has become essential that a competition agency have both economists and lawyers learned in the fields, respectively, of intellectual property and intellectual property rights. Scientific and technical developments in the pharmaceutical and particularly the digital electronics industries have spawned a host of new and thorny issues for competition policy. Advances in digital technology and the growth of the internet have significantly altered the competitive landscape in those and in many other industries, including prominently newspapers, book publishing and distribution,[25] motion picture distribution and exhibition, musical recordings, and general retailing; indeed, few if any sizeable industries have not been affected in some competitively relevant way by digital technology. Dominant firms have emerged in markets with significant network effects. In some there has been a succession of dominant firms—competition being *for* the field rather than *within* the field—often with ambiguous implications for competition policy.[26]

Competition agencies around the world are not of one mind about these developments. They are, however, in almost constant dialogue about them, in part because agencies in multiple jurisdictions are called upon to analyse the competitive implications of the same mergers, the same joint ventures, and business practices of the same dominant firms. Because there are diverse views, and because the same product market may have different participants and market shares in different jurisdictions, each competition agency needs its own ability to analyse the competitive implications of transactions and conduct in which intellectual property and intellectual property rights are important components. Attracting and keeping specialists in these fields is made more difficult by the competition of private sector employers and it is, again, the agency's challenge to provide an intellectually and professionally rewarding experience if it is not consistently to be over-matched by the parties that come before it.

C. Competition Advocacy

The economic analytic capacity of a properly staffed competition agency is also a resource with the potential to improve decision making throughout the Government of which it is a part. Indeed, the agency can probably make a greater contribution to consumer welfare through advocacy within the councils of government than it can through its enforcement of competition law in the private sector because governments typically make decisions heedless of their anti-competitive impact. Each department and agency of government has its own mission and it is rare indeed for one of them to consider whether a decision it is contemplating might better serve the public if altered in some way not inconsistent with its primary goal.

A government regulatory body contemplating a new or changed regulation will ordinarily receive input from the affected industry and perhaps from other interests with a stake in that industry, such as labour unions or suppliers. If it hears anything from anyone expressing concern about the anti-competitive effect its proposed decision is likely to have, it will probably be from a relatively unsophisticated consumer association and, if the experience in the United States is a guide, even that type of input will be rare. As public choice

[25] See Eric M Fraser, 'Antitrust and the Google Books Settlement: The Problem of Simultaneity' 2010 *Stanford Technology Law Review* 4, available at http://ssrn.com/abstract=1417722.

[26] See Michael Katz and Carl Shapiro, 'Systems Competition and Network Effects' (1994) 8 *Journal of Economic Perspectives* 93.

economists have long recognised, consumers are less likely to be represented because they each have a small interest in any particular government decision, so it is not worth their while to organise, whereas other interest groups with a large stake in that decision do find it cost-beneficial to expend efforts to influence the Government.[27]

The large number of significant government regulatory initiatives with adverse effects upon competition and the paucity of protests from consumers mean the gains from sophisticated competition advocacy are potentially very great. Persuading an environmental protection agency, for example, to take a market-oriented rather than a command-and-control approach to regulating the emissions of a particular pollutant may reduce the costs of regulation greatly without at all impairing and indeed perhaps increasing its efficacy.[28]

In the United States, both the Antitrust Division and the FTC have long had active programmes of competition advocacy.[29] They have pointed out the anti-competitive consequences of measures proposed or adopted by legislatures, licensing boards, and other regulatory agencies at both the state and the federal levels. For example, the Antitrust Division recently submitted comments to the Department of Transportation regarding airline alliances[30] and to the Federal Communications Commission regarding its national broadband policy;[31] the FTC recently submitted comments to state legislatures regarding the provision of pharmaceutical services.[32]

Competition advocacy need only be tolerated by the larger government to be cost-effective because even an occasional victory for competition can dwarf the cost of the competition agency's advocacy programme. So much the better, however, if the competition agency's concerns must be addressed by the sectoral regulators and other government departments to whom they are addressed. This is the institutional arrangement long established in Korea, where the FTC has been very influential. In its own words:

> The Korean Competition Law (Monopoly Regulation and Fair Trade Act) requires other ministries to have prior consultation with the KFTC on whether their proposed acts and decrees have any clause having anti-competitive effects on business, which is very unique as a competition advocacy role in Korea. As such ... the competition advocacy role of the competition authorities ... is deemed one of the core functions of the KFTC ...

[27] See Kay Lehman Schlozman and John T Tierney, *Organized Interests and American Democracy* (Longman Higher Education, 1986); Mancur Olson, *The Logic of Collective Action*, 2nd edn (Harvard University Press, 1971); Gary Becker, 'A Theory of Competition among Pressure Groups' (1983) 98 *Quarterly Journal of Economics* 371.

[28] See W David Montgomery, 'Markets in Licenses and Efficient Pollution Control Programs' (1972) 5 *Journal of Economic Theory* 395.

[29] See generally James C Cooper, Paul A Pautler and Todd J Zywicki, 'Theory and Practice of Competition Advocacy at the FTC' (2005) 72 *Antitrust Law Journal* 1091; US Department of Justice Antitrust Division, 'Division Update: Spring 2010', Competition Advocacy and Policy, available at www.justice.gov/atr/public/update/2010/competition-advocacy.html.

[30] See Comments of the United States Department of Justice, Joint Application of American Airlines, Inc et al, D.O.T. OST-2008-0252 (21 December 2009), available at www.justice.gov/atr/public/comments/253575.htm.

[31] See *Ex Parte* Submission of the United States Department of Justice, *In re* Economic Issues in Broadband Competition: A National Broadband Plan for Our Future, F.C.C. GN Docket No 09-51 (4 January 2010), available at www.justice.gov/atr/public/comments/253393.htm.

[32] See, eg, Letter from Todd R Zywicki, Director, Office of Policy Planning, FTC, et al, to Patrick C Lynch, Attorney General of Rhode Island (8 April 2004), available at www.ftc.gov/os/2004/04/ribills.pdf; see also Letter from Arnold Schwarzenegger, Governor of California, to Members of California State Assembly (Veto of Assembly Bill 1960), available at http://gov.ca.gov/pdf/press/vetoes/AB_1960_veto.pdf (vetoing bill in part because study 'from the Federal Trade Commission[] have shown that enactment ... will limit competition').

> Policies, once formulated, are difficult to change. In this regard, the KFTC Chairman can ensure that the views of the competition agency are reflected in the policy-making by attending and expressing his opinions at the Cabinet Meetings.[33]

Few if any other competition agencies share the enviable arrangement that gives the Korean FTC the influence it has within the Government of Korea. Many agencies, however, could on their own initiative advocate competitive alternatives to anti-competitive government decisions, as the competition agencies of the United States have done. When a persuasive case for competition is put before an open-minded decision maker in a programmatic agency, he may be quick to alter his course, to the benefit of consumers. Even if he is not inclined to do so, he may find himself without a convincing reason for insisting upon a course that the competition agency has shown harms consumers.

III. Economic Analysis and the Relationship between Agencies and the Courts

It is not enough that the agency deciding whether to challenge a merger or a business practice as anti-competitive is an expert in economic analysis; the agency must be able to defend its decision to a judge who is unlikely to have access to an economist and is unlikely himself to be an expert in competition law—let alone price theory. In this section we explore the dynamic between the agencies and the courts in a world where competition policy is highly dependent upon economic analysis.

In a simple cartel case, of course, the evaluation of economic evidence is not ordinarily necessary. Because a cartel is in most jurisdictions unlawful regardless of the justification its members offer, cartel cases are not significantly different from any charge of civil or criminal conspiracy to violate any law. The picture becomes considerably more complicated, however, when one considers even a merger, and still more complicated when the case involves a charge of attempted monopolisation or abuse of a dominant position.

The investigation of a merger between firms that are in direct competition will typically require an evaluation of their market shares and, if those are deemed significant, of the dynamics of the market or markets in which the firms compete. This investigation may entail gathering price and cost data not only from the merging parties but also from other firms in the market, interviewing customers about their choice of suppliers and how they would be affected by the proposed merger, investigating whether there are high barriers to entry into the relevant market, and interviewing potential entrants. If the merging parties are large firms, then they may compete in many separate product markets, each of which may require a full investigation. Economists will have to analyse the data that are collected and advise their legal colleagues whether the proposed merger is likely to have adverse consequences for consumers, as expressed in higher prices, lower quality, a slower rate of

[33] Nam Kee Lee, 'Advocacy Role of the Korea Fair Trade Commission in Regulatory Reform' APEC-OECD Co-operative Initiative on Regulatory Reform (19–20 September 2001), available at www.oecd.org/dataoecd/10/45/2731502.doc.

innovation, or otherwise. If the agency decides to block the merger and the parties seek review of that decision in court, then the agency will submit to the reviewing tribunal an evidentiary record replete with economic data and analyses, as well as a legal argument about why the effect of the merger would run afoul of the applicable legal standard (for example, in the United States, that it may 'substantially to lessen competition, or to tend to create a monopoly').[34] In a monopolisation or abuse of dominance case, the amount of industry data and economic evidence and the sophistication of the analyses may be much greater still.

In all but a very simple antitrust case, the reviewing court faces a daunting task. Even if the court is specialised in the review of competition cases, it is unlikely to have at its disposal the same quality and quantity of analytical resources as had the competition authority. If the court hears all manner of matters, as is true in the United States, then it almost certainly will not have the assistance of even one staff economist, nor will the judges likely be familiar with the economic concepts about the application of which the competition authority and the firms are debating.

In these circumstances *de novo* review by the tribunal is almost certainly impractical and almost never expected or required by its legal charter. On the contrary, the reviewing process will be undertaken with some significant degree of deference owed to the factual findings and perhaps also the legal interpretations of the enforcement agency. The issue before the court, therefore, will not ordinarily be whether the proposed merger or allegedly unlawful conduct is in fact anti-competitive but rather whether the competition authority has made a sufficiently persuasive case that it is or may be anti-competitive and harmful to consumers. Nonetheless, most cases worthy of pursuit through the courts are close and are made particularly difficult by the sophisticated lawyers and the expert economic witnesses both sides employ. In addition, because the economic stakes in an antitrust case are ordinarily significant, and sometimes very high indeed, the defendant in an antitrust case will find it worthwhile to invest heavily in the defence or pursuit of its position. The challenge facing the court as a consequence should not be underestimated. Even with the aid of a deferential standard of review, sorting through and making sense of technical evidence is a painstaking and intellectually-daunting proposition.

The task facing the parties is likewise difficult, for they must make their positions understandable and appealing to both the intellect and the intuition of the decision maker. Agencies, which repeatedly appear in court in order to defend their enforcement decisions, must be particularly adept at this type of presentation. No amount of economic evidence will persuade the court unless it is presented by the lawyers in a way that is understood by the judges and fits the governing statute and the precedents and traditions of the court. For this reason it is imperative at the stage of judicial review for lawyers and economists still to work hand in hand, whether on behalf of the competition authority or of the interested companies, in order to make a presentation that is both intellectually honest and potentially persuasive to the judges who are sure to be well trained in law but almost certainly not in economics.

[34] Clayton Act § 7, 15 USC § 18.

IV. Economic Analysis in the Supreme Court: Promoting the Rule of Law

The role of economic analysis in US courts in many ways mirrors the experience in its agencies. We explore this history in the Supreme Court, which ignored economic analysis for many decades but then wholeheartedly embraced it with the help of the agencies. In recent decades the Court has become particularly receptive to economic arguments and has even been willing to overturn several long-established rulings that conflicted with the teachings of modern economics. It is our hope that other countries can learn from the experience of the United States, which struggled for so long without a sensible antitrust regime before arriving at a predictable and sound approach with the aid of economic analysis.

Seventy years after the passage of the Sherman Antitrust Act in 1890, the United States Supreme Court still did not have a coherent understanding of competition and hence of antitrust law—but neither had economists for much of that period. Instead the Court interpreted the Sherman Act in light of a set of changeable social and political goals, such as mitigating the effects on producers of the Great Depression of the 1930s,[35] and protecting small businesses from larger, more efficient, rivals. As late as 1961 the Court attributed these goals to the legislature:

> [W]e cannot fail to recognize Congress' desire to promote competition through the protection of viable, small, locally owned businesses. Congress appreciated that occasional higher costs and prices might result from the maintenance of fragmented industries and markets. It resolved these competing considerations in favor of decentralization.[36]

In the 1960s, there came to the fore a generation of legal scholars who had learned, largely by collaboration with economists, to apply sound economic principles to antitrust law. Professors Phillip Areeda, Robert Bork, Ward Bowman, Richard Posner and others advocated an interpretation of the antitrust laws that promoted economic efficiency in the form of consumer welfare. A decade later the Supreme Court adopted economics as its tool of choice in interpreting the antitrust laws and since then has systematically revisited its old decisions 'in order to bring [them] into alignment with the modern economic understanding of competition' and industrial organisation.[37] For example, in the 1977 case *Continental TV Inc v GTE Sylvania, Inc*,[38] the Court held that non-price vertical restraints, such as a territorial restriction in a contract between a manufacturer and a retailer, would no longer be condemned as a per se violation of Sherman Act § 1, which prohibits any 'contract combination or conspiracy in restraint of trade';[39] henceforth they would be analysed under the 'rule of reason',[40] which entails a close examination and balancing of the likely pro- and

[35] See *Appalachian Coal v United States* 288 US 344, 373–74 (1933) (characterising particular agreements among competitors as 'stabiliz[ing] market prices' and not 'detrimental to fair competition').

[36] *Brown Shoe Co v United States* 370 US 294, 344 (1962).

[37] Douglas H Ginsburg, 'Originalism and Economic Analysis: Two Case Studies of Consistency and Coherence in Supreme Court Decision Making' (2010) 33 *Harvard Journal of Law and Public Policy* 217, 218.

[38] *Continental TV Inc v GTE Sylvania, Inc* 433 US 36 (1977).

[39] Sherman Act USC § 1.

[40] *United States v Trans-Missouri Freight Ass'n* 166 US 290, 355–56 (1897). See also Richard A Posner, 'The Rule of Reason and the Economic Approach: Reflections on the Sylvania Decision' (1977) 45 *University of Chicago Law Review* 1.

anti-competitive effects of the practice.[41] In so doing, the Court overruled its own decision of only a decade earlier.[42] By 1979 the Court had embraced a broad understanding of the Sherman Act inconsistent with much of its prior teaching when it stated, in *Reiter v Sonotone Corp*,[43] that the legislative history of the statute 'suggest[s] that Congress designed the Sherman Act as a 'consumer welfare prescription''[44]—a proposition it took directly from Robert Bork's book, *The Antitrust Paradox*, published the year before.

From *Sylvania* and *Sonotone* forward, the Court's antitrust jurisprudence, which once had been ad hoc and lacking in any consistent understanding of economics, began consistently to follow some simply stated legal norms drawn from, or at least consistent with, a contemporary understanding of price theory. The trend in the Court's adoption of economic principles is clear from the citations to economic sources in its opinions (see Figure 4). Over the last 40 years, the rate of citations to economically-oriented antitrust scholars has increased from 30 per cent to more than 75 per cent.

Once the Court abandoned its concerns with vague social and political goals of the sort set out in *Brown Shoe*,[45] the scope of antitrust liability narrowed; the Court condemned only those transactions and practices that economic analysis showed to be inimical to consumer interests. Gone was the concern with the welfare of producers and with small firms that could not compete with large or more efficient rivals.

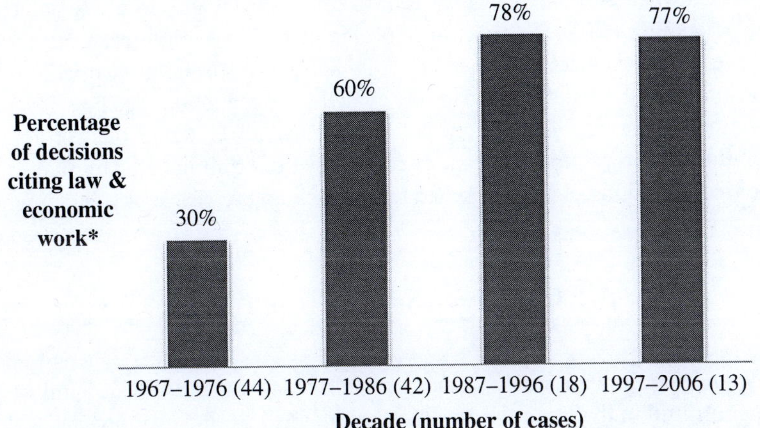

Figure 4: Percentage of Antitrust Decisions of the US Supreme Court Citing Law and Economics Work

41 See, eg, *National Collegiate Athletic Ass'n v Board of Regents* 468 US 85, 119–20 (1984) (weighing pro- and anti-competitive effects).

42 *United States v Arnold, Schwinn & Co* 388 US 365 (1967).

43 *Reiter v Sonotone Corp* 442 US 330 (1979).

44 Ibid 343.

45 *Brown Shoe* 370 US 294.

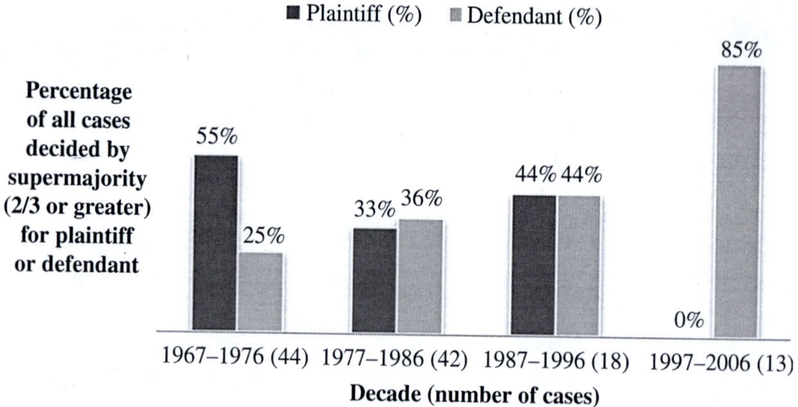

Figure 5: Antitrust Cases in the US Supreme Court Decided by a Supermajority (2/3 or Greater)

Armed with a more principled and hence a more predictable tool for analysing antitrust cases, the degree of agreement among the nine Justices steadily increased, as shown in Figure 5.

This is not surprising when one considers that thoughtful observers are more likely to agree when asked whether a practice is harmful to consumers than they are to agree upon whether the practice is desirable as a socio-political matter. Take a simple example: a merger between retailers that produces efficiencies of scale likely to result in lower prices is clearly good for consumers; if the result is that a locally owned store goes out of business, however, it may be less clear whether it is good for the community overall. However, that communitarian consideration has no place in and cannot practically be accommodated by an economically tractable competition policy, as opposed to, perhaps, an exercise in city planning.

V. A Challenge for the Rule of Law

Predictability and certainty are surely virtues in a rule of law regime. The account we have given of the contribution that economic analysis has made to advancing those values should not be underestimated. Embracing economic evidence allows decision makers to apply a coherent system to each case and also enables private parties better to predict outcomes and thus to avoid litigation. At the same time, one should not think economic analysis invariably indicates how a case should be decided. On the contrary, a complex or novel antitrust case may engender genuine disagreement among disinterested economists on the competitive implications of the business conduct at issue in a particular case. Indeed, some recent cases have prompted various academic economists to submit opposing amicus briefs to the Supreme Court.[46]

[46] Compare Brief of Economists as Amici Curiae in Support of Respondents, *American Needle, Inc v National Football League*, No 08-661 (S Ct Nov. 24, 2009), available at 2009 WL 4247983; *with* Amicus Curiae Brief of Economists in Support of Petitioner, *American Needle, Inc v National Football League*, No 08-661 (S Ct Sept. 24, 2009), available at 2009 WL 3090453.

Once the law is closely tethered to economic analysis, moreover, it becomes a matter of concern that the law itself not be made uncertain by rapid changes in economic thinking. It is neither practical nor consistent with the rule of law for courts to decide cases based upon the latest theory or empirical study to appear in the most recent issue of an economic journal. To be sure, the law must take account of changes in the scientific disciplines upon which it relies, but courts should not rely upon a new theory or empirical study until the theory has been generally accepted or the study replicated and its finding accepted within the relevant scientific community.[47] The Supreme Court made a related point in *Daubert* when it reminded us that 'scientific conclusions are subject to perpetual revision'.[48] The challenge is for competition agencies, and concomitantly for reviewing courts, to incorporate into their enforcement decisions and judicial opinions respectively new but generally accepted developments in economics without creating uncertainty or impairing the agency's or the court's legitimacy as an interpreter of the law.

To take a contemporary example, the Merger Guidelines described earlier in this chapter were issued in 1982, were revised somewhat in 1984 and 1997, and are now being reconsidered by the Antitrust Division and the FTC. Over the years actual practices at the agencies have gravitated away from those prescribed by the Guidelines, as practising lawyers and others who follow such matters closely understand. Beyond revising the Guidelines to reflect recent practice, however, the agencies are now giving active consideration to a significant change: introducing an alternative to defining markets for purposes of evaluating proposed mergers and determining whether a firm has monopolised a particular market.[49]

The Guidelines are screening devices the agencies use for allocating their resources and for notifying the public in advance of the type of transactions likely to trigger close scrutiny. In principle, it is of no great moment to the rule of law that the agencies might change how they identify cases meriting a thorough investigation. In practice, however, the Guidelines have also been influential in the courts; when a merger is challenged in court, the judge, anxious for a ready source of assistance and quick to find it in the Guidelines, may tend to regard the merger as presumptively unlawful, solely because it exceeds the Guidelines' threshold for investigation. Such reliance makes a change in the Merger Guidelines much more consequential than merely a change in the agencies' internal processing rule, and it is not insignificant that the change would be brought about administratively, that is, without the need for legislation. To their credit, the enforcement agencies in the United States will

[47] *Cf New Jersey v Behn* 868 A.2d 329, 343 (NJ Super Ct App Div 2005) ('Science moves inexorably forward and hypotheses or methodologies once considered sacrosanct are modified or discarded. The judicial system, with its search for the closest approximation to the "truth," must accommodate this ever-changing scientific landscape.').

[48] *Daubert v Merrell Dow Pharmaceuticals, Inc* 509 US 579, 597 (1993). See also Gregory J Werden, Luke M Froeb and David T Scheffman, 'A Daubert Discipline for Merger Simulation' (Summer 2004) 18(3) *Antitrust* 89.

[49] The method, proposed by Joseph Farrell and Carl Shapiro, now the chief economists of the FTC and DOJ, respectively, evaluates the likelihood of increased prices from unilateral effects. See Joseph Farrell and Carl Shapiro, 'Antitrust Evaluation of Horizontal Mergers: An Economic Alternative to Market Definition' (2010), available at: http://faculty.haas.berkeley.edu/shapiro/alternative.pdf.

For a critique, see Richard Schmalensee, 'Should New Merger Guidelines Give UPP Market Definition?' (December 2009) 12(1) *Competition Policy International Chronicle* 1, available at www.competitionpolicyinternational.com/should-new-merger-guidelines-give-upp-market-definition. For the authors' response, see Joseph Farrell and Carl Shapiro, 'Upward Pricing Pressure and Critical Loss Analysis: Response' (February 2010) *Competition Policy International Antitrust Journal*, available at www.competitionpolicyinternational.com/assets/Free/Shapiro-FarrellFEB10.pdf.

For its proposed inclusion in the Merger Guidelines, see 2010 Proposed Merger Guidelines § 6.1, available at www.ftc.gov/os/2010/04/100420hmg.pdf.

not make such a change without soliciting and seriously considering comments from interested members of the public. The fact remains, however, that a change in the Guidelines is likely to effect a change in the law as applied, in that it will affect the inferences courts draw and hence their ultimate decision when reviewing a challenged merger.

The dynamic and increasingly mathematical nature of the modern economic techniques now used by competition agencies poses another problem for the rule of law and one for which there is no obvious solution: how is a court to determine whether a competition agency has acted arbitrarily or upon the basis of inadequate evidence? One possibility is to make sure judges are educated in economics. Although we firmly believe that a basic economic understanding is useful for every judge and imperative for a judge reviewing a competition case, we do not think it is practical to expect judges, as they are currently educated and selected, could become sufficiently proficient with contemporary economic tools, such as econometrics, to provide an independent check upon the work of the competition authorities. That is not to say judges should not be expected to know basic economics—at the level, perhaps, of an introductory college-level course—but one should have modest expectations for the degree of facility that can be imparted to a person whose career decision many years earlier was in favour of the law and not of a technical field.

To the extent that reliance upon economics creates these challenges of change and complexity, the case for specialised courts to review the decisions of antitrust agencies becomes more compelling. In the United Kingdom, appeals from the Office of Fair Trading are heard by the Competition Appeals Tribunal (CAT). In order to have the benefit of both judicial and economic experts, the CAT sits in panels comprising one judge and two highly qualified laymen from a roster that includes economists, accountants, and others with relevant backgrounds.[50] The work of the CAT has been admirable and stands in very favourable contrast with some of the decisions of the European Court of First Instance, the jurisdiction of which is almost as broad and diverse as the remit of the European Commission. To take one prominent example, in the *Microsoft v Commission of the European Communities* case,[51] the Court restated each of the charges brought by the competition bureau of the Commission and duly stated with respect to each that it found no 'manifest error', but it provided virtually no analysis of its own to explain its judgment, which appeared therefore more as supineness than as informed deference. Another possibility is to appoint one or more economists to serve as a judge on each multi-member panel reviewing a competition decision. The work of Frederic Jenny, a PhD economist and professor of economics but not a lawyer, is illuminating. He serves as a judge at the Commercial, Economic, and Financial Law Chamber of the Supreme Court of France (*Cour de Cassation*) and gives reason to think even a single judge with a sophisticated understanding of economics can be very helpful to his or her legally trained colleagues in applying the law to the facts of a case. No doubt there are other variations yet to be devised as ways to cope with this difficulty.

In addition, it is a matter of concern to the rule of law that economic analysis is becoming more mathematical and therefore even more difficult for judges to understand. This poses two risks for courts incorporating economics into competition law. First, it may require judges—whether generalists or members of a specialised tribunal—to evaluate evidence in

[50] See Enterprise Act 2002, c. 40, § 12 (Eng.); Competition Appeal Tribunal, 'Who Will Hear My Case?' available at www.catribunal.org.uk/245/Frequently-asked-questions.html.

[51] Case T-201/04 *Microsoft Corp v Commission of the European Communities* [2007] ECR II-3601.

a framework with which they are not adept or even comfortable. Second, it may lead judges to defer too much to the agencies whose decisions they review and enforce, much as the US Supreme Court did when Justice Stewart remarked, as we noted in the first paragraph of this chapter, 'The sole consistency ... in [merger cases is that] the Government always wins.'[52] In this regard, we can only suggest that judges confronting economic evidence couched in mathematical terms consider the view of Professor Ronald Coase, a Nobel laureate in economics and a member of the University of Chicago law faculty. During his long tenure as the editor of *The Journal of Law and Economics* (1964–82) he would not publish articles that relied upon mathematical notation (except, perhaps, in an appendix) on the ground that an author who could not express himself in English probably did not know what he was talking about.[53]

VI. Conclusion

It is our hope that understanding the process by which agencies and courts in the United States incorporated economic analysis into competition law will help the competition communities in other countries, and particularly those with new or young competition agencies, think through the institutional arrangements best suited to their needs. Although there are different ways to organise a competition enforcement agency, we believe highly skilled economists must play a vital and integrated role in each. Sophisticated economic analysis is necessary not only to determine which cases to pursue, but also to marshal the evidence presented to the appellate tribunal that reviews the agency's decisions, and to aid in the advocacy of competition throughout the councils of government.

Reviewing courts, too, should understand and embrace economic evidence. Economic analysis leads to predictability and stability in the law, which are essential elements in a rule of law regime. Just as with the natural sciences, however, courts and agencies should take care before embracing unsettled economic principles.

[52] *United States v Von's Grocery Co* 384 US 270, 301 (1966) (Stewart, J dissenting).

[53] Professor Coase said this to Judge Ginsburg when he was a student in Coase's seminar on law and economics in 1972. See also Gordon Tullock, 'A Comment on Daniel Klein's "A Plea to Economists Who Favor Liberty"' (2001) 27 *Eastern Economic Journal* 203, 204 fn 2 ('As Ronald Coase says, "if you torture the data long enough it will confess." Note: "I have heard him say this several times. So far as I know he has never published it."').

VII. Appendix

Jurisdiction	Enforcement Tribunals	Court Review & Appeals
Australia[54]	— Australian Competition and Consumer Commission.	— **First instance:** Federal Court of Australia (single judge). — **Rehearing:** Federal Court of Australia (Full Court).
China[55]	— **Policy/coordination:** Anti-Monopoly Commission. — **Enforcement:** Anti-monopoly Enforcement Authorities: – Ministry of Commerce – State Administration of Industry and Commerce – National Development and Reform Commission – Civil courts.	— **First:** Administrative reconsideration. — **Appeal:** administrative lawsuits.
India[56]	— Competition Commission of India.	— **First:** Competition Appellate Tribunal. — **Appeal:** Supreme Court of India.
Indonesia[57]	— Commission for the Supervision of Business Competition (Komisi Pengawasa Persaingan Usaha).	— **First:** District Court. — **Then:** Supreme Court of Indonesia (bypassing High Court).
Japan[58]	— Fair Trade Commission of Japan.	— **First:** Administrative hearing procedures. — **Appeal:** Tokyo High Court.
Korea[59]	— Korea Fair Trade Commission.	— **Appeal:** Seoul High Court — **Then:** Supreme Court.
Singapore[60]	— Competition Commission of Singapore.	— **First:** Competition Appeal Board. — **Then:** High Court. — **Then:** Court of Appeal.
Thailand[61]	— Trade Competition Commission.	— Appeal Consideration Commission.
United States	— Department of Justice — Federal Trade Commission	— United States District Court — United States Court of Appeals — Supreme Court of the United States

[54] Brett Bolton and Kate Williams, 'Australia' in 'The International Comparative Guide to: Cartel & Leniency' (Global Legal Group), available at www.iclg.co.uk/khadmin/Publications/pdf/3298.pdf.

[55] Christopher F Corr and Patrick W Ma, 'China' in 'International Comparative Legal Guide to: Merger Control' (Global Legal Group), available at http://www.iclg.co.uk/khadmin/Publications/pdf/3245.pdf.

[56] Vinod Dhall and Sonam Mathur, 'India' in 'The International Comparative Guide to: Cartel & Leniency' (Global Legal Group), available at http://www.iclg.co.uk/khadmin/Publications/pdf/3322.pdf.

[57] Ningrum Natasya Sirait, 'Overview of the Indonesia Competition Law', available at www.jftc.go.jp/eacpf/05/AOTS/indonesia_ningrum.pdf.

[58] Eriko Watanabe, 'Japan' in 'The International Comparative Guide to: Cartel & Leniency' (Global Legal Group), available at www.iclg.co.uk/khadmin/Publications/pdf/3345.pdf.

[59] Sung Bom Park and Paul S Rhee, 'Korea' in 'The International Comparative Guide to: Cartel & Leniency' (Global Legal Group), available at www.iclg.co.uk/khadmin/Publications/pdf/3347.pdf.

[60] 'Competition Law', Singapore Academy of Law, available at www.singaporelaw.sg/content/CompetitionLaw.html.

[61] Fabrice Mattei, 'The New Trade Competition Act Seeks to Eliminate Unfair Trade Practices and Monopolization', available at www.globalcompetitionforum.org/regions/asia/Thailand/thai_cp.pdf.

4

Favouring Dynamic Competition over Static Competition in Antitrust Law[1]

J GREGORY SIDAK AND DAVID TEECE

I. Introduction

In 1988, in anticipation of the centennial of the Sherman Act, David J Teece and his Berkeley colleagues held a conference that led to the 1992 volume *Antitrust, Innovation, and Competitiveness*, with contributions from many of the day's leading scholars in antitrust law and economics.[2] The conference was designed to alert the law and economics community to a set of emerging issues on antitrust and innovation. In hindsight, we believe that the conference was a watershed event. A slow and reluctant awakening to antitrust and innovation issues is now well underway.

In the introduction to the proceedings of the conference, Thomas Jorde and David Teece, as editors, endeavoured to reframe antitrust questions. The issue, they asserted, was that scholars and practitioners needed to take a more dynamic approach to competition in the spirit of Joseph Schumpeter:

> As Schumpeter (1942) suggested…, the kind of competition embedded in standard microeconomic analysis may not be the kind of competition that really matters if enhancing economic welfare is the goal of antitrust. Rather, it is dynamic competition propelled by the introduction of new products and new processes that really counts. If the antitrust laws were more concerned with promoting dynamic rather than static competition, which we believe they should, we expect that they would look somewhat different from the laws we have today.[3]

Jorde and Teece posed the provocative hypothesis that 'antitrust laws may be at odds with technological progress and economic welfare'.[4] In three subsequent articles, Teece and his co-authors made efforts to advance the Schumpeterian agenda.[5]

[1] This chapter originally appeared in (2009) 5(4) *Journal of Competition Law and Economics* 581.

[2] Thomas M Jorde and David J Teece (eds), *Antitrust, Innovation and Competitiveness* (Oxford, Oxford University Press, 1992).

[3] Ibid 5.

[4] Ibid 3.

[5] See Raymond S Hartman, Will Mitchell, Thomas M Jorde and David J Teece, 'Assessing Market Power in Regimes of Rapid Technological Change' (1993) 2 *Industrial and Corporate Change* 317; David J Teece and Mary Coleman, 'The Meaning of Monopoly: Antitrust Analysis in High-Technology Industries' (1998) 43 *Antitrust Bulletin* 801; Christopher Pleatsikas and David J Teece, 'The Analysis of Market Definition and Market Power in the Context of Rapid Innovation' (2001) 19 *International Journal of Industrial Organisation* 665.

The Horizontal Merger Guidelines ('the Merger Guidelines')[6] are the intellectual cornerstone of modern antitrust law, yet they contain little discussion of innovation or dynamic competition. Since the mid-1990s, however, the intellectual winds have slowly begun to change. A milestone in that progression was the publication of an article by Michael L Katz and Howard A Shelanski in 2005 entitled, '"Schumpeterian" Competition and Antitrust Policy in High-Tech Markets'.[7] Antitrust scholars now actively debate the merits of replacing static competition with dynamic competition in antitrust analysis.[8] Moreover, the Federal Trade Commission (FTC) and Department of Justice (DOJ) staff and FTC commissioners also now profess that innovation is important to competition. The agencies promulgated the Intellectual Property Guidelines in 1995 to allow firms more confidence in exercising their intellectual property rights (IPRs),[9] and the Joint Venture Guidelines[10] in 2000 to outline acceptable forms of cooperation among competitors.

Although the guidelines of the antitrust enforcement agencies do not constitute law merely by virtue of their promulgation by the agencies, the courts previously have accepted the revised principles that the agencies have advocated. By embracing the reasoning in the Merger Guidelines promulgated several decades ago by the Antitrust Division and the FTC, the federal courts have caused antitrust case law to ossify around a decidedly static view of antitrust. Put differently, in the years since 1980, the Division and the FTC have successfully persuaded the courts to adopt a more explicitly economic approach to merger analysis, yet one that has a static view of competition. The result is not a mere policy preference. It is law. To change that law to have a more dynamic view of competition will therefore require a sustained intellectual effort by the enforcement agencies (as well as by scholars and practitioners) that, once more, engages the courts to re-examine antitrust law as they did in the late 1970s during the ascendancy of the Chicago School, when antitrust law became infused with its current, static understanding of competition. It appears that, before the Obama Administration took office, the Antitrust Division was attempting to incorporate more dynamic analysis, but the result was inconsistent across different mergers

[6] US Department of Justice (DOJ) and Federal Trade Commission (FTC), 'Horizontal Merger Guidelines' (revised 8 April 1997), available at www.usdoj.gov/atr/public/guidelines/horiz_book/hmgl.html.

[7] See Michael L Katz and Howard A Shelanski, 'Schumpeterian Competition and Antitrust Policy in High-Tech Markets' (2005) 14 *Competition* 47, available at www.law.berkeley.edu/institutes/bclt/pubs/shelanski/katz_Shelanski_Schumpeter__30Nov2006_final.pdf.

[8] See, eg David S Evans and Keith N Hylton, 'The Lawful Acquisition and Exercise of Monopoly Power and Its Implications for the Objectives of Antitrust' (2008) 4 *Competition Policy International* 203; Jonathan Baker, '"Dynamic Competition" Does Not Excuse Monopolization' (2008) 4 *Competition Policy International* 243; Christian Ewald, 'Competition and Innovation: Dangerous "Myopia" of Economists in Antitrust?' (2008) 4 *Competition Policy International* 253; Richard Gilbert, 'Injecting Innovation into The Rule of Reason: A Comment on Evans and Hylton' (2008) 4 *Competition Policy International* 263; Herbert Hovenkamp, 'Schumpeterian Competition and Antitrust' (2008) 4 *Competition Policy International* 273; Thomas K McCraw, 'Joseph Schumpeter on Competition' (2008) 4 *Competition Policy International* 309; Ilya Segal and Michael D Whinston, 'Antitrust in Innovative Industries' (2007) 97 *American Economic Review* 1703. For an earlier Schumpeterian perspective on the Microsoft antitrust case, see Howard A Shelanski and J Gregory Sidak, 'Antitrust Divestiture in Network Industries' (2001) 68 *University of Chicago Law Review*; J Gregory Sidak, 'An Antitrust Rule for Software Integration' (2001) 18 *Yale Journal on Regulation* 1. For a discussion of the role of dynamic competition in the antitrust analysis of patent royalties and standard-setting, see Richard Schmalensee, 'Standard-Setting, Innovation Specialists, and Competition Policy' (2009) 57 *Journal of Industrial Economics* 526.

[9] See US DOJ and FTC, 'Antitrust Guidelines for the Licensing of Intellectual Property' (1995) § 1, available at www.usdoj. gov/atr/ public/guidelines/0558.pdf [hereinafter Antitrust-IP Guidelines].

[10] See US DOJ and FTC, 'Antitrust Guidelines for Collaboration among Competitors (2000), available at www.ftc.gov/os/2000/04/ftcdojguidelines.pdf.

and different doctrinal areas of antitrust law. A necessary but not sufficient condition for infusing antitrust analysis with a dynamic competition perspective is a public process by which the Division and the FTC revisit and restate the Merger Guidelines in a manner that explicitly clarifies and defends the role of dynamic competition. We therefore applaud the announcement of the antitrust agencies in September 2009 to solicit public comment on the possibility of updating the Merger Guidelines.[11] Assuming that the Division and the FTC decide to revise the existing Merger Guidelines, those revised guidelines (and useful complementary undertakings, such as generalised guidelines on market power and remedies) will then require leadership by the enforcement agencies to persuade the courts that antitrust doctrine should evolve accordingly. That neo-Schumpeterian process may take a decade or longer to accomplish, but it is a path that we believe the Roberts Court is willing to travel.

II. Economic Theory and the Structuralist Tradition

Economists have long debated the significance of market structure on various indicia of economic performance, including innovation. As recently as September 2009, for example, the FTC and the Antitrust Division asked whether the Merger Guidelines should 'be updated to address more explicitly…the effects of mergers on innovation'.[12] This assertion of the direction of causation seems to presuppose the relationship between market structure and innovation. Does market structure—and, thus, a merger that contributes to a particular change in market structure from the status quo—determine the level and nature of innovation in a market? Why might we doubt, as a matter of economic theory, that market structure determines innovation? Does a firm's market share provide a reliable proxy for the firm's ability to capture the returns to innovation? Does causation run in the opposite direction, such that innovation determines market structure? Does a failure to evaluate market share and market power in this dynamic context help to explain why evidence of the efficacy of antitrust intervention (in terms of advancing consumer welfare) is both hard to document and a source of bitter dispute among antitrust economists?

A. Static Efficiency and the Disputed Efficacy of Antitrust Intervention

We remain bereft of evidence that antitrust intervention has benefited the consumer. Robert W Crandall and Clifford M Winston of the Brookings Institution 'find little empirical evidence that past interventions have provided much direct benefit to consumers'.[13] They cite, as one of the causes of this unfortunate state of affairs, the 'substantial and growing challenges of formulating and implementing effective antitrust policies in a new economy characterized by dynamic competition, rapid technological change, and important intellectual property'.[14]

[11] FTC and US DOJ, 'Horizontal Merger Guidelines: Questions for Public Comment' (2009), available at www.ftc.gov/bc/workshops/hmg/hmg-questions.pdf [hereinafter Questions for Public Comment].

[12] Ibid 5, question 15.

[13] See Robert W Crandall and Clifford M Winston, 'Does Antitrust Policy Improve Consumer Welfare? Assessing the Evidence' (2003) 17(4) *Journal of Economic Perspectives* 3, 4.

[14] Ibid 23.

The lack of compelling evidence indicating that antitrust has benefited consumers is a matter of concern and motivates our inquiry here. Our working hypothesis is that using static analysis to address antitrust issues in a dynamic economy is unlikely to improve consumer welfare and that a more dynamic analytical framework increases the likelihood of helping rather than hurting consumers. The problem may be that (1) static analysis still permeates much of economic theory; (2) the community of antitrust practitioners seems unaware of a substantial literature, much of it now quite robust, on evolutionary theory and the economic, organisational, behavioural, and strategic management foundations of innovation; or (3) although this new literature has generated useful general descriptions of market and organisational behaviour, those descriptions have only recently caught the attention of antitrust scholars. Due to this recent awareness, (4) the enforcement agencies are not confident about discarding conventional wisdom, despite that fact that many within the agencies know that much of that conventional wisdom is deeply discredited. Consequently, (5) the agencies sometimes strike the pose, not very convincingly, that existing statements of enforcement policy are living documents—sufficiently supple and far-sighted that they already embody dynamic analysis. Some at the enforcement agencies may subscribe to a hagiographic reverence toward the Merger Guidelines; others may see this position as an expedient justification for the maximisation of agency discretion. Alternatively, (6) one hears that the antitrust analysis of dynamic industries (formerly called the 'new economy', before that label became cliché) is no different from the antitrust analysis of less dynamic, 'smokestack' industries undergoing slower rates of technological innovation.[15]

This chapter explains why static analysis appears to dominate, even though thoughtful policy makers are aware of dynamic competition. Unfortunately, policy makers are left wielding static analysis in part because of an incorrect perception that scholars have not yet filled the intellectual void. Indeed, until that perception changes, antitrust analysis is not likely to improve. Indeed, Judge Richard A Posner has observed that 'antitrust doctrine has changed more or less in tandem with changes in economic theory, albeit with a lag'.[16] If scholars do not embrace the now-robust behavioural and evolutionary approaches, antitrust economists will miss an opportunity to analyse dynamic considerations properly. They also risk doing consumers more harm than good.

B. Market Structure as a Determinant of Innovation

Unfortunately, many economists are stuck in a well-travelled and largely irrelevant debate, now a half century old, as to what form of market structure favours innovation. They label this topic the 'Schumpeterian' debate. Regrettably, this nomenclature is all that many have absorbed from the rich work of Joseph Schumpeter, the Austrian School, and the extensive developments in behavioural and evolutionary economics. This so-called Schumpeterian debate casts Schumpeter excessively narrowly and is not of much interest anymore. That debate, however, can still bog down discussions about competition policy and innovation.

A more careful reading of Schumpeter reveals at least three Schumpeterian propositions relevant to antitrust policy. (The first two are discussed in this section, the third in

[15] See Richard A Posner, 'Antitrust in the New Economy' (2001) 68 *Antitrust Law Journal* 925.
[16] Ibid 942.

the next.) The first proposition relates to the impact of market structure on innovation. On this topic, Schumpeter himself articulated conflicting and inconsistent perspectives. In *The Theory of Economic Development*, first published when Schumpeter was only 28-years-old, he spoke in 1911 of the virtues of competition fuelled by entrepreneurs and small enterprises.[17] By the time Schumpeter, at the age of 59, published *Capitalism, Socialism, and Democracy* in 1942, his revised (second) proposition was that large firms with monopoly power are necessary to support innovation.[18] That transformation no doubt partly reflected the dramatic change that had occurred with respect to the principal sources of innovation in the American economy. So, with respect to the impact of market structure on innovation, Schumpeter seems to have maintained two almost diametrically opposite positions. We call his first position Schumpeter I and the second position Schumpeter II. If the popular celebration of new products coming from Silicon Valley is any indicator of informed opinion, Schumpeter I is perhaps more appealing today than Schumpeter II. Indeed, we believe that the debate over whether to favour competition over monopoly (as the market structure most likely to advance innovation) was won long ago in favour of some form of rivalry or competition.

Schumpeter was among the first to declare that perfect competition was incompatible with innovation. He noted that '[t]he introduction of new methods of production and new commodities is hardly conceivable with perfect—and perfectly prompt—competition from the start. And this means that the bulk of what we call economic progress is incompatible with it.'[19] However, the later Schumpeterian notion that small entrepreneurial firms lack financial resources also seems at odds with his earlier views and seems archaic in today's circumstances where the funding of enterprises through venture capital plays such a large role in innovation. The new issues (stock) market has itself funded early stage biotech and internet companies with minimal revenues and negative earnings.

The fact that perfect competition is inconsistent with innovation does not necessarily mean that monopoly is a requirement. Schumpeter himself recognised, as we do, the importance of pluralism and rivalry in the economic system. However, one need not define rivalry as occurring inside some tightly circumscribed 'antitrust market' containing only existing competitors, with their capabilities proxied by existing market shares. Moreover, numerous variables complicate any simple relationship between the generation of monopolistic rents and the allocation of resources to develop new products and processes. We examine some of those variables below. The line of causation that is most commonly discussed in the industrial organisation literature runs only from competition to innovation. Reflecting this, the FTC said on the opening page of its report on innovation in 2003, 'competition can stimulate innovation.'[20] 'Competition amongst firms', the agency reasoned, 'can spur the invention of new or better products or more efficient processes'.[21] Although these statements are undoubtedly correct, they do not recognise that innovation may affect

[17] See Joseph A Schumpeter, *The Theory of Economic Development: An Inquiry into Profits, Capital, Credit, Interest, and the Business Cycle* (1911) R Opie (trans) (Oxford, Oxford University Press, 1963).

[18] See Joseph A Schumpeter, *Capitalism, Socialism and Democracy* [1942] (Re-print: New York, Taylor & Francis, 2005).

[19] Ibid 105.

[20] FTC, 'To Promote Innovation: The Proper Balance of Competition and Patent Law and Policy (2003) 1, available at www.ftc.gov/os/2003/10/innovationrpt.pdf.

[21] Ibid.

competition and market structure. Nor do they suggest what type of market structure is desirable. These statements suggest only that competition can drive innovation.

Despite 50 years of research, economists do not appear to have found much evidence that market concentration has a statistically significant impact on innovation. This relationship probably is not a useful framing of the problem, because market concentration alone is neither theoretically nor empirically a major determinant of innovation. In short, framing competition issues in terms of monopoly versus competition appears to have been unhelpful. At a minimum, doing so has been inconclusive. Rivalry matters, but market concentration does not necessarily determine rivalry. The empirical evidence is still murky. In a review of the literature published in 1989, Wesley M Cohen and Richard C Levin found that a strong linkage does not exist between market concentration and innovation.[22] The endogeneity of market structure is perhaps one reason that we have yet to find a robust statistical relationship between concentration and innovation. In addition, no significant relationship exists between market concentration and profitability. Paul L Joskow argued, in 1975, that 'we have spent too much time calculating too many kinds of concentration ratios and running too many regressions of these against profit figures of questionable validity'.[23]

Some industrial organisation theories suggest that innovation is bound to decline with increasing competition, because the monopoly rents for new entrants will decline with increasing competition.[24] In contrast, Kenneth J Arrow has hypothesised a positive relationship between competition and innovation.[25] However, Arrow sets aside the appropriability problem (that is, how to capture value from innovation) and posits a perfect property right in the information underlying a specific production technique. One can perhaps interpret Arrow's posited property right as a clearly specified and costlessly enforceable patent of infinite duration. His principal focus is on how the (pre-invention) structure of the output market affects the gain from invention. Competition prevails because output is greater under competition than monopoly. Hence, a given amount of reduction in unit costs is more valuable if the market is initially competitive. Protected by a perfect patent, the inventor simply licenses the invention at a price slightly below the cost saving that the invention makes possible. Put differently, competition will prevail and advance innovation when the business environment is characterised by what Teece elsewhere has called a 'strong appropriability regime'.[26] Absent strong appropriability, the presumption that perfect competition is superior to alternative arrangements cannot be built on Arrow's analysis. In fact, it is important to note that despite how Arrow's article is usually interpreted (to claim that competition spurs innovation), his general position in his

[22] Wesley M Cohen and Richard C Levin, 'Empirical Studies of Innovation and Market Structure' in Richard L Schmalensee and Robert D Willig (eds), (1989) 2 *Handbook of Industrial Organisation* 1059.

[23] Paul L Joskow, 'Firm Decision-Making Processes and Oligopoly Theory' (1975) 65 *American Economic Review* 270, 278.

[24] See Morton Kamien and Nancy Schwarz, *Market Structure and Innovation* (Amsterdam, North Holland, 1982); Partha Dasgupta and Joseph E Stiglitz, 'Industrial Structure and the Nature of Innovation Activity' (1980) 90 *Economic Journal*. 26.

[25] See Kenneth J Arrow, 'Economic Welfare and the Allocation of Resources for Invention' in Richard R Nelson (ed), *The Rate and Direction of Inventive Activity* (Cambridge MA, National Bureau of Economic Research, 1962).

[26] See David J Teece, 'Profiting from Technological Innovation: Implications for Integration, Collaboration, Licensing and Public Policy' (1986) 15 *Research Policy* 285.

writings is, much like Schumpeter, that competitive markets provide inadequate incentives for firms to innovate.

As Sidney G Winter observes, Arrow's analysis also sidesteps business model choices.[27] The producer and the inventor are the same. Of course, one must also recognise that business model innovation is important to economic welfare, just as technological innovation is. However, neither the theoretical nor the empirical literature in economics seems to address whether market structure is important to business model innovation.

Historical and comparative evidence suggests that competition and rivalry are important for innovation; but few believe that the world of perfect competition (in which firms compete in highly fragmented markets using identical non-proprietary technologies) is an organisational arrangement that any advanced economy would aspire to create. Nevertheless, many policy debates proceed on the assumption that highly fragmented markets assist innovation. Although rivalry and competition are important to innovation, belief in the virtues of perfectly competitive systems reflects casual empiricism and prejudice rather than careful theorising and empirical study. One can say the same for belief in the virtues of monopoly.

To summarise, the basic framework employed in discussions about innovation, technology policy, and competition policy is often remarkably naïve, highly incomplete, and burdened by a myopic focus on market structure as the key determinant of innovation. Indeed, it is common to find a debate about innovation policy amongst economists, collapsing into a rather narrow discussion of the relative virtues of competition and monopoly, as if they were the main determinants of innovation. Clearly, much more is at work. In subsequent sections, we identify various dimensions of internal firm structure and management that influence the rate and direction of innovation.

C. Why is a Nexus between Market Structure and Innovation Unlikely to Exist?

Why might no nexus exist between market structure and innovation? Consider, first, single-product firms. The notion that the funding of innovation requires the cash flows generated by the exercise of monopoly power assumes both that (1) capital markets are inefficient, and (2) the difference between competitive and monopolistic levels of internal cash flows are sufficient to justify research and development (R&D) programmes that would otherwise lie fallow. However, if capital markets are operating according to what Eugene Fama has called strong-form efficiency,[28] then actual cash flows need not be the source of funding. Firms with high-yield projects will be able to signal their profit opportunities to the capital market, and the requisite financial resources should be drawn forth on competitive terms. Thus, if there is strong-form efficiency and zero transaction costs (its corollary), cash should get matched to projects whether or not the cash is internally generated. Even if one were not to assume strong-form market efficiency, cash can be generated by mechanisms other than the sale of current products. Any source of cash flow can

[27] Sidney G Winter, 'The Logic of Appropriability: From Schumpeter to Arrow to Teece' (2006) 35 *Research Policy* 1100.

[28] See Eugene F Fama, 'Efficient Capital Markets: A Review of Theory and Empirical Work' (1970) 25 *Journal of Finance* 383.

be used to invest in R&D in established enterprises, if management decides to do so. Put differently, cash is fungible inside the corporation.

Of course, the world is not properly characterised by zero transaction costs and strong-form capital market efficiency; but the absence of those stylised conditions does not imply that the availability of internal cash flows from monopoly (as compared to competitive) product market positions is what makes the difference between a firm being able to fund and not being able to fund development projects for new products or processes. Significant innovative efforts almost always involve expenditures in a particular year that may be many multiples of available cash flows. So the availability of marginally higher cash flows occasioned by monopoly power is unlikely to change the sources of funds very much, except in unusual circumstances. Furthermore, even in the absence of adequate internal cash flow, firms may access the capital markets to obtain the requisite financing.

It is also the case that product development goals can be accomplished by a myriad of collaborative organisational arrangements, including research joint ventures, co-production, and co-marketing agreements. With such arrangements, there is the possibility that the innovator's capital requirements for a new project could be drastically reduced.[29] This possibility suggests that inter firm arrangements can harness economies of scale and scope.[30]

Any link between market power and innovation in specific markets is further unshackled if the multidivisional multiproduct firm (rather than the single-product firm) is admitted onto the economic landscape. The multiproduct structure allows the allocation of cash generated everywhere to be directed to high-yield purposes anywhere inside the firm. If a multidivisional multiproduct firm actually operates this way, then the link between market power in a particular market and the funding of innovation in that market collapses.

Put differently, if a multiproduct firm sells products in markets A to Z, then the cash generated by virtue of any market power in market A can fund innovation relevant to market A; but that cash can equally well fund innovative activity for products in market Z. The fungibility of cash inside the multiproduct firm thus unlocks any causal relationship between market structure and innovation. Clearly, Schumpeter's hypothesis is not robust in the presence of multiproduct firms.

Another stream of research implicitly attacks the foundations of the Schumpeterian hypothesis. Since the late 1980s, Michael C Jensen has initiated a provocative body of scholarship in corporate finance that argues that, for firms to operate efficiently, free cash flow ought to be distributed to shareholders rather than be invested internally in discretionary projects.[31] Jensen's basic insight is that the discipline of debt is needed to cause capital to be channelled to high-yield uses in the economy, as well as in the firm. The implicit assumption is that the principal-agent problem is so great that managers will fritter away shareholders' money on unprofitable new projects and products. Accordingly, leveraging the corporation with debt will benefit shareholders—not only because of the tax

[29] See Kyle J Mayer and David J Teece, 'Unpacking Strategic Alliances: The Structure and Purpose of Alliance versus Supplier Relationships' (2008) 66 *Journal of Economic Behaviour and Organisation* 106.

[30] For a managerially oriented analysis of the limits of outsourcing in the context of innovation, see Henry W Chesbrough and David J Teece, 'When Is Virtual Virtuous: Organizing for Innovation' (1996) 74(1) *Harvard Business Review* 65.

[31] See Michael C Jensen, 'Agency Costs of Free Cash Flow, Corporate Finance, and Takeovers' (1986) 76 *American Economic Association Papers and Proceedings* 323.

deductibility of interest, but also because of avoidance of the principal-agent problem that Jensen believes exists if managers are left with cash to reinvest.

There are severe problems with Jensen's thesis, not least of which is that debt holders are generally loss averse and not opportunity-driven. Although it may indeed be the case that free cash flows do sometimes get misallocated by managers, to restrict management access to free cash flow by burdening the enterprise with high debt levels will suffocate R&D, force the firm into equity markets to finance innovation, or both. This effect is not always desirable because the new issues markets, both public and private, are relatively expensive sources of new capital and may not be 'open' when needed to develop products to hit particular market 'windows'. However, as a positive rather than normative matter, to the extent that Jensen's thesis is correct and boards do encourage firms to load up with debt, then Schumpeterian mechanisms will be blunted by financial structure.

To summarise, innovation is risky and costly, and it clearly requires access to capital. On this point we agree with Schumpeter. The necessary capital can come from cash flows or from equity (private or public) or from debt financing. However, at least with respect to early-stage activity, debt financing is unlikely to be viable, unless the firm has other assets to pledge.[32] Nevertheless, certain downstream investments needed to commercialise innovation can be debt financed if they are redeployable. Alternatively, the firm can enter into alliances that reduce the need for new investment in complementary assets.

In short, many factors besides firm size and the presence or absence of market power affect an innovator's capacity to access capital.[33] The firm's financial structure and its multiproduct scope break any simple *ex ante* nexus between market structure and innovation. Hence, at least in today's world of reasonably well developed venture capital and financial markets, we see no a priori reason to expect that circumstances will validate the Schumpeterian hypothesis.

D. Why Market Share is a Poor Proxy for Appropriability

As we discussed above, Schumpeter also developed the thesis that large firms were necessary for innovation. In his view, large firms not only routinised the innovation process, but also developed market power, which generated the high profits necessary for innovators to appropriate sufficient returns to justify the risks associated with investing in R&D.

In the preceding sections we explained why no a priori basis exists to expect there to be a nexus between R&D investment and market share—at least with respect to the large multiproduct firm and firms that have access to venture capital and other sources of cash flow not internally generated. In this section, we elaborate why Schumpeter's appropriability theory, in which high market share is necessary to enable the innovator to appropriate

[32] Oliver E Williamson explains that the decision by firms to use debt or equity to support individual investment projects is likely to be linked to the redeployability of the underlying investment. See Oliver E Williamson, *The Mechanisms of Governance* (Oxford, Oxford University Press, 1996). Because new product development programmes commonly involve investment in assets that are substantially irreversible (like R&D) or non-redeployable (like specialised equipment), or both, debt has only limited value in financing innovation, unless a firm has collateral and is under-leveraged to begin with. Accordingly, the funding sources generally available to support new product development are internal cash flow and new equity.

[33] For an expanded discussion, see Richard H Day, Gunnar Eliasson and Clas G Wihlborg, *The Markets for Innovation, Ownership and Control* (Amsterdam, North-Holland 1993).

(capture) value from innovation, is misguided. We examine the key elements of appropriability and show that market share and market power are not the key to appropriability and stimulating R&D. In fact, high market share may have the opposite effect. The fear of cannibalising one's own market share (which might be called 'anti-cannibalism') might actually dampen or thwart innovation if the new product or innovation displaces sales and profits at a higher rate for the incumbent than for competitors and new entrants.

As already noted, the Schumpeterian thesis is implicitly an appropriability thesis, at least in part. Schumpeter argued that a firm needs market power to enable it to capture sufficient profit to justify the costs and risks of investment in innovative activity. We agree that investors need an adequate return for their investment in risky R&D. However, capturing high market share in a product market and pricing above some hypothetical competitive level is not the only business model available for profiting from innovation.

Elsewhere, Teece has suggested that the two most important factors conditioning appropriability (of the returns from innovation) are not high market share but the efficacy of legal mechanisms of protection (that is, intellectual property) and the nature of the new knowledge that has been created.[34] The ownership of complementary assets also helps govern returns from innovation. Market power is likely to be a second-order factor relative to these considerations. It is as much a result as a cause of innovative activity.

Winter observes that Teece's profiting-from-innovation thesis represents a logical progression from the Schumpeterian thesis.[35] We now outline the elements of this post-Schumpeterian approach.

Consider intellectual property, particularly patents. Patents can be used to exclude competitors and generate profits, even if the firm has low market share. Patents work through technology markets; dominance in a technology market may or may not lead to exclusion from a product market. This distinction provides yet another reason why the Schumpeterian thesis connecting market concentration and market power to innovation is flawed.

Moreover, it is well known that patents do not work in practice as they do in theory. Rarely, if ever, do patents confer perfect appropriability, although they do afford considerable protection in some instances, such as with new chemical products and rather simple mechanical inventions.[36] It is often the case that rivals can 'invent around' many patents at modest costs.[37] In fact, one experienced patent law practitioner we know claims that he can 'invent on demand' by writing a patent application for a client that can invent around any existing patent. Even if our friend is mildly boasting, his comment underscores that patents are often ineffective at protecting innovation. Often patents provide little protection because the legal and financial requirements for upholding their validity or for proving their infringement are high, and they are narrow because prior art is substantial in fields where there is rich innovation.

[34] D Teece, *Profiting from Technological Innovation* (n 26) 26.

[35] See Winter, *The Logic of Appropriability* (n 27) 27.

[36] See Richard C Levin, Alvin K Klevorick, Richard R Nelson and Sidney G Winter, 'Appropriating the Returns from Industrial Research and Development' (1987) *The Brookings Papers on Economic Activity (Microeconomics)* 783.

[37] See Edwin Mansfield, Marc Schwartz and Samuel Wagner, 'Imitation Costs and Patents: An Empirical Study' (1981) 91 *The Economic Journal* 907.

One must also recognise that the degree of legal protection that a firm enjoys is not necessarily an exogenous attribute. The inventor's own intellectual property strategy itself enters the equation. So does the fundamental nature (or lack thereof) of the invention. The inventor of core technology not only can seek to patent the invention, but can also seek complementary patents on new features or manufacturing processes (or both) and possibly on designs. The way that a patent counsel writes the claims in the patent application also matters. Of course, the more fundamental the invention, the higher the probability that a broad patent will be granted and granted in multiple jurisdictions around the world.

Exclusionary rights are not fully secured by the mere issuance of a patent, of course. Although a patent is presumed to be valid in many jurisdictions, validity is never firmly established until a patent has been upheld in court. A patent is merely a passport to another journey down the road to enforcement and possible licensing fees. The best patents are broad in scope, have already been upheld in court, and cover a technology essential to the manufacture and sale of products in high demand.

In some industries, particularly where the innovation is embedded in processes, trade secrets are a viable alternative to patents. Trade secret protection is possible, however, only if a firm can put its product before the public and still keep the underlying technology secret. Usually, only chemical formulas and industrial-commercial processes can be protected as trade secrets after the products embodying them are released to the public. And, of course, the filing of a patent application constitutes public disclosure of the trade secret and consequently forfeits protection under state trade secret law regardless of whether a valid patent subsequently issues under federal law.

The degree to which knowledge about an innovation is tacit or easily codified also affects the ease of imitation, and hence appropriability. Tacit knowledge is, by definition, difficult to articulate. Consequently, it is hard to transfer to others unless those who possess the know-how can demonstrate it to others. It is also hard to protect tacit knowledge using intellectual property law. Codified knowledge is easier to transmit and receive, and it is more exposed to industrial espionage. On the other hand, codified knowledge is often easier to protect using the instruments of intellectual property law.

At the risk of grave oversimplifications, one can divide appropriability regimes into 'weak' regimes (innovations are difficult to protect because they can be easily codified and legal protection of intellectual property is ineffective) and 'strong' regimes (the profits from invention/innovation can be protected because knowledge about the invention/innovation is tacit or they are well protected legally, or both). Despite recent efforts to strengthen the protection of intellectual property, strong appropriability is the exception rather than the rule. This state of affairs has been so for centuries, and it will never be substantially different in democratic societies, where individuals and ideas move with little governmental interference, and where intellectual property protection is inherently limited.

Implicitly, then, appropriability need not depend on market share or market power in product markets. In this article, we do not endeavour to analyse technology markets, but we do note that the 'Schumpeterian thesis', as it has come to be known, references product markets, not technology markets. Because overlaps between technology markets and product technology markets are loose, it is easy to see that the Schumpeterian thesis is flawed on this account alone. Clearly, appropriability for a particular innovation depends on more microanalytic factors than Schumpeter and the subsequent mainstream industrial economics literature have recognised.

Besides the appropriability regime itself, there is yet another class of factors that determines the returns to the innovator. Those factors are complementary assets. Ownership of complementary assets affects returns to innovation even though they are outside the appropriability regime that we define here.[38]

Notably, Schumpeter overlooked complements and complementary assets. He stressed how 'gales of creative destruction' could overturn the existing order.[39] The new would drive out the old. Substitution was the primary consequence of Schumpeterian innovation. Schumpeter's single-minded emphasis on substitution is too narrow, as it ignores complements. Innovation can enhance the value of complements. There are several reasons for this result.

First, as stressed by Teece,[40] innovation is rarely sold (licensed) in disembodied form. To be useful, and to generate a revenue stream, inventions must become embedded in products. To produce and sell products, one usually needs to employ complements. At the most general level, the importance of complementary technologies and complementary assets has been recognised by historians for a long time.[41] The complementarity of factor inputs has been part of the theory of production since the writings of Adam Smith, Augustin Cournot, and David Ricardo. However, it is only relatively recently, after the topic has been embedded in a contracting framework,[42] that the nature and role of complementary assets in the theory of innovation has become better understood.

Once a contracting framework is adopted, it is a small step to recognise that (1) the asset value of complements may rise if the overall demand for complements is enhanced by innovation and (2) if in fact the innovation and the complement are co-specialised to each other, and if the co-specialised asset is not under the control of the innovator, then rents (profits) can be extracted from the innovator by the owner of the co-specialised asset.[43] Complementors are especially important in a multi-sided market, which we will discuss later in the context of antitrust intervention.

E. Innovation as a Determinant of Market Structure

Despite evident theoretical flaws in the Schumpeterian market structure-innovation hypothesis, the received wisdom and dominant logic in industrial organisation studies remain that market structure is the main determinant of innovation. A less familiar logic—but in our view, a far more convincing and empirically supportable logic—runs the other way: innovation shapes market structure. At a general level, the argument was first articulated by Almarin Phillips in his study of the evolution of the civilian aircraft industry.[44]

Phillips' field research led him to conclude that developments in jet engine technology available in the United Kingdom and Germany immediately after World War II were largely exogenous to the development activity in US industry. Boeing and Douglas and other

[38] Teece (n 26).

[39] Schumpeter (n18) 83.

[40] See Teece (n 26); David J Teece, 'Reflections on 'Profiting from Innovation' (2006) 35 *Research Policy* 1131.

[41] See Nathan Rosenberg, 'On Technological Expectations' (1976) 86 *The Economic Journal* 523.

[42] See Winter (n 27).

[43] Teece (n 26).

[44] See Almarin Phillips, *Technology and Market Structure: A Study of the Aircraft Industry* (Lexington, Heath, 1971).

companies in the United States successfully used these technologies to develop the civilian jet aircraft. Domestic market structure did not drive these decisions and developments. Market outcomes in the United States were then very much affected by how and when Boeing, McDonnell, Douglas, Lockheed, and others decided to tap into a largely external reservoir of technological know-how available in the United States, United Kingdom, and Germany.

Boeing did so quickly and successfully. It leveraged its success with the KC-130 jet tanker that it built for the US Air Force into a civilian version, the Boeing 707. Boeing captured the lead in market share globally with this airplane. It maintained its lead until the emergence and growth of Airbus. Philips' historical analysis led him to conclude that

> an important influence on market structures and on research and development programs and innovative behavior of firms stems from the presence or absence of related technological and scientific changes which occur for reasons generally exogenous to market phenomena and the goals of the particular firm.[45]

Studies find that various types of externally shaped and externally funded technological regimes exist.[46] For example, university-funded and government-funded research in science and technology has created vibrant technological environments that fuel venture-funded new businesses. Biotech is a case where US government funds distributed through the National Institutes of Health have helped to create technological opportunities that are then seized upon and developed further by new venture-funded startups.[47] Although most of these companies fail, enough survive to influence the structure of the pharmaceutical industry.

The concept of technological opportunity, although poorly developed in economics, has been used as a surrogate for issues associated with an industry's external reservoir of know-how and ferment in the underlying technological base. However, technological opportunity is a remarkably passive concept that needs further explication. Nelson and Winter claim that knowledge and opportunity are determined by the underlying 'technological regime', and that regimes differ from industry to industry.[48] How and why some firms tap into technological opportunities remains enigmatic. Economic theory—or any other theory, for that matter—poorly explains the microanalytics of these decisions.

The importance of new entrants to innovation is consistent with the importance of 'exogenous factors'—factors outside the market or even the industry. It is well established that new entrants have been responsible for a substantial share of revolutionary new

[45] Ibid 3.

[46] See Keith Pavitt, Michael Robson and Joe Townsend, 'The Size Distribution of Innovating Firms in the U.K.' (1987) 35 *Journal of Industrial Economics* 297; David B Audretsch and Zoltan J Acs, 'Innovation, Market Share, and Firm Size' (1988) 69 *Review of Economics and Statistics* 567; David B Audretsch and Zoltan J Acs, 'Innovation in Large and Small Firms: An Empirical Analysis' (1998) 78 *American Economic Review* 678.

[47] Audretsch's empirical work on innovation rates shows that, 'whereas the large-firm innovation rates are relatively high in rubber, instruments, and chemicals, the small firm innovation rates are relatively high in instruments, chemicals, non-electrical machinery, and electrical equipment'. David B Audretsch *Innovation and Industry Evolution* (Boston, MIT Press, 1995). Relatedly, Audretsch finds that '[t]he small firm innovation rate exceeds the large firm innovation rate in fourteen of the industrial sectors, but the large firm innovation rate exceeds the small-firm innovation rate in four of the sectors.... [T]he relative innovative advantage of large firms tends to be promoted in industries that are capital intensive, advertising intensive, concentrated, and highly unionized'. Ibid 38.

[48] Richard R Nelson and Sidney G Winter, *An Evolutionary Theory of Economic Change* (Boston, Belknap Press 1982).

products and processes. They include the jet engine (Whittle in England, Henkel and Junkers in Germany), catalytic cracking in petroleum refining (Houdry), the electric typewriter (IBM), electronic computing (IBM), electrostatic copying (Haloid), PTFE vascular grafts (WL Gore), the microwave oven (Raytheon), and diet cola (RC Cola). These anecdotes and other evidence further erode any connection between market structure and innovation, which further suggests that (1) incumbency and market share or market power is by no means a prerequisite for innovation and (2) no particular firm size is conducive to technological progress.

In summary, with exogenous factors including technological opportunity playing such a large role, one can readily understand and agree with John Sutton's characterisation that 'there appears to be no consensus as to the form of relationship, if any, between R&D intensity and concentration'.[49] As already noted, Wesley Cohen's and Richard Levin's authoritative study in the Handbook of Industrial Organization likewise concluded that the evidence on the market structure-innovation nexus was mixed.[50] Once one includes control variables, the partial correlation between R&D intensity and concentration is extremely weak.

Sutton speculates that a 'bounds issue'[51] may exist—that is, the relationship between market structure and innovation might well exist in some narrowly circumscribed set of bounds. However, even if Sutton's conjecture is true, it suggests that market concentration may not be particularly helpful in understanding innovation and its determinants. Furthermore, game-theoretic models are unlikely to provide much insight and, to the contrary, may in fact prove empirically empty.[52]

F. Summary and Recapitulation

For almost three-quarters of a century, economists have devoted much effort (we would say too much effort) to exploring relationships between market structure and innovation. One hypothesis, often attributed to Schumpeter,[53] is that profits accumulated through the exercise of monopoly power (assumed to be correlated with large firms) are a key source of funds to support risky and costly innovative activity. As discussed, these predictions as a matter of economic theory are not well grounded in the nature of the (modern) firm.[54]

Nor is there good theory to suggest, alternatively, that perfect competition is the ideal regime. As discussed later, many other factors are at work, particularly factors that are internal to firms. So on a priori grounds one would not expect any relationships between market structure and innovation to be strong. Indeed, the evidence indicates at best a weak

[49] John Sutton, *Technology* and *Market Structure: Theory and History* (Boston, MA, MIT Press 1998).

[50] See Cohen and Levin (n 22).

[51] Sutton (n 49) 5.

[52] See Franklin M Fisher, 'Games Economists Play: A Noncooperative View' (1989) 20 *Rand Journal of Economics* 113 (1989); John Sutton, 'Explaining Everything, Explaining Nothing? Game Theoretic Models in Industrial Organization' (1990) 34 *European Economic Review* 505; Sam Peltzman, 'The Handbook of Industrial Organization: A Review Article' (1991) 99 *Journal of Political Economy* 201.

[53] See Schumpeter (n 18) ch 8.

[54] See Morton I Kamien and Nancy L Schwartz, 'Self Financing of an R&D Project' (1978) 68 *American Economic Review* 252.

effect. Also, as already discussed, causation is more likely to run in the opposite direction, from innovation to market structure.[55]

More formal theoretical modeling on market structure has likewise provided little insight. The industrial organisation textbook by Frederick M Scherer and David Ross has noted that 'through astute choice of assumptions, virtually any market structure can be shown to have superior innovative qualities' and 'to avoid biased inferences, it is necessary to take into account variables other than market structure that affect the pace of innovation'.[56] Interestingly, the main independent variable to which many scholars, including Scherer and Ross, gravitate is technological opportunity—'the rate at which more or less exogenous and cumulative advances in science and technology generate profitable new innovative possibilities'[57] Scherer and Ross further note that 'the structure-to-innovation linkage probably operated over a much shorter time span than the innovation-to-structure linkage'.[58] This second linkage is expected to be stronger in industries with rich technological opportunities. The idea is that concentration is more conducive to innovation in slow-moving fields. That is, technological opportunity, often manifested by radical breakthroughs, favours newcomers, not incumbents. These refinements seem plausible. However, perhaps the biggest reason why three-quarters of a century of scholarly work has failed is that the various economic theories of innovation pay very little attention to factors inside the firm. We commence an effort to remedy that situation in subsequent sections. Accordingly, we find ourselves not in agreement with Schumpeter, that monopoly power is necessary for innovation. So long as rivalry is maintained, it may help; but other factors are likely to be more important. However, as we explain in the next section, there is a third Schumpeterian hypothesis with which we agree.

III. Static Competition and Dynamic Competition

As we discussed above, a third proposition is embedded in Schumpeter. Usually overlooked, but very important, and one with which we agree, it is that dynamic competition should be favoured over its weaker cousin, static competition. Schumpeter observed that

> [t]his kind of competition is as much more effective than the other as a bombardment is in comparison with forcing a door, and so much more important that it becomes a matter of comparative indifference whether competition in the ordinary sense functions more or less promptly; the powerful lever that in the long run expands output and brings down prices is in any case made of other stuff.[59]

55 There is also considerable empirical evidence that augmented R&D activity follows increases in profitability with short lags. See Ben Branch, 'Research and Development Activity and Profitability: Distributed Lag Analysis' (1974) 82 *Journal of Political Economy* 999; Ariel Pakes, 'On Patents, R&D, and the Stock Market Rate of Return' 93 *Journal of Political Economy* 390.

56 Frederic M Scherer and David Ross, *Industrial Market Structure and Economic Performance*, 3rd edn (Houghton Mifflin. 1990) 642, 644.

57 Ibid 645.

58 Ibid.

59 See Schumpeter (n 18) 83.

We will describe both static competition and dynamic competition in turn. In doing so, we recognise that sometimes these styles of competition do not have bright lines separating them. Certainly, Schumpeter did not provide any crisp delineation.

We attempt to give some substance to Schumpeter's intuition. Unfortunately, antitrust economists often unwittingly favour static competition. They are often unaware that there are many ways to conceptualise competition. Dynamic competition is a style of competition that relies on innovation to produce new products and processes and concomitant price reductions of substantial magnitude. Such competition improves productivity, the availability of new goods and services, and, more generally, consumer welfare. Promoting dynamic competition may well mean recognising that competitive conduct may involve holding short-run price competition in abeyance. For example, the argument against generic 'me-too' drugs may be of this kind; generics may lower prices for existing drugs, but they may slow the development of new drugs, yielding a classic trade-off between static efficiency and dynamic efficiency.

Put succinctly, competition policy rooted in static economic analysis sees the policy goal as minimising the Harberger (deadweight loss) triangles from monopoly. A new competition policy, recognising the special power of dynamic competition, would advance the availability of new products and the co-creation of new markets that allows latent demand (and hence new amounts of consumer surplus associated with new demand curves) to be realised by consumers. It would also recognise cost savings flowing from innovation as an indicator of likely future consumer welfare gains. Put differently, the focus of a revised competition policy and merger-guideline framework would still very much be on the consumer, but it would be future-oriented and would recognise that certain business practices might lead to market creation (or at least co-creation) that would yield new demand curves with large gains in consumer surplus (because demand for new products could be satisfied). The minimisation of Harberger deadweight loss triangles would be a secondary focus. Where minimising Harberger triangles today stands in the way of creating new and significant future demand curves, a new competition policy would likely favour the future and recognise the welfare benefits associated with creating or co-creating new markets.

Economists do not embrace the concept of dynamic competition as widely or as wisely as they should, partly because the overwhelming focus in economic research is implicitly inside the marginalist paradigm of static competition. Indeed, a major contribution can come from simply revealing to judges, juries, the enforcement agencies, and legislators that most economic analysis is static—when it should be dynamic—and that, consequently, superficial answers derived from implicitly held static notions about desirable forms of competition may well harm innovation and, in the long run, consumers. This bias stems merely from the analytical tools that economists use for their convenience. Although most economists recognise the importance of innovation, they usually proceed to apply analytical approaches that ignore it or are ill-suited to studying it. Recognising that this state of affairs exists should deflate the hubris with which many antitrust scholars approach alleged restraints of trade. To the extent that they wield analytical tools of static competitive analysis, antitrust analysts are likely to make prescriptions that harm both innovation and competition and thus sap productivity. Needless to say, such prescriptions are likely to harm consumer welfare as well.

To develop policy prescriptions that do more good than harm, economists and antitrust scholars and practitioners need to inquire into the determinants of innovation and the impact of antitrust activity (including merger policy) on innovation. Rapid technological change advances dynamic competition. The problem is that the analytical framework that economists most commonly embrace adheres stubbornly to the view that market structure—and little else—determines the rate of technological change. As already discussed, that framework is grossly inadequate and cannot be supported.

For instance, in merger analysis, as in many forms of antitrust analysis under the rule of reason, one is required to define a market and examine market shares. If a merger would raise concentration above an accepted threshold, the Government may block it. Merger analysis usually proceeds this way, even though a growing number of economists are beginning to think otherwise, particularly in the context of differentiated products. In such cases, that emerging consensus seems to be that the particular firms that one is examining are what matters.

More often than not, however, avid antitrust economists allow the concept of static competition to guide their analysis. Because of its familiarity and simplicity, they inappropriately use the apparatus of static microeconomics to analyse contexts where innovation is important. Innovation is at best an afterthought in static microeconomic theory. The presence of innovation complicates economic analysis. It destroys equilibrium, thereby debasing the value and usefulness of the familiar toolkit that most economists carry. It leads to indivisibilities, rendering marginal analysis of limited value. It generates spillovers and raises 'appropriability' and 'public good' issues. For these and other reasons, the profession tends to resist abandoning the old tools of neoclassical economics. Economists shun dynamic analysis either because they do not understand that framework or because they fear that recognising it will be excessively hostile to well-accepted and well-practiced analytical frameworks. We contend that advocates of competition policy should not accept this state of affairs any longer. We therefore applaud the FTC and the Antitrust Division for asking whether the Merger Guidelines '[s]hould…be revised to explain more fully than in the current [version] how market shares and market concentration are measured and interpreted in dynamic markets, including markets experiencing significant technological change'.[60]

Dynamic competition is powered by the creation and commercialisation of new products, new processes, and new business models. As Schumpeter said, competition fuelled by the introduction of new products and processes is the more powerful form of competition:

> competition from the new commodity, the new technology, the new source of supply, the new type of organization—competition which commands a decisive cost or quality advantage and which strikes not at the margins of the profits and the output of existing firms, but at their foundations and their very lives.[61]

Advocates of strong competition policy must surely favour dynamic competition, for static competition is anemic in comparison. However, by unwittingly using static microeconomic theory, advocates of strong competition policy end up settling for less competition and lower consumer welfare than they would get if they developed policies to favour the dynamic genre. In what follows, we elaborate in more detail upon some of the differences between these modes of competition.

[60] Questions for Public Comment 4(n 11) question 8.
[61] Schumpeter (n 18) 8.

A. Static Competition

Static competition reflects an intellectual framework, less so a state of the world. Static competition manifests itself in the form of multiple providers of existing products offered at low prices, offering an unchanging menu of unimproved products at very good prices. When firms introduce no new products, rapid price reductions driven by innovation do not occur. The constant churn of customers will be commonplace, and profits will be thin. However, fierce competition associated with the introduction of new products, or new features, or new pricing approaches does not exist. Without innovation, all firms have the same technology and the same business models. Markets are in a comfortable but bland equilibrium.

Prices are drawn down to the floor of long-run marginal cost; but that floor becomes their resting place. Firms earn only their cost of capital and cover long-run marginal costs, and consumers are bereft of new products and true bargains. Firms never overcharge customers, but firms offer customers no exciting new products. Agents are nevertheless rational and well informed. Although this static framework has a theoretical simplicity and elegance, the industrial dynamics are overlooked. Absent innovation, new entry is unlikely. If incumbents can satisfy demand, new entrants are not needed. Absent scale economies, no firm is likely to become dominant, and the ecology of firms does not change.

The static economics paradigm infuses at least the undergraduate economics textbooks. Unfortunately, that paradigm tends to spill over into antitrust economics as both an analytical and a normative paradigm. However, that paradigm is not, and has never been, a good abstraction of the economy. Nor has that paradigm ever been a state to which we should aspire.

B. Dynamic Competition

Innovation drives dynamic competition—but not exclusively. The adjective 'dynamic' is a shorthand descriptor for a variety of rigorously competitive activities such as significant product differentiation and rapid response to change, whether from innovation or simply from new market opportunities ensuing from changes in taste or other forces of disequilibrium. Dynamic competition is in fact more intuitive and much closer to today's everyday view of competition than is the stylised notion of static competition routinely depicted in textbooks.

Many times innovation-driven competition has modified, if not overturned, the established order in an industry and has brought forth great price and non-price benefits to consumers. The steamship brought enhanced competition to the sailing ship and to ocean transportation. Steam and sail competed side by side for decades. The great days of sail—the era of the clipper ships—occurred partly in response to competitive pressures from steam ships. Likewise, vacuum tubes got better with competition from the transistor. Competition from refrigeration destroyed the ice-harvesting industry but brought massive cost savings and convenience to consumers. Technological innovation in aircraft jet engines marginalised internal combustion engines and destroyed many of the traditional aircraft manufacturers that were wedded to internal combustion engines. Electronics destroyed the typewriter. Industry after industry can demonstrate gains from dynamic (innovation-driven) competition that overshadow the gains when competition is present but innovation is absent.

Schumpeter's perspective on innovation-driven competition owes its intellectual origins to the economic framework of the Austrian School, founded by Carl Menger in the nineteenth century.[62] The Austrian School's treatment of competition differs significantly from that of neoclassical economics, the focus of which is on a static equilibrium with a minimum number of known exogenous variables. Austrian economics does not purport to compute any equilibrium, because the essence of competition is taken to be the dynamic pattern by which such competition arises, not the equilibrium itself. Friedrich A Hayek, a later leader of the Austrian School and eventual Nobel laureate, argued that 'competition is by its nature a dynamic process whose essential characteristics are assumed away by the assumptions underlying static analysis'.[63] The implication that Hayek recognised is that one cannot regard the wishes and desires of consumers as information given to producers; instead, one must view the task of identifying consumers' preferences as a problem that the process of competition can solve.

With dynamic competition, new entrants and incumbents alike engage in new product and process development and other adjustments to change. Frequent new product introductions followed by rapid price declines are commonplace. Innovations stem from investment in R&D or from the improvement and combination of older technologies. Firms continuously introduce product innovations, and from time to time dominant designs emerge. With innovation, the number of new entrants explodes, but once dominant designs emerge, implosions are likely, and markets become more concentrated. With dynamic competition, innovation and competition are tightly linked.

The model of dynamic competition recognises that competition is a process in which entrepreneurs and entrepreneurial managers are important actors. Unyielding competitive forces defeat stagnation. Maintaining innovation depends upon the existence of entrepreneurs and the institutional structures and public funding that support innovation. Technological innovation comes in waves created by different technologies. These waves cause what Schumpeter famously called, in the most evocative phrase penned by an economist, 'perennial gales of creative destruction'.[64] Entrants introduce a large fraction of radical technologies into an industry. Incumbents do, however, sometimes pioneer, and if they do not innovate, they are often able to imitate or improve on the entrants' products. The benefits of creative destruction may not come immediately; change takes time. Innovation drives competition and competition in turn drives innovation.

Building on work by Burton H Klein,[65] William J Abernathy and James M Utterback refined this paradigm of industrial change, and postulated an innovation cycle.[66] Considerable evidence now supports this paradigm over a wide range of technologies.[67] That evidence implicitly recognises inflection points in technological and market evolution. The advent of new technological ensembles or paradigms is usually marked by a wave of new

[62] See Carl Menger, *Grundsatze Der Volkwirtschaftslehre* (PRINCIPLES OF ECONOMICS) (1871).

[63] Friedrich A Hayek, 'The Meaning of Competition' in *Individualism and Economic Order* (1948).

[64] Schumpeter (n 18) 83.

[65] See Burton H Klein, *Dynamic Economics* (Boston, Harvard University Press, 1977).

[66] See William J Abernathy and James M Utterback, 'Patterns of Industrial Innovation' (1978) 80 *Technology Review* 40.

[67] See, eg Steven Klepper and Elizabeth Grady, 'The Evolution of New Industries and the Determinants of Market Structure' (1990) 21 *Rand Journal of Economics* 27; James M Utterback and Fernando Suarez, 'Innovation, Competition, and Industry Structure' (1993) 22 *Research Policy* 1; Franco Malerba and Luigi Orsenigo, 'The Dynamics and Evolution of Industries' (1996) 5 *Industrial and Corporate Change* 51.

competitors entering an industry to sustain success. Incumbents must master discontinuities as well as incremental change and improvement.

Many other complementary 'models' of innovation exist. At their core, most accept some version of an evolutionary theory of economic change and a behavioural theory of the firm. The methodological imperative of behavioural theory is that internal firm structure (not market structure) and internal processes such as learning, diffusion, sensing, seizing, and reconfiguring affect the firm's behaviour. Some understand evolutionary theory in economics to be economic Darwinism, but the logical structure of an evolutionary theory is much broader than its biological versions.[68] Evolutionary theory draws attention to what went before. As a general principle, novelty arises from changing and combining existing artifacts and structure. 'Descent with modification' crystallises this key point.[69] Selection leaves behind variants that are unfit according to the selection criterion at work. Selection processes include not only births and deaths of individual firms,[70] but also the ability of firms to adapt to the changing environment by modifying strategies and structures.[71]

Scholars disagree about the amount of adaptation that is possible within the firm. Some evolutionary economists see firms as strongly constrained. Strategic management scholars disagree. They claim that firms have much greater capacity for change than what managers actually undertake. All scholars recognise that a failure by the firm to change in the face of changing markets and technologies will diminish prospects for the enterprise.

Another common thread to behavioural or evolutionary mechanisms is that they are probabilistic rather than determinative.[72] Rigorous evolutionary theories will make a probabilistic assertion such as, 'There is a Z probability that individual Y will not replicate (die when the entity has a limited life span) under the selection environment X.'[73]

Because routines that interact in highly complex ways guide business enterprises, managers find it difficult to identify what makes the enterprise successful. This ambiguity surrounding causation becomes a problem when the environment changes, as causal ambiguity makes it difficult for managers or directors to determine what the enterprise should do differently. When Japanese auto manufacturers started to capture market share from the US manufacturers in the 1980s, the US auto industry offered a string of rationales to explain the phenomenon, including a view that the cost of capital was lower in Japan, that unfair trade barriers in Japan prevented exports from the United States, that US firms were falling behind in the use of robotics, and so forth. The US auto industry took nearly two

[68] Hayek argued that evolutionary theory in economics did not borrow from Darwin. To the contrary, Hayek argued, evolutionary concepts about markets contained in Adam Smith's writings influenced Darwin's theory of natural selection. See WW Bartley (ed), *The Fatal Conceit: The Errors of Socialism (The Collected Works of F A Hayek* (Chicago, University of Chicago Press, 1991).

[69] See William H Durham, *Coevolution: Genes, Culture and Human Diversity* (Stanford University Press, 1991). Durham identifies five requirements for an economic theory of change: units of transmission (for example, ideas and values); sources of variation (for example, invention); mechanisms of transmission; processes of transformation; and sources of isolation.

[70] See Michael T Hannan and John Freeman, *Organisational Ecology* (Cambridge MA, Harvard University Press, 1989).

[71] See David J Teece, 'Explicating Dynamic Capabilities: The Nature and Microfoundations of (Sustainable) Enterprise Performance' (2007) 28 *Strategic Management Journal* 1319; Mie Augier and David J Teece, 'Strategy as Evolution with Design: The Foundations of Dynamic Capabilities and the Role of Managers in the Economic System' (2008) 29 *Organisational Studies* 1255.

[72] See Howard Aldrich, *Organisations Evolving* (London, Sage Publications, 1999) 33–50.

[73] See Johann P Murmann, *Knowledge and Competitive Advantage: The Coevolution of Firms, Technology and National Institutions* (New York, Cambridge University Press, 2003) 15.

decades to discover for itself that labour-management issues, and management itself, were key causal factors associated with the industry's decline. Once the industry more accurately diagnosed causation, manufacturers made management and organisational changes that began to make a difference. However, it was too late. The deep recession of 2008–09 drove General Motors and Chrysler into bankruptcy. As Teece explained,[74] often firms must create a breakout structure to unshackle the new from the old. If they fail, the alternative is extinction.

This evolutionary assessment of the extinction of firms requires qualification to take account of the political economy of failure. The recession that began in 2008 introduced a new genre of government regulation in the United States in the automobile and financial services industries. Such regulation replaces extinction with quasi nationalisation. Clearly, an important topic of future research for industrial organisation economists will be what a firm's being 'too big to fail' implies for the evolutionary process by which the firm diagnoses and responds to change. A conscious policy decision to interrupt the evolutionary process that weeds out failing firms and strategies may have short-term appeal because it may appear to be an onramp to a turnpike that promises to speed one past market failure. However, policy makers need to be mindful of two caveats. First, the protection of failed entities will influence the future formulation of strategy, most likely introducing over the intermediate term a new variety of moral hazard. Second, over the longer term, evolutionary processes will continue to operate, such that it would be naïve to suppose that the industrial planning inherent in nationalisation necessarily can insulate the firm from the imperative to evolve in response to new exogenous forces or face new threats of extinction.

In sum, a number of assumptions and propositions characterise dynamic competition. Many are rooted in an evolutionary theory of economic change. As Schumpeter said, 'in dealing with capitalism, you are dealing with an evolutionary process'.[75] Government intervention to regulate failure will not arrest that evolutionary process. Part IV outlines features of evolutionary theory.

IV. Relevant Aspects of Evolutionary and Behavioural Economics

Evolutionary economics and the behavioral theory of the firm are separate but related frameworks. Both have existed for a half-century or longer. Both embrace firms and markets as we see them. Both recognise a capability to discover new technologies and business models in the economic system. Entrepreneurial activity by individuals and enterprises is critical to that capability.

Some endogenous generation of innovative opportunities is accepted in evolutionary theory. Evolutionary theories recognise processes of imperfect learning and discovery on the one hand and selection on the other. Whereas neoclassical theory can recognise unfavourable outcomes caused by bad luck and uncertainty, evolutionary theory also accepts

[74] See Teece (n 71) 1335.
[75] See Schumpeter (n17) 82.

the systematic mistakes associated with ignorance or misunderstanding. Clearly, the canons of rational choice theory and equilibrium economics provide only a very limited basis for the study of innovation.

Neoclassical theory almost completely neglects the specificities of competencies and skills that each firm possesses. The theory especially neglects the relatively tacit and organisational capabilities that cannot be imputed to individuals. This neglect impedes any satisfactory analysis of the innovative capabilities of firms. Neoclassical theory assumes bounded rationality because agents have an imperfect understanding of the environment in which they live and of what the future will deliver. Because of limits to rationality, rules often guide or determine enterprise behaviour. The learning history of the enterprise shapes relatively invariant routines.

Adaptation and learning generate diversity. Managerial action inside firms (at headquarters) and competition among firms in product markets and factor markets act as selection mechanisms that lead to the disappearance of some firms and the rapid growth of others. Managers, for example, act as the proximate agent of selection when they pull resources from underperforming units and reallocate them to growing units. Knowledge of specific technologies determines how technology will advance. Technologies develop along relatively ordered paths shaped by specific technical properties, search rules, technical 'imperatives', and cumulative expertise. Consequently, diversity among firms is a fundamental and permanent characteristic of environments undergoing technical change.

Firms differ because of different technological capabilities with respect to innovation, different degrees of success in adapting to technologies developed externally, and different cost structures. They may also differ because of differing search or sensory procedures and capabilities and differing strategic behaviours. One should expect path dependencies when increasing returns to scale or scope exist. This expectation will especially hold for information goods and for cumulative technological advances. How strong path dependencies will be is mainly an empirical question.

Market concentration is a function of two opposing forces: (1) selection mechanisms that tend to increase the standing of innovating firms, and (2) learning and imitation mechanisms that spread innovations or new knowledge throughout the potential adapters, thereby reinforcing existing disparities through cumulative mechanisms internal to the firm. Abilities to innovate and imitate are firm-specific and depend on a firm's past innovative record. In other words, the firm's learning is cumulative. Chance matters, but it favours firms that are prepared to innovate.

Although innovators themselves can appropriate some of the economic benefits from innovation and the adaptation of new products and processes, learning externalities exist. The ease of imitation depends on the intellectual property regime (strong or weak) and the nature of the relevant knowledge (codified or tacit). Skills and know-how almost always spill over from individual path breakers to the whole industry. Innovation in products and processes is nevertheless to a fair degree endogenous—through in-house R&D and technological acquisition (that is, in licensing), as well as through learning mechanisms.

Firms within an industry face considerable dispersion in costs, profitability, and growth rates. Asymmetries in capabilities are a direct consequence of the cumulative, idiosyncratic, and appropriable nature of technological advances. The more that technological advances accumulate at the firm level, the higher the likelihood that success breeds success. Moreover, the higher the opportunity that exists for technological progress, the higher the possibility of differentials between innovators and laggards. High technological opportunity associated with a high degree of appropriability provides high incentives for firms on or near the frontier to innovate, but possibly low incentives for firms with relatively lower technological capabilities to do so.

'Normal' technical progress proceeds along trajectories defined by an established paradigm, and extraordinary technical advance is associated with the emergence of new paradigms. As others have shown,[76] market processes are generally weak in directing the emergence and selection of radical technological discontinuities. Put differently, when the process of innovation is highly exploratory, its direct response to economic signals is weaker and its linkage with scientific knowledge is greater. In those circumstances, institutional and scientific contexts are more important than the market.

Institutions and markets co-evolve. Industrial, technological, and institutional factors interact. In particular, research and training bodies and the intellectual property system help shape industrial outcomes. The competitive strengths of individual enterprises, as well as the competitive strength of the industry of which they are part, depend on such factors. For instance, according to Johann P Murmann, German firms achieved global superiority in dyestuffs by 1914, not because they had superior strategies and organisation, but because large numbers of new entrants and exits gave the German dye industry more room to experiment with different firm strategies and structures.[77] By 1900, the leading dye firms had all developed in-house R&D capabilities and could match new product introductions by competitors in the United Kingdom and the United States, as well as in Germany. The German firms also patented heavily in the United Kingdom, and their innovative efforts at home drew upon an extremely strong university system in chemistry. Murmann argues that 'Germany had it easier than Britain in bringing forth competitive firms'.[78] The British Government also hindered its domestic industry by imposing higher tariffs on industrial alcohol, an important input in dye making. Strong organisational capabilities in R&D, manufacturing, marketing, management, and strong patent portfolios allowed the German dye industry to capture 70 to 90 per cent of world market share.[79] Strength in the supplier industry and in supporting institutions aids innovation. The German firms actively shaped their selection environment—particularly through education and training, tariffs, and patents.

Indicators of dynamic competition include heterogeneous firms engaging in experimentation and innovation. They develop and introduce new products and processes, and they rework and adjust internal processes. Firms constantly battle unanticipated events. Rivalrous behaviour is the norm. An evolutionary approach underscores the importance of maintaining diversity in the economic system. Competition policy authorities as well as other agencies must be concerned with protecting economic diversity and meaningful variety in organisational forms. Policy makers need not focus on a particular market; their focus should be broader because some of the best candidates for new entry and radical innovation exist outside the market. The propositions derived from behavioural and evolutionary theories of firms and markets promise to expand our understanding of firm behaviour, particularly in domains of rapid innovation. Following Joskow, we believe that the field of

[76] See, eg Giovani Dosi, *Technical Change and Industrial Transformation* (Palgrave Macmillan, 1984).
[77] See Murmann (n 73).
[78] Ibid 51.
[79] Ibid 92.

industrial organisation, to which antitrust economics owes so much, can 'play an important leadership role in the extension and revision of the conventional theory of the firm rather than be its prisoner'.[80] Extensions of and revisions to the theory of the firm, if they recognise the firm as having the potential to create innovation and act as an engine of innovation, will assist in the development of new approaches to antitrust theory that will pave the way for the improvement of actual policy.

V. Implications for Antitrust Law and Merger Policy

Adopting a dynamic view of competition would require significant changes to current antitrust law and merger policy.

A. Framing Dynamic Competition's Animating Force in the Law

Static and dynamic views of competition have elements in common. Current law embraces both. Indeed, Katz and Shelanski observe that 'Judge Learned Hand wrote as early as 1916 that "the consumer's interest in the long run is quite different from an immediate fall in prices" and spoke of competition as a "proper stimulus to maintenance of industrial advance".'[81] In our view, however, when the courts rely on economic theory to inform antitrust law, the law gets a larger injection of static analysis than dynamic analysis.

As discussed, traditional static analysis focuses on detecting market power in product markets. Dynamic analysis views competition through a broader lens and focuses less on outcomes and more on process. Dynamic analysis favours maintaining rivalry but also protects property, including intellectual property. The working assumption in dynamic competition analysis is that IPRs are desirable institutional or legal arrangements providing necessary appropriability mechanisms to advance and reward innovation. Dynamic analysis also recognises that the benefits of dynamic competition do not arrive immediately; firms may need to tolerate some short-run (static) inefficiencies to support innovation. Wooden antitrust policies that fixate on short-run efficiencies are likely to hurt innovation and thereby hurt competition.

If antitrust policy is to favour dynamic competition over static competition, a role for vigorous enforcement still remains, but it proceeds less self-confidently. Uncertainty and complexity are hallmarks of dynamic market environments. In particular, policy makers should use the tools of static analysis sparingly, if at all. Simple rules based on static analysis may well produce policy actions and judicial decisions that impede competition. In particular, policy makers should de-emphasise concentration analysis. To prohibit mergers merely to manage concentration is unlikely to help consumers. More generally, policy should overturn the presumption that more competitors are always better—the goal is not merely lowering price, but also protecting innovation.

[80] Joskow (n 23) 278.

[81] Katz & Shelanski, *'Schumpeterian' Competition*, (n 7) 50 (quoting *United States v Corn Prods Ref Co* 234 F. 964, 1012 (SDNY 1916)).

Policy makers may need to examine barriers to entry over a longer time period and must do so at the firm level. (The strategy literature refers to the firm-level analog to barriers to entry as 'isolating mechanisms.'[82]) Supporting structures and government funding for research also affect entry conditions. Those factors may reflect the capabilities that incumbents have developed that newcomers should not expect to possess. Capabilities are likely to reflect the search for unique advantages. Their possession drives competition.

In stark contrast to the neoclassical assumption of the structure-conduct-performance paradigm, in dynamic contexts conduct in this framework is not a function of market structure. Market conduct is driven more by internal organisational factors: standard operating procedures, investment strategies, and improvement routines. Performance depends on the (relative) organisational capabilities and behavioural traits of the enterprise. Enhanced industrial performance also stems from improvement in individual technologies and expanded use of more productive technologies.

As discussed above, one can observe some typical evolutionary patterns in industry dynamics—perhaps one can call it an industry life cycle. In the early stages of an industry's evolution, firms tend be small, and entry relatively easy, because of the diversity of technologies that firms are using. As the dominant design emerges, however, costs of entry rise as an established scale for competitive activity becomes apparent. Learning becomes cumulative, and established firms experience some advantage over subsequent entrants. After an industry shakeout, established firms settle into a more stable industry structure. However, a new technology with the promise of being superior may soon overturn that stability. With entry and exit, the life of many firms tends to be short.[83]

New technologies can enhance or destroy a firm's competency. The essence of the dynamic competition approach is that technological change itself shapes industry structure. Also, path dependencies and dynamic increasing returns may exist. Put differently, the rate and direction of innovation at the level of the firm do not depend on market structure but on the firm's competencies, the internal and external knowledge upon which the firm can draw, the intellectual property regime, and the firm's complementary assets. Entry conditions are a function of appropriability and 'cumulativeness'. Learning and innovation will also shape the firm's boundaries.

Market concentration is likely to be an outcome of market selection, which in turn depends on the uneven exploitation of learning opportunities. Thus, concentration has little to do with market power. As Giovanni Dosi and his colleagues observe,

> if the degrees of selection are interpreted as a proxy for how well markets work—in the sense that they quickly reward winners and weed out losers—then more efficient markets tend to yield, in evolutionary environments, more concentrated market structures, rather than more 'perfect' ones in the standard sense.[84]

The possibility of innovation rests on the permanent existence of unexploited technological opportunities. A significant body of evidence from the microeconomics of innovation

[82] See, eg Mehmet Oktemgil, Gordon E Greenley and Amanda J Broderick, 'An Empirical Study of Isolating Mechanisms in UK Companies' (2000) 122 *European Journal of Operations Research* 638.

[83] See Paul A Geroski and Joachim Schwalbach (eds) *Entry and Market Contestability: An International Comparison* (Oxford, Basil Blackwell, 1991); Paul A Geroski, 'What Do We Know about Entry?' (1995) 13 *Int'l J Indus Org* 421.

[84] Giovanni Dosi, Orietta Marsili, Luigi Orsenigo and Roberta Salvatore, 'Learning, Market Selection and the Evolution of Industrial Structures' (1995) 7 *Small Business Economics* 411.

indicates that unexploited opportunities do permanently exist and that firms actually explore only a small subset of what is available.[85] Firms are constrained not by nature, but by their own capabilities. Firms therefore almost always have opportunities to sense and seize. This persistence of unexploited opportunities raises the question of why antitrust law would threaten to penalise successful exploitation of opportunities in the first place.

B. Market Definition

Antitrust analysis, particularly with respect to section 2 of the Sherman Act and section 7 of the Clayton Act,[86] typically focuses on market definition. Defining the boundaries of a market is the first step under the Horizontal Merger Guidelines promulgated by the Antitrust Division and the FTC.[87] Economists recognise that market definition is merely an analytical tool. We agree with Janusz Ordover and Daniel Wall that '[a]rguments for and against a merger that turn upon distinctions between broad and narrow markets definitions are, to an economic purist, an inadequate substitute for, and a diversion from, sound direct assessment of a merger's effect'.[88] Indeed, the seminal article on market power, published by William Landes and Judge Richard Posner in 1981, demonstrated analytically why the gaming of market definition in an antitrust case would, under correct economic analysis, be precisely offset by compensating adjustments in the pertinent elasticities of demand and competitor supply.[89] Nonetheless, in practice the courts and agencies have tended to require market definition. Analysing competition in an evolutionary or dynamic manner would appear to support Ordover and Wall's position, as market share or concentration is unlikely to have much power in explaining conduct decisions, including those concerning pricing. No general theorem establishes that higher concentration leads to higher prices or less output. Static models may, however, offer some theoretical support to the notion that equilibrium output falls and equilibrium prices rise as the number of firms decline.

A modicum of empirical work in such markets as telecommunications and airlines supports the structure-conduct-performance paradigm. However, the evidence supporting it is weak, and when innovation is significant, theoretical connections and empirical correlations become even weaker. Fortunately, the Merger Guidelines are clear that, at least in the merger context, market share is only a starting point and market definition is merely a tool. However, even these caveats are too timid in an industry characterised by rapid technological change. As discussed earlier, high market share may simply indicate that selection or competition processes are working well. Also, of course, if the firm is

[85] See, eg Nathan Rosenberg, *Inside the Black Box* (Cambridge, Cambridge University Press, 1982); Christopher Freeman, *The Economics of Industrial Innovation*, 2nd edn (Cambridge MA, MIT Press, 1982); Giovanni Dosi, 'Sources, Procedures and Microeconomic Effects of Innovation' (1988) 26 *Journal of Economic Literature* 1120.

[86] Clayton Act 15 USC §§ 2, 18.

[87] See US DOJ and FTC, 'Horizontal Merger Guidelines'.

[88] Janusz A Ordover and Daniel M Wall, 'Understanding Econometric Methods of Market Definition' (1989) 3 *Antitrust* 20, 20–21.

[89] William E Landes and Richard A Posner, 'Market Power in Antitrust Cases' (1981) 94 *Harvard Law Review* 937.

subject to maximum price regulation or an obligation to serve, its high market share is endogenous to the regulatory regime.[90]

Also, in practice, the hypothetical monopolist test is hard to apply in the context of innovation. When innovation is present, products are likely to be differentiated in quality, and price is not the main or only competitive weapon.[91] Furthermore, innovation can make defining relevant product markets difficult because business executives and government officials alike may not yet know what the future products will be. The use of the hypothetical monopolist test to establish relevant markets may be better suited for commodity products than the products of high-tech companies. With innovation, value disparities are likely to exist among substitute products. Before the dominant design emerges, competition occurs with respect to features and functionalities, not price. Hence, the hypothetical monopolist test might be uninformative or inadministrable before the dominant design emerges. In the case of automobiles, an application of the test circa 1910 might have placed steam cars, electric cars, and internal combustion engine cars in separate markets, despite the fact that competition among these technologies was already fierce and led over the next few years to the obliteration of firms that could not make the transition to designing and producing automobiles propelled by the internal combustion engine.

More importantly, if one is to adopt a forward-looking antitrust analysis, then neither the enforcement agencies nor the courts will likely know which products will be good substitutes in the future. Because innovation produces new products and lowers the cost of existing products, policy makers must include such future products when defining the market, but doing so is quite difficult in many instances, as our discussion of the XM-Sirius satellite radio merger will illustrate.

C. Market Share and Actual versus Potential Competitors

Using the neoclassical framework, antitrust analysts first define a relevant market, identify actual competitors within it, and allocate market shares. That analysis includes actual but not potential competitors in the market. Potential competitors are recognised only when certain conditions of probability and immediacy of entry are met.

In dynamic contexts, potential competitors can have much greater importance. What today appears merely to be a potential competitor can obliterate incumbents tomorrow in acts of Schumpeterian creative destruction. To exclude such a competitor from the boundaries of the market would clearly be a mistake. Yet, that is what the Merger Guidelines still do (as of late 2009).

Proper analysis requires an assessment of capabilities. Existing approaches implicitly proxy capabilities by current market share. In dynamic environments, this method is likely to be highly inadequate. Although capabilities are difficult to quantify, a large literature now exists in the field of strategic management that provides many clues to assessing the capabilities of both actual and potential competitors.[92]

[90] J Gregory Sidak and Daniel F Spulber, Deregulatory Takings and the Regulatory Contract: The Competitive Transformation of Network Industries in the United States (Cambridge, Cambridge University Press, 1997).

[91] See Hartman, Mitchell, Jorde & Teece (n 5).

[92] See, eg Teece, *Explicating Dynamic Capabilities,* (n 71); David J Teece, Gary Pisano and Amy Shuen, 'Dynamic Capabilities and Strategic Management' (1997) 18 *Strategic Management Journal* 509.

Snapshots of market shares, whether present or forward-looking, reveal little if markets are in turmoil, as they frequently are in dynamic contexts. As noted earlier, a distinguishing feature of the Austrian school of economics is its emphasis on disequilibrium. Moreover, a high market share by no means implies market power. Not only is today's market share a poor indicator of the future, but a high market share may indicate not only superior performance, but also strong selection (which is to say competition) at work in the industry.[93]

Accordingly, in both merger analysis and in section 2 cases, when dynamic competition is at work, one must look beyond market share data. Serious consideration of potential competitors and their capabilities is essential, for studies show that new entrants almost always drive innovation in established industries. A focus on capabilities and on potential competition will help to ensure that market analysis is forward-looking.

Furthermore, market share is likely to be irrelevant in regimes of rapid change, because competition for the market is likely to be as significant as competition within it.[94] Market share may be altogether irrelevant in some cases because markets may exist in which innovation is so characteristic and sustained that firms compete not merely for market share, but for markets as a whole. A firm's monopoly today may say little about the firm's prospects one, two, or five years in the future.

One should note that analysts have already begun to develop new approaches to defining markets, in recognition of the fact that doing so at the level of the product is difficult when one cannot predict successful future products with any degree of certainty. Richard J Gilbert and Steven Sunshine, for example, have put potential competition to one side and have focused instead on what they call 'innovation markets',[95] by which they seem to mean R&D markets. Although General Motors used the concept in *United States v General Motors Corp*,[96] the enforcement agencies and the courts seem to have forgotten it, and further development of these ideas has stalled.

Despite the shortcomings of the 'innovation market' approach, which we discuss below, the framework did shift attention from product markets to activity upstream. This shift required antitrust authorities to determine what skills and assets firms need to be able to innovate and which firms possess those skills. Such an inquiry fundamentally differs from examining demand-side substitution, the exercise that is now quite familiar to economists, antitrust lawyers, and courts. The 'innovation market' approach might have been pushed to its logical conclusion. If it had been, it may well have led to the analysis of capabilities, a subject that we now examine.

[93] Katz and Shelanski argue: 'Even absent innovation, there are reasons to be cautious about the interpretation of market share data. In order to generate sensible predictions of the effects of a merger, the measurement and analysis of market shares should always be tied to a coherent theory of competitive effects that fits the facts of the industry under consideration. Put another way, the analysis of market shares can most confidently be used to predict adverse competitive effects of a merger when one has an empirically supported theory that market shares are informative of competitive conditions and that an increase in concentration will harm competition and consumers.' Michael L Katz and Howard A Shelanski, 'Merger Policy and Innovation: Must Enforcement Change to Account for Technological Change?' (National Bureau of Economics, Research Working Paper No 10710, 2004) 29 available at http://papers.ssrn.com/sol3/papers.cfm?abstract_id=583708.

[94] See Teece and Coleman (n 5); Pleatsikas and Teece (n 5); Shelanski and Sidak (n 8)

[95] See Richard J Gilbert and Steven Sunshine, 'Incorporating Dynamic Efficiency Concerns in Merger Analysis: The Use of Innovation Markets' (1995) 63 *Antitrust Law Journal* 569.

[96] *United States v General Motors Corp* 384 US 127 (1966).

D. Analysing Capabilities to Assess Competitor Positions and Economic Power

Edith Penrose observed that analysts should define an enterprise not by its current products, but by its (upstream) 'resources', or what some prefer to call capabilities.[97] She defined the internal resources of the firm as 'the productive services available to a firm from its own resources', particularly those from management experience.[98] 'A firm is more than an administrative unit', Penrose argued, 'it is a collection of productive resources'.[99] She saw that 'many of the productive services created through an increase in knowledge that occurs as a result of experience gained in the operation of the firm as time passes will remain unused if the firm fails to expand'.[100] Penrose saw the capabilities of management, not the exhaustion of technologically-based economies of scale, as determining whether a firm could expand to exploit opportunities. In reality, of course, other assets—such as innovation capabilities—define the firm's resources or capabilities, but it is important to note that Penrose articulated a model that implicitly eschewed market shares as a measure of how well a firm is 'positioned' to compete.

Subsequent research has established that firms exhibit more stability in their capabilities than in their products. In this respect, one can analyse capabilities more easily than products. Capabilities are proxies for the firm's interrelated and interdependent attributes that govern its competitive significance. These capabilities are arguably a better proxy for the firm's competitive position than is its downstream market share.

Strategy refers to the broad set of the firm's commitments that define and rationalise its objectives and the way that the firm intends to pursue them. These commitments may be explicit or implicit in the firm's culture and values. Strategy is often more a matter of faith and determination, not one of calculation. Structure refers to how a firm is organised and governed and how decisions are made and implemented. Although strategy and structure shape capabilities, what an organisation can do well is likely to be partly a function of what it has done well in the past. A firm's R&D activities and success in acquiring external technologies can mould its future capabilities. However, strategy helps determine what capabilities a firm should own and protect. The world is too complicated for a firm to have 'an optimal strategy' and although the firm's capabilities are always in a state of flux, existing capabilities are a good guide to what a company can do in the future.

The capabilities approach would depart markedly from standard antitrust analysis. It would calibrate a firm's competitive standing not by reference to products but by reference to more enduring traits. In a dynamic context, a firm will have a kaleidoscope of products, yet the underlying capabilities are likely to be more stable. For instance, rather than analysing Honda's market share in outboard motors, lawnmowers, and small electric generators, one might shed more light on the antitrust analysis by examining a capability profile or 'market'. Here the relevant capability might centre on small, four-stroke internal combustion engines. A capabilities approach might lead to 'markets' defined more narrowly

[97] See Edith Penrose, *The Theory of the Growth of the Firm* (New York, John Wiley and Sons, 1959).
[98] Ibid 149–50.
[99] Ibid 24.
[100] Ibid 54.

or broadly than how the current Merger Guidelines define product markets. Potential competition (or its absence) would receive more attention.

The tools for assessing capabilities may not be well developed yet, but they are developed enough to allow tentative application. Clearly, product market analysis can be unhelpful and misleading in dynamic contexts. Using the right concepts imperfectly is better than precisely applying the wrong ones. The question arises whether simply doing a better job of analysing potential competition would help. Clearly, doing so might help. In the end, however, one would be forced to examine the capabilities of potential competitors—so one probably could not avoid developing the analytics of a capabilities approach.

The innovation-market approach introduced by Gilbert and Sunshine implicitly recognises that focusing on product-market analysis is inadequate.[101] However, the innovation-market approach focuses too narrowly on R&D as the arena for measuring innovation competition. Even if R&D is defined broadly, it is usually only one element of the resources and problem solving that go into innovation. The resources that firms must commit and the skills that firms must employ to succeed at innovation usually exceed those needed for merely conducting R&D. The resources available in the supporting ecosystem are as important as the firm's capabilities. Furthermore, R&D concentration has little to do with innovation outcomes, except possibly in industries characterised by cumulative technological change. Even there, we can expect the linkage to be weak. The importance of other institutional players in the ecosystem, such as venture capitalists and private equity providers, needs to be assessed as well. The widespread adoption of elements of an open innovation[102] model—in which elements of the innovation process are outsourced—makes these points even more compelling.

E. Merger Analysis

Despite the misgivings of an increasing number of economic scholars, in practice merger policy in the United States, the European Union, and most other jurisdictions that have competition law focuses on how the merging parties' combinations will affect concentration in one or more existing product markets. In effect, enforcement agencies take an increase in concentration as a proxy for a decrease in competition that, if sufficiently large, will increase the prices that consumers face.

i. Schumpeterian Competition and Merger Enforcement

We favour revision of the Horizontal Merger Guidelines. A focus on dynamic competition is likely to be especially relevant in high-technology industries. The evolutionary and behavioural economics approaches outlined here would not abandon antitrust enforcement or even necessarily restrict it. However, those approaches do lead to a more careful framework that recognises uncertainty and complexity and relentlessly asks, does this practice support or discourage innovation? Will this merger assist or burden dynamic competition?

[101] See Gilbert and Sunshine (n 95).

[102] See Henry W Chesbrough, Wim Vanhaverbeke and Joel West (eds), *Open Innovation: Researching a New Paradigm* (New York, Oxford University Press, 2006).

The evolutionary or behavioural economics framework that we advance suggests a number of modifications to how the antitrust enforcement agencies should approach the analysis of a particular merger. First, market structure is not a meaningful concern, at least not until a dominant design has emerged, and the evolutionary paradigm is established and likely to remain for quite some time. Second, if the analysis is to be deflected away from products in the market, the natural phenomena to examine are capabilities. Capabilities transcend products. Other elements of the ecosystem, such as the availability of venture capital and public support, also need to be taken into account.

Third, only if the merger entities are the sole firms with the necessary capabilities to innovate in a broad area should antitrust concerns arise. Katz and Shelanski suggest that, if new product development efforts are underway to create or improve products and processes, and if those products are not yet in the market, then harm can arise from a merger because it may cripple future product-market competition in a market that does not exist.[103] A capabilities approach would soften such concerns. The question should be framed not in terms of whether product-market competition will be impaired, as that is too much of an immediate concern, but in terms of whether capabilities will be brought under unitary control, thereby possibly thwarting future variety in new product development.

As we have stressed earlier, Schumpeterian competition is engendered by product and process innovation. Such competition does more than bring price competition—it tends to overturn the existing order. A framework for antitrust analysis that favours dynamic over static competition would place less weight on market share and concentration in the assessment of market power and more weight on assessing innovation and enterprise-level capabilities.

ii. The Antitrust Division's Spasmodic Attempt to Embrace Dynamic Competition

It appears that, during the George W Bush Administration, the Antitrust Division gravitated toward a more dynamic approach to analysis. In the Oracle-PeopleSoft merger in 2004, the Division advocated a narrow market definition that excluded consideration of dynamic competition. In perhaps the most significant defeat at trial ever experienced by a US antitrust enforcement agency, the Division lost.[104] By October 2007, the Division had experienced a neo-Schumpeterian makeover under its next Assistant Attorney General, Thomas Barnett, who argued that innovation is the major source of consumer-welfare gains.[105] Barnett's view was expressed more officially in the Division's September 2008 report on monopolisation.[106]

Although the implications of Barnett's premise for particular doctrines in the law of monopolisation can (and did) engender controversy, there can be no dispute over the correctness of his basic thesis. Innovation entails the creation of new demand curves for new products, which implies the creation of all the consumer surplus and producer surplus beneath those new demand curves. Producers rarely capture all the gains from a new

[103] See Michael L Katz and Howard A Shelanski, 'Mergers and Innovation' (2007) 74 *Antitrust Law Journal* 1, 8.

[104] *United States v Oracle Corp* 331 F. Supp. 2d 1098 (ND Ca 2004). Teece testified as an expert witness for Oracle.

[105] Thomas O Barnett, 'Maximizing Welfare through Technological Innovation' (2007) 15 *George Mason Law Review* (2007) (article based on October 2007 speech).

[106] US DOJ, Antitrust Division, 'Competition and Monopoly: Single-Firm Conduct Under Section 2 of the Sherman Act' Report (September 2008) 123.

product. Consequently, this net accretion of consumer welfare from product innovation is a bigger prize, probably by an order of magnitude or more, than are the fruits to be gained from haggling over the small Harberger deadweight loss triangles that can arise from marginal changes in price along the extant demand curve of an established product.[107] This theme informs the larger debate over Schumpeterian economics —which posits that competition is a dynamic process and that firms can compete for the market and temporarily achieve a position of dominance. This view of competition is distinguished from static competition in which multiple firms compete simultaneously in the market, primarily on the basis of marginal differences in price as opposed to dramatic differences resulting from innovation and quality improvement.

However, the degree to which the Antitrust Division has advocated the neo-Schumpeterian vision of competition has varied over time and across different doctrinal areas of antitrust law. It remains to be seen whether the Division's advocacy, once more under the guidance of Berkeley economists, will change course during the Obama Administration. (Berkeley economists once again dominate the FTC as well.) In May 2009, Assistant Attorney General Christine Varney, presumably relying on concurring input from chief economist Carl Shapiro, repudiated the report on monopolisation law released less than a year earlier by her Republican predecessor, Barnett.[108] To the extent that neo-Schumpeterian arguments are considered to favour defendants in monopolisation cases, that policy reversal may signal resistance to neo-Schumpeterian arguments.[109] However, as we have stressed, the neo-Schumpeterian approach need not favour defendants or plaintiffs. Rather, it favours dynamic assessments of the consumer-welfare effects of firm behaviour and transactions.

iii. Legitimacy versus Authority: Why Do the Courts and Enforcement Agencies Deny that the Merger Guidelines Bind them?

A factor complicating the neo-Schumpeterian transformation of antitrust law is the fact that the federal courts have, by thoroughly embracing the economic reasoning of the Horizontal Merger Guidelines as promulgated several decades ago by the Antitrust Division and the FTC, caused antitrust case law to ossify around a static view of competition. After three decades, the result of that intellectual accretion is not a mere policy preference that can be altered by speeches or statements of prosecutorial discretion by enforcement officials. Rather, the static view of competition is, by dint of the imprimatur of the federal judiciary, the law. Curiously, the courts pretend otherwise. While it relies on the Guidelines as authority, the DC Circuit continues—as recently as the decision in *FTC v Whole Foods Market Inc*—to assert that 'the Merger Guidelines…"are by no means to be considered binding on the court"'.[110] All of us like to keep our options open, but this kind of statement

[107] The seminal empirical analysis is Jerry A Hausman, 'Valuing the Effect of Regulation on New Services in Telecommunications' (1997) *Brookings Papers on Economic Activity (Microeconomics)* (measuring the forgone consumer welfare from regulatory delay in the introduction of cell phone service and voicemail). See also Jerry A Hausman and J Gregory Sidak, 'Google and the Proper Antitrust Scrutiny of Orphan Books' (2009) 5 *Journal of Competition Law and Economics* 411 (applying the new-product framework to Google Book Search).

[108] Stephen Labaton, 'Administration Plans to Strengthen Antitrust Rules' *New York Times* (11 May 2009) 1.

[109] See, eg Don Clark and Jessica E Vascellaro, 'Silicon Valley Girds for New Antitrust Regime' *Wall Street Journal* (18 May 2009), available at http://online.wsj.com/article/SB124260263059528447.html.

[110] *FTC v Whole Foods Market Inc* 548 F.3d 1028, 1046 (DC Cir 2008) (citing *FTC v PPG Indus Inc* 798 F.2d 1500, 1503 n.4 (DC Cir 1986)).

reduces the intellectual prestige of the judiciary. We see no reason why anyone would find this *ipse dixit* to be credible.

To an economist—which is to say, someone attuned to the information revealed through the evolutionary processes of institutions, including law—the legitimacy of the Merger Guidelines comes from their survival in the face of sustained attempts to refute their intellectual coherence.[111] Legitimacy does not arise from the fact that the Guidelines originated as expressions of bureaucratic authority. If the Merger Guidelines were perceived to be intellectually comparable to the guidelines of the Internal Revenue Service, we believe that the DC Circuit and other federal courts would regard them quite differently.

iv. Self Contradiction and the Consequential Role of the Merger Guidelines in Antitrust Jurisprudence

Merger analysis implicates a larger series of issues that are relevant across all of antitrust jurisprudence. For the Obama Administration, the unanimous en banc decision by the US Court of Appeals for the DC Circuit in *United States v Microsoft Corp* is a useful guidepost for charting the evolution of antitrust jurisprudence over the eight years of the George W Bush Administration.[112] The DC Circuit's *per curiam* opinion in *Microsoft* contains an introductory section that asks whether antitrust law is up to the challenge of evaluating competition in the 'new economy'.[113] This passage alludes to a debate, which transpired before the internet bubble burst, over whether high-tech industries could be analysed under conventional antitrust principles. In *Microsoft* the DC Circuit said: 'We decide this case against a backdrop of significant debate amongst academics and practitioners over the extent to which "old economy" § 2 monopolization doctrines should apply to firms competing in dynamic technological markets characterized by network effects.'[114] In a well-read essay, Judge Richard Posner argued that traditional antitrust analysis was competent for the task.[115] In *Microsoft*, the DC Circuit agreed.[116] And yet, a few pages later, the Court seemed to contradict itself. It announced a new and more permissive liability rule for tying arrangements concerning software integration—a rule that repudiated the Supreme Court's ostensibly regnant rule of per se illegality for tie-ins.[117] The DC Circuit's rationale for so doing was its concern for the dynamic effects on innovation: 'Applying per se analysis to…an amalgamation [of software] creates undue risks of error and of deterring welfare-enhancing innovation.'[118] So troubled was the Supreme Court by the DC Circuit's repeal of the per se rule as applied to software integration that the Court denied cert.[119]

[111] We allude here to Karl Popper's theory that objective knowledge consists of conjectures that have survived empirical attempts to refute them. See Karl Popper, *Objective Knowledge: An Evolutionary Approach* (Oxford, Clarendon Press 1972). As an epistemological matter, we regard the Popperian view of objective knowledge to comport with many of the seminal contributions on the theory of the firm that invoke processes of evolution or survivorship. See J Gregory Sidak, 'Mr. Justice Nemo's Social Statics' (2000) 79 *Texas Law Review* 737.

[112] *United States v Microsoft Corp* 253 F.3d 34 (DC Cir. 2001).

[113] Ibid 49.

[114] Ibid.

[115] Posner, Antitrust in the New Economy, (n 15).

[116] Microsoft 253 F.3d, 50 ('As an initial matter, we note that there is no consensus among commentators on the question of whether, and to what extent, current monopolization doctrine should be amended to account for competition in technologically dynamic markets characterized by network effects.').

[117] Ibid 89–90.

[118] Ibid 90–91.

[119] United States v Microsoft Corp 534 US 952 (2001) (denial of certiorari).

The Antitrust Modernization Commission (AMC) report from April 2007 provides a second major example of self-contradiction regarding the need to revise antitrust principles to accommodate consideration of dynamic efficiency. In its summary of recommendations, the AMC said that 'no substantial changes to merger enforcement policy are necessary to account for industries in which innovation, intellectual property, and technological change are central features'.[120] Nevertheless, the same report recommended two pages later that the Antitrust Division and the FTC 'update the Merger Guidelines to explain more extensively how they evaluate the potential impact of a merger on innovation'.[121] So, again, in one breath the AMC said that antitrust as we know it is competent to analyse innovation issues, while in the next breath it said that the Guidelines should be revised, presumably because the manner in which the enforcement agencies evaluate innovation is unclear or unpersuasive, or both.

If a lesson can be generalised, it is that one should approach with considerable skepticism the august pronouncements of the suppleness of existing antitrust doctrine to accommodate consideration of dynamic efficiency. It is time for the antitrust enforcement agencies and the courts to address forthrightly the challenge of developing more dynamically efficient merger guidelines. Achievement of that goal would lay the foundation for an analogous refinement of substantive rules of liability, defences, and remedies across antitrust law generally.

v. *Intellectual Candor and the Silent Revision of the Merger Guidelines*

Infusing antitrust analysis with principles of Schumpeterian competition is a good thing. However, so is intellectual candor and transparency in the decision making of those who make and enforce antitrust policy. So, while we applaud the evolution toward an antitrust jurisprudence predicated on dynamic competition, we prefer that the process be more transparent and explicit. A recent merger during the George W Bush Administration illustrates the difficulty of trying to revise the Merger Guidelines without announcing that intention.

As we noted earlier, in public remarks in October 2007, former Assistant Attorney General Thomas Barnett strongly endorsed the primacy of innovation over static competition as the engine that produces large gains in consumer welfare.[122] In the Antitrust Division's official actions, that belief manifested itself most tangibly in the decision not to oppose the merger of XM Satellite Radio Holdings Inc and Sirius Satellite Radio Inc, the only US licensed providers of satellite digital audio radio services (SDARS). The horizontal combination of the only two SDARS providers would have constituted a merger to monopoly—if the Antitrust Division had deemed SDARS to constitute a relevant antitrust product market. The Division's press release in March 2008 explaining the basis for not prosecuting the merger accepted dynamic competition arguments concerning market definition, market power, competitive effects, and merger-specific efficiencies.[123] In that respect, the decision not to prosecute may reflect the kind of neo-Schumpeterian analysis that we endorse here.

[120] Antitrust Modernisation Commission (AMC), 'Report and Recommendation 9' (April 2007), available at www.amc.gov/report_recommendation/amc_final_report.pdf.

[121] Ibid 11.

[122] Barnett (n 105).

[123] Statement of the Department of Justice Antitrust Division on Its Decision to Close Its Investigation of XM Satellite Radio Holdings Inc's Merger with Sirius Satellite Radio Inc (24 March 2008) ['Decision to Close Investigation'].

As we have explained, the Merger Guidelines as of this writing in late 2009 still officially embody a static view of competition. Consequently, it is difficult to find language in the Guidelines consistent with the methodology that the Division employed in reaching its decision not to challenge the XM-Sirius merger in 2008. It is, of course, possible that merger enforcement in practice had already deviated from the written Merger Guidelines, just as practice before many federal agencies rests on unwritten norms as much as the written law. In terms of implementing change, the matter would be simpler if the Division had the discretion to change its guidelines at will to reflect a new prosecutorial agenda. A distinguishing characteristic of the rule of law, however, is that it constrains discretion. The complication arises because of the prior success of the Division and the FTC in persuading the federal courts to embed the economic reasoning of the Merger Guidelines into substantive antitrust doctrine—and not doctrine necessarily confined to the law of mergers. (An illustration of that success is that both the majority and the dissent in the recent *Whole Foods* merger decision in the DC Circuit defended its view as consistent with the reasoning of the Guidelines.[124])

The difference between static antitrust analysis and dynamic antitrust analysis is evident in how XM and Sirius urged the Government to define the relevant product market. The Merger Guidelines specify the kind of evidence that may inform market definition: 'Market definition focuses solely on demand substitution factors—ie, possible consumer responses.'[125] Applied here, to expand the product market beyond satellite radio (the narrowest possible set of products), one must demonstrate that satellite radio subscribers shift their demand between satellite radio and other forms of audio entertainment (for example, terrestrial radio) in response to a relative change in the prices of those services.[126] XM and Sirius failed to demonstrate any evidence of buyer substitution in response to changes in relative prices. Through their economists, XM and Sirius argued that such evidence was hard to find because satellite radio prices had not changed between 2005 and 2007. More importantly, they argued that dynamic demand considerations in the satellite radio industry undercut the utility of the demand-side test for market definition contained in the Merger Guidelines. The vast majority of XM's and Sirius's inferences were based on supply-side information, which the Merger Guidelines currently exclude when defining product markets, except in rare cases in which decisions by sellers can serve as a proxy for how buyers would react to a change in relative prices.[127] The fact that entrepreneurs may be designing new audio devices in their garages in Silicon Valley does not inform the ultimate question of whether, over the two years following the announcement of the merger,

[124] cp *FTC v Whole Foods Markets Inc* 553 F.3d 869, 878, 886 (DC Cir. 2008), with ibid 893 (Kavanaugh J dissenting).

[125] US Department of Justice & Federal Trade Commission, 'Horizontal Merger Guidelines' (n 6), § 1.0 (emphasis added).

[126] Ibid § 1.11 ('In considering the likely reaction of buyers to a price increase, the Agency will take into account all relevant evidence, including, but not limited to, the following: (1) evidence that buyers have shifted or have considered shifting purchases between products in response to relative changes in price or other competitive variables; (2) evidence that sellers base business decisions on the prospect of buyer substitution between products in response to relative changes in price or other competitive variables; (3) the influence of downstream competition faced by buyers in their output markets; and (4) the timing and costs of switching products.').

[127] Ibid § 1.0 ('Supply substitution factors—ie, possible production responses—are considered elsewhere in the Guidelines in the identification of firms that participate in the relevant market and the analysis of entry.').

satellite radio customers would substitute away from satellite radio to another audio device in response to a change in relative prices.

Defining markets and measuring post-merger market power are two sides of the same coin. If outside products constrain the price of the merged entity, then the market should be expanded and the merged firm will be more likely to be found to lack market power. Section 7 of the Clayton Act prohibits any merger, 'the effect of [which] may be substantially to lessen competition, or to tend to create a monopoly'.[128] The Division explained that it decided not to challenge the *XM-Sirius* merger 'because the evidence did not show that the merger would enable the parties to profitably increase prices to satellite radio customers for several reasons'.[129] However, two of the four factors that the Division then listed were unrelated to the ability of a merged firm to raise price, such as 'a lack of competition between the parties in important segments even without the merger' and 'efficiencies likely to flow from the transaction that could benefit consumers.'[130] Thus, the Division's competitive-effects conclusion had to rest on two other factors: 'the competitive alternative services available to consumers' and 'technological change that is expected to make those alternatives increasingly attractive over time'.[131]

The XM-Sirius satellite radio merger implicated Schumpeterian competition in several respects, the most significant being whether the relevant product market should be defined strictly in terms of consumer-substitution choices. If the market had been defined to consist exclusively of satellite radio, which was being supplied by only two firms, then analysis of the merger would have been trivial. A merger to monopoly would result and drive the Herfindahl-Hirschman Index (HHI) to its limit of 10,000.

Consequently, the merging parties cast the question as to whether consumers considered iPods, streaming audio over wireless internet, and other kinds of electronic devices to be substitutes for satellite radio. To define the relevant product market, the Horizontal Merger Guidelines evaluate consumer substitution in terms of whether, over a two-year horizon, a five per cent price increase by a hypothetical monopolist of the product in question would be profitable. This exercise is the evaluation of a small but significant non-transitory increase in price (SSNIP). The SSNIP test focuses on consumer substitution. Supply substitution (including entry) is not considered until after market shares are calculated solely on the basis of the static, consumer-oriented market definition. One can dispute whether that approach is good economics; as a matter of law, however, the static approach was the law. The DC Circuit in *Microsoft* and the AMC in its report essentially said that the static perspective reflected in the Horizontal Merger Guidelines was adequate to address technologically dynamic industries, such that a neo-Schumpeterian revision of the Guidelines is unnecessary.

During the review of the *XM-Sirius* merger by the Antitrust Division and the Federal Communications Commission (FCC), however, it became clear that on multiple issues—relevant market, market power, entry, and merger efficiencies—the enforcement agencies were disinclined to challenge the merger and were, in practice, undertaking a dynamic competition analysis without so characterising it. Is this dynamic competition gloss bad?

[128] Clayton Act 15 USC § 18.
[129] Decision to Close Investigation (n 123)
[130] Ibid.
[131] Ibid.

It is not bad if one is a Schumpeterian and considers dynamic competition arguments to be valid. However, there is a cost to pretending that one is not changing substantive rules when one really is.

We recommend transparency and dialogue, which we hope will result from the review of the Merger Guidelines initiated by the FTC and the Antitrust Division in September 2009. The enforcement agencies should be candid and unambiguous about how and when they intend to depart from the old, static competition version of the Guidelines. The federal courts should be clearer about whether they believe that authority or reason legitimates the Guidelines. It remains to be seen whether the Antitrust Division's analysis in the *XM-Sirius* merger represented the adoption of an unapologetically dynamic approach to merger analysis—and to antitrust analysis more generally. As the *Whole Foods* case suggests, however, it is valuable for the antitrust enforcement agencies to revisit the Merger Guidelines explicitly, rather than leave courts, businesses, and the lawyers advising them to speculate on whether—and where—the agencies no longer embrace the explicitly static view of competition articulated in the plain language of the Guidelines.

vi. Symmetric Time Horizons for Merger Analysis

One manifestation of the difference between static analysis and dynamic analysis is the relevant time horizon for evaluating a number of issues that arise not only in mergers, but also in all big section 1 and section 2 cases. Is a two-year period appropriate for the purpose of defining markets and evaluating market power? Should we evaluate substitution from entrants over the same period of time? A major inconsistency in merger and antitrust cases concerns the proper time horizon for evaluating the feasibility of proposed remedies.[132] In a merger case, the antitrust enforcement agency may evaluate market power over two years yet seek conditions on approval of the merger that extend many more years into the future.

This approach to establishing a time horizon is intellectually inconsistent. It is selectively Schumpeterian. We believe intuitively that symmetry ought to exist between the length of time used to evaluate market power and the period of time over which the enforcement agencies and the courts consider themselves professionally competent to fashion sensible remedies. At the very least, some kind of guideline of the enforcement agencies should squarely address the issue of developing an appropriate time horizon, even if the ultimate policy choice differs from our preference that the two time frames be identical.

In broader terms, we recommend that, in addition to revisiting the Horizontal Merger Guidelines, the Antitrust Division and FTC promulgate guidelines of general applicability for market definition, market power, efficiency defences, and remedies.

vii. Mergers Involving Multi-Sided Platforms or Markets

The Horizontal Merger Guidelines look dated in the more nuanced antitrust matters that routinely arise today. For example, a recurring phenomenon in many high-tech mergers is a two-sided market (or, as David Evans prefers to describe it, a multi-sided platform), as in the case of credit cards.[133] In a multi-sided market, two or more sets of consumers exist

[132] See, eg Shelanski and Sidak (n 8) 79–80.

[133] The seminal paper is William F Baxter, 'Bank Exchange of Transactional Paper: Legal and Economic Perspectives' (1983) 26 *Journal of Law and Economics* 541.

for the product. The aggregate demand is the vertical summation of their demand curves. However, the demand curves are not necessarily equidistant from the origin or sloped in the same way. Consequently, in a multi-sided market there will be a different demand elasticity and a different willingness to pay for each set of consumers. These characteristics of multi-sided markets are central to the network neutrality debate and to antitrust issues in network industries such as telecommunications, financial services, and internet search.[134]

It is fanciful to suggest, in a paroxysm of antitrust originalism, that the Merger Guidelines are already capable of addressing this subtlety. Only recently, and principally in the academic literature, have economists derived a SSNIP test for a multi-sided platform.[135] Multi-sided platform interactions are often strong evidence that some important new product has been created—perhaps through innovations in finance or information management or market intermediation. Given the importance and prevalence of multi-sided platforms and markets, and given the potential for multi-sided platforms to create large consumer welfare gains, the Antitrust Division and the FTC should clarify how they will evaluate market definition and market power with respect to multi-sided platforms and markets.

viii. Ancillary Revenue Streams, Bankruptcy, and State Ownership

An issue related to the phenomenon of a multi-sided platform or market is the strategy of companies 'giving away stuff for free'—in essence, Google's business model for search and other web-based services. We call this phenomenon the 'ancillary revenue stream problem'. In a multi-sided market, a company generates revenue from one set of customers and gives away (or subsidises) products or services demanded by another set of customers. This problem is as old as the newspaper subscriptions and newspaper advertisements that provided separate but complementary revenue streams in *Albrecht v Herald Co*.[136]

How does the business model of providing free or subsidised goods dovetail with traditional antitrust case law on a subject like predatory pricing? How does a court apply a predation rule in a market where one set of firms sells the product for a positive price while another firm (following a different business model entirely) gives away the same product for free because it derives an ancillary revenue stream elsewhere?

Consider the much-scrutinised case of *Aspen Skiing*,[137] a 1985 Supreme Court decision now experiencing renewed respectability in light of the laudatory comments directed to the opinion by Assistant Attorney General Varney when she rescinded the Antitrust Division's report on monopolisation in May 2009.[138] In *Aspen Skiing*, the Supreme Court was particularly troubled that the vertically integrated firm would not sell wholesale access to its ski slopes even when the competitor offered to pay the full retail price of a lift ticket.

[134] See J Gregory Sidak, 'A Consumer-Welfare Approach to Network Neutrality Regulation of the Internet' (2006) 2 *Journal of Competition Law and Economics* 349.

[135] See, eg David S Evans and Michael D Noel, 'The Analysis of Mergers that Involve Multisided Platform Businesses' (2008) 4 *Journal of Competition Law and Economics* 663; Elena Argentesi and Lapo Filistrucchi, 'Estimating Market Power in a Two-Sided Market: The Case of Newspapers' (2007) 22 *Journal of Applied Econometrics* 1247; Dennis L Weisman, 'Assessing Market Power: The Trade-Off between Market Concentration and Multi-Market Participation' (2005) 1 *Journal of Competition Law and Economics* 339.

[136] *Albrecht v Herald Co* 390 US 145 (1968).

[137] *Aspen Skiing Co v Aspen Highlands Skiing Corp* 472 US 585 (1985).

[138] Christine A Varney, 'Vigorous Antitrust Enforcement in This Challenging Era, Remarks Prepared for the Center for American Progress (May 11, 2009), available at www.usdoj.gov/atr/public/speeches/245711.htm.

When analysing a case like this one, where the prevailing business practice seems inexplicable when compared with simplistic static models of the firm and its objectives, it is useful to search for an ancillary revenue stream, which may or may not be described in the court's opinion. If an ancillary revenue stream exists, it might provide a simple explanation for firm behaviour that, if viewed narrowly either across transactions or over time, might impress a court as being irrational and non-profit-maximising.

New economic theories of anti-competitive effects tend toward complexity in part because the intellectual pay-off to academic economists within the leading research universities increases with the technical complexity of those novel theories. It is important to remember Occam's razor when evaluating these theories as sources of guidance for enforcement agencies and courts. With all due respect to Assistant Attorney General Varney, we believe that *Aspen Skiing* is, and will forever remain, an incoherent decision because the Supreme Court decided the case on a record that suggests a startling lack of curiosity by the trial court and an equally startling lack of sophistication by defence counsel in explaining the economic justifications for the business practices at issue.

ix. Subtler Counterfactuals in Merger Analysis

The courts and antitrust enforcement agencies should think more precisely about counterfactuals —not only in the context of the Horizontal Merger Guidelines, but in antitrust law more generally. There can be little doubt that, as a positive matter, the Antitrust Division and the FTC already contemplate counterfactuals when reviewing a merger. The intentionally political structure of the FTC surely encourages the consideration of counterfactuals at that agency. However, the consideration of counterfactuals should be coherent and transparent. To take an example relevant to defining markets under the SSNIP test, it is possible that particular sectors of the US economy will experience deflation in the aftermath of the Panic of 2008. If so, then the counterfactual for a proposed merger may be that prices that would otherwise fall might be stabilised.

This concern over the relevant counterfactual was known to the Antitrust Division and the FCC in the XM-Sirius merger. Prices were not likely to rise after a merger—to the contrary, the merging companies 'voluntarily' consented to a temporary price cap.[139] Instead, the more likely competitive effect of the merger would be an increase in the amount of commercial time inserted into the subscription-based programming. Consequently, the proper counterfactual in the XM-Sirius merger was not a price increase, but rather a degradation in product quality while the subscription price remained constant. Of course, one could simply recast that competitive effect as a quality-adjusted price increase: after the merger, the candy bar would get smaller, even if the price on the wrapper did not change.

In a revised set of Horizontal Merger Guidelines, it would also be useful to examine counterfactuals in another way, particularly in the case of financially distressed firms. If the merger were blocked, would an alternative transaction (or set of transactions) having a lesser risk of reducing competition be likely to occur? In the case of XM and Sirius, for

[139] See Farrell Malone and J Gregory Sidak, 'Should Antitrust Consent Decrees Regulate Post-Merger Pricing?' (2007) 3 *Journal of Competition Law and Economics* 471; J Gregory Sidak and Hal J Singer, 'Evaluating Market Power with Two-Sided Demand and Preemptive Offers to Dissipate Monopoly Rent: Lessons for High-Technology Industries from the Antitrust Division's Approval of the XM-Sirius Satellite Radio Merger' (2008) 4 *Journal of Competition Law and Economics* 697.

example, was it plausible for another company to acquire one of the merging firms? Could two alternative acquisitions have occurred, such that each of the only satellite radio companies could have merged with a firm other than its closest competitor? It bears emphasis that this kind of counterfactual inquiry is not a failing-firm defence. Rather, it is a kind of neo-Schumpeterian inquiry, consistent with the grander scope of this article, to scrutinise mergers in a more dynamic sense that recognises that the boundaries of the firm evolve as innovations in technology, finance, information management, or other capabilities reveal that the firm's existing products are more efficiently offered to consumers in combination with other, complementary products.

x. *The Adverse Consequences of Inaction*

For all the reasons discussed above, the antitrust enforcement agencies should revise the Horizontal Merger Guidelines to take dynamic competition concerns explicitly into account. We conclude our discussion of merger enforcement by adding one cautionary tale. If the antitrust enforcement agencies do not exercise leadership by revising the Horizontal Merger Guidelines, the counterfactual is not necessarily the perpetuation of the status quo. It is more likely that sector-specific regulatory agencies will fiddle with merger policy in pursuit of goals far removed from, or even antithetical to, the maximisation of consumer welfare.

The US economy will undoubtedly be more heavily regulated under President Obama than under President George W Bush. The Federal Government will play a greater role in ownership and control of business enterprises. Regulatory agencies are more likely to acquire than relinquish powers. To take one regulatory agency, consider how the FCC has conducted merger analysis in comparison with how the Antitrust Division and FTC conduct it. We foresee a risk of sector-specific regulatory bodies performing considerable amounts of bad antitrust analysis. In the XM-Sirius satellite radio case, the FCC came to the same conclusion as the Antitrust Division that the merger should be allowed. However, the FCC did so by reasoning that contradicted the Antitrust Division's analysis of market definition. To justify continuation of the structural regulation of terrestrial broadcasting, the FCC needed to explain why the merger was not unlawful without saying that terrestrial radio, iPods, and streaming audio over wireless internet are all in the same product market as satellite radio.[140] The FCC, in essence, said that the Antitrust Division reached the correct answer through faulty reason. Such agency conduct diminishes legal clarity and certainty.

Multiply that incident by the number of sector-specific approvals that will be required as the many newly nationalised companies in the United States restructure themselves through mergers or acquisitions. It is unlikely that a coherent merger policy that recognises the role of dynamic competition will emerge if the Antitrust Division and the FTC fail to act.

F. Intellectual Property Issues

Favouring dynamic competition over static competition does double duty. In addition to stimulating competition and innovation, it softens the tension in the patent-antitrust

[140] In the Matter of Applications for Consent to the Transfer of Control of Licenses XM Satellite Radio Holdings, Inc., Transferor, to Sirius Satellite Radio Inc., Transferee, Memorandum Opinion and Order and Report and Order 23 FCCR 12, 384 (2008).

debate. Static analysis views patents with considerable awkwardness and, consequently, fuels tension between the patent system and antitrust.

The DOJ and FTC Intellectual Property Guidelines have endeavoured to reconcile the tension between intellectual property and antitrust by declaring that intellectual property is merely another form of property and by noting that patents imply market or monopoly power only if they enable control of a relevant market, which is rarely the case. Still, justifying the exclusivity provided by the patent system is not easy for many competition policy advocates. In practice, neoclassical economists are often hostile to patents because they believe that other mechanisms solve the appropriability problem naturally, a result that is often not the case.

Embracing dynamic competition eases tension between intellectual property and antitrust concerns. The patent system provides some amount of exclusion, and some amount of exclusion is required to foster innovation, particularly in more competitive market environments. Of course, once antitrust doctrine sees the promotion of innovation as its major goal, innovation and competition snap into greater harmony. However, the harmony is not perfect, as questions remain with respect to the degree of intellectual property protection needed to foster innovation and competition. The cumulative or sequential nature of innovation means that policy makers need to calibrate intellectual property protection in a careful manner. Almost always the number of users of intellectual property will exceed the number of its generators; so the predictable public choice danger is that the users will try to crimp the scope of IPRs provided to the generators.

VI. Conclusion

Antitrust scholars must confront an inconvenient truth: innovation drives competition as much as competition drives innovation. Thus, antitrust analysis must recognise that advancing dynamic competition will benefit consumers most, certainly in the long run if not also in the short run. The law has already begun to move in this direction, as have the enforcement agencies. The pace is glacial, however, in part because antitrust economics has trouble articulating, quantifying, and operationalising dynamic concepts. The Chicago School in large measure inadvertently ignored dynamic competition by embracing static microeconomic theory. The post-Chicago economists have been almost as reluctant to embrace dynamic competition because their tools are inadequate. Fortunately, there has emerged a large body of research in evolutionary economics, the behavioural theory of the firm, and corporate strategy that antitrust policy makers can use to mitigate the harmful unintended consequences of static analysis. If nothing else, a wider appreciation of the importance of dynamic competition for innovation and consumer welfare may temper the hubris that the uninformed sometimes bring to antitrust analysis.

2

Country Chapters

5

Australia

BOB BAXT AND HENRY ERGAS

I. Introduction to Intersection and Concerns

The setting of an appropriate policy or policies in law in Australia has always involved a tortuous process. This is particularly true for changes that are made from time to time in our competition law. In the two parts of this chapter we explore the failure of successive Australian governments to reach an appropriate balance between the regulation of anti-competitive practices and the encouragement of intellectual enterprise and expertise, and the encouragement of joint ventures whether in that field or in other important areas of our economy.

In the first part of this chapter (written by Henry Ergas), the regulation of intellectual property rights (IPRs) in Australia and the nature of constraints imposed upon those rights, including anti-trust prohibitions in the Trade Practices Act 1974 (Cth) (TPA)[1] and those specific to copyright and patent laws are discussed. It will argue that protection of creative endeavours through IPRs does not necessarily lessen competition. It is the ambiguity and inconsistencies between the two legislative regimes that limit innovation and distort competition.

The second part of this chapter, prepared by Bob Baxt, explores similar issues in a discussion of the specific provisions of the TPA and the relevant policy considerations in the 'regulation' of joint ventures. As noted earlier, joint ventures play an important role in Australia's economy. This is particularly so in relation to mining and related activities, but also in encouraging the development of new ideas that are protected by IPRs. The recent introduction of criminal cartel offences in the TPA threatens the continued use of joint ventures and illustrates confusion on the part of the Government. Its approach is too draconian when compared to the more balanced and appropriate rule of a reason approach to such activities in the United States and elsewhere.

II. Interaction of IP and Competition Laws

A. Introduction

IPRs, Professor Cornish reminds us, 'are essentially negative: they are rights to stop others doing certain things'[2]—those things being primarily the use of the ideas (or more properly,

[1] In 2011 the Trade Practices Act became the Competition and Consumer Act 2011 (Cth).
[2] WR Cornish, *Intellectual Property*, 3rd edn (London, Sweet and Maxwell, 1996) 6.

the output of creative endeavour, which may be the expression or material embodiment of an idea, rather than the idea itself) covered in the grant made to a right-owner. As rights to exclude, IPRs sit uneasily with the conventional notion of competition, which centres on the ability of several, possibly many, parties to act as rivals in striving for economic rewards. The uneasy nature of the relationship should not suggest that there is contradiction between IPRs and competition: rather, it is a truism that IPRs, by allowing creators to secure a greater share of the social gain from their creation than they would otherwise, can promote rivalrous investment in creative effort; and that it is this investment that underpins the development of new processes and products which not only contributes directly to increased wellbeing but also, in Schumpeter's famous phrase, is a form of competition 'as much more effective than [conventional price competition] as a bombardment is in comparison with forcing a door'.[3]

This is clearly a gain to society; but it is bought at a cost. Once made, ideas are relatively readily transmitted and used; they are, in economic terms, non-rivalrous.[4] From an economic point of view, therefore, they ought to be used as widely as possible—which implies a price of or close to zero (for the idea itself, though not for its material form). The exclusionary right granted by the IPR, however, enables the right-owner to set a positive price for the protected material, thereby reducing the flow of and output from ideas. To the extent to which ideas themselves serve as the basis for generating further ideas, the social cost of the reduced flow can take the form not only of less income today but also of less growth in income in periods to come. If owners of IPRs could use their exclusionary rights to extend their control even further than the original grant contemplated, securing an income stream in excess of the social gain arising from their creation, the costs to society could be greater yet.

The fact there is consequently a balancing to be sought is nothing new. Arguments that 'public utility requires that production of the mind should be diffused as widely as possible'[5] were common in the English literary property debate of the eighteenth century; so too was the hostility to patents embodied in Blackstone's view that 'mechanical inventions tend to the improvement of arts and manufactures, which employ the bulk of people; therefore they ought to be cheap and numerous'.[6] Although copyright eventually gained widespread acceptance, criticism of the 'monopoly' granted by patents has periodically resurfaced, with even the intellectual grand-father of Chicago economics, Frank Knight, viewing them as an 'exceedingly crude way of rewarding invention'.[7] From this he concluded that 'it would seem to be a matter of political intelligence and administrative capability to replace

[3] JA Schumpeter, *Capitalism, Socialism and Democracy* (New York, Harper and Law, 1944) 84.

[4] This simply means that one person can consume more of an idea without reducing the stock of that idea that is available for others to consume. This does not require that the costs of transmitting information and even less so technology, are zero; this is plainly not the case (otherwise lawyers could not earn as much as they do for mediating the public's access to information that is in the public domain). However, the presumption remains that the costs involved in transfer are low relative to those of first creation. Indeed, a central rationale for IPRs is that in the absence of rights to exclude, third parties could readily and at relatively low cost benefit from the creative effort of others.

[5] The Cases of Appellants and Respondents in the Cause of Literary Property before the House of Lords (1774) 6, cited in B Sherman and L Bently, *The Making of Modern Intellectual Property Law* (Cambridge, Cambridge University Press, 1999) 29.

[6] W Blackstone [as Counsel] in *Tonson v Collins* (1760) 96 ER 189.

[7] FH Knight, 8th impression *Risk, Uncertainty and Profit* (New York, Kelley and Millman, 1957) 372. Knight believed that most of the rewards from patents went to those who put the 'finishing touch' on ideas, rather than the genuine risk-takers.

artificial monopoly with some *direct* method of stimulating and rewarding research'[8]—a view the Nobel laureate in economics, Kenneth Arrow, echoed, some 40 years later, in his classic article of the economics of research and development (R&D).[9]

These arguments, compelling though they may be in the abstract, rest on the assumption that governments, in implementing Knights' 'direct method' of stimulation, will make fewer or less costly errors in allocating resources to creative effort than are caused by the market-oriented mechanism of IPRs. This assumption has merit when applied to pure research, but must surely fail at the more applied end of the spectrum. To begin with, it requires a greater degree of omniscience (and perhaps of omni-benevolence) from public decision-makers than it is safe to assume. Additionally, it underestimates the incentives even owners of monopoly rights have to expand output, say through price discrimination, and hence likely overstates the costs of the alleged monopoly. Finally, it wrongly assumes that IPRs serve only to fund investment in creative effort; in practice, they also act to promote the disclosure of new ideas (particularly in areas where secrecy is a viable alternative) and, by allowing well-defined rights to be traded, to facilitate the allocation of the ownership of creative works to those who can put them to their most highly valued use. As no 'direct method' of stimulation has yet been found that even comes close to matching these effects, calls for a wholesale retreat from IPRs are not likely to command much support.

What can and should command support is the continued investigation of whether the right balance has been struck between vesting ownership rights in creators and promoting the widest use of the results of creative effort. Faced with changes in technology, and more generally in the economic and regulatory environment in which investment in creative effort occurs, the balance that has been struck, and the particular mechanisms that give it effect, need to be open to re-examination.

In reviewing this balance, it is important to note that it is effected at two levels: first, in the conditions attached to the grant of an IPR, and in privileges and obligations the legislation directly governing that right[10] vests in the right-owner; and second, in the constraints on the exercise of that right that may be imposed by other legislation—with the TPA being most directly relevant.[11] In practice, it is the two together that define the bundle of rights available to those who invest in creative effort; and concerns about promoting the widest use of knowledge, and enhancing competition both in its production and in

[8] Ibid 372.

[9] Although often cited by those who support strong IPRs, suggesting that as with so much economic literature, it is far more often cited than read, Arrow's main conclusion is that 'for optimal allocation [of resources] to invention it would be necessary for the government or some other agency not governed by profit-and-loss criteria to finance research and invention'. K Arrow, 'Economic Welfare and the Allocation of Resources to Invention' in *The Rate and Direction of Inventive Activity: Economic and Social Factors* (National Bureau of Economic Research, 1962) 623.

[10] Specifically relevant are the Copyright Act 1990 ('CA'); the Designs Act 2003; the Patents Act 1990 ('PA'); the Trade Marks Act 1995; the Circuit Layouts Act 1989; and the Plant Breeder's Rights Act 1994.

[11] This formulation is not intended to uncritically accept the distinction drawn in EU case law, since *Costen and Grundig v Commission* (56 and 58/64) [1966] ECR 299, as between the existence and exercise of IPRs—the one being protected from other community laws, the other not. As Korah notes, 'in legal theory, it is impossible to draw the line between existence and exercise, except at the extremes. Analytically, the existence of a right consists of all the ways it may be exercised. In ruling that an important difference rests on a distinction which cannot be drawn by logical analysis, the Court created a very flexible instrument for it to develop the law and reduce the value of intellectual property rights'. V Korah, *An Introductory Guide to EC Competition Law and Practice*, 5th edn (London, Sweet and Maxwell, 1994) 190. Having said that, it is neither unreasonable nor illogical to distinguish between the grant of a right and the conditions of its exercise. Each of these may involve a balancing of competition and other considerations.

its exploitation, have been reflected in both of these layers. Indeed, a difficult issue, and one which has commanded far greater attention in North America and Europe than in Australia, is that of the appropriate division of labour as between these levels.

The approach taken here will consequently be to first examine some of the issues that currently arise in respect of the balance struck within two of the main statutory instruments that define IPRs (the copyright and patent statutes respectively); then consider aspects of the treatment of those rights under the TPA; and finally, to examine some of the open questions that arise from the interaction between these.

The overall hypothesis being advanced is a simple one: that in Australia, considerations as to the appropriate balance to be struck in the definition and enforcement of IPRs have very largely, if not entirely, been given effect by embodying specific provisions, aimed at achieving that balance, in the intellectual property system; the bundle of rights thus defined has then been given a relatively wide-ranging, though ambiguous and poorly worded, exemption from the more general statutes aimed at protecting and promoting competition. There has, in other words, been a marked preference for relying on the definition of the rights, rather than on *ex post* constraints on the exercise of those rights, as the primary means of striking a balance between incentives to creative effort and the public interest in wide access to ideas.

Before examining this proposition in more detail, it is useful to consider why that may be the case. At the highest level of abstraction, three factors seem relevant.

The first is the legal tradition, which despite some significant differences relative to the United Kingdom, is probably closer to the formalism Atiyah and Summers, in their classic comparison of the English and American legal traditions, ascribe to the United Kingdom, than to the more instrumentalist approach common in American law.[12] In the intellectual property area especially, this translates into a tendency to interpret rights fairly narrowly and hence to hew closely to the precise definition of the extent of the rights as given in legislation.[13]

A second factor is the economic context. Australia has long relied heavily on imported technology, and well-defined IPRs may have been valuable in facilitating the transactions required. Moreover, a substantial share of the R&D undertaken domestically is publicly funded. Traditionally, this publicly funded R&D was carried out largely in government agencies, notably the Commonwealth Scientific and Industrial Research Organisation (CSIRO); much of this research involved projects where individual end users, for example pastoralists, were price-takers in world markets, and hence did not perceive each other as rivals. As a result, these agencies tended to distribute the results of their research widely, especially within Australia, with IPRs placing little restriction on end users' access to research results. More recently, the Government has placed considerable emphasis on cooperative research (involving both public and private sector participants) in emerging technologies, particularly through the Cooperative Research Centre (CRC) Program,[14] and

[12] PS Atiyah and RS Summers, *Form and Substance in Anglo-American Law* (Oxford, Clarendon Press, 1987).

[13] See, eg J McKeough, 'Horses and the Law: The Enduring Legacy of Victoria Park' in Andrew T Kenyon, Megan Richardson and Sam Ricketson, *Landmarks in Australian Intellectual Property Law* (Melbourne, Cambridge UP, 2009) 53–72.

[14] The CRC Program commenced in 1991. Since then, 168 CRCs have been established, of which 48 currently operate. A CRC may be an incorporated or unincorporated organisation, but must be formed through collaborative partnerships between publicly funded researchers and end users. CRCs must comprise at least one Australian

clear IPRs may have been viewed as useful in facilitating both the initial investments and the commercialisation of any results.

Last but not least, competition policy—both in the sense of 'antitrust' and in the sense of policy aimed at removing statutory obstacles to competition—is a relatively recent arrival on the Australian scene (dating, in the case of the first form, to the early 1970s and of the second, to the early 1990s). In contrast, intellectual property law has roots that stretch back to well before Federation in 1901, reflected in a long legacy of both statute and case law. Concerns about preserving the integrity and clarity of that precedent have weighed on policy-makers whenever questions have arisen of whether and how competition issues relating to the intellectual property laws should be addressed.

Individually and combined, these factors have lead to a marked preference for dealing with any balancing between the competing claims of exclusivity and access through the intellectual property laws themselves, rather than through *ex post* controls on the exercise of the rights once granted. This is a response the intellectual property laws lend themselves to, as they are rich in instruments that can be used to 'fence in' or more generally 'fine tune' the exclusivity provided, including through changes to coverage, originality requirements, duration, the precise content of the reserved rights and the mechanisms for the exhaustion of those rights, statutory exemptions and exceptions, the allocation of burdens in the context of infringement proceedings and the nature and extent of remedies. This multiplicity of defining variables offers (or at least has been thought to offer) the scope to deal in a targeted, well-defined way with the competing considerations of exclusivity and access, without introducing the uncertainties that would arise were an approach based on general concepts and principles—as is largely a characteristic of competition law—superimposed on, and allowed to over-ride or redefine, the rights granted in the intellectual property statutes.

Although this architecture is not *per se* inefficient, its implementation lacks consistency and has in some instances resulted in rules that are at times seriously under- or over-inclusive. A consideration first of copyright and then of patents helps highlight the nature of the resulting issues.

B. Copyright

Copyright is often described as an ownership right that is easily acquired and durable but extremely narrow—easily acquired, because of the absence of registration requirements and because the threshold of creativity required to attract protection is low; durable, because the right persists for far longer than other IPRs; but narrow, because of the limited scope of protection the right offers.[15] The rise of new technologies, which convert an ever-greater part of the stock of copyrightable material into digital form, along with the emergence of copyright as the prime (although by no means sole) form of protection of software in all of its many manifestations, have brought ever greater pressures to bear on this most flexible of rights.

end user (either from the private, public or community sector) and one Australian higher education institution (or research institute affiliated with a university).

[15] SM Besen and SN Kirby, 'Private Copying, Appropriability and Optimal Copying Royalties' (1989) 32 *Journal of Law & Economics* 255.

To understand the form these pressures take, it is important to note a distinctive feature of the Australian copyright regime. In the United States, the desirability of providing scope for limiting the reach of the right-owner's power to exclude is reflected in relatively general provisions relating to 'fair use'. These are set out in section 107 of the Copyright Act (CA) (Title 17 of the United States Code), which exemplifies instances of fair use (by referring to 'purposes *such as* criticism, comment, news reporting, teaching, … scholarship, or research' (emphasis added)) and then lists factors which must be taken into account (although others may also be considered) in determining whether a particular use falls within the provision.[16] A specific provision then allows libraries to provide copies to users, upon request, within limits set out essentially in qualitative terms.[17] A similar, although not identical, approach is adopted in the United Kingdom.[18]

In contrast, the Australian approach is prescriptive. The purposes encompassed by the fair dealing provisions are set out exhaustively, mainly in sections 40–43 of the CA,[19] rather than by example. Additionally, the deeming provision of section 40(3), together with the inclusive definition of a 'reasonable portion' in section 10(2), creates a 'safe harbour' from the operation of the factors identified in section 40(2).[20] The relations between rights-owners and users are then further regulated by the statutory licensing requirements imposed upon rights-owners, along with the jurisdiction vested in the Copyright Tribunal to fix royalties or equitable remuneration in respect of compulsory licenses and to arbitrate disputes in relation to the terms of the licenses or of proposed licensing schemes.[21]

The Copyright Law Review Committee, in its first report on its Simplification reference, recommended a move to a less prescriptive approach to fair dealing.[22] In considering this recommendation, it is important to consider the rationale underpinning the current arrangements. In essence, these arrangements serve to reduce the transaction costs that could arise were the relevant provisions were less clearly specified. By their nature, ownership of the relevant rights is dispersed; so too is the use of the works in which the rights are embodied. At the cost of some arbitrariness, the provisions reduce the uncertainty that bears on the process of determining the scope of the right, be it through contracting,

[16] See generally RP Merges, PS Menell and MA Lemley, *Intellectual Property in the New Technological Age* (New York, Aspen Publishers, 2000) 490–543.

[17] For example, by referring to whether, when the purpose of the copying is replacement, 'an unused replacement cannot be obtained at a reasonable price' (s 108(d)(1)), or whether the effect of any inter library loan scheme in which the library operates makes available 'such aggregate quantities as to substitute for a subscription to or purchase of such work' (s 108(g)(2)). See also, on the economics involved in the application of this provision to libraries, B Kingma, *The Economics of Access versus Ownership* (London, Routledge, 1996).

[18] Section 29 of the Copyright, Designs and Patent Act 1988 provides a general fair dealing exception for research and private study, while ss 37–43 provide exceptions for libraries and archives. As Cornish notes, these provisions embody a 'relatively light legislative hand … [so that] it remains for the Courts to decide how far business, and for that matter government, should be able to take single copies without licence by claiming to need them for these purposes': Cornish, *Intellectual Property* (1996) 436.

[19] Related provisions, of varying importance, are discussed in J McKeough, A Stewart and P Griffith, *Intellectual Property in Australia*, 3rd edn (Sydney, Butterworths, 2004) 246 ff.

[20] The factors set out in s 40(2) of the CA are not exhaustive, and in that sense, a court could look more widely in adjudicating a dispute that involved the copying of more than a 'reasonable portion' of a work. However, the purposes for which the copying may occur are prescribed, and it is in that sense that the Australian provisions are narrower than their counterparts in (say) the United States.

[21] See generally, J McKeough, A Stewart and P Griffith, *Intellectual Property in Australia* (Sydney, Butterworths, 2004) 207 ff.

[22] Copyright Law Review Committee, 'Simplification of the Copyright Act 1968 Part 1: Exceptions to the Exclusive Rights of Copyright Owners' (1998).

litigation or both, and hence likely make for greater use than would otherwise occur.[23] The presumptive rights granted to educational institutions and to libraries are also an important way of recognising the externalities associated with these points of access to the various forms of copyrighted material. Moves away from the current scheme, towards one that is more open-ended, therefore need to be viewed with caution.

Having said that, the Australian approach has imposed some costs in terms of the ability of the copyright system to adapt to change. It is especially in the software area that the consequences for competition of a degree of inflexibility in the system have been apparent. The central element of contention in this respect is the permissible scope of various forms of 'reverse engineering'. Some economic background is needed to make sense of the relevant debate.

Competitive conditions in the supply of software are affected to a greater or lesser degree by what economists refer to as network effects.[24] A *network effect* exists when, other things being equal, consumers would rather join a larger than a smaller network. The most direct way in which a network effect arises is when consumers obtain value as other users adopt the same service, or compatible ones. The classic example of a network effect is that telephone users benefit from being connected to the same network as others: there is little point having a telephone if one is unable to reach, or be reached, by others. Similarly, computer users value the fact that others use the same computer operating system (such as Windows) since this makes the sharing of files possible. As a result, consumers will, all other things being equal, place a greater value on joining whichever network is larger—for example, choosing Windows over other competing programs because of the greater base of other users with whom Windows allows them to interact. One consequence of this is that where network effects are significant, and are appropriable by individual producers (for example, through ownership of IPRs), competition can become 'tippy', with a supplier gaining dominance not because of the inherent merit of its goods or services but because it attains a critical mass at which consumers—who would otherwise have purchased from a competitor—shift towards it in large numbers.[25] The resulting equilibrium can be difficult to shift if challengers to the dominant standard, so as to attract customers, need to compensate users for foregoing the network effects the incumbent product enjoys.[26]

When this set of circumstances holds, IPRs, by precluding competitors from offering users products compatible with those supplied by the incumbent, could impose significant efficiency costs. To begin with, the standard allocative efficiency loss will be greater than is conventionally the case, because the higher price the incumbent (sheltering under the protection of the IPR) can charge imposes welfare losses not only on marginal users but, through foregone network effects, on inframarginal consumers as well. Additionally, there may be dynamic efficiency losses as products that are superior on the merits may

23 This line of argument, drawn by analogy to shifting between property and liability rules, extends back to W Gordon, 'Fair Use as Market Failure' (1982) 82 *Columbia Law Review* 1600; a critique that is fundamentally unconvincing, especially in the light of the Australian experience, can be found in RP Merges, 'Contracting into Liability Rules' (1996) 84 *California Law Review* 1293.

24 A useful overview of this concept, setting out its uses (and frequent abuses) is presented in S Liebowitz and SE Margolis, *Winners, Losers and Microsoft: Competition and Antitrust in High Technology* (Oakland, CA, The Independent Institute, 1999).

25 The concept of tipping was set out in TC Schelling, *Micromotives and Macrobehaviour* (London, WW Norton, 1976) and its consequences for collective action are well explained in J Elster, *Nuts and Bolts for the Social Sciences* (Cambridge, Cambridge University Press, 1989) 101 and follows.

26 See, for eg B Owen and S Wildman, *Video Economics* (Cambridge, MA, Harvard University Press, 1992) 260 and follows.

take longer to displace less meritorious products, if they can displace them at all. From these observations flows an argument, with obvious implications for copyright protection of software, that intellectual property protection should be weaker for products in which network effects predominate.[27] The counter-argument is, of course, that the prospect of the greater gains associated with benefiting from network externalities itself induces added investment in innovation, so that here too, a balancing needs to be effected.

In the United States, these considerations have been reflected in the courts' interpretation of the permissible scope of copyright protection. Both the merger doctrine, which restricts the protection accorded to copyright work in which the idea and the expression have merged, and more importantly the fair use provisions have been interpreted[28] as protecting various forms of reverse engineering when these are used to provide inter-operability and even when the purpose of the reverse engineering is to allow one supplier to substitute for the products of another.[29]

The more limited nature of the Australian fair dealing provisions, and the lower standard of creativity required to attract copyright, have largely ruled out this approach in Australia. The resulting tensions between the copyright provisions and the protection of competition have been addressed by specific amendments to the copyright laws that allow decompilation of computer programs for the purpose of securing inter-operability.

It is too early to judge the effects or effectiveness of section 47D of the amended CA. There remains, at least at this time, some uncertainty as to the meaning of inter-operability, and the scope of the defence it creates.

Moreover, while the overall objective of the inter-operability provisions is a reasonable one, it clearly rests on competition concerns—that is, on the possibility that, at least in certain cases, competition in the supply of software can be materially harmed by the refusal of third party access to the code required to develop inter-operable products. However, the provisions, rather than embodying a competition test or threshold (such as those set out in section 44G(2) of the TPA), apply generally to the relevant class of copyrightable material. They thereby create a default entitlement. Whether such a default entitlement is economically efficient, when compared to a more case-by-case approach, depends on how the costs of the error involved in some possible 'over-inclusiveness' of the default entitlement compare to the costs that would arise in some more case-by-case mechanism (such as might occur under a competition test). To date, no careful analysis has been done of how these costs compare, particularly in the light of the High Court's recent decision in *IceTV Pty Ltd v Nine Network Australia Pty Ltd*.[30]

[27] See J Farrell, 'Arguments for Weaker Intellectual Property Protection in Network Industries' (1995) 3 *Standard View* 46, and more generally JR Church and R Ware, *Network Industries, Intellectual Property Rights and Competition Policy* (Calgary, University of Calgary Press, 1999).

[28] In some cases, it must be said, through reasoning that seems very convoluted indeed, especially when heavy reliance is placed on the filtration tests for identifying protectable material: see for example *Computer Associates Int'l, Inc v Altai, Inc* 982 F.2d 693 (2d Cir 1992).

[29] See for example *Sony v Connectix* US 9th Circuit Court of Appeals, no 99-15852, 10 February 2000.

[30] *IceTV Pty Ltd v Nine Network Australia Pty Ltd* [2009] HCA 14 (22 April 2009). The High Court found that there was no infringement by IceTV of copyright held by Nine Network Australia Pty Ltd ('Nine') in its television programme schedules. The High Court unanimously held that IceTV did not infringe Nine's compilation copyright as there was no substantial reproduction of Nine's programme titles and times in IceTV's subscription-based electronic programme guide for television. The decision has important implications for the treatment of compilations, but also introduces a greater element of 'sweat of the brow' considerations into Australian copyright law than has generally been thought to exist.

C. Patents

As with copyright, the Australian patent system has reflected a mix of competition concerns, which it deals with at varying levels of generality and with varying degrees of success. Two areas (which are far from exhausting the field) are worth considering here: the scope of patentable subject matter; and the restrictions imposed on the exercise of a valid patent.

It has long been accepted that granting patents on 'mere discoveries' would over-extend the scope of the patent right.[31] The costs of granting such patents in terms of restricted access to the raw material of technical progress could be high; the practical difficulties involved in defining and implementing the scope of such patents might impose additional transaction costs that exceeded the benefit resulting from the stimulus they would provide to discovery; and to these costs must also be added the social waste resulting from any 'patent races' the availability of protection for discoveries would create.[32] Moreover, as this is the area where Knight's 'direct method of stimulating and rewarding research' is most likely to be effective in coping with market failure, the case for relying on the patent system seems weak. The resulting exclusion of discoveries from the scope of patentability has been one of the factors cited at times as limiting the degree of monopoly the patent system entails.

This long standing exclusion has recently come under pressure as a result of several factors. Technological change, most notably in biotechnology, but also in some areas of material science and of computing, is blurring the distinction between discoveries and inventions.[33] At the same time, reductions in public interest research funding, and the search for greater market-testing even of public sector research outlays, are pushing an ever greater portion of research into the private domain. Pressures to grant IPRs over forms of knowledge traditionally regarded as not capable of patenting have consequently increased.[34]

In the European Union, restrictions on the scope of patentability are embodied in article 52(2) of the European Patent Convention 1973 which inter alia excludes from being regarded as inventions 'mere discoveries of things already in nature; scientific theories; mathematical methods'.[35] A specific exclusion is also made in Canada by section 27(8) of the Patent Act, which states that 'No patent shall be granted for any mere scientific principle or abstract theorem.' In contrast, in the United States and Australia, the exclusion has been read into the relevant legislation by the courts. In the United States, while the

[31] Patents are 'granted for some production of these elements [the 'first ground and rules for the arts and sciences, or in other words the elements and rudiments of them'] and not for the elements themselves (since)... a principle cannot of itself, apart from a practical application, produce any vendible article or manufacture'; *Buller J, Boulton and Watt v Bull* (1795) ER 662.

[32] See on this R Posner, *Economic Analysis of Law*, 4th edn (London, Little Brown and Company, 1992) 39. Historically, some weight attached to the argument that discoveries, unlike inventions, were more likely to be made in any event; and hence society would derive less benefit (as the effect would be mainly one of timing) from their promotion—see Sherman and Bently, (n 5) 44–47.

[33] See on gene technology, L Palombi, *Gene Cartels: Biotech Patents in the Age of Free Trade* (Cheltenham, Edward Elgar, 2009).

[34] Sherman and Bently (n 5) fn 14.

[35] See also, for the provisions giving effect to these exclusions, the European Patent Office Patent Examination Guidelines arts 52(2) and 52(3).

relatively open-ended nature of the statutory formulation[36] has resulted in considerable expansiveness in the scope of patentability, the inclusion in the patent examination process of a test of utility filters out applications which lack a specified use. In Australia, it is well established that mere discoveries are not proper patentable subject matter;[37] however, the lack of a substantial utility criterion in the examination stage, the presumption in favour of the applicant that is to be given in examination, and the uncertain meaning of the 'artificially created state of affairs' test (that would at least potentially seem to encompass many mathematical algorithms[38]) has the potential to expand the scope of patentable subject matter. Given the relevant case law, this would seem to be capable of being dealt with by changes in the administration of the legislation, and most notably through the inclusion in the examination process of rules specifically aimed at establishing that a credible useful application had been identified. Such a change could better target the patent system to those areas where its benefits are most likely to exceed its costs.[39]

Given greater clarity as to the conditions on which a valid patent can be obtained, the question then turns to the bundle of rights that holders of a patent can exercise. The Australian patent legislation imposes constraints on these rights, both through specific (but seemingly little enforced) restrictions on practices such as tying,[40] and through the provisions allowing for compulsory licensing.[41]

It is apparent from the substance of these provisions that they are to be read as embodying a generic concern about competition and the possible abuse of any market power that obtains to a rights-owner. However, it is equally clear that the specific content of the provisions bears little or no relation to contemporary conceptions of competition policy. The close to *per se* prohibition on tying, for example, is inconsistent with many years of recognition of the efficiency-enhancing impacts tying can have.[42] An even greater gap between the statutory formulation and a concern with competition as a means to securing greater efficiency is apparent in the compulsory licensing provisions, which rather than embodying a test of competitive effect, speak of whether 'an existing trade or industry in Australia, or the establishment of a new trade or industry in Australia is unfairly prejudiced' by a patent right.[43]

Whether these provisions have much practical effect is not known. While there is virtually no case law,[44] it has been said that Australian licensees benefit by bargaining in

[36] 35 USC 101 'Inventions patentable' states 'Whoever invents or discovers any new and useful process, machine, manufacture, or composition of matter, or any new and useful improvement thereof may obtain a patent therefore, subject to the conditions and requirements of this title.' However, it has been held that 'A principle, in the abstract, is a fundamental truth; an original cause; a motive; these cannot be patented, as no one can claim in either of them an exclusive right.' *Le Roy v Tatham* 55 US 156, 175 (1852). See also the United States Patent and Trademark Office (USPTO) Patent Examiners' Manual s 2105: Patentable Subject Matter.

[37] See, for eg *CCOM v Jiejing* 28 IPR 481, 511 and *IBM Corp v Commissioner of Patents* 22 IPR 417, 423.

[38] A contrary view is expressed, but not fully explained, in the Australian Patent Examiners' Manual (revised December 1999) which states (at 8.2.7.4) that 'a mathematical algorithm per se is neither an "artificially created state of affairs", nor is it something having "utility in the field of economic endeavour"'.

[39] A number of changes to the administration of the patent system are proposed in Advisory Council on Intellectual Property, 'Post-Grant Patent Enforcement Strategies: Interim Report' (August 2009). However, these changes do not alter the substantive balance in the current system.

[40] See Patent Act s 144(1).

[41] See notably Patent Act ss 133–35.

[42] WS Bowman, 'Tying Arrangements and the Leverage Problem' (1957) 67 *Yale Law Review* 19.

[43] See Patent Act s 135(1).

[44] See McKeough, Stewart and Griffith (n 18) 382 and following.

these provisions' shadow. Be that as it may, it seems reasonable to suppose that efficient outcomes would be advanced by repealing those provisions (such as Patent Act section 144) that seem obsolete and at least reforming those (notably Patent Act ss 133–35) whose formulation is inconsistent with accepted principles of the current competition law. These could be replaced with a more narrowly defined test for compulsory licensing, based on public interest considerations.[45]

D. The Interaction with the TPA

In short, in both copyright and patent law, competition concerns have largely (if not always well) been addressed through the substantive provisions in the intellectual property statutes. Similar adaptations can be found in other areas of intellectual property, with the 'must fit, must match' exemption in section 72 of the Designs Act 2003 for complex parts used to repair motor vehicles being a case in point: a case that is all the more telling as it reflects a concern to ensure that registered design rights could not be used to increase smash repair costs, while at the same time not undermining the rights of suppliers in other 'after markets' (for instance, for toner or cartridges) to use charges for those parts as a means of price discrimination.

At the same time, the exercise of the rights granted by these statutes has enjoyed exemptions from the reach of the main competition statute, the TPA. The principal instrument granting an exemption is section 51(3) of the TPA, which exempts some aspects of the exercise of IPRs from part IV of the TPA, with the exception of sections 46, 46A and 48. Additionally, section 44B of the TPA exempts 'the use of intellectual property' from the operation of the national third party access regime that is set out part IIIA of the TPA, so long as that 'use of intellectual property' is not 'an integral but subsidiary part' of a service that is otherwise capable of declaration.[46] Finally, section 152AL(6) of the TPA grants an exemption, more limited than that applying under part IIIA, from declaration of a 'use of intellectual property' under part XIC of the TPA (the telecommunications access regime), with that exemption applying only if the intellectual property is not 'an integral but subsidiary part' of a service *and* the service is not a listed carriage service but merely 'a service that facilitates the supply of a listed carriage service' (defined at section 152AL(1)(b) of the TPA).

There is controversy about the precise reach of these exemptions, and notably of those made under section 51(3) of the TPA. The wording of section 51(3), particularly the requirement that the conditions being protected from the TPA must 'relate to' the variously defined subject matter of the right, lends itself to a number of conflicting interpretations. However, what is uncontroversial is that these provisions provide an exemption which has no counterpart in either the European Union or the United States. This naturally raises the question of whether such exemptions can be justified.

[45] See Australian Law Reform Commission, 'Genes and Ingenuity: Gene Patenting and Human Health (2004) c 24.

[46] The key features of part IIIA are discussed in Ergas, 'Access, Property Rights and Welfare: An Examination of Part IIIA of the Trade Practices Act' (2009), available at http://papers.ssrn.com/sol3/papers.cfm?abstract_id=1428184.

From an analytical point of view, it may be assumed that in the absence of section 51(3),[47] the provisions of section 51(1) of the TPA would apply to the intellectual property statutes. As a result, any consideration of, for example, the competitive effects of conduct made in the exercise of an IPR (say, in terms of seeking to impose a particular condition in an intellectual property license) would have to consider as its counter-factual a world in which the rights-owner could simply refuse to license,[48] and secure by its own means as large a share of the differential efficiency contributed by its creative effort as the IPR allows it to do. As a result, the exercise of IPRs would only lessen competition where it served to go beyond the scope of the right granted under the intellectual property statute. If this is accepted, section 51(3) would seem redundant, as the socially desired behaviour (the exercise of the rights within the confines of their grant) would in any event not breach the competition provisions of the TPA.

This line of argument abstracts, however, from important features of the TPA. More specifically, the TPA contains a range of provisions which prohibit certain conduct independently of its assessed effect on competition and subjects other conduct to administrative authorisation, again regardless of its effect of competition. It must be assumed that the logic underpinning these provisions is that the conduct at issue will, in the great majority of cases, be harmful, so that precluding or severely discouraging it will yield net social benefits.[49]

However much merit this argument may have at a general level, it seems open to some question in respect of IPRs. This is mainly because of the great importance that licenses and assignments have to the efficient use of intellectual property. Three factors are at work. The first is that the initial owners of IPRs are often not the parties best placed to exploit the output of their creative efforts. This is most plainly the case with specialised inventors, who remain responsible for some of the most important innovations in industrial use;[50] it also applies to small, research-intensive firms[51] and to public sector research entities. In these circumstances, licenses and assignments are needed to ensure that control over the rights is allocated to the parties that can exploit them most effectively.

Second, in many if not most areas of technology, rights do not map simply into products. Commercial products will often embody technology covered by claims in tens or even hundreds of patents.[52] Also, the inter-dependence between rights is even greater in the innovation process itself, which frequently involves combining technological inputs owned by

[47] And of the qualifier referring to intellectual property in TPA s 51(1)(a).

[48] The necessary qualification is that analogous considerations have not prevented competition laws from being used to trump IPRs both in the EU (V Korah, *An Introductory Guide to EC Competition Law and Practice*, 5th edn (London, Sweet and Maxwell, 1994) 190 and follows) and in the United States (see PE Areeda and H Hovenkamp, *Antitrust Law: An Analysis of Antitrust Principles and their Application III*, revised edn (New York, Aspen Publishers, 1996) 150–204.

[49] This judgment is reinforced by the scope provided under the TPA for parties to in most cases seek approval of that conduct where it yields social benefits that outweigh the conduct's competitive detriment. Given this scope, it can be assumed that the instances in which the conduct is most beneficial will be those in which the parties seek and receive authorisation. As a result, and to the extent to which the authorisation process is efficient (an important caveat), the prohibitions will deter the conduct that is most likely to be harmful, without impeding that which yields the greatest gains.

[50] See J Jewkes, D Sawers and R Stillerman, *The Sources of Invention*, 3rd edn (London, Macmillan, 1993).

[51] On the importance of which, see for example, DC Mowery and N Rosenberg, *Paths of Innovation: Technological Change in 20th-Century America* (Cambridge, Cambridge University Press, 1998) 41 and follows. Interestingly, Mowery and Rosenberg argue that small firms in the US innovation system have generally benefited from weaker rather than stronger IPRs, as weaker rights have reduced the risk they bear of litigation and facilitate their access to technology.

[52] See EW Kitch, 'The Nature and Function of the Patent System' (1997) 20 *Journal of Law and Economics* 265.

multiple rights-owners.[53] Complex webs of cross-licenses are required if these accumulated technical capabilities are to be put to productive use. While this can create important issues associated with 'anti-commons' and 'patent thickets', reducing the clarity of rights is unlikely to assist in resolving those issues.[54]

Third, even independent of the factors set out above, the costs of impeding efficient licensing can be high. As has been noted above, knowledge is non-rivalrous: increased access to it by one party does not reduce the stock available to others. As a result, when parties are forced to 'invent around' existing knowledge, there is a risk that the resources consumed in the process will, in social terms, be largely wasted. Even when the result of 'inventing around' is greater immediate competition, and hence a lower allocative efficiency loss, the benefits can readily be swamped by the productive inefficiency the duplication of outlays entails.[55]

Any assessment of repealing section 51(3) must therefore take account of the effect repeal would have on licensing and assignment decisions. More specifically, it seems reasonable to suppose that the per se prohibitions embodied in the TPA, and the potentially burdensome requirements for administrative review, would catch many license conditions that are usually socially beneficial—for example, tying and exclusive dealing arrangements in patent licenses.[56] Over the longer term, this could both reduce innovation and distort competition as between those (typically smaller and more specialised) firms that depended on licenses and assignments and those which did not.[57]

These considerations gain added weight from the substantial uncertainty that surrounds competition law in general and the TPA in particular. Key concepts that underpin the competition laws such as 'market power', 'conduct that lessens competition' and 'competition on the merits', are notoriously difficult to pin down and even more difficult to properly apply.[58]

[53] See RP Merges and RR Nelson, 'On the Complex Economics of Patent Scope' (1990) 90 *Columbia Law Review* 839.

[54] It is useful in this respect to consider Jaffe and Lerner, *Innovation and its Discontents* (Princeton, Princeton University Press, 2004) and J Bessen and MJ Meurer, *Patent Failure* (Princeton, Princeton University Press, 2008), which both point to economic costs associated with the patent system. Neither of these works sees the solution as lying in less clear rights. Rather, Jaffe and Lerner advocate more stringent patent examination, while Bessen and Meurer argue (as per above) against expanding the field of patentable subject matter to areas where the scope of the exclusive rights is either over-broad (as in algorithms) or unclear (as in business methods).

[55] This is not to deny that duplication can also bring benefits in the form of a wider diffusion of innovative skills, increased product differentiation and the occasional serendipitous discovery. However, the fact remains that, with a non-rivalrous good, the productive inefficiency (a rectangle) associated with duplication will generally outweigh the reduction in deadweight loss associated with increased competition (merely a triangle).

[56] On the economic impacts of which, see Bowman, (n 42), WS Bowman Jr, *Patent and Antitrust Law: A Legal and Economic Appraisal* (Chicago, University of Chicago Press, 1973) 64–139 and P Rey and RA Winter, *Exclusivity Restrictions and Intellectual Property* (1999). These contract provisions can serve four major efficiency enhancing purposes: they can prevent inefficient substitution when the good protected by the IPR is used in variable proportions; they can control double marginalisation; they can enhance the efficiency of metering and hence of price discrimination, which itself can lead to higher output; and in the face of transactions costs that impede complete contracts, they can reduce the risks of post-contract opportunism and better align the incentives of the contracting parties. However, this does not mean that they will invariably enhance efficiency. Moreover, other practices, such as pooling and joint pricing among potentially competing rights-owners of similar patents, clearly have the potential to act as conduits for horizontal price fixing.

[57] The efficiency costs of obstacles to the licensing and assignment of IPRs are well illustrated by reference to the technological histories of the UK, France and the US in C Macleod, 'The Paradoxes of Patenting: Invention and its Diffusion in 18th and 19th Century Britain, France and North America' (1991) *Technology and Culture* 885.

[58] See generally H Ergas, 'Should Developed Countries Require Developing Countries to Adopt Competition Laws? Lessons from the Economic Literature' (2009) *European Competition Journal* 5(2), 347–75.

The most generous interpretation is that, to use WD Gallie's famous classification, these are concepts that are 'essentially contested'. Such 'essentially contested' concepts are not incapable of being the subject of notions of evidence, cogency and rational persuasion, related to 'the rationality of a given individual's continued use (or change of use) of the concept', but it is quite impossible to find a general principle, of overarching and enduring validity, for 'deciding which of two contestant uses of an essentially contested concept really "uses it best"'.[59] They are therefore subject to ongoing definition and redefinition, with the result that—in the case of competition laws—it is adjudication, and the exercise of discretion in the course of adjudication, rather than statute that is the primary force shaping the substance of the prohibitions. As the late Professor William F Baxter, eminent antitrust scholar and Assistant Attorney General for Antitrust in the US Department of Justice in the Reagan years, explained that antitrust law, properly applied, is common law par excellence, for:

> 'An adaptive approach to antitrust law is necessary both because of the diversity and rapidly changing nature of the business conduct to be scrutinised, and because of the continuing progress of economic theory in explaining why firms pursue certain strategies and the competitive consequences of their behaviour.'[60]

The resulting uncertainty is compounded in the case of the TPA. Unfortunately, key sections of the TPA are, to put it simply, in a mess: not least the price-fixing provisions (which have a joint venture defence that seems unworkable) and the provisions dealing with the abuse of market power (which have been the subject of populist tinkering, with consequences that remain highly uncertain). Other sections are simply inconsistent with current economic thinking, such as the per se prohibition on resale price maintenance. Those problems have also been accentuated by fluctuating and unstable application by the enforcement agency[61] and varying, at times questionable, interpretation by the courts.[62]

This tells strongly against merely exposing the exercise of IPRs to full application of the TPA; but it cannot be an argument for indefinitely retaining section 51(3) in its current form. Even abstracting from the errors and inconsistencies in the section's wording and substance—for example, the far narrower exemption that seems to be granted to

[59] Gallie defined the class of concepts that are 'essentially contested' as those that meet seven characteristics: they are appraisive; internally complex; capable of rival possible descriptions, including because of possible differing emphases on the parts; 'of a kind that admits of considerable modification in the light of changing circumstances … and such modification cannot be prescribed or predicted in advance'; capable of both offensive and defensive use; derive their acceptance from 'an original exemplar whose authority is acknowledged by all the contestant users'; and their plausibility of continued use 'enables the original exemplar's achievement to be sustained': WB Gallie, 'Essentially Contested Concepts' (1956) 56 *Proceedings of the Aristotelian Society* 167, 172–80.

[60] WF Baxter, 'Separation of Powers, Prosecutorial Discretion and the "Common Law" Nature of Antitrust Law' (1982) 60 *Texas Law Review* 661, 670. The central role of the common law mechanism of litigation in interpreting and especially reinterpreting antitrust law is also well explained in a paper by Professor Stephen Calkins, former General Counsel of the US Federal Trade Commission: see S Calkins, 'In Praise of Antitrust Litigation' (1998) 72(1) *St John's Law Review* 1.

[61] The Australian Competition and Consumer Commission (ACCC) has alternated between periods of significant activism, particularly under the chairmanship of Professor Fels, a long phase under his successor (Mr Graeme Samuel) of seeming quiescence, especially in terms of court proceedings, and more recently strong and public support for relatively interventionist government proposals, notably to control fuel prices and monitor grocery prices. While such changes in enforcement stance are hardly unique, they are relatively unusual in the Australian environment.

[62] H Ergas, 'Reflections on Expert Economic Evidence'(2007) *The Journal of the New South Wales Bar Association*, Summer 2006–07, reprinted in the *Australian Law Society Journal*, vol 45, Issue 1, 2. Also available at http://papers.ssrn.com/sol3/papers.cfm?abstract_id=1430208.

copyright than to patents[63]—the uneven coverage of the provision (which exempts horizontal price fixing but not resale price maintenance) lacks policy justification. There is consequently a clear case for reform, although that reform should be conditional on a wider and comprehensive reappraisal of the TPA.

The National Competition Council, after considering a number of options in this respect, recommended some tidying up of the provision, along with an exclusion from its effect of 'price and quantity restrictions'.[64] Given that restrictions other than these are unlikely to breach the TPA, this exclusion would seem to swallow the rule. It is consequently questionable whether it would advance the purpose of promoting efficiency in the allocation and use of IPRs. Were that taken as the relevant alternative, it would be preferable to retain the provisions in their current form.

Matters are no less complex in respect of the exempting provisions relevant to parts IIIA and XIC of the TPA. While the policy rationale underlying these exemptions is not spelled out in the explanatory material to the legislation, it may be that it was considered unnecessary to subject IPRs to the access regimes these parts create, as specific arrangements for third party access existed in the intellectual property statutes themselves. While this is broadly correct, the fact remains that (as has been noted above) these arrangements are flawed in some respects.

Again, this is not an argument for removing the exemptions: the structure of parts IIIA and XIC of the TPA are not such as to readily accommodate the special concerns third party access to IPRs entails. However, it does suggest that if the exemptions are retained, consideration will need to be given to placing the access arrangements provided for in the individual intellectual property statutes on a sounder footing. The compulsory licensing provisions of the Patent Act, which (as noted above) hark back to an earlier era of Australian industry protection, are an obvious priority in this respect.

E. Conclusions

The interaction of the competition and intellectual property laws in Australia has generally been viewed through the prism of the exemptions from the competition statutes granted to certain aspects of the exercise of IPRs by section 51(3) of the TPA. This has led to a tendency to under-estimate the role of competition factors in shaping specific provisions of the intellectual property statutes, and hence to overlook the 'IP-specific competition regimes' these provisions embody.

The analysis set out above has highlighted some of the tensions between these regimes and the more general conception underpinning the TPA. It seems reasonable to embody competition concerns in the intellectual property statutes when those concerns form an intrinsic part of the eligibility tests for the right, or when a competition and efficiency test, applied to a particular use of the right, would lead to a bright line rule governing the use of that right. It is recognised that such rules (for example, the deeming provisions

[63] This arises from the operation of the 'relates to' requirement which, in the context of copyright, is specified (in s51(3)(a)(v)) as referring to 'the work or other subject matter in which the copyright subsists'. This appears to exclude copies or reproductions of the work or other subject matter, which would presumably be the main subject of conditions in a license or assignment.

[64] National Competition Council (1999) Review of Sections 51(2) and 51(3) of the Trade Practices Act 1974: Final Report 243.

contained in the Australian fair dealing regime) can have costs of their own, most notably in the greater difficulty imposed on attempts to adjust outcomes to the facts of particular cases. However, where the costs of detailed investigation and adjudication are high, properly chosen and sculpted rules of this kind can reduce the costs of litigation and of legal uncertainty by more than any social losses they impose. Where this balance is best assessed in terms of a particular IPR, and the scope of any resulting rule confined to that right, reliance on provisions in the intellectual property statutes themselves seems clearly warranted.

What is less apparent is the appropriate treatment of provisions which involve, or ought to involve, case-by-case determination of competition matters. Where the provisions themselves need to be adapted to the specific circumstances of an IPR, there are good reasons for embedding the provisions within the statute that defines and regulates that right. This would reduce the risk of statutory inconsistencies arising, as has occurred with respect to section 51(3) of the TPA. Additionally, it could make clearer the scope of the right being granted. However, the provisions themselves, and the tests they embody, ought to reflect the competition tests used more widely in the economy. Whether the procedures for the enforcement and administration of those tests should be the same as those for the competition laws is an open question, and it may well be better, in terms of use of expertise, to rely on specialised processes (for instance, in areas of jurisdiction of the Copyright Tribunal).

Once a greater measure of consistency is achieved between the competition provisions of the intellectual property statutes and the generally accepted concepts of competition policy, the issues associated with section 51(3) of the TPA can be more readily dealt with. It is particularly important to ensure that the provisions of the TPA are not used to trump IPRs, but rather are applied from the premise that the rights grant the rights-owner the scope to secure, at least temporarily, an income stream reflecting the efficiency gain to society from the rights-owner's creative effort.

Some degree of tension between the goals and content of the intellectual property statutes on the one hand, and the competition laws on the other, is inevitable. Additional difficulties arise from the fact that the intellectual property laws are not a field for tidy minds. The fact that the intellectual property laws must adapt to challenges constantly created by rapid technological change leads, especially but by no means solely in the area of copyright, to a considerable degree of complexity in the relevant provisions.[65] In the need to react and respond to changing circumstances, inconsistencies can all too readily arise, and then persist, between the solutions adopted in the intellectual property statutes and the efficiency-oriented tests that should underpin a competition policy approach. Not all of these can or even should be resolved, given the costs the search for complete consistency would necessarily entail. The current situation, however, is one that can and should be improved, not only so as to achieve greater benefit to the community as a whole from creative effort but also so as to place the rights and obligation of owners of IPRs on a more stable, certain and secure basis.

[65] Oakeshott's more general observation rings especially true in this context, to the effect that 'the significance of power is always in relation to its task, and while power to integrate has increased, so has the variety of activities to be integrated. The skill of the bowler is greater, but so also is the versatility of the batsman'. M Oakeshott, *The Politics of Faith and the Politics of Scepticism* (New Haven, Yale University Press, 1996) 64.

III. Treatment of Joint Ventures in Competition Law

A. The Australian Position

The TPA (as it is currently known; its name will change shortly to the Australian Competition & Consumer Act) remains schizophrenic in the way in which it treats joint ventures. This is similar to the unfortunate stance that has been taken in the TPA in dealing with intellectual property and rights and their interface with competition law.

Australia does not adopt a rule of reason approach in dealing with anti-competitive agreements. That approach in the United States (which is copied elsewhere) allows a degree of flexibility in dealing with joint ventures especially in the context of the criminalisation of such activities by the amendments made to the TPA in 2009. The failure of the Government to treat joint ventures in a pragmatic and appropriate fashion illustrates a regrettably narrow approach to the interaction of policies in different areas of the law.

Successive Australian governments have not always properly recognised the role of 'sensible' business policy in their treatment of joint ventures. This has the unfortunate effect of limiting an important part of the Australian economy.

B. Joint Ventures and Australian Competition Law

In fact, the pattern of Australian competition law has always been to treat joint ventures with suspicion. There was no 'joint venture defence' when the TPA was enacted in 1974. The Swanson Committee recognised the need for some qualification which was introduced into the TPA in section 45A(4). This was regarded as totally inadequate, not only in the context of price fixing but in the context of the additional per se offence introduced into the TPA—the prohibition of exclusionary provisions or collective boycotts contained by a combination of sections 45 and 4D of the TPA. The 2007 amendments introduced some further clarification following the review of the TPA by the Dawson Committee in its 2003 Report.[66] Those amendments contained in sections 76C and 76D of the TPA were again guided by suspicion on the part of policy makers about joint ventures. That suspicion has been magnified in the Cartel Act.

Australia, by joining many other western communities in introducing potential jail sentences for cartel conduct, and by limiting the operation of an appropriate rule of reason in the context of joint venture activity, may unintentionally provide further impediments to joint ventures generally, and in particular the development of IPR through joint venture activities.

C. Understanding the Cartel Act

The Cartel Act amends the TPA to establish parallel criminal offences and civil penalty provisions relating to cartel conduct.

[66] Dawson Committee Report on the Trade Practices Act 2003.

Under the Cartel Act, a corporation must not make, or give effect to, a contract, arrangement or understanding that contains a cartel provision. A cartel provision is a provision relating to the following by parties that are, or would for an agreement be, in competition with each other:

— price fixing;
— restricting outputs in the production and supply chain;
— allocating customers, suppliers or territories; or
— bid-rigging.

We note that the Commonwealth Director of Public Prosecutions (CDPP) is the only party that will be able to prosecute criminal cartel proceedings, following its independent review and assessment of the matter. The Australian Competition and Consumer Commission's (ACCC) role in relation to criminal proceedings is to undertake an investigation and gather evidence. We would expect that the vast majority of (if not all) criminal prosecutions under the Cartel Act would arise in circumstances where the ACCC has conducted a comprehensive investigation, has delivered a brief of evidence to the CDPP and has recommended a criminal prosecution having regard to the seriousness of the alleged conduct. To establish a criminal contravention, the CDPP would need to prove each relevant element 'beyond reasonable doubt'.

As for other competition law prohibitions, the ACCC is the only party that can initiate proceedings for civil penalties arising from a contravention of the proposed cartel prohibitions. A Memorandum of Understanding (MOU) has been entered into with the CDPP setting out how the two bodies will work together in relation to the prosecution of cartels. It is not appropriate in this chapter to go into the details of these arrangements.

In my discussion of the legislation I will be referring to the specific sections in the TPA being introduced by the Cartel Act. I make no apology for the fact that the section numbering is bizarre, and a drafting device that is regrettably being used in nearly all the legislation in Australia today. It does create enormous problems for us in providing appropriate advice.

I return now to the elements of these prohibitions with respect to each of the different types of cartel conduct.

i. Price Fixing

A criminal cartel offence will be established with respect to price fixing if the following matters are proved:

(i) There must be at least two parties to the contract, arrangement or understanding are likely to be (but for any contract, arrangement or understanding) in competition with each other: section 44ZZRD(4) (the competition condition).
(ii) The provision in question must have the purpose, or has or is likely to have the effect, of directly or indirectly fixing, controlling or maintaining prices for goods or services: section 44ZZRD(2).
(iii) There must be proof of knowledge or belief that the contract, arrangement or understanding contains a cartel provision: sections 44ZRF(2) and 44ZRG(2).
(iv) There must be an intention to make or give effect to the contract, arrangement or understanding (as provided for in subsection 5.6 of the Criminal Code).[67]

[67] I note that s 84 of the TPA provides that the state of mind of a corporation will be established if a director, employee or agent engaged in the relevant conduct (within the scope of their actual or apparent authority) with

A civil contravention can be established only if items (i), (ii) and (iii) are satisfied.

ii. Preventing, Restricting or Limiting Production, Capacity or Supply

Formally this general prohibition is contained in sections 45 and 4D of the TPA. Under the *Cartel Act* a cartel offence will occur in relation to any of these matters if the following elements are established:

- The competition condition is satisfied.
- The provision has the purpose of directly or indirectly preventing, restricting or limiting the production of goods, the capacity of a party to supply goods or services, or the supply of goods or services to persons or classes of persons: section 44ZZRD(3)(a).
- The knowledge or belief that the contract, arrangement or understanding contains a cartel provision.
- An intention to make or give effect to the contract, arrangement or understanding.

A civil contravention can be established if the first two elements set out above are satisfied.

iii. The Allocation of Customers, Suppliers or Territories

This again is probably covered by the terms in sections 45 and 4D of the TPA. Under the *Cartel Act*, a criminal cartel will occur if there is an allocation of customers, suppliers or territories and the following conditions are established:

1. The competition condition is satisfied.
2. The provision has the purpose of directly or indirectly allocating customers, suppliers, or geographical areas in which goods or services are supplied or acquired: section 44ZZRD(3)(b).
3. The knowledge or belief that the contract, arrangement or understanding contains a cartel provision.
4. An intention to make or give effect to the contract, arrangement or understanding.

A civil contravention can be established if the first two elements set out above are satisfied.

iv. Rigging Bids

These matters are also likely to be covered under the provisions relating to exclusionary conduct, but they can amount to price fixing. There have been one or two interesting cases in this area. A rigged bid will be a cartel offence if the following conditions are satisfied:

1. The competition condition is satisfied.
2. The provision has the purpose of directly or indirectly rigging bids: section 44ZZRD(3)(c).
3. The knowledge or belief that the contract, arrangement or understanding contains a cartel provision.
4. An intention to make or give effect to the contract, arrangement or understanding.

A civil contravention can be established if the first two elements set out above are satisfied.

the relevant state of mind. Knowledge or belief of a corporation can also be proven by having regarding to the 'directing mind and will' type principles set out in pt 2.5 of the Criminal Code.

D. International Treatment of Joint Ventures

As indicated earlier, in the United States joint ventures are treated subject to a 'rule of reason' approach. There is litigation awaiting a decision of the Supreme Court of the United States (the American *Needle* case—*American Needle Inc v National Ball League*[68]). Its decision may have something further to say about these issues.

The Canadian Competition Bureau has adopted a more reasoned and balanced approach to the treatment of joint ventures in its paper 'Competitor Collaboration Guidelines' issued on 23 September 2009. It is a pity that we do not have a more balanced approached such as that enunciated in Canada. Indeed, even the New Zealand Ministry of Economic Development has recently suggested, in promoting cartel laws in that country, that a balanced approach based on the rule of reason may be appropriate in dealing with joint ventures.

E. Does the New Joint Venture Defence in the TPA Apply to the Relevant Cartel Provisions?

Genuine joint venture activities, previously covered by section 77D of the TPA, are quite different. There are two major elements that I wish to discuss in this overview which are relevant to joint venture activity in the context of intellectual property know-how and related matters. In the first place, the joint venture defence only applies to the supply or production of goods or services and not to the acquisition of goods or services. In the second place, it only applies if the cartel provision is part of a joint venture that arises in the context of a contract which contains the relevant cartel provisions.

The additional matters that must be established for the defence to apply in the context of the joint supply or production of goods or services are:

1. that the cartel provision is for the purposes of a relevant joint venture: section 44ZRO(1)(a);
2. that the joint venture is for the production and/or supply of goods or services: section 44ZRO(1)(b); and
3. that the joint venture is carried on jointly by the parties to the contract: section 44ZZRO(1)(c).

Any person who wishes to rely on the defence carries the burden of establishing each of these items.

F. What is a Relevant Joint Venture?

The term 'joint venture' is broadly defined in the TPA to include an activity in trade or commerce carried on jointly by two or more persons.

Whilst there is no case law directly on point, a 'genuine' joint venture is generally understood to involve a collaborative commercial activity in which each participant contributes money, property or skill for mutual gain. This can be distinguished from a so-called 'sham'

[68] *American Needle Inc v National Ball League* 538 F.3d 736 (7th Cir 2008).

joint venture that does nothing productive and is merely designed to restrict output and raise prices.

If a joint venture is not fully documented, one would have thought that the joint venture defence would still apply.

It is not uncommon for joint venture arrangements to develop over time, often resulting in the relationship extending beyond the founding written agreements. This reality was discussed in *Australian Oil & Gas Corporation Ltd v Bridge Oil Ltd*,[69] where Kirby P (then President of the New South Wales Court of Appeal) stated:

> ... A joint venture is a particular and increasingly familiar form of relationship between business parties. Corporations or individuals who enter such ventures normally do so upon the basis of a proposed association, the main features of which are typically defined in a written agreement. Yet, above and beyond the terms of the written agreement will necessarily be a wide range of activities and relationships which are in general contemplation and which the parties cannot predict in their entirety. They therefore cannot be covered exhaustively in the initiating written agreement. The very association of a joint venture will normally imply the acceptance of an ongoing relationship between the parties which is envisaged to be one of contractual harmony. At least at the outset of their relationship—and before disputes bring them to lawyers and before courts or arbitrators—the parties normally contemplate a harmonious and cooperative relationship of mutual advantage. (at 72)[70]

G. What is the Meaning of 'Contract' and the Rules of Statutory Interpretation?

In the first version of the cartel legislation the Explanatory Memorandum described what might be meant by the word 'contract'. The Federal Government intended that this term be given a reasonably broad interpretation as paragraph 4.32 of the first Explanatory Memorandum stated:

> 'Contract' has its ordinary meaning of an agreement binding or enforceable at law. It can apply to a range of agreements, both written and oral, provided they meet the common law criteria for a contract. In the context of the *[TPA]*, the term refers to agreements that are distinct from those covered by 'arrangements' or 'understandings', which apply to agreements that may not give rise to legally enforceable rights.

As a result of representations that I, and others, made to the Government, there were amendments made to the legislation before it was enacted. In effect, the defence will now apply to any arrangement or understanding containing a cartel provision where each party to the arrangement or understanding:

1. intended the arrangement or understanding to be a contract; and
2. reasonably believed that the arrangement or understanding was a contract.

[69] *Australian Oil & Gas Corporation Ltd v Bridge Oil Ltd* (1995) 14 AMPLABull 60.

[70] I note these comments were made in the context of an obiter discussion of whether or not a fiduciary duty should be extended to a commercial context between joint venturers and that there was no oral argument on this issue.

Examples used in the Explanatory Memorandum helped to expand upon these words, but purists may not find them of sufficient clarity and thrust to provide the type of comfort that may be sought by many wishing to engage in joint venture activity in a greenfields project. Relevant explanatory materials to the Cartel Act have been extracted in Attachment 1.

Regrettably, the examples used by the Government in the second Explanatory Memorandum to the Cartel Act do not provide much comfort, in my view, in the framework of Australian legal interpretation.

The practice, which has grown up like topsy in the country, to use end notes, examples and related devices to give extended application to legislative provisions, has proved inadequate and unsatisfactory. The general rules of statutory interpretation do not provide for this type of device to be used in anything other than a very, very rare set of circumstances. In the only reported case in which the examples such as footnotes and marginal notes have been considered by the court, Bergin J in *One.Tel (in liq) v Rich*[71] stated that unless there were clear indications in the relevant statutory document that marginal notes, footnotes and other devices such as examples, are to operate as part of the statute they will not do so. The better view is that section 13(3) of the Australian Acts Interpretation Act 1901 will operate to negate their applicability as part of the statute. That section provides 'no marginal note, footnote, endnote to an Act, and no heading to a section of an Act, should be taken to be part of the Act'.

This view has recently been confirmed by a decision of the New South Wales Court of Appeal in *Harrison v Melham*,[72] although that case dealt more with a statement of the minister as to the meaning of the words in the statute and what their terms mean. Relevantly, the Court held that those statements were of no value in interpreting the relevant statute.

H. Joint Ventures for the Acquisition of Goods and/or Services

As noted earlier, the defence created in the cartel legislation does not extend to joint ventures for the acquisition of goods or services. Part of the reason for this rather strange policy conclusion reached by the Government was a proposition put quite strongly to the Government by the ACCC that joint ventures in this 'space' were likely to be artificial. They were likely to be created for the purposes of avoiding the per se prohibition against collective boycotts/exclusionary activity governed by the previous section 4D of the TPA, now governed by the cartel provisions, and therefore not warranting the opportunity to escape the per se approach.

As a result of submissions put to the Government and to the Economics Committee which reviewed the legislation and recommended that it be passed unchanged, the Government provided what it believed would represent some 'carve outs' from the strict non-application of the joint venture defence to joint acquisition activity by using examples in the revised Explanatory Memorandum. These examples, which I attach to this chapter for information, do not of course provide a satisfactory solution. As explained earlier, the use of examples, side notes and related devices do not work satisfactorily in the Australian system to provide an exception to the strict reading of the legislation (see my discussion above of *One.Tel (in liq) v Rich*).

[71] *One.Tel (in liq) v Rich* (2005) 53 ACSR 623.
[72] *Harrison v Melham* (2008) 72 NSWR 380.

However, an important provision in the cartel legislation for genuine collective acquisition activities in relation to contracts, arrangements or understandings does exist if these acquisitions relate to the collective acquisition of goods or services in a joint venture context.[73] In this context, it is useful to note that the US Competitor Collaboration Guidelines published in 2000 generally regard collective arrangements of this kind as not creating a problem, although difficulties may arise.[74]

This is not surprising and is in line with the general approach in the United States to joint venture activity which is usually approved pursuant to the rule of reason.

Whilst the ACCC has been known to have taken a sympathetic approach to acquisition activity in relation to the medical sector,[75] the ACCC may be flexing its muscles to adopt a significantly tougher stance against joint acquisition activities. From comments made by senior counsel who assisted the Government in drafting the relevant parts of the legislation, 'all joint ventures are price fixing by another name'. This aggressive approach is clearly not one that should be regarded as conducive to a sympathetic approach to joint ventures for the acquisition of services, intellectual property information and related activities.

In the discussion document which in part evaluated the current Australian cartel prohibitions released by the New Zealand Government, the Ministry of Economic Development recognised the possibility that a joint venture might be used as a cover for a cartel, but concludes that:

> [g]enuine joint ventures do not deserve per se condemnation—they need to be assessed individually for their competitive effects. As a general principle, genuine joint ventures should be excluded from the scope of a cartel offence. They should however, still be subject to the competition test in section 27.[76]

The discussion document notes the limitations of the Australian joint venture defence and the criticism that this defence has received. It also notes that the scope of the defence is more limited than that currently found in the New Zealand competition statute. In its discussion of a possible 'joint venture exemption', the discussion document concludes that a 'first-principles joint venture exemption would define a joint venture in economic terms, requiring a significant economic integration of activities. It might also require proof of actual or potential efficiency gains. A joint venture exemption should also include a requirement that the cartel provision in question be reasonably necessary to achieve the commercial objectives of the joint venture.'[77]

Although the discussion document discussed a number of exemptions available in different jurisdictions, it appears to prefer the Canadian approach of incorporating an

[73] See s 44ZZRV.

[74] Stephen Corones in his book *Competition Law in Australia* (Sydney, Law Book Company, 2010) discusses the possible interpretation of s 45A(4) at para 695.

[75] In a now quite dated guide to the operation of the TPA for the health sector (published in November 1995), the then Trade Practices Commission provided a very wide reading of s 45A(4) in relation to the difficulties that were faced by weaker sections of the health sector economy in dealing with larger players. Of course, we now have specific provisions in the TPA which allow for collective bargaining by health funds and other bodies within the health sector. However, these are just examples of why we should not have a per se prohibition against joint acquisition activity, especially joint venture activity in the context of the development of intellectual property. They are not per se illegal, they produce significant benefits, and the onus should be on the ACCC to show that they are anti-competitive.

[76] New Zealand Ministry of Economic Development 'Cartel Criminalisation Discussion Document' (January 2010) para 109.

[77] Ibid para 290.

'ancillary restraints defence' into the statute which, although not limited to joint venture situations, would help to distinguish between legitimate joint venture activities and those established as a cover for a cartel arrangement. In support of this approach, the discussion document notes that the ancillary restraints defence 'does not protect the restraint from a competition test, merely per se condemnation. It will not chill legitimate pro-competitive activity and allows firms to undertake relatively simple assessments to see if they come within its scope.'[78]

I. A Further Australian Problem—the Division of Powers between Commonwealth, State and Territory Governments

When Australia's Constitution[79] was finalised, there was unfortunately (and understandably) not enough future vision adopted in relation to how the Australian economy would develop. The division of powers between the Commonwealth and the states is largely impractical and has served as a particular impediment to the development of a national approach to competition law and IPRs. Historically, national regulation such as in the case of competition law requires the full cooperation of all the states.

Some commentators argue that the only long term solution to the division of powers is to amend our Constitution.[80] However, the attempt to amend the Constitution through constitutional change has proven frustrating and largely ineffective. History provides us with a number of examples where Australia's State and Federal Governments have attempted to address the issues associated with the way in which the Constitution divides the powers of the State and Federal Governments. The history of competition regulation in Australia provides one such example.

My initial experience in the competition law area in Australia arose when I was asked to write a commentary on the now largely forgotten case of *Strickland v Rocla Concrete Pipes*.[81] That case concerned the first modern attempt by Australia to introduce competition law after the Australian Industries Preservation Act 1906 (which was one of the very earliest statutes prohibiting anti-competitive conduct and practices) foundered on constitutional grounds in two famous cases *Huddart Parker & Co Pty Ltd & Appleton v Moorehead*, and the *Attorney-General (Cth) v Adelaide Steamship Co Ltd*.[82]

Sir Garfield Barwick framed the Australian Trade Practices Act of 1965 on that of the UK Restrictive Trade Practices Act of 1956, which in my view was a not a well thought through proposal, and one which nevertheless failed on constitutional grounds. As a result of the hints given in the *Concrete Pipes* case to the Australian Government, a new Bill was passed—the Restrictive Trade Practices Act of 1971 introduced into parliament by the Restrictive Trade Practices Bill (No 2) and the Monopolies Commission Bill 1972.

However, political events intervened, Labour was elected to power in 1972 and it quickly moved to the introduction of the current legislation. This legislation has, however,

[78] Ibid para 275.

[79] *Commonwealth of Australia Constitution Act 1900* (Cth).

[80] See Professor George Williams, 'George Williams: Expensive way to run a country' The Australian, 8 December 2006.

[81] (1971) 124 CLR 468.

[82] *Huddart Parker & Co Pty Ltd & Appleton v Moorehead* (1909) 8 CLR 330 and *Attorney-General (Cth) v Adelaide Steamship Co Ltd* (1913) 18 CLR 30.

been amended and added to over the years, not least as a result of the Hilmer Report,[83] the product of an Independent Committee of Inquiry charged by Professor Frederick G Hilmer which the then Prime Minister Keating established in October 1992.

The Hilmer Report proposed wide ranging and significant reforms impacting the provision of services by government entities and the basis on which these services are subject to competitive forces and, along with a further report commissioned by the Council of Australian Governance (COAG) in August 1994, led to the adoption of a National Competition Policy in April 1995 by all the governments of Australia. The framework for the implementation of this Policy was encompassed in three main agreements—the Competition Principles Agreement 1995, the Conduct Code Agreement 1995 and the Agreement to Implement the National Competition Policy and Related Reforms 1995—which together provided a mechanism for implementing the key elements of the Hilmer reform proposal. These agreements incorporated a system of national competition payments whereby the Commonwealth agreed to provide financial assistance to the States and Territories conditional upon the satisfactory progress of the reforms in accordance with the timetable set out in the agreements. This example demonstrates the complexities involved in effecting national change.

In recent times, other necessary measures have been taken to attempt to harmonise important areas of law. The current Federal Government has taken steps to implement a national consumer law—a law which at present comprises parts IVA, V (with the exception of division 1AA (country of origin representations)), VA and VC of the Trade Practices Act 1974 and equivalent provisions in each of the State and Territory Fair Trading Acts.[84] This initiative was in part in response to a report of the Productivity Commission released on 8 May 2008[85] which was commissioned by the former Treasurer Peter Costello to report on, amongst other things, 'any barriers to, and ways to improve, the harmonisation and coordination of consumer policy and its development and administration across jurisdictions in Australia, including ways to improve institutional arrangements to avoid duplication of effort'.[86]

Originally the state and territory Fair Trading Acts were designed to mirror the consumer protection provisions in Part IVA of the relevant Commonwealth legislation. Over the years they began to diverge. For example Victoria legislated to prohibit 'unfair' terms in consumer contracts whilst the other states kept the prohibition of unconscionable consumer contracts. The Productivity Commission recommended that Australia introduce a new national consumer law. The Federal Government and the State and Territory Governments agreed with the recommendations of the Productivity Commission. As a result the Trade Practices Amendment (Australian Consumer Law) Acts of 2009 and 2010 were passed by the Federal Parliament (with similar action being taken in the states and territories).

[83] Independent Committee of Inquiry, 'National Competition Policy' (August 1993).

[84] See for example, Fair Trading Act 1992 (Australian Capital Territory); Fair Trading Act 1987 (New South Wales); Fair Trading Act 1989 (Queensland); Fair Trading Act 1987 (South Australia); Fair Trading Act 1990 (Tasmania); Fair Trading Act 1999 (Victoria); Fair Trading Act 1987 (Western Australia); and Consumer Affairs and Fair Trading Act 1990 (Northern Territory).

[85] Productivity Commission, 'Review of Australia's Consumer Policy Framework: Inquiry Report', No 45 (30 April 2008).

[86] Ibid vol 1, p vii.

The name of the Trade Practices Act has been changed to the Competition and Consumer Act which became effective on 1 January 2011.

III. Conclusions

In this very short review of the cartel legislation, the joint venture exceptions and the current state of 'indecision' as far as policy is concerned on the interaction between intellectual property and competition law, I hope I have given a picture that we are in a state of some confusion, and the policy regrettably is not very satisfactory in dealing with this area of the law. One consolation is that Graeme Samuel, the Chairman of the ACCC, has indicated that the ACCC rarely faced problems surrounding the interface of competition policy and intellectual property. Perhaps that is because parties are not willing to risk pursuing arrangements that pose competition policy concerns with the ACCC.

It is not possible in a short chapter of this kind to highlight the particular problems that arise in certain types of joint venture activity concerning the development of conflicts and know-how and other arrangements. Certainly, my experience has been that, in the context of tenders being called for the production of plans, where parties have to cooperate to prepare a tender so as to acquire the rights to supply goods or services to the Government, the absence of a clear language in this context is worrying. It may suggest that the joint acquisition of these rights would be regarded as part of a relevant joint venture (because the next stage of the activity would lead to the production or supply of goods and services); but if the defence does not apply, this may constrain parties from running the risk that their joint activity (common prices, terms and conditions, etc) could amount to serious cartel conduct in breach of the Cartel Act. Clarification of this question would be welcomed.

Regrettably, the very unyielding interpretation adopted by the Australian Government in relation to these areas is symptomatic of rather unimaginative initiatives in allowing the rule of reason, and the interpretation by the courts of relevant transactions, to guide us in moving forward.

Trade Practices Amendment (Cartel Conduct and Other Measures) Act 2009—Explanatory Material Extracts

---

Explanatory Memorandum

Price of goods or services collectively acquired; or joint advertising of price for re-supply of goods or services collectively acquired

4.45 Current subsection 45A(4) provides that current subsection 45A(1) does not apply to a provision of a contract, arrangement or understanding in relation to the price for goods or services to be collectively acquired, or for the joint advertising of the price for the re-supply of goods or services collectively acquired. In each case, if a relevant is exempted from subsection 45A(1), it may still be prohibited by the TP Act if the provision has the purpose, effect or likely effect of substantially lessening competition.

4.46 As noted earlier in this explanatory memorandum, s 45A is deleted by the Bill. [Schedule 1, item 21]

Exceptions

4.47 Exceptions apply to the cartel criminal offences and civil penalty prohibitions to reflect the existing exemption in current subsection 45A(4) [Schedule 1, item 19, s 44ZZRV]. As s 44ZZRE, in effect, quarantines expressions used in Division 1 of Part IV from applying to the rest of the TP Act, the language used in the exception has been simplified to the extent possible.

4.48 The exception applies in relation to a contract, arrangement or understanding containing a cartel provision if the cartel provision meets the purpose/effect test, and the cartel provision relates to the price for goods or services to be collectively acquired, whether directly or indirectly, by the parties to the contract, arrangement or understanding, or the cartel provision is for the joint advertising of the price for the re-supply of goods or services collectively acquired.

4.49 Where the exception applies to the criminal offences, a note is inserted specifying that a defendant bears an evidential burden of proof of establishing the matters contained in the exception. [Schedule 1, item 19, subsection 44ZZRV(1)]

4.50 Where the exception applies to the civil prohibitions, a subsection specifies that a person wishing to rely on the exception in relation to a contravention bears an evidential burden of proof of establishing the matters contained in the exception. [Schedule 1, item 19, subsection 44ZZRV(2)]

4.51 Similar exceptions are also included in the Schedule version. These exceptions do not refer to the evidential burden on the defence in relation to criminal prosecutions, because the Schedule version operates independently of the Criminal Code. [Schedule 1, item 126, s 44ZZRV]

Supplementary Explanatory Memorandum

Collective acquisition of goods or services and re-supply exception

1.11 Example 1.3 demonstrates that s 44ZZRV (while also not specifically stated to apply to joint ventures) may also apply to enable a joint venture to make acquisitions without breaching the criminal offences or civil penalty prohibitions in the Bill. Unlike the joint venture exceptions, the exception provided under s 44ZZRV is not limited to joint ventures established under a contract only, but alternative prerequisites regarding the scope of the exception apply.

Example 1.3

The exception in s 44ZZRV provides that the criminal offences and civil penalty prohibitions in the Bill do not apply to a contract, arrangement or understanding containing a cartel provision, in so far as the cartel provision has the purpose, effect or likely effect of fixing prices (broadly speaking), and either the cartel provision relates to the price of goods or services to be collectively acquired, whether directly or indirectly, to the parties to the contract, arrangement or understanding, or the cartel provision is for the joint advertising of the price for the re-supply of goods or services so acquired. That is, the exception does not exclude its application to joint ventures, and could be relied upon by joint ventures engaged in marketing activities regarding goods or services collectively acquired.

Second Reading Speech

Exceptions

The Trade Practices Act currently provides a number of exemptions and defences to the prohibitions against anticompetitive behaviour. Similarly, the bill provides for specific exceptions to the new prohibitions. These fall into six categories:

1. conduct notified under the collective bargaining regime in the act;
2. contracts containing cartel provisions subject to the notification provisions or a grant of authorisation;
3. contracts, arrangements or understandings between related bodies corporate;
4. joint ventures contained in contracts;
5. anti-overlap exceptions; and
6. the price of goods or services collectively acquired, and the joint advertising of the price for resupply.

The exceptions are intended to ensure that the prohibitions do not prevent legitimate business activities that are beneficial to the economy or in the public interest.

6

China

MICHAEL JACOBS AND XINZHU ZHANG

I. Introduction

Over the past several decades, the competition law community has recognised that intellectual property (IP) law and antitrust law share the fundamental goals of enhancing consumer welfare and promoting innovation. Indeed, the modern understanding of these two disciplines regards IP and antitrust as working in tandem to help bring new and better technologies, products and services to consumers at lower prices.

In China, anti-monopoly laws and institutions have developed only recently. IP and anti-monopoly laws have therefore not been used to achieve the goals of promoting innovation and competition. With the enactment of the Trademark Law of 1982, China began to install a systematic legal framework for IP, at an early stage of the period of economic reform and opening up. However, a comprehensive antitrust regime was established only recently, after the Anti-Monopoly Law (AML) took effect in 2008. While the extent to which China's IP laws are and will be actively enforced is a matter of conjecture, the creation of institutions for IP protection has contributed significantly to the inflow of foreign direct investment (FDI) and technology transfer, the driving forces of China's sustained economic growth.

As China's economy continues to open and expand, disputes regarding IP infringement have increased. Since China's entry into the World Trade Organisation, it is estimated that the infringement damages paid by Chinese firms to international companies that manufacture DVDs, TV sets, digital cameras, MP3, cars, telecommunications equipment and so on, have surpassed one billion dollars.[1] The huge losses incurred from infringement have placed a heavy burden on some Chinese firms and affected certain industries quite severely. They have also alerted the Chinese authorities to the importance of IP protection, the urgency of prohibiting the abuse of IP, and the relationship between IP protection and the maintenance and promotion of competition.

Over the past few years, while the Chinese Government has continued its efforts to enhance the protection of IP, for example by creating the Steering Group of Intellectual Property Protection in 2004, it has strengthened regulations prohibiting the abuse of IP, especially with respect to IP restraints on competition. The milestone AML enacted in 2007 articulates clearly for the first time the fundamental legal principles guiding anti-monopoly enforcement at the intersection of IP and antitrust. Moreover, the Outline of the National

[1] Xiantao Huang, *Patent: Strategy, Management and Litigation* (China, Law Press, 2008) 3.

Intellectual Property Strategy released on 5 June 2008 indicates that preventing abuses of intellectual property rights (IPRs) forms part of the core of the Chinese national IP strategy.

While a discussion of the misuse of IPRs can be quite broad, this chapter focuses on one aspect of a significant question regarding the relationship between antitrust and IP laws: whether and on what terms courts and competition regulators should compel a dominant firm to license its powerful IP to a smaller rival. As many would know, this question has already generated substantial controversy, largely because the relevant law in the United States and Europe provide markedly different answers to it, differences that have been highlighted and will doubtless be exacerbated by the decision of the European Court of First Instance in the *Microsoft* case.[2]

Modern economic theory suggests that, as a remedy for the abuse of powerful IP, compulsory licensing can serve two main purposes. The first relates directly to consumer welfare and would compel licensing in order to improve health or save lives. The second, the focus of this chapter, would seek to remedy the anti-competitive misuse of IP by a dominant firm, which has foreclosed smaller rivals from market access or otherwise harmed consumers. This use of compulsory licensing aims to promote competition, or to remedy the effects of IP misuse, rather than to address consumer welfare directly.

In standard economic terms, compulsory licensing provides a remedy for static inefficiency—the deadweight loss incurred when an IP owner appropriates rents by excluding others from the relevant market and charging a monopoly price. This remedy, however, comes at a cost: dissipating rents through compulsory licensing will reduce returns from research and development (R&D), discouraging innovation and creating dynamic loss. The dynamic loss will occur in several ways: the dominant firm will refrain from investing further and in the future; its rivals will be spared the need to invent around the dominant IP, and will thus forego efforts that could result in welfare-enhancing products; and other firms in other markets, now and in the future, will also be more reluctant to invest. A comprehensive approach to compulsory licensing must therefore attempt to balance static gains against dynamic losses.

What is the best balance? At the present time, there may not be one universally acceptable response. In some ways, the answer is country-dependent, since it hinges in an important sense on 'local' conceptions of the value of IP, the place of the dominant firm, the efficacy of market mechanisms, and the importance of long-term incentives for economic growth. The approaches of the United States and the European Union are representative. Relevant case law in the United States values the dominant firm, trusts in market mechanisms, and places great importance on maintaining incentives for innovation. It is willing to tolerate short-term consumer harm in exchange for what it perceives to be the greater long-term benefit of strong incentives to invest. Consequently, compulsory licensing is rarely imposed by antitrust courts or advocated by enforcers. In contrast, EU law focuses on the short run inefficiency of monopolistic distortion and the attendant and immediate harm to consumers, while placing much less weight on incentives to innovate. Therefore, compulsory licensing has been ordered more frequently.

China has not yet produced a case or administrative decision involving compulsory licensing. However, it faces the challenge of designing a sound compulsory licensing regime if it wants to make full and wise use of the newly enacted AML to prohibit the misuse of

[2] Case T-201/04, *Microsoft Corp v Commission of the European Communities.*

IP to restrain competition and to encourage investment in innovation. It is a difficult task, which will require not simply balancing IP protection and the promotion of competition, but will entail 'political' aspects of IP regulation that may affect policy in a developing country like China. For example, since most patents with high technical content in China have been granted to non-residents, authorities may be inclined to tilt the balance in favour of compulsory licensing, simply on grounds of perceived national advantage: Chinese consumers will benefit; foreign firms will suffer. At the same time, however, the Chinese Government is committed to a national strategy of creating an innovation-oriented country to sustain high economic growth and enhance long-term international competitiveness. This strategy contemplates, and is intended to encourage, a nation of inventors, local inventors, who will want and need the same kinds of strong IP protection and valuable incentives that compulsory licensing may prevent and discourage.

This chapter first compares the US and EU approaches to compulsory licensing of 'powerful' IP, and then expands the discussion to include the Chinese context. It has modest aims. It will neither attempt to resolve the larger dispute about compulsory licensing, nor will it choose sides. Rather, it will describe the basis for the dispute, demonstrate that the opposing arguments are irreconcilable, and argue that these irreconcilable differences bear significantly on two fundamental issues in global competition law today: the prospect (and wisdom) of international convergence around a single approach to complicated antitrust questions; and the choices that newer competition law regimes, such as China's, must face in fashioning substantive rules in areas where international consensus is, and will likely remain, absent.

This chapter argues that the antitrust laws of the United States and Europe differ in their approaches to compulsory licensing not because they follow different schools of economic thought, but because the different political and cultural beliefs that inform and animate them lead inevitably to different answers. These political and cultural beliefs have little to do with economics. Indeed, they are persuasive precisely because economic theory lacks explanatory power in this area. The beliefs themselves reflect divergent opinions about the relative importance of the long term in antitrust analysis, about faith in the workings of complex regulatory regimes, and about confidence in the ability of markets to reach socially beneficial outcomes. And because these beliefs are primarily political—grounded, that is, in different historical experiences and cultures—it follows that the legal rules that emanate from them are (a) unlikely ever to converge, and (b) contingent, appropriate that is for the systems that embrace them, but not necessarily for anyone (or everyone) else.

II. Compulsory Licensing and the Long Term

IP law is intended primarily to promote innovation.[3] Starting with a definition of the various rights, IP law allows owners and creators to appropriate rents from their works and inventions by excluding others from copying, making, selling or using them. The efficient

[3] We do not attempt to have an exhaustive survey of the literature on economics of compulsory licensing. Please see US Department of Justice and Federal Trade Commission, 'Antitrust Enforcement and Intellectual Property Rights: Promoting Innovation and Competition' (2007) and the references therein. Available at www.justice.gov/atr/public/hearings/ip/222655.htm.

extent and duration of the exclusionary period of any IPR is determined with reference to two trade-offs. One is static loss against dynamic gain. Static loss can arise from the power to exclude, in those few cases where the invention generates market power, and from the attendant ability of the powerful firm to raise price above competitive level.[4] However, by allowing the patent owner to retain supernormal profits, IP law makes it worthwhile for inventors to commit significant resources to risky projects of research and development. The dynamic gain from those projects that result in successful innovation has been characterised by Schumpeter as the source of true economic advance.

The other trade-off is between static inefficiency and the disclosure of information. In return for the right to exclude others, an inventor must disclose the technology behind its patent. In contrast, if an inventor relies on trade secrets, it can also exclude others from using the technology—as long as it can protect the secret—but it need make no public disclosure of the relevant information. Since the informational gain to society from inventions dependent upon trade secrets is small (or non-existent), the level of inefficiency that is tolerated in markets dominated by the holder of a powerful trade secret should arguably be less than the inefficiency tolerated in markets dominated by patented inventions.

In the field of IP, compulsory licensing is usually intended to remedy an 'anti-competitive' refusal to license powerful (market-dominating) IP.[5] From an economic perspective, the main benefit of compulsory licensing is the reduction of ex post static inefficiency incurred when the owner of a dominant product protected by IP law appropriates rents by charging monopoly prices. However, dissipating those rents through compulsory licensing will also reduce returns from research and development (R&D) investments, which will ex ante discourage innovation and create dynamic losses. Moreover, on the margin, compulsory licensing may encourage IP owners to rely more often on trade secrets to protect their IP, which will reduce the disclosure of socially valuable information.

Therefore, whether the compulsory licensing of 'dominant' IP constitutes a sound legal approach in general hinges on a comparison of short run versus long run effects. Long-run effects, however, are notoriously difficult, impossible, to measure. Short-run effects, though, and especially those that have already occurred, are largely amenable to measurement. For this reason, an institutional preference for resolving difficult competition law problems by reference to their short-term or static effects underlies much of competition law analysis in the United States and Europe. Thus, in both jurisdictions, regulators and courts assess the legality of competitor collaborations—contractual arrangements, joint ventures, and mergers—in part by comparing their past, present or near-term anti-competitive consequences with their immediate or near term benefits. Conduct of dominant firms that might harm competition is usually subject to the same form of analysis.

In one important area, however, the European approach diverges from that of the United States. In the United States, a dominant firm possessed of powerful IP can refuse to license

[4] If rent-seeking is considered, the social loss approaches to the producer surplus. If transaction cost of rent-seeking is taken into account, the social cost is even higher. There are other short run inefficiencies as well, which are analysed in a large literature on economics of open access to essential facilities. For a good summary, see Jean-Jacques Laffont and Jean Tirole, *Competition in Telecommunications* (Cambridge MA, MIT Press, 2000). In the IP context, an obligation to open access to the property is equivalent to a requirement for compulsory licensing. Because of this access requirement, compulsory licensing also may reduce efficiency in the short run by facilitating the entry of inefficient producers and by promoting licensing arrangements that result in higher prices.

[5] Compulsory licensing is not the only remedy of abuse of IPRs. Changing the breadth of IPRs can make inventing around easier.

that property to its rivals, or would-be rivals, even though access to the property is arguably necessary to foster or preserve competition in the short term. If it has previously licensed that property, the dominant firm can refuse to continue licensing it, as long as its refusal arises plausibly from the (presumptively valid) everyday desire to appropriate for itself the full value of its invention or creation, and even if the refusal would impede competition in the short run.

In Europe, the dominant firm operates under a more intrusive rule. Although the applicable law appears similar in certain superficial respects to that of the United States, IP licensing decisions come under much stricter regulatory and judicial scrutiny. Thus, while the dominant firm with powerful IP can normally refuse to license its property to rivals, it is required to license in 'exceptional circumstances'. The European Court of First Instance's *Microsoft* ruling has significantly expanded the set of so-called 'exceptional circumstances' to include relatively unexceptional situations in which smaller rivals demonstrate, or argue, that they need access to the relevant IP in order to compete 'effectively' with the dominant firm in a neighbouring or secondary market, in which access to the IP would (or might) enable them either to develop a 'new' product or to make 'technical improvements' to their existing ones.

Even before the recent *Microsoft* opinion, this difference in approach to compulsory licensing was the subject of heated debate both within and between US and EU antitrust circles. The *Microsoft* case has provided additional fuel for the antagonists. For the most part, however, the argument has concerned itself with practical matters: is the US law sensible? Can refusals to license do more economic harm than good? Are courts and regulators competent to define and administer workable standards for compulsory licensing in general and for remedial orders in particular? While these are certainly important questions, the discussion has thus far overlooked the fundamental factor accounting for the difference between the European and American views.

In important respects, antitrust law in the United States is animated by a deep-seated faith in the long term. A central tenet of this faith holds that a rule of law encouraging the possession and retention of monopoly power will create strong incentives over the long-term for vigorous competition, as each firm strives to become a monopolist, and—therefore—very few succeed. Those few firms that do succeed, lawfully, will in turn encourage others to continue trying, provided of course that the successful receive their just rewards.

Another important article of faith holds that since innovation is the best engine of long-term economic growth, antitrust law should foster and protect incentives to innovate. An important way to achieve this goal is to allow dominant firms with valuable IP to realise the full value of their inventions. Those firms will then continue to invest in invention, their rivals will need to invent to keep up with them, and—in the long term—social investment in invention will remain at usefully high levels, all to the benefit of consumers.

This faith in the long term comes with both a corollary and a cost. The corollary requires a minimum of regulatory intervention in the short term, since unwarranted intervention—in the form of compulsory licensing, for example—would, among other things, discourage future investment in invention and deprive society of the valuable long term benefits that it would otherwise receive. The cost comes in the short run, since an institutional reluctance to intervene in markets dominated by powerful firms necessarily results in consumers' paying more than they would under a more aggressive enforcement regime. The United States accepts this cost, regarding it as necessary to encourage investment in innovation.

In contrast, the European regime does not trust so completely in the workings of the long term. Rather, in its approach to regulating the dominant firm, to merger review, and to the specific issue of compulsory IP licensing, it looks primarily to the short term needs of consumers. It is therefore less tolerant of dominant firms in general, more apt to challenge their conduct, and more skeptical of appeals to the social value of encouraging firms to strive for dominance and of ensuring long-term incentives to invest in innovation.

III. The Relevant Case Law and the Relevant Differences, Briefly Discussed

Two strains of case law are relevant to this discussion. The more general pertains to the liability of the dominant firm for refusing to deal with its smaller rivals. The more particular covers the refusal of the dominant firm to license its powerful IP to smaller rivals. In both the United States and Europe, these areas of law are regarded as related but distinct.

A. The US Case Law

In both areas, US law divides itself into two parts: (1) refusals to begin a course of dealing (or licensing) and (2) refusals to continue a course of dealing already begun. With regard to the former, the law provides a simple and readily comprehensible rule. It imposes no duty whatsoever on the dominant firm either to initiate a course of cooperative conduct with its rivals, or to respond positively to its rivals' requests for cooperation.

With regard to the latter, the law is somewhat more complicated. Prior to the Supreme Court's opinion in the *Trinko* case[6], the freedom of the dominant firm to discontinue a course of cooperative conduct with its smaller rivals was constrained—significantly in the view of some—by the Court's ruling in *Aspen Ski Co.*[7] That case upheld a finding of liability against a dominant ski resort which had ceased cooperating with its smaller rival in the sale of an all-area, six-day lift ticket, refusing even to sell its own lift tickets at retail to the smaller firm, on the grounds that:

(a) the cooperation had begun when the relevant market was competitive;
(b) consumers preferred the market with cooperation to the market without;
(c) the defendant's behaviour could plausibly be characterised as predatory—'[t]he jury may well have concluded that [the defendant] elected to forego . . . short-run benefits because it was more interested in reducing competition . . . over the long run by harming its smaller competitor';[8] and
(d) perhaps most importantly, the dominant firm had failed to offer a valid business justification, an efficiency defence, for its conduct.

[6] US Supreme Court, *Verizon Communications Inc v Law Offices of Curtis V Trinko, LLP*, 540 US 398 (2004).
[7] US Supreme Court, *Aspen Skiing v Aspen Highlands Skiing*, 472 US 585 (1985).
[8] *Aspen Ski Co* 472 US 585, 608 (n 7 above).

The Court's opinion in *Aspen* was controversial, and had more than its share of critics, but until *Trinko* it played an important, if controversial role in antitrust jurisprudence.

Trinko limited *Aspen*, condemning it to a fate almost worse than death—irrelevance. It located *Aspen* 'at or near the outer boundary' of section 2 liability. It referred to its holding as 'a limited exception' to the general right of a dominant firm to refuse to deal with its rivals.[9] It also confined its future applicability to cases whose fact patterns neatly matched *Aspen's* own. In particular, the Court observed, the defendant in *Aspen* terminated 'a voluntary *(and thus presumably profitable)* course of dealing', refusing to provide its competitor with 'a product that it already sold at retail', facts that now seem—after Trinko, that is—essential to plausible refusal-to-deal claims, whose future in general has been cast into grave doubt.

The US law regarding a dominant firm's refusal to license powerful IP to rivals is somewhat less clear, but not much. The Supreme Court has not ruled on the relevant issues, but a handful of appeals courts have. From these rulings, several salient points have emerged. First, it seems clear—as it is with refusals to deal in general—that a dominant firm has no obligation to cooperate with rivals in the first instance, and can reject with impunity their requests for access to valuable IP. No reported case in the United States imposes antitrust liability for a unilateral refusal to sell or license a patent and several expressly decline to do so.

The most notable of these is the Second Circuit's 1981 opinion upholding Xerox' refusal to license its plain-paper copying technology to SCM, which claimed that compulsory licensing would create competition in a market without any. Xerox had steadfastly refused to license its technology to SCM, a refusal vindicated on appeal: to rule otherwise, wrote the Court, 'would severely trample upon the incentives provided by our patent laws and thus undermine the entire patent system'.[10]

In regards to refusals to continue licensing IP to one's rivals, the law is slightly less clear. Among circuit courts that have ruled on the issue, small differences in opinion exist. Thus, in the *Image Technical Services* case, in which Kodak was sued for, among other things, having stopped licensing patented copier parts to rivals in the after-market for service, the Ninth Circuit held that a monopolist's desire to exclude others from its lawfully obtained intellectual property 'is a presumptively valid business justification for any immediate harm to consumers'.[11] On the Ninth Circuit's view, plaintiffs could rebut the presumption of validity by showing, through proof of the monopolist's subjective intent, that the claimed desire to exclude was 'pretextual', a cloak for some different and noxious anticompetitive intention.

Three years later, on nearly identical facts, the Federal Circuit adopted a modified version of the Ninth Circuit's test, in a case brought against Xerox by rivals in a parts and service after-market. Although relatively small, the Federal Circuit's modification makes a world of difference. Its test eschews any inquiry whatsoever into the monopolist's subjective intention in refusing to license its rival. Thus, under this test, unless the monopolist has (a) obtained its IP unlawfully (that is, by committing fraud on the patent office, or (b) brought 'sham litigation' to enforce its patent, its claimed desire to exclude others from

[9] *Trinko* 540 US, 409 (n 6 above).
[10] *SCM Corp v Xerox Corp*, 645 F.2d 1195 (2d Cir 1981), cert denied, 102 S Ct 853 (1982).
[11] *Image Technical Servs v Eastman Kodak Co*, 125 F.3d 1195, 1216 (9th Cir 1996).

using its IP provides an unassailable defence to antitrust claims brought by disappointed rivals.

It is easy to over-emphasise the difference between the Ninth and Federal Circuits' respective approaches to the issue of the monopolist's subjective intent. Focusing too closely on their differences, however, can obscure the large common ground shared by the two opinions. Both make it very difficult for plaintiffs to prevail. Each recognises the validity and importance of the monopolist's desire to use the exclusionary power in its valuable IP for its own exclusive benefit. Also, each creates a strong presumption favouring the use of that power and disfavouring rivals' attempts to interfere with it. For another, firms possessed of powerful IP and well-advised by counsel are not likely to run afoul of Kodak in the future. They can easily create a paper trail of bona fide memoranda announcing the high importance attached to capturing all available benefits from valuable IP.

B. The European Case Law

Until recently, reasonable people could disagree about whether EU law regarding the ability of the dominant firm to refuse to deal with smaller rivals differed materially from its counterpart in the United States. In general, that is in cases not involving powerful IP, European courts had adopted a relatively strict version of the so-called essential facilities doctrine. Thus, a dominant firm possessed of powerful property (such as a fleet of trucks which were arguably indispensable for the nationwide home delivery of newspapers) was not required to afford a smaller rival access to that property, since the rival had failed to show, as the law required, that the denial of access 'was likely to eliminate *all* competition on the part of the smaller firm' (emphasis added).[12] While not so protective of the dominant firm's interests as US law, the requirements of (i) indispensability and (ii) the likelihood that, without access, all competition in the relevant market would be eliminated nevertheless provided the dominant firm in Europe with a large degree of freedom.

As to the compulsory licensing of IP, the pre-*Microsoft* legal regime approached access requests cautiously. After affirming in the *Volvo* case[13] the inventor's exclusive right to refuse to allow others to reproduce its patented property, the European Court of Justice (ECJ) expanded the rights of access-seekers, but gradually and only in 'exceptional circumstances'. In *Magill*,[14] holders of what might be termed 'weak' copyrights in separate, weekly listings of television programmes, were made to license their copyrighted material to a firm seeking to publish a new product that would collect all of the listings in one comprehensive guide. The following four factors dictated the outcome:

(1) The copyright holders were the only sources of the information indispensable to the compilation of a comprehensive guide.

(2) The copyright holders' refusal to license 'prevented the appearance of a new product'.

(3) There was no good business justification for the copyright holders' refusal.

[12] *Oscar Bronner GmbH & Co. KG v Mediaprint Seitungs- und Zeitschriftenverlag GmbH & Co. KG and others* (C-7/97), 26 November 1998, [1998] ECR I-7817, [1999] 4 CMLR 112, [1999] CEC 53.

[13] *Volvo AB v Erik Veng (UK) Ltd* (238/87), 5 October 1988, [1988] ECR 6211, [1989] 4 CMLR 122, CMR 14498.

[14] Joined Cases C-241/91 and C-242/91 *Magill* [1995] ECR I-00743.

(4) Through the refusal, the copyright holders effectively reserved for themselves and eliminated *all* competition in, the market for weekly programme guides.

The holding in *Magill* was ratified by the opinion in the *IMS Health* case, another dispute involving the refusal of a dominant firm to license 'weak' but arguably indispensable copyrighted material to a smaller rival. The Court in IMS held that the refusal to grant a license to indispensable IP would constitute an abuse of a dominant position under the following circumstances:

(a) the access-seeker 'intends to offer a new product or service not offered by the copyright owner and for which there is potential consumer demand';
(b) the refusal 'is not justified by objective considerations' [valid business justifications]; and
(c) the refusal reserves the relevant market for the dominant firm 'by eliminating *all* competition on that market'.

The *Microsoft* opinion has changed European law dramatically by expanding each of the three criteria set forth in *IMS*. First, Microsoft interpreted the 'new product' requirement broadly, allowing it to encompass potential improvements to rivals' existing products already competing in the same market as those offered by the dominant firm. Second, it held that unproven claims about the general tendency of sharing obligations to affect innovation on the margin were not sufficient to constitute an 'objective justification' for a refusal to license. Rather, it held that such a justification required the dominant firm to 'prove' the extent to which its incentives to invest in innovation would be weakened. Third, it changed the requirement that the refusal eliminate 'all' competition in the relevant market, into one that asks whether the refusal eliminates 'effective' competition in that market. Collectively, these changes create a large and uncomfortable gap between the now relatively permissive European regime and the relatively restrictive American one.

IV. The Difference between EU and US Competition Law in Regards to Protecting Consumer Welfare

Since both regimes explicitly identify the protection of 'consumer welfare' as the main objective of competition law, the existence of such a significant difference in approach seems fundamental, remarkable, and unsettling. The difference is fundamental because it suggests that there might be, for the very same conduct, different and competing time frames within which to assess consumer welfare. It is remarkable because it implicitly asks even now, at this relatively late and sophisticated point in antitrust history, on which time frame the analysis should focus. It is unsettling because the lack of consensus on such a basic matter suggests that there are fixed limits to the ability of economic analysis to solve some of antitrust law's most pressing problems, and that perhaps one can and indeed must resort to some other, explicitly political calculus to answer these questions.

In this regard, the European approach focuses on the immediate and obvious benefits to consumers that flow from requiring dominant firms to license their valuable IP to smaller rivals. In the short term, smaller rivals can improve upon the relevant technology, and offer consumers a greater choice of products, or at least a greater quantity of roughly similar products at (necessarily) lower prices. Access to the dominant technology could well enable the smaller rivals to remain viably competitive in the short term and protect them from having to cede the market to the dominant player then and for the foreseeable future. Consequently, in the short term, prices will fall, output will rise, choice may expand, and dominance will be checked. Consumers benefit. While the European position would certainly acknowledge the possibility that compulsory licensing might at the margin dampen long-term incentives to innovate, it appears agnostic about this possibility, according it (non-dispositive) weight and only then when the dominant firm can 'prove' that the licensing in question would weaken its incentives to invent.

In this area, the United States sees consumer welfare in an entirely different light. It postulates that in the long run consumers benefit enormously from innovation; that ongoing innovation requires a set of incentives and protections that enable inventors to capture the full value of their inventions; and that legal rules that either discourage the incentives or weaken the protections will ultimately serve to diminish investment in invention and thus run counter to consumers' long-term interests. Put another way, the US view rejects the notion that compulsory licensing truly serves consumer welfare. While it would admit, as it must, that compulsory licensing affords consumers greater choice and lower prices in the short term, it insists that in the long run those benefits are illusory. Eventually, goes the argument, a regime that requires dominant firms to provide rivals with access to valuable IP will sap innovation incentives across the board—incentives not only of the incumbent dominant firm, but also of its smaller rivals and of would-be dominant firms now and in the future. In the long term, these weaker incentives will lead to fewer valuable inventions and a serious net loss of consumer welfare.

Three things about these different approaches should be clear. The first is that each relies on assumptions that economics cannot validate. The second is that their respective costs and benefits are incommensurable, so they cannot be usefully compared. The third follows from the first two: that their foundations are political, historical and cultural, valid for each country or regime, but not perhaps fully instructive for others.

Economics cannot help determine whether either the EU or the US approach to compulsory IP licensing is sensible. Of course, economics can confidently evaluate improvements to consumer welfare in the short term: compulsory licensing should yield greater choice and increased output. This is not problematic. The problem lies instead in attempting to conduct the trade-off between those short-term improvements and the supposed longer term harms. So, again, economics can confidently predict that compulsory licensing will reduce returns to invention and that therefore, on the margin, there will be less investment in invention in the future, a decrease likely to harm consumers. However, how much less investment will there be? How much less must there be before useful innovation is decreased? Is there a positive correlation between amounts invested in innovation and valuable invention? What if there is currently over-investment in innovation? If so, then maybe decreased incentives would, over time, reduce investment to the socially efficient level. The point is that economics is unable to provide answers to these fundamental questions.

Even if the long-term incentive effects of a more frequent compulsory licensing regime could be measured in some manner, other significant problems of measurement and comparison would remain. For example, the short-term benefits of lower prices and greater choice are not readily commensurable with the long-term benefits of higher incentives to invest in invention. Investments do not always yield inventions, for one thing. For another, there are at least four types of relevant investors, each with a slightly different set of incentives:

1. Dominant incumbents.
2. Smaller rivals (that would, under US law, for example, have incentives to invent around, or over, the incumbent's IP).
3. Existing potential entrants into the relevant market, and other IP markets.
4. Future inventors.

Comparing all of these uncertain potential long-term losses to the more definite gains obtainable in the near term would almost certainly be an exercise in futility.

These observations cut three ways. First, they mean that the US bias in favour of protecting the dominant firm's incentives to innovate inevitably lacks an empirical foundation, and may (or may not) be misplaced. Second, they mean that the European tendency to compel licensing more frequently does not, because it cannot, weigh off the losses of the likely but unquantifiable disincentives to invest that flow from compulsory licensing. It, too, may be misplaced. Consequently, except at the most basic level—that of identifying the very general incentive effects of the relevant legal rules—economic analysis is unhelpful. Third, if economic analysis does not dictate the choice of a legal rule in this area something else must, something non-economic—in other words, something political.

There is not the space here to rehearse the obvious and various historical differences between the United States and Europe that might account for their differing choices about how to treat the compulsory licensing of powerful IP. Nearly from its inception, the United States has enjoyed a national market in goods and services relatively free of local interference. The European Union is still in the process of developing such a market. The United States has very little history of state-owned firms; the vast majority of its monopolists gained their dominance on the merits. In Europe, by contrast, many of today's monopolists—in transport, electricity, and telephony, for example—were yesterday's state-owned companies.

For a variety of reasons, over the past century markets have worked more effectively in the United States than in Europe. They have been fluid, and Americans in general seem to trust their workings. Over the long term, the United States has been inventive: from a social perspective, investments in innovation seem to have paid big dividends to society. Europe has had very different experiences with markets, with local protectionism, with dominant firms and with invention. Given these differences, and others, it would be odd indeed if the two legal regimes supplied identical rules to the resolution of problems whose answers are not apodictically ordained by economics.

This conclusion holds several important implications for larger issues central to competition law. Before discussing them, however, it bears noting that the issue of compulsory licensing is not the only area of competition law whose questions are answered by resort to historical and cultural referents. The obligation of the dominant firm to license its valuable IP to smaller rivals is simply one of a much bigger set of questions pertaining to what kinds of behaviour constitute an abuse of dominance, or monopolisation. This large question can arise in many settings and business contexts, but in every case its resolution necessarily begins with certain basic assumptions about the dominant firm in general.

The United States not only accepts dominance, but welcomes it. The Supreme Court has recognised that the possibility of dominance creates incentives, again in the long term, for every business to invest in assets that might enable it to achieve the monopoly rents available to dominant firms. Of course, if most firms compete to become dominant, then very few will actually succeed; and the result will be an economy that promotes consumer welfare. Markets can almost always be trusted to work. However, in those relatively rare circumstances when a firm does outstrip its rivals, its success will both identify it as a boon to consumers and serve as a pleasant reminder to others, in the long run, that large rewards can accompany dominance fairly earned. Moreover, if smaller firms cannot match the dominant firm's appeal to consumers, no tears will be shed on their behalf: in the long term, other challengers will enter the market, and the dominant firm, like so many before it, will lose its power to a rival with even more appeal to consumers.

Recently, the United States Supreme Court, without a dissenting voice, referred to the 'mere possession of monopoly power' as 'an important element of the free-market system', observing that 'the opportunity to charge monopoly prices—at least for a short period —is what attracts "business acumen" in the first place; it induces risk taking that produces innovation and economic growth'. [*Trinko*] Restated, the Court's view tolerates certain short-run costs associated with the lawful possession of monopoly power, and imposes a significant burden on those who would complain about monopoly conduct, because it regards those costs (and that burden) as indispensable and unavoidable by-products of an incentive system crucial to the production of 'innovation and economic growth'.

The European Union is suspicious of dominance, rues its arrival, and encourages its demise. It defines dominance more broadly, and limits its exercise more strictly than does the US. Opinions of important appellate courts do not contain, as *Trinko* did, judicial praise for the beneficial economic role played by the dominant firm. There is less confidence that competition can undo dominance, and more fear that dominance will become and remain entrenched for the long term. Thus, as demonstrated by *Microsoft*, there is a preference in Europe for short-term 'fixes' to the 'problem' of dominance, for regulation now rather than competition later, and for the preservation (and even the support) of smaller, less efficient rivals, in the hope that they can somehow check the power of the dominant firm and protect consumers from future abuse.

We have drawn these differences broadly, but they are no less real for that. Significantly, like the narrower dispute about the proper approach to IP licensing, these different beliefs about the nature of the dominant firm and its relationship to the competitive process reflect views that arise largely from divergent experience with markets and dominant firms, and from the differing biases that those experiences have generated. Importantly, these differences exist and endure because in large measure economics offers no testable hypothesis about whether in the long run dominance should be encouraged or constrained.

V. The Broader Implications of these Differences

First, the differences in approach are important. Among other things, they have significant practical implications for the enforcement of competition law, not just in Europe and the United States, but in the world at large. In product markets that are truly international, the most aggressive competition law regime can effectively create rules of worldwide application. Now that European law has made it relatively easier for smaller firms to compel dominant rivals to afford them access to valuable IP, it will be difficult, if not impossible, for jurisdictions with different views on this issue, and the companies doing business in them, to avoid the impact of the European rule. For practical reasons, dominant firms will not often adopt a range of country-by-country licensing practices, and European law will thus become the de facto rule in many jurisdictions that might otherwise prefer their own, distinct approach to this issue. To that extent, European law may create a significant negative externality, serving the short run interests of Europeans, but in the process imposing significant costs upon other countries' perceived interests.

Second, the differences in approach are irreconcilable. Antitrust analysis in the United States exalts the social and economic importance of the need to maintain, and even to expand, long-term incentives to innovate. They play a role that is at once powerful and unquestioned. Although it may be both distant and unknowable, the long term is very much alive in US antitrust law. In Europe, the long term occupies a subordinate status. There seems to be no regulatory or judicial presumption that current legal rules will meaningfully affect incentives for long-term innovation. Indeed, the efficacy of such incentives is, in court, a matter that must be established by proof, rather than through an a priori presumption.

Moreover, the differences are irreconcilable because the values that explain them are incommensurate. The European regime places a high value on the short-term benefits that consumers will likely realise from a legal rule that would sometimes afford smaller firms access to the powerful IP of their dominant rivals. The US approach regards those benefits as detriments in sheep's clothing, seeing them as deeply corrosive of more highly valued long-term incentives to innovate. How can one reasonably compare the value of the short-term benefits favoured by Europe to the value of the longer-term benefits preferred by the United States? Any attempt at such a comparison would require something akin to 'judging whether a particular line is longer than a particular rock is heavy'. [Scalia J, concurring in *Bendix Autolite v Midwesco Enterprises*[15].] Nor can one assess, except by resort to a distinctly political calculus, whether the short-term benefits are somehow more important or desirable than those in the longer term. Measurement and comparison are simply not helpful. Without a useful metric, or a workable set of shared values, the different approaches cannot be reconciled.

Third, the fact that the differences are political, non-economic and irreconcilable suggests that the two regimes are highly unlikely to converge in the future on a means of resolving them. The differences are apt to be durable. While the United States and European Union, and other members of the world's antitrust enforcement community have in recent years quite usefully adopted convergent approaches to the prosecution of international criminal cartels and the procedures for reviewing multi-jurisdictional mergers, there seem to be distinct limits to the possibility of future convergence around a resolution of the issues discussed in this chapter.

Finally, this analysis contains an important lesson for the world's new and emerging competition law regimes. The fact that the two most developed systems disagree markedly in their approaches to the issues discussed here, and that they disagree for reasons of policy, history, and culture, suggests that certain aspects of competition law—not by any means all or even most, but some—are contingent, and properly variable. Those aspects of the law do not admit of one 'right' response, or perhaps of any 'right' response. Rather, they admit of several responses, each contestable, all debatable, none paramount or universally conclusive.

[15] *Bendix Autolite v Midwesco Enterprises* 486 US 888, 897 (1988).

This is not to say that each nation, or each antitrust regime, ought to go its own way in fashioning rules for the compulsory licensing of dominant IP. It may be that current institutional mechanisms preclude a uniform approach to this issue. However, in a world in which countries fully respected one another's economic histories and values, one country might well take into account another's history and values when applying its legal rules to that other country's firms. Those US firms with dominant IP, for example, rose to dominance in a climate that encouraged them to invest and promised them, through the applicable legal rules, that they alone would reap the benefits of those investments.

Without that climate and those rules, it seems fair to say, some of the valuable IP produced by US firms would not have found its way to market. Consequently, it might be appropriate, respectful, and properly sensitive for antitrust regimes outside the United States to recognise that imposing compulsory licensing obligations upon such firms serves not only to reject the US rule of law, and to defeat the initial expectations of the inventing firms, but also to disregard the culture and history from which those firms arose. Of course, this kind of recognition and respect must run in both, or all, directions. US and European courts and regulators should acknowledge and respect Chinese economic history as well, and bring to their tasks an informed understanding of the remarkable changes that the Chinese economy has undergone in the past three decades.

Moreover, it should be noted that in both the United States and the European Union, the issue of compulsory licensing applies only in circumstances where the relevant IP has enabled a firm to become or remain 'dominant' in a properly defined antitrust market. Neither regime even contemplates the possibility that compulsory licensing might be imposed on a non-dominant firm. Thus, while the two regimes differ significantly regarding their approach to compelling **dominant** firms to share their valuable IP, they agree that non-dominant firms are to be free of any such compulsion.

VI. The Legal Framework for Compulsory Licensing of IP in China

In this section we briefly describe China's legal framework regulating the intersection of IP laws and competition laws, particularly with respect to compulsory licensing. Since the relevant substantive rules are scattered in a variety of laws, which is a unique feature of China's legal rules governing both IP and competition, it is helpful to clarify the relationship between these two bodies of law. Civil law, contract law, IP law and competition law provide the main statutory rules for compulsory licensing of IP in China.

An IPR, defined legally as the ownership of IP, is a civil right under Chinese law. According to article 71 of China's Civil Law, the owner of IP has the authority to lawfully possess, utilise, benefit from, and dispose of his or her IP in accordance with laws. This means that the refusal to license IP is a legal right of the owner. There may be three legal ramifications of refusals to license IP. One is that refusals to license are legal as long as they are justified by valid reasons. The second is that they may constitute an abuse of IP law alone, unrelated to competition concerns. In this case compulsory licensing may be explored but not for the purpose of addressing abuses of market power. The third is that a refusal to license may be an abuse of market power and compulsory licensing may be used to prohibit or remedy such an abuse in IP-related markets.

Thus, the fundamental legal principle for compulsory licensing in China is that refusal to license IP is a right of the owner guaranteed and protected by civil law and IP law. However, this right is not absolute and receives protection only if the owner does not abuse it. If the owner of IP abuses the right to refuse to license, with the purpose or effect of eliminating or restricting competition, antitrust liability may arise and compulsory licensing may be ordered.

A. China's Laws on the Intersection of IP and Competition

i. IP Laws

To facilitate the development of a market-oriented economy, China has created a systematic legal framework to protect IP.[16] However, the legal rules guiding compulsory licensing of IP have emerged only gradually. The main body of laws covering compulsory licensing includes the Patent Law, the Rules for the Implementation of the Patent Law, Regulations on the Protection of Layout-Designs of Integrated Circuits, and Measures for the Implementation of the Patent Compulsory Licensing.[17]

China enacted its first Patent Law in 1984.[18] At that time, China had not yet fully achieved the institutional capacities and economic conditions necessary for installing a sound legal system for the protection of IP. Understandably, as a result, compulsory licensing of IP was not approached in a sophisticated fashion. Largely influenced by the country's eagerness to join the Paris Convention on the Protection of Industrial Property (Paris Convention), the compulsory licensing rules in the Patent Law, which were largely borrowed from the Paris Convention, provided that compulsory licensing should be imposed only if a patent owner had not fulfilled its obligation to use or practice the patent within a specified period of time (the carrying-out rule) or a technically more advanced patent depended for its practice on an existing patent (the dependence rule). The law did not deal with whether compulsory licensing should be imposed to prohibit or remedy anti-competitive conduct.

The 1984 Patent Law and the ensuing Measure for Implementation, released in 1985, failed to address several key issues. Besides, the Chinese Government pledged then to fulfill its commitment to the Memorandum of Understanding between the People's Republic of China and the United States of America on Protection of Intellectual Property Rights. The Patent Law was revised in 1992, in light of the Agreement on Trade-Related Aspects of

[16] After 30 years of efforts, China has created a legal system that is in accordance with international practice. The Trademark Law, the Patent Law, the Copyright Law, Regulations on Computers Software Protection, Regulations of the People's Republic of China on Customs Protection of Intellectual Property Rights, Regulations of the People's Republic of China on Protection of New Varieties of Plants, The Regulations on the Protection of Right of Dissemination via Information Network, Regulations on Collective Copyright Management, Regulations on the Protection of Layout-Designs of Integrated Circuits, Regulations on Protection of World Exposition Symbols, Regulations on Protection of Olympic Symbols, Regulations on Protection of Traditional Arts and Crafts constitute the main body of China's IP laws. In addition, General Principles of the Civil Law also contain rules on IP protection.

[17] Article 22 of the Copyright Law enacted in 2001did provide rules on compulsory licensing but they were unrelated to competition concerns. Regulations for the Protection of Computer Software published in 2001 did not contain explicit rules on compulsory licensing.

[18] For a more detailed account of the evolvement of compulsory licensing of IPRs in China, please refer to Xiuqin Lin, *Patent Compulsory Licensing under the TRIPs Agreement* (China, Law Press, 2006).

Intellectual Property Rights (TRIPs) reached at the Uruguay Round of negotiations. The rules respecting compulsory licensing left the dependence rule unchanged—compulsory licensing may still be imposed under this circumstance. The carrying out rule was replaced by a procedure governing refusals to license. In particular, if any entity 'qualified' to exploit the invention in question has requested a license from the patentee of that invention on 'reasonable terms', and has been unable to obtain such a license within a reasonable period of time, the Patent Office may, upon application of that entity, grant it a compulsory license to exploit the patent. Again, the 1992 Patent Law did not mention explicitly whether compulsory licensing was predicated on the patentee's 'dominance', or 'abuse' of dominance, and made no mention of competition concerns.

In order to join the World Trade Organization, China revised its Patent Law again in 2000, to make it accord more closely with TRIPs. While refusals to license and 'dependent' patents still constituted the main circumstances where compulsory licensing might be imposed, significant changes were made to the relevant substantive rules. The precondition for compulsory licensing of technical advancements was amended to require 'significant and breakthrough' technical advancements. More importantly for our purpose, article 72 (4) of the Measure for Implementation issued in 2001 raised the possibility that compulsory licensing could be explored to remedy a practice determined to be anti-competitive after judicial or administrative process. This was the first appearance in the Patent Law of language permitting compulsory licensing to be used to address competition problems.

The latest revision of the Patent Law was published in 2008, after the enactment of the Anti-Monopoly Law. There are now six circumstances in which compulsory licensing may be explored. In particular, article 48 of the new Patent Law stipulates that compulsory licensing of IP shall be imposed to remedy certain kinds of anti-competitive conduct.[19]

Compulsory licensing to address competition concerns is also mentioned in the Regulations on the Protection of Layout-Designs of Integrated Circuits issued in 2001, which stipulate that compulsory licensing may be imposed upon the holder of rights in layout-design, in order to address unfair competition concerns.[20] Because the AML had not been enacted when these regulations were issued, this area of competition law was regulated by the Anti-Unfair Competition Law, which listed 11 types of 'unfair' competition behaviours, five of which were declared to be 'anti-competitive' conduct.

ii. Contract Laws

Another body of law that contains rules against misuse of market power conferred by IP is contract law. In particular, article 329 of the Contract Law enacted in 1999 states that any contracts that illegally monopolise technologies, hinder technical progress or infringe upon technological products of others are invalid. Because this rule is too general, the Supreme

[19] The Patent Law of the People's Republic of China. (...the Patent Administration Department under the State Council may… grant a compulsory license for the exploitation of an invention patent or utility model patent: (1)… ; or (2) The patentee's act of exercising the patent right is determined as monopoly in accordance with the law and the negative impact of such an act on competition needs to be eliminated or reduced.)

[20] Regulations on the Protection of Layout-Designs of Integrated Circuits (…that there is unfair competition on the part of the holder of the right of layout-design and there is a need to give remedy, the intellectual property administration department of the State Council may grant a non-voluntary license to exploit the layout-design.)

People's Court issued a judicial interpretation on 16 December 2004,[21] which listed six restrictive terms involved in IP contracts, including quantity restriction, limitation of territory for use of technology, price-fixing, restriction of distribution channels, unreasonable grant-back, non-competition clause, tie-in, and no challenge clause. Neither Contract Law nor the Judicial Interpretation of the Supreme Court explicitly mentioned whether compulsory licensing could be used to remedy anti-competitive conduct in the field of IP.

The Regulation on Import and Export of Technologies issued by the State Council in 2001, and the two versions of the Foreign Trade Law issued in 1994 and 2004, also contain rules against IP restraints on competition. In particular, article 30 of the Regulation on Import and Export of Technologies provides that if the owner of IP prohibits a licensee from challenging the validity of the IPRs in the licensing contract, forces the licensee to accept a bundle of licenses, requires exclusive grant-back clauses, or distorts fair competition in foreign trade, the Administration of Foreign Trade under the State Council has the authority to adopt measures to address the harm. Again, however, the laws make no mention of compulsory licensing.

iii. Competition Laws

Before the AML was enacted, statutory rules against anti-competitive conduct were scattered among several sets of laws and regulations. These included the Anti-Unfair Competition Law, the Price Law, and the Tendering and Bidding Law, which were enacted by the People's Congress, China's national legislative assembly, as well as Regulations on Telecommunications and Regulations on Electricity, which were issued by the State Council. The larger body of competition law in China also encompassed a variety of regulations issued at the ministerial level, and laws and regulations issued by local governments. In general, unlike the laws and regulations promulgated by the People's Congress and the State Council, these laws and regulations impose rules against monopolistic conduct under specific circumstances in particular jurisdictions. However, none of them addresses the competition problems that might arise with respect to IP, let alone those pertaining to compulsory licensing.

In 2007, China enacted the AML, the first comprehensive competition law in China's history. Among other things, the AML explicitly promulgates the legal principles guiding antitrust enforcement related to IP. Article 55 of the AML stipulates that while the law shall not interfere with the conduct of business operators to exercise their IPRs under relevant laws and administrative regulations, it prohibits business operators from eliminating or restricting market competition by abusing their IPRs.

The first part of article 55 means that the law shall not apply to the exercise of IPRs, so long as the relevant conduct does not constitute an abuse of the power conferred by those rights. The second part implies that misuse of IPRs is not exempt from coverage by the AML. Thus, the anti-competitive misuse of IPRs may result in liability, if the antitrust enforcement agencies can establish that the owner of the IP has otherwise violated the law. According to article 3 of the AML, anti-competitive conduct includes 'monopolistic agreements' among business operators, abuse of dominant market positions by business operators, and concentrations of business operators that eliminate or restrict competition

[21] Interpretation of the Supreme People's Court Concerning Some Issues on the Applications of Laws for the Trial of Case on Disputes Over Technology Contracts.

or might eliminate or restrict competition. Although it is not yet clear, these acts may constitute the kind of 'abuse' prohibited by article 55.

Until recently, neither the AML nor the other competition laws had directly addressed refusals to license IPRs. Article 17 of the AML prescribes some general circumstances under which antitrust liability may flow from the refusal to license IP that possesses market power. Article 17 (1) of the AML may impose liability if the licensing fee for the relevant IP is 'too high', and thus unfair. Since charging high prices for licensing is closely related to refusals to license, this article may be interpreted to require compulsory licensing when the owner of 'dominant' IPRs seeks to charge the monopoly price to would-be licensees.

Under Article 17 (3), unilateral refusals to license IP without justifiable reasons may result in liability, which means that under the injunction requirement of article 15,[22] compulsory licensing may be used to remedy an 'anti-competitive' refusal to license. Under article 17 (5), which sets forth the rule against tie-ins, certain kinds of conditional licensing may be subject to antitrust liability. Finally, article 17 (6) proscribes unjustified discrimination. However, it is important to emphasise that the AML has adopted the general principle that rule of reason analysis governs the establishment of liability under these rules, which suggests that refusals to license may be justified by 'valid' reasons.

B. Institutions for Antitrust Enforcement in IP

Since China has not yet produced a single case or administrative decision dealing directly with compulsory licensing, it is not possible to analyse the relevant enforcement policies or activities. Instead, we shall provide a brief discussion of the enforcement institutions with the authority to deal with IP restraints on competition and with compulsory licensing.

i. Administration Enforcement

The State Intellectual Property Office (SIPO), an administrative agency under the State Council, is charged with enforcing IP law. In particular, SIPO is responsible for investigating and deciding issues arising out of claims for compulsory licensing, including the appropriate licensing fees and the length of the license. This grant of authority suggests that all issues relating to compulsory licensing, even those arguably pertaining to anti-competitive conduct, may fall within the jurisdiction of SIPO. IP laws require, however, that a case alleging that misuse of IP has restrained competition should be decided according to the relevant competition laws.

Based on the AML and the authorisation by the State Council, the power to enforce the AML is shared by the Ministry of Commerce (MOFCOM), the National Development and Reform Commission (NDRC), and the State Administration for Industry & Commerce (SAIC), which are in charge of dealing with merger control, price agreements and price abuse of dominant position, and non-price abuse of dominance, respectively. Since compulsory licensing would usually be imposed to remedy the abuse of market power, both the NDRC and the SAIC may have authority to deal with questions of compulsory licensing.

It is worth noting that since both the Patent Law and the AML prescribe legal liabilities for anti-competitive conduct, there may be some overlapping jurisdiction between the IP

[22] Article 47 of the AML stipulates that where any business operator abuses its dominant market status in violation of this Law, it shall be ordered to cease doing so.

administrative body and the antitrust enforcement agencies regarding the resolution of cases that could result in compulsory licensing.

ii. Court Enforcement

Since administrative enforcement co-exists with court enforcement, there are two possibilities for private actions in IP and anti-competition cases in China. One is that a private plaintiff may choose to file a civil lawsuit without pursuing an administrative action. The other is that a plaintiff might lodge an administrative lawsuit after the relevant agency has made a decision with which the plaintiff disagrees.[23]

Private actions for IP cases are tried before the Third Civil Division of the Supreme People's Court, the 31 Higher People's Court (which is one level in importance below the Supreme Court and one level above the Intermediate Court) at the provincial or municipality level, and the intermediate courts situated in the capital cities of the provinces, autonomous regions and municipalities. The second trial is taken as the final appeal.[24] Because of the need for judicial expertise in IP cases, the Supreme People's Court has specially designated 48 intermediate courts and a small number of basic courts as the courts of first instance.

In comparison with the enforcement of IP laws, where both administrative enforcement and private actions regularly occur, the AML, which has only a short history of enforcement, is expected to be enforced mainly by administrative agencies. However, there is the possibility that private actions may be brought alleging anti-competitive conduct involving IP. Indeed, article 50 of the AML establishes civil liability for antitrust violations.[25] More importantly, the Provision on the Subject Matter of the Civil Case issued by the Supreme People's Court in 2008 stipulates explicitly that anti-competition cases in IP shall be tried by the Third Civil Division. However, it seems that civil lawsuits against anti-competitive conduct are likely to develop very slowly in China. Indeed, only recently, in March 2011 has the Supreme People's Court promulgated regulations setting forth the rules applicable to the commencement and trial of private actions under the AML. While these regulations clarify the relevant procedures and reinforce the role of the private action in the overall enforcement scheme, they have yet to receive much practical application.

C. The Draft 'Anti-Pricing Monopoly Regulation'

On 12 August 2009, the NDRC released for public comment a set of regulations, whose stated purpose is 'preventing and prohibiting pricing monopoly activities, protecting fair

[23] Article 58 of the 2008 Patent Law stipulates that if the holder of IPRs is not satisfied with the compulsory licensing decision made by the SIPO, it can start an administrative lawsuit against it. Similarly, article 53 of the AML provides that where any party concerned objects to the decision made by the anti-monopoly authority in accordance with this Law, it may first apply for an administrative reconsideration; if it objects to the reconsideration decision, it may lodge an administrative lawsuit in accordance with law.

[24] Before the 1990s, there was no special trial court for IP cases. Rather, the cases were divided as civil, criminal and administrative cases and reviewed by the civil division, the economic division, and the administrative division, respectively. In 1993 the Beijing Intermediate People's Court created the first division dealing with civil and administrative IP cases. In 1996 the Shanghai Supreme People's Court established the IP trial division dealing specifically with the cases of second instance and a trial de novo. In 2000 the Supreme People's Court restructured the IP Division to the Third Civil Division, which is called the IP Division by outsiders.

[25] See article 50 of the AML (where any loss was caused by a business operator's monopolistic conducts to other entities and individuals, the business operator shall assume the civil liabilities).

competition and safeguarding the interests of consumers and the public'. These regulations were published in final form in early 2011. Although it is not perfectly clear, the regulations are apt to apply to compulsory licensing of IP by the dominant firm. For the reasons discussed below, the text of the regulations is quite worrisome in this regard, and others, though their real effect will be determined more by their enforcement than by their wording.

Article 1 of the Regulation, quoted in part above, suffers from one of the same problems that afflicts the AML itself. The three stated goals of the pricing regulation—prohibiting 'monopoly pricing', 'protecting fair competition', and safeguarding consumer interests—can often be at cross purposes. 'Monopoly pricing' may, in the short term, strike some as 'unfair' and will certainly—again in the short term—result in wealth transfers from consumers to monopolists. However, it may also be, will often be, the fair and necessary social price for encouraging and rewarding invention. For the same reason, a dominant firm's refusal to license its powerful IP to smaller rivals, which effectively places an infinite price on the desired license, may seem unfair to rivals and harmful to consumers, again in the short term. However, the social benefits likely to be lost by a regime that is quick to compel licensing on grounds of 'fairness'—whatever that might mean—are very likely to be significant.

The Anti-Pricing Regulation (APR) applies to two types of conduct: (1) monopoly pricing agreements, and (2) abusive monopoly pricing by the dominant firm. In each case, the regulations are troubling in regard to IP licensing, among other things. Articles 6 and 7 presumptively proscribe joint pricing decisions by competing firms. In many cases of course, joint pricing ought to be suspect, but in some cases—pricing of a new product by joint venture partners, or of a patent package by the members of a patent pool—there can be good reason, and social benefit, from collective pricing activity. Article 10 of the APR makes it possible for firms engaging in joint pricing conduct to offer a 'reasonable explanation' for their behaviour, but at this point it is entirely unclear what kinds of explanations will be deemed 'reasonable'.

Articles 11 and 12, which together forbid abusive monopoly pricing by a firm with 'a dominant market position', are more worrisome still. Three of the five described offences might bear on IP licensing. Article 11 (1) prevents a dominant firm from selling 'products' (it is not clear whether the 'licensing' of an IP 'right' will constitute the 'sale' of a 'product', but for present purposes we assume that it will) at 'unfairly high prices'. Article 11 (3) prevents a dominant firm, 'without valid justification' (a phrase whose meaning is completely unclear), from 'refusing to deal' with a counterparty by setting 'excessively' high prices. Article 11 (5) prevents a dominant firm from engaging in any 'other pricing conduct' that might, after the fact, be judged 'abusive' by the Price Authority.

Article 12 sets forth a series of four factors relevant to the determination as to whether a dominant firm has in fact sold its products at 'an unfairly high price'. The first would ask whether 'the selling price is obviously higher than cost'; the second would inquire into whether the selling price has been 'increased by a percentage above the normal level, where the cost is basically unchanged'; the third would examine whether the selling price has been increased 'by a percentage obviously larger than the increase of the cost'; and the fourth would ask whether 'the selling price is obviously higher than that of the same kind of product of other business operators'.

It does not require much legal training to see that the terminology used in article 12 is dangerously vague. In the case of a dominant firm with powerful IP, the sunk costs of R&D will invariably outweigh the marginal costs of producing the next unit of product.

If marginal costs are the relevant measure for article 12, then every firm with powerful IP will violate it. However, article 12 is silent as to the appropriate measure of cost. It is also silent, as it must be perhaps, as to the meaning of its 'obviousness' test, which lies at the heart of the section: 'obvious' to whom? 'Obviously' high? Obviously 'excessively' high? Obviously 'unfairly' high? Who can tell? In a market dominated by the IP of a powerful firm, what is the 'normal' pricing level? Is it the monopoly price normally prevailing in that market, or is it instead a hypothetical price that might prevail if the actual monopoly were somehow a competitive one? Or is it something else entirely? If there are no other firms that sell 'the same kind' of product (but what does that mean?), does article 12 not apply?

The last sentence of article 12 sets out an escape clause that makes the Regulation inapplicable when buyers can obtain 'the same kind of product or substitutes from other business operators at a reasonable price'. This clause offers no hope, and more confusion, for firms with powerful IP. It will often be the case that they are dominant precisely because they have invented a product for which there is no good substitute. However, if there happens to be a competing product available, how can the dominant firm know whether the regulator will decide—after the fact—that its sale price was 'reasonable', whatever that means? As a more general matter, the escape clause seems silly, a truism, since it effectively says that where competitive pricing exists, abusive pricing does not, a declaration that is not particularly helpful to the business community.

The first paragraph of article 14 prohibits a dominant firm, 'without a valid justification', from refusing to deal with a counterparty by setting an 'excessively' high price, which the second paragraph defines as 'a price at which the transaction counterparty could not achieve normal profit after normal production and sales'. Like the preceding sections of the regulation, this section depends for its enforcement on terms with no clear or fixed meaning—'normal' profit', 'normal production and sales'—and consequently leaves the business community without any guidance as to permissible pricing behaviours. At the same time, it grants the regulator an enforcement discretion which is both dangerously vague and unlimited.

Article 26 is equally unsettling. It provides that the pricing regulation is 'not applicable' to business conduct of firms exercising their IPRs 'in accordance' with IP law and relevant regulations, but 'is applicable' to the conduct of firms that 'abuse their intellectual property rights to eliminate or restrict market competition'. No definition of 'abuse' is set forth, nor is compulsory licensing discussed or described. However, the section seems to suggest that IP can be priced 'abusively'; and that doing so will offend the APR.

Finally, while the APR proscribes the kind of conduct discussed above, and permits the relevant agencies to punish offending firms in accordance with section 51 of the AML, it provides no guidance to administrative agencies about how they might establish a regime of 'fair' or 'normal' pricing, in order to remedy instances of 'abusive' pricing conduct. This omission is understandable in a sense: there is no effective way for any administrative agency to act as an ongoing price-setter or adjuster. It is far easier (misguided, but easier) to punish unfairly 'high' prices than to set prices that are 'fair', or at least 'fairly' high. To this extent, the APR violates the antitrust maxim that no competition law regime should proscribe conduct that it cannot effectively remedy; and will likely present a host of intractable difficulties to regulatory bodies.

The APR may well pose a serious roadblock to everyday and socially beneficial conduct. It will impede, and may even seriously punish, proper refusals to license IP. It will require firms to guess at the meaning of words that have none, and to risk liability for being unable to divine their meaning. It will require the regulator to make critical factual determinations—about pricing levels, 'normal' markets—without reference to useful or knowable criteria.

VII. Inadequacies in China's Legal Framework for Compulsory Licensing

China introduced legal rules regarding compulsory licensing in 1984, but there has yet to be a case or decision dealing with this issue, which seems unusual given the growing number of complaints about IP restraints. One possible reason for the lack of a reported decision is that a contestable case has yet to arise. A more likely explanation may be that China's legal framework is inadequate to deal with the complicated issues involved in claims for compulsory licensing, and particularly with those relating to promoting competition and innovation in the field of IP. While the legal framework is evolving and being improved continuously, the current situation suggests that the main challenges for China's legal rules on compulsory licensing lie in addressing inadequacies in some of the applicable legal standards and in resolving the potential for conflict and confusion arising from overlapping agency jurisdiction.

As described in the last section, Chinese IP laws and competition laws both express the fundamental legal principle that the exercise of IPRs is subject to legal control. More specifically, both the Patent Law and the AML make certain refusals to license IP remediable by compulsory licensing. However, the current IP laws and competition laws still cast some shadow over the enforcement of antitrust rules in the field of IP, in particular regarding the imposition of compulsory licensing, and of the terms on which compulsory licensing might be ordered.

An important problem stems from the lack of comprehensive statutory criteria for assessing the extent to which the use of IPRs might restrain competition· Article 55 of the AML stipulates that any anti-competitive conduct in the use of IP shall be regulated by the AML. Article 17 of the AML specifies six categories of restraints on competition, but these categories are general in nature and not placed into the context of IP use. The interpretation by the Supreme People's Court of the Contract Law prescribes, in the context of IP, six circumstances under which a case may be established on account of illegally monopolising a technology and impeding technical progress. However, the interpretation does not discuss some important circumstances. For instance, there is no discussion of patent pools or cross-licensing, which raise important questions about the relationship between IP and competition law. The Foreign Trade Law also pinpoints in the context of foreign trade some IP restraints, but again these references offer little guidance about enforcing the AML in IP-related cases.

One may argue that this lack of specificity does not constitute a serious problem as article 17 (7) of the AML provides that the law shall apply to unspecified restraints on competition. However, the vagueness of such a clause is apt to create uncertainty in the business community and to raise the likelihood of enforcement error: both Type I and Type II errors are more likely because the 'unspecified' circumstances are incapable of accurate prediction, may raise difficult factual or substantive questions, and may not be readily amenable to reasoned analysis. Further, since China follows the statutory law tradition and its enforcement capability is still being developed, the specification of circumstances attracting enforcement of the AML is necessary to enhance enforcement efficiency and effectiveness by describing the prima facie case and allocating the burden of proof efficiently.

Second, until recently, there have been no explicit legal rules governing compulsory licensing in the software industry. As is well known, many IPRs in the software industry are protected by copyright, and compulsory licensing has been one of the controversial issues in the Microsoft cases worldwide. However, neither the Copyright Law nor the Regulation on the Protection of Software, which are the main bodies of law regulating the software industry in China, provides legal rules to deal with competition issues in general and compulsory licensing in particular. For example, it is unclear whether China's competition agencies may require the owner of the interface code of a software system to provide access to its rivals and, if so, under what circumstances and terms. The open access issue can be analysed under the general guidance of the AML. Indeed, one can analogise a denial of access to a refusal to deal under the essential facility doctrine. However, given the specific features of the software industry and the complicated issues involved, it is doubtful that the existing IP laws and competition laws are adequate to deal with such cases.

Third, there are many uncertainties regarding the application of article 17 of the AML to the field of IP. For instance, article 17 (1) provides that antitrust liability may be imposed if a seller sets a high price that is unfair. In the context of IP this suggests that the licensor may be unable to set the license fee or royalty at the monopoly price level, even if it has done nothing to restrain competition. This provision is particularly worrisome. Licensees are naturally inclined to complain that license fees are too high; and if their complaints find a receptive audience within the relevant enforcement agency, owners of IPRs will run the risk of being denied adequate compensation for their investments in R&D, which would likely, as discussed earlier, discourage investment in and development of innovations.

As is well known, the central economic feature of innovative activities is that inventors almost always have to incur large amounts of sunk costs, and bear the substantial risk of research or market failure, facts which are often played down by rivals and sometimes by enforcement agencies. Thus, allowing inventors to fully appropriate monopoly rents from successful inventions is necessary to compensate them for their risk-taking and to induce them, and others, to take comparable risks in the future. Indeed, temporary supernormal rents are exactly the incentives necessary for making investments in innovation that dramatically improve consumer welfare, and that spur dynamic competition in invention. Therefore, charging monopoly prices per se should not be deemed to be a violation of the AML.

Another problem with article 17 (1) of the AML is that it may place an IP owner's legal right of exclusion at risk. Article 17 (3) of the AML specifies that refusals to license IP without reasonable justification are a restraint of competition. However, in many cases refusals to deal may result from the parties' inability to agree on appropriate compensation for the relevant license. Such refusals could also be viewed as equivalent to charging monopoly, or infinitely high, prices. Thus article 17 (1) and (3), if inappropriately applied, may endanger the exclusionary right of an IP holder, which stands at the centre of IP law.

We are not arguing that IPRs are absolute or unqualified, or that all refusals to license are per se legal. Rather, we worry about the uncertainties and social harms that may result if these rules are inappropriately applied. Fortunately, the AML has adopted the general principle of rule of reason analysis to assess claims of anti-competitive conduct. This should make it possible to avoid the unfortunate consequences of bad decision-making. However, it should also encourage the enforcers of IP laws and competition laws to issue guidelines clarifying these important issues.

Fourth, neither IP law nor competition law specifies a methodology for establishing license fees, in those cases where compulsory licensing is imposed. Article 57 of the Patent Law stipulates that if compulsory licensing is ordered, the licensee should pay 'reasonable' usage fees to the licensor. The usage fees shall be negotiated by the licensor and the licensee. If they cannot agree upon a reasonable fee, they can apply to SIPO for an administrative ruling. If they are not satisfied with the ruling, they can file an administrative lawsuit in court. However, no guideline has been released either for administrative ruling or court review. A host of difficult questions exists: what constitutes a reasonable license fee; on what basis should the license fee be determined; should the license fee be cost-based, and if so, on what cost; should the inventor receive a 'fair' return on its initial investment; should payment consist of a lump sum fee, an annual royalty, or a combination of the two—a two-part tariff; and so on.[26]

In fact, ordering a dominant firm to license its powerful IP to rivals amounts to a declaration that the IP is an essential facility. Declaring certain IP to be an 'essential facility' requires courts or agencies to determine the 'proper' amount of the licensing fee, and other terms and conditions of the license, initially and then repeatedly over time. Compulsory licensing necessarily forces the IP and antitrust enforcement agencies to perform the regulatory function of setting prices, a role to which they are ill-suited. As the practice of interconnection pricing has demonstrated vividly worldwide, it is a daunting task for regulators simply to set initial access prices (licensing fees), due to the complex trade-offs that must be made. On the one hand, they may be tempted to set a low licensing fee in order to promote short-term competition (service competition) and thus to enhance short-run consumer welfare. On the other, they may want to set a high licensing price to promote longer-term investment (facilitate-based competition) and innovation. The trade-off is complicated by specific features of certain kinds of IP, particularly where the marginal costs of use or production are almost zero, and marginal cost pricing is unremunerative and therefore inefficient.[27]

Finally, potentially serious problems of overlapping and conflicting jurisdiction exist. SIPO and the competition policy agencies share the enforcement power over anti-competitive conduct in IP, in particular in imposing compulsory licensing to remedy IP restraints on competition. Indeed, the Patent Law grants SIPO general jurisdiction over compulsory licensing. At the same time, the AML bestows competition agencies with the power to forbid anti-competitive conduct, including unreasonable refusals to deal. In the context of IP, this power enables the enforcement agencies to explore compulsory licensing as a remedy for refusals to license IP. This structure of shared power contains an obvious potential for administrative conflict that could lead not only to the squandering of scarce administrative resources but also to incompatible enforcement standards.

[26] Michael L Katz and Carl Shapiro, 'On the Licensing of Innovations' (1985) 16(4) *Rand Journal of Economics* 504; Morton I Kamien, Shmuel S Oren and Yair Tauman, 'Optimal Licensing of Cost-reducing Innovation' (1992) 21 *Journal of Mathematical Economics* 483.

[27] Reiko Aoki and John Small, 'Compulsory Licensing of Technology and the Essential Facility Doctrine' (2004) 16(1) *Information Economics and Policy* 13 (Arguing that charging royalty, which is at odds with the marginal cost pricing principle, mat be more efficient.)

In addition, there may be overlapping and conflicting jurisdiction among competition agencies. As described in the last section, the NDRC and SAIC have the power to prohibit monopolistic agreements and abusive conducts in price and non-price fields, respectively. While it may appear that their respective areas of authority powers are separate and distinct, many cases involve both price and non-price conducts, creating the potential for jurisdictional conflicts to arise with some regularity. For example, suppose certain competitors agree to create a patent pool. The agreement provides that each member can use the patents in the pool royalty-free but may not license them to third parties; and that each member may unilaterally license its own (non-pooled) IPRs to third parties but may charge no less than the licensing fee specified in the agreement. Clearly, both refusals to license and price agreements are involved in this case. The NDRC may deal with this case as to the price agreement, while the SAIC may regulate the non-price conduct. However, it is hard to think of a situation where different enforcement agencies might usefully share jurisdiction over the same case, not least because of the high coordination costs involved.

VIII. Relevant Factors in Determining China's Compulsory Licensing Policy

Thus far, we have discussed the basic economic trade-offs between short-run and long-term efficiencies, US and EU case law, and China's legal framework for compulsory licensing in the field of IP. We now move to the analysis of factors necessary to the formation of a coherent compulsory licensing policy in China's context. Fundamental economic principles suggest that imposing compulsory licensing in China should take due account, but without exaggeration, of special 'developing country' issues, including inter alia, the high proportion of IPRs granted to non-residents, and current institutional enforcement capacity.

A. High Proportions of Patents Granted to Non-Residents

As in other developing countries, most patented technologies and copyrighted IP practised in China are developed abroad, in part because of China's current comparative disadvantage in R&D investment. Even though the overall proportion of patents granted to non-residents was only 14.26 per cent in 2007, the total inventions patented to foreign firms and individuals were 52.99 per cent (patents are divided into three categories in China—inventions, utility models, and design patents; the latter two types have lower technical content than the first type), while at the same time the percentage of utility model and design patents granted to non-residents was 1.1 and 9.34, respectively (see Table 1). This suggests that most patents granted to local residents are utility model and design patents with relatively low technical content, while most patents owned by foreign companies or individuals have relatively high technical content, and therefore have more commercial value. From an economic perspective, the distribution of patents granted to residents and non-residents will have a profound impact on the basic trade-offs involved in establishing a policy for compulsory licensing.

Table 1: Patents Granted to Non-Residents in China (%)

	Total	Invention	Utility Model	Design Patent
1985	19.57	5.00	6.67	55.26
1986	11.67	7.14	2.06	67.81
1987	6.02	26.30	1.58	33.49
1988	5.47	39.80	0.76	23.12
1989	9.63	52.97	1.00	22.31
1990	14.54	70.06	1.23	21.52
1991	13.97	68.20	0.73	15.79
1992	10.05	65.05	0.46	13.74
1993	8.44	59.82	0.51	12.17
1994	8.13	57.28	0.63	16.50
1995	8.47	54.91	0.91	14.97
1996	7.87	53.14	0.59	12.48
1997	9.03	56.15	0.57	12.34
1998	9.59	65.03	0.55	11.10
1999	8.04	59.45	0.49	8.97
2000	9.60	51.30	0.61	8.62
2001	13.11	66.89	0.63	8.56
2002	15.33	72.67	0.68	8.04
2003	17.91	69.31	0.89	8.24
2004	20.45	63.04	0.86	10.23
2005	19.81	61.16	1.53	10.54
2006	16.47	56.60	1.25	9.84
2007	14.26	52.99	1.10	9.34
2008	14.46	50.28	0.85	7.74

Source: World Patent Report: a Statistical Review 2008, WIPO Statistics Database.

As discussed earlier, the purpose of the patent system is to provide incentives for firms to invest in R&D by permitting monopoly rents in return for disclosure to the public of the underlying technology. However, this may not be the primary function of the patent system in China under current circumstances. Since high-value technologies patented in China have mostly been invented abroad where firms make R&D investment decisions based on projected profits from larger markets—typically the United States, European Union or Japan—reducing monopoly rents from sales in China might not cost China much in innovation, as lost sales there would likely be small compared to those made in the other countries. Similarly, the information disclosure function of the patent system would not be affected too much. Since technologies are usually patented abroad, firms and individuals in China can obtain the relevant information from the patent documents disclosed in those other countries.

However, this does not mean that foreign inventors will decline to seek patent protection in China. Since the information contained in foreign patent applications is available elsewhere and to others, if an inventor does not obtain a patent in China, someone else could do so and exclude the inventor from the market. If no one obtains a patent, rents that might have been available will be dissipated because the technology will be used on a royalty-free basis.

Some might suggest that restricting the market power of patents in developing or technology-importing countries could lead to static gains locally—consumers would get something for nothing, or for very little—while the dynamic loss from discouraging innovation or less information disclosure would likely be small. It might seem to follow then that China would benefit from a strategy that provided relatively little protection to IP and that adopted lenient rules that would require more compulsory licensing of powerful IP.

While we can understand this so-called developing country argument, we believe it to be short-sighted and incomplete. First, the profile of the patent grant is changing in China. While until recently, IPRs for most core technologies were owned by foreign companies or individuals, this situation is changing as China becomes more economically developed. Indeed, from 1998 to 2008, more than 50 per cent of invention patents were granted to non-residents each year, with the proportion peaking at 72.67 per cent in 2002. Since then, however, it has decreased for six consecutive years, falling to 50.28 per cent in 2008. Given the trend of China's economic growth and the national strategy to develop an innovation-oriented country, the proportion of patents granted to non-residents is likely to decline further in the future. In fact, while one must be cautious in interpreting the relevant statistics, Table 2 shows that patents granted to residents already constitute a significant part of the total in China: it is still lower than in Japan, France, Germany and Korea, but higher than in the United States and Canada. Under such circumstances the disincentive effect will certainly loom larger in the years to come, a fact that poses a strong challenge to the standard developing country argument.

Table 2: Patents Granted to Non-Residents by Office in 2007 (%)

Japan	15.85
France	13.95
Germany	21.54
Republic of Korea	25.38
Russian Federation	30.26
United Kingdom	30.50
China	37.57
United States of America	47.09
New Zealand	75.88
Norway	81.62
Thailand	36.82
Canada	87.55
Australia	90.06
Singapore	93.01
Mexico	96.21
Hong Kong (SAR), China	98.84

Source: World Patent Report: a Statistical Review 2008, WIPO Statistics Database.

Second, a parochial approach to IPRs might diminish the long-run attractiveness of China for FDI. In 2007, for example, China received 74.8 billion dollars of FDI,[28] making it the largest recipient of FDI worldwide. This fact may suggest that China has already installed a pro-innovation legal framework for IP protection which has contributed to China's attractiveness to incoming foreign investments and technology transfers. However, for those who may wonder about the Chinese Government's enforcement intentions with regard to IPRs, this high level of investment may make it seem that the strength of IP protection is irrelevant to FDI inflow. In fact, strong IPRs alone are not sufficient incentives for firms to invest in a foreign country. They are only one component of a larger regulatory system, which includes tax laws, investment regulations, production incentives, trade policies, and competition rules. However, since weaker protection of IP and the threat of compulsory licensing tend to lower the expected returns of foreign investments, they could well affect FDI in the long run.

Third, adverse selection effects might cause firms with dominant core technologies either to leave China or to refrain from entering. If a foreign firm with dominant technology expects that its IP may be declared an essential facility and made subject to compulsory licensing, it might well choose to avoid China's market because it would not expect to realise a fair return on investment. Under this circumstance, foreign capital with high technological content would not flow to China, leaving China with only low technical FDI. This result would defeat the main incentive behind efforts to attract FDI, and harm technical progress in China.

Finally, independent innovation might be suppressed. The developing country argument builds upon the assumption that patents owned by non-residents are disproportionately numerous and more valuable. However, independent innovation is very important for China as a means of upgrading industries and enhancing its international competitiveness. One could argue that independent (home-grown) innovation is too demanding in terms of funding requirements and technological support. Since China still has a relatively weak technological sector, it can afford only a relatively low level of R&D investment.[29] Thus, some might argue, China should not engage much in independent innovations. However, independent innovations include, more generally, not only original inventions but also integrated innovations, combination innovations, improvement innovations, and in-draught assimilation innovations. Indeed, until recently China has adopted the low-risk bearing innovation strategy of promoting integrated innovations and in-draught assimilation innovations based upon innovations embodied in FDI. In light of this, since FDI would be discouraged by weak IP protection and unwarranted compulsory licensing, independent innovation would be suppressed.

B. Enforcement Capability

Even if economic conditions warrant compulsory licensing due to IP restraints on competition, China needs to take serious account of its enforcement capacity as the already

[28] *China Statistic Yearbook 2008* (National Statistic Bureau, China Statistic Press).

[29] For example, China's R&D investments in 2006 are 50.1 billion dollars which are 0.96% of gross domestic product (GDP). In contrast, the US, Japan, and Korean's R&D investments are 285, 131.7, and 22.4 billion dollars and 2.52%, 3.28%, and 2.17% of GDP, respectively.

complex economic trade-offs are complicated further by enforcement issues. In fact, weak enforcement capacity may counsel in favour of a policy of less compulsory licensing.

First, the legal rules regulating compulsory licensing are inadequate. As discussed earlier, the criteria in the current statutory rules in regard to compulsory licensing as a remedy for anti-competitive conduct are incomplete. Since China follows the statutory law tradition, clear and comprehensive rules are essential to guide and facilitate the enforcement agencies in establishing a prima facie case and place the burden of proof efficiently. Furthermore, confusion and inconsistencies plague China's current competition laws on compulsory licensing. The Chinese Government clearly needs to publish regulations and guidelines to address these issues.

Second, the jurisprudence and capability of economic analysis are still being developed. While we have argued that economics has limits in dealing with the long-term effects of compulsory licensing of IP, we do not mean to suggest that economic analysis has no place in such cases. Among other things, our argument suggests that sound decision-making in the area of compulsory licensing is difficult and complex, and necessarily forces competition agencies to exercise regulatory functions. In fact, as decisions governing compulsory licensing are based on the rule of reason, economic analysis is indispensable to the decision-making process. However, economic analysis has come to anti-competition cases only recently in China; and, as experience in the United States and European Union demonstrates, it takes a long time and lots of resources to develop.

Finally, there are problems in the allocation of enforcement responsibilities. One obvious problem is that too many government agencies have jurisdiction over competition policy in IP, particularly as to compulsory licensing. As discussed before, there are potential overlapping and conflicting jurisdictions between the IP administration and competition agencies, and between the competition agencies themselves. Indeed, the existence of overlapping and conflicting jurisdiction, coupled with a lack of clarity as to the particular responsibilities of relevant administrative agencies, is often an institutional problem in China that hinders the efficiency and effectiveness of law enforcement.

Another governance problem is the absence of institutions that might ensure independence of decision making on issues pertaining to the compulsory licensing of IP. As we have argued, compulsory licensing of IP is a complex and subtle issue not only because there are complicated economic trade-offs to make but also because other, non-economic factors might influence the decision making process. Under such circumstances, good governance is especially necessary to ensure commitment to independent decision making.

IX. Conclusions and Recommendations

The question of whether and on what terms to require dominant firms to license their powerful IP to rivals lies at the centre of the intersection between antitrust and IP law. Not only is it extremely important, but it is also unanswerable, that is, beyond the competence of economics to answer. It is one of those few but crucial problems that seem intractable to economic analysis, and whose solution therefore requires antitrust enforcers to draw on local history, politics and culture. If this prospect is unsettling, because it is indeterminate and relative, it is nevertheless unavoidable (which may also be unsettling), since no better method for solving these problems exists.

Most of the problems arising in competition law can best be solved using accepted methods of economic analysis. For most countries, in the large majority of cases, and for the vast majority of businesses, a competition law regime driven mainly by political principles and concerns would be confusing and inconstant, and could thus deter more competition than it protected. Newer competition law regimes should be encouraged to use all of the economic tools available to the more experienced regulators. However, as to some issues—again, those discussed here, in which economics lacks explanatory power—developed competition law regimes seem to lack an objective basis for arguing that the history and politics of their own countries or regions should serve as the universal or international standard. As to those issues, newer regimes should presumably be largely free to develop their own answers on their own terms, but with reference to and regard for the approaches of more experienced and developed systems.

There are limits to economics, even in a field as heavily and beneficially influenced by that discipline as competition law. Even after three decades of growing influence, during which economics has reshaped and refined competition law in the United States and Europe, some of the law's most important problems—compulsory licensing among them—remain resistant to economic analysis. For those problems, politics and history—messy, individuated, idiosyncratic, and un-scientific—are the answers of last resort. However, they have limits as well: no one answer fits all countries; different legal systems cannot completely converge; the respective values of older systems and newer ones might conflict; and many inventing companies have invested large sums in research in reliance on the legal protections afforded them by their national competition law regimes.

In China's context, since compulsory licensing of IP is so complicated and subtle an issue, it may be too soon to recommend any specific approach. Certainly, more discussion and research are needed. However, certain preliminary steps should be taken. First, the Chinese authorities regulating issues involving IP and competition law should issue specific regulations and guidelines to clarify the meaning and likely application of the legal rules guiding law enforcement. Second, the administration of law enforcement should be improved to facilitate the coordination of enforcement agencies, avoid conflicts between them, and ensure their independent decision making on compulsory licensing. Finally, efforts on capacity-building in law enforcement should be stressed.

7

India

VINOD DHALL AND AUGUSTINE PETER

I. Introduction

India is a developing country, but with a long tradition of scientific inquiry. There was, however, consistent decline in India's economic and scientific prowess during the eighteenth and nineteenth centuries and continuing into the first half of the twentieth century until the country gained independence and started a new run on the path of economic and scientific development. The economic policies immediately after independence were aimed at 'capsuling' generations of lost growth into a few decades. The economic and technological policies visualised by independent India were aimed at making the country self reliant through an import substituting strategy, with the State (public sector) given the responsibility to build and control the 'commanding heights' of the economy. Intellectual property (IP) laws inherited from the colonial past were not found to be suited to national interests and were either amended or repealed and substituted by new laws enacted to complement the self reliance and import substituting objectives. Import, in general, and import of technology in particular, was restricted to the bare essentials. However, as time passed, especially by the end of 1970s, it was realised that countries that were at similar stages of development as India in the early 1960s had achieved much faster growth and export capability through an export oriented strategy. This prompted a shift in India as well in the 1980s towards relaxing the restrictions on industry, investment and trade. In 1980s the reform was essentially limited to deregulation of procedures. This was followed in 1991 by comprehensive liberalisation of the economy, which included opening up to foreign investment and technology transfer as well.

While the IP laws pre-dated India's independence, the anti-monopoly law was only enacted in 1970. The Patents Act 1970 and other IP laws supplemented the broader economic policy framework to make it a coherent one. The first anti-monopoly law, the Monopolies and Restrictive Trade Practices Act (MRTP) 1969 reflected India's abhorrence of monopolies and large business empires and had a structuralist approach; but over time it was seen to obstruct growth. A modern competition law was enacted in India only in 2003 and was made enforceable (except the provisions relating to combinations) in May 2009. Since the implementation of the competition law is at an early stage and since final decision in no case has yet been issued by the Competition Commission of India (CCI), there has been no instance of formal interface as yet between the competition law and IP laws. Therefore, periodical reference would also be made to the erstwhile MRTP Act and the jurisprudence that went with it.

This chapter is organised as follows: the first part is the Introduction. The second part touches on the industrial and technology policies pursued by the Government since independence. The third part analyses the IP laws and competition law in the country. The fourth part looks at the interface between competition law/policies and IP laws/policies. The chapter ends with concluding remarks and suggestions relating to better management of the interface between the competition law and the IP laws.

II. The Industrial and Technology Policies of India

The dynamics of Indian economic development in recent years cannot be appreciated without reference to her colonial past, characterised by resource drain and very low rates of growth in gross domestic product (GDP), and the period of planned economic development that followed independence in 1947. Post independence, economic planning was primarily aimed at building a foundation on which India could build a self reliant economy with stress on growth and distribution. The early years concentrated on creating the necessary industrial infrastructure to facilitate future growth. The developmental efforts were however interrupted thrice by wars, with China in 1962, and with Pakistan in 1965 and again in 1971.

Three distinct phases may be viewed in India's economic development after independence:

(1) the initial socialist period with state control of the 'commanding heights' of the economy: 1950–51 to 1980–81;
(2) the period of domestic economic de-regulation: 1981–82 to 1990–91; and
(3) the period of liberalisation: 1991 onwards.

A. Phase I: The Socialist Phase

Although the development process only started with the launch of the first Five Year Plan in 1951, the Industrial Policy Resolution of 1948 had already envisaged a mixed economy for the country; it visualised four categories of industries viz:

(i) state monopolies (defence, atomic energy, railway);
(ii) mixed sectors (aircraft, ship building, telecom equipment, mineral oil, coal, iron);
(iii) industries subject to controls (18 sectors); and
(iv) sectors generally open to private enterprise.

The approach was formalised in 1952, with the Industries (Development and Regulation) Act of 1952 which further entrenched the role of the State and the public sector, as well as the mixed sectors. The State monopoly sectors were increased from six to 17, and the mixed sectors from six to 12. The strategy was two pronged: first, to maintain government control over the economy and second, through the first, to promote import substitution and self reliance. The Import Control Order (1955) and the Industrial Policy Resolution of 1956 reiterated and re-enforced this economic philosophy. Stiff labour protection laws were enacted, which in later years were found difficult to be rolled back, and became a stumbling block in the reform process. State presence in the economy was further enhanced through nationalisation of several enterprises and reservation of sectors/products for the public sector and small scale sector. The MRTP Act 1969 and the Patents Act 1970 were enacted as part of these policies.

While the economic growth during the initial years of planned development was certainly superior to that in the colonial days (1.5 per cent), the rate of 3.5 per cent, also known as the Hindu rate of growth, fell short of the growth performance of medium and large economies internationally. India ranked 60th in the global growth ranking of 74 large and medium countries for which GDP figures were available for 1960 onwards. Only 19 per cent of these countries had a worse growth performance.[1] As the restrictive regime tightened its grip, the growth rate fell to an average of 2.9 per cent per annum, well below the rate of around 3.5 per cent during the period 1950–51 to 1965–66. In global growth ranking, India fell to the bottom 15 per cent at 64th position out of a set of 74 countries for which data is available.[2]

B. Phase II: De-Regulation, 1980–81 to 1990–91

Starting around 1980, the policy witnessed a gradual and subtle shift from the import substitution to a more liberal regime through de-regulation of domestic economic policies and processes. These reforms were limited to internal deregulation and there were differences of opinion as to whether these could at all be termed as reforms. However, the de-regulation resulted in a structural break in the Indian economy, as pointed out by Ahluwalia,[3] Ray,[4] and Virmani,[5] among others. Several intellectuals and economists like Bhagwati and Desai[6] and Ahluwalia[7] have tried to explain the causes of industrial stagnation in India in terms of the policies then pursued, including doubts about the effectiveness of the import substituting approach.

The de-regulation measures included 'broad-banding' of the products that a firm could produce based on the license obtained, enabling it to reap economies of scale and scope, specifying minimum economies of scale (MES), expansion of the positive list of MRTP exempt industries, and raising of the investment thresholds (above which a licence was required even for industries in the positive list); raising of investment thresholds for the purpose of monopoly control; and revision of investment limit for the small scale sector. Reforms in corporate and personal income tax were also initiated during this period. The import policy witnessed slow but steady transition with products under open general license (OGL) increasing progressively from 76 items in 1979 to 1939 items in April 1990. The shift from the import substituting strategy to an export neutral regime was subtle and without much fanfare. This phase was transitory, but it prepared the economy for the comprehensive liberalisation that was to come in 1991.

[1] Arvind Virmani, *The Dynamics of Competition: Phasing of Domestic and External Liberalization in India*, Working Paper No 4/2006-PC (Planning Commission, Government of India, 2006).

[2] Ibid.

[3] IJ Alhluwalia, *Productivity and Growth in Indian Manufacturing* (Delhi, Oxford University Press, 1991).

[4] Amit Shoon Ray, *Emerging Through Technological Capability: An Overview of India's Technological Trajectory*, Working Paper No 227 (New Delhi, ICRIER, 2008).

[5] Virmani, *The Dynamics of Competition* (2006).

[6] J Bhagwati and P Desai, *India: Planning for Industrialisation* (London, Oxford University Press, 1970).

[7] IJ Ahluwalia, *Industrial Growth in India* (New Delhi, Oxford University Press, 1985).

C. Phase III: Liberalisation from 1991

The economic reforms from 1991 were comprehensive and 'big bang', unlike the 'reform-by-stealth' of the 1980s. These reforms included liberalisation of industrial, trade, investment, technology, exchange rate, fiscal, monetary and capital market policies. Industrial licensing was abolished except in a select set of industries. Regulatory structures in place were either abolished altogether (eg, the Controller of Capital Issues, who determined the quantum and issue price of shares issued by companies, and the Directorate General of Technical Development, responsible for technology transfer policy), or overhauled (eg, the Chief Controller of Imports and Exports was transformed into the Directorate General of Foreign Trade). The new capital market regulator, the Securities and Exchange Board of India (SEBI), was established through the SEBI Act. The MRTP Act 1969 was drastically amended, with the asset ceiling for treatment as monopoly undertaking being removed altogether, and the provisions related to mergers being taken off the statute. The process of pruning of the small scale reservation list was accelerated. Tariffs were brought down even more steeply than was warranted by India's commitments under the Uruguay Round. Liberalisation of the foreign investment regime included raising of the foreign investment limit from generally 40 per cent to over 50 per cent, and even to 100 per cent in select sectors. Foreign direct investment approval procedures were liberalised with the automatic approval process put in place for many sectors. Foreign investment was largely de-linked from foreign technology transfer. The Foreign Exchange Regulation Act (FERA) 1974 was substituted by the much less restrictive Foreign Exchange Management Act (FEMA). The capital market was opened up to Foreign Institutional Investors. Interest rates were de-regulated. Privatisation of public sector undertakings in a selective manner was also initiated. Private enterprise and initiative began to receive greater recognition.

III. Evolution of the Technology Policies

Even though a formal technology policy in the form of a Scientific Policy Resolution came out only in 1958, efforts to build India into a technologically advanced nation were discernable since the beginning of the planning process in 1951. The Industrial Policy Statement of 1980, which focused attention on promoting competition in the domestic market, also recognised the need for technological upgrading and modernisation; thus foreign investment and technology transfer received special attention. Efficiency and productivity became important objectives. Although productivity was not high by international standards, by the mid 1980s India had a large network of basic industries, with different degrees of self-reliance in a large number of products. Besides, the country also witnessed the emergence of new industrial centres and a new generation of entrepreneurs. The number of skilled manpower also registered substantial increase.

The Technology Policy Statement of 1983 made a clear statement of its basic objective: 'the development of indigenous technology and efficient absorption and adaptation of imported technology appropriate to national priorities and resources'.[8] The effort was to achieve breakthroughs in indigenous technological development. Considerable resources were allocated

[8] Technology Policy Statement of 1983, Government of India.

for this purpose. The new Science and Technology Policy 2003 complemented the liberalised economic policies. The policy differentiated between fundamental research and development (R&D) and commercial R&D. The private sector was encouraged to create Scientific and Industrial Research Organisations (SIRO) for undertaking more fundamental R&D in a non-commercial manner. The emphasis shifted from indigenisation to productivity.

Table 1 below gives the highlights of policy liberalisation having implications for technology development.

R&D expenditure as a share of GNP is considered an indicator of efforts at innovation. R&D expenditure in India, as a share of gross national product (GNP), rose consistently from 0.17 per cent in 1958–59 to 0.91 per cent in 1988–89, the major share of which was borne by the Government.[9] However, the immediate post reform period witnessed a declining trend in this regard, with the share falling to a level of 0.71 per cent in 1995–96 and then rising marginally to 0.80 per cent.[10] This could probably be explained by the fact that imports of disembodied technology emerged as the most preferred mode of technology acquisition for Indian manufacturing during 1991–2001.[11] Pradhan and Puttaswamaiah[12] note that on account of the policy initiatives there has been a perceptible decline in the average import coverage ratio for capital goods from 77 per cent in 1986–90 to 21 per cent in 1991–95 and further to eight per cent in 1996–2000. The average effective rate of protection (ERP) fell steeply to 33 per cent in 1996 from 79 per cent in 1980–90.[13]

Table 1: Post 1991 Liberalisation: Highlights

- Technology import through foreign direct investment (FDI) freely allowed in all sectors except a small negative list based on environmental, scale economies and security reasons.
- Automatic approval for foreign investment subject to certain ceilings.
  Foreign technological collaboration of up to US$2 million allowed the automatic approval route in all industries if royalty payment was limited to eight per cent on sales.
- Royalty payment allowed up to 10 years from the date of agreement or seven years from the date of commercial production, whichever is earlier.
- In the case of foreign financial collaboration (without technology transfer), royalty payment of up to two per cent for exports and one per cent for domestic sales on use of trademarks and brand name under automatic route permitted.
- The wholly owned subsidiaries (WOS) permitted under automatic route to make royalty payment up to eight per cent on exports and five per cent on domestic sales to their parent companies without any restrictions on the duration of royalty payment.
- Quantitative restrictions on capital imports removed (2001), facilitating embodied technology import.
- Import of second hand capital goods permitted provided they have a minimum residual life of five years.

[9] Even as late as 1998–99, 75.5% of the national R&D expenditure in India was borne by the Government (Ray, 'R&D and Technological Learning in Indian Industry' (2008)).

[10] R&D Statistics, Department of Science & Technology, Government of India, various issues.

[11] Jaya Prakash Pradhan and S Puttaswamaiah, *Trends and Patterns of Technology Acquisition in Indian Organized Manufacturing: An Inter-industry Exploration*, Working Paper No 157 (Gujarat Institute of Development Research Gota, Ahmedabad, 2005).

[12] Ibid.

[13] DK Das, '*Quantifying Trade Barriers: Has Protection Declined Substantially in Indian Manufacturing*', ICRIER Working Paper No 105 (New Delhi, 2003).

The National Science Foundation's Report[14] on Asia's rising science and technology strength noted that substantial differences in R&D-to-GDP ratios exist among the five major Asian economies. In 2003, Japan and South Korea had the highest values: 3.15 and 2.63 respectively. The ratios were lower in Taiwan (2.45) and Singapore (2.13). China's ratio showed the sharpest increase since 1995, closely followed by Singapore's, and showed further growth in 2004, to 1.23. The Report did not give corresponding figures for India, due to data inadequacies, although the figures available (which may not be strictly comparable) indicate that the ratio is below one per cent. Even within this low share, the contribution of central and state government laboratories and industrial R&D in public sector enterprises in India is as high as four-fifths of the total, with the private sector contributing only 20 per cent.[15] On the other hand, the corresponding share of the private sector in the East Asian countries, even in the early 1990s, was much higher: eg Singapore (60 per cent in 1992), Korea (around 80 per cent in 1992) and Taiwan (50 per cent in 1993).

High-technology manufacturing exports provide an indication of a country's ability to produce technologically sophisticated goods that can compete in the international market.[16] As per the compilation of the NSF Report, while the high-technology exports worldwide grew from $474 billion in 1990 to $1.9 trillion in 2003, exports by Asia's high-technology manufacturing industries grew especially rapidly since 1990, contributing to the region's strong economic performance. In 2003, Asia accounted for 43 per cent of world high-technology exports, up from 33 per cent in 1990. In 2001, China displaced Japan as Asia's leading exporter of such goods. The growth in Asia's share of world activity during the 1990s was also driven by increased exports from Singapore, South Korea, and Taiwan. Among Asian economies, China's success as a high-technology exporter is the most prominent. In 2003, China accounted for 12 per cent of world high-technology exports, up from five per cent in 1990. Singapore was third at six per cent in 2003. South Korea and Taiwan each had about five per cent. India's position was not indicated by the NSF 2007 Report.

It is expected that India's position is much behind the above mentioned five Asian countries. This could probably be explained by the following factors:

(a) The R&D efforts in India have been largely in the public sector, whose productivity is generally lower compared to that of the private sector; the effect on competitiveness, especially at the international level, was therefore not commensurate with the R&D efforts.

(b) The concentration of the R&D efforts during this period was largely on self reliance, and not on frontier technologies. International competitiveness was not one of the motives.

(c) The policy restrictions inhibited the flow of the best technologies into the country or of their whole-hearted transfer; this resulted in poor and inadequate absorption. Naturally their impact on exports was also negligible. This observation underlines the need for continuous incentivising of innovation in industry.

[14] The National Science Foundation (NCF), 'Asia's Rising Science and Technology Strength: Comparative Indicators for Asia, the European Union and the United States', Special Report (NSF, August, 2007) ('NCF 2007 Report').

[15] R&D Statistics 2004–05, Department of Science & Technology, Government of India.

[16] NCF 2007 Report.

Ray,[17] in an interesting observation, contends that the technological trajectory of the Indian Electronics and Electricals sector was oriented towards high total factor productivity (based on *know-how* capabilities), with little emphasis on acquisition of adaptive and designing (*know-why*) capabilities and, therefore, IP policy had perhaps a little role to play in this regard. The pharmaceutical industry, on the other hand, focused on building up of *know-why* oriented technological capability, even at the cost of immediate productivity gains in the short or medium terms. In the case of pharmaceutical industries, the IP regime did matter. He concludes that the process revolution in the Indian pharmaceutical industry reflecting significant learning and technological catch up can be largely attributed to the Patents Act of 1970 allowing only process (and not product) patents for pharmaceutical substances.

IV. Evolution of Competition Law and Intellectual Evolution of Competition and IP Laws

Competition law and IP laws both seek to promote economic advancement, innovation and technological progress and consumer welfare; in this sense the two laws complement each other, even though there might be apparent conflict between them. However, these common goals are pursued by each through different instruments: IP laws grant the exclusive legal right to the exploitation of an innovation for a limited period of time, while competition law seeks to remove impediments to the efficient functioning of markets. In the long term, the benefits from the two laws converge. In the nearer term, a balance needs to be struck between the two instruments, in order to ensure that both laws can play their complementary roles in incentivising innovation and economic growth. The balancing of the two laws needs an understanding that an IP is comparable to any other property, and that possessing an IP does not automatically confer market power. However, in certain circumstances, an intellectual property right (IPR) could be exercised in a manner that could be anti-competitive. In such cases, it becomes necessary to establish as to when the exercise of an IPR ceases to be legitimate and violates the principles of competition law.

A. Evolution of Competition Law in India

The Monopolies and Restrictive Trade Practices (MRTP) Act 1969 was the first competition related legislation in India. The Act drew inspiration from the mandate enshrined in the Directive Principles of State Policy in the Constitution of India that mandates the State to: prevent the concentration of economic wealth and means of production and to ensure equitable distribution of the material resources of the country. The Mahalanobis Committee on Distribution of Incomes and Levels of Living had in its report in 1960 highlighted the growing income inequality in India after independence. Following this, the Monopolies Inquiry Committee (MIC) was appointed by the Government to

[17] Ray (n 4).

inquire into the extent and effect of concentration of economic power in private hands. The MIC was also to suggest legislative and other measures to protect essential public interest and mechanisms for enforcement of the legislation. The MIC found that there were adverse social effects of economic concentration and the government policies were one of the contributing factors of economic concentration. The MIC inter alia recommended:

— An autonomous Commission headed by a judge to implement an anti-monopoly law.
— All proposals for expansion by dominant enterprises to be approved by the proposed Commission.
— IPRs to be under the purview of the proposed law.

The focus of the MRTP Act was, therefore, more on the control of monopolies and the prohibition of monopolistic and restrictive trade practices—it was a product of the regime of licensing and controls.[18]

After the working of the MRTP Act for over six years, in 1977, a High Powered Expert Committee (Sachar Committee) was set up, inter alia, to consider and report changes necessary in the MRTP Act. In pursuance of the Sachar Committee's report, two important amendments were carried out in the MRTP Act in 1984: (1) unfair trade practices (UTPs) were brought within the purview of the Monopolies and Restrictive Trade Practices Commission (MRTPC). These included misleading advertisement and false representation; bargain sale, bait and switch selling; offering of gifts or prizes with the intention of not providing them and conducting promotional contests; and hoarding and destruction of goods. (2) Several restrictive trade practices (RTPs) were deemed to be anti-competitive and required to be registered, and the burden of proving that these RTPs were eligible for the 'gateways' of exemption was placed on the defendant; these RTPs included, for example, cartels, exclusive supply and exclusive distribution, tying, resale price maintenance, and predatory pricing.

When comprehensive liberalisation was undertaken in the early nineties, one of the first measures was to amend the MRTP Act by removing the restrictions placed on the growth of large companies, as well as the requirement of prior approval of the Government for expansion of monopolistic/dominant undertakings. Also, public sector undertakings were brought under the purview of the Act.

However, as the reform process progressed, it was realised that the MRTP Act was not in tune with the new market-oriented environment, and a new competition law was needed to maintain and sustain competition in the markets where the Government's role had now been withdrawn. The Government set up a High Level Committee on Competition Policy and Law in 1999 (the Raghavan Committee). This Committee observed that the MRTP Act fell short of addressing competition issues and that the law would be ineffective in an era of globalisation and liberalisation. The Committee found it more expedient to have a new competition law altogether. The Government accepted the Raghavan Committee's recommendation leading to the enactment of the Competition Act 2002.

Like most modern competition laws, the Competition Act 2002 addresses the following competition issues:

[18] S Gopalakrishnan, 'Competition Law: An Analytical Perspective' (September 2008) *Chartered Secretary*. Available at www.icsi.edu.com.

i. Anti-Competitive Agreements

Section 3[19] of the Competition Act 2002 recognises an anti-competitive agreement as an arrangement or understanding between businesses which has or is likely to have an appreciable adverse effect on competition in Indian markets. It deals severely with hard core horizontal agreements which are presumed to be anti-competitive, while all other agreements are to be analysed under the rule of reason. From the perspective of this chapter, notably, the Act exempts from the provisions of section 3 any reasonable restriction for protecting an IPR.

ii. Abuse of Dominance

Unlike the MRTP ACT, the Competition Act has no problem with mere possession or acquisition of dominance, but it has strict provisions against the abuse of dominance (section 4[20]). A dominant position[21] has been defined similar to the EU definition as a position of strength enjoyed by an enterprise in a relevant market in India, which enables it to operate independently of competitive forces prevailing in that market. Dominance has to

[19] 3. Anti-competitive agreements.-

(1) No enterprise or association of enterprises or person or association of persons shall enter into any agreement in respect of production, supply, distribution, storage, acquisition or control of goods or provision of services, which causes or is likely to cause an appreciable adverse effect on competition within India.

(2) Any agreement entered into in contravention of the provisions contained in sub-section (1) shall be void.

(3) Any agreement entered into between enterprises or associations of enterprises or persons or associations of persons or between any person and enterprise or practice carried on, or decision taken by, any association of enterprises or association of persons, including cartels, engaged in identical or similar trade of goods or provision of services, which-

(a) directly or indirectly determines purchase or sale prices;

(b) limits or controls production, supply, markets, technical development, investment or provision of services;

(c) shares the market or source of production or provision of services by way of allocation of geographical area of market, or type of goods or services, or number of customers in the market or any other similar way;

(d) directly or indirectly results in bid rigging or collusive bidding, shall be presumed to have an appreciable adverse effect on competition:

Provided that nothing contained in this sub-section shall apply to any agreement entered into by way of joint ventures if such agreement increases efficiency in production, supply, distribution, storage, acquisition or control of goods or provision of services. Explanation.-For the purposes of this sub-section, 'bid rigging' means any agreement, between enterprises or persons referred to in sub-section (3) engaged in identical or similar production or trading of goods or provision of services, which has the effect of eliminating or reducing competition for bids or adversely affecting or manipulating the process for bidding.

[20] 4. Abuse of dominant position.- (1) No enterprise shall abuse its dominant position.

(2) There shall be an abuse of dominant position under sub-section (1), if an enterprise,-

(a) directly or indirectly, imposes unfair or discriminatory-

(i) condition in purchase or sale of goods or service; or

(ii) price in purchase or sale (including predatory price) of goods or service.

Explanation.-For the purposes of this clause, the unfair or discriminatory condition in purchase or sale of goods or service referred to in sub-clause (i) and unfair or discriminatory price in purchase or sale of goods (including predatory price) or service referred to in sub-clause (ii) shall not include such discriminatory condition or price which may be adopted to meet the competition; or

(b) limits or restricts-

(i) production of goods or provision of services or market therefore; or

(ii) technical or scientific development relating to goods or services to the prejudice of consumers; or

(c) indulges in practice or practices resulting in denial of market access; or

(d) makes conclusion of contracts subject to acceptance by other parties of supplementary obligations which, by their nature or according to commercial usage, have no connection with the subject of such contracts; or

(e) uses its dominant position in one relevant market to enter into, or protect, other relevant market.

[21] Competition Act 2002 s 4 [Explanation (a)].

be determined based on the set of factors specified in the Act.[22] The Act lists the abuses of dominance, and once a dominant enterprise indulges in any of the listed practices, it would amount to abuse of dominance. Although there is no mention of an effects analysis in section 4, an effects analysis could be read into the formulation of some of the abuses.

iii. Regulation of Combinations

The Competition Act 2002 seeks to regulate large mergers above the given thresholds, called combinations, which includes mergers, amalgamations and acquisitions (sections 5 and 6). It prescribes a compulsory notification regime, and the enterprises are required not to complete the merger until the CCI decides the matter. The CCI can approve, reject, or modify the merger. The CCI's assessment of the anti-competitive effects of the merger is to be based on the factors listed in the Act. The thresholds are prescribed in terms of assets and turnover of the combined entity, and there are separate thresholds for the domestic nexus (in India) of the combined entity.

iv. Competition Advocacy

The Competition Act 2002 mandates the CCI to undertake competition advocacy by creating awareness and imparting training in competition issues. It also provides that the Government may refer any policy on competition to the CCI for its opinion, although the opinion is not binding on the Government. Competition advocacy[23] would encompass non-enforcement activities which are geared towards promoting a competition culture and achieving competition neutrality across the economy, mainly through interaction with government departments and agencies and sector regulators and by increasing public awareness of the benefits of competition.

Although the Competition Act was enacted in January 2003, and the CCI was set up in October 2003, the CCI could not commence enforcement due to certain constitutional challenges to the validity of the Competition Act followed by a lengthy process of amendments to the Act. Meanwhile, the CCI undertook extensive competition advocacy, and other preparatory measures for the eventual enforcement of the Act, which commenced finally in May 2009, but without the merger regulation provisions. Merger regulation was brought into force with effect from 1 June 2011.

B. Evolution of IP Laws in India

Most IP legislations in India have colonial origins and their subsequent versions have partaken generously from their English counterparts. However, subsequent to India becoming a member of the Agreement on Trade Related Aspects of Intellectual Property Rights (TRIPS), Paris and Berne Conventions, IP legislations have reflected the minimum uniform standards expected of member countries under these international treaties. The development of various forms of IP under these legislations in India is briefly described below.

[22] Ibid s 19 (4).
[23] Ibid s 49.

i. Patents

A patent is a negative territorial right granted to a person in return for disclosing a new, non-obvious product or a process which is capable of industrial application. Such a product or process is considered an invention. The current legislation for patents in India, the Patents Act 1970, was preceded by the Patents and Designs Act 1911, which for all practical purposes replicated the provisions of the 1907 Act of the United Kingdom.[24] In 1948, a Committee under Dr Bakshi Tek Chand, a retired Judge of the High Court of Lahore, was appointed to review the status of patent laws in India, with a view to ensuring that the system of patents was made more responsive to Indian interests. The Committee submitted its report in 1950 observing thus:

> The Indian Patents System has failed in its main purpose, namely, to stimulate inventions among Indians and to encourage the development and exploitation of new inventions for industrial purposes in the country so as to secure the benefits thereof to the largest section of the public.

A Bill based on the recommendations of this Committee was introduced in the Parliament in 1953, but it lapsed due to the dissolution of the lower house of the Parliament, the Lok Sabha. Following this, Rajagopala Ayyangar J was appointed in April 1957 as a one-man Committee to advise on revision of the law relating to patents and designs. The following were his primary recommendations:

1. For drugs, pharmaceuticals and chemicals, only process patents should be given.
2. Provisions relating to compulsory licensing should be widened.
3. Public health concerns should be given high consideration.

The Ayyangar Committee recommendations led to the enactment of the Patents Act 1970.

In light of economic liberalisation from 1991, and with India joining the World Trade Organisation (WTO) on 1 January 1995 which included TRIPS, a few significant changes were necessary, and this gave rise to three amendments in the Patents Act 1970, in the years 1999, 2002 and 2005, each of whose purpose was to fulfil India's obligations under TRIPS.

The Patents (Amendment) Act 1999 introduced a transitional facility to receive and hold product patent applications for pharmaceutical and agricultural chemical products until 1 January 2005.[25] This facility was incorporated because India had sought time until 2005 to introduce its product patent regime. Until such time, the application would be granted 'Exclusive Marketing Rights' (EMRs) for five years or until the grant of patent or rejection of the application, whichever was earlier.

One of the significant changes introduced under the Patents (Amendment) Act 2002 was to extend the term of the patent from 14 years from the date of grant to 20 years from the date of filing of the application. In addition, compulsory licensing provisions were amended to convey to patentees that mere importation of the patented invention into India would not amount to working of the invention. Manufacture within the territory of India would be primarily deemed as working, in the absence of which the compulsory licensing mechanism could be set in motion. Further, this mechanism could be triggered if it is established that a patent impedes protection to public health and nutrition or if a patented invention is not made available to the public at reasonably affordable prices.

[24] Under the Patents and Designs Act 1911, the expression 'exclusive privileges' was substituted with 'patent'.
[25] Popularly known as 'Mailbox Applications'.

The Patents (Amendment) Act 2005 finally re-introduced the product patent regime for pharmaceutical substances and agricultural products and the concept of EMRs was completely done away with. Further, the Intellectual Property Appellate Board was set up as the first appellate forum for appeals from decisions of the Controller of Patents and for institution of proceedings for revocation of a patent.

In the last half a decade, judicial guidance on certain critical aspects of patent law has increasingly contributed to increased levels of IP awareness. Further, this has translated into the evolution of indigenous IP jurisprudence which considers conditions peculiar to India.

ii. Copyrights

The premise underlying the law of copyright is the same as patents—it gives authors/creators an incentive to create and protect the product of their efforts. Copyright is a bundle of rights which entitles the holder to the right to adapt, distribute, and reproduce and a host of other rights. Unlike patents, copyright law recognises neighbouring rights such as the rights of the performing artist (such as actors, musicians and singers, etc) and the rights of broadcasting organisations.

India's first copyright legislation was the Copyright Act of 1914 (1914 Act), which substantially resembled the United Kingdom's copyright law of 1911. This law was repealed and replaced by the Copyright Act of 1957. The 1957 Act was amended in the years 1983, 1984, 1994 and 1999 to accommodate the international conventions on copyright.

Subsequent to the Copyright (Amendment) Act of 1983, serious concerns were raised by the international community about rampant piracy in India, to address which, provisions to prevent and deter widespread piracy of films and records were introduced through the Copyright (Amendment) Act of 1984.

Of all the past amendments, the one in the offing, the Copyright Amendment Bill 2009 is expected to bring in a slew of changes, the most prominent being the preservation of rights of creators of the work. The proposed provision on this point prevents authors/creators from assigning away all their rights with respect to technologies/media which are either non-existent or not foreseeable at the time of assignment of the rights.

iii. Trademarks

A trademark is any sign that distinguishes the goods of a given enterprise from goods of its competitors.[26] There was no statute governing trademarks in India prior to 1940; consequently, disputes such as passing off were dealt with by applying section 54 of the Specific Relief Act 1877. However, the Specific Relief Act is not designed to address concerns arising out of misappropriation of commercial goodwill and reputation. To overcome this difficulty, the Indian Trademarks Act was passed in 1940 which was replaced by the Trade and Merchandise Marks Act 1958. This Act was to provide for registration and better protection to trademarks and for prevention of the use of fraudulent marks on merchandise. To bring trademark law in line with TRIPS, the Trade and Merchandise Marks Act 1958 was again replaced by the Trade Marks Act 1999. Besides according protection to service marks and collective marks, the 1999 Act also distinguished between well known trademarks and trademarks in general, and also provided for special treatment and rights envisaged for well known trademarks.

[26] World Intellectual Property Organisation, *Introduction to Intellectual Property—Theory and Practice* (London, Kluwer Law International, 1997).

iv. Geographical Indicators (GI)

Prior to the Indian Geographical Indications of Goods (Registration and Protection) Act 1999, there was no composite legislation to protect the interests of the producers of agricultural goods or handicrafts. The 1999 Act seeks to protect producers of such goods and prevent unauthorised users from manufacturing protected goods. The Act was promulgated pursuant to TRIPS which allowed member countries to provide for *sui generis* protection to their indigenous manufactures, but it also required member countries to recognise protection to goods coming into India from abroad if such goods were given protection in their home jurisdictions.

v. Industrial Designs

The Designs Act of 1911, modelled on the British legislation on the subject, lost its relevance as it did not address several critical aspects of designs. Following the enactment of the Industrial Designs Act 2000, protection is granted to a non-functional, ornamental and aesthetic design which appeals to the eye.

V. Interface between Competition Law and IPRs

As the enforcement of the Competition Act 2002 only commenced in May 2009, so far very few occasions have arisen to test the interface between the new competition law and the revised modern IP laws of India, and to smoothen out the contradictions, if any. Under the erstwhile MRTP Act too very little is available by way of views on IP related issues. Thus, at this point in time, we are constrained to examine the interface between the competition law and the IP laws mainly on the strength of the laws themselves.

It is noteworthy that the MRTP Act 1969 had reference only to patents and not to any other IPRs or the laws governing those rights. Section 15 of the MRTP Act specified that:

> No order made under this Act with respect to any monopolistic or restrictive trade practice shall operate so as to restrict-
>
> (a) the right of any person to restrain any infringement of a patent granted in India, or
> (b) any person as to the condition which he attaches to a license to do anything, the doing of which but for the license would be an infringement of a patent granted in India.

Despite the above provision in section 15 of the MRTP Act, no case alleging monopolistic or restrictive practices arising on the strength of a patent seems to have been decided by the MRTPC. On the other hand, there were some decisions of the MRTPC related to 'trade marks' and 'copyrights' with the focus however on UTPs, which are more akin to consumer complaints. These cases were: *Vallal Peruman v Godfrey Philips Ltd*[27] and *Manju Bhardwaj v Zee Telefilms.*[28]

In *Vallal Peruman*, the MRTPC applying the principle, followed by the European Court of Justice, held that if a certificate of registration is held by the undertaking, it has a right

[27] *Vallal Peruman v Godfrey Phillips (India) Ltd* (1995)CTJ 21 (MRTPC).
[28] *Manju Bhardwaj v Zee Telefilms Ltd* (1996) CTJ 230 (MRTPC).

to use the trademark so long as the trademark is used strictly in conformity with the terms and conditions subject to which it is granted. If, however, while presenting the goods and merchandise for sale in the market, the holder of the certificate misuses the same by manipulation, distortion, contrivances and embellishments, etc so as to mislead or confuse the customers, the holder would be exposing him or herself to an action under section 36A(1) of indulging in UTP. The provisions of the MRTP Act would be attracted only where there is an abuse in the exercise of the rights protected and granted under IP legislation. This view of the Court was reiterated in *Manju Bhardwaj*.

In *State of Andhra Pradesh v Mahyco Monsanto*,[29] the respondents were a joint venture (JV) between an Indian company and a US company which had in the year 1996 developed a bollworm insect resistant cotton seed. This JV entered into sub-license agreements with a number of seed companies with restrictive conditions. The respondents would charge a one-time fee of INR 5 million and then would charge trait value on future sales. It was argued by the applicants that there were many anti-competitive conditions which put restrictions on the licensee to assign, transfer or sub-license without the consent of the licensor. The MRTPC prima-facie found the respondents to be indulging in restrictive trade practices under section 2(o) of the Act which had the effect of preventing, distorting and restricting competition. It was also contended and proved that the respondents were charging INR 90/kg in China and for the same seed the trait value in India was INR 900 for less than half a kilogram. This was imposing unjustified costs on Indian consumers. The Commission passed a temporary injunction in the applicant's favour, restraining the respondent party from the restrictive trade practice on the grounds that it was prejudicial to public interest; the Commission directed the respondents to charge trait value as was being done in China.

Unlike the MRTP Act, the Competition Act 2002 acknowledges not only patent rights, but a range of IPRs; accordingly section 3(5) carves out an exception for the rights conferred under the following six laws:

- — The Copyright Act 1957.
- — The Patents Act 1970.
- — The Trademarks Act 1999.
- — The Geographical Indications of Goods Act 1999.
- — The Designs Act 2000.
- — The Semi-Conductor Integrated Circuits Layout-Designs Act 2000.

Section 3(5) states that nothing in section 3 shall restrict the right of any person to restrain any infringement of, or to impose reasonable conditions, as may be necessary, for protecting any of his or her rights which have been or may be conferred upon him or her under the above mentioned laws. Thus, the Act recognises the incentives that IPRs provide for creativity and innovation and consequently for economic growth, and it protects IPR holders so long as the restrictions they place are 'to restrain any infringement' of the IPR or 'to impose reasonable conditions as may be necessary for protecting' the IPR. If the restriction satisfies these criteria, it would be exempt from the prohibitions of section 3 altogether, and presumably there would be no ground for the CCI to proceed to examine the anti-competitive effects of the impugned restriction. On the other hand, if the restrictions are not justified by the objective of preventing the infringement of the IPR or are

[29] *State of Andhra Pradesh v Mahyco Monsanto* RTPE 02/2006 [MRTPC].

unreasonable for protecting the IPR, these would be subject to the rigours of section 3; in the case of a hard core horizontal agreement covered by section 3(3), this would lead to a presumption of having anti-competitive effect. In the case of other agreements, horizontal or vertical, the anti-competitive effect would still be subject to the rule of reason analysis.

The expressions 'reasonable conditions' or 'to restrain any infringement' have not been explained or defined in the Act nor has the CCI explained these in its Regulations or otherwise. However, in its advocacy booklet on IPRs,[30] the CCI has given a non-exhaustive list of conditions that may give rise to competition concerns. Some of these conditions are as follows:

— Patent Pooling
— Tie-in arrangements.
— Royalty payments after expiry of the patent period.
— Prohibiting the licensee to use a rival's technology.
— Prohibiting the licensee from challenging the validity of an IPR.
— Fixing exclusive grant back requirements.
— Fixing selling price of the licensee.
— Restricting the territory or class of customers.
— Coercive package licences.
— Restricting sale of products to those provided by the licensor.
— Imposing trademark use requirements.

The above list of restrictions giving rise to competition concerns provides an insight into the early thinking of the CCI on the issue of anti-competitive use of IPRs in agreements, wherein it has relied on IPR-related approaches in other jurisdictions. Naturally, it will take time for the CCI to evolve its own thinking in this area. No specific case on the issue of IPRs has been decided by the CCI so far, and therefore no further guidance is available on this vexed subject.

It is worth noting that the exception under section 3(5) extends only to the rights conferred by the laws listed in that section, and it does not cover mere know-how, unlike in the European Union, or other IP laws. Restrictions placed for the protection of mere know-how or other IPs would thus be subject to examination under section 3 just like any other agreement, with no consideration to the exception of section 3(5). This does not mean, however, that enterprises cannot put up protection of their know-how or other IPR as a normal defence under the Competition Act.

It is clear from section 3(5) that the benefit of this exception does not extend to abuse of dominance under section 4 of the Act. (This contrasts with section 15 of the MRTP Act which allowed the benefit for both restrictive trade practices and monopolistic trade practices.) Under section 4 of the Competition Act, an abuse of a dominant position occurs when the dominant enterprise:

1. directly or indirectly, imposes unfair or discriminatory condition or price [section 4(2)(a)];
2. limits or restricts production of goods or provision of services or market or technical or scientific development to the prejudice of consumers [section 4(2)(b)];

[30] The original document can be found at: www.competition-commission-india.nic.in/advocacy/Intellectual_property_rights.pdf

3. denies market access in any manner [section 4(2)(c)];
4. makes conclusion of contracts subject to acceptance by other parties of supplementary obligations which, by their nature or according to commercial usage, have no connection with the subject of such contracts [section 4 (2)(d)];
5. uses its dominant position in one relevant market to enter into, or protect, other relevant market(s) [section 4(2)(e)];

Thus, if a dominant enterprise imposes restrictions in an agreement that would be 'reasonable conditions' for the protection of the IPR or are incorporated 'to restrain any infringement' of the IPR, the enterprise could still benefit from the exception of section 3(5). However, if it abuses its dominance by indulging in a practice listed in section 4 of the Act, the shelter of section 3(5) would not be available to it. This would not however, prevent the dominant enterprise from putting up the defence that the restriction imposed by it unilaterally is reasonable and objectively justifiable; that defence should then be considered as part of the overall analysis, even if it would not provide an escape route from section 4 itself. The spirit of the exemption under section 3(5) that respects the special importance of IPRs, even if not specifically listed in section 4, is a factor that the CCI would do well to keep in mind when dealing even with an abuse of dominance case.

It may be noted that the Act nowhere presumes that the mere holding of an IPR leads to a dominant position. Dominance is to be determined on the basis of a host of factors listed in section 19(4) of the Act such as market share, size and resources of the enterprise or its competitors, dependence of the consumers, and entry barriers. The particular IPR may be contributing to one or more of these factors which must be taken into consideration, but by itself the IPR cannot be presumed to confer dominance.

In the event that the CCI finds that there has been a violation of section 3 (anti-competitive agreements) or of section 4 (abuse of dominance) by an enterprise holding an IPR, the CCI is empowered to pass inter alia any or all of the following orders as given under section 27[31] of the Act against the IPR holder:

1. Direct the enterprise to discontinue and not to re-enter into such agreement.
2. Direct that the agreement shall stand modified to a particular extent.

[31] 27. Orders by Commission after inquiry into agreements or abuse of dominant position.-Where after inquiry the Commission finds that any agreement referred to in section 3 or action of an enterprise in a dominant position, is in contravention of section or section 4, as the case may be, it may pass all or any of the following orders, namely:-

(a) direct any enterprise or association of enterprises or person or association of persons, as the case may be, involved in such agreement, or abuse of dominant position, to discontinue and not to re-enter such agreement or discontinue such abuse of dominant position, as the case may be;

(b) impose such penalty, as it may deem fit which shall be not more than ten per cent. of the average of the turnover for the last three preceding financial years, upon each of such person or enterprises which are parties to such agreements or abuse:

Provided that in case any agreement referred to in section 3 has been entered into by any cartel, the Commission shall impose upon each producer, seller, distributor, trader or service provider included in that cartel, a penalty equivalent to three times of the amount of profits made out of such agreement by the cartel or ten per cent. of the average of the turnover of the cartel for the last preceding three financial years, whichever is higher;

(c) award compensation to parties in accordance with the provisions contained in section 34;

(d) direct that the agreements shall stand modified to the extent and in the manner as may be specified in the order by the Commission;

(e) direct the enterprises concerned to abide by such other orders as the Commission may pass and comply with the directions, including payment of costs, if any;

(f) recommend to the Central Government for the division of an enterprise enjoying dominant position;

(g) pass such other order as it may deem fit.

3. Direct the enterprises concerned to abide by such other orders as the Commission may pass and comply with the directions, including payment of costs, if any.
4. Pass such orders as it deems fit.

In case of abuse of dominant position under section 4, the Commission is also empowered under section 28 of the Act to direct the division of the dominant enterprise to ensure that such enterprise does not again abuse its dominant position; this is however, a remedy rarely resorted to in practice by competition authorities, and so should be the case under the Competition Act. The power of ordering division of an enterprise in section 28 also encompasses the power of the CCI to order transfer or vesting of property, rights, liabilities or obligations, which would include IPR as well.

As a WTO member, India is obliged to comply with the provisions of TRIPS, which establishes minimum universal standards in all areas of intellectual property and backs these up through an enforcement mechanism. The TRIPS agreement in article 40[32] permits Member States to apply their national laws appropriately to prevent:

1. abuse of IPR by intellectual property holders;
2. practices which unreasonably restrain trade; and
3. practices which adversely affect international technology transfer, particularly the anti-competitive licensing practices [articles 8(2) and 40 of TRIPS].

Thus, a Member State may adopt, consistently with the other provisions of TRIPS, appropriate measures to prevent or control the above practices in the light of the relevant laws and regulations of that Member State. The IP laws in India, which predate the Competition Act, do not contain references to that Act; nonetheless, several of them do reflect the above TRIPS principles.

The Patents Act 1970 in section 83[33] specifically declares inter alia that a patent is not granted merely to enable the patentee to enjoy a monopoly, and that the patent right is not to be abused by the patentee and he or she is not to resort to practices which unreasonably restrain trade or adversely affect the international transfer of technology.

Further, section 140[34] prohibits insertion of anti-competitive conditions like tying-in, exclusive dealing, exclusive grant back, prohibiting a challenge to the patent, and coercive

[32] Article 40(2) of TRIPS. Nothing in this Agreement shall prevent Members from specifying in their legislation licensing practices or conditions that may in particular cases constitute an abuse of intellectual property rights having an adverse effect on competition in the relevant market. As provided above, a Member may adopt, consistently with the other provisions of this Agreement, appropriate measures to prevent or control such practices, which may include for example exclusive grantback conditions, conditions preventing challenges to validity and coercive package licensing, in the light of the relevant laws and regulations of that Member.

[33] Patents Act 1970 s 83. General principles applicable to working of patented inventions. Without prejudice to the other provisions contained in this Act, in exercising the powers conferred by this Chapter, regard shall be had to the following general considerations, namely,-

(a) that patents are granted to encourage inventions and to secure that the inventions are worked in India on a commercial scale and to the fullest extent that is reasonably practicable without undue delay; and

(b) that they are not granted merely to enable patentees to enjoy a monopoly for the importation of the patented article.

[34] Ibid s 140. Avoidance of certain restrictive conditions. (1) It shall not be lawful to insert-

(i) in any contract for or in relation to the sale or lease of a patented article or an article made by a patented process; or

(ii) in a licence to manufacture or use a patented article; or

(iii) in a licence to work any process protected by a patent, a condition the effect of which may be-

package licensing into a contract for the sale or lease of a product, or in a license to manufacture a patented article or work a patented process. Any such condition shall be void under the Patents Act and the contract shall operate as if that condition did not exist.

On the lines of section 140 of the Patents Act, section 42 of the Indian Designs Act 2000[35] too prohibits insertion of anti-competitive conditions like exclusive supply and tying-in in any contract for sale, lease or license of a design. In the Semi-Conductor Integrated Circuits Layout Design Act 2000,[36] section 51 is also similar to the compulsory licensing clause of the Patents Act. Under this law the Government may, with the permission of the Board, be allowed use of a protected product so as to remedy an anti-competitive practice.

(a) to require the purchaser, lessee, or licensee to acquire from the vendor, lessor, or licensor, or his nominees, or to prohibit him from acquiring or to restrict in any manner or to any extent his right to acquire from any person or to prohibit him from acquiring except from the vendor, lessor, or licensor or his nominees, any article other than the patented article or an article other than that made by the patented process; or

(b) to prohibit the purchaser, lessee or licensee from using, or to restrict in any manner or to any extent the right of the purchaser, lessee or licensee, to use an article other than the patented article or an article other than that made by the patented process, which is not supplied by the vendor, lessor or licensor or his nominee; or

(c) to prohibit the purchaser, lessee or licensee from using or to restrict in any manner or to any extent the right of the purchaser, lessee or licensee to use any process other than the patented process, and any such condition shall be void.

35 Indian Designs Act 2000 s 42. Avoidance of certain restrictive conditions.-(1) It shall not be lawful to insert-

(i) in any contract for or in relation to the sale or lease of an article in respect of which a design is registered; or

(ii) in a licence to manufacture or use an article in respect of which a design is registered; or

(iii) in a licence to package the article in respect of which a design is registered, condition the effect of which may be-

(a) to require the purchaser, lessee, or licensee to acquire from the vendor, lessor, or licensor or his nominees, or to prohibit him from acquiring or to restrict in any manner or to any extent his right to acquire from any person or to prohibit him from acquiring except from the vendor, lessor, or licensor or his nominees any article other than the article in respect of which a design is registered; or

(b) to prohibit the purchaser, lessee or licensee from using or to restrict in any manner or to any extent the right of the purchaser, lessee or licensee, to use an article other than the article in respect of which a design is registered which is not supplied by the vendor, lessor or licensor or his nominee, and any such condition shall be void.

36 Semi-Conductor Integrated Circuits Layout Design Act 2000 s 51. Power of the Board to permit certain uses.-(1) Notwithstanding anything contained in this Act, the Appellate Board may on an application made in the prescribed manner before it on behalf of the Government or by any person authorised by the Government and after giving notice of such application to the registered proprietor of a layout-design and providing the opportunity of being heard to the parties concerned permit the use of such registered layout-design by the Government or by such person so authorised, as the case may be, subject to any or all of the following conditions as the Board deems fit under the circumstances of such use, namely:-

(a) that the use of the layout-design shall be for non-commercial public purposes or for the purposes relating to national emergency or of extreme public urgency;

(b) that the duration of the use of the layout-design shall be limited for a period specified by the Board.

(c) that the use of the layout-design shall be non-assignable and non-transmissible;

(d) that the use of the layout-design shall be to the extent which the Board deems necessary to remedy the anti-competitive practice;

(e) that the use of the layout-design shall be predominantly for the supply of semiconductor integrated circuits or articles incorporating semiconductor integrated circuits in domestic market of India:

Provided that Board shall not permit the use of a registered layout-design, by any such person authorised by the Government, under this sub-section unless the Board is satisfied that such person so proprietor of such layout-design on reasonable commercial terms and conditions for permitted use of such layout-design and such efforts had not been successful within prescribed period: authorised has made efforts to enter into agreement with the registered:

Provided further that the first proviso shall not be applicable in a case where the person so authorised produces to the Board a certificate issued by the Government to the effect that such use is required due to national emergency or any other circumstances which the Government considers to be of extreme urgency or of public non-commercial use.

As visualised in TRIPS, the Patents Act 1970 permits issue of compulsory licenses (albeit subject to certain safeguards) and stipulates the conditions to be observed in the compulsory license. Section 84(1)[37] allows a compulsory license to be issued after the elapse of three years only on the following grounds:

1. that the reasonable requirements of the public with respect to the patented invention have not been satisfied; or
2. that the patented invention is not available to the public at a reasonable affordable price; or
3. that the patented invention is not worked in the territory of India.

In considering the grant of a compulsory license, the Controller of Patents is required to take into account factors such as the nature of the invention, time that has elapsed since the sealing of the patent, the ability of the applicant to work the invention and his or her capacity to take the risk, and whether the applicant has made efforts to obtain license from the patentee on reasonable terms and conditions. However, these conditions shall not apply in cases of national emergency, extreme urgency, public non-commercial use, or most relevantly for us, in case of establishment of anti-competitive practices adopted by the patentee. In such cases the waiting period of three years and the other conditions of section 84(1) shall not apply. Clearly then, the Patents Act itself empowers the Controller of Patents to remedy an anti-competitive practice through the issue of a compulsory license.

The non-voluntary licensing mechanisms of the Act provide certain opportunities to the Government, as well as the general public, to have reasonable access to patented products at reasonable rates. The Act specifically bars granting of patents that amount to 'ever-greening' [section 3(d)[38]]. Under section 100[39] of the Patents Act, the Government also has power to use the invention for government purposes and under section 102[40] of the Act to acquire a patent for a public purpose.

[37] Patents Act 1970 s 84. Compulsory licences. (1)At any time after the expiration of three years from the date of the sealing of a patent, any person interested may make an application to the Controller alleging that the reasonable requirements of the public with respect to the patented invention have not been satisfied or that the patented invention is not available to the public at a reasonable price and praying for the grant of a compulsory licence to work the patented invention.

[38] Ibid s 3. What are not inventions?: The following are not inventions within the meaning of this Act,-

(d) the mere discovery of any new property or new use for a known substance or of the mere use of a known process, machine or apparatus unless such known process results in a new product or employs at least one new reactant;

[39] Ibid s 100. Power of Central Government to use inventions for purposes of Government. (1) Notwithstanding anything contained in this Act, at any time after an application for a patent has been filed at the patent office or a patent has been granted, the Central Government and any person authorised in writing by it, may use the invention for the purposes of Government in accordance with the provisions of this Chapter.

[40] Ibid s 102. Acquisition of inventions and patents by the Central Government. (1) The Central Government may, if satisfied that it is necessary that an invention which is the subject of an application for a patent or a patent should be acquired from the applicant or the patentee for a public purpose, publish a notification to that effect in the Official Gazette, and thereupon the invention or patent and all rights in respect of the invention or patent shall, by force of this section, stand transferred to and be vested in the Central Government.

Competition law issues could also arise with respect to the Copyright Act 1957 and the Trade Marks Act 1999. The Copyright Act in section 31[41] allows the Copyright Board to permit the complainant to re-publish a work after having satisfied itself that as alleged by the complainant a work has been withheld from the public, which in competition terms may amount to refusal to deal or refusal of access. Similarly, section 31A[42] of the Act empowers the Board to grant a license to the applicant for publishing a work whose owner is either dead or unknown or cannot be found, or if the owner of copyright in such work cannot be found.

The Trade Marks Act 1999, unlike other IP laws, contains no specific provision to deal with anti-competitive practices or situations. However, this has not prevented the courts from redressing anti-competitive actions. For example in the *Hawkins Cooker Ltd v M/s Murugan Enterprises* case,[43] Murugan Enterprises owned a trademark 'Mayur' under which it sold gaskets for pressure cookers manufactured by Hawkins. The defendants used the word 'Hawkins' so as to show compatibility of its gaskets with the Hawkins cookers. The Court held that no reasonable person or purchaser could assume a trade connection between the 'Mayur' brand of gaskets and the 'Hawkins' brand of pressure cookers. Further, the Court opined that in this case Murugan Enterprises neither sought to benefit from Hawkins' trademark nor did it try to show a connection between the two; thus, this was not a trademark infringement case as long as the defendant did not start selling the gaskets it produced under the Hawkins trademark.

VI. Conclusions and Observations

We saw that the Competition Act and several IP laws contain provisions to deal with the interplay of competition law and the IP laws. The Competition Act recognises the importance of IPRs and accordingly gives them special treatment in the assessment of their

[41] Copyright Act 1957 s 31. Compulsory licence in works withheld from public - (1) If at any time during the term of copyright in any Indian work which has been published or performed in public, a complaint is made to the Copyright Board that the owner of copyright in the work-

(a) Has refused to republish or allow the republication of the work or has refused to allow the performance in public of the work, and by reason of such refusal the work is withheld from the public, or

(b) Has refused to allow communication to the public by [(Note: Subs. for 'radio-diffusion' by Act 23 of 1983, S.2 (w.e.f. 9-8-1984)) broadcast] of such work or in the case of a [(Note: Subs. by Act 38 of 1994, S.2 (xii) (w.e.f. a date to be notified)) sound recording] the work recorded in such [(Note: Subs. by Act 38 of 1994, S.2 (xii) (w.e.f. a date to be notified)) sound recording,] on terms which the complainant considers reasonable;

The Copyright Board, after giving to the owner of the copyright in the work reasonably opportunity of being heard and after holding such inquiry, as it may deemed necessary, may, if it is satisfied that the grounds for such refusal are not reasonable, direct the Registrar of Copyrights to grant to the complainant a licence to republish the work, perform the work in public or communicate the work to the public by [(Note: Subs. for 'radio-diffusion' by Act 23 of 1983, S.2 (w.e.f. 9-8-1984)) broadcast], as the case may be, subject to payment to the owner of the copyright of such compensation and subject to such other terms and conditions as the Copyright Board may determine, and thereupon the Registrar of Copyrights shall grant the licence of the complainant in accordance with the direction of the Copyright Board, on payment of such fees, as may be prescribed.

[42] Ibid s 31-A. Compulsory licence in unpublished Indian works- (1) Where in the case of an Indian work referred to in sub clause (iii) of clause (I) of Section 2, the author is dead or unknown or cannot be traced, or the owner of the copyright in such work cannot be found, any person may apply to the Copyright Board for a licence to publish such work or a translation thereof in any language.

[43] *Hawkins Cooker Ltd v M/s Murugan Enterprises* [2008(36) PTC 290(Del)].

anti-competitive effects. On the other hand, in line with the TRIPS principles, several IP laws themselves contain safeguards against the anti-competitive use of IPRs; each law empowers its authority to issue remedial orders.

It goes without saying that each authority has the domain knowledge in its assigned area of responsibility. While the IP authorities have the technical skills to deal with issues like patents, designs and copyrights, they may not have the skills for competition analysis, which may reside in the CCI. This raises the spectre of conflicting orders from different authorities, lack of clarity about jurisdiction, confusion about the principles that will be followed by the CCI and the IP authorities, unnecessary litigation and associated costs, and even undesirable practices like forum hunting by parties. Clearly, there is, or soon will be, the need for bringing clarity in the demarcation of the roles of the CCI and the IP authorities.

The need for coordination between the CCI and the IP authorities exists at least at two levels. At one level, it relates to individual cases before the CCI or the IP authorities, mutual consultation should be encouraged and would in fact be necessary to bring to bear the knowledge and skills of both authorities to the resolution of a particular case. At a broader level, which may be referred to as the policy level, the two sets of authorities should agree broadly about their respective jurisdictions and responsibilities, and broad approaches to the issues that arise in the intersection between competition law and the IP laws.

Fortunately, a very useful provision has been incorporated in the Competition Act: section 21[44] provides that where during the course of a proceeding before a statutory authority (that would include an IP authority) a competition law issue is raised by any party, the authority may make a reference to the CCI for its opinion. The CCI shall give its opinion within 60 days. Thereafter, the statutory authority shall consider the opinion and give its finding, recording the reasons for the same. The reference can also be made *suo moto* by the statutory authority. A mirror image of this provision exists in section 21A[45] of the Competition Act allowing the CCI to make reference to a statutory authority to obtain its opinion and consider it before passing orders in the case. Abundant use should be made of these two consultative provisions by the IP authorities and the CCI to understand the interplay between their respective IP laws and the competition law in individual cases. Experts from the two sides could also be heard in suitable cases; for this a specific

[44] Competition Act s 21. Reference by statutory authority- (1) Where in the course of a proceeding before any statutory authority an issue is raised by any party that any decision which such statutory authority has taken or proposes to take, is or would be, contrary to any o the provisions of this Act, then such statutory authority may make a reference in respect of such issue to the Commission.

(2) On receipt of a reference under sub-section (1), the Commission shall, after hearing the parties to the proceedings, give its opinion to such statutory authority which shall thereafter pass such order on the issues referred to in that sub-section as it deems fit:

Provided that the Commission shall give its opinion under this section within sixty days of receipt of such reference.

[45] Ibid s 21A. Reference by Commission- (1)Where in the course of a proceeding before the Commission an issue is raised by any party that any decision which, the Commission has taken during such proceeding or proposes to take, is or would be contrary to any provision of this Act whose implementation is entrusted to a statutory authority, then the Commission may make a reference in respect of such issue to the statutory authority:

Provided that the Commission may, suo motu, make such a reference to the statutory authority.

(2) On receipt of a reference under sub-section (1), the statutory authority shall give its opinion, within sixty days of receipt of such reference, to the Commission which shall consider the opinion of the statutory authority, and thereafter give its findings recording reasons therefore on the issues referred to in the said opinion.

enabling provision exists in section 36[46] of the Competition Act. Presumably, there would be nothing in the IP laws that prevent the IP authorities from seeking and / or hearing competition law experts to understand the competition issues in any particular case.

At the broader policy level, it would be beneficial to create a platform where the CCI and the IP authorities could meet regularly to better understand the intent and purpose of each other's laws, and to arrive at mutual understanding about demarcating their respective roles and the mechanisms for cooperation with each other in individual cases. Apart from formal mechanisms, frequent informal consultations can go a long way in removing misconceptions about each other and in promoting harmonious working relationships.

Sections 21 and 21A of the Competition Act are enabling provisions. Their spirit is to encourage mutual consultation in practice, which is a regular feature in many other jurisdictions. Unfortunately, there are no provisions in the IP laws corresponding to sections 21 and 21A of the Competition Act. That might be explained by the fact that the Competition Act 2002 had not appeared on the statute book at the time the IP laws were enacted. It would be useful now to consider the insertion of such provisions in all of the IP laws.

While granting IPRs, especially patents, the patent authorities could take care that the patent is not over-broad so that inventing around the patent is still possible and exercise of the exclusive right is limited to legitimate horizons. At the same time, undue restriction of the patent could act as a serious disincentive for innovators. A reasonable balance has to be struck, and the process of consultation between the competition and IP authorities could help. In general, it would also be advisable for the CCI to exercise forbearance and defer, as far as possible, to the powers given to the IP authorities under their respective jurisdictions to remedy anti-competitive situations.

Valentine Korah has observed that the conditions in a developing country are generally different from those in the developed economies. The markets are more concentrated and entry barriers are high. Resources are not easily available for local firms to invest in research and development, and to develop new products. On the other hand labour and other costs are cheaper than in the developed world. In such conditions, patent and other IP authorities are generally advised to be mindful of the competition perspective in the grant of patent

[46] Ibid s 36. Power of Commission to regulate its own procedure.-(1) The Commission shall not be bound by the procedure laid down by the Code of Civil Procedure, 1908 (5 of 1908), but shall be guided by the principles of natural justice and, subject to the other provisions of this Act and of any rules made by the Central Government, the Commission shall have powers to regulate its own procedure including the places at which they shall have their sittings, duration of oral hearings when granted, and times of its inquiry.

(2) The Commission shall have, for the purposes of discharging its functions under this Act, the same powers as are vested in a civil court under the Code of Civil Procedure, 1908 (5 of 1908), while trying a suit, in respect of the following matters, namely:-

(a) summoning and enforcing the attendance of any person and examining him on oath;

(b) requiring the discovery and production of documents;

(c) receiving evidence on affidavits;

(d) issuing commissions for the examination of witnesses or documents;

(e) subject to the provisions of sections 123 and 124 of the Indian Evidence Act, 1872 (1 of 1872), requisitioning any public record or document or copy of such record or document from any office;

(f) dismissing an application in default or deciding it ex parte;

(g) any other matter which may be prescribed.

(3) Every proceeding before the Commission shall be deemed to be a judicial proceeding within the meaning of sections 193 and 228 and for the purposes of section 196 of the Indian Penal Code (45 of 1860) and the Commission shall be deemed to be a civil court for the purposes of section 195 and Chapter XXVI of the Code of Criminal Procedure, 1973 (2 of 1974).

and other IPRs lest these create monopolistic positions and deny access to essential knowledge and skills. In the words of Valentine Korah:

> Where, in a particular sector, entry barriers are high any market power conferred by an IPR is likely to last longer than in a large developed country. This may tilt the balance some way towards granting compulsory licences where this would not be done in a more developed country. The need for access is likely to be more important and last longer.[47]

The essential facilities doctrine has been invoked in several competition law cases related to IPRs, for example Microsoft, Magill, and Commercial Solvents in the EU to mandate access to a facility essential to compete. Also, the

> US and EC courts have developed a duty in exceptional circumstances for dominant firms to supply or license which illustrates the tension between property rights given to induce investment and competition which requires the possibility of access to markets.[48]

At the same time, in the United States, recent court pronouncements have curtailed the reach of the essential facilities doctrine.[49] While section 4 of the Competition Act allows the CCI to invoke the essential facilities doctrine, it may like to take care not to over-stretch it to the point where the exercise of IPRs gets unduly diluted.

The Indian economy has travelled a long distance since liberalisation commenced in 1991. Besides being a more mature economy, there is greater capability within the economy for technological innovation and for operationalising innovations. The need for a balanced approach that will protect competition but not disincentivise innovation is quite clear.

In India, it has been noticed that differences in technology policies relating to different sectors have differing impacts on their total factor productivity (TFP),[50] which is particularly evident in the case of two select sectors viz pharmaceuticals and electronics and electrical (E&E). With the Patents Act 1970 envisaging a process patent regime from the early 1970s, the pharmaceutical industry acquired substantial technological capability of process development through reverse engineering. The learning process has been largely *know-why* oriented in the pharmaceutical sector, while in E&E it has perhaps been more *know-how* oriented. The de-regulation phase of the Indian economy starting in the early 1980s resulted in the TFP growth taking an upward trend; a structural break in India's growth was also noticed. With the modernisation of the Patents Act, in particular with the amendment in 2005, India is well positioned to join the industrialised economies in the innovation and acquisition of technological capabilities. Implementation of the IP laws and the Competition Act 2002 in a coordinated manner would better serve the objectives of innovation, diffusion, and rapid economic growth with fair trade.

[47] Valentine Korah, 'Competition Law and Intellectual Property Rights' in Vinod Dhall (ed), *Competition Law Today* (New Delhi, Oxford University Press, 2007) 134.

[48] Ibid 135.

[49] *Verizon Communications v Law Offices of Curtis V Trinko, LLP* 540 US 398 (2004); 157 L.Ed.2d 823 (2004).

[50] AS Ray, 'R&D and Technological Learning in Indian Industry' (2008) 29(2) *Oxford Development Studies* 155; AS Ray and S Bhaduri, 'R&D and Technological Learning in Indian Industry' (2001) 29(2) *Oxford Development Studies*; S Bhaduri and AS Ray, '*Exporting through Technological Capability: Econometric Evidence from India's Pharmaceutical and Electrical/Electronics* Firms' (2004) 32(1) *Oxford Development Studies* 87.

8

Indonesia

NINGRUM SIRAIT AND CENTO VELJANOVSKI

I. Introduction

This chapter traces the development and enforcement of intellectual property (IP) law and its interrelationship with the more recent evolving competition law in Indonesia. The chapter is organised as follows: section II provides a brief overview of the basic policy considerations surrounding the interrelationship between IP laws and competition law; section III provides background to the structure of the Indonesian economy, and the role that intellectual property rights (IPRs) play in the economy; section IV describes the main elements of Indonesia's IP law; section V looks at the treatment of IP and licensing and franchise agreements under competition law and section VI looks more generally at the policy and administrative issues surrounding IPRs and competition law.

II. Overview

IPRs grant exclusive rights to their owners protected by the law. This has led to the view that IPRs are monopoly rights,[1] and therefore in conflict with competition laws. However, this is to confuse private ownership with monopoly. An IPR is an exclusive right but not necessarily a monopoly right.

At their simplest, IPRs simply recognise legal ownership in IP on a par with that of real property, and thereby provide the basis for a market economy. The recognition and development of IPR laws has taken on heightened importance given the move in many advanced economies from an industrial to a knowledge and services base.

The overriding policy premise is that the commercial exploitation of patents and other IPRs is an important contributor to the economic growth and innovation, therefore a major engine for competition. These dynamic efficiency concerns—the way competition encourages innovation, and in turn creates new and enhanced competition—provide the economic justification for defining and protecting IPRs.

[1] ZU Purba, *Peta Mutakhir Hak Kekayaan Intelektual Indonesia*, Direktorat Jenderal Hak Kekayaan Intelektual, Departemen KeHAKIman dan Hak Asasi Manusia (2000) 1.

Among the theories which have been advanced for the creation and enforcement of IPRs are:

1. the protection of private property rights;
2. to reward inventive and creative activity; and
3. to encourage inventive and creative activity.

None of these theories provide a basis for actual IPR laws, and some are highly contentious.

For the economist, the economic and empirical justification for IPRs is that they stimulate inventive and creative activity by rewarding it.[2] The widespread claim is that patents are necessary to encourage innovation, and hence dynamic efficiency. There is, unfortunately, little evidence that this is the case.[3] Studies have found that apart from the chemical and pharmaceuticals sectors, patents are rarely the principal means of appropriating the returns from research and development (R&D). Indeed some economists, most notably the British economist Arnold Plant in the 1930s, argue that the incentive effects of patents and other IPRs are in practice overwhelmed by the monopoly losses (see below). However, more significantly, Plant claimed that what today is referred to as the first mover advantages of inventors were sufficient to generate an adequate return, and that therefore there was no real risk of the under-provision of R&D. If correct it would undermine the case for patent protection and patent law. It is notable that Professors Landes and (now judge) Posner's,[4] two highly regarded law and economics scholars, treatise on the economic foundations of IP law does not rely on the incentive effects of patents to explain its rationale, structure and effects.

There is also a darker side to the patent system. The two guiding principles of patent law developed in Britain in the eighteenth century were 'that patents should be granted only for new and important discoveries, and that the breadth of the patent holder be proportional to the size of the discovery made.'[5] These principles are reflected in patent laws across the world, including Indonesia. However, there are increasing concerns that the patent system has become a source of inefficiency which has reduced the pace of innovation.

Changes to US patent law in the 1980s expanded the scope of patent protection, made it easier to patent by relaxing the novelty and non-obviousness requirements, and strengthened the patent owner's rights. This, in turn, led to an explosion in the number of patents and in patent litigation.[6] There is growing evidence that US patent law and litigation are being used to foreclose markets and reduce competition. Some argue that the US patent system has become a threat rather than a stimulus to the innovation process.

While this is a matter of general and policy concern, it also has an impact on the transfer of IPRs to developing economies and the response in those countries to the enforcement of those IPRs.

[2] A Plant, 'The Economic Theory Concerning Patents for Inventions' (1934) 1 *Economica* 30; A Plant, 'The Economic Aspects of Copyright in Books' (1934) 1 *Economica* 167, both reprinted in A Plant, *Selected Economic Essays and Addresses* (London, Routledge Kegan Paul, 1974); M Boldrin and DK Levine, 'The Case Against Intellectual Property Law' (2002) 92 *American Economic Review (Papers & Proceedings)* 209.

[3] F Leveque and Y Meniere, *Patents and Innovation: Friends or Foes?* (Paris, Cerna, 2006).

[4] WM Landes and RA Posner, *The Economic Structure of Intellectual Property Law* (Cambridge MA, Harvard University Press, 2003).

[5] AB Jaffe and J Lerner, *Innovation and Its Discontents: How our Broken Patent System is Endangering Innovation, Progress and What to do About It* (Princeton University Press, 2004) 8.

[6] 'The Cost of Ideas' The Economist (London 13 November 2004).

Notwithstanding this, the principle focus of this chapter is not the efficacy of patents and other IPRs, but the way these may be exploited to reduce the competitiveness of markets and harm consumers. IPR laws do not operate independently and the rights conferred under these laws cannot be exercised unhindered. In most jurisdictions, including Indonesia, IPRs are subject to competition law which seeks to ensure that markets based on IPRs operate competitively. If a patent or copyright is genuinely unique and novel and achieves considerable market penetration, especially where it provides an essential input for a patent holder's competitors, then there will be an incentive to exploit the patent in a way inconsistent with competitive markets. The case law in many countries shows that patents and copyright holders have sometimes acted in an anti-competitive and abusive manner to extract monopoly profits, and/or foreclosed markets to competition by the refusal to licence, exclusive licensing and/or discriminatory licensing terms.[7] Indeed, some of the recent major competition decisions in the United States, Europe and in Asia are investigations and prosecutions of firms that have exploited or foreclosed markets using their IPRs, eg IBM, Microsoft, and Intel[8] prosecutions to name several of the most prominent.

Thus, the rights of IPRs must be qualified by laws which deal with market power abuses and practices. Competition law qualifies the rights of patent and other IPR holders where their exploitation of those rights reduces competition. In doing so, the substantive competition law and its enforcement must draw a balance between the benefits of the exploitation and licensing of IPRs and their effects on competition, whether defined in static terms (as competition laws are generally), or the more difficult to define dynamic efficiency benefits of innovative and creative activity.

Drawing this balance is not easy in theory or practice. The presumption of most competition laws is that the commercial exploitation of IPRs is legitimate and fosters economic growth and greater consumer welfare. Yet, it is often difficult to distinguish from market power abuses since rights holders will inevitably claim that any interference with their IPRs will harm consumers and reduce future innovation and R&D in the sector.[9] This, as we have seen, may or may not be true. Resolving these claims in Western competition law jurisdictions has been complex, time consuming, highly contentious, and raised challenges to competition law enforcement.

These issues are often problematic even in jurisdiction with well developed competition laws. For example, how are markets to be defined where future competition is considered a major consideration? How are static efficiency losses for the excessive exploitation of a patent holder's market power to be traded-off from the alleged incentive for greater future competition? And how is the factual basis for both propositions to be quantified and validated—static consumer welfare loss as balanced against future dynamic efficiency gains?

[7] On the European competition law position see SD Anderman, *EC Competition Law and Intellectual Property Rights—The Regulation of Innovation* (Oxford, Oxford University Press, 1998); SD Anderman and J Kallaugher, *Technology Transfer and the New EU Competition Rules—Intellectual Property Licensing after Modernisation* (Oxford, Oxford University Press, 2006).

[8] *Microsoft v Sun Microsystems* (Case COMP/C-3/37.792) [2004]. *STM/Intel/JV* (Case COMP/M.4751) [2007]. European Commission, 'Commission Initiates Formal Investigations against IBM in Two Cases of Suspected Abuse of Dominant Position' (2010), available at http://europa.eu/rapid/pressReleasesAction.do?reference=IP/10/1006&format=HTML&aged=0&language=EN&guiLanguage=en.

[9] US Department of Justice and Federal Trade Commission, 'Antitrust Guidelines for the Licensing of Intellectual Property 1995' (Washington, 1995) available at www.justice.gov/atr/public/guidelines/0558.htm. For recent extensive review of US law and policy, see US Department of Justice and Federal Trade Commission, 'Antitrust Enforcement and Intellectual Property Rights: Promoting Innovation and Competition' (Washington DC, 2007) available at www.usdoj.gov/atr/public/hearings/ip/222655.pdf.

Some economists and lawyers have suggested the use of the 'innovation market'[10] concept to sit beside the standard approach to market definition based on short-term price increases (the so-called SNIPP test[11]), while others regard this as simply not useful. Even in the area of pricing, IPRs pose a major impracticable difficulty. For example, there has been considerable focus on the use of IPRs in setting industry and product standards. This requires a degree of industry cooperation which hints at lessening competition. However, there is also the prospect that royalty rates are set too high for key patents and other IPRs. If there are concerns then setting the appropriate royalty rate is a matter of judgment and often cannot be reduced to a mechanical formula. However, where a competition authority intervenes, setting the Fair, Reasonable and Non-Discriminatory royalty or charge (or FRAND) is intractable.

In developing economies, and especially those with low R&D investment and innovation such as Indonesia (see next section below), another layer of issues arise. There are basic questions regarding the legitimacy and coherence of both IPR and competition laws, the effectiveness and integrity of the enforcement agencies and courts, and the way the law is enforced. Further, since many developing economies are net importers of technology and goods and services protected by IPRs, there are distributional issues associated with the terms of trade and pricing of IPRs, such as we have seen in the pharmaceutical sector where the costs of patented medicines to developing countries has been controversial and often highly regulated by national health services and governments irrespective of the operation of competition law. There is also the different international treatment of IPRs. The European Community (EC) operates with the concept of IPR exhaustion which allows goods once they have been sold in the EC to be re-exported or exported to any of its other Member States, whereas most other countries (eg the United States) prohibit such parallel/grey importing.

III. Country Background

Before describing Indonesia's IPR and competition laws, it is useful to put these in the context of the structure of the Indonesian economy, and data on the role played by IPRs.

A. Economic Environment

Indonesia comprises over 13,000 islands with an estimated population of 228 million. It is ranked as a 'lower middle-income country'[12] with around 21.4 per cent of the population

[10] RJ Gilbert and SC Sunshine, 'Incorporating Dynamic Efficiency Concerns in Merger Analysis: The Use of Innovation Markets' (1995) 63 *Antitrust Law Journal* 569.

[11] This stands for Small Non-transitory Increase in Permanent Price. It asks whether a hypothetical monopolist of a product or service can profitably raise prices by 5% or 10% above the competitive price. If it can then this defines the relevant product market. The test is a feature of most competition laws.

[12] According to the World Bank, the average income of a citizen in a lower middle-income economy country is between $976–$3,855. World Bank, 'Country Classifications', available at www.data.worldbank.org/about/country-classifications.

living below the poverty line of $1.25 a day, according to a survey conducted in 2005.[13] The Indonesian economy in 2007 was dominated by three sectors—energy (52.4 per cent), agriculture (23.4 per cent) and transport and storage (12.9 per cent).[14] Mineral resource development has displaced agriculture, including forestry and fishing, as the main sector. Indonesia is a resource-rich country, has the world's tenth largest reserves of natural gas, and is the only Asian member of the Organization of the Petroleum Exporting Countries (OPEC). Tourism also contributes significantly to the economy.

Indonesia suffered badly during the Asian crisis of the late 1990s. Its Gross Domestic Product (GDP) per capita fell by over 13 per cent in 1998, more than any other Asian economy. It also experienced significant net outflows of foreign direct investment which persisted until 2003. The decline was arrested in 2004, but the latest available data indicates that it remains below the annual average for the previous decade (1990–97).

As a response to the economic crisis in 1997 and in order to relax the extensive regulations on domestic competition and trade in Indonesia (and perhaps to limit the power of the political elite), the Indonesian Government set out a reform package which included tariff reductions, removal of trade restrictions and elimination of some state-owned monopolies. Many new laws were adopted as part of the commitment of the Letter of Intent to the International Monetary Fund (IMF) bail-out programme, including a new competition law.

These reforms have generated stimulus for the Indonesian economy. There has been a substantial increase in exports and investment, the latter largely financed by private investment from the United States, Japan, the United Kingdom and Hong Kong.[15] However, the level of investment still remains low compared to the Asian (tiger) economies such as China and India.

Table 1: Indonesia's Economic Performance, 2002 to 2008

	2002	2003	2004	2005	2006	2007	2008
PDB Growth (%)	4.5	4.8	5.0	5.6	5.5	6.1	6.0
Investment Growth (%)	4.7	0.6	14.7	10.8	2.9	10.7	20.5
Export Growth (%)	1.5	6.8	6.1	19.7	13.1	6.3	9.1
Inflation (%)	11.8	6.8	6.1	10.5	13.1	6.3	9.1
Exchange Rate (Rp/US)	9.3	8.6	8.9	9.7	9.2	9.2	9.7
GDP/ Capita (in million RP)	8.5	9.4	10.6	12.7	15.0	17.5	21.7

Source: B Pasaribu, 'Industrial Policy and Competition Policy. Are they always conflicting?', UNCTAD 1GE Meeting, Geneva, 7–9 July 2009.

[13] United Nations, *Statistical Yearbook for Asia and the Pacific 2008* (New York, United Nations, 2008) Table 17.1.

[14] Measured as a percentage by sector in 2007. Data from Organisation for Economic Co-operation and Development (OECD), *Air for Trade at a Glance 2009: Maintaining Momentum* (Paris, OECD, 2009) 200.

[15] World Bank, *World Development Indicators 2000* (Washington, World Bank, 2001).

The private sector is highly fragmented and consists mainly of businesses with less than 20 employees (99.85 per cent in 2005). This fragmented industrial structure is grossly inefficient, and reforms have sought to help small and medium sized enterprises (SMEs) grow.

B. IP Investment and Protection

Indonesia has a low level of R&D investment compared to other Asian countries and one-twentieth of the Organisation for Economic Co-operation and Development (OECD) average (Table 2 below).

The protection of IPRs in Indonesia is weak by international standards. Its IP protection was ranked 67 out of 134 countries, according to the Global Competitiveness Index 2009–10 (Table 3 below).[16] This was the lowest of any South East Asian country (at 81). However, this was a significant improvement compared with 2008/09 rankings.

Table 2: R&D as % GDP

Country	1995	2002/05
Japan	2.98	3.19
Korea	2.68	2.99
Taiwan	1.81	2.45
Singapore	1.10	2.36
Hong Kong	0.30	0.74
China Coast	0.93	1.59
All China	0.60	1.34
Malaysia	0.20	0.63
Thailand	0.10	0.25
Phillipines	0.70	0.30
Indonesia	0.10	0.50
India	0.50	0.61
OECD average	2.07	2.25

Source: GA Hu and GH Jefferson, 'Economic Integration, Technologic Development and Public Policy in Asia' (Asia Development Bank, 2007).

[16] World Economic Forum, *The Global Competitiveness Report 2009–10 and 2008–09* (World Economic Forum, 2009) 173. The number next to the indicator shows the rank (score) achieved out of all the countries taken into account in a survey (one being the highest). The data used in the Report was taken from various international agencies, private sources and national authorities.

Table 3: Global Competitiveness Index, Asia 2009/10

Country	Overall	Institutions	Innovations	IPRs	IP protection
Indonesia	54	58	39	81	67
Singapore	3	1	8	4	1
China	29	48	26	39	45
Japan	8	28	4	19	14
Korea	19	53	11	48	41
Australia	15	12	20	13	12
India	49	54	30	54	61
Thailand	36	60	57	73	77
US	2	34	1	30	19

Source: World Economic Forum, The Global Competitiveness Report 2009–10 (New York, World Economic Forum, 2010).

According to the International IP Watch List, IP infringement in Indonesia is significant particularly for CDs, DVDs, clothing and software (the highest estimated business losses, see Table 4 below). Furthermore, high unemployment (around 9.1 per cent in 2007)[17] and low standard of living make piracy an attractive and profitable business.

Indonesia has been on the Office of the United States Trade Representative's Special 301 Priority Watch List for violations of IPRs rights since 2001. The 2007 watch list claimed that Indonesia had improved its position.[18] Nonetheless, the 2009 watch list states that Indonesia had 'high copyright piracy levels, including involvement by organized crime' which continue to plague the market.[19] The US Government continues to raise the IP infringement concerns with the Indonesian Government, and to work with it to strengthen its IPR regime.

In late 2008, the Indonesian Government announced a change in import licensing procedures on a broad range of products including electronics, household appliances, textiles, footwear, toys, and food and beverage products. The measure, known as Decree 56, includes a requirement for pre-shipment at importers' expense and a restriction on imports to five designated ports and airports. The Indonesian Government is considering extending these licensing provisions to additional products.[20]

There have also been claims of widespread drug counterfeiting. According to the International Pharmaceutical Manufacturers Group (IPMG), 25 per cent of Indonesia's US$2 billion pharmaceutical drugs market is pirated, counterfeited, or contains unregistered drugs. These counterfeit medicines are either illegally manufactured in the home country or illegally imported from western countries. In recent years, Indonesia (and a

[17] Based on a survey of people aged 15 plus. Source: Federal Statistical Office (FSO), *Country Profile: G20–Advanced Industrial and Emerging Countries—Indonesia* (Jakarta, FSO, 2009).

[18] Out-of-Cycle Review has examined the effectiveness of IPR protection in Indonesia and has reported improvements. International Intellectual Property Alliance (IIPA), *Special 301 Report on Copyright Protection and Enforcement* (Washington DC, IIPA, 2007).

[19] IIPA, *Special 301 Report on Copyright Protection and Enforcement* (Washington DC, IIPA, 2009) 2.

[20] World Trade Organization (WTO), 'Committee on Import Licensing: Import Licensing System of Indonesia' (Geneva, WTO, 2009) 1.

Table 4: Losses Due to Copyright Piracy (est US$m), 2007/08

Country	Business Software				Records & Music				Books		Total	
	Losses		Levels		Losses		Levels		Loss	Loss	Loss	Loss
	2008	2007	2008	2007	2008	2007	2008	2007	2008	2007	2008	2007
India	1384	1013	68	69	36.2	13.8	55	55	NA	38	1420	1194.7
Indonesia	299	226	85	84	20.0	20.2	95	92	NA	32	319.0	278.2
Thailand	335	253	76	80	21.7	20.7	50	50	37	35	458.1	308.7
Malaysia	184	156	59	59	26.2	16.0	60	45	NA	9	210.2	181.0
Hong Kong	135	134	48	51	NA	NA	NA	NA	NA	4	135.0	215.8
Japan	748	876	21	23	NA	NA	NA	NA	NA		748.0	876.0
Singapore	98	95	36	37	NA	NA	NA	NA	NA	2	98.0	97.0
Taiwan	111	118	39	40	4.4	4.9	22	21	NA	16	115.4	341.8

Source: IIP A Special 301 Report on Copyright Protection and Enforcement (Washington DC, IPPA, 2007).
Note: data not available for Motion Pictures and Entertainment Software, hence not included. Indonesia was on the priority Watch List.

number of other developing countries) has made use of compulsory licensing to enable the supply of more affordable generic drugs.[21] However, access to medicines is being affected by new developments such as free trade agreements (FTAs) with developed countries. These FTAs restrict parallel imports and technology licensing. Higher IP standards can prevent or delay the competition from the generic drugs, forming a barrier to the access to medicines. However, one must exercise caution in interpreting these figures and claims, as apart from data and estimation problems there are tricky issues regarding parallel imports which are legal in some jurisdictions such as the European Union.

Table 5 below shows the number of prosecutions for the infringement from 2005 to 2007 for counterfeit drugs and for illegally imported products such as food related products and cosmetics in Indonesia.[22] The low level of prosecutions suggests that the problem is either not significant or that there is a massive under-enforcement of the law. The government enforcement agencies, such as the Trademark Office (supported by international organisations such as the World Intellectual Property Organization Intergovernmental Committee) are reportedly reluctant to conduct regular enforcement actions because of the presence of organised criminal gangs.[23]

The attitude of the Government and institutions towards IPRs is similar for the other developing countries. There is often a reluctance to deal with the problem, the enforcement is poor and there is a lack of awareness that violating IPRs is wrong. In Indonesia, IPR laws are enforced by the special Commercial Court which is a branch to general court. The enforcement has been generally not effective.

Table 5: Number of Prosecuted Cases, 2005–07

	2005	2006	2007
Illegally imported products	37	13	19
Counterfeit drugs	14	15	2
Total	51	28	21

Source: NADFC, Combating Counterfeit Drugs in Indonesia (Jakarta, NADFC, 2007).

IV. Intellectual Property Law

Indonesia has enacted three major pieces of IPR legislation covering copyrights, patents and trademarks[24]:

— Copyright: Law No 6 of 1982 as amended by Law No 7 of 1987 and Law No 12 of 1997, and lastly by Law No 19 of 2002.

[21] In October 2004, Indonesia issued a compulsory license to manufacture generic versions of lamivudine and nevirapine, until the end of the patent term in 2011 and 2012 respectively. The license is for government use, and includes a royalty rate of 0.5% of the net selling value.

[22] National Agency of Drug and Food Control (NADFC), 'Combating Counterfeit Drugs in Indonesia', First ASEAN Conference on Combating Counterfeit Medical Products (Jakarta, NADFC, 2007).

[23] This is true for, for example, Harco Glodok in Jakarta which is one of the largest markets for counterfeit and pirated goods, particularly well-known for pirated optical discs.

[24] A Heroepoetri, *Aspek Hukum Hak Kekayaan Intelektual dan Masyarakat Adat* (Jakarta, WALHI, 1998) 1.

- Patents: Law No 6 of 1989 (as amended by Law No 13 of 1997) and latest by Law No 14 of 2001.
- Trademarks: Law No 19 of 1992 (as amended by Law No 14 of 1997) and latest by Law No 15 of 2001.[25]

A. Copyright

Copyright protects the rights of authors of creative works. The duration of a copyright varies between 25 to 50 years. The copyright on photography and typographical arrangements of a published work is valid for 25 years and copyright on other works for 50 years (sections 26 and 27). The State can hold copyright in works from prehistoric remains, historical and other national cultural objects. Copyright held or implemented by the State is for an indefinite period, except copyright regulated under article 10(1) which is valid for 50 years.

B. Patents

Patents protect inventions. An invention is defined as any activity that solves a specific problem related to technology, either in the form of a product or process, or an improvement and development of a product or a process. An invention must be novel when the patent application is filed, and not similar to nor part of any previous invention (section 3). A simple patent can be applied to inventions in the form of a new product or process, having simple quality of invention but with practical use value (section 6).

Under Indonesian law, a patent will not be granted for any invention of the following:

1. A process or product, which awards and/or contravenes the law, public order or morality.
2. A method of examination, treatment, medication, and/or surgery applied to humans and/or animals but without reaching out any product used in or related to the aforesaid method.
3. A theory and method in the field of science and mathematics.

The life of a patent is 20 years from the date of the registration (section 8). A simple patent is granted for a period of 10 years from the date of application (section 9).

C. Trademark

The Law on Trademarks recognises three types of trademarks—trademark, service mark and collective mark. A trademark is a mark used on goods traded by an individual or by several persons collectively or by a legal entity to distinguish the goods from other goods of the same kind. A service mark is a mark used for services traded by an individual or by several persons collectively or by a legal entity to distinguish the services from other services of the same kind. Collective mark is a mark used on goods and/or services of the

[25] The first law recognising trademarks in Indonesia was Law No 21 of 1961 on Company and Commerce Trademark.

same characteristics traded collectively by several persons or legal entities to distinguish the goods and/or services from others of the same kind (some experts are of the opinion that collective mark cannot be categorised as a separate mark, as it consists of service mark and trademark).

A trademark is registered in the General Register of Marks for a specific period for own use or to grant permission for one person, a number of persons collectively or a legal entity. The owner of the mark can be one person or a number of persons collectively or a legal entity.

A registered mark is protected for 10 years from the application filing date (section 7). The period of protection can be extended for further 10-year periods at the request of the mark owner. The request must be submitted to the Office of Trademarks, at least six months and not more than 12 months prior to the expiration of the protection period (section 35).

V. Competition Law

A. Indonesia's Competition Reforms

Indonesia enacted its competition law in 1999—Law No 5/1999 on The Prohibition of Monopolistic Practices and Unfair Business Competition (Undang Undang Tentang Larangan Praktek Monopoli dan Persaingan Usaha Tidak Sehat).[26] It has as its stated objectives:

- — Safeguarding the public interest.
- — 'Improving the efficiency of the national economy as a means of improving people' welfare.
- — Creating effectiveness and efficiency in business operations.
- — Providing equal business opportunities to small, medium and large scale businesses.
- — Preventing monopolistic practices and unfair business practices.[27]

Law No 5/1999 is seen as a significant tool to increase domestic and international competition.[28] It is part of a general international trend of adopting competition laws to improve economic growth and productivity.[29]

The law also established the Commission for the Supervision of Business Competition—the Komisi Pengawas Persaingan Usaha or KPPU. The KPPU is responsible for enforcing the law, and imposing sanctions and penalties for violations of the law.[30]

[26] It was noted that during the period of President Habibie government transition, 69 laws were enacted. Kompas Daily, *Pemerintah Habibie Menggolkan 69 Undang-undang*, 24 September 1999.

[27] See art 3(a), (b), (c) (d) of Law No 5/1999.

[28] EM Fox, 'Equality, Discrimination and Competition Law: Lessons from and for South Africa and Indonesia' (2000) 41 *Harvard International Law Journal* 589.

[29] RH Lande, 'Symposium Creating Competition Policy for Transition Economics' (1997) *Brooklyn Journal of International Law* 339.

[30] Law No 5/1999 constitutes 51 articles: Chapter I, General Provisions (one article), Chapter II: Principles and Purposes (two articles), Chapter III: Prohibited Agreement (13 articles), Chapter IV: Prohibited Activities (eight articles), Chapter V: Dominant Position (five articles), Chapter VI: Commission for The Supervision of Business Competition (eight articles), Chapter VII: Case Handling Procedure (nine articles), Chapter VIII: Sanctions

There are a number of exemptions in the operation of competition law under Article 50 for specific actions or agreements as authorised under the Ministerial Decree, and other specific agreements[31] and entrepreneurs.[32] These exemptions[33] are based on different factors such as constitutional protections, the existence of laws which regulate specific sectors (that is sectoral regulation of the transport, drinking water, electricity, and telecommunication sectors)[34] and the exercise of powers by administrative bodies.[35] For example, section 33 of the Indonesian Constitution 1945[36] protects micro, small and medium enterprises (MSME), and there are laws which support cooperatives[37], small and medium enterprises,[38] and small-scale home industry enterprises.[39]

Article 50(b) exempts 'agreements related to intellectual property rights such as license, patent, trade brand, copyright, industrial product design, integrated electronic series, trade secrets, and contracts related to franchise'. KPPU issued guidelines on IPRs[40] in January 2010.[41]

B. Intellectual Property Right Guidelines

IPR license agreements must be registered at the Directorate General of Intellectual Property Rights and placed in the General Registry for payment of a fee. Failure to register a license means that it cannot benefit from an Article section 50(b) exemption.

A license agreement is prohibited when it contains provisions which directly or indirectly inflict loss to the Indonesian economy, or limit the capacity of the Indonesian economy to exploit and develop technology. The registry and request for registration of license agreement containing such provisions must be refused by the Directorate General of Intellectual Property Rights.

(three articles), Chapter IX: Exemptions (two articles), Chapter X: Transitional Provisions, Chapter XI: Closing Statement.

[31] Article 50 (b-g) of Law No 5/1999.

[32] Article 50(h) of Law No 5/1999.

[33] As an example, in the United States labour and insurance services are exempt under the McCarran-Fergusson Act in addition to other exemptions for agriculture and fishery, small and medium enterprises, export and sport associations and others. Japan has exempted agriculture and cooperatives.

[34] The KPPU has issued guidelines on Article 50a on exemption for government regulation; and article 51 on the exemption for state-owned enterprises.

[35] T Jorde et al, *Gilbert Law Summaries - Antitrust*, 9th edn (Harcourt Brace, 1996) 114.

[36] See *Laporan Kebijakan Persaingan Indonesia* (Indonesian Competition Report), Elips Project, 2000.

[37] See Law No 25/1992 on Cooperative.

[38] See Law No 20/2008 on Micro, Small and Medium Enterprises.

[39] R Brazier and S Sianipar (eds), *Undang-Undang Antimonopoli Indonesia dan Dampaknya Terhadap Usaha Kecil dan Menengah* (The Asia Foundation, 1999).

[40] Commission Regulation No 2 of 2009 on the Guidelines on the Provisions of Article 50(b) (IPR Guidelines).

[41] The European Commission has issued a number of notices and guidelines on the application of competition law to IPRs. Commission Regulation (EC) No 2659/2000 on the application of Article 81(3) of the Treaty to categories of research and development agreements [2000] OJ L 304, pp 7–12. European Commission, Guidelines on the applicability of Article 81 of the EC Treaty to horizontal cooperation agreements (2001/C 3/02) [2001] OJ C 3, pp 2–30; European Commission Directive 2004/48/EC on the enforcement of the intellectual property rights, [2004] OJ L 195, pp 16–25. Commission Regulation No 772/2004 on the application of Article 81(3) of the Treaty to categories of technology transfer agreements [2004] OJ L 123, pp 11–17.

The exemptions under competition law are not absolute and must pass a rule of reason requirement. To determine whether the exemption applies, the following must be satisfied:

1. If there is a refusal to license, it is necessary to determine whether or not the IPR is an 'essential facility'. If not, an exemption can be granted, but otherwise the refusal will be in breach of competition law.
2. The agreement must be an IPR license agreement. If it is not an IPR license agreement there is no exemption.
3. It must comply with patent law, ie has it been registered? If not, the exemption is not applicable.
4. It must not contain clauses which are clearly anti-competitive.

Under the IPR exemption guidelines, IPR license agreements are considered exclusive dealing if they contain clauses on:

— pooling licensing and cross licensing;
— tying arrangement;
— limitation in raw material;
— limitation in production and selling;
— limitation in the selling price and reselling price;
— grant back.

The existence of one or more of the above clauses does not indicate that the IPR license agreement is anti-competitive. Each clause must be assessed individually for its anti-competitive nature.

C. Licenses Pooling and Cross Licensing

License pooling is where a number of separately owned licences which relates to a specific production process or a standard are pooled. Cross-licensing is where parties licence IPRs to one another to enable R&D activities. By pooling licenses and/or cross licensing, firms can reduce the transaction cost and facilitate production.

Clauses related to license pooling and cross-licensing are not anti-competitive per se as they can improve business efficiency and facilitate competition. However, if such arrangements result in production or marketing of a product being controlled by one or several licensors in a way that makes it difficult for other firms to compete effectively, the clause may be deemed anti-competitive.

D. Tying and Bundling

While product bundling and tie-in sales are not inherently anti-competitive, the consumer must be given the option to unbundle and buy one product only. Thus, forced bundling is regarded as anti-competitive.

E. Limitations in Raw Material

A licensor can place limitations on the licensee regarding the quality of raw materials used. This can enhance technology, maintain safety, and protect trade secrets. On the other hand such a limitation can restrict competition and foreclose markets. Therefore, the clause which obligates the licensee to use raw material from a source exclusively determined by the licensor, where the same raw material is available from other sources, can be regarded as anti-competitive.

A licensor can place restrictions on the licensee in production process and product selling. Where the object of such restrictions is to protect know-how, or to prevent the illegitimate use of technology, such restrictions will not be regarded as anti-competitive. However, if the licensing terms limit the production process or production sales or the sales of competing products owned by the licensor, which hampers the licensee to effectively use the technology, they may be anti-competitive.

F. Limitation in Production and Sales

A licensor can place territorial and quantity restrictions on the licensee's technology. However, license terms placing territorial and product quantity restrictions on what can hamper the licensee from undertaking technological innovation in such way that the product development becomes inefficient, can be considered anti-competitive.

G. Limitation in Sales and Reselling Price

A licensor can set the price at which his/her products can be marketed, given the investment it has made. However, resale price maintenance and price floors which adversely affect competition will be treated as anti-competitive.

H. Grant-Back

Grant-back is where a licensee is required to disclose and transfer information to licensor on any improvement or development made to the licensed products, including the know-how related to the development.

In assessing whether a clause on grant-back is anti-competitive or not, consideration is to be given to whether it hampers the licensee in mastering the technology and the legitimacy of transferring new technology in intellectual work that he/she did not invent. Therefore, a clause in a license agreement containing the obligation of grant-back may be regarded as anti-competitive.

The KPPU Guidelines also contain a number of benchmarks to ensure the application of the Article 50(b) by answering the following questions:

— **Is there agreement reached or a form of refusal to license?** When the refusal to license does not involve an IPR regarded as an essential facility, it can be granted an exemption. If it relates to an essential facility there will be no exemption.

— **Is exemption sought for a license agreement?** Exemption can only be granted for a license agreement. For other matters related to IPRs, exemption is based on a competitive assessment.

— **Has the license agreement been registered with the Directorate General of Intellectual Property Rights?** A license agreement must be registered with the Directorate General of Intellectual Property Rights to be eligible for exemption; even in the related provision, IPR can have influence on its enforceability to the third party.[42] The Directorate General is required to assess whether the provisions of a registered license is anti-competitive to avoid conflict competition law.[43] An unregistered license is subject to a full competitive assessment before it can be exempt.

— **Does the license agreement contain anti-competitive provisions? Where this is the case exemption is not granted.** The easiest to identify are those which are exclusive, such as pooling and cross-licensing, tying arrangement, limitation on raw materials, limitation of production and sales, limitation of sales and reselling price, and grant-back. If such exclusivity is found, it is necessary to examine the background, purpose, and reason of the inclusion of the provision.

I. Competition Cases Related to IPR Issues

There have only been three competition law investigations involving IPRs to date. These decisions shed little light on the operation of the Article 50(b) exemption process, or the treatment of IPR agreements.

The first case concerned trade secrets in the music industry (Case No 19/KPPU-L/2007). This alleged market control and collusion by EMI Music South East Asia, EMI Indonesia, Arnel Affandy, Dewa 19, and Iwan Sastrawijaya. It concerned damages and collusion involving the company's trade secret. PT Aquarius Musikindo claimed damages from EMI Music South East Asia, PT EMI Indonesia, Arnel Affandi, SH, and Dewa 19 for violating Article 23 of Law No 5/1999. The case illustrated that Dewa 19 moved from PT Aquarius Musikindo to EMI Music South East Asia which involved PT EMI Indonesia, inflicting an alleged loss to PT Aquarius Musikindo in excess of Rp 4,2 b. The defendants claimed that their agreement should be exempt because it was related to the trade secret registered under Indonesian IPR law and therefore Law No 5/1999 did not apply. Apart from the attempted use of the IPR exemption provisions, the case provided no precedent or substantive analysis of the application of competition law to IPRs. The case went for appeal to the District Court in Jakarta and to the Supreme Court. In late 2010, the Supreme Court reached its final decision and affirmed the KPPU's decision.

In the second case (Case No 03/KPPU-L/2008), exemption was sought for exclusive broadcasting rights for English Premiere League 2007–10. Indovision, Telkomvision, IndosatM2 and a group of consumers submitted complaints to the KPPU alleging violations of Articles 16 and 19 (a) of the Anti-Monopoly Act. The KPPU held that the exclusive agreements between ESS and AAMN violated Article 16. The exclusive agreement barred other operators from acquiring such rights. During the hearings evidence was given and it was accepted that such content was critical to the pay TV operators, and that the exclusive right was sold to AORA thereby causing consumer loss to former Astro's subscribers. The attempt to seek exemption under Article 50(b) failed.

[42] See article 47(2) of Law No 19 of 2002 on Copyright.

[43] Vide provisions related to IPR, among others: 1) section 47 Article (1) of Law No 19 of 2002 on Copyright (Copyright Law) asserts, 'A licensing agreement not contain any clauses, which may cause detrimental effect on the economy of Indonesia or to contain any clauses, which cause unfair business competition as provided for in the prevailing laws and regulations.' 2) article 71(1) of Law No 14 of 2001 on Patent (Patent Law) asserts that a licensing agreement does not contain any provisions that may directly or indirectly damage the Indonesian economy, or to contain restrictions, which obstruct the ability of the Indonesian people to master and develop technology in general and relating to the patented invention in particular.

In Case No 17/KPPU-I/2010, the KPPU found that Pfizer Group (and four affiliated companies) and PT. Dexa Medica had participated in a price-fixing scheme involving patented medicines using Amlodipine Besylate supplied to both by Pfizer LLC in violation of Article 5 (which prohibits fixing), article 11 (which prohibits cartels), article 16 (which prohibits restrictive agreements with foreign parties) and Article 25(1) (which prohibits the abuse of dominant position). The KPPU found that the price of patented drugs Norvask and Tensivak were over 13–14 times higher than the average international price. The KPPU ordered both companies to revoke certain supply agreements, cease further communications, and that Pfizer lower its price of Norvask by 65 per cent and PT Dexia Medica its price of Tensivak by 60 per cent.

Both Norvask and Tensivak used active extract Amlodipine Besylate which had patent protection from 3 April 1987 until 2 April 2007[44] and therefore had a monopoly of their respective patented medicines. Pfizer and Dexa argued that when patents ended, new products entered the market that increased competitiveness in the industry. Therefore, after 2007, the market has been competitive as proved through the increasing number of players in the market.

Both parties also argued that the KPPU's decision contradicts Article 50 (b) which regulates exemption on IPRs. According to KPPU Guidelines No 2/2009 on IPRs, patented products are exempted. Otherwise, they argued that if patented medicines were not exempt it would subvert the purpose of patent law to give firms the incentive to invest in innovation. The parties appealed the decision to the District Court in Jakarta, arguing that they had no incentive to form a cartel agreement during the patent right protection when the inventor enjoyed the profits of their innovation.

VI. Policy Issues

A. Competition Principles

The concerns relating to the application of competition law where IPRs are concerned can be divided into general and what might be termed Indonesian-specific. The general concern is whether standard competition law principles are appropriate to deal with IPRs and innovation markets. Here, views are sharply divided. There are those who contend that there is nothing fundamentally different about the competition issues surrounding IPRs, and that standard competition law principles are appropriate with suitable amendment. This has led to a range of guidelines on the application of competition law.

Others argue that there is something fundamentally different about innovation and the exploitation of IPRs which calls for a different approach to competition law (See Sidak and Teece in chapter four of this volume). This has several sub-themes or factions. The most liberal are those who hold that monopoly is necessary for innovation—that the lure of monopoly profits acts as the engine for innovation, and that therefore a more liberal approach should be taken to the exploitation of IPRs. The most forthright advocates of

[44] See arts 1(1), 10, 16, 69 and 70 of Law No 14, n 43 above.

this approach draw on the work of Joseph Schumpeter.[45] However, the correlation (let alone causation) of high market concentration and greater R&D is generally weak, or at best unsupported by evidence. Others see major differences between innovation; and static efficiency and competition in goods and service markets. They have called for the development of new antitrust principles, such as the use of innovation markets, and more focus on dynamic efficiency factors. For many competition laws this creates a tension with the competition focus and efficiency objective of fostering R&D which is often not present as a goal.

In the context of the development of Indonesia's competition law, these tensions play out in terms of its objectives, principles and enforcement. A brief comment is warranted on each.

i. Confused and Conflicting Objectives of Competition Law

Indonesia's competition law has multiple objectives with very unclear guidance as to how these are to be balanced in any overall assessment. Thus, while economic efficiency may be seen as an objective of US antitrust (although this is a highly contentious claim), it is not for EC competition laws and those of Indonesia. Thus, there are limits to the extent to which dynamic efficiency claims can be taken into account.

ii. Redistribution and Trade Effects

As has been shown above, Indonesia is not a major originator of IPRs and therefore is a net importer of innovative and IPR protected technologies. To the extent that there are competition concerns arising from technology transfer and licensing, and standard setting, Indonesia gains from access but may be significantly disadvantaged by the terms and conditions of licenses. This raises a wider issue for competition law—the potential transactional redistributive effects of enforcing IPRs and the extent to which these are subject to domestic competition law.

One manifestation of this is the stark differences between EC and US law concerns, IPR exhaustion and the consequent parallel importation of goods. Within the EC, once an IPR is brought into the EU it can then be freely re-exported to the 27 Member States without the rights holders' agreement. Thus, parallel importing (otherwise known as grey imports) is legal within the EU. In the healthcare sector the position is similar in Indonesia where parallel imports are exempt from the operation of criminal sanctions (Patent Law No 14/2001 chap XV Article 135). The grounds for this are that IPR restrictions on the free flow of goods within the EC violate the single market objective of the Union, and are also anti-competitive. Although the latter is contested in recent cases, it points to one significant tension between the way IPRs are treated outside the EC and within the EC.

iii. Administration of Competition Law

Competition law is a legal and administrative innovation for Indonesia. The KPPU is the first independent regulatory commission. As such there have been a number of teething problems as one would expect. Indonesia's competition law has a number of acknowledged

[45] JA Schumpeter, *Capitalism, Socialism and Democracy* (USA, Routledge, 2003).

weaknesses. Some of the institutional problems with the implementation of the competition law in Indonesia are as follows:

— Industrial economics and competition law are fairly young fields of study which many authorities are not familiar with.
— The administrative sanctions decided by the KPPU do not comply with the Indonesian legal system.
— Interpretation and enforcement problems.
— Low public and business awareness as to the role, responsibilities and the powers of KPPU.
— Perceived lack of independence of the KPPU. The concept of regulatory independence is not well established in Indonesia. As a result, the public sees the KPPU as part of the Government, and under the influence of politicians.

Further, there has not been a significant level of enforcement as yet. During the period 2000 to 2008 the KPPU received 231 complaints and made 46 decisions finding infringements in 70 per cent of the latter. This is not a high prosecution rate. One other concern is a major source of anti-competitive practice is the government itself through its activities and ownership of state entities. While these are subject to the competition law, there has not as yet been significant enforcement against this sector.

The enforcement of IPR laws in Indonesia has been negligible despite the fact that they have been in operation for over a decade. IPR law enforcement has been placed in the special Commercial Court which is a branch of the general courts. Enforcement has been mediocre in the sense that many violations of patent or trademark rights have not been stopped. Sanctions under IPR laws include revoking or nullifying the granted rights but most claims seek compensation via claims for damages. Now the Government of Indonesia is in the process of decentralising IPR registration to make it easy to apply by opening regional offices.

VII. Conclusions

IPR and competition laws in Indonesia are still at a formative stage, but their significance is increasing. There is a substantial interaction between the two which has yet to be tested. In common with other developing economies, the poor enforcement of IPRs is exacerbated by a poor understanding from the business, especially when it comes to the exemption from competition law. The Article 50(b) Guidelines have affected the way businesses deal with competition issues. Critical questions for the future are whether the Guidelines should be (a) applied automatically or based on KPPU approval; or b) assessed ex post when the KPPU mounts an investigation. These issues are at present unclear and need to be resolved if businesses are to be given certainty and adequate guidance as to the operation of the competition rules with respect to IPRs.

9

Japan

H STEPHEN HARRIS, JR AND HIROSHI OHASHI

I. Introduction

Since the 1950s, economists have understood that innovation is critical to economic growth. Greater economic activity and a higher quality of life are crucially dependent on a steady supply of new technologies along with that of new goods and services. In Japan, the rapid progress of demographic ageing and declining birthrates make innovation far more important as a means of compensating for the shrinking labour force. Perhaps reflecting this environment, as shown in Table 1, the recent share of total research and development (R&D) expenditure in the gross domestic product (GDP) of Japan is the highest at 3.67 per cent. It is interesting to note that as of 2007, the Government accounted for 17.4 per cent of the total R&D expenditure, the lowest proportion as compared to that in the United States, European Union, China, and Korea (Table 1). While the recent economic crisis may alter the way the Government aids research and development, Table 1 illustrates the fact that the private sector plays a key role in innovation activities, ultimately bringing about economic growth in Japan. In order to further spur innovation and technological progress in Japanese private sectors, a competition policy, which presumably influences a firm's innovation activities, is considered to be of critical importance.

This chapter is organised as follows. The first section provides an overview of Japan's anti-monopoly act, followed by a brief account of the structure of Japanese antitrust enforcement. The third and fourth sections summarise Japan's intellectual property laws

Table 1: R&D Expenditure and GDP, Japan and Other Countries

	Countries (fiscal yr)							
Trillion JPY (%)	**Japan 2007**	**U.S. 2007**	**E.U.-27 2006**	**Germany 2006**	**France 2006**	**U.K. 2006**	**China 2006**	**Korea 2006**
Total R&D Expenditure (in trillion JPY)	**18.9**	**43.4**	**31.3**	**8.6**	**5.5**	**5.0**	**4.4**	**3.3**
(% Public R&D)	(17.4)	(27.7)	(34.2)	(27.8)	(38.4)	(31.9)	(24.7)	(23.1)
(% Per GDP)	(3.67)	(2.68)	(1.84)	(2.54)	(2.10)	(1.78)	(1.42)	(3.23)
GDP (in trillion JPY)	**516**	**1,618**	**1,704**	**339**	**264**	**279**	**308**	**103**

and their relation to the anti-monopoly act. The fifth section lists some important anti-monopoly cases related to intellectual property. The sixth section describes the recent amendments to the anti-monopoly act enacted in January 2010, and the final section concludes the chapter.

II. Overview of Japan's Anti-Monopoly Act[1]

The Act on Prohibition of Private Monopolization and Maintenance of Fair Trade (Act No 54 of 14 April 1947; hereafter AMA) aims

> to promote free and fair competition in markets, to stimulate the creative initiative of entrepreneurs, to encourage business activities, to heighten the level of employment and actual national income, and thereby to promote the democratic and wholesome development of the national economy as well as to assure the interests of general consumers. (Article 1.)[2]

Drafted under pressure from the occupation forces, many provisions of the AMA resemble the US federal antitrust laws, namely, the Sherman Act,[3] the Clayton Act,[4] and the Federal Trade Commission Act.[5] The AMA comprises four major categories of regulations:

1. Prohibition of unreasonable restraint of trade (latter clause of article 3).
2. Prohibition of private monopolisation (former clause of article 3).
3. Prohibition of unfair trade practices (article 19).
4. Regulations on mergers and acquisitions (chapter 4).

The regulations on the unreasonable restraint of trade control horizontal anti-competitive activities, including cartels and bid-rigging. The regulations on private monopolisation prohibit any exclusion or control of the business activities of other firms that leads to a substantial restraint of trade in a relevant market. Unfair trade practices refer to certain business activities defined in article 2.9 of the Act, and are designated by the Japan Fair Trade Commission (hereafter, JFTC), the primary regulator on the AMA. Conducts subject to the regulations of unfair trade practices include activities such as abuse of superior bargaining position, unjust low price sales, and refusals to sell. It has been widely believed that it is easier to establish a violation of unfair trade practices, which requires 'a tendency to impede fair competition' than to establish a violation of the provisions prohibiting unreasonable restraint of trade or private monopolisation, which requires 'a substantial restraint of trade'. The JFTC also regulates business combinations, including mergers and acquisitions. It is interesting to note that the JFTC and courts have not made any formal decision on business combination cases since the year 1970, when Fuji and Yawata merged

[1] The overview of the AMA is available for example in Kawai, K, F Hirano, K Fujii, 'Japan' in Shaun Goodwin (ed), *The Public Competition Enforcement Review*, 2nd edn (London, Law Business Research, 2010). Available at www.papaphilippou.eu/media/documents/LBR_The_Public_Competition_Enforcement_Review_2010.pdf and A Inoue, *Japanese Antitrust Law Manual: Law Cases and Interpretation of the Japanese Antimonopoly Act* (The Netherlands, Kluwer Law, 2007).

[2] Unauthorised English translation of the Act is available at www.jftc.go.jp/e-page/legislation/ama/amended_ama.pdf.

[3] Sherman Act 15 USC §§ 1-7 (2000).

[4] Clayton Act 15 USC §§ 12-27 (2000).

[5] Federal Trade Commission Act 15 USC §§ 41-58 (2000).

into Nippon Steel, then the second largest steelmaker in the world.[6] Instead, almost all business combination cases have been dealt with in informal consultations, which are not stipulated in the AMA, but strongly encouraged by the JFTC in practice.

III. Structure of Japanese Antitrust Enforcement

In the United States, the Government delegates antitrust enforcement to two agencies: the Antitrust Division of the Department of Justice (hereafter, DOJ), and the Federal Trade Commission (hereafter, US-FTC). While the AMA emulated the American antitrust laws, antitrust enforcement in Japan does not resemble the practices in the United States. Unlike the case of the United States, in Japan there is only one antitrust agency—the JFTC, which was established by the AMA (article 27). The JFTC was apparently modeled after the US-FTC: it is an independent agency under the Prime Minister's Office. The JFTC has five commissioners, including one chairperson who is appointed by the Prime Minister with the consent of both House of the Diet (article 29). Each commissioner has a five-year term (article 30), and they are protected against pay cuts (article 36) or removals without cause or their consent (article 31). Decisions are made by a majority vote; however, minutes of meetings of the Commission have not been published.

Having only one antitrust agency responsible for enforcing the Act helps promote the development of a uniform national competition policy. Under the structure of the AMA, almost all basic antitrust violations are covered by the regulations on unreasonable restraint of trade, private monopolisation and mergers. It has long been argued that unfair trade practice regulations are not needed in Japan as the country has one regulatory agency, and these regulations were originally expected to serve merely a supplemental role in antitrust enforcement. Otherwise, the regulations on unfair trade practices would engender unnecessary confusion in the application and enforcement of the AMA, because violations covered by the regulations on private monopolisation are also covered by those on unfair trade practices. Furthermore, it has often been considered that the unfair trade practices category of regulations required a lower standard of anti-competitive effect than those required under the unreasonable restraint of trade and private monopolisation categories, as unfair trade practices in general did not require adverse effects on competition in the relevant market, whereas unreasonable restraint of trade and private monopolisation do require the adverse effects. As such, there were fewer sanctions concerning unfair trade practices than other regulations: while the JFTC can issue a cease-and-desist order on unfair trade practices, it is bound to order a surcharge payment if it found a violation of the provisions governing unreasonable restraint of trade and private monopolisation (but only when related to controlling business entities). The new amendments enacted in January 2010 have expanded the coverage of surcharges on unfair trade practices, as discussed in further detail later in the chapter.

[6] The case of Hiroshima Dentetsu is an exception, which was settled in the consent order. The Fuji-Yawata merger case is recently reviewed in Satoshi Myojo and Hiroshi Ohashi, 'Evaluating Merger Remedies in a Dynamic Environment: Revisiting the Steel Merger in 1970' CIRJE WP 609 (University of Tokyo, 2009). They find that the merger enhanced the production efficiency and far exceeded the welfare loss associated with an increase in market power.

IV. JFTC Procedures for Antitrust Cases

The JFTC's current legal procedures for handling cases are shown in Figure 1. If a preliminary finding indicates that a violation exists, the JFTC initiates a formal investigation. The 2005 amendments have enabled the JFTC to exercise compulsory criminal investigations on cartel cases. After a formal investigation, if the JFTC finds a violation, it issues a formal order—a cease and desist order and/or a surcharge order—after having provided the respondent firm with an opportunity to present views and submit evidence. Subsequently, the JFTC initiates a formal Shinpan hearing upon the request of the respondent. The Shinpan hearing adopts the adversary system, in which independent referees, who are members of the JFTC staff, make a judgment. The structure of the Shinpan hearing has long been criticised as being rather inquisitorial, because within the JFTC staff, no clear firewall has been erected between Shinpan referees and Shinpan prosecutors.[7]

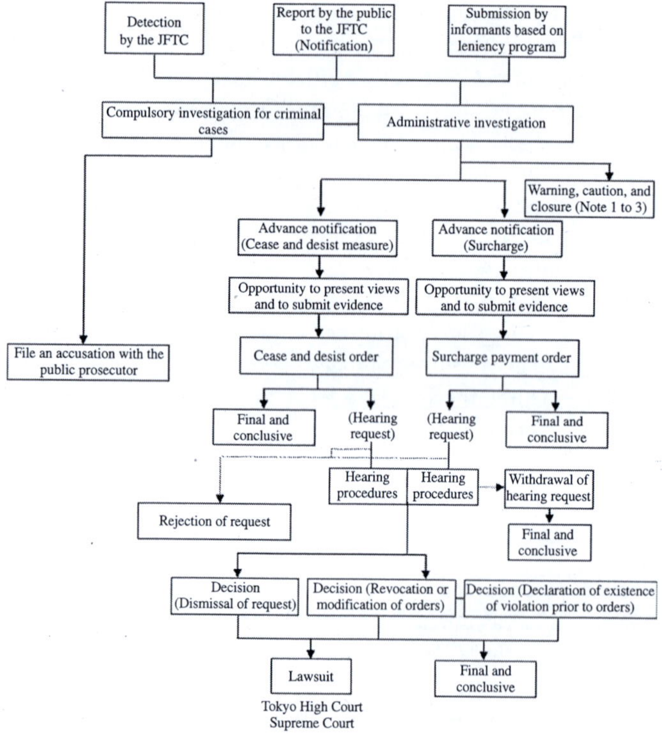

(Note) 1. Warning: A case where there is no evidence to take a legislative measure but is a suspicion of violation
2. Caution: A case where there is no evidence to suspect the existence of violation but is a possibility that could lead to violation in the future
3. Closure: A case where the investigation is terminated because there is no conduct violating the Antimonopoly Law

Figure 1: JFTC Procedures for Handling Illegal Cases Based on the Anti-Monopoly Act

[7] See, eg Masahiro Murakami, *Dokusen Kinshiho Kenkyu* (Anti-monopoly Law in Japanese) (Tokyo, Kaobundao, 1997).

During the formal hearing, the respondent firm may challenge the JFTC's fact finding and application of the law, and make a remedial proposal. If the JFTC finds that the remedy proposed by the respondent is appropriate, the JFTC drops the case, and orders the firm to perform the remedy. If the JFTC finds that a violation exists, the JFTC issues a formal decision at the end of the Shinpan hearing procedure, ordering the firm to perform the remedy.

If the parties are dissatisfied with the decision delivered after the Shinpan hearing, they may enter into litigation at the Tokyo High Court, which has exclusive jurisdiction to revoke the JFTC judgment. Under the judicial review, the Court is bound by facts found in the JFTC's decision if such facts are 'supported by substantial evidence' (article 80). If the courts find that a reasonable person would reach the same conclusion based on the same facts as the JFTC did, the courts should abide by the JFTC's findings. Thus, under the judicial review, the plaintiff would argue that the facts on which the JFTC's decision is made are not supported by substantial evidence. The plaintiff may also file an appeal against the judgment of the Tokyo High Court with the Supreme Court.

The Japanese Government has proposed significant changes to the procedures for challenging orders issued for antitrust violations by the JFTC. The Cabinet submitted a bill of amendments to the AMA to the House of Representatives (Shugiin) in March, 2010[8]. The bill provided for the abolition of the administrative hearings on alleged antitrust violations that currently are conducted by the JFTC, and will establish certain due process rights for parties being investigated prior to the issuance of a JFTC order.

In addition to abolishing JFTC hearings and revising the process for court review, the bill would provide certain due process protections for parties under investigation by the JFTC, including requiring that the JFTC:

- provide an explanation of the content of an anticipated order
- allow the parties informally to present arguments and evidence to the JFTC
- allow them to review evidence obtained by the JFTC from the party and its employees, absent legitimate reason for refusing access to those materials.

The ability to review such evidence is regarded as important for parties' to prepare to challenge the order in the Tokyo District Court.

A. Sanctions

The AMA is normally enforced by the JFTC through administrative procedures, such as cease and desist orders and surcharge payment orders; however, criminal and civil procedures in court may also be instituted in court in some cases, as is briefly summarised in Table 2.

The surcharge system was introduced in 1977. Surcharges are a rigid administrative fine. There are two aspects to the rigidity: first, the JFTC is obliged to issue a surcharge order if it is applicable, as listed in Table 2. Second, the amount of the surcharge is calculated according to a formula, namely, as a percentage (stipulated in the Act) of the profit received

[8] The bill has not been in process as of May 2011.

Table 2: Sanctions under the Current AMA

		Unreasonable restraint of trade	**Private monopolisation**	**Unfair trade practices**
	Cease and desist order	Y	Y	Y
	Surcharge	Y for price fixing cartel	Y	Y+
Criminal Sanctions		Y	Y	N
Civil Procedure	Injunctive relief	N	N	Y
	No-fault compensation	Y	Y	Y

Note: Y (or N) refers to the fact that a particular sanction is applicable (or not applicable) to certain anti-competitive behaviour.
+: Surcharges applies to certain types of unfair trade practices, including concerted refusal to deal, discriminatory pricing, unjustly low price sales, and resale price maintenance.

from the sales of products or services related to the anti-competitive activity involved.[9] The percentage of surcharge rate differs by the capital or total amount of contribution and lines of business, not by the severity of damages or the amount of excessive profit accrued by the alleged anti-competitive behaviour. Also note that in calculating the surcharges, the JFTC takes into account only domestic sales. Thus, it is currently impossible for the agency to collect fines from those foreign companies, for example, that participate in cartel activities by not selling to Japan. We believe that the current surcharge system is out of date in the era of a globalised economy where cross-border transactions are common. While it is often argued in Japan that a discretionary administrative fine is against transparency and predictability from the respondents' point of view, we think it worthwhile to reconsider introducing a discretionary surcharge system. Such a system is more in line with the original purpose of the surcharge, in that it accounts for the difference in the amount of disgorged undue profit. Of course, calculating the appropriate amount of a discretionary surcharge requires the economics discipline.

B. Civil Procedure

The no-fault compensation suit is a private lawsuit specifically prescribed under article 25 of the AMA. The damage award is not trebled: instead, single damages are payable. A firm whose interest is seriously injured by unfair trade practices may seek injunctive relief from the court for suspension of such conduct (article 24 of the Act). Both of these private actions have not worked properly. It is presumably because plaintiffs, under the civil litigation procedures in Japan, do not have sufficient capacity to collect evidence to prove violations. As we will discuss below, these private actions can in principle be a complement to, rather than a substitute for, JFTC's enforcement, and thus should be activated effectively.

[9] Note that a reduction or exemption through an application of the Leniency Program and coordination with criminal penalties should be considered as an exception.

V. Overview of Japan's Intellectual Property Laws

Japan has enacted intellectual property statutes, including the Patent Act,[10] the Utility Model Act,[11] the Copyright Act,[12] the Trademark Act,[13] the Design Act,[14] and the Unfair Competition Act.[15] Japan has also entered into most of the important international conventions related to intellectual property rights (IPR).[16]

Textually, the IPR laws of Japan closely resemble those of other developed countries. The Patent Act, for example, provides for the patenting of inventions of products and processes, if the inventions satisfy the statutory requirements of novelty, utility and inventiveness.[17]

Like most such laws, with the notable exception of the US Patent Act,[18] the Patent Act gives priority to the first to file an invention, not the first to invent or use an invention, although an independent inventor who used the invention prior to the filing of the patent may continue to use the invention on a non-exclusive basis.[19] Until a decision rendered by the Japan Supreme Court in 1998, Japanese courts rarely applied the doctrine of equivalents, also engendering significant criticism. That may have changed with the Supreme Court's 1998 decision in *Tsubakimoto Seiko Co Ltd v THK K.K.* Japan Supreme Court Case No 1994 (o) 1083, decided 24 February 1998.[20]

Some differences, however, stand out, including the lack of any requirement in the Japan law to disclose the best mode of practice of an invention, and apparently no Japanese court has ever invalidated a patent for a failure to disclose the best mode.[21]

The Japan Patent Office (JPO)[22] examines all applications and grants or denies patent applications. During the 1990s, various countries, principally the United States, alleged that the JPO showed favouritism towards Japanese patentees, those complaints have now waned and Japan's patent issuance regime is now regarded as generally fair and effective. The court enforcement of patent rights were also broadly criticised as offering insufficient damages, and inefficient and costly procedural hurdles, including the length of litigation,

[10] *Tokkyo Ho*, Law 121 (1959).

[11] *Jitsuyo Shin'an Ho*, Law 123 (1959).

[12] *Chosakuken Ho*, Law 48 (1979), amended by: Law 49 (1978); Law 46 (1984); Law 62 (1985); and Law 64 (1986).

[13] *Shohyo Ho*, Law 127 (1959).

[14] *Isho Ho*, Law 125 (1959).

[15] *Fusei Kyoso Boshi Ho*, Law 14 (1934), as amended by Law 66 (1990) (which incorporated trade secret provisions into the Act).

[16] These include: Trade Related Aspects of Intellectual Property Rights 1994; The Paris Convention for the Protection of Industrial Property 1883; The Patent Cooperation Treaty 1970; The Nice Agreement Concerning the International Classification of Goods and Services for the Purposes of the Registration of Marks 1991; The Trademark Law Treaty 1994; The Protocol Related to the Madrid Agreement Concerning the International Registration of Marks 1989; The Berne Convention for the Protection of Literary and Artistic Works (Paris Act) 1971; The Universal Copyright Convention 1971; The WIPO Copyright Treaty 1996; and The Convention Establishing the World Intellectual Property Organization 1967.

[17] Patent Act art 29.

[18] US Patent Act 35 USC §§ 1-376 (2000).

[19] Patent Act arts 72 and 79.

[20] An English translation of this decision is available at www.okuyama.com/doe.htm.

[21] See James A Forstner, 'International Business Implications of the US Best Mode Requirement' (1993) 21 *American Intellectual Property Law Association Quarterly Journal* 157, 158–59.

[22] *Tokkyocho* or JPO. See generally the overview of the JPO's structure and activities on the JPO website at www.jpo.go.jp/.

high filing fees, limited discovery, and the absence of judicial authority to increase damages for willful infringement.[23]

Those concerns have been addressed substantially by two rounds of amendments to the Japan Code of Civil Procedure[24] in 1998,[25] 2004,[26] and 2006, as well as by 1999, 2007, and 2009 amendments to the Patent Act. The 1998 civil procedure reforms permitted plaintiffs to file intellectual property cases before the Tokyo or Osaka District Court, which each have a specialised intellectual property division and thus have more experience and expertise to handle intellectual property cases. They also sought to address concerns about the length of intellectual property litigation by concentrating formal hearings within shorter time periods and encouraging more expeditious handling of such cases, and by providing for meaningful preliminary hearings to focus the claims and defences and to permit the judges to meet with the parties, examine documentary evidence and discuss the issues on which the court should hear from witnesses. The 1998 amendments further empowered the courts to set specific time limits for submission of parties' arguments and evidence, and the power to reject claims or defences not raised early in the case, and increased the obligation of parties to produce documents and the rights of the parties to seek information and documents, though the amendments, and courts interpreting the amendments, imposed a stringent level of specificity for such requests to be effective, which limited their effectiveness.

The 2004 amendments to the Code of Civil Procedure added procedures to further expedite cases, especially in complex litigation such as patent cases, urging disposition of cases within two years, and requiring courts and parties to seek to establish a schedule for all proceedings, with recommended deadlines.[27] The amendments also gave the Tokyo and Osaka District Courts exclusive jurisdiction over first-instance intellectual property cases and further expanded the rights of parties to seek information and documents from opponents. They also empowered the courts, in complex cases such as intellectual property litigation, to appoint 'expert commissioners' to provide their views in writing or orally, and even to participate in settlement conferences.[28]

Of the numerous rounds of recent amendments to the Patent Act, those that became effective in 1999 were the most relevant to the handling of intellectual property litigation and other issues that may bear on the intersection between antitrust and intellectual property law. Specifically, those amendments augmented the courts' power, under the amended Code of Civil Procedure, to order a party to produce documents needed to prove infringement, and incorporated into the patent law the in camera procedure found in the 1998 amendments to the Code of Civil Procedure.[29] The Patent Act amendments also require a

[23] See Scott K Dinwiddie, 'A Shifting Barrier? Difficulties in Obtaining Patent Infringement Damages in Japan' (1995) 70 *Washington Law Review* 833.

[24] An English translation of the Code of Civil Procedure is available at www.japanlaw.co.jp/procedure/civilcode.html.

[25] See generally Shoichi Okuyama, Izumi Sato and Alan J Kasper, 'The New Code of Civil Procedure in Japan, Toward More Effective Resolution of IP Disputes' (October 1997), available at www.sughrue.com/files/Publication/8341f83f-a239-45c7-a8a7-e1b82afcab1b/Presentation/PublicationAttachment/f649debe-b64e-4d33-bbf8-e42218ba8e1a/new_code.htm.

[26] See generally Carl F Goodman, 'Japan's New Civil Procedure Code: Has It Fostered a Rule of Law Dispute Resolution Mechanism?' (2004) 29 *Brooklyn Journal of International Law* 511.

[27] Luke Nottage, 'Civil Procedure Reforms in Japan: The Latest Round' (2004) 18 *Journal Japan Law* 203, 206.

[28] The use of such commissioners (*senmon i'in*) is subject to veto by the parties.

[29] Patent Act art 105(1) and (2).

defendant to explain its acts that purportedly rebut an allegation of infringement, absent a proper reason for refusing to do so, providing plaintiffs with a more detailed understanding of the defendants' theory of the case at an early stage in the litigation.[30]

According to various sources, these reforms appear to have reduced the duration of district court intellectual property litigation and increased damages awards during recent years. From 1999 to 2005, the average deliberation period of resolved intellectual property suits in Japan decreased from an average of 23.1 months to 13.5 months.[31] The average amount of damages awarded in 'major lawsuits' regarding infringement of patents and utility models also increased from an average of JPY 14.81 million (approximately US$145,000) in the 1975–79 period, to an average of JPY 111.36 million (approximately US$1,100,000) during the 1998–2000 period.[32]

VI. The Anti-Monopoly Act and IP Laws in Japan

The key article of the AMA that addresses IP rights is article 21, which reads as follows: 'The provisions of this Law shall not apply to such acts recognizable as the exercise of rights under the Copyright Law, the Patent Law, the Utility Model Law, the Design Law or the Trademark Law.'

Despite the fact that this article is included in chapter VI entitled Exemptions, exercise of an intellectual property right is not automatically exempted from the AMA. While relatively rare, there are instances of the JFTC and the courts of Japan applying the AMA to various kinds of conduct involving intellectual property rights, the most prominent examples of which are discussed in the next section.

The JFTC has issued several guidelines over the years to provide guidance on the extent to which the AMA may be applied to intellectual property-related activities. The most comprehensive such document is the Guidelines for the Use of Intellectual Property under the Anti-Monopoly Act (the 'IP Guidelines')[33] which the JFTC promulgated in 2007. The IP Guidelines replaced the JFTC Guidelines for Patent and Know-How Licensing Agreements under the Anti-Monopoly Act ('Patent and Know-How Guidelines'). The IP Guidelines expressly recognise that legal protection of intellectual property rights 'may encourage entrepreneurs to conduct research and development and may serve as a driving force for creating new technologies and products based on the technologies'. As such, the JFTC recognises that the exercise of intellectual property rights 'can be seen as having pro-competitive effects'.[34]

[30] Ibid art 104.

[31] David W Hill and Shinichi Murata, 'Patent Litigation in Japan' (2007) 1 *Akron Intellectual Property Journal* 141, 147.

[32] Ibid 149.

[33] An unofficial translation of these guidelines is available on the JFTC website at www.jftc.go.jp/e-page/legislation/ama/070928_IP_Guideline.pdf.

[34] IP Guidelines part 1. *cf* Antitrust Guidelines Issued by the US Department of Justice and Federal Trade Commission § 2.0, which states that 'the Agencies recognize that intellectual property licensing allows firms to combine complementary factors of production and is generally procompetitive'.

The IP Guidelines also recognise, however, that certain common licensing conduct may violate the AMA. They seek to reconcile this view with article 21 of the AMA, quoted above, by explaining that:

> [Article 21] means that the [AMA] is applicable to restrictions pertaining to the use of technology that is essentially not considered to be the exercise of [IP] rights. An act by the right-holder to a technology to block other parties from using its technology or limit the scope of use may seem, on its face, to be an exercise of rights. The provisions of the [AMA] apply even to this case if it cannot be recognized substantially as an exercise of a right. In other words, any act that may seem to be an exercise of a right cannot be 'recognizable as the exercise of the rights' provided for in the aforesaid Article 21, provided that it is found to deviate from or run counter to the intent and objectives of the intellectual property systems, which are, namely, to motivate entrepreneurs to actualize their creative efforts and make use of technology, in view of the intent and manner of the act and its degree of impact on competition. The [AMA] is applicable to this kind of act.

When determining whether or not any specific act is recognisable as an exercise of the right, attention must be paid to the exhaustion of a right. After a party owning the right to technology legally distributed any product based on the technology in the Japanese market at its own discretion, its right is not infringed by any other party trading in the product in the Japanese market. In other words, the patent or other rights have been exhausted. There is no difference, in the principles of application of the [AMA], between the cases where the right-holder imposes restrictions on another party that deals in the product that it has distributed at its own will and where a supplier, in general, imposes restrictions on the dealers that deal in its products.[35]

In emphasising that the pro-competitive benefits of IP must be balanced against the risk of anti-competitive harm, the JFTC references article 10 of the Intellectual Property Basic Act[36] which prescribes that

> In promoting measures for the creation, protection and exploitation of intellectual property consideration shall be paid to secure the fair exploitation of intellectual property, consideration shall be paid to secure the fair exploitation of intellectual property and public interests and to promote fair and free competition.[37]

Specific types of conduct that the IP Guidelines regard as potentially raising concerns under the AMA include refusals to license, excessive royalties, agreements not to challenge the validity of licensed intellectual property rights, and license provisions related to 'platform functionality'. These will be addressed in turn.

With regard to refusals to deal, the IP Guidelines provide that:

> In a case in which an entrepreneur conducting business activities in a particular technology or product market collects all of the rights to a technology that may be used by its actual or potential competitors but not for its own use and refuses to license them to prevent the competitors from using the technology, this activity may fall under the exclusion of business activities of other entrepreneurs [and thus possibly constitute private monopolization under the AMA].[38]

Similarly, the IP Guidelines indicate that a refusal by members of a patent pool to grant licenses to new entrants or existing entrepreneurs without reasonable grounds may

35 IP Guidelines part 2(1).

36 Intellectual Property Basic Act No 122 of 4 December 2002.

37 IP Guidelines part 2(1) fn 6.

38 Ibid part 3(1)(c).

constitute an unreasonable restraint of trade under the AMA, if the refusal substantially restrains competition in the field of trade of the product in question.[39] A refusal to license may also constitute an unfair trade practice under the AMA. The IP Guidelines state that:

> In a case where an entrepreneur acquires the rights to a technology from the right-holder, with the recognition that a competitor uses the licensed technology in its business activities and that it is difficult for the competitor to replace the technology with an alternative, and the entrepreneur refuses to grant a license for it in order to block the competitor from using the technology, this conduct impedes the use of the technology with the intent of interfering with the competitor's business activities. It is found to deviate from or run counter to the intents and objectives of the intellectual property systems. It is therefore considered to constitute an unfair trade practice if it degrades the competitive function of the competitor and tends to impede fair competition.[40]

The IP Guidelines also recognise that a refusal to license IP rights by a participant in standard-setting activities may constitute an unfair trade practice when the participant had previously vowed to grant a license on advantageous terms, where it is difficult for entrepreneurs to switch to another technology.[41] Similarly, refusing to license to a particular entrepreneur without reasonable grounds, while licensing to a number of other entrepreneurs competing in the same product market, may also constitute an unfair trade practice.[42]

The IP Guidelines do not contain several of the criteria that the European Union has imposed to limit the applicability of antitrust law in refusals to grant access to essential facilities, including intellectual property licenses, which are intended to limit interference with independent decisions on which counterparties to deal with to only 'extraordinary cases'. These criteria include findings of indispensability of access to the facility, that the party seeking access will produce a new product, that, absent access, all competition will be excluded, and that there are no objective grounds for refusing to deal.[43] Nor do the IP Guidelines restrict the application of antitrust law to rare cases involving changes in prior courses of dealing, as in the Aspen Skiing US Supreme Court decision.[44] The absence in the IP Guidelines of such criteria and recognition of the extremely limited circumstances in which compulsory licensing (or other forced dealing) should be imposed as a competition remedy has caused some concern about whether such remedies will be applied only in extremely limited circumstances, as under EU and US law. Of particular concern in this regard is a passage that states that the imposition of 'prohibitively expensive' royalties is, in some cases, 'in effect equivalent to a refusal to license' and will be analysed under the AMA in the same fashion, as a possible instance of private monopolisation.[45]

The IP Guidelines recognise that, generally, the imposition by a licensor of an obligation of licensees not to contest the validity of IPRs may 'promote competition by facilitating

[39] Ibid part 3(2)(d).

[40] Ibid part 4(2)(i), referencing paras (2) and (15) of the General Designation.

[41] Ibid part 4(2)(ii).

[42] Ibid part 4(2)(iii), referencing para (4) of the General Designation.

[43] Case C-418/01 *IMS Health GmbH & Co OHG v NDC Health GmbH & Co KG* [2004] ECR I-5039 (Judgment of Court (Fifth Chamber) of 29 April 2004), available at http://eur-lex.europa.eu/LexUriServ/LexUriServ.do?uri=CELEX:62001J0418:EN:HTML (29 April 2004).

[44] *Aspen Skiing Co v Aspen Highlands Skiing Corp* 472 US 595 (1985). See also *Verizon Communications Inc v Law Offices of Curtis v Trinko LLP* 540 US 398 (2004) (noting that the Supreme Court has never recognised the essential facilities doctrine and stating that Aspen Skiing is 'at or near the limit of §2 [of the Sherman Act] liability', but acknowledging that Aspen Skiing established that '[t]he high value that we have placed on the right to refuse to deal with other firms does not mean that the right is unqualified').

[45] IP Guidelines part 3(1)(i).

transactions and is unlikely to reduce competition directly'.[46] However, the Guidelines go on to state that such no-contest provisions 'may constitute an unfair trade practice when it is found to tend to impede fair competition by continuing rights that should be invalidated and by restricting the use of the technology associated with the said rights'.[47]

Under US law, such no-contest provisions are unenforceable,[48] but no court has held that such an agreement violates the Sherman Act, and generally has not regarded them as constituting patent misuse.[49]

The IP Guidelines include a new provision that regards as an unfair trade practice a licensor of technology that serves a 'platform function', such as a computer operating system, and incorporates into the platform function certain functions supported by existing applications, but does not support competing applications.[50] The description of the circumstances that would constitute such an unfair trade practice are exemplified by the JFTC's view of the effect of Microsoft's bundled license in the JFTC Microsoft matter, discussed below.

VII. IP-Related AMA Cases in Japan

There is very little court case law related to the application of the AMA and virtually none related to the AMA in the intellectual property context. Accordingly, most of the decisions that provide useful guidance are administrative decisions of the JFTC. The following are brief summaries of several such decisions.

In 1997, the JFTC considered a complaint regarding a patent pool operated by an association formed by 10 leading manufacturers of pachinko (Japanese pinball) machines. The pool members, which manufactured approximately 90 per cent of the pachinko machines made in Japan, assigned to the association a substantial portfolio of patents on technologies essential to the manufacture of pachinko machines and adopted a policy of granting no licenses to any of those patents to any entity that was not a member of the pool. The JFTC found that this joint refusal to license substantially restrained competition in the market for the manufacture of pachinko machines and concluded that the conduct constituted private monopolisation in violation of article 2, paragraph 5 of the AMA. The JFTC ordered the pool members to abolish the no-license policy and to cancel all decisions taken in accordance with it.[51]

In an oft-forgotten early case against Microsoft, the JFTC considered a Microsoft Japan licensing policy that offered licenses in Japan to the Excel spreadsheet application only on the condition that licensees also took licenses to the word processing application and the Outlook scheduling management program. At the time, in Japan, Ichitaro, produced by Just Systems, was the most popular word processing application, and Organizer, produced by Lotus, was the most popular scheduling management program. In 1998, the JFTC

[46] Ibid part 4(4)(vii).

[47] Ibid referencing para 13 of the General Designation.

[48] *Lear v Adkins* 95 US 653 (1969).

[49] See, eg *American Equip Corp v Wikomi Mfg Co* 630 F.2d 544, 548 (7th Cir 1980).

[50] IP Guidelines part 4(5)(v).

[51] JFTC, 6 August 1997, Case—Patent Pool of Pachinko Makers, *Shinketsushu*, 44, 238. The *Pachinko Manufacturers* decision is used as an illustrative example in the IP Guidelines part 3(1)(i)(a).

found that this conduct constituted an unfair trade practice under Item 10 of the General Designation (tie-in sales), and issued a recommendation decision to Microsoft Japan, to take remedial measures. Microsoft Japan accepted the recommendation. Therefore, the JFTC issued a cease and desist order requiring Microsoft Japan to cease imposing the conditions on separate licenses of Excel, to accept proposals by PC manufacturers to amend existing contracts of Word, Excel and Outlook to allow licenses for one or two of those applications, and not tie licenses to PC manufacturers of any other software to licenses for Word or Excel.[52]

In 2000, the JFTC found that a publisher of a newspaper, Hokkaido Shimbun, in the northernmost Japanese island, Hokkaido, had attempted to prevent a new entrant into the Hokkaido newspaper market by filing applications for a large number of trademarks on possible names of newspapers that could be used by the new entrant. The JFTC also found that Hokkaido Shimbun had persuaded a news agency not to provide news to the new competitor, and had asked local companies not to advertise in the new paper. The JFTC found that this conduct constituted private monopolisation and required several remedial measures, including the withdrawal of the trademark applications.[53]

The JFTC considered an agreement entered into by Konami Corporation, a manufacturer of software games, and the Professional Baseball Organization of Japan (PBOJ), granting Konami the exclusive merchandising rights to the intellectual property covering baseball team names, player names and logos of the 12 professional baseball teams, for the three-year period. The agreement required Konami to grant sub-licenses to the intellectual property rights to competing software developers unless there was a reasonable basis to refuse such sub-licenses. Nevertheless, Konami refused to accept applications for sub-licenses. The JFTC found that the use of the IP rights covered by the agreement between Konami and PBOJ were indispensable to the creation and sale of game software related to professional baseball. Accordingly, the agency issued a warning to Konami, stating that Konami should not engage in any of the conduct described above.[54]

In 2003, the JFTC found that Twentieth Century Fox Japan (Fox Japan), the distributor in Japan of movies supplied by the related company Fox International Ltd Inc to movie theatres. In conjunction with licensing the intellectual property of the movies for showing by the theatres, Fox Japan fixed the admission charges for theatre patrons to view the movies, or limited discounts on those charges, through a related movie distribution contract. The JFTC found that the conduct constituted an unfair trade practice, namely dealing on restrictive terms in violation of article 13 of the Designation of Unfair Trade Practices. The agency ordered Fox Japan to cease the described activities and delete the offending provisions from the distribution contract.[55]

Following almost four years of hearings, in 2008, the JFTC issued a decision (shimpan shinketsu) finding that Microsoft Corporation's use of a non-assertion of patents (NAP)

[52] See Osamu Igarashi, 'Non-Price Restriction Conducts in Japan' presented at 5th APEC Training Program on Competition Policy (6–8 December 2004) and available at www.jftc.go.jp/eacpf/05/APECTrainingProgram December2004/Igarashi_NonPriceRestriction.pdf.

[53] The *Hokkaido Shimbun* decision is referenced as an example of private monopolisation in the IP Guidelines part 2(2) Note 4(3).

[54] See JFTC Press Release, 22 April 2003, available at www.jftc.go.jp/e-page/pressreleases/2003/april/03422Konami.html.

[55] See JFTC Press Release, 8 October 2003, available at www.jftc.go.jp/e-page/pressreleases/2003/october/031008-1.html.

clause in its software licenses, which prohibited licensees from asserting certain IPRs against Microsoft and its customers, violated the AMA's prohibition against dealing on restrictive terms, consistent with the provision in the IP Guidelines part 4(4)(vii) and paragraph 13 of the General Designation, discussed above. OEM (Original Equipment Manufacturer) PC manufacturers had complained to the JFTC that they were concerned about actual and potential use of their patented technologies in future versions of the Microsoft Windows Operating System (OS). The JFTC concluded that OEMs had 'core' technologies related to PC audio-visual applications, and that the OEMs' incentives and ability to expand those technologies were substantially impaired as a result of the Microsoft NAP clauses.[56]

The JFTC decisions that have been issued in the intellectual property field are consistent with the IP Guidelines, but are too sparse in analysis and too few in number to provide much needed detailed guidance on JFTC enforcement policy in this complex area.

VIII. New Amendments to the AMA

Amendments to the AMA were passed by the Diet on 3 June 2009. There are a number of elements to the recent AMA amendments, the principal of which involve the following:

1. Expanded coverage of anti-competitive activities that face surcharges.
2. Increased penalties on cartel participants.
3. An increase in the number of potential leniency applicants accepted under the existing programme.
4. Revision of the rules governing business combinations.
5. Special rules of the document production order issued by courts.

The JFTC issued a surcharge order against private monopolisation, but only for the activities that 'control' business entities and not for exclusionary conduct. Perhaps in line with the global trend toward fines against abuses of dominant market positions, the 2009 amendments authorise surcharges on the exclusion of private monopolisation that are as high as six per cent. The amendments also authorise the imposition of surcharges against certain types of unfair trade practices. These practices include concerted refusal to trade, discriminatory pricing, and unjustly low price sale and resale price maintenance. If the violators are subject to another charge under unfair trade practices, they will be subject to surcharges, with the rate ranging from one to three per cent. The amendments also allow for a surcharge order of one per cent upon the abuse of a superior bargaining position. The amendments increase the amount of surcharges for unreasonable restraint of trade by 50 per cent for those that lead the formation of a cartel and also increase criminal penalties. For business combinations, the amendments bring about two major changes: one is that firms are required to declare a certain amount of share acquisitions prior to the merger, and the other is that the minimum notification thresholds for both the acquirer and target have been altered. It is said that these changes to the regulations on business combinations are aimed at bringing Japanese regulations more on par with international best practices,

[56] See JFTC Press Release, 8 October 2003, available at www.jftc.go.jp/e-page/pressreleases/2003/october/031008-1.html.

and also at allowing the JFTC to review international business combinations in a more appropriate way.

In view of the fact that the number of petitions for civil injunctive relief against unfair trade practices remains low, the new amendments introduce special rules, similar to those of the Patent Act, by which the court can issue an order to produce documents unless there is a justifiable reason for refusing such production. The amendments also introduce provisions that allow the judge to issue a confidentiality order to those litigants who touch upon trade secrets. It remains to be seen to what extent the amendments make injunctive relief more accessible to private parties.

IX. Law and Economics of Japan's Antitrust Enforcement

While the AMA emulates the US antitrust laws, antitrust enforcement in Japan is distinctly different from its American counterpart. Unlike the United States, which has two agencies—Antitrust Division and the US FTC—the JFTC is the only antitrust agency in Japan and it was established by the AMA. As described above, judicial remedies have not functioned effectively, and injunctive relief and private damages actions have not worked well. In essence, the JFTC effectively creates and maintains a jurisdictional monopoly in antitrust enforcement. Many Japanese textbooks on the AMA often describe this situation as JFTC-centrism or Kotorii-Chushinsyugi in Japanese.[57] This JFTC-centrism may conceivably have engendered two controversial issues that are often discussed in the political science literature on the legislative-agency relationships: bureaucratic discretion and congressional control.[58] The first view—bureaucratic discretion—derives from the assumption that agencies are independent of the legislature. This independence affords agencies a degree of discretion. This discretion allows the agents to pursue their own private goals, which may or may not be aligned with the public purpose for which they were originally developed. The second view rests on the opposite assumption, namely, that agencies are controlled by the Congress: the Congress or some politicians therein possess sufficient rewards and sanctions to create an incentive system for agencies.

The underlying assumptions of both theories do not exactly capture the facts associated with the JFTC that were described earlier. Although the JFTC is an independent agency, as legally stipulated in the Act, several factors could influence the Diet's incentive system for the JFTC. We discuss two of them here. First, in the budgetary process, each agency (including the JFTC) competes with the others for budgetary favour. The politicians pursuing their own electoral goals would 'favor those agencies that provide the best clientele service'.[59] Second, and the factor that Weingast and Moran[60] claims as the most effective means of influence, is that the Congress controls who gets appointed. As explained in

[57] For example Kanai, T, N Kawahama and F Sensui, *Dokusen-Kinshi ho* (Anti-monopoly Law in Japanese) (Kobun-do, 2008).

[58] The following discussion has been inspired by BR Weingast, and MJ Moran, 'Bureaucratic Discretion or Congressional Control? Regulatory Policymaking by the Federal Trade Commission' (1983) 91(5) *Journal of Political Economy*, and Y Miwa and Mark Ramseyer, 'Toward a Theory of Jurisdictional Competition: The Case of The Japanese FTC' (2005) 1(2) *Journal of Competition Law and Economics* 247.

[59] Weingast and Moran, 'Bureaucratic Discretion or Congressional Control? (1983) 769.

[60] Ibid.

section III, the Act requires that the JFTC commissioners be approved by both the Houses of the Diet. This factor, along with the budgetary process discussed above, could in theory provide the Diet with leverage to control the agency's decision.

While we ultimately need a new theory that encompasses the two existing theories to understand the genesis of decision making by the JFTC, such research is beyond the scope of this chapter. Instead, in what follows, we provide an exploratory analysis based on the premise that the monopolistic agency is controlled by the legislature. Note that the analysis undertaken in this chapter should be considered as merely preliminary, and a formal analysis needs to be conducted for a better grasp of the legislature-agency relationships in Japan's antitrust enforcement.

In the antitrust context in Japan, and perhaps in other countries, it is reasonable to assume that few politicians specialise in anti-monopoly law. Therefore, the politicians have to rely on quantitative signals to assess the performance of the antitrust agencies. Such signals may include the number of cases filed or the amount of surcharges collected. If a rival agency existed, or private actions or injunction relief were made easily accessible, the politicians may well assess the effectiveness of JFTC's enforcement by comparing the relative performance of the alternative agents. If there is only one agency, politicians have no means for comparison. In such a case, at first glance, the best strategy for the monopolistic agent would be inactive enforcement and to report to the politicians that they have earned such high regard that no firms broke the law. However, this strategy entails the risk of a (wrong) signal being sent out to politicians—namely, that the agency is not working actively enough to implement enforcement actions. In view of this possible concern, the JFTC may wish to increase the number of cases, but at the same time, to minimise the efforts put in to do so. To resolve this trade-off, as the hypothesis goes, the monopolistic agent would focus on cases where it is easier to establish violations.[61]

Consistent with the hypothesis, Figure 2 shows that the regulations on unfair trade practices are enforced far more frequently than those on private monopolisation in the study period from 2003 to 2009: the number of cease and desist orders issued in cases involving unfair trade practices during this period is greater than that during any another period. Note that, as discussed in section III, it has been considered to be easier to establish cases against unfair trade practices than against private monopolisation.[62] Therefore, the observation found in Figure 2 is consistent with the hypothesis that the JFTC maximises both its slack and the number of cases filed (and also the number of cases completed, as those cases tend to be quickly resolved). Note that Figure 2 does not

[61] One could also argue that the agency may prefer the cases that involve neither criminal penalty nor surcharges, because such cases would elicit less opposition from the parties. This argument however does not explain why the agency prefer unfair trade practices to exclusionary private monopolisation, both of which had no consequence of criminal and surcharge penalties prior to the 2009 amendments. Indeed, it is increasingly common that a party fights against a cease and desist order, as the order considerably damages its company image.

[62] It is also intriguing to ask why the number of bid-rigging cases is so high in Japan. While it has been said that bid rigging, also known as Dango, exists in the awarding public works projects in Japan (for example, J McMillan 'Dango: Japan's Price Fixing Conspiracies' (1991) 3(3) *Economics and Politics* 201), it is not clear whether Figure 2 reflects the actual distribution of illegal activities, or the JFTC spare resources more than proportionally on bid-rigging investigations. According to Miwa and Ramseyer, 'Toward a Theory of Jurisdictional Competition' (2005), the latter hypothesis may also sound reasonable, because bid-rigging is not an area where the JFTC enjoys the monopoly; the Ministry of Justice can also file criminal charges on its own. The JFTC may have to compete with the Ministry on the bid-rigging cases.

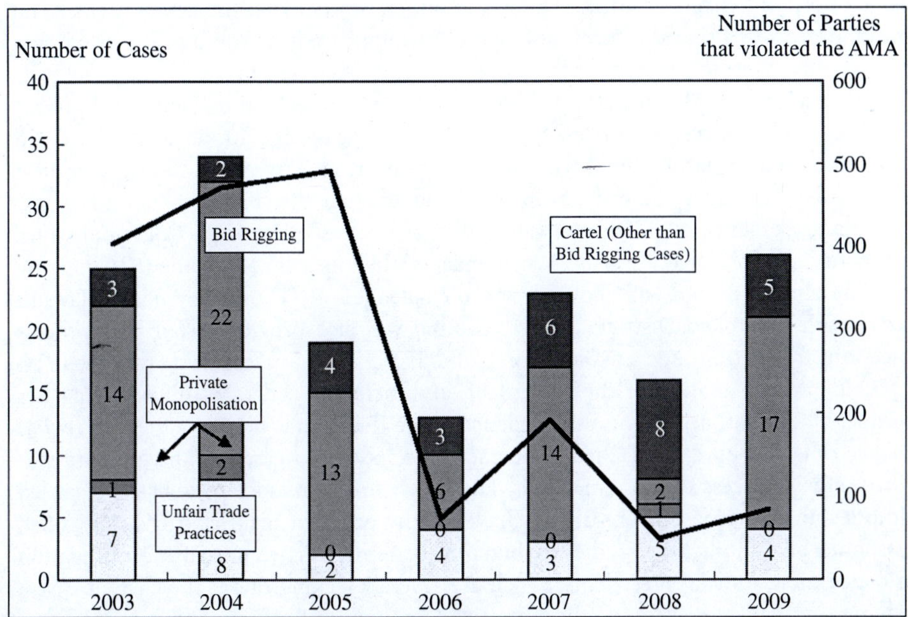

Figure 2: Number of Parties that violated the AMA

include administrative warnings, on which the JFTC often relies when they do not have sufficient evidence to establish the cases against unfair trade practices. While the administrative warning enables the JFTC to make the suspected parties voluntarily correct their business activities, it lacks transparency, and there is no way for the parties to contest warnings under the AMA.

The amendments to the AMA passed in June 2009 witness how the jurisdictional monopolist as an agent is vulnerable to congressional influence. To see this, think about the economic environment surrounding Japan: the worst global economic slump since the Depression has hit the Japanese economy hardest. Both the manufacturing production and export volume had experienced the worst slowdown since the Second World War and, as a consequence, the unemployment rate has risen steeply. Japanese politicians are currently very keen on protecting the small and medium sized businesses (SMEs), especially when the general election for the House of Representatives is just around the corner. It is commonly believed that the decision to extend coverage of surcharges to include unfair trade practices, in particular, the activities of unjustly low price sales and abuses of superior bargaining positions, were the result of strong political influence.

We expect that the 2009 amendments could fundamentally alter the way the JFTC enforces the AMA. First of all, once surcharges are introduced on unfair trade practices, the agency may have to define such practices to be on a similar level as 'substantial restraint of trade', which refers to the unreasonable restraint of trade and private monopolisation. This prompts the JFTC to consider the validity of the threshold conditions required for the imposition of injunctive relief under article 24, in which a private party is allowed to seek injunctive relief only for unfair trade practices.

A second point is related to the Diet resolution accompanying the amendments. The resolution promised that the current Shinpan hearing procedure would be reviewed over the year, with a view to changing the existing procedure. As noted above, a bill was submitted by the Cabinet in March 2010, consistent with the Diet resolution. Under the current AMA, the JFTC issues cease and desist orders or surcharge orders (administrative fines) to parties accused of violating the AMA, with no prior hearing. Parties that choose to contest a JFTC order may, after the order is in place, request that the JFTC conduct a hearing. A lawsuit to challenge a JFTC order can be filed with the Tokyo High Court only after the conclusion of the JFTC hearing. When enacted, the bill will abolish the JFTC hearing procedure altogether and will allow parties to challenge a JFTC order by filing a lawsuit directly with the Tokyo District Court.[63] The bill will also provide certain due process protections for parties under investigation by the JFTC, including requiring that the JFTC (i) provide an explanation of the content of an anticipated order, (ii) allow the parties informally to present arguments and evidence to the JFTC, and (iii) allow them to review evidence obtained by the JFTC from the party and its employees, absent legitimate reason for refusing access to those materials. The ability to review such evidence is regarded as important for parties' to prepare to challenge the order in the Tokyo District Court, and should allow judicial remedies to function better. If this results in more litigation and hence more judicial precedents, which are severely lacking under the current AMA, replacing the JFTC's practice of administrative warnings and informal consultations, we anticipate that the degrees of transparency and accountability in Japan's antitrust enforcement will be significantly enhanced.

In the era of a globalised economy and dynamic innovative markets, economic activities that the antitrust authorities have to monitor are ever expanding over geographical regions and over types of goods and services. While, as Figure 3 shows, the JFTC's budgetary and personnel resources are on the increase over the years, it is next to impossible for the JFTC alone to quickly and thoroughly respond to anti-competitive activities and restore free and fair competition in every corner of the markets related to Japanese interests. In this sense, the idea to maintain JFTC-centrism or Kotorii-Chushinsyugi appears to be contrary to the global economic trend. To bring Japan closer to the goal of AMA cited in the introduction of this chapter, we believe it essential to invite private parties and the courts to be more actively involved in the AMA enforcement process, or introduce 'competition' in the enforcement procedure. As David Teece convincingly argues in this conference, competition spurs innovation, burgeoning entrepreneurs and new businesses. We agree. We believe that introducing competition in Japan's antitrust enforcement further improves transparency and accountability, increases the opportunity to introduce rigorous economic analysis by private and academic economic consultants, into cases under the AMA, and eventually ensure the further penetration of economics further into the law-dominated organisation, as indicated in Table 3. The first thing the JFTC should do perhaps is to create a position of the chief economist inside the organisation.[64]

[63] See Figure 4 summarising the changes that are expected to result from passage of the bill, available on the JFTC website at www.jftc.go.jp/en/pressreleases/uploads/2010-Mar-12_3.pdf.

[64] The *Global Competition Review* has mistakenly published the name of a commissioner since the 2007 issue.

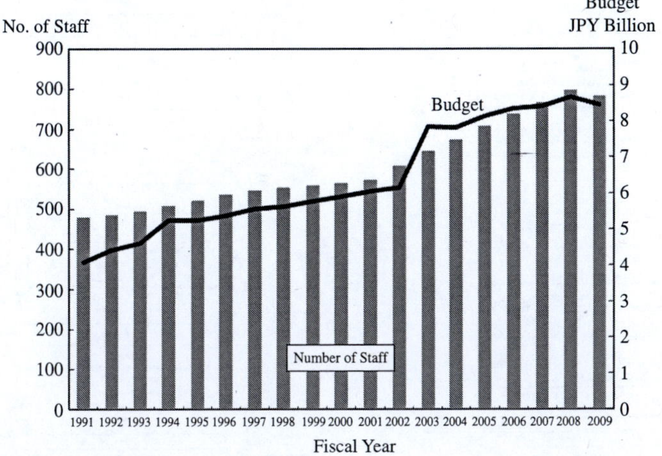

Figure 3: Staff and Budget 1991–2009

Table 3: Number of Economists in Major Jurisdictions, 2007

	No Competition Staff	% Economists	No Economics PhD
US	1165	15	853
EC	633	35	17
Japan	601	5	5
Korea	439	13	11
UK	373	25	10
Australia	335	43	8
Russia	305	36	13
Canada	273	31	12
Netherland	225	27	7
Germany	220	35	16

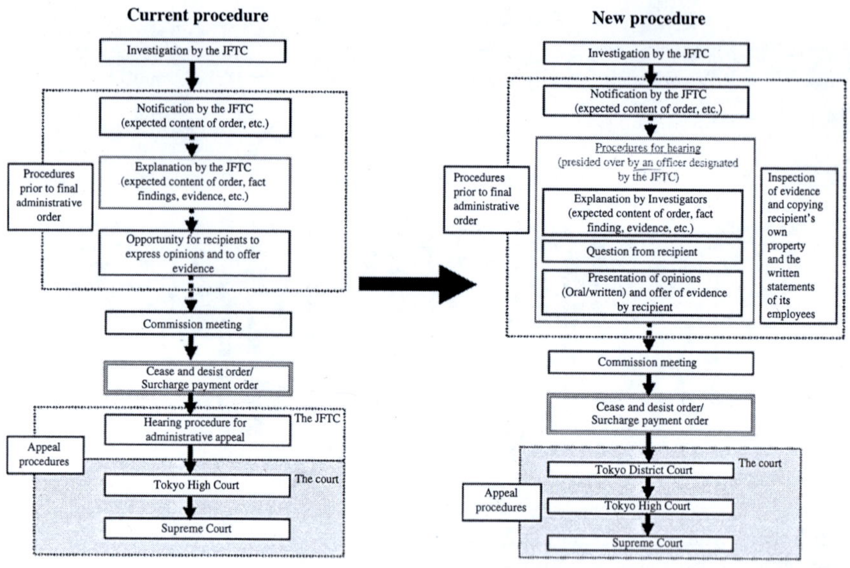

Figure 4: Revision to Shinpan Procedure (in a bill submitted in March 2010)

10

Singapore

ASHISH LALL AND DARYL LIM*

I. Introduction

Singapore is a young nation and a recent entrant to the interface between intellectual property rights (IPRs) and competition law ('the Interface'). Singapore started developing its intellectual property (IP) regime from the 1980s, partly because of pressure from major trading partners to provide stronger protection for IP originating from these countries and partly because it was determined to move up the value chain as a matter of economic strategy.[1] The history of competition law in Singapore is even more recent. Singapore introduced a general competition law regime following the recommendations of the Economic Review Committee in 2003 and in keeping with its obligations under the US-Singapore Free Trade Agreement.[2] Substantive portions of the Competition Act came into force in stages from 2006 and it is administered by the Competition Commission of Singapore (CCS).[3]

Singapore has ramped up its research and development (R&D) as it seeks transition to an innovation-based economy. There has been a significant increase in R&D inputs in recent years, both in terms of dollars and personnel. In 2008, the total number of (full time equivalent) researchers was 27,841 and gross domestic expenditure on R&D was US$6.6 billion

* Ashish Lall contributed the economic framework section of the chapter. Daryl Lim contributed the legal framework section of the chapter. Daryl attributes his best thoughts here to discussions with his colleagues at the Federal Trade Commission in Washington DC during his summer internship on the staff of Commissioner William E Kovacic, as well as to his participation in the Asian Competition Forum's 5th Annual Conference in Hong Kong, both in 2009. He gratefully acknowledges the pioneering work of Professors R Ian McEwin, George Wei, Ng-Loy Wee Loon and Burton Ong. All errors and omissions remain his own.

[1] Ng-Loy Wee Loon, *Law of Intellectual Property of Singapore*, revised edn (Singapore, Sweet & Maxwell Asia, 2009) 16 ('Singapore is an expert in using the IP system as a tool to achieve significance for Singapore when it became clear in the mid-1980s that software could be protected within the copyright regime. To encourage the growth of the software industry here, a major revamp of its copyright law was undertaken and the result was the Copyright Act passed in 1987.... The same focused approach is taken with patents: the moment the policy-makers saw the need to move Singapore into emerging fields such as biotechnology, a new Patents Act was passed in 1994.').

[2] Cavinder Bull, 'Competition Policy and Law' in Cavinder Bull and Lim Chong Kin (eds), *Competition Law and Policy in Singapore* (Singapore, Academy Publishing, 2009) 7 ('A number of FTAs concluded by Singapore included provisions relating to the regulation of competition issues. One of the landmark FTAs was the United States Singapore (USSFTA) which set out extensive competition-related obligations.... In particular, Article 12.2 of the USSFTA requires Singapore to (a) adopt or maintain measures to proscribe anti-competitive business and (b) establish an authority responsible for the enforcement of the measures to proscribe anti-competitive business conduct'.) Competition law was also introduced due to the recommendations of the Economic Review Committee in 2003 to 'create a level playing field for businesses, big and small, to compete on equal footing'. See ibid 9.

[3] Cap 50B, 2006 rev ed. For a comprehensive summary of the CCS, see Bull, 'Competition Policy and Law' (2009) 14–17.

(current purchasing power parity (PPP) adjusted dollars); with the private sector accounting for about two-thirds of the expenditure.[4] Singapore's ability to attract researchers from other countries shows up in bibliometric studies which show that Singapore has a very high rate of growth in the number of publications in areas such as nanotechnology and biotechnology.

This chapter argues that the key to navigating the Interface in Singapore includes understanding the nature of IP markets in Singapore and fostering synergies between the key institutions responsible for the IP and competition regimes. As Singapore adopts a regulatory self-assessment system, firms with substantial IPRs in Singapore need to fully understand the Interface to avoid what may be costly mistakes.[5] The discussion of the economic framework first provides background on the economic structure of Singapore, illustrating the role of location and legacy in sectors that continue to be important today. The second part discusses Singapore's innovation performance based on international innovation rankings, as well as on standard measures such as patents, R&D expenditures and personnel. It suggests that Singapore is not yet an innovation-based economy despite the recent increase in innovation inputs. The discussion of the legal framework first surveys IP issues arising from anti-competitive agreements, abuse of dominance, as well as mergers and acquisitions. The second part highlights the challenges and opportunities relevant to Singapore as a small open economy trying to move up the technology value chain and concludes by suggesting a number of ways Singapore can better navigate the Interface.

II. The Economic Framework

A. Singapore's Economic Structure

In 1965, Singapore's per-capita gross domestic product (GDP) was $2,667 (in 1990 PPP adjusted international dollars). By this measure, average incomes in Singapore were the third highest in Asia after Japan and Hong Kong. Between 1965 and 2008, average incomes in Singapore grew by about 3.5 per cent per annum (Table 1) and in 2008 Singapore's per-capita GDP ($28,289) was below only that of Hong Kong ($29,825), Norway ($29,140) and the United States ($31,328).

Table 1: Comparisons of Prosperity

GDP per capita (PPP) growth, CAGR	**Singapore**	**Hong Kong**	**Ireland**	**Norway**	**Switzerland**	**Taiwan**	**Japan**	**South Korea**	**United States**
1965–1985	7.2%	5.0%	3.1%	3.5%	1.5%	7.1%	4.9%	7.1%	2.2%
1986–1997	5.8%	4.1%	5.7%	2.6%	0.6%	4.6%	2.6%	7.1%	1.9%
1997–2008	3.3%	3.1%	4.7%	2.0%	1.5%	3.7%	1.0%	3.8%	1.7%

[4] See Organisation for Economic Co-operation and Development (OECD), *Main Science and Technology Indicators* (Paris, OECD, 2010) vol 2010/1.

[5] See Bull (n 2) 20 ('To minimize the regulatory and compliance burdens on business, the CCS emphasises the need for self-assessment and voluntary compliance by businesses'.).

Table 1: *(Continued)*

1965–2008	3.6%	3.5%	3.2%	2.1%	0.9%	4.1%	1.7%	4.4%	1.5%
2008 GDP per capita '000 of *1990 PPP US$'*	29.2	30.4	28.3	29.5	24.9	22.2	23.1	20.0	31.4

Source: Total Economy Database (January 2009), The Conference Board and Groningen Growth and Development Centre.

Economic growth is accompanied by structural change, however many of the sectors which continue to make significant contributions to the Singapore economy have legacies related in one way or another to Singapore's location on international shipping routes and the foresight of Sir Stamford Raffles who founded Singapore in 1819 and established it as a free port. Examples include shipping, ship-repair and associated services such as finance and insurance; petroleum refining and the associated petro-chemical value chain. The availability of engineering skills which facilitated structural change toward manufacturing after 1965 is also attributed to the presence of rubber milling and tin refining in the late nineteenth and early twentieth century. The growth of many of these sectors was due to technological changes and fortuitous events that took place elsewhere, but which had a considerable impact on the development of Singapore.

Factors which contributed to the development of the port and ancillary activities include the opening of the Suez Canal in 1869, which gave Singapore an edge compared to other ports in the Malayan peninsula such as Penang and Malacca.[6] A second development was the advent of the steamship. The increase in vessel size reinforced the importance of larger ports such as Singapore and led to the development of a hub and feeder system. By the First World War, Singapore's port was the seventh busiest in the world in terms of shipping tonnage handled. After independence, the Government made an early bet by setting up a container terminal in the early 1970s; much before container shipping was well established. In 2010, Singapore's port was the second busiest container port in the world (after Shanghai), handling about 28.4 million twenty-foot equivalent units (TEUs).

Singapore is also a leading centre in the world for ship repair, tanker repair and the construction of petroleum drilling rigs and support ships. The development of these industries can also be traced back to the early twentieth century. By 1913, Singapore had five dry docks—the fifth (King's dock) was built to the specifications of the Admiralty as the British established a naval base in the north of Singapore in 1928. When the British left Singapore in 1967, the shipyard was taken over by the Government which used the infrastructure for the ship repair industry.

The development of related industries and other 'clusters', although linked to the development of the port, are also explained by Singapore's vast hinterland. Huff argues that in the late nineteenth century and until 1960, Singapore was a 'staple port' or one which exported surplus natural resources from the hinterland.[7] In the late nineteenth century, tin was exported

[6] The historical overview draws heavily on A Lall, 'Canada's Pacific Gateway' (Paper prepared for Vancouver Conference under Government of Canada's Asia-Pacific Gateway and Corridor Initiative, Vancouver, BC, Canada, 2–4 May 2007).

[7] WG Huff, *The Economic Growth of Singapore: Trade and Development in the Twentieth Century* (Cambridge, Cambridge University Press, 1994).

from the Malayan peninsula and, later in the 1920s, rubber from Malaya and petroleum from the Dutch East Indies. Favourable geography was a necessary condition for staple ports and this led to an expansion of facilities required to handle a greater volume of goods and shipping. Other requirements included entrepreneurial, investment, management and mercantile functions connected with the staple—which essentially turned the port into a commercial centre.

Between 1874–77 and 1896–99, Malayan tin production increased more than sixfold, growing from one fifth to over one half of world output due to demand for tin plate in the West, which was attributed to two innovations: canned food and the use of barrels for transporting petroleum. By 1899–1900, the world's largest and most technically sophisticated tin smelting facility was located in Singapore and the port was also the world's largest exporter of tin.

In the inter-war period, Singapore was the largest centre in the region for re-milling small-holder rubber. The demand for rubber and petroleum increased due to demand for motorised transport. Between 1913 and the 1930s, the United States imported half to three quarters of world rubber production. The auto industry accounted for three quarters of rubber imports into the United States. The market for petroleum also got a boost due to the conversion of mercantile marine fleet to oil-fired ships. After the First World War, oil majors developed production facilities in British Borneo and the Dutch East Indies and used Singapore to collect, blend and distribute products such as petrol, kerosene and fuel oil for bunkering. Oil companies were drawn to Singapore because of its local and international geographical advantage and freedom from regulation. Petroleum exports were four times greater in volume in the 1950s than in 1937–38. The Royal Dutch Shell Group maintained its headquarters for its Far East shipping fleet in Singapore. In 1959 Caltex started marketing operations; oil refining started in 1960 and by 1980 Singapore was the largest bunkering centre in the world.

Government built on legacy industries such as shipping, ship-repair and petroleum refining and the linkages of tin refining and dry docks to the local engineering industry provided a skill base which allowed Singapore to move to a model of export-led growth based on heavy foreign direct investment (FDI) after the 1960s.

Between 1988 and 2001, the ratio of Singapore's total trade (goods and services) to GDP fluctuated between 3.0 and 3.5, however, since 2002, this ratio has increased more or less monotonically and it stood at about 4.5 (3.5 for goods and one for services) in 2008. Total merchandise trade increased from US$43 billion in 1980 to $658 billion in 2008, representing an annual growth of 10.2 per cent. Export growth of goods (at 10.75 per cent per annum) outpaced growth in imports (9.69 per cent) over the period of 1980 to 2007. Entrepöt trade is an important component of Singapore's trade. In 2008, re-exports accounted for 42.62 per cent of Singapore's total exports. Growth in re-exports accounted for 51.13 per cent of total export growth between 1990 and 2008. Singapore's re-exports are dominated by high-tech products, and this pattern has become more pronounced over time. The share of high-tech products in total re-exports increased from 63.22 per cent in 1995 to 67.17 per cent in 2008. The other important product category is petroleum and related products.

Foreign investment accounts for about 80 per cent of gross fixed capital formation in Singapore. This is one of the highest rates in the world, with only Hong Kong relying even more on foreign capital to finance investment. As a proportion of GDP, FDI inflows doubled from 82 per cent in 1991 to 171 per cent in 2007. Traditionally, manufacturing and financial services attracted most of the FDI inflows. Since 2004, finance has outpaced

Table 2: Profitability of FDI in Selected Industries

Industry	Return on Investment		FDI Inward Stock	
	2001–07 average	2007	in 2007 (S$ mill)	Growth (01–07)
Banking Services	41.3%	35.1%	11,319	–4.5%
Instrumentation, Photographic & Optical Goods	40.6%	40.9%	2,765	–26.0%
Pharmaceutical Products	22.4%	38.9%	47,435	19.4%
Water Transport Services	21.5%	19.2%	26,941	12.1%
Insurance Services	20.4%	–2.8%	10,059	–1.0%
Refined Petroleum Products	20.1%	41.9%	14,148	2.8%
Chemicals & Chemical Products	18.8%	17.0%	6,837	42.1%
Electronic Products & Components	18.6%	17.6%	28,241	–15.3%
Transport Equipment	18.0%	25.0%	3,564	30.3%
Wholesale Trading Services	16.6%	23.4%	72,116	10.6%
Machinery & Equipment	14.8%	16.6%	5,180	32.5%
Other Financial Services	12.7%	27.1%	13,450	–27.1%
Warehousing, Post & Courier Services	11.6%	10.8%	3,187	2.6%
Rental & Leasing Services	7.6%	5.0%	5,511	–22.6%
Real Estate Services	7.2%	26.3%	12,179	6.8%
Business Services	6.8%	13.8%	16,239	28.3%
Hospitality and Food Services	5.1%	8.4%	3,006	–5.6%
Investment Holding Services	4.6%	6.5%	157,363	–0.6%
Information and Communications Services	3.8%	15.4%	4,754	36.9%
All Industries/Total	14.00%	17.8%	457,024	3.5%

Sources: Foreign Equity Investment in Singapore (2005–2007 editions), all published by the Singapore Department of Statistics.

manufacturing as a target for FDI. Western foreign firms continue to dominate investments in the manufacturing sector with the United States continuing to be the leading investor. In 2007, local investment accounted for 28 per cent of gross fixed investment in the manufacturing sector; the United States accounted for 29 per cent; Japan for 16 per cent and European countries for another 18 per cent. These shares have remained remarkably stable since 1997. Table 2 shows that foreign investors continue to be attracted to Singapore due to the high returns they obtain from their investments.

While Singapore maintains an open trading environment, the domestic economy is not led by the local private sector, but is one in which the Government and multinationals play a substantial role. Local small and medium scale enterprises (SMEs) only dominate general manufacturing and real estate and business services; all other sectors are dominated by foreign firms or large (generally government-linked) local firms. There are various estimates of the number of government-linked companies (as many as 600) and their contribution to GDP (from 13 to 60 per cent), however they are just estimates as

Table 3: Financial Statistics of Singapore's 1,000 Largest Companies

	2008 Financial Indicators, S$ per employee			
	GLC	**Non-GLC**	**Foreign**	**All Firms**
Revenues	542,321	381,369	2,387,977	905,950
Net Income	105,632	48,817	132,375	80,461

Source: Singapore Top 1000, provided by the DP Information Network Pte Ltd.
Note: Domestic firms include government linked companies (GLC) and private domestic firms (non-GLC).

many government-linked companies are exempt from filing public accounts.[8] Table 3 shows that foreign firms generate higher revenues and net income per employee than either government-linked or local private firms.

Singapore is often cited as an example of 'state capitalism' where government uses various tax and other incentives to both attract foreign investment and to direct investment to 'targeted' sectors. The process of structural change is more a matter of state direction rather than an outcome of market forces. Young argues that this fast pace of structural change comes at the cost of low total factor productivity, which is the driver of sustainable economic growth.[9] At an aggregate level, however, the structure of the economy shows remarkable stability. Over the period 1990–2008, the share of the manufacturing sector in total output (or GDP) has remained at about 25 per cent and this is not by accident but by design. Over the same period, the employment share of manufacturing declined from 30 to 20 per cent, reflecting the shift to higher value-added sectors (or sectors with higher capital intensity). However, the most important sectors continue to remain the same and include petroleum, chemicals, pharmaceuticals, electronics, transport equipment and machinery and equipment. In 2007 these sectors accounted for 85 per cent of the gross output of the manufacturing sector and 88 per cent of manufacturing exports. The share of the services sector in GDP increased from 60 to 66 per cent and the employment share of services increased from 62 to 67 per cent. Wholesale and retail trade was the largest service sector contributing to 16 per cent of output and 14 per cent of employment in 2008, while financial services accounted for 13 per cent of output.

While Singapore's broad strategy remains the same, over the years government has used various policy levers to encourage the transition to higher value added industries in manufacturing, followed by a push toward the service sector and more recently toward innovation-intensive sectors such as biotechnology, water and clean technologies. Often, these and other changes are driven by exogenous factors and events; for example, the deregulation of telecommunication in 2000 was brought forward by two years to remain competitive with Hong Kong.

B. International Innovation Rankings

In recent years there has been a proliferation of rankings and their popularity has risen as well. It would appear that everything can be reduced to a single number, including measures of the quality of governance and judicial systems. Nonetheless, there appears to be considerable

[8] See G Hopf, *Saving and Investment: The Economic Development of Singapore 1965–1990* (Saarbrücken, VDM Verlag Dr Müller, 2009) 260–64.

[9] A Young, 'A Tale of Two Cities: Factor Accumulation and Technical Change in Hong Kong and Singapore' in OJ Blanchard and S Fischer (eds), NBER Macroeconomics Annual 1992 (Cambridge, MA, MIT Press, 1992).

interest in rankings and countries such as Saudi Arabia and Kazakhstan have used them to set national objectives. Saudi Arabia, for example, sought to be ranked in the top 10 in the World Investment Report, the World Bank Doing Business Rankings or the World Economic Forum Global Competitiveness Rankings by 2010.[10] The Saudi Government also hired strategy consulting firm Monitor Group to help it achieve this objective. Generally, rankings are of limited use from a prescriptive or policy viewpoint; however they could be used as a quick-and-easy benchmarking tool. Unfortunately, as is shown below using innovation rankings, this can sometimes prove challenging. Data, methods of aggregation and metrics differ across rankings and understanding these requires deconstructing the rankings. Doing so, however, defeats the purpose of constructing them in the first place.

The World Bank's 'Knowledge Index' and 'Knowledge Economy Index' measure a country's ability to generate, adopt, and diffuse knowledge.[11] The former is based on three pillars: use of information and communications technology (ICT); education and human resources and the innovation system. The latter includes an additional pillar: economic incentive and institutional regime. Use of ICT is measured by per-capita penetration of computers, telephones and the internet. Educational attainment is measured using adult literacy rates, as well as enrolment in secondary and tertiary education. The innovation system measure is based on US patent grants, royalty payments and bibliometric data. These three measures are aggregated to arrive at the Knowledge Index. In 14th place, Taiwan was the highest ranked Asian country in 2009, while Singapore ranked 26th. Singapore's ranking was dragged down by the education metric on which it ranks 70th. Adding the economic pillar which includes measures of tariff and non-tariff barriers, the quality of regulation and the rule of law, helped Singapore's standing as its rank in the Knowledge Economy Index was 19th, or second in Asia, just after Taiwan (18th).

Most other cross-country comparisons of innovation use the notion of innovation inputs and outputs and in addition some include measures of the innovation environment. The Economist Intelligence Unit-Cisco Innovation Index uses this approach.[12] Innovation output is measured by patents granted by the European, Japanese and US patent offices. Innovation inputs include measures of R&D expenditure, educational and technical skills and the quality of ICT infrastructure. The innovation environment is measured by factors such as policies towards trade and investment, the political environment, taxes, availability of financing, the labour market and infrastructure. In constructing the index of 'innovation enablers', innovation inputs are given a higher weight (75 per cent) than indicators of the innovation environment. Based on 2004–08 data, Singapore ranked second (after Denmark) on environmental factors, but its overall rank on both enablers, as well as output or 'innovation performance', was 16th. Japan was in first place whereas Taiwan was ranked seventh and South Korea 11th.

In 2009, The Boston Consulting Group (BCG), the National Association of Manufacturers, and the US Manufacturing Institute released an international innovation index comparing innovation inputs and performance across countries.[13] The scope of both measures is very wide and includes measures of economic growth, employment growth, the level

[10] www.saudincc.org.sa/getdoc/f4e88d1e-96b5-4ad5-b3b1-3fd84a693e31/How-Competitiveness-is-Assessed.aspx.

[11] go.worldbank.org/JGAO5XE940.

[12] Economist Intelligence Unit (EIU), *A New Ranking of the World's Most Innovative Countries* (London, EIU, 2009).

[13] Boston Consulting Group, *The Innovation Imperative in Manufacturing: How the United States Can Restore Its Edge* (Boston, BCG, 2009).

of taxation, high-tech exports and labour productivity. Singapore ranked first overall on innovation inputs, but it ranked ninth on innovation output and performance. While it is highly implausible that Singapore is the most innovative country in the world, these results point to Singapore's inefficiency in producing innovation outputs. For example, Singapore's innovation input score was 2.74, whereas that of Hong Kong was 1.61. Yet, Hong Kong's (ranked sixth overall) innovation performance score was 1.97 compared to Singapore's score of 1.92.

INSEAD (The European Institute of Business Administation) and the Confederation of Indian Industry released their third global innovation rankings for the year 2009–10.[14] Innovation inputs were measured using five pillars: institutions, human capacity, general and ICT infrastructure, markets sophistication and business sophistication. Innovation outputs included scientific outputs, creative outputs and benefits to social wellbeing. Many of the measures drawn from the Global Competitiveness Report data and data on creative outputs are drawn from the United Nations Conference on Trade and Development (UNCTAD) which includes production and exports of tangible products or hardware used in creative industries including compact discs, music players, etc.[15] Overall, Iceland was ranked the most innovative country and Hong Kong was third, followed by Singapore (seventh), United States (11th) and Japan (13th). Singapore's rank on the input and output pillars was third and 12th respectively.

The 2009 Innovation Index of the Information Technology and Innovation Foundation (ITIF) in the United States also gives a large weight to indicators of economic performance.[16] These include general economic business environment indicators such as trade balance, foreign direct investment, corporate tax rates and the World Bank's doing business rankings and new business registration data. Singapore was ranked first—or the most innovative country in the world; South Korea fifth and the United States sixth. Singapore had low ranks in areas such as e-government (21st), scientific publications (22nd) and broadband (14th).

Generally, Singapore ranks reasonably well (in the top 20) in international innovation rankings and its standing is higher in indices which include either general economic metrics such as tax rates, economic growth, export performance and ability to attract FDI or business environment metrics, such as the costs of doing business. Singapore also does well in rankings which include measures of government support for innovation. However, Singapore tends to perform better on measures of innovation inputs than on outputs. The next section provides comparative data on more specific metrics of innovation outputs such as patents, trademarks and copyright registrations.

C. Innovation Metrics

Innovation is a complex phenomenon and not just restricted scientific R&D activities. Firms may make process and organisational innovations and increasingly customers and

[14] INSEAD, Global Innovation Index Report 2009–2010, available at www.globalinnovationindex.org/gii/main/home.cfm. Note that there is a lot of volatility in the rankings compared to the previous year 2008–09. For example South Korea was ranked 20th in 2009–10, as opposed to sixth in 2008–09 and Iceland was ranked 20th in 2008–09 and first in 2009–10.

[15] The Global Competitiveness Report is an annual publication of the World Economic Forum.

[16] RD Atkinson and SM Andes, *The Atlantic Century: Benchmarking EU and US, Innovation & Competitiveness* (Washington DC, The Information Technology and Innovation Foundation, 2009).

other business partners are playing an important role in collaborative or open innovation. Ultimately, to fuel economic growth, innovation should lead to commercialisation or the introduction of profitable new products, services, or methods of delivery. Singapore is moving toward an innovation-based economy and government has devoted a considerable amount of funds to R&D since 2000. Innovation is difficult to measure so researchers rely on readily available IP registration data as measures of output and R&D expenses and personnel as measures of inputs into the innovation process.

Table 4 shows Singapore's global share of IP including patents, trademarks, industrial designs and utility models or petty patents. While Singapore's share is small, it appears to have made some progress. Its share of approved patents increased from 0.18 per cent in 2001 to 0.62 per cent in 2007—a factor of three. Approved trademarks also increased from 0.24 per cent in 2001 to 0.66 per cent in 2007.

Table 5 shows the average (2001–07) number of approved patents, trademarks and industrial designs and also presents more recent data on a per-capita basis (per 10,000 population). So, for example, about 748 patents on average were granted to Singapore residents over the period 2001–07, which translates to about 1.62 patents per 10,000 population. In general, Singapore looks somewhat similar to Ireland; it does better than Hong Kong on all measures except industrial designs, but is generally behind OECD and Scandinavian countries. US-registered patent data (Table 6) show that Singapore's patenting rate per-capita (per-million population) is comparable to countries such as Denmark and the Netherlands. However, countries like Finland, Israel, Switzerland, Japan, South Korea, and Taiwan continue to outperform Singapore. Singapore has shown strong growth, but on this measure, countries such as India and China have outpaced Singapore by a factor of two to three. Despite the recent push towards new areas such as biotechnology, Singapore has a strong focus on electrical engineering, which is very similar to South Korea and Finland (Table 7).

Singapore amended its IP laws about a decade ago and trademarks, industrial designs and patents can since be registered at the Intellectual Property Office.[17] Table 8 provides data on filings and approvals in Singapore and filings and approvals by Singapore residents. In other words it asks: which are the top five countries that file (and get approved) for intellectual property in Singapore? In which countries do Singapore residents file (and get approved)? For patents, the United States and Japan and the top applicant countries in Singapore, whereas for trademarks and industrial designs, Singapore residents are the top applicants followed by either the United States or Japan. Singapore residents show a clear domestic preference for obtaining trademarks and industrial designs, but they prefer to file for patents in the United States.

Singapore has made great strides in strengthening its research inputs, particularly over the last decade or so. Table 9 shows a consistent increase in both spending and personnel since 1994. Research scientists and engineers per-thousand of the total labour force increased at an average annual rate of 5.9 per cent from 1994 to 2008 and R&D expenditures per capita grew at 10.8 per cent per annum over the same period. In absolute terms, however,

[17] Utility models or petty patents are not recognised in Singapore and Singaporean residents are not significant users of utility models. Over the period 2000–07 Singaporean residents accounted for a total of 51 filings and 26 approvals. The most important location was China, which accounted for about 60% of both filings and approvals, followed by Germany and Australia. See World Intellectual Property Organization (WIPO) Utility Model Database http://wipo.int/ipstats/en/statistics/models/.

Table 4: Global Share of Singapore-owned Intellectual Property

Year	Share of Applications				Share of Approvals			
	Patents (%)	Trade marks (%)	Industrial Designs (%)	Utility Models (%)	Patents (%)	Trade marks (%)	Industrial Designs (%)	Utility Models (%)
2001	0.0518	0.1514	0.1091	0.0012	0.1878	0.2439	0.0672	0.0014
2002	0.0610	0.2017	0.0866	0.0039	0.2878	0.3075	0.1159	0.0031
2003	0.1201	0.2878	0.1636	0.0034	0.4844	0.4663	0.1513	0.0027
2004	0.1234	0.2669	0.2164	0.0000	0.3802	0.4945	0.2017	0.0000
2005	0.1056	0.2650	0.1582	0.0010	0.3796	0.5055	0.2266	0.0008
2006	0.1303	0.2691	0.1149	0.0019	0.3463	0.4727	0.1261	0.0005
2007	0.2035	0.3745	0.1548	0.0107	0.6208	0.6632	0.2302	0.0066

Source: *WIPO Patents, Trademarks, and Industrial Designs Database 2008.*

Table 5: Comparison of Granted Intellectual Property to Residents

Country	*2001–2007 average*			*per 10,000 population in 2008*		
	Patents	**Trademarks**	**Industrial Designs**	**Patents**	**Trademarks**	**Industrial Designs**
Denmark	2,131	8,107	610	3.89	14.78	1.11
Finland	4,103	4,850	842	7.82	9.25	1.61
France	23,302	47,695	32,543	3.73	7.63	5.21
Germany	50,430	137,664	52,008	6.10	16.66	6.29
Hong Kong	312	6,937	2,275	0.44	9.88	3.24
Ireland	872	2,285	164	2.10	5.50	0.39
Japan	192,448	109,090	38,637	15.12	8.57	3.04
Netherlands	8,488	5,761	1,525	5.10	3.46	0.92
Norway	1,151	2,464	286	2.48	5.30	0.62
Singapore	748	5,740	564	1.62	12.46	1.22
South Korea	60,385	45,630	29,887	12.48	9.43	6.18
Sweden	7,606	11,187	1,160	8.41	12.37	1.28
Switzerland	8,501	49,882	11,704	11.21	65.79	15.44
United Kingdom	13,314	40,136	4,605	2.18	6.59	0.76
United States	142,258	206,385	22,372	4.68	6.79	0.74

Source: WIPO Patents, Trademarks, and Industrial Designs Database 2008.

Table 6: US Patent Ownership, 2008

	Utility patents owned	**Per million population**	**Avg. Annual Growth 1999–2008**
World	157,772	23.10	0.31%
United States	77,501	246.16	–0.88%
Japan	33,682	264.89	0.88%
Germany	8,915	108.50	–0.51%
South Korea	7,549	156.19	8.35%
Taiwan	6,339	275.92	6.00%
France	3,163	50.74	–2.10%
United Kingdom	3,094	50.26	–1.61%
Netherlands	1,329	80.10	0.71%
China	1,225	0.91	29.01%
Israel	1,166	162.63	5.01%
Switzerland	1,112	146.94	–1.55%
Sweden	1,060	114.60	–3.10%
Finland	824	154.72	2.65%
India	634	0.53	19.26%
Singapore	399	84.23	11.32%

(Continued)

Table 6: *(Continued)*

	Utility patents owned	Per million population	Avg. Annual Growth 1999–2008
Denmark	391	71.48	–2.44%
Hong Kong	311	44.29	7.74%
Norway	273	56.73	2.20%
Ireland	164	36.32	6.67%

Source: USPTO Databases.

Table 7: WIPO-Registered Patent Applications by Field of Technology (2002–06)

	Electrical Engineering (%)	Mechanical Engineering (%)	Instruments (%)	Chemistry (%)	Other Fields (%)	Total Applications (%)
World	31.32	23.20	17.30	23.82	4.37	3,236,551
China	28.47	17.80	17.54	32.65	3.54	146,646
Denmark	8.88	22.49	21.04	44.70	2.90	3,594
Finland	46.61	23.21	9.96	18.58	1.65	28,837
Germany	18.03	35.55	15.33	27.60	3.49	159,822
Ireland	17.86	20.08	23.56	33.31	5.19	2,408
Japan	36.67	24.29	17.29	17.42	4.33	1,344,446
Netherlands	38.32	16.22	16.61	25.57	3.29	58,829
Norway	15.06	36.30	15.75	28.12	4.77	3,097
Singapore	49.95	12.32	19.30	15.94	2.49	6,695
South Korea	49.61	19.32	12.29	13.11	5.65	372,435
Sweden	23.68	26.24	20.40	26.92	2.77	24,904
Switzerland	10.43	22.86	24.00	38.74	3.97	15,077
United Kingdom	19.55	22.42	20.55	31.59	5.89	49,405
United States	30.70	17.29	18.95	28.88	4.17	757,589

Source: WIPO Statistics Database, July 2009.

Table 8: Intellectual Property filed in Singapore and by Singaporeans (2001–08)

Patents filed in Singapore				Patents filed by Singaporeans			
Top Country Appliers		*Top Country Holders*		*Top Countries Applied*		*Top Countries Held*	
USA	29.58%	USA	32.47%	USA	39.63%	Singapore	46.79%
Japan	11.86%	Japan	17.94%	Singapore	33.67%	USA	38.71%
Singapore	7.05%	Germany	16.03%	EPO	5.97%	EPO	5.75%
Germany	4.40%	Singapore	5.54%	China	4.58%	Japan	1.66%
Switzerland	3.26%	UK	5.17%	Australia	3.20%	China	1.13%
All others	43.85%	All others	22.84%	All others	12.95%	All others	5.96%
Total Filed	61,065	Approved	47,354	Total Filed	12,785	Approved	5,236

(Continued)

Table 8: *(Continued)*

Industrial Designs filed in Singapore				**Industrial Designs filed by Singaporeans**			
Top Country Appliers		*Top Country Holders*		*Top Countries Applied*		*Top Countries Held*	
Singapore	23.12%	Japan	23.62%	Singapore	71.72%	Singapore	73.85%
Japan	22.18%	Singapore	22.02%	USA	7.76%	USA	5.47%
USA	8.44%	USA	8.87%	China	5.96%	China	5.35%
Switzerland	8.08%	Switzerland	7.83%	Japan	2.17%	France	3.52%
Netherlands	3.71%	Netherlands	3.79%	OHI (EU)	1.85%	Australia	2.20%
All others	34.46%	All others	33.86%	All others	10.55%	All others	9.60%
Total Filed	13,588	Approved	13,236	Total Filed	4,381	Approved	3,947

Source: WIPO Patents, Trademarks, and Industrial Designs Database 2008.

Table 9: Innovation Input Trends in Singapore

Year	**Research scientists & engineers per 1,000 labour force**	**GERD per capita (current S$)**
1994	38.50	342.76
1995	47.70	385.72
1996	50.10	488.02
1997	53.40	553.50
1998	57.80	638.30
1999	62.60	669.47
2000	66.10	745.53
2001	65.90	784.59
2002	67.50	811.06
2003	73.80	800.71
2004	80.90	932.94
2005	90.10	1,035.36
2006	87.40	1,115.21
2007	90.40	1,392.29
2008	87.60	1,546.84

*Source: A*Star's 'National Survey of R&D in Singapore 2008'.*

some corporations have a larger R&D spend than Singapore. In 2007, gross expenditure on R&D (GERD) in Singapore was S$6.34 billion, with the private sector accounting for about two-thirds (S$4.23 billion) of the expenditure. In contrast, Sony Corporation which was ranked 20th in a global survey of corporate R&D spending, reported R&D spending of about S$6.8 billion in 2007.[18]

[18] B Jaruzelski and K Dehoff, 'Beyond Borders: The Global Innovation 1000' *Strategy+Business*, issue 53, reprint No 08405 (Booz & Company, 2008) www.strategy-business.com.

In 2008, the Government's share in total R&D spending in Singapore was about 18 per cent, which was higher than in OECD countries and slightly lower than in Taiwan (Table 10). In comparison, the share of higher education in total R&D spending (9.9 per cent) was almost equivalent to that of South Korea and among the lowest in comparison to all OECD and Scandinavian countries. About half of all R&D spending is focused on the electronics sector and within that sector an overwhelming proportion of the expenditure is on semiconductors. Further, most of the R&D expenditure is on experimental development, rather than on applied or basic research—basic research is minimal. There is little evidence that private R&D spending has gone into 'new' areas like biotechnology, where the Government has made major investments. As shown in Table 11, countries such as Taiwan and South Korea also have a focus on electronics, whereas OECD countries such as Germany, Japan, the United Kingdom and the United States have a much more diverse research portfolio. Tables 12 and 13 show that Singapore compares quite well to OECD countries on both R&D researchers and personnel, but the focus appears to be on the former as Singapore's researcher population (10.22 per 1,000 employed workers) places it in the top four, ahead of every Asian country except Japan. Singapore also has comparatively more public institute research personnel per 1,000 employed workers than any other country except the United Kingdom.

Table 10: Comparison of R&D Spending

Country	Year	Private Sector	Higher Education	Government & Public Institutes	Total Spending as % of GDP
Denmark	2007	64.92%	27.49%	7.59%	2.54%
Finland	2008	72.31%	19.01%	8.68%	3.41%
France	2007	63.18%	19.17%	17.66%	2.08%
Germany	2007	69.95%	16.33%	13.72%	2.53%
Ireland	2008	66.96%	26.04%	6.99%	1.42%
Japan	2006	77.16%	12.69%	10.15%	3.39%
Netherlands	2007	60.42%	26.55%	13.04%	1.73%
Norway	2007	51.25%	32.83%	15.93%	1.57%
Singapore	2008	71.83%	9.96%	18.21%	2.77%
South Korea	2006	77.26%	9.95%	12.79%	3.23%
Sweden	2007	72.73%	21.07%	6.20%	3.63%
Switzerland	2004	73.74%	22.90%	3.36%	2.90%
Taiwan	2006	67.50%	12.23%	20.27%	2.58%
United Kingdom	2006	61.65%	26.12%	12.22%	1.78%
United States	2007	71.91%	13.26%	14.83%	2.68%

*Sources: OECD Science & Technology Indicators 2009 and A*Star's 'National Survey of R&D in Singapore 2008'.*

Table 11: Comparison of Private R&D Spending

	Year of Data	Aerospace (%)	Electronics (%)	Office Machinery and Computers (%)	Pharmaceuticals (%)	Scientific Instruments (%)	Other Manufacturing (%)	Services (%)	Total Spend (mill. US$) (%)
Denmark	2006	0.00	4.08	0.00	28.78	6.67	26.94	33.54	3,155
Finland	2004	0.40	49.51	0.10	4.93	2.79	27.76	14.52	3,782
Germany	2005	5.14	8.49	1.41	8.77	6.76	59.35	10.09	43,304
Ireland	2005	0.19	12.57	5.80	20.07	9.35	18.41	33.60	1,300
Japan	2003	0.45	13.08	12.71	7.51	4.27	52.83	9.14	84,180
Netherlands	2006	0.71	21.81	0.00	10.05	2.79	42.74	21.90	6,125
Norway	2004	0.27	6.18	0.13	3.58	5.43	49.13	35.28	1,698
Singapore	2006	0.63	40.99	0.00	7.69	2.25	15.75	32.68	3,144
South Korea	2006	0.80	47.94	1.54	2.17	1.35	39.15	7.06	27,725
Sweden	2003	3.24	22.10	1.01	19.52	5.52	38.18	10.42	7,713
Switzerland	2004	0.00	8.59	0.00	36.90	5.64	29.30	19.57	5,515
Taiwan	2006	0.00	52.12	14.96	1.12	2.77	21.57	7.46	11,173
United Kingdom	2005	16.21	6.12	0.45	25.39	3.35	27.97	20.51	20,512
United States	2006	6.61	12.47	2.94	15.71	9.04	24.12	29.11	247,669

Source: OECD Science & Technology Indicators 2009.

Table 12: Comparison of Researchers (Full Time Equivalent per Thousand Employees)

Country	Year	Private Sector	Higher Education	Government	Public Institutes	Overall
Finland	2007	8.83	4.87	1.80	0.14	15.64
Japan	2006	7.53	2.87	0.52	0.13	11.05
Denmark	2007	6.35	3.15	0.78	0.07	10.35
Singapore	2007	6.07	2.70	0.59	0.86	10.22
Taiwan	2007	6.05	2.55	1.39	0.06	10.05
Sweden	2007	6.06	3.28	0.44	0.01	9.79
United States	2005	7.62	1.26	0.33	0.42	9.64
Norway	2006	4.79	3.23	1.45	—	9.48
South Korea	2006	6.72	1.23	0.61	0.09	8.65
Germany	2007	4.40	1.71	1.08	—	7.19
Switzerland	2004	3.03	2.95	0.10	—	6.08
Ireland	2006	3.43	2.29	0.24	—	5.96
United Kingdom	2006	3.00	1.50	0.29	1.08	5.86
Netherlands	2007	3.05	1.30	0.80	—	5.15

Sources: OECD Science & Technology Indicators 2008/2; Taiwan Science & Technology Indicators 2008 (National Science Council of Taiwan); Yearbook of Manpower Statistics 2008 (Singapore Ministry of Manpower).

Table 13: Comparison of R&D Personnel (Full Time Equivalent per Thousand Employees)

Country	Year	Private Sector	Higher Education	Government	Public Institutes	Overall
Finland	2007	12.81	6.62	2.94	0.19	22.56
Sweden	2007	13.44	3.88	0.75	0.02	18.08
Denmark	2007	10.49	4.34	1.18	0.10	16.11
Japan	2006	9.64	3.72	0.98	0.22	14.57
Norway	2007	6.72	4.44	2.23	—	13.39
Taiwan	2007	9.12	1.93	1.78	0.06	12.89
Germany	2007	8.05	2.46	2.01	—	12.52
Switzerland	2004	7.92	4.39	0.19	—	12.51
Singapore	2007	7.09	2.88	0.91	1.17	12.06
United Kingdom	2006	4.77	3.45	0.64	1.82	10.68
Netherlands	2007	5.75	3.47	1.42	—	10.64
South Korea	2006	7.42	1.91	0.82	0.12	10.27
Ireland	2007	5.34	2.83	0.59	—	8.77

Sources: OECD Science & Technology Indicators 2008/2; Taiwan Science & Technology Indicators 2008 (National Science Council of Taiwan); Yearbook of Manpower Statistics 2008 (Singapore Ministry of Manpower).

Singapore has also taken many steps to provide an attractive environment for science-related investments. In terms of IPRs, Singapore's legal regime of protection is 'TRIPS-plus', and the country has recently emerged as one of only three Asian countries (along with Japan and Taiwan) on the list of the top 25 countries in the world with the lowest software piracy rates. The Agency for Science, Technology and Research (A*STAR) is the national research body that oversees public sector R&D activities in Singapore. It not only manages R&D activities, but has education and commercialisation arms as well. Singaporean firms, however, both government-linked as well as private, do not stack-up internationally. The 2008 R&D scoreboard produced by the UK Government ranked 1,400 firms based on their 2007/08 R&D investment.[19] Only two Singaporean firms appear on that list—Creative Technologies was in position 966 and government-linked Singapore Technologies Engineering was in position 1204.

D. Appraisal

Singapore has a successful economic model and a government which places a very high priority on economic prosperity. In addition, it has been successful in capitalising on its location advantage and built on its legacy of being open to foreign trade and investment. The efficiency-driven model has served Singapore well and continues to provide economic gains, however the move toward an innovation-driven economy has yet to take root. Singapore performs very well on innovation measures that take into account the business environment and indeed the Government has provided support for innovation through higher expenditures and attempting to fill the manpower gap by recruiting scientists and engineers from other countries. Therefore, on the innovation input side, Singapore is well ahead of Asian peers and looks like an OECD country. However, this is not the case on the output side. Output metrics show that Singapore has some way to go in comparison not only to OECD and Scandinavian countries, but also to Taiwan and South Korea which outperform Singapore despite their lower GDP per-capita.

III. The Legal Framework

A. The Law

The Competition Act is largely based on UK legislation,[20] and seeks to promote the efficient functioning of the markets in Singapore and to enhance the competitiveness of the economy through prohibiting anti-competitive activities that unduly prevent, restrict or distort competition.[21] Within a relatively short amount of time, Singapore has installed

[19] UK Department for Business, Innovation & Skills, '2008 R&D Scoreboard' (2008), available at www.innovation.gov.uk/rd_scoreboard/downloads/2008_RD_Scoreboard_analysis.pdf.

[20] R Ian McEwin et al, 'Competition Law' in *Singapore: Principles, Practice and Procedure* (Singapore, LexisNexis, 2007) 1 ('The [Competition] Act is largely based on the Competition Act 1998 (UK) … and Enterprise Act 2002 (UK).').

[21] Vivian Balakrishnan (then-Senior Minister for Trade and Industry), 'Second reading speech for the Competition Bill' Hansard vol 78 col 863 (19 October 2004) ('Sir, the objective of the Bill is to promote the efficient functioning of our markets and hence enhance the competitiveness of our economy. The Bill seeks to prohibit anti-competitive activities that unduly prevent, restrict or distort competition.').

the institutional framework and expertise mirroring the best practices from the world's leading competition authorities.[22] One example of this is the CCS IP Guidelines, which incorporates a distilled blend of EU and US jurisprudence, firmly grounded in contemporary economic analysis.[23]

Singapore's competition law is concerned with total welfare rather than simply consumer welfare.[24] Flowing from this, the effectiveness of anti-competitive agreements, for example, are assessed not merely on the basis of trade-offs between consumer benefit and harm. Instead, the CCS may accept producer efficiency arguments showing producer benefits even if consumers do not visibly benefit from the process.[25]

i. Anti-competitive Agreements

Section 34 of the Competition Act prohibits agreements or concerted practices between undertakings and to decisions by associations of undertakings with the object or effect of appreciably 'preventing, restricting or distorting' competition within Singapore.[26] Entities engaging in commercial or economic activities[27] which knowingly cooperate[28] or concur in any form[29] to substitute competitive risks with the benefits of collusion are thus prohibited.

[22] Ibid ('MTI subsequently studied the competition legislation of various jurisdictions, including the UK, Australia, Ireland, the United States and Canada.').

[23] See, eg Commission Regulation (EC) 772/2004 (OJ L 2004 L 123/11) on the application of Article 81(3) of the Treaty to Categories of Technology Transfer Agreements (27 April 2004) and the 1995 Antitrust Guidelines for the Licensing of Intellectual Property issued by the US Department of Justice and the Federal Trade Commission (6 April 1995); see also the Antitrust Enforcement and Intellectual Property Rights: 'Promoting Innovation and Competition: A Report Issued by the US Department of Justice and the Federal Trade Commission' (April 2007).

[24] Competition Bill Consultation Paper, issued 12 April 2004 by Singapore's Ministry of Trade and Industry, available at www.ccs.gov.sg/archival-First.htm, Annex C (The Relationship between Competition Law and Intellectual Property rights) para 7–10 ('In considering whether a business activity involving the exercise of IPR would have any competition concerns, the Competition Commission of would adopt an "economics-based" or "rule of reason" approach. This means that the Competition Commission would take a holistic view and look at the overall net welfare effects of the activity to decide whether a particular use of an IPR reduces welfare in Singapore.').

[25] Bull (n 2) ('For instance, in the European Community, Article 81(3) of the EC Treaty requires that consumers receive a "fair share" of any efficiency benefits before agreements can enjoy the exemption from Article 81(1) prohibiting anti-competitive agreements. What this means is that the positive effects of an agreement must compensate for the negative effects on consumers [referring to the European Commission, Guidelines on the Application of Article 81(3) of the Treaty [2004] OJ C101/97.] Singapore has however, deliberately removed that specific requirement of consumers receiving a fair share of any efficiency benefits from its Net Economic Benefit test which is similar to Article 81(3). … This strongly suggests that the CCS will consider the impact of an agreement on the total welfare of society (that is, consumer as well as producer welfare) instead of just focusing on consumer welfare. Practically what that means is that the CCS will be more open to accepting efficiency arguments arising from restrictive agreements that may benefit producers but that do not provide any benefits to consumers.').

[26] Section 34 of the Competition Act. For a generic introduction to s 34, see Richard Whish, 'Anti-Competitive Agreements' in Cavinder Bull and Lim Chong Kin (eds), *Competition Law and Policy in Singapore* (Singapore, Academy Publishing, 2009) ch 3.

[27] CCS, 'CCS Guidelines on the Section 34 Prohibition' (July 2007), available at http://app.ccs.gov.sg/cms/user_documents/main/pdf/S34_Jul07FINAL.pdf para 2.6.

[28] Ibid para 2.17 gives factors to be considered in establishing whether a concerted practice exists.

[29] Case T-41/96 *Bayer AG v Commission (ADALAT)* [2000] ECR II-3383, [2001] 4 CMLR 126 [69] (noting that the concept of an agreement 'centres around the existence of a concurrence of wills between at least two parties, in the form in which it is manifested being unimportant as long as it constitutes the faithful expression of the parties' intention').

Agreements running afoul of the Act attract financial penalties[30] and can be declared void.[31] At the Interface, the main focus of section 34 is on anti-competitive clauses in licensing agreements.

The CCS IP Guidelines provide some guidance on the CCS' possible approach to IP rights.[32] They set out a three-step process to assessing licensing agreements. First, agreements between competitors are more likely to be anti-competitive.[33] The CCS is, in particular, concerned with restraints between competitors that fix prices, divide markets, limit outputs or reduce incentives to carry out independent R&D.[34] The CCS IP Guidelines focuses on anti-competitive effects toward technological innovation,[35] and expressly excludes trademarks.[36]

[30] Section 69 of the Competition Act.

[31] Section 34(3) of the Competition Act; Whish (n 26) 109 ('Where a provision is void as a result of the operation of section 33(3) of the Act, it would be a matter of contract law to determine whether the loss of that provision leads to the consequence that the agreement in its entirety becomes unenforceable.').

[32] CCS, 'CCS Guidelines on the Treatment of Intellectual Property Rights' (July 2007) ('CCS IP Guidelines'), available at http://app.ccs.gov.sg/cms/user_documents/main/pdf/IPR_Jul07FINAL.pdf; Burton Ong, 'The Interface between Intellectual Property Law and Competition Law in Singapore' in Steven D Anderman (ed), *The Interface between Intellectual Property Rights and Competition Policy* (Cambridge, Cambridge University Press, 2007) 402 ('Guidelines issued by the CCS are policy statements which reflect the Singapore competition regulator's analytical approach towards the interpretation and application of the statutory prohibitions found in the Competition Act 2004. The contents of the CCS Guideline of the Treatment of intellectual Property Rights have no legal force on their own, are non-exhaustive in character, and may be revised by the CCS should the need arise. The Guideline sets out how the CCS views the interface between IPRs and competition law, indicating some of the factors and circumstances which it may consider when assessing agreements and conduct involving intellectual property. The scope of the Guideline is limited to intellectual property rights granted under the Patents Act, Copyright Act, Plant Varieties Protection Act, Layout-Designs of Integrated Circuits Act, and the Registered Designs Act, as well as trade secrets.'); Bull (n 2) 20 ('Following the enactment of the Competition Act, the CCS developed 13 sets of guidelines relating to the implementation and enforcement of the law. These guidelines cover the major aspects of the work of the CCS, such as the three prohibitions, market definition, investigation, enforcement and notification procedures. These guidelines are of particular importance as they clarify the interpretation of the Competition Act by the CCS when competition law is new in Singapore with no precedents.').

[33] CCS IP Guidelines para 3.2; Ong (n 32) 404 ('The CCS IP Guidelines set out the following general framework for assessing licensing agreements under the section 34 prohibition. Step 1: The nature of the relationship between the parties to the licensing agreement—whether they are competitors or non-competitors—needs to be ascertained. The parties will be treated as being in a competitive relationship if they would have been actual or potential competitors in the absence of the licensing agreement. Step 2: The CCS will consider if the restraints in the licensing agreement restrict actual or potential competition that would have existed in their absence, taking into account their impact on inter-technology and intra-technology competition. Step 3: The pro-competitive benefits of the licensing agreement will be factored into the CCS analysis and weighed against its negative effects on competition. The licensing agreement will not fall within the scope of the section 34 prohibition, if on balance, it may have a net competitive benefit. This would be the case if the agreement "contributes to improving production or distribution or promoting technical or economic progress and it does not impose on the undertakings concerned the possibility of eliminating competition in respect of a substantial part of the goods or services in question"'.).

[34] Ibid para 3.4.

[35] See ibid para 1.2 ('For purposes of these guidelines, the term "intellectual property rights" refers to the rights granted under the Patents Act, Copyright Act, Plant Varieties Protection Act, Layout-designs of Integrated Circuits Act, Registered Designs Act and trade secrets.'); para. 2.3 ('These guidelines address mainly issues relating to technology transfer and innovation.').

[36] Ibid para 1.2 and para 3 of the explanatory policy paper which accompanies it. ('The CCS has indicated that the Guideline is only intended to deal with the competition-related issues concerned with technology transfer and innovation aspects of IPRs. This Guideline is not intended to regulate the product differentiation performed by trademarks and geographical indications. The intellectual property rights statutorily granted under the Trade Marks Act and Geographical Indications Act are therefore not within the scope of this Guideline.')

Agreements between non-competitors are regarded to have more adverse impact on competition where one or more of the undertakings enjoy 'high market power' and 'forecloses access to, or increases competitors' cost to obtaining inputs',[37] preventing licenses from licensing competing technologies.[38] Second, agreements imposing actual or potential restraints on competition that would not otherwise have been there are more likely to be anti-competitive.[39] Third, agreements without countervailing net economic benefits are more likely to be anti-competitive.[40] The Guidelines also state how the CCS will approach the common varieties of licensing clauses, including restrictions on independent R&D,[41] grantbacks,[42] territorial and field-of-use restrictions,[43] geographical exclusivity[44] and technology pools.[45]

Parties whose market shares fall below *de minimis* levels generally need not be concerned that their agreements will run afoul of competition law.[46] Parties whose market shares exceed these levels may still be excused if their agreement passes muster under a rule of reason analysis.[47] Agreements that improve production and distribution, facilitate technology transfers and encourage innovation in related markets may be allowed, notwithstanding being tainted by prima facie anti-competitive effects.[48] With technology firms increasingly integrating functions in a lattice of horizontal and vertical structures over related markets, it may be a challenge to determine whether agreements made by entities within this type of corporate structure are exempted as being made within a single economic entity.[49] Vertical agreements where the IP licensing restraints are merely ancillary to the agreement, such as

[37] Ibid para 3.7.

[38] Ibid para 3.8.

[39] Ibid para 3.2.

[40] Ibid para 3.2. Net economic benefits is read according to para 9 of the Third Schedule of the Act.

[41] Ibid para 3.22.

[42] Ibid para 3.2 (stating that direct or indirect restrictions may have anti-competitive effects since they reduce potential competition in technology or innovation markets).

[43] Ibid para 3.24 (stating that field-of-use or territorial restrictions may promote technology transfer and would be favorably regarded).

[44] Ibid para 3.25 (stating that territorial exclusivity may provide the incentive to invest in the licensed technology or to develop it).

[45] Ibid at para 3.26 (Technology pools are cross-licensing agreements. Licensing of essential and complementary technologies are regarded as pro-competitive, but may raise competition concerns if they consist of essential or substitute technologies as efficiency gains are reduced and the arrangement may amount to price fixing.)

[46] Ibid para 3.14 (Noting that where the licensing agreement is made between competitors, their aggregate market share should not exceed 25% of any of the relevant markets; where the licensing agreement is made between non-competitors, the market share of each of the parties should not exceed 35% of any of the relevant markets; where it may be difficult to classify the status of the parties to the licensing arrangement as competitors or non-competitors, the 25% threshold will be applied.)

[47] Ibid para 3.16. Para 10.4 states that there must be an objectively determined direct causal link between the agreement and claimed efficiencies which is of sufficient value to outweigh the anti-competitive effects of the agreement.

[48] Ibid para 3.2 ('The CCS will consider if an agreement that falls within the scope of the section 34 prohibition, may, on balance, have a net economic benefit. An agreement may have a net economic benefit, where it contributes to improving production or distribution or promoting technical or economic progress and it does not impose on the undertakings concerned the possibility of eliminating competition in respect of a substantial part of the goods or services in question.') [Footnotes omitted].

[49] Ibid para 2.7. The Guidelines states that s 34 does not apply to entities which form a single economic unit. Whish, 'Anti-Competitive Agreements' (2009) 75 ('[S]ince entities in the same economic unit form a single undertaking, it follows that an agreement between those entities is not entered into *between* undertakings.').

franchise agreements, will also be exempted from review.[50] Licenses or assignments of IP, while not exempted, are recognised as being pro-competitive.[51] However, bundling or tying agreements will still be scrutinised.[52] In any case, vertical agreements may still be subject to the prohibition against the abuse of dominance where one or more licensing parties are dominant.

ii. Abuse of Dominance

Firms with substantial market power must avoid conduct distorting market competition, either through unilateral or collective exercise of their market power.[53] Market power is assessed in the market for the technology, the market for products and services embodying the technology, as well as markets for R&D.[54] Market power accruing from the IP itself is not objectionable.[55] The CCS IP Guidelines allow even 'persistently high' market shares resulting from the owner's use of his or her IP to deter entry in the short term, as long as competitors may 'in the long term be able to enter the market with its own innovation'.[56] As Burton Ong observes:

> This complicates the traditional approach of assessing an undertaking's market power with direct reference to its share of the relevant market. To what extent can an IP-owning undertaking argue that, despite having the sizeable share which has traditionally been used as an indicator for market dominance, it should not be treated as a dominant undertaking simply because its advantages are time-limited by the finite duration of its IPRs?[57]

Being dominant or maintaining dominance through successful innovation or economies of scale or scope are acceptable. It is only where the IP owner attempts to leverage its IP to extend its market power to the detriment of market competition resulting in a loss of

[50] Ibid para 3.11 ('The exclusion covers agreements which concern the purchase or redistribution of products, such as a franchise agreement where the franchisor sells to the franchisee products for resale. This includes IPR provisions contained in the franchise agreement, such as the trademark and know-how which the franchisor licenses the franchisee in order to market the products.').

[51] Ibid para 3.4 ('IP licensing is viewed as pro-competitive "in the vast majority of cases" because they lead to more efficient exploitation of the IP, promote innovation by giving incentives to IP owners and reduce transaction costs in some circumstances.').

[52] McEwin et al, (n 20) 49 ('Section 34 of the Act prohibits product and service bundling. Bundling occurs when a company conditions the sale of one product or service on the customer's purchase of a second product. This is often known as "tie" or "bundle" arrangement.').

[53] Section 47 of the Competition Act; McEwin et al (n 20) 76 ('The elements that must be proved to find an abuse of a dominant position are: there must be more or more undertakings who are dominant in a relevant market anywhere in the world there must be an abuse of that dominant position which has an effect in Singapore.').

[54] CCS IP Guidelines para 2.7; Ng Ee Kia, *Market Definition*, in Cavinder Bull and Lim Chong Kin (eds), *Competition Law and Policy in Singapore* (Singapore, Academy Publishing, 2009) 54 ('According to the CCS, a technology market consists of the intellectual property that is licensed and its close substitutes, that is, technologies that licensees can switch to in response to an increase in the license fee or royalty of the intellectual property.... An innovation market, on the other hand, consists of the research and development (R&D) directed at bringing about new or improve products and/or better processes, and the close substitutes that could significantly constrain the exercise of market power with respect to that R&D.').

[55] CCS IP Guidelines para 2.5 ('The possession of an IPR does not necessarily create market power in itself, as the "legal" monopoly required for market power to subsist—the latter only arises when there are insufficient actual or potential close substitutes from alternatives supplied by the intellectual property owner's competitors.').

[56] Ibid para 4.3 ('[I]n markets where undertakings regularly improve the quality of their products, a persistently high market share may indicate no more than persistently successful innovation.').

[57] Ong (n 32) 408–09.

total welfare that the CCS will intervene.[58] This includes predatory behaviour,[59] refusals to license essential IP,[60] and tying arrangements.[61] In justifying their right to exercise the right to exclude conferred by IP, IP owners facing abuse of dominance allegations should be aware of the riposte that the CCS IP Guidelines recognise entry barriers arising from network effects which commonly permeate high technology markets.[62] The CCS IP Guidelines allows high market shares if market power is curtailed by low entry barriers.[63] There is no express prohibition against excessive pricing in Singapore. As Richard Whish notes:

> This is a sensible position for the CCS to have taken, since it is certainly not the function of a competition authority to establish itself as a price regulator: in competitive markets, it is the market itself that should determine what the price should be.... It may be that the courts in Singapore would interpret the deliberate deviation from the wording of Article [102 TFEU] and the Chapter II prohibition in the UK as indicating that exploitatively high prices—simply overcharging customers—are excluded from the Act; however, where an excessive price is simply a different way of achieving the effect of a refusal to supply, it may be more difficult for the CCS to ignore a claim that the price in question is abusive.[64]

An issue that may arise in the context of the abuse cases is the difficulty of defining the relevant geographic market because of Singapore's small, open economy. As Michael Gal notes, by excluding imports, the market power of domestic firms may be artificially high.[65]

[58] McEwin et al (n 20) 90 ('[I]t is important to note that, unlike the US and Australia, there is no need to prove a causal link between being dominant and abuse. So a firm that is dominant in a market does not have to use the market power conferred by that dominance to abuse its position. So the market in which the abuse occurs can be separate from the market in which the firm is dominant'.); see also Ong (n 32) 409 ('The CCS IP Guidelines suggest that the real competition-related concerns involving the exercise of an IPR by a dominant undertaking arise primarily in situations where "the dominant undertaking attempts to extend power into a neighbouring or related market, beyond the scope granted by IP law". This form of leveraging is exemplified in tying arrangements where the dominant undertaking, an IP licensor, imposes a condition on IP licensees that it will only grant licenses if the licensee agrees to buy another product not covered by the IPR... Similarly, a dominant undertaking which occupies a position of market dominance by virtue of its IPR ownership may, in limited circumstances, also engage in abusive conduct if it refuses to license its intellectual property rights. Such conduct might qualify as an abuse of a dominant position if the refusal "concerns an IPR which relates to an essential facility with the effect of (likely) substantial harm to competition, and where the dominant undertaking is not "able to justify its conduct"'.).

[59] McEwin et al (n 20) 80 ('(T)he EU and UK are not only concerned with exclusionary conduct but also with exploitative or unfair conduct. … The Singapore Competition Act on the other hand is primarily concerned with exclusionary conduct…').

[60] Ibid 96 ('A dominant firm can abuse its dominant position by restricting access to a new technology. For example, the European Commission found that IBM had abused its dominant position by withholding critical information from competition which made it difficult for competitors to offer new IBM-compatible equipment in time to compete with new IBM products. In the Magill case the [European Court of Justice] ordered[ed] television companies, who formerly published their own individual program guides, to supply another company and each other with their copyrighted programming in advance of broadcast.').

[61] Ibid 100 ('The theory behind the prohibition is that a dominant firm can use its market power in one market to lever that power into another market. ... In the *Microsoft II case*, the European Commission imposed a substantial fine because Microsoft tied its Windows Media Player (where it faced competition) to Windows operating system (a market in which it was dominant). Microsoft was ordered to un-tie the two products and to offer a Windows operating system without Windows Media Player.').

[62] CCS, 'CCS Guidelines on the Section 47 Prohibition' (July 2007). Available at:http://app.ccs.gov.sg/cms/user_documents/main/pdf/s47_Jul07FINAL.pdf para 3.12.

[63] Ibid para 3.11.

[64] Whish (n 26) 147–48 (noting that the absence of an expression prohibition should be understood in the open ended nature wording of para 11.1 of the CCS Section 47 Guidelines).

[65] Michal S Gal, *Competition Policy for Small Market Economies* (Cambridge, MA, Harvard University Press, 2003) 60, quoted in Ng Ee Kia, (n 54) (2009) 47 ('It is important, especially for small economies, to give due

Getting data on the likelihood of consumers switching to imports and market entry by foreign suppliers, as Ian McEwin notes, may be difficult as a practical matter.[66]

Internal checks and balances within the IP regime sidestep the requirement to measure switching costs and the likelihood of market entry.[67] Consistent with Singapore's liberal trade policy, its IP laws generally encourage parallel imports of genuine goods without the consent of the IP owner. These policies prevent owners from segmenting domestic and overseas markets and promote price competition both through the provision of direct substitutes as well as through the threat of entry by competitors,[68] since '[t]he threat of import competition can constrain a dominant firm, even if there are currently no imports. In fact the dominant firm may be pricing at a level to deter imports'.[69]

Once a trademark owner has placed its goods on the market anywhere in the world, or allows their goods to be so sold, his or her rights are exhausted and can be imported for resale in Singapore in competition with more expensive versions of the same products.[70] Consent is deemed to have been given even if conditions against resale were contractually undertaken by distributors or retailers of those goods.[71] As Loy Wee Loon has rightly argued, trademark owners should be treated as having enjoyed the first mover advantage conferred by trademark law, and not be able to hide behind the guise of associated companies to artificially extend its entitlement to create scarcity and hold up prices.[72] Only where the condition of the goods have changed or are defective in a way that harms the

consideration as to whether imports should be included when defining the relevant market in order to prevent the market power of domestic firms from being systematically exaggerated.').

[66] McEwin et al (n 20) 88 ('As Singapore is a small open economy open to international trade, defining the geographic market may be problematical at times. For example, it may be difficult to get data on whether consumers will switch purchases outside Singapore or identifying which suppliers outside Singapore are likely to export or otherwise enter Singapore if domestic price is raised.').

[67] Ong (n 32) 377–78 ('While competition may be used as an instrument to address conduct involving the exercise of intellectual property rights which curtail competition market processes, similar pro-competitive outcomes may also be facilitated from within the law of intellectual property through its internal checks and balances which circumscribe the extent of the right holder's ability to exercise his proprietary rights.').

[68] Ng-Loy (n 1) 12 ('In parallel importation, products made by the IP right proprietor (or by his licensee) and put on the market in one country, are lawfully purchased by a trader who then imports them into another country for resale. Parallel importation thrives as a trade usually because of different price structure for the product in different markets/countries. The price of the imported products in the second market/country is usually lower than that of products put onto that market by the IP right proprietor himself or by his licensee. Naturally, the IP right proprietor is opposed to this leakage of products from his lower-priced markets/countries into his higher priced markets/countries.').

[69] McEwin et al (n 20).

[70] Ng-Loy (n 1) 312 ('Section 29(1) sets out what is called the principle of *international exhaustion* of the rights in a registered trade mark—the registered proprietor's right in the goods marketed with the registered trade mark are exhausted once the goods are sold anywhere in the world by the registered proprietor or with his consent.').

[71] Ibid 312 ('[T]he proprietor is deemed to have given consent to the sale of the goods even where he has imposed conditions on the further movement of the goods, for example, by restricting sale of the goods to a particularly territory.').

[72] Ibid 312–13 ('[A] trade mark proprietor should not be allowed to get around the principle of international exhaustion of rights in s29(1) by registering the mark in different countries in the names of different subsidiaries or associated companies. Whatever may be the corporate structure used by the trade mark proprietor in its global marketing strategy, the fact remains that goods are made by any one of the entities within the same corporate structure are made under the control of the trade mark proprietor and to this extent, these goods if imported into Singapore should be regarded as parallel imports for the purposes of s29(1).').

reputation or distinctiveness of the trademark can the Singapore owner prevent the sale of those goods.[73]

Copyright and patent laws have similar provisions.[74] In the case of copyright law, copyright owners are also prohibited from using copyright in accessories to prevent imports of products which would otherwise be permitted.[75] Competitors of pharmaceutical patent owners can manufacture generic versions of the patent drug for regulatory approval to shorten the lag between the patent's expiry and the available of generic substitutes.[76] A more tenuous example is the ability of patients requiring specific drugs which enjoy patent protection in Singapore, but are not locally available to import those drugs. It has been argued that this puts pressure to make those drugs available.[77] However, the patent owner

[73] Section 29(2) of the Trade Marks Act; Ng-Loy (n 1) 315 ('Section 29(2) sets out a scenario where the principle of international exhaustion of rights will not apply. This is where "the condition of the goods has been changed or impaired after they have been put on the market". The reference to the phrase "condition of the goods" is probably a reference to the physical condition of the goods found inside the packaging. This means that repackaging of the goods which does not involve any change to the goods themselves ... would not qualify as a change to the "condition of the goods" for the purposes of s 29(2). ... Section 29(2) applies where the change or impairment to the condition of the goods occurs after the goods have been put on the market. This subsection cannot deal with cases where the quality difference between the imported goods and domestic goods exist before the imported goods were put on the market and is, in fact, a difference introduced by the trade mark proprietor himself.').

[74] Ong (n 32) 385 ('The net effect of [Section 25 of the Copyright Act] is to make it permissible for persons to import copyright-protected articles into Singapore which have been lawfully made abroad with the consent of the copyright holder, or anyone authorised by him, in the country where the article was made. In other words, as long as the copyright was not violated in the country where the article was manufactured, the article will not be treated as an infringing article if it is brought into Singapore, even if the copyright holder in Singapore is not the importer. This approach eliminates the problem arising from situations where the copyright owner has licensed his copyright to different and independent entities in different jurisdictions. Further, any conditions placed on the manufacturer of those goods on where the goods can be sold and so forth are disregarded. If, on, the other hand, where the imported articles were made under a compulsory license in the country of manufacture, these articles will probably be considered as having been made without the requisite "consent" of the relevant copyright holder.'); see also Ng-Loy (n 68) 418–19 ('There are three features to note about the principle of exhaustion of patent rights in Singapore. First, importation is permitted even if the proprietor in Singapore is different from the proprietor of the patent in the country of manufacture. ... Secondly, ... this defence has no application to cases where the infringing act relates to the use of the patented process in Singapore.... Thirdly, any condition imposed by the patentee restricting the resale of the product outside the territory of manufacture/first sale shall be disregarded for the purposes of determining if the product was produced by or with his consent.').

[75] Ong (n 32) 385 ('The liberal approach towards parallel imports extends to accessories which accompany parallel imports... no copyright infringement arises from the importation or use of accessory articles which accompany non-infringing imported articles. In these circumstances, copyright holders cannot assert their copyright in instruction booklets, packaging, labels, pamphlets, brochures, warranties, manuals or other works ancillary to the main product as a means of keeping parallel imports of the main product from entering the Singapore market.').

[76] George Wei, *Some Thoughts on Intellectual Property Right: A Monograph for Gerald Dworkin* (Singapore, George Wei, 2009) 214–15 ('The Bolar provision refers to a provision in US patent law allowing third parties to manufacture generic drugs shortly before expiration of the patent for the purposes of obtaining marketing approval for the US market. Rather than forcing the third party to wait until the patent rights have expired, the Bolar provision allows this limited use of the patented drug pre-patent expiry so that the third party can gear up in anticipation of the time when the drug is patent free from protection.'); see also Ong (n 32) 401 ('This facilitates immediate competition between "branded" drugs manufactured by patent holders and generic versions of these drugs to take place after the 20-year period of exclusivity ends, rather than giving the former a post-patent window period in which they are the sole-suppliers of the drug while generic drug manufacturers are held back by the marketing approval process.').

[77] Ibid 214–15 ('The Patents (Amendment) Act 2004 also creates a new provision in section 66(2)(i) covering importation, use and disposal of any pharmaceutical product (made with consent of the patentee) required for the use of a specific patient in Singapore. Thus suppose that a patented drug is available only in US. A patient in Singapore needs the drug for treatment. So long as the drug was made by or with the consent of the patentee or his licensee, it can be imported into Singapore for that patient's use. The relevant authority (Health Science

may find it nonetheless more desirable to limit sales in the short term to countries outside Singapore by segmenting markets for profit or other strategic reasons. Parallel import of patents were also narrowed in other respects, allowing owners of pharmaceutical patents to prohibit imports made in breach of contract with a foreign licensed distributor where first sale in Singapore had not been made.[78]

Like parallel imports, compulsory licensing offers consumers and downstream technology users access to IP that would otherwise be embargoed by the owner.[79] The Patent Act thus allows the High Court to grant compulsory licenses where it is necessary to remedy an anti-competitive practice. This happens where there is a market for the invention in Singapore, but it is either not being supplied or not being supplied on reasonable terms and the patentee has no valid reason for failing to supply the market.[80] It is not clear whether anti-competitive acts that result in failure to supply overseas markets would invoke compulsory licensing powers, the view on this seems that it will be unlikely.[81] Another area of ambiguity is whether compulsory licensing under the Patent Act will be invoked upon a finding of anti-competitive abuse under competition law or whether competition related conduct under patent law encompass broader or distinct considerations.[82] This debate is not limited to Singapore. In the US, for example, patent law embraces the doctrine of patent misuse, and an alleged infringer or party unrelated to an infringement action can request that the court prohibit a patent owner from enforcing its patent rights because of misuse. While the view espoused by the penultimate appellate court, the Court of Appeals for the Federal Circuit, is that patent misuse is limited to addressing anti-competitive conduct whose analysis is informed by antitrust principles, others have challenged this view as

Authority) must grant approval for the use of the product by the patient.'); see also Ong (n 32) 390 ('The secondary, and perhaps unintended, effect of this defence is the imposition of additional competitive pressures on firms which supply the same patented pharmaceutical products in Singapore. These imported pharmaceutical products may be brought into Singapore as non-infringing articles even if exporting them from their country of origin resulted in a breach of the license conditions under which they were manufactured.').

[78] Ong (n 32) 389 ('The breadth of the defence was reined in by legislative amendments in 2004 which introduced section 66(2A): in response to pressure from the United States, the section 66(2)(g) defence is not available to patented pharmaceutical products when the product has not previously been sold or distributed in Singapore with the consent of the Singapore patent proprietor or his licensee, where the import of the products would result in their being distributed in breach of a contract between the Singapore patent proprietor and a foreign licensed distributor, and where the importer has actual or constructive knowledge of these matter.').

[79] Ibid 379 ('The availability of compulsory licences under the various intellectual property regimes also enables third parties to gain access to protected subject matter and, in limited cases, offer consumers an alternative avenue for goods and services which are identical to those supplied by the intellectual property right owner.').

[80] Section 55 of the Patents Act.

[81] Wei (n 76) 214 ('Another point worth a mention is that the former restriction in section 55(4) that the grant of compulsory licences to cases where the need is to supply the patent invention predominantly in Singapore was removed. How this will be interpreted may [be] a matter of some importance. Will the new provisions apply where the allegation concerns an anti-competitive act that affects the ability of Singapore manufacturers to supply an overseas market? This seems unlikely.').

[82] Ibid 214 ('Does this mean that section 55 is only relevant after the Competition Commission has made a finding that the patentee has behaved in an anti-competition manner? This seems unlikely as there is no mandatory link between anti-competitive behaviour under section 55 and the work of the Competition Commission. And yet, it seems a little odd that the court might take its own view of what an anti-competitive act in respect of patent behaviour when the term "anti-competitive" has no general definition of meaning in the Patents Act and when the term requires careful appraisal of the exercise of power and market efficiency.').

detracting from the view taken by the US Supreme Court which allows non-competition related considerations to invoke the patent misuse defence.[83]

It may fairly be expected that there will be more cases brought under the Patents Act, with the right to private action filtered through the CCS as well as a higher threshold of proof for anti-competitive harm.[84] In Singapore, patent law recognises that licensors may impose 'tie-up' contracts requiring licensees to continue paying royalties after the patent has expired. These contracts which inhibit the dissemination of the patented technology to others who could use it to offer consumers competing products or build upon that technology in related markets. On the application of the licensee, the court may vary the contract to the extent that it has been infected by the post-expiration condition.[85] Another form of anti-competitive agreements are 'tie-in' licenses requiring licensees to purchase products or services connected to the patented technology in order to be allowed to use that technology. In such instances, courts may not only void the clause, but immunise all infringers from liability until the infected clauses are removed.[86] The Patent Act, however, was amended to bring agreements containing 'tie-up' and 'tie-in' clauses under the Competition Act.[87] With this amendment,

[83] Bruce D Abramson, *The Secret Circuit: The Little Known Court where the Rules of the Information Age Unfold* (New York, Rowman & Littlefield, 2007) ('In its decision establishing the patent misuse doctrine, the US Supreme Court did not require a finding of either an antitrust violation or an anticompetitive effect. The Federal Circuit, in its recent decisions, however, has almost uniformly required proof of an anticompetitive effect before the doctrine can be invoked. Those recent decisions cannot be squared with the patent misuse doctrine established by the Supreme Court.'); see also Daryl Lim, *Patent Misuse and Antitrust: An Empirical Study* (Edward Elgar, 2011, forthcoming) (providing empirical data supporting this observation and discussing the role of the Court of Appeals for the Federal Circuit in shaping conventional wisdom about patent misuse in US patent law).

[84] Bull (n 2) 23 ('The interests of parties who have been harmed by anti-competitive activities are also taken into account by the Competition Act, which provides for third-party rights of private action. However, these parties may seek redress in the courts for the harm they have suffered after the CCS has made a finding of infringement of the Competition Act. This approach allows the harmed parties to seek the relevant compensation while at the same time preventing businesses from being burdened by frivolous claims.').

[85] Section 52 of the Patents Act; Ng-Loy Wee Loon (n 1) 402 ('These contracts are objectionable because they thwart the rationale underlying the patent system—a monopoly is given for a limited period of time to reward the patent proprietor but after the expiry of this period, the invention should fall into the public domain free for all to use and to build on. For this reason, the Patents Act frowns upon an attempt by the patent proprietor to prolong his monopoly over his invention. Therefore, there is specific provision which safeguards the interests of licenses who find themselves in this position. Section 52 allows the licensee of such a contract to terminate the "tie-up" contract when the patent is no longer in force. Further, the licensee can apply to the High Court under this provision to review any term or condition in this contract on the basis that it would be unjust for him to continue to comply with this term or condition. The court may then vary this term or condition as it thinks just as between the parties.').

[86] Section 51 of the Patents Act; Ng-Loy Wee Loon (n 1) 425 ('Section 51 deals with what are called "tie in" contracts. These are contractual agreements used by the patentee to tie his licensee, or a person seeking a supply of his patented invention, to acquire things a person seeking a supply of his patent invention ("tie in") from him. Here, the patent proprietor is attempting to extend his monopoly beyond the market for his invention to an adjacent market. The penalty for engaging in such anti-competitive practice is severe. Under s51, not only is this clause void, but the existence of such a contract also provides a defence to any person sued for infringement by the patent proprietor.').

[87] Agreements made after December 1, 2008 bearing 'tie-in' and 'tie-up' clauses will be reviewed by the CCS, likely under section 47. This limits scrutiny to conduct by patentees in a dominant position, and raises the bar from one of a per se prohibition to analysis under the rule of reason. At the same time, the CCS is not limited to simply voiding the offending contractual terms, but has the flexibility to impose additional penalties such as fines. See Section 50A of the Patents Act and the Second Reading Speech on Patents (Amendment) Bill 2008 by Senior Minister Assoc Prof Ho Peng Kee http://app2.mlaw.gov.sg/News/tabid/204/currentpage/16/Default.aspx?ItemId=78 ('In reality, these agreements may not always be anti-competitive. For example, "tying" arrangements may not be anti-competitive if there are alternative products on the market that serve the same purpose as the patented product. Also, agreements that require a patent licensee to pay royalties after the expiry of the patent may not amount to an abuse of monopoly rights by the patent owner since licensees may, for commercial reasons, prefer to distribute the royalties payable over a longer time period .... This will give

the role of private parties in bringing allegations of anticompetitive abuses of patent rights before the courts will likely diminish further in favour of enforcement by the CCS.

iii. Mergers

The Competition Act prohibits mergers that substantially lessen competition[88] and the CCS' Merger Guidelines expressly note that IP is an entry barrier relevant to the analysis.[89] So a merger between two undertakings that consolidates ownership of patents that prevent challenges to their monopoly may be anti-competitive. In most cases, patents are the source of this anti-competitive effect. One outcome may simply be to block the proposed merger on the basis that the likelihood of concentrating technology which is not readily duplicated in the hands of a single entity would make it likely for it to engage in monopolistic behaviour and unlikely for new entry to challenge that market position.[90] Another outcome would be to allow the merger to proceed, but to require remedial measures to address the anti-competitive effect, for example, an undertaking by the new entity to provide non-discriminatory licenses for a reasonable royalty to third parties seeking access to the technology.[91] These compulsory licenses may be made available worldwide, and even on a royalty free basis.[92] In cases where the IP forms but a component of the firms' overall portfolio, such licenses may be treated as routine steps in the merger review process. However, careful thought should be given before imposing compulsory licensing obligations on firms whose entire asset base is made up of IP. This may amount, in effect, to a state-sanctioned divestiture of the undertaking's key strategic assets to competitors and in doing so, undermine both the incentives put in place by the IP regime, as well as sever the synergies inherent in an integrated firm structure.

IV. Policy

The Singapore Government is mindful that competition law imposes compliance costs, and will likely be cautious in regulating the exploitation of IPRs.[93] Singapore's ability to propel its economy in 30 years from simple manufacture and unskilled labour, to one with

businesses greater flexibility in structuring new commercial agreements and put Singapore on par with jurisdictions such as the UK and US, where such agreements are regulated by competition law.')

[88] McEwin (n 20) 166 ('History has shown us that dominant firms in a given market can and do often abuse their dominance and financial might by snapping up would-be competitors and libraries of intellectual property to halt the commercialization of technology that may hurt their dominance.').

[89] CCS, 'CCS Guidelines on the Substantive Assessment of Mergers' ('CCS Merger Guidelines') (July 2007), available at: http://app.ccs.gov.sg/cms/user_documents/main/pdf/substantiveassessmerger_Jul07FINAL.pdf para 7.6.

[90] Federal Trade Commission, 'FTC Challenges Thoratec's Proposed Acquisition of HeartWare International' (30 July 2009), available at www.ftc.gov/opa/2009/07/thoratec.shtm.

[91] See, eg Boston Scientific's Acquisition of Cardiovascular Imaging Systems (9 March 1995), West Publishing citations to court opinions (5 July 1995) and *Ciba-Geigy/Sandoz Ltd Merger US v 3D Systems* (3 January 2001), available at www.cptech.org/ip/health/cl/us-at.html; see also CCS Merger Guidelines (Mentioning 'an amendment to intellectual property licenses' as a possible remedy).

[92] *US v Halliburton Company* (where the 'DOJ alleged that the merger of Halliburton and Dresser would combine two of the four companies that were developing drilling tools for oil and natural gas projects and their merger would likely lead to "a slowdown in the pace of ... innovation".').

[93] Bull (n 2) 10 ('The Singapore government recognized that there is a need to balance regulatory and business compliance costs against the benefits from effective competition.').

a high degree of sophistication in life sciences and biomedical sciences, has been the product not only of long-range planning facilitated by the current administration's durability, but also the Government's ability to convince its people of the merits of respecting IPRs.[94] Singapore leads the Asia-Pacific in its multilateral commitments to ever higher minimum standards of IP protection, and has committed itself to bilateral Free Trade Agreements such as those with the United States which surpass its multilateral obligations.[95] Today, Singapore has been held up as an IP haven in Asia, with more than 7,000 multinationals.[96] The World Intellectual Property Organization (WIPO) chose Singapore as its hub for alternative dispute resolution. The 2009 World Competitiveness Report of the World Economic Forum ranked Singapore in overall third position with a first position for IP protection.[97]

Reinforcing this commitment to ensuring returns on IP investments is Singapore's status as an export oriented economy, highly dependent on international trade and foreign investments.[98] Singapore sits at the heart of Asia-Pacific and is the gateway to the East and West. Unlike many developing countries past and present, Singapore regarded foreign multinational corporations (MNC) as a boon to national development.[99] MNCs have also played a critical role in technology transfer and which would be most affected

[94] Ng-Loy Wee Loon, 'Singapore' in Paul Goldstein and Joseph Straus (eds), *Intellectual Property in Asia: Law, Economics, History and Politics* (Berlin, Springer, 2009) 250 ('Singapore's ability to successfully implement IP protection is tied to Singapore's unique cultural and political landscape. The country enjoys a high level of respect for the rule of law and low rates of corruption. The public perception towards IP is generally favourable.... Another reason Singapore has been able to accomplish long-range objectives is Singapore's exceptional political stability. The People's Action Party (PAP) has been the ruling party since the beginning of nationhood (1965), and it enjoys an overwhelming majority: there are only two opposition members in the entire 84-member Parliament. This consistent majority means that legislators can take a long-term approach, and also that the process of lawmaking is relatively efficient.').

[95] Ibid; see also Report of the Economic Review Committee of Singapore (2003) 52 ('We will continue to support the World Trade Organization (WTO) as it remains the foundation for world trade, and protects small countries like Singapore against unfair unilateral trade practices. However, a purely multilateral approach has its limitations. We are therefore supplementing it with bilateral FTAs with key trading partners.').

[96] Ng-Loy (n 93) 234, 235 ('Singapore's rapid technological development and industralisation programme is heavily dependent on MNCs rather than on indigenous firms.... The strategy was to embark on an industralisation program that was export-oriented. Foreign investors were actively wooed to develop their manufacturing operations in Singapore for export to the world markets—both in low-technology, labour-intensive technologies ... and in higher-technology industries. The electronics sector began during these early years with American MNCs setting up in Singapore: Texas Instruments in 1968, National Semiconductor in 1969, Hewlett Packard in 1970 etc.'). Note, however, Ng-Loy (n 1) 50–51 ('It would be very naïve, though, to attribute Singapore's success in attracting FDI solely or primarily on its strong IP infrastructure.... A strong IP infrastructure is a very important, but certainly not a sufficient factor to pull in FDI. If it were otherwise, China with its problematic track record in IP enforcement would have attracted far less FDI.').

[97] www.weforum.org/documents/GCR09/index.html.

[98] McEwin (n 20) 5 ('Singapore is a relatively small economy but open to international competition. What does this mean for competition law? ... [I]nternational trade increases the size of market demand and so in open economics, in order to compete internationally, firms must be of a sufficient size to compete on export markets and with imports. So firms that would be too small in a closed economy reach efficient size through exporting.').

[99] Lee Kuan Yew, *From Third World to First: The Singapore Story* (1965–2000) 76, 85–86 ('If MNCs could give our workers employment and teach them technical and engineering skills and management knowhow, we should bring in the MNCs ... We did not have a group of ready-made entrepreneurs such as Hong Kong gained in the Chinese industrialists and bankers who came fleeing from Shanghai, Canton and other cities when the communists took over [China]. Had we waited for our traders to learn to be industrialists, we would have starved. It is absurd for critics to suggest in the 1990s that had we grown our own entrepreneurs we would have been less at the mercy of the rootless MNCs.').

by IP-oriented competition enforcement. The Economic Strategy Committee reaffirmed in 2009 that:

> Singapore should entrench its position as a location of choice for the world's leading companies, including MNCs, global mid-sized industry leaders, and Asian enterprises seeking to internationalise. MNCs must remain key players in our economy. They are a major source of new technologies, and allow Singapore to stay plugged into the developed country markets—which although slow growing, will remain sizeable sources of sophisticated demand.[100]

As a result, while Singapore's competition policy may mirror those in the European Union and United States in many ways, it can be expected to diverge where foreign precedents are inconsistent with local policy interests, as commentators such as Bruce Owens have noted.[101] Indeed, the CCS itself has declared that:

> The Commission notes that competition law is a new area of law in Singapore. While some of the [EC and US] cases cited in this decision may be persuasive or useful in assisting the Commission in reaching this decision on the single economic entity argument, they are not binding. The value of any foreign competition case law will depend very much on the overall context and the extent to which the facts of these cases are applicable to the local context and the facts of the present application by the Parties.[102]

Singapore has firmly committed itself to providing robust IP rights to maintain its attractiveness to foreign IP-related investors,[103] as well as tap into the wellspring of the technology transfer process.[104] With this know-how, Singapore pushed itself up the value chain from manufacturing to high technology and into R&D intensive industries where

[100] Economic Strategies Committee, Key Recommendations 23 (1 February 2010), available at www.esc.gov.sg/attactments/ESC%20Report%201%20Feb%202010.pdf.

[101] Bruce Owen, *Imported Antitrust* in John M Olin Program in Law and Economics Working Paper No 281 (Stanford Law School, March 2004) 12–13 ('While US federal antitrust enforcement policy is now largely welfare-oriented, it is oriented toward the welfare of domestic consumers. It is ambivalent at best toward domestic producer welfare and it is largely antagonistic to the economic welfare of foreign consumers.... For this and other reasons, the adoption of domestic consumer welfare as the sole objective of competition policy in every nation on the globe clearly is incompatible with global welfare optimism because such policies fail to internalise economic effects that spill over national borders. [footnotes omitted]'); Cavinder Bull, 'Preface' in Cavinder Bull and Lim Chong Kin (eds), *Competition Law and Policy in Singapore* (Singapore, Academy Publishing, 2009) ix ('In the meantime there will be a natural reliance on cases from other jurisdictions, in particular the European Union and the United Kingdom. American case law may also prove to be significant. However, one cannot assume that the CCS will follow a particular case or practice from mature competition law jurisdictions. While Singapore will typically borrow from the lessons and wisdom of other jurisdictions, it will also have to chart its own course as competition law is applied to its own unique situation and economic circumstances.'); see also Ong (n 32) 375 ('Despite the strong influence of UK laws on the domestic legislative framework which Singapore has enacted, a number of substantive modifications have been made by the legislature to further specific policy objectives which reflect domestic commercial and socio-economic conditions. Singapore has a small domestic market of less than 4 million consumers, but a relatively large, open and export oriented economy.').

[102] Qantas & Orangestar Co-operation Agreement CCS 400/003/06 (10 January 2007) at para 28, available at http://app.ccs.gov.sg/public_reg_Notified_agreement_Qantas_Orangestar_Agreement.aspx.

[103] Second Reading of the Patent Bill 1994 Hansard vol 62 col 1445 (21 March 1994) ('[W]e live in a global economy where trade is driven by desire, potential for profit, which in turn is determined by the element of competitiveness. Inventions and innovations sharpen this competitive edge. More countries are therefore improving their industrial property systems, particularly their patent systems to encourage invention and innovation, and to assist in the recoupment of continuing investment costs for development of products and services.').

[104] Ng-Loy (n 93) 240 ('The idea behind the strategy to deepen the technology base in Singapore was to move Singapore up the value-chain in manufacturing, especially in emerging fields. The policy-makers firmly believed that a solid IP infrastructure, particularly a sound patent system, was needed to achieve this goal.').

IP protection remains, in a self-reinforcing cycle, at the forefront of economic policy.[105] To impose robust scrutiny on IP conduct under its competition law would unravel these carefully cultivated efforts.[106]

The question that arises is how the overlay of competition law, which necessarily restricts the commercial freedom over and above the IP laws, would affect Singapore's competition policy with respect to IPRs. In this regard, Burton Ong makes the observation that:

> The basic objectives of the Commission in this respect are no different from those which inform its more experienced counterparts. The ultimate goal is to adopt a competition policy which strikes an optimal balance between, on the one hand, the incentives for innovation generated by the availability of intellectual property rights against, on the other hand, the exclusionary effects which these limited legal monopolies have on competition and further innovation by third parties.[107]

The Competition Act incorporates features which recognise the expertise of sectoral regulation in dealing with anti-competitive effects arising from commercial activity in those sectors.[108] Some commentators have suggested that IP law and policy will inform the enforcement of competition law at the Interface in a similar fashion,[109] and it is possible that the CCS will be primarily responsible for the oversight of anti-competitive exploitation of IPRs with guiding input from the Intellectual Property Office of Singapore. This would be a sensible approach. Enforcement of competition law done with an informed appreciation of the nature and scope of the internal checks and balances underlying the IP regime and the IP policies animating the law will a major step forward in getting the balance right.

[105] Wei (n 76) 6 ('Strong intellectual property protection is a core component of Singapore's economic and industrial strategy for her next stage of growth. … Singapore's progress in information technology is well known and few will doubt the resolve to maintain that progress and to develop other areas of 'creative' industry such as design and the performing arts'.); see also Ng-Loy Wee Loon (n 93) 241 ('To maintain Singapore's competitiveness in this new millennium the current phase of economic planning is to work toward graduating Singapore into a "knowledge-based, innovation driven economy".').

[106] As Burton Ong observes: '[E]xogenous derogations from the legal monopoly which IP owners receive from the law of intellectual property would probably not occur in too many cases, given that those who administer Singapore's competition law framework have emphasised that the incentive-reward functions of the law of intellectual property should not be unnecessarily disrupted by the legal uncertainties that would result'. Ong (n 32) 401.

[107] Ong (n 32) 376–77.

[108] Bull (n 2) 11 ('In addition, certain exclusions from sections 34, 47 and 54 are set out in the Third and Fourth Schedule to the Competition Act. A number of the exclusions relate to activities in sectors that have recently been liberalized, and are in transition to a more competitive market environment. There are considerable technical matters affecting competition in these sectors and as such, sectoral regulators, with their industry knowledge and expertise, are deemed to be better positioned to address and balance competition goals with other policy concerns.').

[109] Ong (n 32) 395 ('It is interesting to note that the legislature chose to vest the function of determining when a compulsory license is an appropriate remedy to the court—rather than the competition regulator, the Competition Commission of Singapore—and *to internalise compulsory licensing as one of the features of the patent law system rather than delegating this remedial device to those responsible for administering the competition law regime*.) (emphasis added) and fn 76 ('In contrast, the compulsory licensing under the UK Patents Act 1977 is a lot broader, and more complex as a result, in that it permits compulsory licenses to be sought on competition-related grounds … and non-competition related grounds'.); see also Ng-Loy Wee Loon (n 1) 426–27 ('[I]n determining whether the exercise of a patent right by the proprietor is anti-competitive or not under the Competition Act, the CCS may defer to the guidance provided by the provisions in the Patents Act targeted at anti-competitive behaviour (ss 51, 52 and 55). If that is the case, it means that the extent of 'external' control of the patent proprietor's behaviour under the Competition Act would not be very different from the 'internal controls' provided for in the Patents Act.').

Singapore's policy toward IP is strongly utilitarian.[110] IPRs are not granted to gratify a creator's moral claims over his or her creation, or even to reward IP owners as an end in itself. Instead, the goal is to foster creativity, innovation or entrepreneurship which builds upon what has been developed for the betterment of Singapore in the technological, social and economic sense.[111] The temporary monopoly given to owners to control and commercialise their IP is therefore, at least notionally, calibrated to the level that is sufficient to induce his or her participation in this endeavour while providing competitors the ability to build upon the IP owner's contribution and, in time, compete with the IP owner. As Burton Ong notes, pro-competitive policy levers within IP law 'confine the exclusive rights enjoyed by the intellectual property owner to subject matter within reasonable limits, seeking at the same time to make it possible for his rivals to offer consumers competing, alternative products and services'.[112] To this end, a number of layers of internal checks and balances have been woven into the fabric of Singapore's IP laws.[113]

As IP rights expand, however, their potential for anti-competitive externalities increase. For example, copyright has expanded to protect more functional subject matter such as software and databases. The underlying source code may be near impossible to reverse engineer or license fees and may be prohibitively expensive.[114] Database owners may

[110] Wei (n 76) 14 ('Singapore clearly strongly subscribes to the utilitarian justification for strong intellectual property protection.').

[111] Ng-Loy Wee Loon (n 1) 355 ('Like copyright, the aim of the patent regime is not just about providing an incentive to the individual inventor/company. The other aim is to use the patent system to encourage investors to add their new and inventive findings to the common pool of technological knowledge that can be used, and improved upon by other inventors. That is why the patent monopoly, just like the copyright monopoly, has a limited duration. In the case of the patent, it generally lasts for 20 years from the date of filing the patent application.').

[112] Ong (n 32) 378–79.

[113] A number of examples may be given. First, boundaries between the various species of IPRs serve as the first line of defence to limit the rights of IP owners in favour of market competition. The boundary between copyright law and patent law draws the line between protecting expressions and protecting ideas. The boundary between patent law and trademark law draws the line between protecting functional aspects of products and protecting distinctive aspects of products. The boundary between copyright and trademark law similarly draws the line between protecting a sign as a form of creative expression and a sign as an indicator of source. The boundary between copyright law and the law of registered designs draws the line between protecting the copyright owner's rights in his or her two dimensional images and protecting ability of competitors to offer substitutes for three-dimensional works which embody those two dimensional designs. The second layer of anti-competitive checks and balances restraining the ability of IP owners to distort market competition exists within each IPR. Each species of IP is an ecosystem that attempts to balance competing interests by calibrating the scope and length of protection in line with the specific goals of each ecosystem, as well as in relation to the other species of IPRs. Patents, for example, protect ideas, the raw material needed for innovation and competition. The requirements are therefore higher than for other IPRs. Patents must be novel with respect to prior art worldwide, inventive and capable of industrial application. Applicants must also disclose and support claims as broad as their desired legal monopoly, so that a person ordinarily skilled in the field of endeavour can work the invention. This makes the invention accessible for public benefit once the patent monopoly expires. Third, exceptions and defences respectively carve out categories of conduct that do not fall within the scope of the IP owner's exclusionary right to begin with, or which excuse otherwise infringing activity from liability. An example is the defence of fair dealing under copyright law. Fair dealing is available to all types of copyrighted works and is a complete defence to allegations of infringement, incorporating concept of 'fair use' from United States jurisprudence. Courts in the United States have interpreted fair use to include even commercial use, with the 'transformative' nature of that use being a key factor informing the overall fair use inquiry. See *Campbell v Acuff-Rose Music, Inc* 510 US 569 (1994). If courts in Singapore here take the same approach, there will be greater leeway in developing substitutes and derivative works. Copyright also allows reverse engineering of software so that downstream competitors are allowed to reproduce copyrightable code to uncover interface information required to offer interoperability in ancillary markets. For a discussion of these internal checks and balances, see generally Ng-Loy (n 1); Ong (n 32) 378–79; and Wei (n 76).

[114] See Daryl Lim, 'Beyond Microsoft: Intellectual Property, Peer Production and the Law's Concern with Market Dominance' (2008) 18 *Fordham Intellectual Property Media & Entertainment Law Journal* 291.

similarly refuse to license competitors in secondary markets.[115] As a result, competitors may therefore be excluded from the market or forced to compete with a severe disadvantage. George Wei raised concerns that the expansion of IPRs may eviscerate defences and exceptions built into the IP regime to check precisely these negative externalities:

> Then there are those who argue that even existing exceptions and limitations in copyright law such as fair dealing or fair use type exceptions will count for nothing in the digital world if electronic works are subject to copy-protection that prevents all unauthorized access: even when the copying may fall within fair dealing/use exceptions. Not only is there a threat that technology may render the exception worthless, the technological restraints are now backed up by fearsome laws forbidding the sale or use of counter-technology. Contractual terms may also be used by copyright owners in attempts to circumvent statutory exceptions and the like.[116]

However, the upward march of copyright may be inevitable:

> There is no retreat from the growth of copyright over functional works. Business needs shape the law. As economies become more technology dependent, the case for exclusive rights in database and software industries will be more compelling. To reduce the commercial risks from misappropriation in already risky ventures, businesses appreciate and, in some cases, demand the security that copyright provides in safeguarding their investments. This is not ideal, as it trades one form of risk for another—the risk that information gets balkanised by copyright owners controlling access to interface information or raw data.[117]

Similarly, patent rights may extend to genes,[118] business methods[119] or basic research tools[120] which block the arteries of commerce and innovation. The narrowing of the right of the public and competitors to IP-related content has been a constant feature in IP policy debates. Where such debates reach an impasse between those favouring stronger IPRs and those favouring weaker rights, competition law can, in appropriate cases, help refocus the debate on market effects in terms of price and visible competition rather than arguments between competitors hinged on speculative threats to innovation incentives. Exacerbating the controversy in recent years are two of the most serious challenges facing Interface policy in the United States and the European Union today. These are patent hold-ups in standard setting in the IT industry, and brand name drug companies paying off generic drug companies in the pharmaceutical industry to stay out of their markets. Both are key industries for Singapore, and she may soon have to confront the same difficult issues herself.

[115] See, eg Nine Network Australia Pty Ltd v IceTV Pty Ltd [2009] HCA 14 (where the High Court of Australia found no infringement of copyright in television programme schedule because mere effort was not sufficient to qualify for protection); Lotus Development Corporation v Borland International, Inc 516 US 233 (1996) (establishing a distinction in copyright law between the interface of a software product (which is protected) and its implementation (which is not protected)); see also Daryl Lim, 'Re-Defining The Rights And Responsibilities Of Database Owners Under Competition Law' (2006) 18 *Singapore Academy of Law Journal* 418 (examining the applicability and effect of competition law to databases in Singapore).

[116] Wei (n 76) 19.

[117] Daryl Lim, 'Copyright Under Siege: An Economic Analysis of the Essential Facilities Doctrine and the Compulsory Licensing of Copyrighted Works' (2007) 17 *Albany Law Journal of Science and Technology* 481, 555–56.

[118] See, eg *In re Deuel* 51 F.3d 1552, 1557 (Fed Cir 1995) (holding that DNA sequences can be 'new chemical entities' in structural terms). However, see *Association for Molecular Pathology v USPTO* Case No 09 Civ 4515, (SDNY 29 March 2010) (holding that isolated gene sequences and diagnostic methods using such gene sequences are not patentable subject matter).

[119] See, eg *Bilski v Kappos* 130 S Ct 3218 (2010) (affirming that business methods are patentable subject matter).

[120] Robin Feldman, 'The Open Source Biotechnology Movement: Is it Patent Misuse?' (2004) 6 *Minnesota Journal of Law Science and Technology* 1.

Standard setting, even amongst competitors, is recognised as generally pro-competitive because it allows the selection and establishment of a uniform technology denominator which reduces transactions costs and promotes the roll-out of offspring technology.[121] However, the standard setting process has been hijacked by firms who lure the standard setting organisations (SSOs) into adopting the standard, either through failure to disclose relevant patents or reneging on assurances that the technology will be licensed on reasonable and non-discriminatory terms. In doing so, they 'hold-up' users of the technology for supernormal profits. There is a great controversy whether and to what extent these patent owners are entitled to those profits, and whether remedying the situation by patent law, competition law or through more SSO oversight may in fact exacerbate the problem by imposing heavy diligence burdens on firms which may end up being deterred in participating in the standard setting process altogether.[122]

At the core of the reverse payments problem is that pharmaceutical consumers are denied access to cheaper drugs because patent owners are paying off potential competitors to delay the introduction of substitutes beyond the expiration date of patents covering 'blockbuster' drugs. US cases have held that the exclusive right granted under patent law enables patentees to settle their infringement suits on terms that stop competitive products that infringe. Anti-competitive effects of these settlements are within the exclusionary scope of the patent and are therefore allowed under antitrust law.[123] In the United States, other means of introducing cheaper substitutes, such as authorised generics and approved biologics also face challenges in their introduction.[124]

The Interface is an evolving landscape, rapidly expanding over subject matter and geography even as technology and business strategies change. Within a brief decade, EU competition law has been confronted by the challenge of devising a legal answer to broadcast companies refusing to license their TV listings, to software companies refusing to license application programming interface information in Europe. Within half that time, it now must address the competition challenges raised by the worldwide digitisation of books[125]

[121] McEwin et al (n 20) 48–49 ('An agreement on technical or design standards may lead to an improvement in production by reducing costs or raising quality, or it may promote technical or economic progress by reducing waste and consumers' search costs. The agreement may, however, have an appreciable adverse effect on competition in particular, if it includes restrictions on what the parties may produce or is, in effect, a means of limiting competition from other sources, for example by raising entry barriers. Standardisation agreements which prevent the parties from developing alternative standards or products that do not comply with the agreed standard may also have an appreciable adverse effect on competition.').

[122] Daryl Lim, 'Misconduct in Standard Setting: The Case for Patent Misuse' *IDEA: The Intellectual Property Law Review* (2011, forthcoming).

[123] See, eg *Arkansas Carpenters Health and Welfare Fund v Bayer AG* (*In re Ciprofloxacin Antitrust Litigation*) 604 F.3d 98 (2d Cir 2010) *en banc* hearing denied 625 F.3d 779 (2010). The size of the payment in the *Cipro* case, however, is larger than the projections of the amount the generic would have made if it won the lawsuit and entered the market and is evidence that the parties may have entered into the agreement even though they believed the patent was invalid. The decision attracted a number of amici briefs requesting an *en banc* review, including one filed on behalf of 86 law professors, as well as others by 39 attorney generals, the Federal Trade Commission, and the Department of Justice.

[124] Tom Rosch, 'Pay-for-Delay Settlements, Authorized Generics, and Follow-on Biologics: Thoughts on the How Competition Law Can Best Protect Consumer Welfare in the Pharmaceutical Context' (Remarks at the World Generic Medicine Congress Washington, DC, 19 November 2009), available at www.ftc.gov/speeches/rosch/091119worldgenerics.pdf.

[125] Ian Traynor, 'Brussels Tries to Fight Google Book Plan by Overhauling EU Copyright Law' *The Guardian UK* (7 September 2009), available at www.guardian.co.uk/business/2009/sep/07/brussels-google-copyright-law-campaign. For a US perspective, see Lalit K Jha, 'New Google Book Settlement Still Raises Antitrust Concerns: US'

and global technology mergers.[126] While jurisprudence at the Interface faced its share of teething problems moving through the first generation of cases, moving from the first generation of the Interface to the second generation will be more complicated—many devices are multifunctional and integrated, and the geopolitics of technology and globalisation can make national enforcement a dicey international affair.[127]

The first Interface case in Singapore is likely to be technically demanding and politically sensitive. Because of its push for foreign technology giants, the potential defendants in competition law cases will likely be sophisticated and well-funded, and the CCS should expect more push back compared to early price-fixing cases where the defendants were found with clear and convincing evidence of their infringement.[128] However, if done well, businesses will know what can be done and what has to be accepted and Singapore can benefit from clear and well-reasoned enforcement at the Interface. As IP is territorial and businesses and foreign investments are mobile, the Interface is a zero-sum game between countries and the country that gets it right will have a feather in its cap.[129] How then should Singapore proceed?

To develop a sophisticated approach to dynamic efficiency considerations, the debate needs first to be informed by more empirical evidence to find out what is really happening on the ground in Singapore. The IP Academy, a think tank in Singapore, did a study on the economic contribution of copyright-based industries in Singapore.[130] This is a step in the right direction. International organisations such as WIPO and the International Competition Network can be valuable resources to better understand the intricacies of the Interface.

Second, the choice of laws and synergy between relevant institutions need to be considered. The CCS prudently focused its early enforcement efforts on 'hardcore' infringements of competition law—price fixing agreements, in sectors with limited potential for spill over, while carefully defining and expanding the corpus of articulated competition policy decisions. In later higher stakes litigation, these early cases will be a valuable guide for the public. A significant challenge, as Burton Ong notes, is to determine how exactly

(5 February 2010), available at www.business-standard.com/india/news/new-google-book-settlement-still-raises-antitrust-concerns-us/85033/on.

[126] Paul McDougall, 'Oracle Sun Merger Wins EU Approval' *InformationWeek* (21 January 2010), available at www.informationweek.com/news/government/enterprise-apps/showArticle.jhtml?articleID=222400062.

[127] US Department of Justice, Assistant Attorney General for Antitrust, Thomas O Barnett, 'Issues Statement On European Microsoft Decision' (17 September 2007), available at www.justice.gov/atr/public/press_releases/2007/226070.htm ('We are, however, concerned that the standard applied to unilateral conduct by the CFI, rather than helping consumers, may have the unfortunate consequence of harming consumers by chilling innovation and discouraging competition.').

[128] See, eg 'CCS Fines 16 Coach Operators and Association $1.69 Million For Price-Fixing' (3 November 2009), available at http://app.ccs.gov.sg/cms/user_documents/main/pdf/EBAAPressrelease031109.pdf; 'CCS Fines Pest Control Operators for Bid-Rigging',(9 January 2008) available at http://app.ccs.gov.sg/cms/user_documents/main/pdf/ID_030108WoodstockCCSRegister.pdf.

[129] www.ipacademy.com.sg/section/aboutus/history.html ('The value of IP cannot be underestimated. With globalization and rapid technological advancements, IP will continue to increase in strategic importance against traditional advantages such as geographical location and abundance of natural resources. Those who are able to maximize their intellectual assets will have a clear advantage.').

[130] Wei (n 76) 6 ('One of the first research exercises carried out by the IP Academy was in fact a study on the economic contribution of copyright-based industries in Singapore. Using the WIPO classification framework for creative industries, the 2004 Report strongly supported the positive impact made by Singapore's copyright-based industries to the nation's economy The preliminary findings indicated that in 2001, copyright-based industries generated "approximately $8.6 billion in value added" representing some 5.6% of Singapore's GDP.').

IP related cases differ from the precedents sent in place by separately developing non-IP case law.[131] The CCS and courts will have to determine how to approach the various branches of IP, each which has different checks and balances and are guided by different policy considerations.[132] The CCS IP Guidelines expressly recognise that while both categories of cases share common characteristics, IP is costly to develop and susceptible to free-riding.[133] Enforcement based on policy purporting to promote innovation can be a speculative enterprise, and the different considerations undergirding the various sectors of IP industries make enforcement of competition law a considerably more challenging task than in 'brick-and-mortar' industries.

The combination of Singapore's relatively small jurisdiction and the right private action, allowed only after the CCS has itself decided to proceed against potential offenders, conspires to make any cases at the Interface few and far between. However, even if such cases do come before the courts, they may not be the best forum to seek a remedy to the problem because of the fast moving nature of technology industries. As Frank Easterbrook put it:

> Competition is the long-run solution to monopoly. Perhaps antitrust law speeds up the arrival of the long run. Perhaps it does not. Unless we know it does, judges ought to apply their talents in other fields, where they have a comparative advantage over other institutions. ... For the law to have a comparative advantage, legal processes must be able to beat market processes to a conclusion in assessing novel business practices... If rivals will undo a monopoly or evade a questionable practice before judges can decide the case, there is little point in incurring the costs of litigation and suffering the inevitable mistaken judgments.[134]

The higher cost of litigation inherent in requiring expert economic witnesses in competition litigation, rather than resolving those issues as part of patent infringement suit, which though costly would be more streamlined and relatively cheaper. Courts, parties and institutions in Singapore are more familiar with IP laws and commercial certainty is aided by a considerable corpus of case law, policy statements and detailed legislation. Falling back directly upon IP policy as a first line of defence to calibrate intervention makes the outcome more sensitive to innovation considerations as well as attenuates the negative effect

[131] Ong (n 32) 401–02 ('The challenge ahead for the Competition Commission of Singapore (CCS) is to fit IP-related instances of commercial conduct which raise competition related concerns within the general competition law framework, while administering block exemption schemes for those transactions which are recognised to be pro-competitive on the whole. One of the more contentious issues here is the extent to which IP-related transactions or commercial conduct should be differentiated from similar situations involving non-IP proprietary interests when brought under the scrutiny of competition law, bearing in mind the special policy considerations which underline the various intellectual property systems and the internal checks and balances that exist within each of them.').

[132] CCS IP Guidelines para 2.4 ('Although there are clear and important differences in the purpose, extent and duration of protection provided under the IP regimes mentioned in paragraph 1.2, the general analytical principles to be applied are the same.').

[133] Ibid para 2.2 ('IP has certain characteristics that may make it difficult for IP owners to restrict access to, and therefore, exercise their rights over it. For example, IP is costly to develop, but often easy and inexpensive to copy, thus making it difficult to prevent others from free-riding on the discovery in the absence of IP law. The use of IP is also typically non-rivalrous, meaning that one person's use does not reduce its use by another person. While these characteristics will be taken into account in competition analysis, they do not warrant the application of fundamentally different analytical principles to IPRs.').

[134] Frank H Easterbrook, 'Comment: Comparative Advantage and Antitrust Law' (1987) 75 *California Law Review* 983, 985.

of false positives, since the remedies under the IP laws are generally less drastic than under competition law.[135]

To succeed in this enterprise, it is crucial to develop the correct competition culture. This involves retaining a core group of competent people, not just in the CCS but in the private sector as well, since Singapore's laws develop in an adversarial way.[136] The right synergy also needs to be developed between lawyers and economists. As Ian McEwin noted, lawyers reason from case to case and draw principles from there—they think from small to big.[137] In contrast, economists work from theories based on assumptions to explain results in specific cases, so they think from big to small, and sometimes two minds do not meet. However,

> At the same time, the complexity of competition economics should not be exaggerated. There is much common sense involved in economic analyses based on sound methodologies. The focus on economic insights should not be confused with applying complex, mathematical formulas and/or econometrical calculation models in competition assessment. The strength of economics lies in econometric analysis. This means that economists should try to help 'de-esoterise' market effects of [IP] and competition law…. (but) [c]ompetition policy should not retreat to purely econometric standards in its attempt to use scientific means to resolve or mask what is an inherently normative dispute requiring a measure of 'hunch, faith and intuition'.[138]

V. Conclusions

Singapore is not yet an innovation-driven economy, but it is in the process of transition toward one. In many instances, firms locate in Singapore due to its traditional strengths such as the business friendly environment; its location and openness to immigration; its multicultural society, etc and not because Singapore has a 'creative' workforce. Most of the private research and development expenditure is focused on the electronics sector and in particular on semiconductors, which is a 'traditional strength' and research is primarily experimental or applied. Very few dollars are spent on basic research. There is little public data about the exact size of the various 'new' sectors such as biotechnology, clean technology, nanotechnology and interactive digital media but these are likely to be small because they are 'new' to Singapore.

[135] IP remedies generally consist of injunctions and restitutionary damages. In contrast, punitive fines generally have accompanied orders to modify the offending license or cease the offending activity in more mature competition jurisdictions. Section 69(4) of the Competition Act allows the CCS to impose a fine of up to 10% of the turnover in Singapore for each year of infringement for up to three years if it is satisfied that the breach was either negligent or intentional.

[136] (n 117) 554. (Discussing the development of 'lexonomists', who 'have the expertise to make sure that competition law is grounded in logical analysis and provide tools to assess the relative merits of competing economic hypotheses and legal theories.').

[137] McEwin et al (n 20) 6–7 ('Common law lawyers often argue by analogy. This means focusing on particular facts and then developing the principles. … Economists on the other hand, use deductive reasoning (that is, top-down). Economists build abstract models based on assumptions which describe a link between conduct and the effect of that conduct. … The difference in methodology can lead to considerable difficulties in competition law. Lawyers dismiss economic modeling because the assumptions of the economic model rarely match the facts of a particular case.').

[138] Daryl Lim (n 135) 551–53 [footnotes omitted].

One of the more significant drivers of Singapore's success is its ability to eclectically emulate the best practices of more experienced countries, and then internalise and institutionalise those practices within a relatively short amount of time. In less than 20 years, Singapore has moved from a jurisdiction sparse in IP protection and rife with piracy to a technologically-driven economy offering one of the highest levels of IP protection in the world.[139] Singapore's IP laws try to balance the rights to investment returns with policies designed to disseminate and encourage third-party innovation. Looking ahead, there are a number of tasks for competition jurisprudence to resolve. Singapore will benefit from the experience elsewhere but must decide how best to address the Interface, either from within the IP system or within competition law, or a cocktail of both. However, 'competition law is an area of where law in which there is little scope for absolute concepts or sharp edges'[140] and the actual contours of the law will not be known until the courts in Singapore have had the opportunity to decide on cases dealing with the Interface.

[139] Ng-Loy (n 93) 237 ('The change in Singapore's attitude towards IP started in the mid-1980s, corresponding to the shift in the country's focus toward higher-technology industries such as the software industry… the need to provide the legal framework necessary for the development of a strong software industry in Singapore, so that major international computer companies and software houses planning to set up software development centers in Singapore could be assured that their products would be adequately protected.'); see also 'Second Reading of the Copyright Bill' Hansard vol 48 col 11–12 (5 May 1986).

[140] *Racecourse Association v OFT* [2005] CAT 26, Case Nos 1035/1/1/04 at [167] ('[C]ompetition law is not an area of law in which there is much scope for absolute concepts or sharp edges.').

11

South Korea[1]

SANG-SEUNG YI AND SEONG-WOOK HEO

I. Introduction

Thirty years have passed since the enactment of the Korean competition law, the Monopoly Regulation and Fair Trade Act (MRFTA) in 1980, and the subsequent establishment of the Korea Fair Trade Commission (KFTC) in 1981 as the principal enforcer of the law.[2] However, it has taken more than two decades of institution building (and the further development of the market economy in Korea) for the KFTC to begin implementing the competition law in earnest. In the area of merger control, which is the focus of the current chapter,[3] a total of 5,506 mergers were reported to the KFTC during its first 20 years (1981 to 2000), but in only 13 cases (0.24 per cent) corrective remedies were imposed in order to address anti-competitive concerns.[4] However, the majority of the remedies were either price controls[5] or market share restrictions[6] and only four (three horizontal and one vertical; all small-scale) mergers were prohibited and partial divestiture was ordered in only two cases.

[1] We thank seminar audience at Symposium on 'Getting the Balance Right: Intellectual Property, Competition Law and Economics in Asia' (September 2009, Singapore), the Seventh CPRC International Symposium on 'The Role of Competition Policy in the Development of East Asian Economies' (February 2010, Tokyo), and the Second Asian Competition Policy Workshop (June 2010, Hong Kong) for comments and Rangwon Suh for excellent research assistance. The origin of the ideas developed in the current chapter can be traced to section VII of Sang-Seung Yi and Youngjin Jung, 'A New Kid on the Block: Korean Competition Law, Policy and Economics' (Competition Policy International, Volume 3, No 2, Autumn 2007, 153–83), available at http://papers.ssrn.com/sol3/papers.cfm?abstract_id=1075324.

[2] The MRFTA was passed into law on 31 December 1980 and KFTC began humbly as a small division of the Economic Planning Board in May 1981. Information about the KFTC, including MRFTA, merger guidelines, and annual reports, can be accessed in English at http://eng.ftc.go.kr/. For a brief overview of the history of the Korean competition law over the past 30 years, see section 2 of Yi and Jung, 'A New Kid on the Block' (2007).

[3] See Yi and Jung (n 1) for an assessment of the KFTC's track record in other areas of competition law, such as cartel enforcement, competition advocacy and abuse of dominance.

[4] KFTC, 'A Twenty-Year History of the KFTC' (2001) (in Korean).

[5] For example, in the 1999 merger between Hyundai Automobile and (then-bankrupt) Kia Automobile, the KFTC allowed the merger on the condition that the combined firm not raise domestic prices for trucks at higher rates than export prices. KFTC Decision 99-43, 'Concerning Violation by Hyundai Automobile of Article on Combination of Enterprises' (Apr. 1999). We discuss this case in more details later.

[6] In the 2000 merger between SK Telecom and Shinshegi Telecom, the KFTC ordered that the combined firm reduce its market share below 50 per cent by June 2001. KFTC Decision 2000-76, 'Concerning Violation by SK Telecom of Article on Combination of Enterprises' (May 2000).

The KFTC itself is aware of its limited role in the merger area in the past and in particular the inadequateness of its past remedies. For example, in its own evaluation of its first 20 years, the KFTC candidly admitted that it had not been very active in enforcing the merger law.[7] However, in the subsequent 10 years, the KFTC has become far more active and has increasingly favoured structural remedies over price controls.

The main theme of the current chapter is to examine the KFTC's track record in the merger area over the past 30 years through the lens of dynamic competition. To begin with, viewed from the conventional perspective with emphasis on concentration and *static* competition, there is no question that the KFTC has moved in the right direction in the past 10 years. In addition, the KFTC's adoption of market definition tools[8] originally developed by the United States Department of Justice in its 1982 Horizontal Merger Guidelines[9] is certainly a welcome development which brought more rigor and coherence into merger analysis.

However, from the *dynamic* competition perspective, our assessment is that the KFTC has moved in the right direction in some aspects, but in the wrong direction in other more crucial aspects. Specifically, when the merging firms largely cater to domestic consumers in Korea, where neither actual nor potential competition from foreign firms typically pose significant threats to the Korean firms, we welcome the KFTC's more activist policy. However, when the merging firms compete both in Korea and abroad, the KFTC's narrow focus on *static* anticompetitive effects in the *domestic* market and insufficient attention to the *dynamic* competition that the merging firms face in *foreign* markets is a step backwards and could hinder dynamic efficiencies.

To put the matter differently, we believe that with the increasing sophistication of its staff in conducting antitrust analysis in the past ten years (certainly a welcome development in its own right), the KFTC has unfortunately suffered from the 'static competition bias'[10] and has lost sight of the 'big picture' of examining the competitive effects of a merger across all markets from a dynamic competition perspective. In particular, we argue that the KFTC has gotten trapped in the market definition mould under the US Horizontal Merger Guidelines, which typically define relevant markets within the short-term time horizon of one to two years and examine competitive effects in *each* relevant (product or geographical) market *separately*.

[7] KFTC, 'A Twenty-Year History of the KFTC' (2001) (in Korean).

[8] The 2007 version of the M&A review guidelines (first enacted in 1998) can be downloaded at http://eng.ftc.go.kr/files/static/Legal_Authority/Guidelines%20for%20M&A%20Review(2007).pdf.

[9] The most recent version of the Guidelines (revised in 2010) can be found at www.justice.gov/atr/public/merger-enforcement.html.

[10] See Evans and Hylton (2008) for an argument that the increasing reliance on economics in antitrust has certainly helped improve antitrust analysis considerably, but at the same time, it has had the side effects of shifting the focus away from dynamic competition to static competition, because economists have not yet developed useful analytical tools for examining dynamic competition. David S Evans and Keith N Hylton 'The Lawful Acquisition and Exercise of Monopoly Power and Its Implications for the Objectives of Antitrust' (2008) 4(2) *Competition Policy International* 203–41 (http://papers.ssrn.com/sol3/papers.cfm?abstract_id=1275431). Sidak and Teece (2009, 620) make a related argument that the United States 'federal courts have, by thoroughly embracing the economic reasoning of the Horizontal Merger Guidelines as promulgated several decades ago by the Antitrust Division and the FTC, caused antitrust case law to ossify around a static view of competition'. J Gregory Sidak and David F Teece 'Dynamic Competition in Antitrust Law'(2009) 5(4) *Journal of Competition Law and Economics* 581–631.

In order to address this 'staticisation' problem, we propose that the KFTC (and other competition authorities in an export-oriented economy) break out of the traditional market definition mould and expand the 'competitive arena' beyond the conventional 'relevant (geographical) markets' under the hypothetical monopolist test. To be specific, we advocate that a competition authority uses the total *national* social welfare standard over *all* geographical markets combined (which recognises fixed-cost savings and other gains by the merging firms in the foreign markets as efficiencies, and weighs them against anti-competitive effects in the domestic market) as opposed to the narrow consumer welfare standard in *each* geographical market concerned (which does not). In other words, we propose that a competition authority in an export-oriented economy, or more generally, any competition authority which reviews a merger with global operations, consider the total national social welfare standard over *all* geographical markets combined (which considers gains in the foreign markets as legitimate efficiencies to be weighed against anti-competitive losses in the domestic market) as the proper welfare standard in evaluating mergers.

We make a case for our proposition by way of examining four horizontal mergers, two mergers in the KFTC's first 20 years and two mergers in its second 10 years. Before presenting our analysis, we first give a brief overview of Korean competition law and economics in section II. Section III then reviews the four mergers that we examine. Section IV is the main part of the current chapter which makes our key proposal that a competition authority in an export-oriented economy should consider the total national social surplus over *all* geographical markets combined as the proper welfare standard in merger review. Section V concludes.

II. Overview of Korean Competition Law Enforcement[11]

The enactment of MRFTA in 1980 was not easy. The proponents of the law had to overcome opposition not only from *chaebol*, the family-controlled large business conglomerates that continue to dominate the Korean economy to this day, but from 'growth-first' intellectuals and government bureaucrats who argued that the Korean economy was not mature enough to have competition law as the guiding principle of the economic policy. The original MRFTA was modeled after the Japanese law, as many Korean administrative laws at that time were. However, Japanese influence has faded over time. Instead, since the KFTC began implementing competition law in earnest after the 1998 economic crisis was over, jurisprudential developments in the United States and European Union have greatly influenced the KFTC's enforcement of the Korean competition law.

In our view, cartel enforcement is the area where the KFTC has achieved the most significant success. An important impetus was the reform of the leniency program in 2005 which guaranteed that the first cartel member that reports the wrongdoing along with credible evidence to the KFTC would receive full exemption from the administrative fines.[12] The new leniency program was pivotal in uncovering cartels in numerous industries such

[11] This section is based on Yi and Jung (n 1) and adds new developments since 2007.

[12] Other important factors were the increase in the maximum level of surcharges on cartels (from 5% to 10% of relevant sales); stepping up of criminal prosecutions of the wrong-doers; and the elevation of the KFTC's cartel team to a new Directorate.

as flour, sugar, petrochemicals, fire insurance and elevators. The success of the leniency program coupled with the KFTC's strong stance against collusion has resulted in record fines against cartels. Indeed, according to Connor's (2007) study,[13] since 1990, the KFTC has been responsible for a striking 85 per cent of all cartel fines in Asia.[14]

Another area of success is competition advocacy. The KFTC has effectively used its statutory right (MRFTA Article 63) to consult government ministries *before* they enact laws or regulations that might restrict competition. Developing countries that consider enactment of competition law (or have recently begun to implement competition law) could learn from the Korean experience and include a similar article to let the competition authority to ensure that other government agencies do not limit competition.

In contrast, merger control and abuse of dominance enforcement have been anemic until recently. Since we examine the KFTC's major merger decisions in the next two sections, here, we briefly review the KFTC's track records on the abuse of dominance. The first significant abuse of dominance case undertaken by the KFTC is Posco refusal to deal case in 2001.[15] When Hyundai Motor Group built its own cold coil plant at its affiliate Hysco in 1998 and demanded Posco, the only integrated steel mill in Korea at that time, to supply hot coils instead of cold coils as it used to, Posco refused. The KFTC ruled that this unilateral refusal to deal restricted competition in the cold coil market. However, in 2007, the Korean Supreme Court reversed, because it could not find any anti-competitive effects in the cold coil market, as Hysco profitably operated at full capacity by using imported hot coils from Japan.[16]

Among all Asian competition authorities, the KFTC has been truly the most aggressive one in pursuing dominant multinationals in the so-called new economy sector. In early 2006, after more than four years of investigation, the KFTC ruled that Microsoft had abused its dominant market position by tying its Windows Media Player (WMP) and Windows Messenger to its Windows PC operating system, and tying Windows Media Services to its Windows Server operating system.[17] The KFTC levied a fine of 32.4 billion KRW against Microsoft. It was also the first competition authority in the world to rule against the inclusion of messengers in Windows OS and media servers in Windows Server OS. While Microsoft vehemently argued that competition was vibrant (for example, a Korean messenger and a Korean media player released long after the alleged tying took place have replaced Microsoft's messenger and media player as the top programs in Korea), it withdrew its

[13] John M Connor, 'Global Antitrust Prosecutions of International Cartels: Focus on Asia' SSRN Working Paper (5 November 2007) 21, available at http://ssrn.com/abstract=1027949.

[14] The KFTC is also the first Asian competition authority to introduce extraterritorial application of competition law to foreign cartels, beginning with an 11 billion KRW fine against the graphite electrode cartel in 2002 and a 4 billion KRW surcharge against the vitamin cartel in 2003.

[15] KFTC Decision 2001-068, Concerning Abuse of Market Dominant Position by POSCO (Apr 2001).

[16] Korean Supreme Court Decision 2002du8626 (Nov 2007). In 2003, at the request of a study group at the Supreme Court, the first author of the current chapter (Yi) wrote an economics analysis paper which made basically the same arguments that the Korean Supreme Court adopted in its 2007 decision. Sang-Seung Yi (2003), 'An Economic Analysis on the Refusal to Supply by Posco' (in Korean). An expanded version with extensive commentaries on the Korean Supreme Court Decision was published as Sang-Seung Yi 'An Economic Analysis of the Main Issues and the Significance of Posco's Refusal to Deal' (2010) 49(4) *Korean Economic Journal* 243–80.

[17] KFTC Decision 2006-042, Concerning Abuse of Market Dominant Position, etc by Microsoft Corporation and Microsoft Korea Yuhan Hoesa (Feb 2006). The first author of the current paper (Yi) was the main testifying economics expert for Microsoft both before the KFTC and before the Seoul High Court.

appeal to the Seoul High Court in September 2007, after its decisive defeat earlier in the same month in the European Court of First Instance ('CFI') in related cases.[18]

In 2008, the KFTC levied a fine of 26.0 billion KRW on Intel for giving loyalty rebates to computer manufacturers with the purpose to exclude rival AMD.[19] Notably, the KFTC made its decision *before* the EC reached a similar ruling in 2009.[20] While the Japanese FTC was the first competition authority to make a ruling against Intel, its 2005 decision only contained 'recommendations' without fines that Intel 'halt the practice of requiring PC makers to limit the use of competitors' chips in exchange for monetary rebates.'[21]

Most recently, in 2009 the KFTC fined 273 billion KRW against Qualcomm for discriminatory licensing and loyalty rebates with the purpose of extending its monopoly power in the mobile radio interface technology market to the chipset market.[22] The fine was not only the largest on a single company in the KFTC's history, but the KFTC was the *first* competition authority in the world to take action against Qualcomm's alleged abuse of dominance.

III. The Four Mergers

A. Hyundai-Kia Merger (1999)[23]

In 1998, Hyundai Automobile was the number 1 car maker in Korea with a 39.1 per cent share for passenger cars, 58.3 per cent for buses and 50.3 per cent for trucks, respectively, while the then-bankrupt Kia[24] was the number three car maker with 16.5 per cent, 15.9 per cent and 44.3 per cent shares, respectively. As shown in Table 1 below, Hyundai's acquisition of Kia created an extremely concentrated industry structure, with the post-merger Herfindhal-Hirschman Index (HHI) close to 4,500 with an accompanying increase in HHI close to 1,300 in the passenger car sector. The bus market was even more concentrated than

[18] CFI upheld EC's 2004 decision against Microsoft's WMP 'tying' and its refusal to supply interoperability information to Sun Microsystems. (Judgment of the Court of First Instance in Case T-201/04, *Microsoft Corp v Commission of the European Communities*, Sep 17 2007, available at http://curia.europa.eu/jurisp/cgi-bin/form.pl?lang=EN&Submit=rechercher&numaff=T-201/04). EC's 2004 decision is available at http://ec.europa.eu/comm/competition/antitrust/cases/decisions/37792/en.pdf. CFI was renamed as General Court in November 2009.

[19] KFTC Decision 2008-295, Concerning Abuse of Market Dominant Position by Intel Corporation, Intel Semiconductor Limited and Intel Korea, Inc (Nov 2008). This case is currently under appeal before the Seoul High Court.

[20] The EC's 2009 decision and related material are available at 'The Intel Case' (http://ec.europa.eu/competition/sectors/ICT/intel.html). The EC's fine of EUR 1.06 billion is far larger than the KFTC's.

[21] JFTC's press release, 'JFTC rendered a recommendation to Intel K.K.' (March 8, 2005) available at http://www.jftc.go.jp/e-page/pressreleases/2005/March/050308intel.pdf For Intel's decision to comply with the JFTC's recommendation, see News.com, 'Intel to abide by Japan FTC recommendations' (April 1 2005) available at http://news.cnet.com/Intel-to-abide-by-Japan-FTC-recommendations/2100-1014_3-5649589.html.

[22] KFTC Decision 2009-281, Concerning Abuse of Market Dominant Position by Qualcomm Inc, Qualcomm Korea and Qualcomm CDMA Technology Korea (Dec 2009). The first author of the current chapter (Yi) testified for Texas Instruments against Qualcomm before the KFTC. This case is currently under appeal before the Seoul High Court.

[23] Factual descriptions of this merger are based on KFTC Decision 99-43, 'Concerning Violation by Hyundai Automobile of Article on Combination of Enterprises' (April 1999) and the accompanying press release.

[24] The bankruptcy of Kia in early 1997 was an important precursor to the financial crisis at the end of 1997 that plunged the Korean economy into a deep recession in 1998.

Table 1: Market Shares and Concentration Ratios in the Korean Automobile Industry, 1998

	Passenger Cars	Buses	Trucks
Hyundai	39.1%	58.3%	50.3%
Kia	16.5%	15.9%	44.3%
Daewoo	36.8%	25.8%	4.6%
Samsung	7.3%	0.0%	0.5%
Others	0.0%	0.0%	0.2%
Imports	0.3%	0.0%	0.1%
Sum (Total units sold in Korea)	100.0% (570,056)	100.0% (75,185)	100.0% (136,739)
Post-merger HHI	4,499	6,171	8,970
HHI increase	1,290	1,854	4,457

Source: KFTC Decision 99-43, 'Concerning Violation by Hyundai Automobile of Article on Combination of Enterprises' (April 1999). The market shares are based on number of cars sold, not revenue.

the passenger car market and the truck market was virtually a merger to monopoly (with the combined Hyundai-Kia controlling close to 95 per cent of market share).

The KFTC determined that the merger was anti-competitive on three grounds. First, as shown above, the merger increased the concentration in the relevant markets to very high levels. Second, new entry was difficult because massive investments were required but the Korean car industry already suffered from excess capacity (with capacity utilisation of only 47.3 per cent in 1998). Third, actual foreign competition in the Korean market was minimal (with foreign firms controlling only 0.3 per cent for passenger cars in 1998).[25]

Nonetheless, the KFTC approved the merger with minimal conditions for five reasons. First, Kia was bankrupt and there was no willing buyer in the first two rounds of international auctions for Kia. As a result, Kia's assets would exit the market unless Hyundai took them over. Second, Daewoo had made significant inroads since 1995 (with shares jumping from 20.5 per cent to 36.8 per cent from 1995 to 1998 in the passenger car markets) and as a result, Hyundai/Kia's combined share had dropped significantly (from 74 per cent in 1995 to 56 per cent in 1998) in the passenger car market. According to the KFTC, the emergence of a strong domestic competitor had a significant potential to limit the exercise of market power by the combined Hyundai/Kia.[26] Third, imports from Japan were scheduled to be liberalised from June 1999, which were expected to further constrain Hyundai/Kia's

[25] Foreign cars accounted for somewhat higher shares before the economic crisis hit Korea, but were still negligible with 0.7% in 1997, 0.8% in 1996 and 0.6% in 1995 (in terms of units). The market share of foreign cars has increased over time, but at a slow pace. In the first 3 quarters of 2010, it reached 7% of all passenger cars sold in Korea, a record. Source: The Korea Automobile Importers and Distributors Association (KAIDA), available at /www.kaida.co.kr/statistics/home.action?programId=365 (in Korean).

[26] This key source of domestic competition was soon weakened in the aftermath of the 1998 economic crisis. Daewoo Motor's market share has fallen from 36.8% in 1999 to 10.0% in 2002 in the wake of Daewoo Group's

market power.[27] Fourth, foreign car markets were very competitive and Hyundai/Kia exported more than half of its cars. (The proportions of Korean automobiles exported were 68 per cent for passenger cars, 54 per cent for buses and 25 per cent for trucks). The KFTC claimed that the vibrant competition in the foreign markets would restrict price increases in the domestic markets.[28] Fifth, the combined Hyundai/Kia would have a total capacity of 2.6 million cars and thus would be in a position to realise economies of scale. Automobile industry participants often claimed that a firm needed at least a capacity of two million cars in order to reach a minimum efficient scale. Before the merger, Hyundai had five automobile platforms[29] and Kia had eight, but the KFTC Decision stated that the combined firm could integrate them and use common parts, streamlining both future model developments and part procurement processes.

The KFTC ruled that the efficiency effects from the merger outweighed the anti-competitive effects in the passenger car and bus markets.[30] However, given the almost monopoly position of the combined Hyundai/Kia and the relatively low export proportion in the truck market, the KFTC determined that anti-competitive effects dominated efficiency effects in that market. As a result, the KFTC did not impose any conditions in the passenger car or bus market, but ordered the combined Hyundai/Kia not to raise domestic truck prices at higher rates than export prices for the next three years. Notably, the KFTC did not order a partial divestiture (the sale of Hyundai's or Kia's production facilities for trucks to third parties), probably because at the time it made its decision (March 1999), Korea had not still recovered from the severe recession of 1998 and Kia desperately needed a quick infusion of capital and thus could not wait for a buyer of its truck capacity.

B. SK Telecom-Shinsegi Telecom Merger (2000)[31]

There were five mobile telephone network operators in Korea in 1999. SK Telecom was the former state monopoly using cellular technology from April 1984 and Shinsegi began operation as the second cellular licensee in April 1996. In October 1997, three Personal Communication System (PCS) licensees began providing services, bringing full competition to the Korean mobile telephony market. Fierce competition among the five carriers for recruiting subscribers (both through massive investments in networks and through heavy

bankruptcy in 2000. Daewoo Motor, a member of Daewoo Group, subsequently went into court receivership and then was acquired by GM in 2002.

27 This prediction was not realised, because even after 10 years, Japanese cars accounted for only 1.9% of all passenger cars sold in Korea in 2009. Source: KAIDA, available at http://www.kaida.co.kr/statistics/home.action?programId=365 (in Korean).

28 The KFTC Decision did not explain why vigorous competition in the foreign markets would constrain price increases in Korea. (The KFTC defined Korea as the relevant geographical market.) We examine this issue below.

29 According to Wikipedia (http://en.wikipedia.org/wiki/Automobile_platform), an automobile platform is a shared set of common design, engineering, and production efforts, as well as major components over a number of outwardly distinct models and even types of automobiles, often from different, but related marques. Platform sharing is practiced in the automotive industry to reduce the costs associated with the development of products by basing those products on a smaller number of platforms. This further allows companies to create distinct models from a design perspective on similar underpinnings.

30 The KFTC Decision simply stated (without any meaningful analysis) its conclusions on balancing of anti-competitive and pro-competitive effects in the three relevant markets.

31 Source for the facts: KFTC Decision 2000-76, 'Concerning Violation by SK Telecom of Article on Combination of Enterprises' (May 2000).

promotions including handset subsidies) in the explosively growing market[32] resulted in heavy losses for the new entrants. By the end of 1999, Shinsegi had suffered a cumulative loss of 479 billion KRW (roughly 479 million US dollars, assuming an exchange rate of 1,000 KRW for one US dollar) and the three PCS carriers each had lost from 286 billion to 539 billion KRW.

SK Telecom, on the other hand, was profitable with accumulated profits of 1.39 trillion KRW. Three things set SK Telecom apart from its competitors:

(i) It had a high-paying business customer base.[33]
(ii) It had already made the bulk of its network investments (while the newcomers had to make huge investments building up networks).[34]
(iii) The spectrum it used (800MHz for cellular technology) was more cost efficient in call transmission so as to require only 1/3 to 1/2 base stations than the PCS spectrums bands (1.8 MHz) do for comparable call quality.[35]

In 1999, Korea was preparing for the assignment of 2MHz band spectrum for the second-generation ('2G' or 'IMT-2000') digital mobile telephony services, which would require even more massive investments than the first generation ('1G') analog services. Given the huge losses that the new entrants had suffered (for example, Shinsegi had lost more than half of its total capital of 800 billion KRW) and the resulting high debt burdens (Shinsegi's debt ratio was 575 per cent at the end of 1999 and 9.8 per cent of its total revenue was used to pay interests),[36] it was widely believed that not all of them could raise new capital to finance investments to provide 2G services on a full scale.

Hence, the environment was ripe for industry consolidation. The question was what form it would take: would the new entrants merge among themselves or would SK Telecom, the number one carrier, take over some of the weaker competitors? It was SK Telecom which made the first move. In December 1999, SK Telecom announced that it would acquire 51.2 per cent of Shinsegi's stocks from its two major shareholders (Posco and Kolon) for cash payments of 1.1 trillion KRW and 6.5 per cent of SK Telecom's new shares.[37] This five-to-four merger would result in a post-merger HHI of 3,882 with an increase of 1,213, with the combined firm controlling 56.9 per cent of subscribers, as shown in Table 2 below.

The KFTC identified three anti-competitive concerns (the first two of which are, in our view, legitimate, but the third is not). First, because SK Telecom's price was regulated by the Ministry of Information and Communications, it might not be able to raise prices directly. However, the loss of competition between SK Telecom and Shinsegi could still

[32] The number of mobile subscribers grew from 3.2 million in December 1996 to 23.4 million in December 1999, a sevenfold increase in just three years. (The population of Korea is roughly 50 million.)

[33] The average revenue per user (ARPU) was 39.6 thousand KRW for SKT, but the average ARPU for the four competitors was only 32.3 thousand KRW.

[34] By the end of 1999, SK Telecom had already allocated 72.9% of its machinery as expenses, but the four competitors depreciated only about 17% (the three PCS entrants) and 32.3% (Shinsegi) of their assets.

[35] As a result, the cost per one minute of talk was 144 KRW for SKT, but it was 160 KRW for the four competitors in 1999.

[36] Three PCS carriers were in a similar predicament: the debt ratios and the interest-service ratios were 151% and 11.8% for KT Freetel; 196% and 16.5% for LG Telecom; and 192% and 9.0% for HansolM.com. In contrast, SK Telecom's debt ratio was only 66% and it paid only 3.1% of its total revenue for interests.

[37] In 2001, KT Freetel acquired HansolM.com, resulting in a three-firm structure that continues to this day.

Table 2: Market Shares and Concentration Ratios in the Korean Mobile Telephony Industry, 1999

SK Telecom	42.7%
Shinsegi	14.2%
KT Freetel	18.3%
LG Telecom	13.3%
HansolM.com	11.5%
Sum	100.0%
Post-merger HHI	3,882
HHI increase	1,213

Source: KFTC Decision 2000-76, 'Concerning Violation by SK Telecom of Article on Combination of Enterprises' (May 2000). The market shares are based on the numbers of subscribers. SK Telecom's and Shinsegi's market shares in terms of revenue are higher: 46.5 and 14.5 per cent respectively (in 1999). Hence, revenue-based calculations would result in even higher post-merger HHI (4,252) and increase in HHI (1,349) than reported in the table.

harm consumers by delaying price cutting, by reducing the quality of current services or by delaying the launch of new services. Second, the combined firm would have a monopsonistic power over the purchase of cellular handsets and SK Telecom might favour its own handset manufacturer over competitors.[38] Third, because SK Telecom had advantages over competitors in terms of financial situation, distribution network, research and development (R&D) capabilities and the cost efficiency of spectrum, the combined firm might be able to attract more subscribers at the expense of the other three competitors.

The KFTC accepted some of SK Telecom/Shinegi's arguments on efficiencies (namely, cost savings from integrating the two cellular networks and sales forces; price reduction/ volume increase for handset purchases (from the supra-competitive levels); and realising R&D synergies) but decided that anti-competitive effects dominated the pro-competitive effects. The KFTC imposed two remedies. First, the combined firm was ordered to limit its purchase of cellular handsets from its affiliate to 1.2 million units per year from 2000 to 2005. Second, it was further ordered to reduce its market share in terms of subscribers to below 50 per cent by June 2001.

The first remedy and the theory of anti-competitiveness that underlies it (monopsonistic power over cellular handsets) appear to be well grounded in economic theory and reasonable. However, the second remedy and the liability theory (a form of 'efficiency offence') are hard to justify. In particular, the limit on market shares violates the core principle of competition law: the combined firm was ordered to reduce its marketing campaign and efforts to recruit new subscribers. This remedy seems to be motivated by the fact that the Korean law has explicit clauses on the presumption of anti-competitive merger: if the combined firm's market share exceeds 50 per cent of the total market and is above 1.33 times of the second largest firm's share, that merger is presumed to be anti-competitive (MRFTA articles 4 and 7). Ordering the combined firm to reduce its market share below 50

[38] As mentioned above, SK Telecom and Shinsegi used cellular technology and the other three competitors used PCS technology. Cellular handsets could not be used for PCS services (and vice versa). Hence, the combined firm would be a monopsonist over the purchase of cellular handsets. In 1999, SK Telecom procured 5.3% of its handsets from SK Teletek (an affiliate) and 12.0% in Jan/Feb 2000.

per cent by June 2001 creates the temporary appearance that the presumption clause of the law was not violated. However, even from the perspective of evaluating the effectiveness of the remedy (assuming that it was a right remedy), it had no lasting effect: the combined firm was simply ordered to reduce its market share below 50 per cent by a certain point in time, but with no follow-up measures. By May 2002, the combined SK Telecom/Shinsegi's market share had climbed back to 53.4 per cent.

C. Muhak-Daesun Merger (2003)[39]

Traditionally, each Korean province has had a local *soju* (Korean hard liquor) brand. There is also a national brand called Jinro. In 2002, Muhak, a leading *soju* producer in Gyeongnam province launched a hostile takeover of Daesun, a rival *soju* manufacturer in the neighbouring metropolitan city of Busan by acquiring 41 per cent of Daesun's stocks. Table 3 below summarises market shares in Gyeongnam, Busan and Korea as a whole.

On the surface, it was clear that this merger would create anti-competitive effects in the two regions. Daesun sold its *soju* only in Busan and Gyeongnam and Muhak's revenue from *soju* sales outside of Busan and Gyeongnam accounted for only 1.1 per cent of its total revenue. Hence, both in the Busan and Gyeongnam regions, a very dominant firm (with market share of about 85 per cent) would merge with one of the two significant competitors. In each region, the combined firm would face Jinro only, with about three to seven per cent of market share. One would normally expect such a loss of competition to generate substantial anti-competitive effects. However, matters were more complicated due to the unique history of the *soju* industry and government tax regulations. First, because of tax regulations, Jinro had to set its prices uniformly across Korea. As a result, contrary to the KFTC's simplistic assertion that this three-to-two merger would increase the risk of collusion in Busan/Gyeongnam regions, localised coordinated effects between the combined firm and Jinro were not feasible. (In other words, Jinro could not raise its prices in Busan and Gyeongnam only in explicit/tacit coordination with the combined firm.) Rather, coordination between the Muhak/Daesun and Jinro would require Jinro to raise it prices

Table 3: Market Shares and Concentration Ratios in the Korean *Soju* Industry, 2001

	Korea as a whole	Busan Metropolitan City	Gyeongnam Province
Jinro	52.3%	7.2%	2.7%
Muhak	8.5%	7.1%	84.3%
Daesun	8.4%	84.4%	12.9%
Seven others	30.8%	1.3%	0.0%
Sum	100.0%	100.0%	100.0%
Post-merger HHI	3,231	8,426	9,455
HHI increase	143	1,198	2,175

Source: KFTC Decision 2003-27, 'Concerning Violation by Muhak on Combination of Enterprises' (January 2003).

[39] Source for the facts: KFTC Decision 2003-27, 'Concerning Violation by Muhak on Combination of Enterprises' (January 2003).

in all provinces. However, in each province, it faced a different competitor (a total of seven in addition to Muhak/Daesun). Since sales in the Busan/Gyeongnam regions accounted for only 1.8 per cent of Jinro's total revenue, unless the other *soju* producers also participated, it did not make sense for Jinro to raise prices on a *national* scale in coordination with the combined firm's price increases in the Busan/Gyeongnam provinces. In sum, it was not clear if the usual coordinated effects (between Jinro and the merged firm in the Busan/Gyeongnam regions) would materialise as a result of Muhak-Daesun merger.

Second, unilateral effects (ie the anti-competitive effects arising from the loss of competition between Muhak and Daesun) were certainly a serious concern. The key question here was if Muhak/Daesun would be able to raise its profits by unilaterally increasing their prices, holding Jinro's prices fixed. (Notice that the above analysis casts doubt on the possibility that Jinro would raise its price in coordination with Muhak/Daesun.) The KFTC simply stated that Muhak and Daesun had competed head to head for a long time and the loss of competition between the two could not be offset by Jinro, as there was a strong preference for local brands in the two regions. The KFTC was clearly right about the loss of head-to-head competition between Muhak and Daesun. However, its observation on Jinro's potential to rein in the combined firm was conclusory and was not based on any real analysis. A closer look reveals that Jinro's competitive threats to Muhak/Daesun could not be dismissed, because as the following data show, Jinro's market share was as high as 40 per cent in the two regions in the recent past.

Furthermore, in the region of Jeonnam, when the local brand (Bohae) pursued a high-price policy from 1997, Jinro had more than tripled its market share (from seven to over 25 per cent), as shown in Table 5 below.

Table 4: Market Shares in Busan and Gyeongnam Regions, 1993–2001

	Busan								
	1993	1994	1995	1996	1997	1998	1999	2000	2001
Daesun	58.9	58.1	53.6	53.5	73.9	79.8	81.5	84.0	85.0
Muhak	3.1	2.6	3.1	2.8	5.1	7.2	7.9	7.9	7.1
Jinro	33.0	34.4	40.7	37.2	18.0	9.7	7.4	6.5	6.6
	Gyeongnam								
	1993	1994	1995	1996	1997	1998	1999	2000	2001
Muhak	63.5	58.4	53.7	68.2	68.9	81.1	84.0	85.2	83.5
Daesun	13.7	14.2	12.5	8.1	10.2	9.7	10.9	10.7	13.0
Jinro	19.8	23.8	30.1	21.7	20.3	9.1	5.1	4.1	3.4

Source: KFTC; shares based on volume of sales.

Table 5: Market Shares in Jeonnam Region, 1993–2002

	1993	1994	1995	1996	1997	1998	1999	2000	2001	2002 (May)
Bohae	83.7	83.9	82.1	88.9	91.1	93.7	91.2	90.0	80.3	74.1
Jinro	11.7	12.7	14.0	9.1	6.9	5.8	7.0	8.9	18.8	25.3

Source: KFTC; shares based on volume of sales.

Hence, without a more rigorous analysis, one could not say that the merged firm would be able to engage in profitable unilateral price increases in the Busan/Gyeongnam regions. Such analyses took place in the appeals process in the form of a geographical market definition exercise. Daesun, whose management resisted the hostile takeover attempt by Muhak, submitted an economic analysis report to the Seoul High Court that defended the KFTC's position that the relevant geographical markets were the Busan and Gyeongnam regions.[40] This study was based on a survey of *soju* consumers in the two regions and explicitly applied the critical loss analysis technique for market definition.[41]

According to Daesun's economic report, the combined firm could increase its profits by raising their prices by 10, 15 and 'more than 20 per cent' (but not by five per cent). Muhak's economic experts[42] criticised several aspects of Daesun's economic analysis. The most important one was about the classification of the two firms' costs (based on accounting data) into fixed and variable costs. Muhak's experts argued that the time horizon for determining if a cost is variable should be one to two years under the hypothetical monopolist's small but significant and non-transitory increase in price (SSNIP) test, which the critical loss analysis technique operationalises by using data on consumer switching ('actual loss') and accounting profit data ('critical loss'). Under the one to two-year criterion, several costs that Daesun's experts classified as variable should be re-classified as fixed costs.

In particular, while Daesun's experts classified all labour costs as variable, Muhak's experts argued that salaries for regular workers (as opposed to temporary workers who could be fired when their contracts expired) were better classified as fixed costs in Korea under the one to two-year time horizon of the SSNIP test, because under the Korean labour law, it is impossible to lay off workers in Korea unless the company faces the dangerous prospects of bankruptcy. After such re-classification, no price increase was profitable for the combined firm. Daesun's experts countered that the time horizon under the critical loss analysis should be 'a sufficiently lengthy period of time during which a hypothetical monopolist is expected to exercise its monopoly power'.[43] Such a claim is not based on the hypothetical monopolist test, which is operationalised to be over a one to two-year time

[40] Jeon, Seonghoon and Shin, Kwangshik, 'An Economic Analysis of Geographic Market Definition Relevant to Muhak-Daesun Merger'(2006) 14(4) *The Korean Journal of Industrial Organization* 17–66 (in Korean).

[41] It was the KFTC staff who first applied the critical loss analysis for market definition in Korea. In a 2002 merger between two bread producers (Paris Croissant-Samlip), the KFTC staff used consumer survey results and a certain assumption on costs (5% of total sales were profits, 35% were variable costs and the remaining 60% were fixed costs) to conclude that factory-produced breads (which consumers buy at supermarkets) and bakery-produced breads (which consumers buy at bakeries) constituted the same relevant product market. Since the merged firm's market share in the 'all bread market' was less than 30%, the KFTC allowed the merger and no decision was made public. A review of the internal KFTC memo dated July 2002 showed that the KFTC staff used the critical loss analysis methodology (without explicitly saying so) to examine if the two types of breads belonged to the same relevant market (although it simply stated its cost assumption without much analysis). Because the KFTC did not publish its findings, it was not widely known that the KFTC staff used the critical loss analysis in as early as 2002. It was the Daesun's outside experts who explicitly introduced and applied the critical loss analysis for the first time in the 2004 Muhak-Daesun merger (see the paper in the above footnote). After that, the critical loss analysis became widely publicised and used. For example, the KFTC used the critical loss analysis to define the relevant product market in its 2006 decision on the merger between a local beer producer and a *soju* producer. KFTC Decision 2006-009, 'Concerning Violation by Hite Beer of Article on Combination of Enterprises' (January 2006).

[42] The first author of the current chapter (Yi) served as the testifying expert for Muhak in the appeals process.

[43] *Muhak v KFTC* 2003 nu 2252 (Seoul High Court. October 2004) 36.

horizon. However, the Seoul High Court accepted Daesun's position (without providing any analysis) and upheld the KFTC's ban of the merger.

Setting aside these differences in expert opinions about the merged firm's ability to engage in profitable unilateral price increases in the Busan/Gyeongnam regions, the KFTC's structural remedy (prohibition of the merger) is the right one *if* one accepts the KFTC's view that the loss of head to head competition between Muhak and Daesun would result in significant anti-competitive harm in the two provinces.

D. DCC-CCC Merger (2006)[44]

Carbon black is mainly used as a reinforcing filler in rubber products (such as tyres) and for special purposes such as laser printer/photocopier toner.[45] In 2006, DC Chemicals (DCC), a Korean producer of carbon black, acquired 100 per cent of stocks of Columbian Chemicals Company (CCC), a global carbon black firm with operations in nine countries (Korea, United States, Spain, Hungary, Italy, United Kingdom, Canada, Brazil and Germany). DCC's capacity in 2004 was about 0.2 million tons per year and CCC's global capacity was 1.1 million tons. CCC's Korean subsidiary (Columbian Chemicals Korea (CCK)) had a capacity of 0.1 million tons. Hence, in terms of size, the Korean portion (CCK) was about 1/10 of the total transaction.

The KFTC defined two separate relevant product markets, one each for the two types of carbon black ('carbon black used to reinforce rubber products' and 'specialty type carbon black'). The KFTC also defined the relevant geographical market as Korea. There was little controversy on the matter of product market definition. Not only was there little demand substitutability between the two uses of carbon black, but there was poor supply substitution between the two types of carbon black, because producing the high valued-added specialty type required sophisticated technology and equipment.

Geographical market definition was somewhat more complicated. Carbon black is bulky and thus costly to transport (especially over the land). Hence, the volume of internationally traded carbon blacks for reinforcing rubber was not high (except between neighbouring nations with short sea transport). For example, Korea imported only about 1.3 thousand tons of carbon black for reinforcing rubber products, less than 0.4 per cent of Korea's total usage in 2004. While imports (especially from China) were rapidly increasing at the time (for example, the import volume more than doubled to 2.9 thousand tons), they accounted still a very small portion (less than one per cent) of total usage in Korea in 2005. Hence, the KFTC's geographical market definition of Korea for carbon black used to reinforce rubber products was reasonable.[46]

[44] Source for the facts: KFTC Decision 2006-173, Concerning Violation by Columbian Chemicals Acquisition LLC of Article on Combination of Enterprises (August 2006). The first author of the current chapter (Yi) served as the economics expert witness for DCC at the KFTC stage.

[45] http://en.wikipedia.org/wiki/Carbon_black.

[46] One issue was how to treat exports. Korea exported a significant volume of carbon black for reinforcing rubber products. For example, in 2004, it exported 91 thousand tons out of 444 thousand tons produced (20% exported). DCC's expert (Yi) argued that exports should be included in addition to sales in Korea in conducting competitive analysis. The reasoning began with the observation that average export prices were already about 10% lower than average domestic prices. (An indication that domestic producers had excess capacity and were 'dumping' abroad (ie, selling the product abroad at prices lower than domestic prices, as long as the export prices were above unit variable costs for export volume).) Hence, it was likely that in response to a SSNIP by a hypothetical

The more expensive specialty type carbon black, on the other hand, was more actively traded internationally. For example, both imports (8.9 thousand tons) and exports (12.4 thousand tons) accounted for significant portions of Korean consumption (18.1 thousand tons; imports accounting for 49.4 per cent) and production (30.5 thousand tons; exports accounting for 40.7 per cent) in 2004. Hence, one could arguably expand the geographical market beyond Korea (especially to include neighbouring Japan and China) for specialty type carbon black. However, this issue was moot, because neither DCC nor CCK produced much specialty type carbon black (each about four per cent of sales in Korea) and thus DCC's acquisition of CCC did not raise any anti-competitive concerns in the market for specialty type carbon black regardless of geographical market definition.

Within the relevant geographical market of Korea, DCC's acquisition of CCC would result in a three-to-two merger with the post-merger HHI of 5,287 and the increase in HHI of 1,847 in the market for carbon black used to reinforce rubber products, as shown in Table 6 below. (As mentioned above, the DDC-CCC merger would raise the HHI by only a small margin (to be precise, 33) in the market for special type carbon black.)

The KFTC ruled that the merger raised the risk of tacit/explicit collusion in the market for carbon black used to strengthen rubber products, because the number of competitors would be reduced from three to two. The KFTC also argued that the combined firm could profitably raise its prices even in the absence of coordination with KCB, because KCB's capacity was limited.[47] Due to environmental regulations, new entry into carbon black

Table 6: Market Shares and Concentration Ratios for Two Types of Carbon Black in Korea, 2005

	Carbon black used for reinforcing rubber products	Specialty type carbon black
DCC	39.8%	4.0%
KCB	36.3%	49.0%
CCK	23.2%	4.2%
Imports	0.7%	42.8%
Sum	100.0%	100%
Post-merger HHI	5,287	
HHI increase	1,847	33

Source: KFTC Decision 2006-173, Concerning Violation by Columbian Chemicals Acquisition LLC of Article on Combination of Enterprises (August 2006). In calculating the post-merger HHI, we count imports (0.7 per cent) as one company in the case of carbon black used to reinforce rubber products. In the case of specialty type carbon black, because we do not have information about imports, we leave the post-merger HHI as blank.

monopolist over all carbon black sold in Korea, the hypothetical competitor which controls exports would profitably divert its exports to internal sales in Korea, defeating the price increase. (This issue would be important in determining if KCB, the second largest domestic producer, would be in a position to defeat unilateral price increases by the combined firm, by diverting its exports to sales in Korea.) The KFTC simply excluded exports and just looked at domestic sales in computing market shares (and available capacity for KCB) without much analysis.

[47] According to the KFTC, KCB's spare capacity was only 7% of DCC-CCK's sale volume in Korea. As discussed in the above footnote, the KFTC rejected DCC's arguments that KCB could profitably divert its export volume to domestic sales in response to DCC-CCK's unilateral price increases.

production was difficult. Imports of carbon black used to reinforce rubber products were minimal and because the demand from China was growing rapidly, the KFTC argued that it was unlikely that imports could defeat DCC-CCK's unilateral (or in coordination with KCB) price increases. The KFTC acknowledged that the three tyre companies, which accounted for about 70 per cent of demand for all carbon black used for strengthening rubber products, were 'large buyers that may constrain the ability of the merging parties to raise price'. DCC argued that the presence of powerful buyers in Korea was the critical difference from the situation in the United States in the early 1980s, when the FTC blocked two competing mergers among carbon black producers.[48] In the United States at the time, there were more than 10 tyre sellers, with the largest one accounting for less than 20 per cent of market share. In Korea, on the other hand, the two top tyre companies each had about 40 per cent purchase share of carbon black used to strengthen tyres (hence, each had roughly 30 per cent of demand for all carbon black used to reinforce rubber products, because tyres accounted for about 70 per cent of rubber products for which carbon black was used as a strengthening material).

A comparison of long-term supply contracts between CCK and Kumho Tire and between CCC and a US tyre company clearly showed that Kumho Tire enjoyed far better terms than the US company. For example, while Kumho Tire could demand price reduction from CCK by obtaining a written offer from a competitor, the US company was obliged to pay CCC a cost-adjusted price for the duration of the contract (about three years). Nonetheless, the KFTC determined that the merger would strengthen the bargaining power of the carbon black companies vis-à-vis tyre companies and thus was anti-competitive.

The KFTC accepted several arguments advanced by DCC concerning the merger-specific efficiency effects. First, DCC could consolidate input (FCC-Oil) purchase with CCK and use larger container ships to transport the input to Korea with significant cost savings. Second, DCC and CCK could each specialise their plants to specific grades and types of carbon black (which vary depending on the precise requirements of the buyer) and thus

Table 7: Purchase Shares of Carbon Black Used to Strengthen Tyres in Korea, 2005

Hankook Tire	46.0%
Kumho Tire	40.5%
Nexen Tire	13.5%
Sum	100.0%

Source: KFTC Decision 2006-173, Concerning Violation by Columbian Chemicals Acquisition LLC of Article on Combination of Enterprises (August 2006).

[48] The FTC blocked both Columbian Enterprises, Inc's acquisition of Continental Carbon Company and Bass Brothers Inc's acquisition of Ashland Oil Inc's Carbon Black Division on the grounds that the acquisitions would substantially increase concentration and eliminate competition in the carbon black industry. (At the time, Columbian was the second largest, Ashland the third largest, Continental the sixth largest, and Bass (through its Sid Richardson Carbon and Gasoline Co Inc subsidiary) the seventh largest carbon producer in the United States.) *Columbian Enterprises, Inc* Dkt 9177, 106 FTC 551 (1985); *Bass Brothers Enterprises, Inc* Dkt 9178, 108 FTC 51 (1986); *FTC v Bass Bros Enters, Inc* 1984-1 Trade Cas (CCH) ¶¶66,041 (ND Ohio 1984). See US FTC's 1984 Annual Report (available at www.ftc.gov/os/annualreports/ar1984.pdf) and FTC Chairman Timothy Muris's August 2001 speech before the American Bar Association (available at www.ftc.gov/speeches/muris/murisaba.shtm).

realise economies of specialisation/scale. Third, DCC planned to produce specialty type carbon black in Korea by using CCC's technology, bringing in more competition in that market. Fourth, the combined firm could realise synergy effects by combining the R&D personnel. Fifth, the combined firm could apply DCC's patented dryer technology to CCK's Korean plant to reduce costs. However, the KFTC did not accept cost savings from applying that technology to CCC's *foreign* plants (the combined capacity of which was about nine times as large as CCK's Korean plant) as merger-specific efficiencies, on the theory that

> if one approves a merger by accepting efficiency effects that take place in the foreign countries when a Korean company acquires a global firm with both Korean and foreign operations, then one cannot resolve the anticompetitive effects in the domestic market.

On the matter of balancing anti-competitive and pro-competitive effects, the KFTC stated (without much analysis) that if prices of carbon black (used for strengthening rubber products) rose just by 10 per cent, the anti-competitive effects would far more outweigh the claimed efficiency effects. Having ruled that the merger would substantially lessen competition in the market for carbon black used for reinforcing rubber products in Korea, the KFTC gave DCC a choice of remedies: either (i) DCC sell 100 per cent of CCK's stock (held by CCC); or (ii) DCC sell one of the two Korean plants of its own to a third party within a year.

DCC appealed the KFTC's decision to the Seoul High Court, but the Court rejected DCC's protests that complying with the KFTC's Remedy would wipe out substantial portions of the efficiencies from the merger and that the KFTC was basically forcing it to abandon the entire transaction. In the midst of the 2008/2009 financial crisis, DCC withdrew its appeal to the Korean Supreme Court and abandoned the entire deal.

IV. Our Analysis

Viewed from a traditional perspective, with its emphasis on concentration and static competition, a comparison of the KFTC's decisions and imposed remedies in the above four mergers shows that the KFTC has moved in the right direction. In particular, assuming that the KFTC's analysis of competitive effects in the four cases is correct, the KFTC's imposition of structural remedies in the 2003/2006 merger cases (divestiture or ban of the merger) is clearly a significant improvement over the behavioral remedies (price controls or market share restrictions) in the 1999/2000 merger cases.

Including the four mergers we have examined, for many products/services in Korea, import competition does not meaningfully constrain domestic firms. Hence, the traditional SSNIP test would define Korea as a separate geographical market in most cases (as the KFTC did in the four mergers). The standard approach is then to examine *each* relevant geographical market *separately* and weigh anti-competitive effects against efficiencies in *each* market.[49]

[49] This is the case unless the market is found to be worldwide.

When the merging firms largely compete for domestic customers, surely there is nothing wrong with the KFTC focusing on the competitive effects in Korea, as there is only one relevant geographical market (ie Korea). In both the 1999 SK Telecom-Shinsegi merger and the 2003 Muhak-Daesun merger, the merging firms compete in the domestic market, and there is neither the presence of foreign firms in Korea nor real prospect of the merging firms to move out to foreign markets on a significant scale.[50] Given the serious anti-competitive concerns the KFTC raised in the SK Telecom-Shinsegi merger, the remedy imposed (temporary reduction of market share to below 50 per cent) is hard to justify. In contrast, assuming that the KFTC's theory of anti-competitiveness is correct, its ban of the 2003 merger between Muhak and Daesun seems to be the right remedy. That is, when the merging firms largely compete in the domestic market, the KFTC's shift to tough structural remedies (prohibition of the merger or divestitures) from hard-to-justify behavioural remedies (in particular, limits on market shares) is a welcome development.

When the merging firms operate *globally*, however, we believe that the KFTC's narrow focus on the domestic market is wrong-headed, especially from the perspective of promoting *dynamic* competition. In both the Hyundai-Kia and DCC-CCC mergers, the merging parties operated both in the Korean market and in markets overseas. It has been rarely the case that a merger between two Korean firms (or a Korean firm and a multinational firm that operates in Korea), which operate globally, creates competitive concerns in foreign markets,[51] but it does so often in Korea. This seems to be the case for both Hyundai-Kia and DCC-CCC mergers.

At the same time, however, both mergers seemed to be driven by the desire to realise economies of scale or scope to compete more effectively in overseas markets. The domestic Korean market is relatively small in size and thus the 'domestic' portion of the merger may not be big. (For example, CCK accounted only for about 1/10th of CCC's global capacity.) Furthermore, in many cases (including the Hyundai-Kia and DCC-CCC merger), actual or potential foreign competition in Korea is not significant so that it is reasonable to define Korea as a separate geographical market from the foreign markets.

Under the traditional approach which examines *each* relevant market separately, in the foreign market the merger in question would be deemed to create few, if any, anti-competitive concerns, but some efficiency gains. In the Korean market, however, the merger would create anti-competitive concerns, but the efficiency gains that the firms assert that they would gain in the overseas market do not directly translate into savings that can be passed through to domestic consumers (at least in the short term horizon under the merger guidelines). Indeed, the KFTC decision on the DCC-CCC merger specifically mentioned that it would not count cost savings in CCC's *foreign* plants as merger-specific efficiencies.

[50] SK Telecom has made some limited attempts to move out to foreign markets, but so far, it has not succeeded. For example, SK Telecom's Helio MVNO joint venture with Sprint launched in 2006 in the US failed, costing SK Telecom hundreds of millions of dollars by 2008. For details, see http://en.wikipedia.org/wiki/Helio_(wireless_carrier).

[51] Some segments of IT industries have become exceptions to this general rule, as Korean firms have gained global dominance. For example, the combined worldwide market shares of Samsung Electronics (40.7%) and Hynix Semiconductor (20.9%) in the DRAM sector exceeded 60% in the third quarter of 2010. ('Samsung, Hynix Strengthening Leadership in Chips' *Korea Times* (8 November 2010 ww.koreatimes.co.kr/www/news/tech/2010/11/133_75959.html).

In such a situation, the standard approach would call for divestiture in Korea that would preserve the competitiveness of the Korean market at the pre-merger level. This is exactly the approach that the KFTC took in the DCC-CCC merger. As we saw in section III, after determining that the anti-competitive effects in the *domestic* market outweigh the efficiency gains in the *domestic* market, the KFTC ordered DCC to sell CCK or one of its own two Korean factories as a condition for acquiring CCC. DCC protested that doing so would deprive it of the economies of scale/scope from the merger, which were needed to compete with top multinational firms in the global market, but to no avail. As previously mentioned, the appellate court's upholding of the KFTC's remedy and the 2008/2009 economic crisis forced DCC to abandon the entire transaction.

One can find a clear contrast between the Hyundai-Kia and DCC-CCC mergers both in terms of the KFTC's competitive effects analysis and in terms of the imposed remedies. While the KFTC's analysis was cursory, it recognised that combining Hyundai's and Kia's production capacities would allow the combined firm to reach a minimum efficient scale to successfully compete in the highly competitive global market by integrating the automobile platforms of the two companies. The KFTC also asserted (without explanation) that vigorous competition in the foreign markets would constrain price increases in the domestic market. We believe that the KFTC had a *dynamic* competition perspective in mind when it made this assertion. That is, despite its dominant position in the domestic market (its market share has increased from 55.6 per cent in 1999 to 75.9 per cent in 2009[52]), Hyundai-Kia has continued to develop new car designs, improve the quality and cut costs in order to compete in the foreign markets. (As of 2009, including foreign production, Hyundai-Kia's foreign sales accounted for about 75 per cent of its total number of cars sold, a significant increase from about 55 per cent in 2000.[53]) In the mid 1980's, Hyundai cars were synonymous with cheap but poor quality cars in the US.[54] After more than a decade of endeavours, however, Hyundai has recently achieved high ratings in consumer satisfaction and quality surveys.[55] Along with the quality improvements of its cars,

[52] Hyundai-Kia's gains have largely come at Daewoo Motor's expense, whose market share has fallen from 36.8% in 1999 to 7.2% in 2009. After Daewoo Group's bankruptcy in 2000, Daewoo Motor went into court receivership and was then acquired by GM in 2002. Recall that the KFTC cited the rise of Daewoo Motor as a significant competitive threat to Hyundai-Kia. However, this key source of *domestic* competition was soon weakened in the aftermath of the 1998 economic crisis. (Sources for market shares: Kia's Annual Reports from 2002 to 2009, available in Korean at the Financial Supervisory Service's online repository of corporate filings (http://dart.fss.or.kr).

[53] Author's calculations from Kiwoom Security's data reported in its Sector Brief on the Korean automobile industry (in Korean, searchable at Kiwoom Security's bulletin board on industry analysis, http://bbn.kiwoom.com/bbs.corpAnalDetail.do; no direct URL link is available). In 2000, Hyundai-Kia exported about 52% of its cars and sold the remaining 48% in Korea. In 2003, Hyundai began production overseas. As of 2009, domestic sales account for 26%, exports 48% and foreign production 26% of Hyundai/Kia's total production.

[54] Hyundai's first export model, Excel, was an instant hit in the United States in its first 2 years (over 0.5 million cars sold in 1986 and 1987) by filling a void in the entry-level market that was being ignored by the United States automakers. However, the United States consumers were soon disillusioned with the poor quality of Excel and Hyundai has had to take dramatic measures (such as providing a 10-year, 100,000-mile powertrain warranty to the United States buyers) to overtime the perception problem. Boston Globe, 'Hyundai's "overnight" success a 20-year project' 1 March 2010, http://www.boston.com/cars/newsandreviews/overdrive/2010/03/hyundais_overnight_success_a_2.html

[55] For example, Hyundai Accent, the successor model to Excel, was the highest ranked model in the sub-compact car segment in J.D. Power and Associates' 2010 US Initial Quality Survey. Overall, Hyundai was ranked #7 (out of 33 brands), below some Japanese brands (Acura #2, Lexus #4 and Honda #6), but ahead of many others (Infiniti #9, Nissan #15, Mazda #19, Toyota #21, Subaru #22, Suzuki #24, and Mitsubishi #32). JD Power and Associates, Press Release, 'JD Power and Associates Reports: Domestic Brands Surpass Imports in Initial Quality for the First

Hyundai-Kia has achieved a record high market share in the US: 7.1 per cent in 2009 (a 2 per centage point increase from that in 2008).[56]

The success of Hyundai-Kia illustrates the importance of *actual* competition in *foreign* markets. An analyst solely focused on the *domestic* market would have been concerned that the combined Hyundai-Kia might turn into a 'sluggish and content' monopolist with poor innovation incentives, because both *actual* and *potential* import competition in the *domestic* market may not be adequate. As we discussed in section III, after 10 years of liberalisation of imports from Japan, Japanese cars accounted for only 1.9 per cent and all imports only 7 per cent in the first 3 quarters of 2010. And the 1998 economic crisis forced Samsung Group to sell the majority stakes at Samsung Motor to Renault and Daewoo Motor was put into a court receivership after the Daewoo Group went bankrupt in 2000, significantly weakening the two *domestic* rivals to Hyundai-Kia. Indeed, the success of Hyundai-Kia is somewhat of an enigma, because it has long struggled with militant labor unions[57] and has also suffered from poor corporate governance.[58]

However, as the KFTC pointed out, the Hyundai-Kia merger probably allowed the combined firm to achieve economies of scale by sharing underlying 'platforms', thereby allowing it to better compete with foreign firms in the foreign markets. As a result, while the loss of domestic competition from Hyundai-Kia merger surely resulted in consumer welfare loss from the *static* point of view, from a *dynamic* perspective, Korean consumers probably have gained from the introduction of new and improved cars at lower prices (although at any point of time, they pay higher prices than foreigners do for the same cars at any point of time). One piece of evidence for Hyundai-Kia's exercise of *static* market power is that its export prices are significantly below the prices it charges in Korea for the same model. For example, in 2008 Korean consumers were outraged when they learned that they had to

Time in IQS History' 17 June 2010, available at http://businesscenter.jdpower.com/news/pressrelease.aspx?ID=2010099 Hyundai and Kia cars have also been picked as 'Best Buys' by a United States consumer magazine. In November 2010, Hyundai Genesis (in the luxury car category) and Sonata (family car) and Kia's Sorento R (compact SUV) and Soul (compact car) were named 2011 Automotive Best Buys by Consumers Digest. Chosun Ilbo, 'Hyundai, Kia Cars Picked as Best Buys in US' 5 Nov 2010, http://english.chosun.com/site/data/html_dir/2010/11/05/2010110500324.html. Hyundai Sonata was also chosen as one of Car and Driver's '2011 10 Best Cars' for the first time in the company's history. '2011 Hyundai Sonata—10 Best Cars: The Student Has Suddenly Become the Teacher' November 2010 http://www.caranddriver.com/features/10q4/2011_10best_cars-10best_cars/2011_hyundai_sonata_page_8

[56] Reuters, 'Hyundai targets 4.5 percent rise in US market share' 15 Feb 2010, http://www.reuters.com/article/idUSTRE61E3PH20100215 and 'Kia aims to grow US market share in '10' 12 Jan 2010, http://www.reuters.com/article/idUSTRE60B31120100112.

[57] Since the mid 1980's to 2008, Hyundai's workers had went on annual wage strikes that inflicted heavy costs to the firm. Only in 2009 and 2010, Hyundai and its unions successfully negotiated wage increases and thus avoided strikes. (Reuters, 'Militant South Korean union stumbling' 11 Aug 2009, http://www.reuters.com/article/idUSTRE57A1FR20090811; CNN Money, 'Hyundai smokes the competition' 5 Jan 2010, http://money.cnn.com/2010/01/04/autos/hyundai_competition.fortune/index.htm; Trading Markets, 'Hyundai Moter Union Accepts Wage Deal, Averts Strike for 2nd Yr' 21 July 2010, http://www.tradingmarkets.com/news/stock-alert/hymzy_hyundai-motor-union-accepts-wage-deal-averts-strike-for-2nd-yr-1057751.html.)

[58] A striking demonstration of the lack of proper corporate governance at Hyundai/Kia is that Chairman Chung was convicted in 2007 for embezzling more than US $100 million from the company to set up a slush fund and for other charges and was sentenced to 3 years in prison (suspended over the same period; he spent 2 months in jail after his arrest in April 2006). Associated Press, 'Hyundai Chairman Chung Mong-koo Convicted of Embezzlement' 5 Feb 2007 (http://www.foxnews.com/story/0,2933,250262,00.html) and Associated Press, 'Hyundai chairman's prison term suspended' 6 Sep 2007 (http://www.msnbc.msn.com/id/20620766/ns/business-world_business#). As discussed in the main text, both *domestic* and *import* (actual or potential) competition in the *domestic* market is inadequate. As such, it is our view that Hyundai-Kia's success could not have been possible without the competitive pressure from *actual foreign* competition in *foreign* markets.

pay 40 per cent more for the new Genesis sedan than American consumers.[59] According to some industry analysts, Hyundai earned a profit margin of some 10 per cent on cars built and sold in Korea, but just 2 per cent for the same vehicles built and sold in the United States.[60]

Despite the high prices that they pay for Hyundai-Kia cars at any given point of time, Korean consumers have clearly benefited over time from Hyundai-Kia's introduction of new cars with better features. Even if not, Hyundai-Kia's gains (profits and cost savings) in foreign markets are certainly a social surplus for Korea. Such gains should be taken into account by competition authorities in reviewing mergers.[61]

In the DCC-CCC merger, DCC claimed that its acquisition of CCC, which is a parent company of CCK, was done with global markets in mind, not Korea. But as we have seen, the KFTC defined Korea as a *separate* geographical market (justifiable under the traditional SSNIP test) and ordered DCC to divest either CCK's Korean plant or one of DCC's two Korean plants. DCC claimed that combined operation of the Korean plants was essential for achieving synergy effects globally.

But unlike in its 1999 approval of the Hyundai-Kia merger, the KFTC only looked at the effects in Korea in reviewing the 2006 DCC/CCC merger. The KFTC could have been right in that Korean consumers could have suffered in the short term from the loss of competition between DCC and CCC. However, along the lines of Hyundai-Kia merger, it is possible that DCC/CCC's gains in the foreign markets (and potential long-term consumer gains in Korea) could outweigh short term losses.

Just like the combined Hyundai/Kia has continued to innovate (based on the economies of scale/scope realised from the merger) in order to meet the competitive threats in the foreign markets (despite its dominant position in smaller domestic market), it is certainly possible that the combined DCC/CCC could have achieved similar *dynamic* efficiencies over time (again based on the economies of scale/scope realised from the merger that is crucial for competing effectively in the foreign markets). If so, while Korean consumers could suffer a *short-term* welfare loss from the loss of competition between DCC and CCC, it is possible that they could gain a *longer-term* benefit from the combined firm's realisation of *dynamic* efficiencies. At a minimum, we believe that the KFTC should have recognised cost savings at CCC's foreign plants of as legitimate merger-specific efficiency gains.

In sum, we believe that with the increasing sophistication of its staff in conducting antitrust analysis in the past 10 years (certainly a welcome development in its own right), the KFTC has unfortunately suffered from the 'static competition bias' and has lost sight of

[59] Yonhap News, 'S Koreans reimport Hyundai Genesis from cheaper US market' 7 Aug 2008, http://english.yonhapnews.co.kr/business/2008/08/07/11/0503000000AEN20080807004700320F.HTML. According to this article, the 3.8-liter Genesis was sold for US $57,000 (with a 5-year, 60,000-mile powertrain warranty) in Korea but only for $32,000 (with a much longer 10-year, 100,000-mile powertrain warranty) in the United States. While some of the price difference is due to import duties and engine-displacement taxes in Korea and for some features that are optional in the United States but standard in Korea, still some Korean consumers found it worthwhile to re-import the Genesis sedan through 'gray importers' even after paying for shipping costs from the United States to Korea.

[60] Yonhap News, 'S. Koreans reimport Hyundai Genesis from cheaper US market' 7 Aug 2008, http://english.yonhapnews.co.kr/business/2008/08/07/11/0503000000AEN20080807004700320F.HTML.

[61] Of course, we do not mean to be nationalistic. Hyundai-Kia's gains in the US were accompanied by increases in US consumer surplus by promoting competition among car makers. Therefore, Hyundai-Kia's continued innovations have increased total global social surplus.

the 'big picture' of examining the competitive effects of a merger across *all* markets from a *dynamic* competition perspective. In particular, we argue that the KFTC has gotten trapped in the market definition mould under the United States Horizontal Merger Guidelines, which typically define relevant markets within the short-term time horizon of one to two years and examine competitive effects in *each* relevant (product or geographical) market *separately*.

In order to address this 'staticisation' problem, we propose that the KFTC (and other competition authority in an export-oriented economy) break out of the traditional market definition mould and expand the 'competitive arena' beyond the conventional 'relevant (geographical) markets' under the hypothetical monopolist test. To be specific, we advocate that the competition authority to use the total *national* social welfare standard over *all* geographical markets combined (which recognises fixed-cost savings and other gains by the merging firms in the foreign markets as merger-specific efficiencies, and weighs them against anticompetitive effects in the domestic market) as opposed to the narrow consumer welfare standard in *each* geographical market concerned (which does not).[62]

In other words, we propose that a competition authority in an export-oriented economy, or more generally, any competition authority which reviews a merger with global operations, consider the total national social welfare standard over *all* geographical markets combined (which considers gains in the foreign markets as legitimate efficiencies to be weighed against anticompetitive losses in the domestic market) as the proper welfare standard in evaluating mergers.

We believe that taking our proposal could be particularly important when innovations are undertaken with *all* markets in mind (or even strongly, with foreign markets in mind, where the merging firms face strong competitive pressure which is absent in the domestic market). Our approach is different from the well-known proposal to examine *potential* competition in the *domestic* market more seriously,[63] because foreign competition—a major source of potential competition for many developing markets and small-sized developed markets—may not materialise in the domestic market even in the relatively long term (which has been the case in the car market in Korea). Rather, in our story, *actual* foreign competition in *foreign* markets serves as a stimulant for dominant domestic firms (which compete in foreign markets) to undertake innovative activities that ultimately benefits domestic consumers (although they suffer short-term losses at any given point of time).

Dennis Carlton (2007) makes a strong case for why the short-run total social surplus standard is better than the short-run consumer surplus standard in promoting dynamic efficiencies.[64] In this context, the current paper can be viewed as expanding Carlton's argu-

[62] If there existed a *global* competition authority, it could use total *global* social welfare standard (which consists of merging firms' profits both in the domestic and in the foreign markets, consumer surplus both in the domestic and in the foreign markets (and possibly the profits of all "impacted" firms such as input suppliers, complementary good providers, distributors and competitors of the merging firms both in the domestic and in the foreign markets). In the absence of such a global agency, we advocate the national agency in the merging firms' country to use total *national* social welfare standard (which consists of merging firms' profits both in the domestic and in the foreign markets, consumer surplus in the domestic market (and possibly the profits of all "impacted" national firms such as input suppliers, complementary good providers, distributors and competitors of the merging firms both in the domestic and foreign markets). A national agency in a foreign market would look at the effects on consumer surplus (and possibly the profits of all "impacted" firms such as input suppliers, complementary good providers, distributors and competitors of the merging firm) in that foreign market.

[63] See Sidak and Teece (2009) for an analysis on the importance of potential competition in dynamic contexts.

[64] Carlton, Dennis W (2007) 'Does Antitrust Need to Be Modernized?' (2007) 21(3) *Journal of Economic Perspectives* 155–76.

ments to a setting with multiple relevant (product or geographical) markets, in which a market-specific structural remedy is not at hand due to the fact that the synergy effects from the merger are intricately linked across relevant markets. In such a situation, we advocate expanding the short-run total social surplus standard so that gains and losses across *all* relevant markets are summed together (which we call a total *national* social surplus standard for an export-oriented economy) in order to evaluate the overall competitive effects of the merger.

V. Concluding Remarks

For a relatively young agency with only a 30-year history, the KFTC has achieved some remarkable success in cartel enforcement and competition advocacy. In the case of merger control, the KFTC's focus on the domestic market and the shift from price controls/market share restrictions to structural remedies such as divestitures and a complete ban on mergers is the correct approach when the merging firms largely cater to the *domestic* customers (as in the case of SK Telecom-Shinsegi and Muhak-Daesun mergers). However, when the merger is pursued with *global* markets in mind, we believe that the KFTC's adherence to traditional market definition and its attempts to restore competition to the pre-merger level in the *domestic* market through structural remedies runs the risk of jeopardising the entire merger, when the synergy effects are linked between the domestic and foreign market operations (as illustrated by the abandoned DCC-CCC merger).

As an alternative, we urge that the KFTC (and other competition authorities reviewing mergers with both domestic and global operations) to break out of the traditional market definition mould and focus more on an overall competitive effects analysis. To be specific, when there are several geographical/product markets, we advocate 'summing' the gains/losses across *all* markets in examining the effects of mergers, when remedies tailored to specific markets are not at hand. We believe that our approach could be potentially fruitful for export-oriented economies/industries. Any short term consumer losses in the domestic market can be outweighed by the merging firms' gains in the foreign markets. On the other hand, under the conventional approach which looks at effects in separate markets in isolation, competition authorities are likely to block mergers that result in short-term consumer losses in the domestic market.

In sum, we welcome the KFTC's more aggressive merger enforcement in markets where firms mostly cater to domestic demand (with little foreign competition present). However when domestic firms compete with foreign firms in foreign markets so that the main source of competitive pressure comes from actual (or potential) competition in the foreign markets but the merged firm faces insufficient actual (or potential) domestic or import competition in the domestic market, we believe that the KFTC's narrow look at the short-term competitive effects in the domestic market only is misguided and a step backwards. It needs to undo the error of getting trapped in the market definition mould by examining the overall competitive effects of the merger across all relevant markets (and not just in the domestic market).

12

Thailand: Medicines, Competition Law and Compulsory Licensing

R IAN MCEWIN AND SAKDA THANITCUL

I. Introduction

Implementing and administering an intellectual property right (IPR) regime is costly, particularly a patent system where considerable technical expertise is required. As the vast majority of patents in developing countries are held by companies from developed countries, it is understandable why developing countries are reluctant to enforce IPRs. Implementation and enforcement only raises prices for local consumers and may provide negligible incentives for indigenous research.

Obviously, a country will only start to protect local innovation once it has started to develop its own research and development industry (and so needs to protect it). However, governments in developing countries, where IPRs are enforced, may threaten compulsory licensing as a way of increasing local bargaining power over the prices paid for imports or the royalties paid to overseas licensors. Compulsory licensing can also help to develop local manufacturing industry as part of a country's industrial policy.

Nowhere has the debate on the intersection between competition law and IPRs been more heated than when dealing with access to medicines and the promotion of generic drug competition through the compulsory licensing of drug patents. In this debate, views about the role of IPRs, and so their dilution, reflect fundamental differences about the policy basis for intellectual property law. On the one hand, there is the 'privilege' view that IPRs are not 'property rights' as such, but rather rights granted by government to serve public goals such as providing incentives for innovation but also subject to limitations in order to serve other public policy objectives such as health. On the other hand:

> The alternative perspective views patents not as a privilege, but rather, as a privileged property right, or an uber-right that is stronger than other property rights. All rights have exceptions, including property rights. Nonetheless, those who subscribe to the uber-right view likely see any possible limitation on patent rights as extremely suspect. While they recognize that property rights may be limited, they nonetheless analogize legal exceptions such as compulsory licensing to stealing. They suggest that limits on patents should be exercised with caution because the nature of the patent right is based entirely in the right to exclude.[1]

[1] Cynthia M Ho, 'Unveiling Competing Patent Perspectives' (2009) 46 *Houston Law Review* 1047, 1056.

Health organisations, not surprisingly, argue the patents as privilege view. As Ho notes, the UN Commissioner for Human Rights argues patents are a privilege that must be 'subject to limitations in the public interest' and the United Nations suggests that certain human rights, such as the right to health, are 'inalienable and universal' rights that must be recognised over state-granted rights such as patents.[2] According to this view, to the extent that there are 'actual or potential conflicts', patent rights should yield to the right to public health.

The United States Trade Representative defines compulsory licensing as where 'a government conditionally authorizes third parties (or the government itself) to use a patented product without the authorization of the patent holder'. Julian-Arnold estimated in the early 1990s that the patent laws of more than 100 countries provided for compulsory licensing.[3] He found the most common reasons for compulsory licensing were non-use, national security, where food or medicines were involved, the inability to work follow-on patents (also called 'dependent patents') and anti-competitive practices.

Countries are limited in their ability to grant compulsory licenses by the Paris Convention and the Trade-Related Aspects of Intellectual Property Rights (TRIPS) Agreement. Under the Paris Convention, compulsory licenses may be issued where the patentee has abused his or her exclusive rights. Compulsory licenses must be non-exclusive and non-transferable (except when the IPR is sold). Article 31 of the TRIPS Agreement (reaffirmed in the Doha Declaration and Public Health 2001) allows for compulsory licenses for national emergencies, situations of extreme urgency, anti-competitive practices, public non-commercial use, and dependent patents (as non-limiting grounds).

Compulsory licensing weakens the patent system and so undermines incentives to innovate (in the country conducting the research and development (R&D)). While a developing country might be able to use competition law to stop anti-competitive practices in its own country, problems of proof and jurisdiction may make it difficult to curb anti-competitive conduct originating overseas. Compulsory licensing could be used to remedy anti-competitive practices outside the country involving IPRs. For example, compulsory licensing could be used to deter collusion between overseas pharmaceutical companies that raise the price in the developing country or to remedy an overseas dominant firm's unilateral refusal to license.[4]

Compulsory licenses are often used to curb anti-competitive practices. In 2002 the US Department of Justice made Microsoft provide uniform licenses to original equipment manufacturers (OEM), with rates published on the web, dealing with the protocols that products needed to inter-operate with Windows. In 2007, the US Federal Trade Commission (FTC) ordered Rambus (a computer chip maker) to license patented technology. Rambus had concealed essential patents it held from an industry-wide standards setting organisation. The FTC imposed a compulsory license by setting a maximum royalty rate.[5] In the European Union, competition law has been used to force compulsory copyright licenses.[6]

[2] Ibid 1054.

[3] G Julian-Arnold, 'International Compulsory Licensing: The Rationales and the Reality' (1993) 33 *IDEA: The Journal of Law and Technology* 349.

[4] See Makan Delrahim, 'US and EU Approaches to the Antitrust Analysis of Intellectual Property Licensing: Observations from the Enforcement Perspective' (US Department of Justice, 2004). Available at www.usdoj.gov/atr/public/speeches/203228.pdf.

[5] In the matter of Rambus Inc, Docket No 9302, Opinion of the Commission on Remedy, 5 February 2007.

[6] Case C-418/01 *IMS Health GmbH & Co OHG v NDC Health GbH & Co KG* [2004] ECR I-5039.

Many developing countries have used compulsory licensing for a number of reasons including national emergencies. Thailand issued compulsory licenses on drugs to promote greater access to medicines (although some also say to help Thailand develop a generic drug industry). Faced with compulsory licensing, the reaction of one multinational pharmaceutical company, Abbott Laboratories Ltd, was to refuse to continue to register new drugs in Thailand. This cross-border refusal was challenged in Thailand on competition law grounds. This chapter examines that decision in Thailand's context as a developing country dealing with the intersection between IPRs and competition law.

II. Thailand: Economic Background

Thailand is a middle-income country that has only recently introduced intellectual property (patents 1979 and competition laws 1999). Thailand has a population of slightly over 66 million with a gross national income (GNI) per capita of $9,947.[7] Its gross domestic product (GDP) in 2007 was US$54,583.79 billion, with an annual growth rate in recent years of slightly less than four per cent. Between 1977 and 2004 increases in total factor productivity (TFP) added about one per cent to Thailand's aggregate growth.[8] The source of this growth was mainly the movement of rural workers into more productive manufacturing jobs. By comparison, TFP increases per annum between 1975 and 2000 for other East Asian economies were as follows:

— China (3.9 per cent).
— Indonesia (0 per cent).
— South Korea (1.1 per cent).
— Malaysia (0.9 per cent).
— Singapore (1.8 per cent).
— Taiwan (2.4 per cent).
— Thailand (1.4 per cent).

These figures suggest that Thailand has considerable scope for improving its productivity via better technology and education.[9]

The World Economic Forum's Global Competitiveness Report 2008–09 placed Thailand in the 'second stage of development' along with Malaysia and Brazil, whereas Hong Kong, Japan, Korea, Singapore were placed in the third (and highest stage). Thailand's overall

[7] GNI per capita is based on purchasing power parity (PPP). PPP GNI is GNI converted to international dollars using PPP rates. An international dollar has the same purchasing power over GNI as a US dollar has in the United States. GNI is the sum of value added by all resident producers plus any product taxes (less subsidies) not included in the valuation of output plus net receipts of primary income (compensation of employees and property income) from abroad. Data are in current international dollars. Source: World Bank, International Comparison Program database at http://ddp-ext.worldbank.org/ext/ddpreports/ViewSharedReport?REPORT_ID=9147&REQUEST_TYPE=VIEWADVANCED.

[8] Office of the National Economic and Social Development Board (Thailand) and the World Bank, 'Towards a Knowledge Economy in Thailand' (2008) vi. Growth in total-factor productivity represents output growth not accounted for by the growth in inputs and so includes improved technology and knowledge of workers (ie improved human capital).

[9] Ibid 9.

competitiveness ranking was 34th out of 134, but had fallen six places from the previous year. The Report commented that its competitive strengths were market size, an efficient labour market (due to strong employer-employee relations), and good transport infrastructure. Its competitive weaknesses included low technological readiness (66th) with low penetration rates for internet, broadband and mobile phones, concerns about the soundness of the banking sector and a weakening of government institutions.[10]

In 2008, in a major joint report by the Thai Office of National Economic and Social Development and the World Bank, it was noted that Thailand's technological capacity lagged for four main reasons:

— 'The business sector, and in particular the medium and large-sized firms responsible for most technology development, are unmotivated, unwilling or unable to invest substantially in R&D whether in-house or through outsourcing … Absorbing technology from abroad is viewed as the lower cost and preferred route to technology upgrading.'

— 'Numerous government programs to encourage R&D and technology developments have failed to produce the desired effect.'

— 'The supply of S&T (science and technology) workers as a percentage of university graduates is below that of Thailand's principle competitors. But perhaps more serious are the deficiencies in the training of these workers, which reflects the quality of Thailand secondary education and universities, even the leading ones. None of Thailand's tertiary institutions are ranked among the leading universities of East Asia.'

— 'Although technology development in Thailand has derived benefits from globalisation this has been in the form of technology that is embodied in equipment. FDI by MNCs has transferred amazingly little tacit knowledge and disembodied technology through vertical or horizontal spillovers. Only a handful of companies have set up research facilities in Thailand and the scope of the research carried out is limited. Thailand has a substantial diaspora of S&T workers in the U.S, in Taiwan (China), Singapore and Malaysia. However this diaspora has not been a source of local entrepreneurship, venture capital, angel investors or a vehicle for the technological leadership unlike the Chinese and Indian diasporas.'[11]

Quality education has been a low priority of successive Thai Governments. For a long time the Thai education system has stressed basic literacy (for which it measures well in international comparisons) but also rote memorisation. By contrast, other Asian countries such as China, India, Singapore and Taiwan have invested substantially in university education and promoted higher-value skills. As a result, they have developed innovative companies able to compete internationally. Thailand, on the other hand, has continued to rely on low-value, export-oriented manufacturing. Large Thai conglomerates (grown big through government licenses) have been more concerned with shielding local industries from international competition than developing competitive, export-oriented products.

[10] www.weforum.org/en/initiatives/gcp/Global%20Competitiveness%20Report/index.htm.

[11] Office of the National Economic and Social Development Board (Thailand) and the World Bank, Towards a Knowledge Economy in Thailand' (2008) 106–07.

III. Thailand's Intellectual Property Laws

Thailand's legal system was originally based on the common law system but changed to a civil law system in 1924. Thailand introduced patent protection relatively recently. In 1979 the Patents Act (BE 2552) was introduced which followed the World Intellectual Property Organisation (WIPO) model for developing countries. Initially the Act provided 15 years protection (after filing) for inventions and seven for product designs. Exclusions included agricultural machines, pharmaceuticals, animals and plants. The 1979 Act allowed for compulsory licensing (section 46) where the patentee did not make the product available to local producers within three years of the patent grant and the needs of the Thai economy were not met—unless there were legitimate reasons. Licensing could not contain conditions, restrictions or royalties detrimental to the development of industry and commerce. Also, competition law (the Price-Fixing and Anti-Monopoly Act 1979) prohibited these conditions, etc in licenses where consumer interests might be adversely affected.

In 1992, a new Patent Act (No 2 BE 2535) brought Thai patent law into conformity with TRIPs—patents were now protected for 20 years and designs for 10 and the exclusions were limited. The Act was further amended in 1999 to allow for, inter alia, national treatment and compulsory licensing, parallel importing and the extension of patentability to drugs, food, beverages and life forms.

Endeshaw examined patenting in the Association of Southeast Asian Nations (ASEAN) between 1997 and 2007. With the exception of Singapore, he found a continuing trend in foreign penetration of each country's patent system. After examining WIPO statistics for ASEAN countries he concluded that:

> Overall, the general picture that emerges from the contrast between resident and non-resident applications and grants in IP rights in ASEAN is an absolute domination by non-residents. In spite of the relatively high figures for residents in Thailand and Indonesia with respect to trade and service marks, the overwhelming sway in IP right by non-residents is very clear. Even in the case of Thailand and Indonesia, it would not be surprising if the resident applications were from foreign rights holders doing business in the two nations.[12]

It is not surprising that a lack of domestic innovation results in limited domestic protection of IPRs. In 2009 the Office of the United States Trade Representative (USTR) placed Thailand on its Priority Watch List in the 2009 'Special 301 Report'. This Report is an annual review of the global state of IPR protection and enforcement. In the Report, the USTR expressed that it had concerns about the lack of progress since the previous year in addressing widespread problems of piracy and counterfeiting in Thailand as demonstrated by 'the lack of sustained and coordinated enforcement efforts, and, in particular, the lack of successful prosecutions'. It was noted that the US pharmaceutical industry was continuing to be concerned about the uncertain climate for their industry there.

The Pharmaceutical Research and Manufacturers of America (PhRMA) in its Special 301 Submission in 2010 pointed to a lack of patent examiners and the use of compulsory licensing as a 'cost containment tool'. It said:

> In 2009, PhRMA welcomed Thailand's announcement that it intended to foster a better environment for intellectual property industries and increase dialogue between healthcare stakeholders

[12] Assafa Endeshaw, *Intellectual Property in Asian Emerging Economies* (Ashgate, 2010) 71.

> and the Royal Thai Government. However, to date, there has been little action taken on these pledges … PhRMA does agree that reforms are needed to improve the Thai patent registration system which has a backlog of patent applications in the thousands. Effective reform will start with ensuring there is an adequate number of patent examiners and that all patent examiners are sufficiently trained. When these resources are available there can then be additional reforms to create a predictable and efficient patent system that stimulates and rewards innovation … Other actions by the Thai government indicate that the use of compulsory licensing remains a cost containment tool to be used when negotiating with individual PhRMA member companies.[13]

IV. Thailand's Competition Law

Unlike intellectual property law, competition law is not subject to an international agreement that prescribes minimum standards with which World Trade Organisation (WTO) Members must comply. While the United Nations General Assembly agreed on a 'Set of Multilaterally Agreed Equitable Principles and Rules for the Control of Restrictive Business Practices' in 1980, the WTO dropped negotiations on competition policy in 2004. So, countries have considerable discretion in setting competition law standards.

Thailand's first competition law was the Price-Fixing and Anti-Monopoly Act 1979. The Act had two objectives—consumer protection and price regulation.[14] Next, the Trade Competition Act (BE 2542) was enacted in 1999. Thanitcul notes that the Trade Competition Act was based on competition laws in South Korea and Taiwan.[15] The prime objective is to protect the competitive process.

Exemptions from the Trade Competition Act were given for the central, provincial and local governments, state enterprises, farmer's co-operatives, etc and businesses exempted by Ministerial Regulation. Thanitcul notes that the exemption for state enterprises was the most controversial (as they competed against private companies in the electricity, telecommunications and railways sectors). Export cartels were not exempted.

The Trade Competition Act includes: abuse of dominant position (section 25); mergers (section 26); horizontal and vertical restraints (section 27); abuse of dominant position (section 25) and unfair trade practices (section 29).

Abuse in section 25, includes *exploitative* conduct (ie setting high prices) and vertical restraints such as:

> 2. Unreasonably fixing compulsory conditions, directly or indirectly, requiring other business operators who are his customers to restrict services, production, purchase or distribution of goods …

The use of the term 'unreasonably' suggests vertical restraints (such as licensing) are subject to a kind of *rule of reason*. It could be argued that 'unreasonably' only applies to the

[13] Available at http://keionline.org/sites/default/files/PhRMA_USTR-2010-0003-0245.1.pdf.

[14] Sakda Thanitcul, 'Competition Law in Thailand: A Preliminary Analysis' (2002) 1 *Washington University Global Studies Law Review* 171.

[15] Ibid.

'fixing compulsory conditions'—if so then the remainder of the conduct in section 2 might constitute *per se* offences.[16] Section 25 (3) goes on to say:

> 3. Suspending, reducing or restricting services, production, purchase, distribution, deliveries or importation without justifiable reasons ...'.

Refusals to supply, then, are subject to a *rule of reason* to establish whether there are 'justifiable reasons'.

In January 2007, the Cabinet approved a new definition of dominant market position under the Act. A dominant market position occurs:

— where a business operator selling any product or providing any service, which in the previous year had a market share of 50 per cent or more and whose sale proceeds amounted to one billion Baht or above; or

— where the first three ranked business operators of any product or service, during the previous year had a market share of 75 per cent or more and whose sales proceeds were one billion Baht or more. This excludes a business operator whose market share in the past year was less than 10 per cent, or a business operator whose sales proceeds in the past year were less than one billion baht.

Section 28 contains an unusual and unique competition law provision. It says:

— A business operator who has business relations with business operators outside the Kingdom, whether it is on a contractual basis or through policies, partnership, shareholding or any other similar form, shall not carry out any act in order that a person residing in the Kingdom and intending to purchase goods or services for personal consumption will have restricted opportunities to purchase goods or services directly from business operators outside the Kingdom.

Apparently, it was introduced to allow wealthy Thais to buy luxury cars directly from foreign manufactures without having to go through local Thai dealers. It effectively allows for parallel imports and so promotes competition by preventing foreign producers from price-discriminating against consumers in Thailand. Presumably this would have allowed the import of the drugs that Abbott refused to register (as the patent on those drugs was not registered then it would be open to a parallel importer to register).

Section 29 is a 'catch-all' provision dealing with *unfair business practices*—which can also cover exclusionary conduct. It says:

> Section 29 A business operator shall not carry out any act which is not free and fair competition and has the effect of destroying, impairing, obstructing, impeding or restricting business operation of other business operators or preventing other persons from carrying our business or causing their cessation of business.

This is broad and could allow other objectives (eg protecting small businesses) rather than economic goals such as efficiency. Section 29 does not require market dominance. Instead, practices where there is *unequal bargaining power* may be proscribed. Deunden Nikomborirak, in describing action taken by the Trade Competition Commission under

[16] The meaning of *rule of reason* varies—some see it as a kind of cost-benefit analysis (with and without non-economic elements) while here is means more examining whether conduct is justified without a detailed weighting of costs and benefits.

section 29 rather than section 25 against Honda (who allegedly had 80 per cent market share and engaged in exclusive dealing by stopping retailers from selling competing brands) said:

> [t]he fact that this case was handled differently from the whiskey and beer abuse of dominance case raised suspicions of selective enforcement of the competition law in favour of powerful local businesses and against foreign companies with little or no political connections.[17]

Nikomborirak goes on to argue that the Act's implementation 'has been opaque, selective and arbitrary' due to political intervention, a lack of 'due process' in administering the law and a lack of a competition constituency among non-governmental organisations (NGOs), academics and the media.

V. TRIPS and Compulsory Licensing

The TRIPS Agreement established minimum standards for intellectual property protection (based on IPR standards applicable in developed countries) that had to be complied with by all WTO Members by 1 January 2006. In exchange for taking on these obligations, developed countries had to provide better access to developing country exports—particularly for agricultural products, textiles and clothing and a commitment by developed countries to stop imposing unilateral trade sanctions for inadequate IPR protection. Bhagwati has said that developing countries did not believe they would get better access to agriculture and textiles without TRIPS; that the United States would 'punish' developing countries that did not protect US IPRs; that IPRs would attract foreign investment and that IPRs would help developing countries such as India develop of its own creative industries.[18] World Bank economist Michael Finger estimates that the cost of TRIPS compliance would exceed $150 million per country. However, developing countries accepted TRIPS because they believed it was in their mutual interest.

TRIPS contains several articles of direct relevance to the compulsory licensing debate. They are:

> Art 8.2 … appropriate measures, provided they are consistent with the provisions of this Agreement, may be needed to prevent the abuse of intellectual property rights by rights holders or the resort to practices which unreasonably restrain trade or adversely affect the international transfer of technology.

This is a broad provision, which could include, potentially, all kinds of anti-competitive conduct. Article 31 deals specifically with compulsory licensing:

> Art 31 Other Use Without Authorization of the Right Holder
>
> Where the law of a Member allows for other use of the subject matter of a patent without the authorization of the right holder, including use by the government or third parties authorized by the government, the following provisions shall be respected:
>
> (a) authorization of such use shall be considered on its individual merits;

[17] Deunden Nikomborirak, 'The Political Economy of Competition Law: The Case of Thailand' (2006) *Northwestern Journal of International Law & Business* 597, 605.

[18] Jagdish Bhagwati, 'Comment on Hoekman' in Susan Collins and Barry Bosword (eds), *The New GATT: Implications for the United States* (Brookings Institution Press, 1994).

(b) such use may only be permitted if, prior to such use, the proposed user has made efforts to obtain authorization from the right holder on reasonable commercial terms and conditions and that such efforts have not been successful within a reasonable period of time. This requirement may be waived by a Member in the case of a national emergency or other circumstances of extreme urgency or in cases of public non-commercial use …

(c) the scope and duration of such use shall be limited to the purpose for which it was authorized, and in the case of semi-conductor technology shall only be for public non-commercial use or to remedy a practice determined after judicial or administrative process to be anti-competitive …

(f) any such use shall be authorized predominantly for the supply of the domestic market of the Member authorizing such use …

(k) Members are not obliged to apply the conditions set forth in subparagraphs (b) and (f) where such use is permitted to remedy a practice determined after judicial or administrative process to be anti-competitive. The need to correct anti-competitive practices may be taken into account in determining the amount of remuneration in such cases …

Article 40.2 gives countries considerable discretion in specifying anti-competitive practices that constitute an abuse of IPRs:

> Art 40.2 ' … nothing in this agreement shall prevent Members from specifying in their legislation licensing practices or conditions that may in particular cases constitute an abuse of intellectual property rights having an adverse effect on competition in the relevant market. As provided above, a Member may adopt, consistently with the other provisions of this agreement, appropriate measures to prevent or control such practices, which may include, for example, exclusive grantback conditions, conditions challenging challenges to validity and coercive package licensing, in the light of the relevant laws and regulations of that Member.

At the time TRIPS was signed in 1994, patent protection for pharmaceuticals was minimal in developing countries. So developing countries could make and (more likely) buy generic drugs (especially from India) at a small percentage of the price of branded drugs. TRIPS meant that developing countries had to grant pharmaceutical patents. The necessary consequence was less competition from generic drugs. However, under TRIPS, as article 31 above indicates, countries can issue compulsory licenses on a number of grounds including public interest, anti-competitive conduct and for non-commercial government use.

TRIPS required countries to notify and negotiate with affected patent-holders but, as mentioned above, allowed this to be waived in the event of a 'national emergency' or where it was for *government use* (ie non-commercial) (see article 31 (b)).[19] In addition, article 31(k) also allowed for the waiver of the negotiating requirement, after a judicial or administrative process has determined that a practice is anti-competitive.

TRIPS also imposed a condition that goods produced under a compulsory license must be mainly for the domestic market (article 31(f)). However, this limitation is subject to article 31(k), which waives this requirement where a practice is anti-competitive. Of course, if a country did not have a domestic pharmaceutical industry then it was not possible to issue compulsory licenses. As Abbott and Van Puymbroeck put it:

> If a developing country does not have the industrial capacity to produce a particular medicine itself under a compulsory license, or if it has insufficient capacity, it has no recourse but to import

[19] It is worthwhile repeating that compulsory licensing is not restricted to developing countries. Both France and Belgium have introduced compulsory licensing of pharmaceuticals for public health purposes.

> the drug. However, if it wishes to import a generic drug that is produced under compulsory license, the amount of product that is available for export is limited by the 'predominantly for the supply of the domestic market' condition in paragraph (f) of Article 31 of the TRIPS Agreement.[20]

In 2001, a joint submission by African and South American countries, as well as a number of Asian countries including India, Indonesia, the Philippines and Thailand said:

> …a common understanding that confirms the right of governments to ensure access to medications at affordable prices and to make use of the provisions in the Agreement whenever the scope or exercise of IPR result to barriers to access to medicines … Article 7 is a key provision that defines the objectives of the TRIPS Agreement. It clearly establishes that the protection and enforcement of intellectual property right do not exist in a vacuum. They are supposed to benefit society as a whole and do not aim at the mere protection of private rights.[21]

As a condition of joining the Doha Round of trade negotiations, developing countries insisted on the removal of constraints in TRIPS in relation to public health. In 2001, a Ministerial Declaration on the TRIPS Agreement and Public Health[22] was made which said that TRIPS 'can and should be interpreted and implemented in a manner supportive of WTO Member' rights to protect public health and, in particular, to promote access to medicines for all' (para 4). The Declaration then went on to allow countries to establish 'legal machinery to manufacture generic substitutes for costly patented medicines under domestically issued compulsory licenses to obtain imports from countries able and willing to assist them without interference from the relevant patent holders' (para 6). Paragraph 6 essentially diluted the requirement that products be primarily for the domestic market.

In summary, as Reichman put it:

> In other words, the scheme ultimately negotiated under the auspices of paragraph 6 of the Doha ministerial Declaration envisioned a process of back-to back compulsory licenses that would enable any country needing medicines at lower prices than those charged by local patentees to seek assistance from other countries able and willing to produce the drugs for export purposes, without interference from patentee in either country.[23]

In 2002, Sykes predicted that:

> The precise impact of the Doha declaration on the policies of developing nations remains to be seen, but it is likely that the declaration will embolden them to enact measures that will reduce the returns to pharmaceutical patent holders, at least with respect to drugs that are used to treat certain diseases. Such measures will likely include the award of compulsory licenses for the production of patented medicines (with minimal royalties payable to the patent holder) and the allowance of 'parallel imports' of medications from nations where prices are lower.[24]

[20] Frederick M Abbott and Rudolf V Van Puymbroeck, 'Compulsory Licensing for Public Health, A Guide and Model Documents for Implementation of the Doha Declaration Paragraph 6 Decision' (World Bank Working Paper No 61, 2005) 8–9.

[21] WTO, Trips Council 'Submission by the Africa Group et al' IP/C/W/296 (29 June 2001).

[22] See www.wto.org/english/thewto_e/minist_e/min01_e/mindecl_trips_e.htm.

[23] Jerome H Reichman, 'Comment: Compulsory Licensing of Patented Pharmaceutical Inventions: Evaluating the Options' (2009) 37(2) *Journal of Law, Medicine and Ethics* 249.

[24] Alan O Sykes, 'TRIPS, Pharmaceuticals, Developing Countries and the Doha Solution', John M Olin Law & Economics Working Paper No 140 (The Law School, The University of Chicago, 2002) 2.

With respect to TRIPS, the World Health Organization summarised the Agreement as follows:

— In case of public non-commercial use or government use, TRIPs does not require countries to provide for the right of injunction, only for payment of compensation. Again, this is important for the actual implementation of a CL for public use. This is practiced in the US; the US Government cannot be sued for infringement of a patent, it can only be sued about the amount of compensation paid. Under US law, the same applies to contractors acting on behalf of the US Government.

— A decision to issue a CL must be subject to review, but this does not have to be a judicial review; TRIPs only requires that the review is independent, so countries may opt for an administrative review, which is less burdensome and much faster. It seems advisable for developing countries to provide for an administrative review only, to prevent patent holders from blocking the use of a CL by initiating time-consuming court procedures.

— A compulsory license shall be predominantly for the supply of the domestic market. A CL therefore would hardly interfere with practices of differential or tiered pricing. However, 'predominantly' is not exclusively, so some export is still possible. Public interest groups advocate that export to a market where a CL has been issued, should be allowed; otherwise, countries with small markets, where local production is not viable, would not be able to use CL provisions effectively.

— If a CL is issued to remedy anticompetitive practices, many of the conditions do not apply, such as the requirement to first try to obtain a voluntary license. Also, the restriction on export no longer applies; this is important for the US, which frequently issues compulsory licenses to remedy such practices.[25]

VI. Pharmaceutical Industry Competition, Competition Law and Licensing

Sykes argues that there is a strong case for protecting pharmaceutical IPR rights:

> The case for protecting the rents of patentholders is particularly strong in the pharmaceutical sector. Even though the rents earned on pharmaceutical patents in developing countries are in general a modest fraction of global patent rents, they may be vital to the incentive for research and development in certain key areas … Pharmaceuticals are unusual in the extent to which R&D and regulatory approval costs are a large part of their total production cost … Without some period of restricted competition, the developers of new drugs will be unable to recoup R&D and regulatory approval costs, and the incentive to develop new drugs will greatly diminish.[26]

However, the pharmaceutical industry has come under considerable competition law scrutiny in the last 10 years, particularly in the United States and Europe. In July 2009, the European Commission adopted the Final Report in its competition inquiry into

[25] http://apps.who.int/medicinedocs/en/d/Jh1459e/6.3.html.

[26] Sykes, 'TRIPS, Pharmaceuticals, Developing Countries and the Doha Solution' (2002) 16.

the pharmaceutical sector, pursuant to article 17 of Council Regulation (EC) 1/2003.[27] The Report noted considerable delays in the entry into the market of generic drugs and examined the practices used by pharmaceutical companies to extend the commercial life of their patented drugs. These included: the filing of patent 'clusters' or 'thickets' (eg a company files many patents around the original patent—many well after the initial patent to create uncertainty for generic competitors as to whether they can produce a generic without infringing a new patent; lengthy litigation (to raise the entry costs of new generic competitors) and patent settlement agreements (which slowed down the entry of generics). The Commission announced it would increase its competition scrutiny of pharmaceutical companies particularly where there was evidence that companies were using patents to block innovation—including where a refusal to license blocked innovation.

One of the more controversial practices identified by the Commission is the use of reverse payment settlement agreements, ie those involving a form of value transfer by an originator to a generic company to slow entry. This is an issue that has attracted significant attention from competition authorities in other jurisdictions, in particular in the United States. The US FTC has been particularly concerned about non-compete agreements between brand-name and generic firms, in which the brand-name firm pays the generic company not to enter the market or for a certain time. This allows the brand-name pharmaceutical prices to remain high—and for the potential new entrant to share in the monopoly profits. In a 2010 Report, the US Federal Trade Commission said 'Pay-for-delay agreements are estimated to cost American consumers $3.5 billion per year'.[28] The Report noted that a 2003 appellate court decision had held that such agreements were automatically (or per se) illegal,[29] but that some subsequent decisions had allowed them and so 'Following those court decisions, patent settlements that combine restrictions on generic entry with compensation from the brand to the generic have re-emerged.'[30]

Pharmaceutical companies compete mainly on the basis of developing new products rather than on price. This creates particular challenges for market definition for competition law purposes. As Balto and Mongoven put it:

> Unlike many consumer products, pharmaceutical products are not substitutable for each other because of consumer preferences for design, conveniences, style, prestige, or any other factor short of efficacy. For instance, although a sport utility vehicle may be substitutable for a van for certain consumers, and thus may be available to defeat a price increase, a drug to aid liver function van never be a substitute for a heart drug. No matter how high prices are raised for a heart drug, drugs with other therapeutic effects cannot be substituted. The outcome of the efficacy requirement is that the relevant product market … will be limited to drugs in an individual therapeutic category.[31]

Because pharmaceutical competition is mainly on the basis of product, not price, and the need to recoup large R&D and regulatory approval costs, IPRs assume a more important role for competition law purposes in pharmaceuticals than in most industries. Competition in

[27] See Communication from the Commission, 'Executive Summary of the Pharmaceutical Sector Inquiry Report'. Available at http://ec.europa.eu/competition/sectors/pharmaceuticals/inquiry/communication_en.pdf.

[28] Federal Trade Commission (FTC) Staff Study, 'Pay-for-Delay: How Drug Company Pay-Offs Cost Consumers Billions' (Report) (FTC, January 2010), available at www.ftc.gov/os/2010/01/100112payfordelayrpt.pdf.

[29] *In re Cardizem CD Antitrust Litigation* 332 F.3d 896 (6th Cir 2003).

[30] FTC Staff Study, 'Pay-for-Delay' (2010) 1.

[31] David A Balto and James F Mongoven, 'Antitrust Enforcement in Pharmaceutical Industry Mergers' (1999) 54 *Food and Drug Law Journal* 255, 258.

pharmaceuticals can be inhibited in a number of different ways. For example, IPR holders may collude on price or agree to terms in licensing agreements that inhibit innovation or distribution. Licenses could impose territorial restrictions, include non-compete clauses, set standards that exclude competitor technologies, impose competitor boycotts, etc. Refusals to license can result in competitive harm. Here there are differences between jurisdictions. In the United States there seems to be a consensus that unconditional refusals to license do not violate antitrust laws[32] but conditional licenses may. In Europe compulsory licensing may be forced in exceptional circumstances. In the 2008 Microsoft decision, the Court of First Instance said:

> [A] simple refusal, even on the part of an undertaking in a dominant position, to grant a licence to a third party cannot in itself constitute an abuse of a dominant position within the meaning of Article 82. It is only when it is accompanied by exceptional circumstances such as those hitherto envisaged in the case law that such a refusal can be characterized as abusive and that, accordingly, it is permissible, in the public interest in maintaining effective competition on the market, to encroach upon the exclusive right of the holder of the intellectual property right by requiring him to grant licenses to third parties seeking to enter or remain on that market.[33]

Developed countries such as Australia, Canada, Germany, Ireland, Italy, New Zealand, the United Kingdom and the United States[34] have often used compulsory licensing, and not only to correct competition problems. Government use licenses are a common feature of patent laws in developed countries. For example, in the United States, under 28 US Code Section 1498, the US Government may use patents or authorise a third party to use patents for virtually any public purpose. The US Government does not have to seek a government use license or negotiate with the patent holder. The patent holder is entitled to 'reasonable and just compensation' but cannot seek an injunction.[35]

Compulsory licensing has been particularly important in correcting competition (and potential) competition problems in mergers between pharmaceutical companies in the United States. Pharmaceutical company mergers are examined in three contexts. First, mergers where the merging companies supply competing products and second, where one of the merging companies supplies a product and the other merging party is researching a competing product. Third, where the merging firms do not currently compete in a final product market but compete in an innovation market to develop IPRs (ie both are researching to produce products that would compete but for the merger). Essential Action's Access to Medicines Project has documented the use of licensing in the United States to correct competition law problems. For example:

> Novartis (1996): Ciba-Geigy and Santos—two companies based outside of the United States—sought approval to merge into the company now known as Novartis. Both of the merging companies held important patents on emerging gene therapies. As a condition of merger approval, the merged enterprise was required to license gene technologies to Rhone Poulenc, on a worldwide basis. It was also required to issue a non-exclusive worldwide license to an exceedingly broad-based patented

[32] For example, see the Supreme Court's decision in *Trinko* 540 US 398 (2004).

[33] Case T-201/04 *Microsoft v Commission* [2007] ECR II 3601 [691].

[34] United Nations Development Programme (UNDP) 2001 Health Intervention and Technology Assessment Program (HITAP)July 2009 5–6.

[35] See International Centre for Trade and Sustainable Development (ICTSD)/United Nations Conference on Trade and Development (UNCTAD), 'Non-Voluntary Licensing of Patented Inventions: Historical Perspective, Legal Framework under TRIPS, and an Overview of the Practice in Canada and the USA' (ICTDS/UNCTAD, 2003).

> invention, the Anderson patent, which covers the entire category of gene therapy treatment involving cell modification that takes place outside the body. Royalty rates ranged from 1 to 3 percent.[36]

In general, for competition law purposes, generic drugs have been put in different relevant antitrust markets. In the United States, the FTC has often found that brand-name and generic drugs are not in the same market due to significant differences in price between them.[37] There is evidence that brand-name drug prices increase following the introduction of generics.[38] Further evidence of this is the recent entry into generics by major pharmaceutical companies. As a recent *New York Times* article noted:

> ... some drug companies are pursuing a two-tiered strategy in developing markets: selling their own lines of more expensive brand-name products to the more affluent, as well as offering mid-priced branded generic lines that include prescription and over-the-counter medicines for the broader market.[39]

Given the widespread use of compulsory licensing, it is worthwhile asking the question: does compulsory licensing of pharmaceuticals across borders actually reduce incentives to innovate? The answer to this depends, partially, on whether a particular health issue or disease is global or limited to a limited number of countries (and whether the disease is in the developed or undeveloped world). The economic incentives to find a drug against AIDS (a global disease) will come mainly from the richer developed countries—not from developing countries with limited markets and limited ability to pay. Diseases limited to poorer developing countries will not provide much in the way of economic incentives for the major pharmaceutical companies. As Lybecker and Fowler note:

> Although the industry claims that compulsory licensing reduces the incentive to conduct R&D in such diseases, as long as there are large emerging markets (ie China and India) with similar disease burdens, it is hard to imagine that the actions of Thailand will influence the industry's decision to research treatments in these disease areas.[40]

Chien examined the relationship between compulsory licensing and innovation. She found that the degree to which a firm can predict compulsory licensing ('predictability') and the relative importance of the market ('importance') are significant factors. She finds that 'only those drug licenses issued predictably in significant markets are likely to harm innovation'.[41] Also, there is the issue of whether pharmaceutical production in developing countries is cheaper. Kapan and Laing (2005) argue that:

> The idea that local production of medicines should be encouraged in developing countries to provide increased access is attractive since we might expect that many of the costs involved will be lower than in developed countries. It is clear, however, that investments in local medicine

[36] Essential Action's Access to Medicines Project 'US Competition Policy and Pharmaceutical Patents', May 2008 available at www.essentialaction.org/access/index.php?/archives/153-US-Competition-Policy-and-Pharmaceutical-Patents.html.

[37] Balto and Mongoven, 'Antitrust Enforcement in Pharmaceutical Industry Mergers' (1999) 259.

[38] FM Scherer, 'Pricing, Profits and Technological Progress in the Pharmaceutical Industry' (1993) 7 *Journal of Economic Perspectives* 97.

[39] Natasha Singer, 'Drug Firms Apply Brand to Generics' *New York Times* (New York 16 February 2010), available at www.nytimes.com/2010/02/16/business/16generic.html.

[40] Kristina M Lybecker and Elizabeth Fowler, 'Compulsory Licensing in Canada and Thailand: Comparing Regimes to Ensure Legitimate Use of the WTO Rules' (2009) 37 *Journal of Law, Medicine and Ethics* 222.

[41] C Chien, 'Cheap Drugs at What Price to Innovation: Does Compulsory Licensing of Pharmaceuticals Hurt Innovation?' (2003) 18(1) *Berkeley Technology Law Journal* 3, 4.

> production will be efficient only if pharmaceuticals can be produced more cheaply locally than they can be imported on the open market. This sets up the inherent tension between a health policy directed to the access problems of making available low cost and quality-assured medicines and an industrial (primarily private sector) policy of optimizing profits and growth by promoting a local industry whose products may be more expensive than those on the international market.[42]

In addition to developing countries obtaining better market access to developed country markets, some argue that better IPR protection results in greater foreign investment in developing countries—particularly for inventions relevant to that developing country—say anti-malarial drugs in tropical countries. As stressed above, IPRs are not needed in countries that have no demand for the resulting products—so there is likely to be more research and development in a developing country that will ultimately buy the resulting product. However, even if there is a local market in a developing country for the resulting product, the company producing the product will still produce in the country that is the most cost-effective or where production compliance and regulatory standards have already been met—and so not necessarily the developing country. However, if a developing country can manufacture drugs more cheaply then it would be in that country's interest to have IPRs because IPRs may be a pre-condition for exporting to countries that have strong IPR protection.

Scherer concluded that developing country losses from the transfer of monopoly rents to developed countries as the result of better patent protection are likely to be considerably greater than the benefits they receive from any new drugs.[43] Sykes argues, first, that even if Scherer is right, when the impact on developing countries is taken in isolation, the 'odds that such patents will nevertheless increase global welfare appear particularly favorable in this sector' and, second, that as

> the incidence of disease is not uniform around the globe … a high percentage of the individuals infected by HIV are located in developing countries. And as the Doha declaration itself acknowledges, diseases such as malaria and drug resistant tuberculosis are endemic in developing nations … it follows that economic incentive to do research on such diseases will critically depend on the ability of pharmaceutical companies to earn rents on sales in the developing world.[44]

Finger is skeptical that developing countries will benefit from TRIPS. As he puts it:

> Its coverage of the development dimension is thus limited to the development dimension of the trade-related aspects of intellectual property. This leaves out a lot of people. In Senegal, for example, of some 30,000 musicians who complain about counterfeit reproductions and radio stations who play their music without paying royalties, less than 10 enjoy international sales. For the other 29,990, intellectual property rights is not trade-related, it is strictly a domestic issue. TRIPS provides no basis for the 29,990 to petition for better enforcement of copyright on their behalf. Knowledge has an important role in development, and intellectual property rights have a role in turning knowledge into a commercial asset, in helping poor people to earn more from knowledge. Development institutions should lead here, trade negotiations cannot.[45]

[42] Warren Kaplan and Richard Laing, 'Local Production of Pharmaceuticals: Industrial Policy and Access to Medicines' (The World Bank, January, 2005) 1.

[43] Frederic M Scherer, *Industry Structure, Strategy and Public Policy* (New York, HarperCollins College Publishers, 1996) 362–66.

[44] Sykes (n 24) 18.

[45] J Michael Finger, 'The Doha Agenda and Development: A View From the Uruguay Round' (Asian Development Bank, 2002) 26.

However, on the other hand, Sykes argues that:

> It is sometimes asserted that research on these health problems is lacking because developing countries are poor and hence pharmaceutical companies do not expect to make enough selling new drugs to recoup their investments in research … but one cannot simply presume that the lack of research is because comparatively low GDP per capita in developing countries makes profitable drug research infeasible. When willingness to pay for effective drug therapies is aggregated across countries containing hundreds of millions if not billions of people, the total profit potential can be substantial. This is all the more true when the governments of developing countries become actively involved in financing drug treatments. Thus it is likely that the dearth of research is attributable in significant part to heretofore weak intellectual property protection for pharmaceutical in developing countries. Many developing countries have no patent protection for pharmaceuticals at all … Such a situation has all the elements of a classic collective action problem … if each individual nation is nevertheless a relatively modest fraction of the collective market. Thus, each nation may be tempted not to afford patent protection, secure in the knowledge that it will reap the full benefits of lower domestic prices as a result while its policy will reap the full benefits of lower domestic drug process as a result while its policy will have only modest impact on global research initiatives … The TRIPS agreement has the potential to change this situation dramatically … TRIPS is in principle a vehicle for overcoming at least part of the collective action problem that may have been acute in the past. (pp 21–22.)

Stronger IPRs tend to be associated with increased knowledge flows and foreign direct investment (FDI) towards middle income and large developing countries (like Thailand), but not towards poor countries.[46] In a Discussion Paper for the Health, Nutrition, and Population Family (HNP) of the World Bank's Human Development Network, Kaplan and Liang conclude that:

> Producing pharmaceuticals is a complex process that requires a reliable, high quality supply of raw materials, technical expertise and a stable supply of electricity, gas and other utilities, plus sufficient human resource capacity with Ph.D-level scientists and expertise in pharmaceutical process and regulation. Pharmaceutical plants are capital intensive and take many years to develop and tend to be located in countries with good infrastructure, reliable utilities and access to technical expertise … Based on the qualitatively and quantitatively limited data sets available to us, our preliminary conclusions are:
>
> 1. In many parts of the world, there is no reason to produce medicines domestically since it makes little economic sense.
> 2. In the local pharmaceutical manufacturing sector, local production is often not reliable and, even if reliable, it does not necessarily mean that medicine prices are reduced for the end user.
> 3. If many countries adopt local production, the result may be less access to medicines, since production facilities in many countries may mean forgoing economies of scale.
> 4. It may be possible for small country markets to be coordinated or otherwise joined together to create economies of scale.
> 5. Regarding state-controlled local production, the WHO considers state-owned production to be 'ill advised'. Profit margins on bulk generic drugs are low, so public production must be as efficient as private manufacturing if losses are to be avoided.

[46] World Bank, 'Global Economic Prospects 2008: Technology Diffusion in the Developing World' (World Bank, 2008), available at http://econ.worldbank.org.

6. For many countries, technical expertise, raw materials, quality standards, and production and laboratory equipment need to be imported, with the result that foreign exchange savings may be small or non-existent.
7. Few developing countries have the capacity to produce active ingredients for pharmaceutical manufacture.[47]

VII. Compulsory Licensing of Pharmaceuticals in Thailand

As mentioned above, many countries have issued compulsory licenses for pharmaceuticals.[48] Some have been for health reasons, some to address competition concerns. In South Africa, a complaint was lodged in 2002 with the South African Competition Commission against GlaxoSmithKline and Boehringer Ingelheim. The complaint alleged that the companies had abused their dominant positions in relation to the anti-retroviral drugs ritonavir, lamivudine, ritonavir+lamivudine and nevirapine. The Commission found that the companies abused their dominant positions by:

— denying a competitor access to an essential facility
— excessive pricing
— engaging in an exclusionary act.

The Commission referred the matter to the Competition Tribunal for determination. A final settlement allowed for a voluntary license granted to Aspen Pharmacare in October 2001 in respect of the public sector to also be extended to the private sector; a further grant up to three more voluntary licenses on terms no less favourable than those granted to Aspen Pharmacare; allow the licensees to export the anti-retrovirals (ARVs) to sub-Saharan African countries; allow the importation of the drugs for distribution in South Africa if the licensee did not have manufacturing capability in South Africa; permit licensees to combine the relevant ARV with other ARV medicines; and charge royalties of no more than five per cent of the net sales of the relevant ARVs.

However, compulsory licensing of pharmaceuticals on competition grounds has also occurred in developed countries. For example, in 2007 the Italian Competition Authority accepted a commitment made by the Merck Group, in response to an investigation for abuse of dominance, to grant free licenses to allow the manufacture and sale in Italy of the active ingredient Finasteride and related generic drugs (used in the treatment of hypertrophy of the prostrate) two years before the 2009 expiration of the Complementary Protection Certificate. This decision was seen by the Italian Competition Authority as part of its efforts to increase competition in pharmaceuticals by encouraging greater use of generic products.

Section 51 of Thailand's Patent Act provides for implementing compulsory licenses for public non-commercial government use. The Thai Ministry of Health and The National Health Security Office describes section 51 as follows:

> 2.1 In order to carry out any service for public consumption or which is of vital importance to the defense of the country or for the preservation or realization of natural resources or the

[47] Warren Kaplan and Richard Laing, 'Local Production of Pharmaceuticals: Industrial Policy and Access to Medicines' HNP Discussion Paper (Washington, DC, The International Bank for Reconstruction and Development/The World Bank, 2005) 33–35.

[48] See www.cptech.org/ip/health/cl/recent-examples.html for a summary.

> environment or to prevent or relieve a severe shortage of food, drugs or other consumption items or for any other public service, any ministry, bureau and department of government may, by themselves or through others, exercise any right under Section 36 by paying a royalty to the patentee without the requirement for prior negotiation on the permission, the royalty fees or the term of patent use (Thai Patent Act section 51).

Between November 2006 and January 2007, Thailand issued compulsory licenses on public use grounds for Merck's anti-retroviral Stocrin (efavirenz), Abbott Laboratories' anti-retroviral Kaletra (lopinavir/ritonavir), and Sanofi-Aventis' heart disease drug Plavix (clopidogrel). The licenses allowed the Government Pharmaceutical Organization (GPO) to import or manufacture cheaper generic versions of these drugs for use in the public health system and thereby increase competition (and through lower prices—improved patient access).[49] The Thai Ministry of Health said that TRIPS article 31(b) permits governments to use a patent without prior negotiations on royalties or term.[50] High prices were used as the main reason for the compulsory licenses. The Thai Ministry of Public Health and the National Health Security Office note:

> The only reason for the implementation of the Government Use of Patents is to allow universal access to essential medicines by all the beneficiaries of the National Health Security System, which are all publicly financed schemes. This is the goal of the previous as well the new Thai Constitution of 2005, and the National Health Security Act of 2002.[51]

The licenses were issued (with a 0.5 per cent royalty) under section 51 of the Thai Patent Act (BE 2522) (AD 1979) as amended by the Patent Act (No 3 BE 2542) (AD 1999). Section 51 allows for government use of patents in the *public interest*.[52] As the Report by the Health Intervention and Technology Assessment Program (HITAP) in 2009 said:

> A primary distinction between public sector and private sector compulsory licenses would be in the nature or purpose of the use of the patent. Government use is confined to 'public, non-commercial purposes'. Article 31 of TRIPS sets forth a number of conditions for use of a patent without the authorisation of the patent holder, which applies to both compulsory and government use licenses. There is however, an important distinction; that is, where the government uses a patent for public purposes, the requirement for prior negotiations with the patent holder for a voluntary license is waived. This waiver allows for speedy action; permitting a 'fast-track' process, which is of importance when life-saving medicines are required urgently. In the public health context, this form of compulsory licenses enable domestic production and/or importation of generic medicines by both the private and public sectors, as means of overcoming patent barriers to access to medicines.[53]

[49] See Lybecker and Fowler, 'Compulsory Licensing in Canada and Thailand' (2009) 229 for a full description of the sequence of events.

[50] The Ministry of Public Health and the National Health Security Office, 'Facts and Evidences on the 10 Burning Issues, Related to the Government Use of Patents on Three Patented Essential Drugs in Thailand' (February 2007), available atwww.cptech.org/ip/health/c/thailand/thai-cl-white-paper.pdf.

[51] See The Ministry of Public Health and the National Health Security Office, 'The 10 Burning Questions on the Government Use of Patents on the Four Anti-Cancer Drugs in Thailand' (2008), available at www.moph.go.th/hot/Second_white_paper_on_the_Thai_CL_%5BEN%5D.pdf.

[52] Article 46 of the Patent Act 1979 provides that a compulsory license to the private sector may be granted on two grounds: (1) where no production of the patented product or application of the patented process has taken place in the country without legitimate reason; or (2) where no product produced under the patent is sold in the domestic market, or where the product is sold at unreasonably high prices or does not meet the public demand, without legitimate reason.

[53] Health Intervention and Technology Assessment Program, Department of Health Thailand (July, 2009) 7, available at www.hitap.net/backoffice/report/pdf_reports/CL.pdf.

HITAP concluded that the number of patients with access to efavirenz and lopinavir/ritonavir increased by 17,959 and 3,421 respectively over a five-year period. The increases were 40,947 for clopidogrel, 8,916 for letrozole, 10,813 for docetaxel, 1.846 for imatinib and 256 for erlotinib. The Report concluded that:

> … there is also a need for a wide range of measures to support the effective use of government use licenses, including strengthening the country' information systems relating to public health, insurance programs and intellectual property, so as to ensure the speedy registration and importation of the generic drugs under the government use licenses. (p x.)

Abbott, the patent holder for LPV/r (sold under the brand name Kaletra), announced it would no longer register new drugs for sale in Thailand. This included a new version of Kaletra that did not need refrigeration (and so was more suitable for developing tropical countries like Thailand). Thai activists complained to the Trade Competition Commission that Abbott's refusal to supply infringed sections 25 and 28 of Thailand's Trade Competition Act.

In April 2007, the US Trade Representative placed Thailand on its 301 Priority Watch List, citing 'further indications of a weakening of respect for patents, as the Thai Government announced decisions to issue compulsory licenses for several patented pharmaceutical products'.

In December 2007, the Thai Trade Competition Commission decided that Abbott's withdrawal of its drug registration application did not breach the Trade Competition Act (BE 2542). The main reason given was that Abbott was not a (market) dominant business operator as defined in sections 25(3) and 3 of the Trade Competition Act (BE 2542) (see below). In February 2008, the new Thai Minister of Public Health, Chaiya Sasomsab, announced that he was reviewing the compulsory licenses that had been issued, as well as four more proposed compulsory licenses for cancer drugs. In March the Minister recommended that the compulsory licenses remain in place, but that the licenses could be revoked by the Minister of Commerce, the Minister responsible for competition law.

Lybecker and Fowler argue that industrial policy was an important reason for the decision. In other words, they argue that the Thai Government wanted to develop a generic drug industry. As they put it:

> … there are reasons to question the government's claim that the compulsory licenses are motivated by the need to safeguard public health. Thai officials point to high prices as the impetus behind the licensing decision. However, in 2002 Auditor-General Jaruvan Maintaka issued a report saying the GPO sold about 60% of its medical products to government agencies at above market prices. In some cases, products were marked up by 1,000 percent … While the compulsory license does not appear to be motivated by finding a reliable supply, neither does price seem to be the primary objective, since cheaper drugs are available through other channels. If price and supply security are not motivating the licence decision, then other potential motives deserve scrutiny. It is worth noting that that the Government Pharmaceutical Organization is not run as a nonprofit entity, but rather as an increasingly profitable enterprise … Thai government officials would like to see the GPO compete with India's generic industry and become a 'regional hub for the manufacture and export of copy medicines'. India is currently the principle supplier of essential medicines for developing countries, exporting an estimated two-thirds of the drugs it produces. Realistically, industrial policy may be more important than public health to the compulsory license strategy.[54]

[54] Lybecker and Fowler (n 40) 228–29.

Locally-made pharmaceutical drugs amount to 65 per cent of the Thai market, imports making up the remaining 35 per cent (Lybecker and Fowler). The compulsory licensing scheme introduced in 2006, involved compulsory licenses issued to the GPO for pharmaceuticals *for government use.* As most pharmaceuticals are supplied through a Universal Health Insurance Scheme, this means that the majority share of the pharmaceutical market in Thailand is now solely supplied by the GPO. Other Thai drug companies cannot manufacture for government use in the Thai market and so provide competition. The position in Thailand contrasts with Malaysia which introduced *government use compulsory licenses* on three AIDS drugs in 2003, but imported generic drugs from India rather than granting a monopoly over these government use drugs to a single supplier in Malaysia (or having a competitive bidding arrangement for the license).

VIII. The Trade Competition Commission's Decision in Abbott[55]

On 24 January 2007, the Department of Disease Control under Thailand's Ministry of Health issued a Ministerial Regulation on compulsory licenses for patents for two antiretroviral drugs: Lopinavir and Ritonavir, sold by Abbott Laboratories Limited under the name 'Kaletra'. Dissatisfied, Abbott responded by withdrawing a number of registration applications for new medicines in Thailand. The withdrawn drugs included 'Zemplar' for treating chronic kidney failure; 'Sindax' for treating heart failure; 'Humira' for treating reheumatoid arthritis; 'Aluvia' for treating HIV/AIDS; 'Brugen' for relieving pain and inflammation; 'Abbotic' an antibiotic; and 'Clivarin' for preventing coagulation.

In response, the AidAccess Foundation, the Foundation for Consumers, the Thai Network for People Living with HIV/AIDS, and the Thai NGO Coalition on Aids filed a complaint to the Trade Competition Commission accusing the Abbott Laboratories Limited of violating section 25 (market domination) and section 28 (restriction of an opportunity to purchase goods or services outside the Kingdom of Thailand) of the Trade Competition Act.

On 27 December 2007, Mr Santichai Santawanpas, the Director of the Office of Trade Competition Commission, notified Mr Nimitr Tianudom, the Director of AidsAccess Foundation, that the Trade Competition Commission had concluded that the defendant's withdrawal of its drug registration application did not violate either section 25 or section 28 of the Trade Competition Act (BE 2542) for the following reasons.

'Market Domination' required a business operator in the market of any goods or service to have a market share in the previous year of over 50 per cent and a sales volume of at least 1 billion baht. However, Abbott had a turnover less than the specified threshold in 2006. Also, the drug in dispute was not in the market at that time because the drug had not yet obtained the necessary approval. So it was decided that Abbott's action did not suspend distribution or importation without justifiable reasons in order to reduce the quantity to that lower than

[55] This section is based on Sakda Thanitcul, *Explanation and Case Study on Thailand Competition Act B.E.2542* (Bangkok, Winyuchon, 2008) 326–29.

the market demand. So the Trade Competition Commission unanimously decided that Abbott did not violate the provision on market domination under section 25(3).

With respect to section 28, the Trade Competition Commission decided that the defendant's withdrawal of registration with the Food and Drug Administration did not constitute an action that restricted any person residing in the Kingdom from buying purchase goods or services for personal consumption directly from business operators outside the Kingdom of Thailand. Apart from the fact that the registration application concerned a drug safety procedure specified by the Food and Drug Administration, it was not apparent that consumers had ever placed an order for the drug directly to the parent company in the United States as these medications are normally prescribed by a doctor in hospital. So, the Trade Competition Commission unanimously decided that Abbott's action did not violate section 28.

There was some disagreement within the Commission. The Trade Competition Commission had established an ad-hoc sub-committee which consisted of representatives from consumer groups and the Ministry of Commerce. The members held differing opinions on the dominance issue. On the one hand, representatives of the Department of Trade Negotiations said that the defendant would have market domination once the sales volume of the drugs exceeded 1 billion baht. On the other hand, representatives of consumers and scholars on drugs argued that a firm would be dominant if it was the sole producer of any drug used to treat a particular disease. Three members of the Committee were of the view that the withdrawal violated the Trade Competition Act, while the other three members believed it did not. The Trade Competition Commission decided Abbott was not dominant because its sales were under 1 billion baht. As a result, the issue of market definition was not determined. So it is a moot point whether the relevant market in this case covered second-line ARVs exclusively, or extended to other HIV/AIDS related drugs or to all other drugs owned by the defendant as a patent holder.

IX. Conclusion

In Thailand, government compulsory licensing of intellectual property on public health grounds has been used to promote generic drug competition in order to reduce the price of certain drugs to the Thai public health insurance schemes. Some have argued, also, that compulsory licensing has been used to develop a Thai generic drug industry. As there is limited R&D in pharmaceuticals in Thailand, the decision would not lead to a decision to pull current R&D out of Thailand. However, the decision could have an impact on future R&D decisions by multinationals. However, the threat of compulsory licensing may make multinational companies more likely to invest in R&D in countries making the threat. Whether Thailand's use of compulsory licensing did in fact chill current or future innovation in Thailand in other industries is undecided. However, given Thailand's poor record on innovation, it seems unlikely.

Competition law sometimes used compulsory licensing to correct domestic abuses of IPRs, including refusals to deal. The issue is really about what is meant by 'abuse'. Is charging high prices an abuse? The jurisprudence in competition law in developed countries focuses on whether the alleged abusive conduct affects competition by driving out efficient competitors, preventing their entry or dictating the terms of competition. Compulsory licensing was used in Thailand on public health grounds to lower the prices of certain drugs—which is not an 'abuse' under current developed-country competition law standards, but could be potentially in some countries, including the European Union.

In Thailand competition law was used, unsuccessfully, to try to remedy a refusal to register new drugs resulting from Thailand's decision to compulsory license certain drugs. While not unusual in domestic competition law jurisprudence, this was a novel use of competition law as it was a refusal across country boundaries. The use reflects the fact that national interest is often paramount in cases involving the intersection of intellectual property law and competition law across countries.

13

Vietnam: A Review of the Legal Framework and Enforcement

DOAN TU TICH PHUOC AND BUI NGUYEN ANH TUAN

I. Introduction

Generally, developing countries regard competition and intellectual property (IP) laws as being two of the most sophisticated economic policies to implement. Developed and industrialised countries did not introduce them until their economies were relatively advanced.[1] Moreover, as Villila has succinctly stated, 'No policy is an island.'[2] The intersection of those two laws, together with closely related policies such as industrial and trade policies, are of critical importance for economic development in developing countries in an age of globalisation.

In the context of a developing country like Vietnam, a full application of 'cutting edge' trade-offs between competition and IP policies in developed countries is not necessarily appropriate or beneficial to promote growth and development. An 'aggressive' competition policy may lead to the breakdown of firms which gain economic power from IP protection, so attract more competition in the market. However, the consequence of this policy would be that incentives to innovate are inevitably reduced to some extent. On the other hand, an overemphasis on protecting intellectual property rights (IPRs) may lead to the exercise of monopoly power by IP owners and so, in many cases, prove to be harmful to consumer welfare, particularly in the pharmaceutical and agricultural sectors. Moreover, as argued in previous chapters of this book, a static view of the state of competition in the IP field is misleading in the sense that this view does not take into account of the specific characteristics of the markets, such as product competition and the possibility of technology and consumption pattern changes as a result of the introduction of newer, better, technologies.

How to balance the intersection between competition and IP policies from a dynamic, rather than static, approach is a topic that has only recently arisen and discussed by both academic scholars and practitioners. This has been the case not only in developed countries, but also in developing countries where neither competition policy nor IP policy existed until recently.

[1] See further HJ Chang, *Kicking Away the Ladder—Development Strategy in Historical Perspective* (London, Anthem Press, 2002).

[2] T Välilä, 'No Policy is an Island—On the Interaction between Industrial and other Policies' (2008) 29:1 *Policy Studies* 101.

This chapter briefly reviews and analyses the interaction between competition and IP policies in Vietnam. Some policy recommendations are proposed that can be expected to be effective and, importantly, feasible in the context of the country.

II. Overview of the Economy

A. Overview

In the last 25 years, Vietnam has recuperated from the destruction caused by war, the collapse of its biggest sponsor, and the termination of its centrally-planned economy. Economic reform started in 1986 when the Communist Party initiated the *Doi Moi*[3] policy, which officially and gradually liberalised a variety of economic activity. Since then, Vietnam has achieved remarkably high growth rates (seven to eight per cent annually and is consistently ranked as the world's second fastest growing economy) except for several years after the Asian financial crisis in 1997 and the global economic downturn in 2008–09.[4] However, the two crises have exposed serious structural inefficiencies in Vietnam's economy. Vietnam is still a developing country in its initial stage of development with gross domestic product (GDP) of approximately US$96bn in 2009. This translates to merely US$1,100 per capita in terms of purchasing power parity, which remains low in comparison with other countries in the region.

Vietnam's macroeconomic environment is relatively stable. After the 1980s, Vietnam managed to lower its inflation rate from the previous high hundreds of per cent annually and has kept it within a controllable range for most of the time since 1996 (see Appendix 1). Normally, the fiscal deficit stays at a level of less than five per cent of GDP, though in the last two years (2008 and 2009), in dealing with an economic downturn, the deficit rose above that threshold. Total public and external debt is controlled at a level of about 43 per cent and 35 per cent of GDP respectively.

The private sector has led economic growth. From 1992 to 1997, the growth in this sector was four to five percentage points higher than that of total GDP. Industry structure has changed remarkably with the expanding share of the secondary (manufacturing) sector at the expense of the primary sector (see Appendix 2). Such a transitional transformation is a typical and virtually universal feature accompanying economic development, especially for an agriculture-based economy at the initial stage of industrialisation. In terms of ownership structure, after *Doi Moi*, other types of enterprises other than those in the state-owned sector (private enterprises, foreign-investment enterprises) have emerged and have gradually increased their proportion of output and employment (see Appendix 3).

Today, Vietnam is regarded as an open economy, with total trade volume (export plus imports) growing to 145 per cent of GDP, from a base of 19 per cent 20 years ago. Its trade openness has reached a relatively high level compared to neighbouring countries (see Appendix 4). In global trade, Vietnam has played an increasingly important role, with its share in world trade tripling from 0.1 per cent in 1988 to 0.9 per cent in 2008.[5] Vietnam has become a leading exporter in a number of products, particularly agriculture-related ones.

[3] Which means 'renovation' in Vietnamese.

[4] Data in this section are from the General Statistic Office of Vietnam, unless identified otherwise.

[5] Authors' calculation, based on data from Vietnam General Statistic Office and the World Trade Organisation (WTO).

In terms of foreign direct investment, foreign direct investment (FDI) companies cumulatively generated 35 per cent of the country's total industrial output, 27 per cent of non-oil exports, 25 per cent of total tax revenue and nearly 13 per cent of Vietnam's GDP in 2008. Vietnam is ranked third in attracting FDI among Southeast Asian countries. A low-cost workforce is an important contributing factor to this foreign investment. Much of the investment has come from neighbouring countries such as Singapore, South Korea, Taiwan and Japan. However, there is no reliable research or statistical indicator to indicate whether IPRs have been important to this investment.

B. Market Structure

In general, the Vietnam economy is characterised by a large number of small and medium sized enterprises (SMEs) with little capital and a small number of state-owned enterprises (SOEs) which hold most of the capital. While around 90 per cent of all enterprises in Vietnam are considered to be SMEs,[6] total SME capital accounts for just 20 per cent of the total business capital value of all enterprises. More importantly, the SOEs are dominant players in most of the important sectors that the Government has deemed 'strategic', such as electricity, petroleum and mineral exploration, tobacco, cement and shipping.

i. Declining Industrial Concentration

The first indicator of increased competition is a decline in the level of concentration[7] (see Table 1). All measures of concentration show a decrease in concentration as measured by the Herfindahl–Hirschman Index (HHI). The HHI shows that firm-size distribution has become less unequal over time. Over a span of seven years from 2000 to 2006, average CR4[8]

Table 1: Concentration of Vietnamese Manufacturing Industries, 2000–06

Year	Average CR4 (%)	Average HHI
2000	37.22	1,151
2001	35.13	999
2002	35.12	832
2003	32.37	684
2004	33.13	682
2005	30.89	631
2006	29.41	470

Source: Authors' compilation from General Statistic Office (GSO) data.

[6] In Vietnam, a SME is defined as an organisation whose legal capital is less than US$700,000 and which employs less than 300 staff.

[7] Care must be taken in interpreting this information. Vietnam shares the same problem with other developing countries in the early stage of development in collecting and maintaining official database of market share. Certain statistics are available at ministries in charge of specific sectors or tax departments or from private sources such as market research firms. Even these data are not easily retrievable, inconsistent and there is no system to double-check their accuracy. However, results calculated in this section by using official data of the General Statistic Office (GSO) may provide a picture of the overall market structure.

[8] CR stands for Concentration Ratio and CR3, CR4 are the combined market share of 3 and 4 largest firms of the industry or market.

declined from 37.22 per cent to 29.41 per cent and average HHI declined from 1,151 to 470. In comparison with other economies in the equivalent stage of development as in Table 2, industries in Vietnam seem to be less concentrated. For instance, CR3 of South Korea in 1981, Taiwan in 1981 and Japan in 1980 are 62, 49 and 56 per cent respectively.

However, a handful of industries have increased concentration, most notably tobacco and textiles (where CR4 increased by 27 and 26 per cent respectively). Almost all other industries show significant declines. While industry data is not a reliable guide to market competition, it seems that industries are becoming more competitive. Industries that experienced the most significant changes are summarised in Table 3.

Table 2: Industries with Most Significant Declines in Concentration in 2000–06

	Industry	Change CR4 (%)	Change HHI
1	Office computing machinery	–47.57	–8,881
2	Paper	–37.58	–634
3	Petroleum products	–23.94	–1,275
4	General machinery	–18.96	–272
5	Motor vehicles	–15.93	–445

Source: Authors' compilation from GSO data

Table 3: R&D and Patent Application Status in South East Asian Countries

SE Asian Country	Annual R&D Budget (USD), % of GDP	No patent applications, no granted per year	% patents granted to citizens
Brunei	$1.5M (2003), 0.026% (2002)	23 app, 23 granted (2005)	0%
Myanmar	----	----	----
Cambodia	$12M (2002), 0.053% (2002)	----	----
East Timor	----	----	----
Indonesia	$55M (2004), 0.054% (2001)	3492 app, 2902 granted (2003)	----
Lao PDR	$0.6M (2002), 0.036% (2002)	7 app, none granted (2005)	n/a
Malaysia	$600M(2002), 0.69% (2002)	4800 app, 6749 granted (2006)	1.5% (2005)
Philippines	$48M, 0.3% (2004)	2431 app, 1666 granted (2005)	0.9% (2005)
Singapore	$4B, 2.25% (2004)	9164 app, 7390 granted (2006)	5.8% (2006)
Thailand	$300M (2004), 0.24% (2002)	6340 app, 533 granted (2005)	14% (2005)
Vietnam	$71.3M (2002), 0.5% (2003)	1864 app, 649 granted (2005)	3.9% (2005)

Source: Kilgour L (2008)[9]

[9] L Kilgour, 'Building Intellectual Property Management Capacity in Public Research Institutions in Vietnam: Current Needs and Future Directions' (2008) 9(1) *Minnesota Journal Law, Science and Technology* 317.

Industries that experienced a decrease in CR4 have seen significant growth in the last decade and most of them are light industries. The emergence of new entrants (particularly private and foreign firms) following deregulation led to a more competitive market structure which had previously been under the control of a few big state enterprises. For instance, from 2004 to the end of 2006, in the five industries that experienced the largest decrease in CR4, the net number of new entrants increased by as much as 125 per cent (from 2,464 to 5,489 enterprises).

On the other hand, CR4 rose in some other industries. There are three possible explanations for this:

1. The number of firms withdrawing from the industry or re-structuring were larger than the number of new entrants due to unfavourable markets conditions.
2. A small number of highly efficient firms expanded their market share at the expense of less efficient firms, for example in the textile industry.
3. In some industries, the Government simply combined a number of formerly independent SOE firms operating in the same industry to form a big state firm (for instance, in the tobacco industry). This occurred in a wide range of industries (19 in all), ranging from military-related products to publishing, tobacco, postal services, etc.

ii. Ownership of Dominant Firms

As far as ownership of the top-three firms is concerned, the biggest proportion (over 50 per cent) is not surprisingly controlled by the State, and foreign-invested enterprises come second with around 30–35 per cent. Less than 20 per cent of them are privately owned (see Figure 1). These original findings are important and provide new evidence of the dominance of the state-owned sector in Vietnam. Despite the fact that markets have been gradually

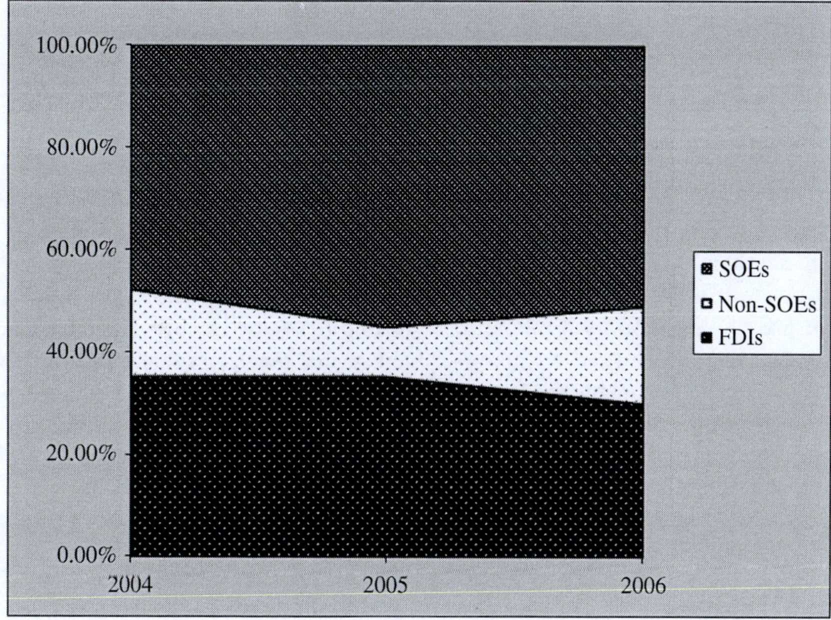

Figure 1: Ownership of Top-Three Firms in All Industries

Source: Authors' compilation from GSO data.

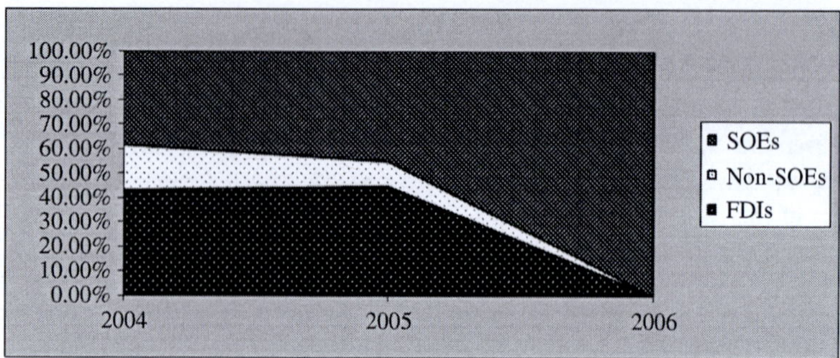

Figure 2: Ownership of Top-Three Firms in 20 Most Concentrated Industries
Source: Author's compilation from GSO data.

liberalised and entry barriers notably reduced, the vast majority of over 120,000 private enterprises are still of SME size—of which 91 per cent having charter capital of less than VND10 billion (equivalent to merely US$500,000) and 98.77 per cent employing less than 300 employees. Meanwhile, 76 state-owned corporations and business groups alone account for up to 40 per cent of GDP and 28.8 per cent of domestic revenues (excluding crude oil and tariff revenues).[10]

A noteworthy fact is that, in 2004–05, the proportion of non-state sectors in the top-three firms of the 20 most concentrated industries was more or less the same as the average of the whole economy. However, by the end of 2006, all the top-three firms in the 20 industries were SOEs (see Figure 2). This finding is important in the sense that alongside other indicators of the dominance of SOEs, it shows the prompt impact in the change of market structure in industries assigned to be controlled by the so-called Korean style economic groups (*tap doan kinh te*) formed recently by administrative decrees of the Government.[11]

C. R&D Expenditure

Although its economy is largely based on agriculture activities, science and technology (S&T) has long been regarded as the important factor for development. However, there is a lack of authoritative and reliable data available on the total expenditure on research and development (R&D) in the country or even that type of data for each sector.

As a matter of fact, innovation is not currently regarded as part of Vietnam's core development policy. However, the Government has begun considering whether to strategically invest in R&D to 'position itself for future moves up the value chain'.[12] The table below shows that in the Southeast Asia region, Vietnam spends much less than Singapore and Malaysia in terms of annual budget for R&D as a percentage of GDP, but much more than other countries in the region. However, the number of patent applications and number of patents granted per year in the country is by far the least, if not counting poorer countries of Myanmar, Cambodia, East Timor, Lao PDR or the small-sized economy of Brunei.

[10] Report by the Prime Minister on 30th May 2008 at the third session of the 12th National Assembly.

[11] Currently, there are eight 'pilot' economic groups occupying key industries (electricity, post and telecommunication, rubber, textile and garment, shipping, insurance, coal and mineral, and petroleum and gas). Several other giant SOEs in selected industries are in the process of transforming into economic groups. Those economic groups are receiving huge investment and support from the State.

[12] 10th National Congress of the Communist Party of Vietnam (CPV)'s documents.

According to an empirical study on the impacts of the IP system on economic growth using publicly available data, Trần Ngoc Ca et al[13] argue that it is very difficult to use econometric models to separate the impact of IP policy on economic growth. The main findings from the study are as follows:

> [I]n the case of Vietnam, the impact of IP policy is not significant and effective due to some possible reasons: (i) The lack of public awareness about IP; (ii) The capacity of IP creation is weak. In industrial sector, as a consequence of low budget for R&D activities, the number of patents, utility solutions and industrial designs submitted to the NOIP is very small. Economic agents inclined to focus on creating and registering for trademark protection rather than creating other IP assets such as patents or designs. (iii) the inappropriate enforcement of IP laws and regulations. There are many infringements happened in the domestic markets without strong punishment to the violators. The court system is still not familiar with civil and criminals lawsuits relating to IP.

Although the econometric regression models' results have not showed a significant impact of IP on socio-economic development, specific cases might show a relatively strong relationship between IP system and their business performance. So, in evaluating the impact of IP on economic growth, it is preferable to conduct small scale surveys of specific industries or specific activities, such as exportation or FDI attraction. Take the export indicator for example. In Vietnam, exports of primary goods and material account for a large proportion of total exports, therefore, it would not be surprising if the IP system has a small impact on export activities. However, it is undeniable that in many cases, IP assets, particularly trademarks, are of significant importance to a company penetrating into new markets overseas.

One survey by the National Institute for Science and Technology Policy and Strategy Studies (NISTPASS) on the impact of the IP system on FDI in the Vietnamese motorbike manufacturing industry shows that FDI firms, especially large companies such as Honda, Yamaha, etc perceive the importance of IPR issues. Those companies frequently have to deal with infringements of their product designs once they are launched to market and cause large economic damage in the context of weak enforcement of IPRs in the country.[14] Another survey of FDI companies operating in different sectors found that, in evaluating the decision to invest in Vietnam, FDI firms consider that IPRs and related activities are not among the most important issues.[15] A consequence is that few foreign firms invest in technology-intensive sectors, but rather almost all of them focus on labour-intensive industries to make use of the advantage of cheap labour in the country. Recent research also shows that the FDI firms are least effective in terms of efficiency (evaluated by ICOR (Incremental Capital Output Ratio) and TFE (Total Factor Efficiency))[16] in comparison with its state-owned and domestic private counterparts. Nonetheless, up to the present date, there is no reliable research focusing on the impact of the IP system toward business performance.

In a study on the links between innovation and export of Vietnam's SME sector, Nguyen Ngoc Anh et al[17] found that innovation as measured directly by 'new products', 'new

[13] Tran Ngoc Ca et al, 'Impact of the Intellectual Property System on Economic Growth' (WIPO—UNU Joint Research Project, 2007).

[14] NISTPASS, 'Learning Via Networking with Multinationals: Closing the Knowledge Gap in Small Developing Economy: The Study of Vietnamese Auto-Motor Industrial Sector' (Research Working Report, IDRC, 2006).

[15] HT Nguyen et al, 'FDI in Vietnam' in S Estrin and KE Meyer (eds), *Investment in Emerging Economies* (Cheltenham, UK, Edward Elgar, 2004).

[16] http://phapluattp.vn/20100303115828110p0c1013/canh-bao-hieu-qua-cua-fdi.htm.

[17] Nguyen Ngoc Anh et al, 'Innovation and Export of Vietnam's SME Sector' (2008) 20(2) *The European Journal of Development Research* 262.

production process' and 'improvement of existing products' are important determinants of exports by Vietnamese SMEs. Evidence of the endogeneity of innovation was found. The study showed that all three measures of innovation, namely product innovation, process innovation and modification of existing product, are important determinants of exporting. This finding is important in the sense that in case endogeneity is not taken into account, biased estimate of innovation may be a result. As part of the process of joining the WTO and fully integrating with international markets, Vietnam was required to build and enhance a wide range of market-oriented legal systems. Among them was the introduction of competition and IP laws which are of crucial importance. Laws covering both were passed in the same year (2005). Not long afterwards, governmental decrees guiding the enforcement of competition and IP law were promulgated. The following part discusses in detail the essences of two laws, as well as their intersections in Vietnam.

III. Background to Competition Law and IP and their Intersection in Vietnam

A. IP Laws

In the past, IP protection was not considered important in the centralised economic system run by the Vietnamese Government. It was believed that creative ideas belonged to the public and should be used to serve people in general. Although the country had joined international agreements on IP protection decades ago (as a member of the Paris Convention and Madrid Treaty since 1949 and the Stockholm Convention on the foundation of the World Intellectual Property Organisation (WIPO) since 1976), it delayed domestic regulations in the field until the introduction of a market economy following the *Doi Moi* policy. The first invention patent was granted in 1984 and the Ordinance on Intellectual Property Protection was issued in 1989. Legal documents were not systemised and only met international standards on IP protection when the country submitted its application to join the WTO.

The Civil Code (1995) was the first law that provided detailed provisions on IP protection in part 4 with 61 articles concerning IP rights and technology transfer. In 2005, Vietnam revised this part of the Code to constitute the first Intellectual Property Law. The Law regulated protection measures for IP rights, including copyrights, industrial property rights and rights to plant varieties:

- Copyrights are the rights of organisations and individuals to works created or owned by them and related rights of organisations, individuals to performances, phonograms, broadcasting programmes, satellite signals carrying encrypted programmes.
- Industrial property rights are the rights of organisations and individuals to inventions; industrial designs; layout-designs of semi-conductor integrated circuits; trademarks; trade names, geographical indications, business secrets created or owned by them and rights to repression of unfair competition.
- Rights to plant varieties are the rights of organisations and individuals to the new plant varieties which are created or discovered and developed by and fall under the ownership right of such organisations or individuals.

The IP provisions broadly followed international laws and agreements, especially after they were amended in 2008 to meet the requirements of the Berne Convention and the Trade-Related Aspects of Intellectual Property Rights (TRIPS) Agreement when the country became an official member of the WTO. The Vietnamese Government is currently in the process of preparing for new guidelines.

B. Competition Law

The Competition Law was passed in the National Assembly in December 2004 and took effect from July 2005. The Law included the following provisions:

- — Prohibition of competition restriction agreements, abuse of dominant or monopoly position and economic concentration when the combined market shares of undertakings exceed 50 per cent of the total market.
- — Prohibition of unfair competition practices that go against business ethics and harm consumers and other businesses.
- — Establishment of Competition Authority and Competition Council under the Ministry of Trade (ie Ministry of Industry and Trade now) to enforce the law nationwide.
- — Establishment of competition procedure to review and apply remedies to violations of the law.

The Vietnamese Competition Law was developed with help from the Organisation for Economic Co-operation and Development (OECD) and the United Nations Conference on Trade and Development (UNCTAD) and followed their suggested model of competition law for developing countries.

It was officially stated that the main purpose of the law was to create an environment of fair competition and to promote a competitive market structure in Vietnam. On the other hand, some people believe that one of the reasons behind the introduction of the law was the Government's concern about threats from larger multinational companies that could enter the domestic market after it opened its economy in accordance with WTO commitments. This was on the basis that in many countries, competition law had proved itself as an effective tool in deterring market power and protecting local SMEs as well as consumers.

Meanwhile, similar to China's Unfair Competition Act 1993, the Competition Law of Vietnam included a provision requiring all government entities not to intervene unreasonably with market activities and to create negative impacts on competition. The provision is typical for competition acts in transitional countries where government entities ran the economy in the past and do not want give up their involvement in business life. However, this attempt to prevent this from happening has not worked well in practice.

IV. Intersection Issues

Vietnamese laws cover a number of horizontal and vertical issues, namely compulsory licensing and licensing contracts and unused patent. However, but the laws fail to provide a systematic approach to the intersection area, as well as enforcement proxies for IP and competition authorities to deal with relevant cases.

A. Compulsory Licensing

Regulations on compulsory licenses were first introduced in the Civil Code 1995. Article 802 of the Code (under part 4 on IP protection) provides that:

> On the basis of the request of the person who has the need for use, the authorized State agency may issue a decision compelling the owner of an invention, utility solution or industrial design to transfer with remuneration the right to use the industrial property right in the following circumstances:
>
> — The owner of the property does not use or use the property not in conformity with the requirement of social and economic development of the country without any plausible reason.
> — The person who has the need to use the property right, after exhausting his/her means to come to an agreement with the owner of the property and having offered the reasonable price, still is refused by the author to sign a contract on the transfer of the right to use the industrial property objects.
> — The use of the industrial property objects aims to meet the needs of national defense and security, medical treatment for the people and other urgent needs of society.

Since part 4 of the Code was split and developed by the Intellectual Property Law 2005, the new law provided more detail about compulsory license issues. General principles of compulsory licensing are stated in section 7.3 as follows:

> In the circumstances where the achievement of defense, security, people's life-related objectives and other interests of the State and society specified in this Law should be guaranteed, the State may prohibit or restrict the exercise of intellectual property rights by the holders or compel the licensing by the holders of one or several of their rights to other organizations or individuals with appropriate terms.

Under IP law, compulsory licensing can be applied to owners of inventions and plant varieties. Inventions are subjected to compulsory licensing following a decision from a competent authority regardless of the consensus of the owner in the following cases:

— When it is necessary to serve public interests, non-commercial purposes, national defence and security, disease prevention and treatment, nutrition for people or other urgent needs of the society.
— When the owner of the invention or his/her exclusive licensees fail to fulfill the obligations to use such invention to serve public and national interests within four years from the registration date and three years from the date of granting the patent.
— When a person fails to reach a reasonable agreement with the owner within a reasonable time for negotiation on price and conditions.
— When the owner of a dependent invention, which makes an important technical advance and economic significance, fails to request the owner of the main invention to license such principal invention with reasonable price and conditions.
— When the owner of the invention is considered to be exercising anti-competitive practices prohibited by competition law.

On the other hand, the law also limits compulsory licensing as follows:

— Compulsory license is not exclusive, ie the licensee shall not enjoy an exclusive right of using the invention.
— Compulsory license is limited in scope and duration that is sufficient to meet licensing objectives, and largely for the domestic market.
— The licensee is not allowed to transfer the use of license, unless he/she sells all of his/her business.

— The licensee has to pay the owner a reasonable licensing fee based on the economic value of the invention in real conditions and compliant with the compensation bracket set by the competent authority.
— The owner of the main invention may request the grant-back licensing of a dependent invention with reasonable price and conditions.

In any case, the owner of the invention has the right to request the termination of the compulsory license when the bases for licensing no longer exist and are unlikely to recur, provided that such termination shall not be prejudicial to the licensee.

Compulsory licensing on plant varieties is provided in article 195, with conditions and limitations similar to those applied to invention.

B. Licensing Contract

In order to prevent IP owners from misusing or abusing his/her exclusive rights, IP Law does not allow any contract term that imposes unreasonable restrictions on a licensee, particularly those that do not derive from the rights of the licensor by nature as follows:

— Prohibiting the licensee to improve the industrial property object (trademark excluded), compelling the licensee to transfer or grant-back to the licensor any improvements of the industrial property object free of charge.
— Directly or indirectly restricting the licensee to export goods produced or services related to licensing contract to a country/territory where the licensor neither holds the respective industrial property rights nor has the exclusive right to import such goods.
— Compelling the licensee to purchase raw materials, components or equipment from the licensor or a third party designated by the licensor exceeding the purpose of ensuring the quality of goods produced or services provided by the licensee.
— Depriving the right of the licensee to file complaint or lawsuit against the validation of the related IP rights of the licensor.

Any clauses in the contract falling into the above categories shall be ex-officio invalid.

C. Unused patent and technical restrain agreement

Unused patents can be named as evidence of some breaches of competition rules in Vietnam. Vietnamese Competition Law does not mention specific usage of 'patent' or IPR, but sets out a general prohibition against agreements to restrain technical developments or technology in Article 8.4. Then in Article 13.3 it also states that sole action of a dominant enterprise that bring similar restrictive result as an 'abuse of dominant position'.

These articles are clarified in the first guideline of the Competition Law, the Decree on Competition.[18] Section 17.1 of the guideline defines that 'an agreement to restrain technical developments or technology means reaching agreement to purchase an invention, patent, utility solution or industrial design in order to destroy it or keep it from being used'. Similarly, the abuse of dominant position in form of restraining technical or technological development is described in Section 28.3 (b) as the 'practices of Purchasing an invention, patent, utility solution or industrial design in order to destroy it or keep it from being used'.

[18] The Decree number 116/2005/ND-CP of the Vietnam Government Providing detailed regulations and guidelines for implementation of a number of articles of the Competition Law, dated 15 September 2005.

With narrow approach to 'purchase' practices, the guideline fails to deal with a broader and more complex category of patent misuses, which in several cases may trigger compulsory licensing. For example, an agreement between parties not to use their previously owned or separately developed patents shall not be sanctioned under Section 17.1 as no purchase would take place in the market. Section 28.3 (b) also has problem in referring to 'purchase' as an abusive practice. Obviously, market power of an IPR owner is formulated by the monopolistic usage of the IP; then no dominant position could exist when it is still in transaction and the buyer has no intention to use it in the market.

D. Exemption

Other relevant provisions might be found in the Competition Law regarding exemptions. Normally, Vietnamese Competition Law prohibits horizontal agreement between competitors whose combined market shares in a relevant market exceed 30 per cent. Article 10 of the Competition Law provides that horizontal agreements shall enjoy exemption if they meet one of the following conditions in order to reduce costs to benefit consumers:

- Rationalising the organisational structure, business model, raising business efficiency.
- Promoting technical and technological advances, raising goods and service quality.
- Promoting the uniform application of quality standards and technical norms of products of different kinds.
- Harmonising business, goods delivery and payment conditions, which have no connection with prices and price factors.
- Enhancing the competitiveness of small and medium-sized enterprises.
- Enhancing the competitiveness of Vietnamese enterprises on the international market.

The law does not offer an automatic exemption for the above mentioned cases, and require undertaking parties to apply for an approval before entering the agreement. This means that members of horizontal agreements related to IP may use business efficiencies as a defense in their application process for an exemption.

E. Unfair Competition

Competition law and IP law in Vietnam also share common regulations on unfair competition, which normally does not fall into the intersection area between the two laws. The right against unfair competition is often considered as an IP matter in the form of enhanced protection granted to IP owners. In the 1990s, WIPO undertook a number of activities dealing with the topic of protection against unfair competition and the WIPO Model Provisions on Protection against Unfair Competition were published in 1996. Vietnam has followed some Eastern European countries in covering unfair competition in a general competition law, in which a number of provisions in chapter 3 (from article 39 to 48) specify unfair competition practices that harm competitors and/or deceive consumers.

Chapter 3 unfair competition practices relating to IP include: misleading indications (article 40) and infringement of business secrets (article 41).

- Commercial indications are known as external characters or signs enclosed with a certain good, service or business entity that can be used by consumers to recognise the supplier of the good or service, or the mentioned business entity.

— Business secrets are known as uncommon and confidential information and know-how that are applicable to business and create certain advantages for the owner out of other competitors.

Two other unfair competition practices were also added to the IP Law in 2005, as follows:

— Using a trademark that is registered and/or protected with another member of the Paris Convention on Industrial Property Protection without the consent of the overseas owner.
— Registering or possessing a domain name for the purpose of misleading or exploiting reputation of a certain trademark, trade name or geographical indication.

There is no doubt that the above provisions enhance protection of IP rights. While IP law traditionally covers a handful of IP objects, namely invention, copyright, trademark and plant variety, unfair competition provisions (which are normally covered outside competition law in other countries) give a broader scope of protection for other objects like commercial indications, business secrets, domain names and overseas trademarks. In this respect, Vietnamese Competition Law functions like an alternative and broader protection for IP rights.

V. Procedures to Deal with Intersection Issues and the Entities in Charge

A. Competition and IP Law Enforcement Authorities

In Vietnam, the Ministry of Industry and Trade (MOIT) is the government body in charge of the competition law enforcement. Under the Ministry, the VCA investigates anti-competitive practices, then reports to the VCC for reviewing and deciding on remedies.

Meanwhile, IP law is enforced by three other ministries: the Ministry of Science and Technology takes responsibility for industrial property protection; the Ministry of Culture, Sport and Tourism handles copyright matters; plant varieties issues belong to the Ministry of Agriculture. In addition, the law also authorises other government entities to deal with IP infringement, including the police, customs, market inspectors and the courts.

B. Authority and Procedure for Compulsory Licensing

According to IP regulations, different government entities may be involved in compulsory licensing decisions:

— Where compulsory licensing is required in the public interest, national defence and security, people's nutrition or state of emergencies like epidemics or widespread diseases, the ministry in charge of a specific area (ie Ministry of Defence, Ministry of Healthcare, etc) can make the decision of compulsory licensing on its own or based on a request from interested parties.
— Where compulsory licensing results from the misconduct of the IP owner, including refusals to deal, inactivation or other anti-competitive conduct, the Ministry of Science and Technology can make decisions on invention licensing; the Ministry

of Agriculture and the Ministry of Healthcare can make decision on plant variety licensing for agricultural and medical plants.

— However, IP Law does not mention the role of the competition authority regarding anti-competition aspects of the compulsory licensing process.

To initiate the procedure, interested parties may submit an application to the specific ministry in charge of compulsory licensing. The ministry in charge verifies the application within an appropriate time (15 days for plant varieties and two months for inventions), in which it may review an applicant's capacity to utilise new technology and to compensate a potential licensor, or require re-negotiation between licensor and licensee(s). It may also consult with other government entities before issuing a final decision. The ministry can turn down the application where it has reason to believe that the applicant does not meet the necessary requirements and conditions. The applicant must be informed about denial rejection in writing.

Table 4: Procedures to Decide Compulsory Licensing in Vietnam

	Compulsory licensing based on public interest, national security, people nutrition	***Compulsory licensing on invention based on misconducts of owners***	***Compulsory licensing on plant varieties***
Competent authority	Ministries in charge of the related area.	Ministry of Science and Technology (NOIP).	Ministry of Agriculture (for agricultural plants) and Ministry of Healthcare (for medical and herbal plants).
Initiation	Application from interest parties to the ministry in charge.	Application from interest parties to NOIP.	Application from interest parties to the Ministry of Agriculture (Cultivation Dept) or Ministry of Healthcare.
Procedure	— Consultation with NOIP. — Final decision.	— Notification to the owner of the invention. — Feedback from the owner. — Request of re-negotiation between the owner and the applicant(s) (if necessary). — Final decision. — Registration on the National Record on IP transfer and publicise in the IP Official Gazette.	— Verification on the proposed duration and scope of utilising plant varieties. — Verification on the applicant's financial capacity of compensating licensor (licensing fee).
Duration	2 months	2 months	15 days
Application fee	Yes	Yes	No
Licensing fee	Yes	Yes	Yes

C. Procedure for Exemption on Horizontal Agreement

As mentioned in Part IV.D of this Chapter, IP law and competition law do not have specified regulations dealing with IP related horizontal agreements such as patent pool and cross licensing. However, an exemption may be granted for these kinds of agreements where they contribute to economic efficiency. To secure an exemption, involved parties are required to submit an application to the Ministry of Industry and Trade before entering the agreement. An application is reviewed by the VCA, then submitted to the Minister for final decision within 60 days.

D. Case Studies

Although provisions on compulsory licensing have been imposed since 1995, up to now no decision has been made following the above procedure. In addition, no exemption application has been submitted to a competition authority regarding patent pool or cross licensing.

i. The Tamilflu Case

The only case in which a compulsory license was almost decided was reported in 2005, when Vietnam was seriously impacted by the bird flu epidemic. The Government was forced to destroy more than 45 million of domestic poultries and the economic loss was estimated to be around 0.5 per cent of GDP.[19] Concern about human infection increased nationwide after 42 death cases and the flu antidote quickly became in short supply. The Vietnamese Government ordered 25 million tablets of Tamilflu, one of the most effective antidotes for bird flu, from F Hoffmann-La Roche Ltd. However, the Swiss pharmaceutical company who owned the antidote patent was not able to provide that amount to meet the order from Vietnam. In November 2005, the Ministry of Healthcare held a meeting with company representatives and required it to transfer the Tamilflu patent to domestic companies for mass production, otherwise compulsory licensing would be ordered.[20] It was clear that the company accepted the request from the Ministry and committed to providing technical support to domestic producers in order to avoid compulsory licensing. In fact, no action was taken after that as bird flu was prevented successfully in the next year (2006) and Tamilflu soon became oversupplied without any additional supplies from domestic pharmaceutical companies.

ii. Son Vu Case

Apart from inventions and plant variety for which no compulsory licensing has been made, other IPRs are sometimes exploited by the owners to deter market competition and the case of Son Vu Company was an example. In 2004, Son Vu Company registered its trademark of ceramic tiles with traditional patterns that have been commonly using for more than 200 years by local households of the Phu Phong Village in the central province of Binh Dinh. After its trademark registration, in 2005 Son Vu sued a number of local competitors in court for 'infringement of protected trademark' and required the defendants to stop

[19] Vietname Government report in April 2005 summarising a two-year fight with bird flu (2004–05).

[20] Notification No 8186/QLD-DK of the Drug Administration Agency under the Ministry of Healthcare of dated 9th November 2005.

producing their traditional products. The provincial court accepted Son Vu's arguments based on its certification of a trademark granted by NOIP. According to a local newspaper, this case had a serious impact on the business of more than 500 households with 7,000 workers.[21] The defendants then appealed the verdict to the Supreme Court and requested NOIP to reconsider the trademark protection granted to Son Vu. In October 2006, NOIP invalidated Son Vu's trademark.

iii. Vien Son Case

A second case of trademark abuse related to parallel import issue, where an importer named Vien Son was appointed by the Kingmax Technology Inc (Taiwan) as the exclusive dealer of its popular PC memory (RAM) products in Vietnam. Vien Son was also authorised to register and use the Taiwanese's trademark Kingmax in Vietnam. Following its registration of the Kingmax trademark at NOIP in November 2006, Vien Son successfully prevented other competitors from importing Kingmax products. Vien Son requested the relevant authorities (customs and market inspectors) to confiscate their competitor's goods because they infringed Vien Son's IPRs. One of the competitors complained and NOIP decided to invalidate Vien Son's Kingmax trademark. Vien Son did not accept NOIP's decision and took action against NOIP in the Administrative Court of Ho Chi Minh City in 2008. In the first verdict, the Court agreed with Vien Son's stand that it had been legally authorised by the trademark holder to register and use the trademark in Vietnam; therefore, the NOIP's decision to invalidate was overturned. After that, the NOIP appealed the verdict to the People's Supreme Court in Hanoi. In January 2009, the Court of Appeal (under the Supreme Court) denied Vien Son's petition and agreed with NOIP's decision. The Court agreed with NOIP that the case reflected collusion between the domestic dealer and its overseas partner to use IPRs to restrain parallel imports. Such an agreement was unacceptable as it not only deterred competition in the market, but also enabled the foreign company to manipulate the domestic market with low-grade products under the umbrella of IP protection.

iv. Megastar Case

In early May 2010, six domestic cinemas filed a complaint dossier with VCA regarding the abuse of dominant position of foreign investment company Megastar in the imported film distribution market. The company allegedly exploited its market power there as an IP right holder in a monopolisation attempt in another market, namely cinema screening. According to the complaint dossier, Megastar is one of major film distributors in the Vietnamese market and has exclusive contracts with several Hollywood studios that enable the company to bring blockbuster films such as Avatar or Transformers to the domestic market. The company also manages seven cinemas in major cities in Vietnam. Megastar is alleged to have abused its exclusive distribution right of highly profitable films to impose unfair terms and conditions in its contracts with local cinemas, including price maintenance (requiring contractors to pay Megastar a fixed fee per member of the audience almost equal to the regular ticket price), tying sales (supplying highly profitable films on condition that lower quality films be taken) and other competition restrictions such as not to screen contracted films at the same time as Megastar' cinemas, which then enjoyed

[21] Binh Dinh Newspaper dated 26th October 2006.

the best showing schedule for audiences. Having experienced losses with new distribution contracts and failing to negotiate with Megastar, local cinemas decided to join together to submit the complaint dossier to VCA, which then decided to launch a preliminary investigation. However, the plaintiffs did not seem to have a strong point on the relevant market definition, ie imported film distribution, where the defendant enjoyed a dominant position. In a media interview recently, legal counsel for the plaintiff admitted difficulties in defining the relevant market and the defendant's dominant position in the case.[22] Market power of Megastar should not be examined by its annual sales volume or the number of films it had imported and distributed, but from its control over certain films which are irresistible to the public. If thousands of youths could go and queue for *Avatar* or *Harry Potter* but no other films, then it might be suggested that each film constitutes a separate market without any substitutable product, and one which holds its copyright and/or related rights actually plays a monopoly role. A broader definition of relevant market and its dominant position should be considered to cover such cases where market power is created through copyright or IP ownership in general.

VI. Conclusions and Recommendations

A. Main Findings

As a part of efforts to build up a market economy, Vietnam has adopted international laws, including IP and competition laws. The introduction of these laws were also responses to international requirements for the country's integration into the world economy, especially in WTO negotiations. However, the adoption of international models sometimes means a lack of compatibility with other sections of the country's legal system. Vietnam's provisions on compulsory licensing and other issues in the intersection between IP law and competition law are to some extent incompatible. When compulsory licensing was first introduced in the Civil Code 1995, it was considered as part of a 'standard IP law' from international models and was explained in light of public interest with no link to competition matters. Only after the promulgation of the Competition Law in 2004 were there new additions to the compulsory licensing section to deal with anti-competitive conduct by IP owners. As a result, the Competition Law covers a narrow scope of intersection issues, applying to agreements and/or sole action of purchasing patent with no intention to use in the market. Moreover, nonuse of inventions or patents should not be considered unlawful per se, since it may be efficiency oriented decision when the application of the patent is not profitable as expected. An IP monopoly does not always create a market power that threatens the soul competition in the market.

This has led to a suggestion that more specific tools should be developed to assess relevant market and market power in IP related cases. Vietnamese Competition Law uses an approach to market definition based on the universally accepted SSNIP test to examine the substitutability of potentially competing products, and it proved to be ill-suited in for exceptional fields like IP transactions, where every IP is somehow unique and not able to

[22] *Phap Luat Thanh Pho Ho Chi Minh* (Ho Chi Minh City Legal) Newspaper dated 15th May 2010.

be substituted or replaced by other IPs. On the other hand, its advantages are temporary, and could be shortly eliminated by the development of new technologies. Enforcement practices, especially in the Megastar case, show that the traditional SSNIP test may be insufficient in identifying market power gained through IP ownerships. In order to examine an IP's impacts on competition, the competent authority should take into account also its applicability and profitability in the market, trends of technology development and consumer loyalty, which are not mentioned in the current laws.

Legal inconsistencies can be found within the compulsory licensing provisions, where procedures applied to inventions and plant variety are different and handled by separated government agencies. The situation has partly resulted from the law making tradition of the country in which drafting work are assigned to ministries who are in charge of relevant matters and so there is a lack of connection with each other. On the other hand, the role of the competition authority in dealing with competition aspects of all the procedures is still unclear.

Inadequacies in the laws regarding the intersection have led to insignificant enforcement where no compulsory licensing case for inventions and plant varieties has been reported in the last 15 years. Meanwhile, other IPRs such as trademarks may be abused to deter competition like in the Son Vu and Vien Son cases, where they were finally handled as disputes in IP registration, but not matters of the Competition Law even though there were evidences of damage to the industry and competitors. Even though correction can be made with the withdrawal of IP certificates from undertakings, it still takes time to reach a final decision (normally one year for an invalidation procedure), while no remedy is available to recover lost competition in the market.

After 25 years of economic renovation, Vietnam remains a developing country whose main exports are agricultural or labour-intensive products and there is insignificant expenditure on R&D. The implementation of the IP law has contributed little to science and technology innovation where the patent granted for invention was 666 in 2008 and 706 in 2009—and where about 95 per cent belong to foreign holders (see Table 6 below). From 1981 to 2009, the number of residential patents was a mere 389, while according to WIPO's statistics the numbers in Korea and China were 61,115 and 46,590 respectively in 2008. The Ministry of Science and Technology has recorded no technology transfer contract since 2007, when the Law of Technology Transfer was promulgated, requiring high value technology transfer to be registered to this government entity.[23] This means that the implementation of IP laws has so far not achieved its goal of encouraging innovation and promoting technology exploitation and transactions which are vital for improving a developing country like Vietnam.

Meanwhile, applications for trademark registration have always exceeded 20,000 annually over the past five years (see Table 5 below). The overwhelming number of trademark registrations suggests that IP law and regulations has been preferred mostly as a marketing tool to introduce consumer and luxury goods to the new market. Imported products of well-known brands or trademarks are often charged with a premium to Vietnamese consumers. Thus, it is believed that current implementation of IP law in Vietnam which focused too much on trademark protections may protect only foreign companies in the domestic market.

[23] Information from the Department of Technology Appraisal, Examination and Assessment under the Ministry of Science and Technology of Vietnam.

Table 5: Number of IP Registrations Applied and Accepted at NOIP from 2006 to 2009

No	Registration Type	Application				Protection Title Granted			
		2006	2007	2008	2009	2006	2007	2008	2009
1	Invention & utility solution	2411	3080	3484	3143	739	810	741	770
2	Industrial design	1604	1908	1753	1899	1175	1370	1337	1236
3	National trademark	23,086	27,110	27,724	28,677	8,840	15,860	23,290	22,730
4	International trademark	4,071	4,920	7,386	6,324	3,417	4,422	3,631	4,147
5	Geographical indication	5	4	8	6	2	7	2	2
6	Integrated circuit	1	1	1	3	0	0	0	0

Source: NOIP.

Table 6: Number of Invention Patents Granted from 1981–2008

Year	Holder		
	Vietnamese	Foreigner	Total
1981–89	74	7	81
1990	11	3	14
1991	14	13	27
1992	19	16	35
1993	3	13	16
1994	5	14	19
1995	3	53	56
1996	4	58	62
1997	0	111	111
1998	5	343	348
1999	13	322	335
2000	10	620	630
2001	7	776	783
2002	9	734	743
2003	17	757	774
2004	22	676	698
2005	27	641	668
2006	44	625	669
2007	34	691	725
2008	39	627	666
2009	29	677	706
Total	**389**	**7,777**	**8,166**

Source: NOIP.

B. How Should the Intersection be Treated?

Since foreign companies have been slow to transfer technology to Vietnam, provisions on compulsory licensing should be used to help the country access the advanced technologies it needs for economic development. Government agencies may decide which technology is suitable for Vietnam and require the IP holder to transfer it to a domestic institution who has capacity of exploiting and developing the technology. Although current licensing procedures require an application from a potential licensee at the beginning, in fact another option could be to allow a ministry on its own initiative to force a compulsory license based on certain economic considerations and assign itself as the direct licensee, then redistribute it to domestic companies based on public bidding and following supervision. However, as foreign subsidiaries in Vietnam usually do not hold IP rights but their mother companies overseas, such compulsory licensing may require ministries to assert extra territory jurisdiction over this—which most government entities in Vietnam are reluctant to claim at the moment. Investment incentive to encourage the needed technology may be another policy alternative.

Given the fact that other IP rights could be used for anti-competitive purposes, it is suggested that the scope of compulsory licensing should be widened to cover other kinds of IP, including copyright and related rights. The government entities in charge could make decisions on licensing such objectives based on their consideration of promoting competition in the market, as well as other remedies for the misconduct of the IP owners, such as boycott, refusal to deal or abuse of bargaining power. In this process, the VCA should play a much more active role in reviewing the competition impact of each case and be able to decide by itself whether to issue a compulsory license in the case of an abuse of market power resulting from exclusive IP rights. Otherwise, the ministries in charge of compulsory licensing in current procedures could be required to consult with the VCA on competition matters before making a decision regarding compulsory licensing. The VCA also need to monitor IP registration processes regularly and access to the registration database if necessary to find out whether potential anti-competitive conduct has occurred after IP certificates have been granted (which is what happened in the Son Vu and Vien Son cases).

Unlike other forms of anti-competition practices, potential misconduct by IP owners takes root from a lawful monopoly which may benefit the economy in general. Therefore, it may be inappropriate for the government to apply severe sanctions to the undertakings which are still under its protection. Instead, compulsory licensing and other remedies would seem to be useful alternatives to deal with specific cases and competition agencies should be given a broader power to decide such remedies, which have not been provided by current laws.

In order to increase VCA's involvement in dealing with compulsory licensing and other intersections between IP and competition laws, detailed provisions should be added to both laws, giving VCA more flexible tools to analyse and evaluate the impact on competition of the use of IPRs rather than simply relying on fixed market share and simply defining markets on the basis of the SSNIP test.[24] The VCA needs to develop its expertise to evaluate both economic and technology aspects of each case and make a balance between competition effectiveness and the benefits to IP owners.

[24] Article 4 of the Decree No 116/2005/ND-CP of Vietnam Government dated 15th September 2005 providing detailed regulations and guidelines for implementation on a number of articles of the Competition Law.

In any change of the competition law and policy in the future, exercises of IPR should be stated clearly as an exceptional case of market power, where a rule of reason approach is used and economic efficiency is taken into account. Technical tools and measures could be helpful in accessing any market power arising from IP ownership based on its novelty and distinctiveness, duration and scope of protection, and the possibility of more advanced IP coming to the market.

In addition, the trademark cases indicate that the authority may consider options of parallel imports or exhaustion of rights to prevent the abuse of trademark and brand powers, and allow the country more freedom in importing necessary products. In Vien Son case, the Appeal Court agreed with the NOIP opinion in favour of parallel import; however, since case law is unpopular in Vietnam, a statutory supplement may be required.

C. Policy Recommendations

A better harmonisation of IP and competition law is necessary to make better use of both in order to improve economic efficiency. However, as Vietnam has followed the Civil Law tradition, all the above measures must be supported by additional provisions in the laws before any improvement can be made. The legislative amendment process is normally time-consuming and law makers are unlikely to accept a new proposal in a near future after the amendment of the IP Law in June 2009. Therefore, a sub-law guideline (in the form of a Government Decree) could be an option. The guideline could contain the following provisions:

- — Basic principles of covering the intersection between IP law and competition law favouring dynamic competition.
- — Detailed guidelines dealing with the intersection, including both horizontal and vertical transactions related to IPRs, with list of hardcore conducts in IP transaction, where the harm on competition may outweigh business efficiency.[25]
- — Better prescription of the functions and responsibilities of government agencies in charge of the intersections and the way they should work together to deal with specific issues such as compulsory licensing.
- — Better economic and technological criteria and measures to analyse the market power of the IP owner and competitive impacts of IPR exercises.
- — More detailed guidance on the appropriate remedies, both structural and behavioural, that can be applied to allow for competition where IPRs are concerned.

VI. Appendix

1. Vietnam Civil Code 2004.
2. Vietnam Competition Law 2004.
3. Vietnam Intellectual Property Law 2005.
4. Vietnam Law on Technology Transfer 2007.

[25] Initial references can be taken from the Technology Transfer Block Exemption and R&D Block Exemption Regulations of the European Commission ((EC) No 772/2004 and 1217/2010).

5. Decree No 116/2005/ND-CP of Vietnam Government dated 15th September 2005 providing detailed regulations and guidelines for implementation on a number of articles of the Competition Law.
6. Decree No 103/2006/ND-CP of Vietnam Government dated 22nd September 2006 providing detailed regulations and guidelines for implementation on a number of articles of the Intellectual Property Law.
7. Annual reports of Vietnam National Office of Intellectual Property 2007, 2008 and 2009.

Appendices

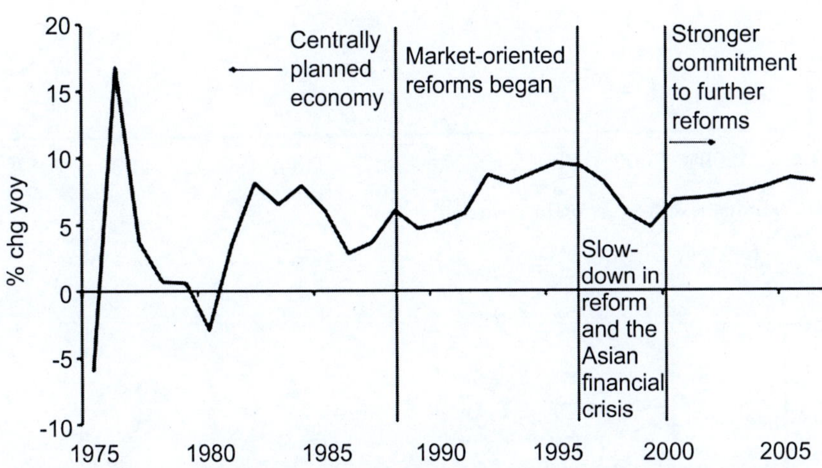

Appendix 1: Vietnam Economy's Growth Rate 1987–2008

Source: Qiao (2008)[1]

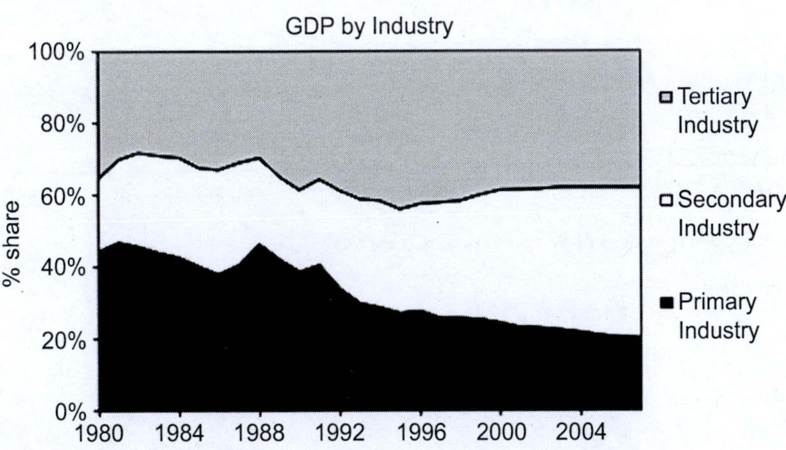

Appendix 2: Structural Changes in the Vietnamese Economy 1986–2004

Source: Qiao (2008)

[1] H Qiao, 'Vietnam: The Next Asian Tiger in the Making' (Goldman Sachs Global Economics Paper No 165, April 2008).

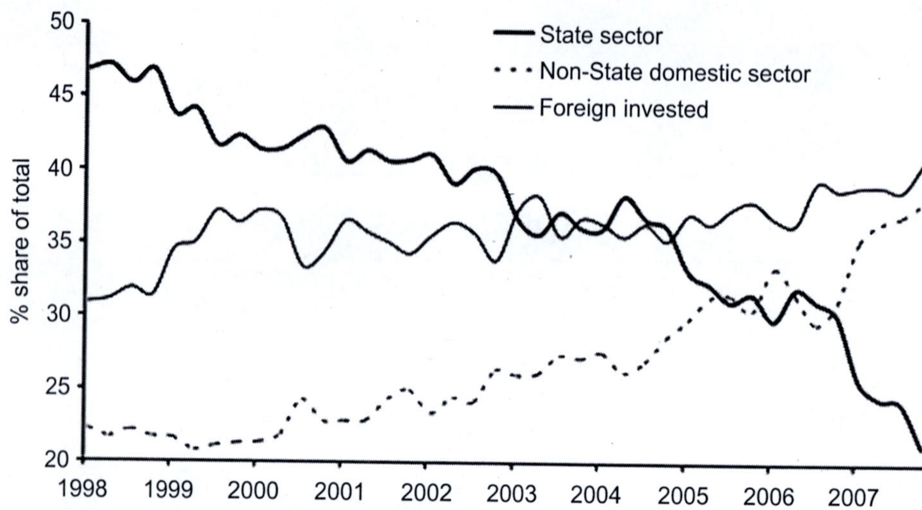

Appendix 3: Industrial Production by Ownership

Source: Qiao (2008)

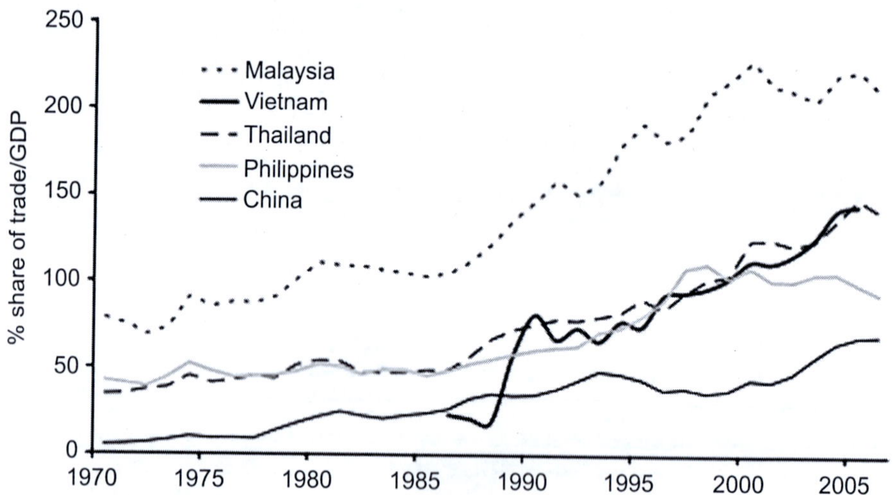

Appendix 4: Trade Openness of Selected Asian Countries

Source: Qiao (2008)

INDEX